Handbook of Research on Opinion Mining and Text Analytics on Literary Works and Social Media

Pantea Keikhosrokiani
School of Computer Sciences, Universiti Sains Malaysia, Malaysia

Moussa Pourya Asl
School of Humanities, Universiti Sains Malaysia, Malaysia

A volume in the Advances in Web Technologies
and Engineering (AWTE) Book Series

Published in the United States of America by
IGI Global
Engineering Science Reference (an imprint of IGI Global)
701 E. Chocolate Avenue
Hershey PA, USA 17033
Tel: 717-533-8845
Fax: 717-533-8661
E-mail: cust@igi-global.com
Web site: http://www.igi-global.com

Library of Congress Cataloging-in-Publication Data

Names: Keikhosrokiani, Pantea, DATE- editor. | Pourya Asl, Moussa, DATE-
   editor.
Title: Handbook of resesarch on Opinion mining and text analytics on literary
   works and social media / Pantea Keikhosrokiani, and Moussa Pourya Asl, editors.
Description: Hershey, PA : Engineering Science Reference, [2022] | Includes
   bibliographical references and index. | Summary: "This book uses
   artificial intelligence and big data analytics to conduct opinion mining
   and text analytics on literary works and social media, focusing on
   theories, method, applications and approaches of data analytic
   techniques that can be used to extract and analyze data from literary
   books and social media, in a meaningful pattern"-- Provided by
   publisher.
Identifiers: LCCN 2021047654 (print) | LCCN 2021047655 (ebook) | ISBN
   9781799895947 (hardcover) | ISBN 9781799895961 (ebook)
Subjects: LCSH: Text processing (Computer science) | Content analysis
   (Communication)--Data processing. | Social media--Data processing. |
   Literature--Data processing. | Artificial intelligence. | Data mining. |
   Big data.
Classification: LCC QA76.9.T48 O65 2022 (print) | LCC QA76.9.T48 (ebook)
   | DDC 005.52--dc23/eng/20211120
LC record available at https://lccn.loc.gov/2021047654
LC ebook record available at https://lccn.loc.gov/2021047655

This book is published in the IGI Global book series Advances in Web Technologies and Engineering (AWTE) (ISSN:
2328-2762; eISSN: 2328-2754)

British Cataloguing in Publication Data
A Cataloguing in Publication record for this book is available from the British Library.

All work contributed to this book is new, previously-unpublished material. The views expressed in this book are those of the
authors, but not necessarily of the publisher.

For electronic access to this publication, please contact: eresources@igi-global.com.

Advances in Web Technologies and Engineering (AWTE) Book Series

Ghazi I. Alkhatib
The Hashemite University, Jordan
David C. Rine
George Mason University, USA

ISSN:2328-2762
EISSN:2328-2754

MISSION

The **Advances in Web Technologies and Engineering (AWTE) Book Series** aims to provide a platform for research in the area of Information Technology (IT) concepts, tools, methodologies, and ethnography, in the contexts of global communication systems and Web engineered applications. Organizations are continuously overwhelmed by a variety of new information technologies, many are Web based. These new technologies are capitalizing on the widespread use of network and communication technologies for seamless integration of various issues in information and knowledge sharing within and among organizations. This emphasis on integrated approaches is unique to this book series and dictates cross platform and multidisciplinary strategy to research and practice.

The **Advances in Web Technologies and Engineering (AWTE) Book Series** seeks to create a stage where comprehensive publications are distributed for the objective of bettering and expanding the field of web systems, knowledge capture, and communication technologies. The series will provide researchers and practitioners with solutions for improving how technology is utilized for the purpose of a growing awareness of the importance of web applications and engineering.

COVERAGE

- Ontology and semantic Web studies
- Web Systems Architectures, Including Distributed, Grid Computer, and Communication Systems Processing
- Metrics-based performance measurement of IT-based and web-based organizations
- Web systems engineering design
- IT readiness and technology transfer studies
- Knowledge structure, classification, and search algorithms or engines
- Security, integrity, privacy, and policy issues
- Case studies validating Web-based IT solutions
- Integrated Heterogeneous and Homogeneous Workflows and Databases within and Across Organizations and with Suppliers and Customers
- Radio Frequency Identification (RFID) research and applications in Web engineered systems

IGI Global is currently accepting manuscripts for publication within this series. To submit a proposal for a volume in this series, please contact our Acquisition Editors at Acquisitions@igi-global.com or visit: http://www.igi-global.com/publish/.

Titles in this Series

For a list of additional titles in this series, please visit: http://www.igi-global.com/book-series/advances-web-technologies-engineering/37158

Security, Data Analytics, and Energy-Aware Solutions in the IoT
Xiali Hei (University of Louisiana at Lafayette, USA)
Engineering Science Reference • © 2022 • 218pp • H/C (ISBN: 9781799873235) • US $225.00

Emerging Trends in IoT and Integration with Data Science, Cloud Computing, and Big Data Analytics
Pelin Yildirim Taser (Izmir Bakircay University, Turkey)
Information Science Reference • © 2022 • 334pp • H/C (ISBN: 9781799841869) • US $225.00

App and Website Accessibility Developments and Compliance Strategies
Yakup Akgül (Alanya Alaaddin Keykubat University, Turkey)
Engineering Science Reference • © 2022 • 322pp • H/C (ISBN: 9781799878483) • US $225.00

IoT Protocols and Applications for Improving Industry, Environment, and Society
Cristian González García (University of Oviedo, Spain) and Vicente García-Díaz (University of Oviedo, Spain)
Engineering Science Reference • © 2021 • 321pp • H/C (ISBN: 9781799864639) • US $245.00

Integration and Implementation of the Internet of Things Through Cloud Computing
Pradeep Tomar (Gautam Buddha University, India)
Engineering Science Reference • © 2021 • 357pp • H/C (ISBN: 9781799869818) • US $245.00

Design Innovation and Network Architecture for the Future Internet
Mohamed Boucadair (Orange S.A., France) and Christian Jacquenet (Orange S.A., France)
Engineering Science Reference • © 2021 • 478pp • H/C (ISBN: 9781799876465) • US $225.00

Challenges and Opportunities for the Convergence of IoT, Big Data, and Cloud Computing
Sathiyamoorthi Velayutham (Sona College of Technology, India)
Engineering Science Reference • © 2021 • 350pp • H/C (ISBN: 9781799831112) • US $215.00

Examining the Impact of Deep Learning and IoT on Multi-Industry Applications
Roshani Raut (Pimpri Chinchwad College of Engineering (PCCOE), Pune, India) and Albena Dimitrova Mihovska (CTIF Global Capsule (CGC), Denmark)
Engineering Science Reference • © 2021 • 304pp • H/C (ISBN: 9781799875116) • US $245.00

701 East Chocolate Avenue, Hershey, PA 17033, USA
Tel: 717-533-8845 x100 • Fax: 717-533-8661
E-Mail: cust@igi-global.com • www.igi-global.com

List of Contributors

Table of Contents

Section 1
Reviews, Techniques, and Approaches

Section 2
Opinion Mining and Literary Studies

Chuu Htet Naing, School of Computer Sciences, Universiti Sains Malaysia, Malaysia
Xian Zhao, School of Computer Sciences, Universiti Sains Malaysia, Malaysia
Keng Hoon Gan, School of Computer Sciences, Universiti Sains Malaysia, Malaysia
Nur-Hana Samsudin, School of Computer Sciences, Universiti Sains Malaysia, Malaysia

Nurul Najiha Jafery, Faculty of Electrical Engineering, Universiti Teknologi Mara, Malaysia
Pantea Keikhosrokiani, School of Computer Sciences, Universiti Sains Malaysia, Malaysia
Moussa Pourya Asl, School of Humanities, Universiti Sains Malaysia, Malaysia

Nikmatul Husna Binti Suhendra, School of Computer Sciences, Universiti Sains Malaysia,
Malaysia
Pantea Keikhosrokiani, School of Computer Sciences, Universiti Sains Malaysia, Malaysia
Moussa Pourya Asl, School of Humanities, Universiti Sains Malaysia, Malaysia
Xian Zhao, School of Computer Sciences, Universiti Sains Malaysia, Malaysia

Nurfatin Binti Sofian, School of Computer Sciences, Universiti Sains Malaysia, Malaysia
Pantea Keikhosrokiani, School of Computer Sciences, Universiti Sains Malaysia, Malaysia
Moussa Pourya Asl, School of Humanities, Universiti Sains Malaysia, Malaysia

Md Habib Al Mamun, School of Computer Sciences, Universiti Sains Malaysia, Malaysia
Pantea Keikhosrokiani, School of Computer Sciences, Universiti Sains Malaysia, Malaysia
Moussa Pourya Asl, School of Humanities, Universiti Sains Malaysia, Malaysia
Nur Ain Nasuha Anuar, School of Humanities, Universiti Sains Malaysia, Malaysia
Nurfarah Hadira Abdul Hadi, School of Humanities, Universiti Sains Malaysia, Malaysia
Thasnim Humida, Dept. of Mass Communication and Journalism, Begum Rokeya University,
Rangpur, Bangladesh

Detailed Table of Contents

Section 1
Reviews, Techniques, and Approaches

Chapter 1

    David Valle-Cruz, Autonomous University of the State of Mexico, Mexico
    Asdrúbal López-Chau, Autonomous University of the State of Mexico, Mexico
    Rodrigo Sandoval-Almazán, Autonomous University of the State of Mexico, Mexico

This chapter presented an analysis of the application of lexicon-based political sentiment analysis in social media. The aim is to identify the most frequently used lexicons in political sentiment analysis, their results, similarities, and differences. For this, the authors conducted a systematic literature review based on PRISMA methodology. Afinn, NRC, and SenticNet lexicons are tested and combined for data analysis from the 2020 U.S. presidential campaign. Findings show that political sentiment analysis is a new field studied for only 10 years. Political sentiment analysis could generate benefits in understanding problems such as political polarization, discourse analysis, politician influence, candidate profiling, and improving government-citizen interaction, among other problems in the public sphere, enhanced by the combination of lexicons and multimodal analysis. The authors conclude that polarity was one of the critical dimensions identified for finding variations in the behavior and polarity of sentiments. Limitations and future work also are presented.

Chapter 2

    Santoshi Kumari, RUAS, India

A huge amount of unstructured data is generated from social media platforms like Twitter. Volume of tweets and the velocity with which they are generated on various topics presents extensive challenges in data analytics and processing techniques. Linguistic flexibility for writing tweets presents many challenges in preprocessing and natural language processing tasks. Addressing these challenges, this chapter aims to select, modify, and apply information retrieval and preprocessing steps for retrieving, storing, organizing, and cleaning real-time large-scale unstructured Twitter data. The work focuses on reviewing the previous research and applying suitable preprocessing methods to improve the quality of data by removing unessential data. It is also observed that using tweeter APIs and access tokens provides easy access to real-time tweets. Preprocessing methods are fundamental steps of text analytics and NLP tasks to process unstructured data. Analyzing suitable preprocessing methods like tokenization, removal of stop word, stemming, and lemmatization are applied to normalize the extracted Twitter data.

In recent years, data analysis has been widely applied in many different domains. Text data plays an important role in prediction of various insights. The data produced in the form of user reviews, satisfactory forms, movie reviews, after sales product reviews, and similar kinds of representations serve as inputs for textual data analysis. In previous years, however, companies relied on paper-based satisfactory surveys, agent reports, etc. for business development or product outreach development purposes. As these methods involve human intervention, there is always a very high chance of false inputs. Hence, the development of computational intelligence-based strategies such as textual and sentimental analysis have been of enormous help for such companies. Automated tools and software have helped various business organizations and firms to develop their business, find their faults and bugs, and relieve themselves from their limitations. This chapter discusses the basics of textual analysis, approaches for textual analysis, as well as the tools, solutions, and some limitations of applying textual analysis.

Comparative opinion contains contrasting views of products (e.g., which aspect of a product is better or worse). Most existing works for comparative opinion mining focus on single comparative sentences but have yet explored the benefits of additional comparative details in neighbouring sentences of a comparative sentence. Motivated by the needs to exploit these supporting details, this chapter proposes an approach to identify the link between a comparative sentence and its neighbouring sentences. As contextual similarity between comparative sentence and neighbouring sentence is crucial to determine their relatedness, contextual features of these two sentences are exploited to measure the similarity between them. Then, linear-chain conditional random field (CRF) is used to identify neighbouring sentence that is related to comparative sentence. Detection of supporting neighbouring sentence using linear-chain CRF with optimized contextual features (cosine similarity, Wordnet similarity, and comparative keywords) outperforms sentence similarity baseline by 4% in accuracy and 0.06 in F-score.

Semantic similarity is a fundamental concept in computational linguistics. The models used for the representation of text have a major role in similarity computation. The text with multilingual and multimodal components shows the need for computing similarity based on different characteristics of text. This chapter studies various aspects of semantic similarity of linguistic units, cross-level similarity, semantic models, and similarity measures. One of the main motivations of this chapter is to analyze semantic similarity models such as geometric models, feature-based models, graph-based models, vector space models, and formal concept analysis models. In addition, a composite summary score based on words and hashtags is applied for the tweet summarization task which is effective when compared with other measures.

Chapter 6

Nikhil V. Chandran, Kerala University of Digital Sciences, Innovation, and Technology, India
Anoop V. S., Kerala University of Digital Sciences, Innovation, and Technology, India
Asharaf S., Kerala University of Digital Sciences, Innovation, and Technology, India

Social media platforms have incorporated more than half of the world's population, making it one of the most data-rich domains recently. The sentiments expressed by social media users hold great significance for various reasons, such as the identification of public opinion on a product or towards a governmental policy, to name a few. There are different domains where companies use social media sentiments to gather feedback from customers to provide them with better products and services. Only a few attempts have been reported on aspect-based sentiment analysis literature on sentiment analysis and opinion mining. This chapter proposes a framework for aspect-based sentiment analysis for social media using a topic modeling-powered approach. The experiments conducted on real-world datasets show that the proposed framework outperforms some existing works on aspect-oriented sentiment analysis.

Section 2
Opinion Mining and Literary Studies

Chapter 7

Chuu Htet Naing, School of Computer Sciences, Universiti Sains Malaysia, Malaysia
Xian Zhao, School of Computer Sciences, Universiti Sains Malaysia, Malaysia
Keng Hoon Gan, School of Computer Sciences, Universiti Sains Malaysia, Malaysia
Nur-Hana Samsudin, School of Computer Sciences, Universiti Sains Malaysia, Malaysia

Descriptions of love can be found in a wide range of literature. The meaning of love that a reader grasps from reading a literary work is mostly the result of self-understanding and is very likely different from the one that the author tried to express. Therefore, it is interesting to explore what love is from the authors' perspective to help readers have a deeper understanding of the meaning of love written by the author. The goal of this study is to build a text analysis framework to identify common words or phrases describing love in romance literature. The proposed analysis is divided into three types, namely 1) text classification and sentiment analysis, 2) key phrase extraction, and 3) topic modeling. The evaluation is performed on 10 romance books. The results of each analysis method are measured using performance metrics as well as presented using visuals like word cloud and histogram.

Chapter 8

Nurul Najiha Jafery, Faculty of Electrical Engineering, Universiti Teknologi Mara, Malaysia
Pantea Keikhosrokiani, School of Computer Sciences, Universiti Sains Malaysia, Malaysia
Moussa Pourya Asl, School of Humanities, Universiti Sains Malaysia, Malaysia

The rapid advancements in data science techniques and approaches have influenced disciplines, such as literary studies, that are particularly engaged in qualitative text analysis. This chapter aims to apply natural language preprocessing (NLP) to identify the connection between theme and sentiment in a corpus of six life writings by or about Iraqi people. To do so, the study uses Latent Dirichlet Allocation (LDA) from topic modeling and the two models of Gensim and Mallet. It also implements TextBlob dictionary to calculate the polarity and subjectivity scores to measure the sentiment for detected themes. Nine topics are extracted from both models. The extracted themes point to the prevalence of traumatic events that the authors have personally endured. Gensim works better than Mallet as it has high coherence score and relevant terms. In sentiment analysis, most of the themes appeared as positive. The application of LDA using Gensim also revealed that the selected life writings are shaped and influenced by the authors' personal feelings. It is hoped that the analytical models can encourage future studies to improve existing qualitative methods in literary studies.

Chapter 9

    Nikmatul Husna Binti Suhendra, School of Computer Sciences, Universiti Sains Malaysia, Malaysia
    Pantea Keikhosrokiani, School of Computer Sciences, Universiti Sains Malaysia, Malaysia
    Moussa Pourya Asl, School of Humanities, Universiti Sains Malaysia, Malaysia
    Xian Zhao, School of Computer Sciences, Universiti Sains Malaysia, Malaysia

Text mining is an important field of study that has proved beneficial for scholars of various disciplines. Literary scholars use text mining to examine the data produced by creative writers, literary readers, publishers, and distributing companies. The produced data are generally in unstructured form that cannot be used to extract useful information. Text mining can discover the unstructured data and convert it to interesting information through several processes. This chapter proposes a text mining technique by using topic modelling and sentiment analysis to retrieve information about the attitude of the user-readers toward the four volumes of KL Noir books on the Goodreads website. The main significance of this approach is to gain the trends by analyzing the book reviews written on Goodreads.

Chapter 10

    Nurfatin Binti Sofian, School of Computer Sciences, Universiti Sains Malaysia, Malaysia
    Pantea Keikhosrokiani, School of Computer Sciences, Universiti Sains Malaysia, Malaysia
    Moussa Pourya Asl, School of Humanities, Universiti Sains Malaysia, Malaysia

With the development of online social network platforms and social cataloging applications, large amounts of datasets are being generated daily in the form of users' reviews, evaluations, and instant messages. Readers of literary books from around the world now use social media to express their thoughts and feelings about literary works. Collecting and analyzing textual data to gain insight about the readers' interest poses a huge challenge to literary scholars and publishing industries. In this study, the authors aim to apply text analytics methods to analyze and interpret reader responses in the form of book reviews. To this end, they focus on readers' responses and reviews to Yōko Ogawa's The Housekeeper and the Professor (2003) as documented in Goodreads, a social cataloging website that allows readers across the globe to interact with each other about books. The collected data are preprocessed and explored and visualized to gain insight on public opinion about the novel. Finally, the authors analyze the collected data on Goodreads platform by using topic modelling and sentiment analysis in this chapter.

Md Habib Al Mamun, School of Computer Sciences, Universiti Sains Malaysia, Malaysia

Pantea Keikhosrokiani, School of Computer Sciences, Universiti Sains Malaysia, Malaysia

Moussa Pourya Asl, School of Humanities, Universiti Sains Malaysia, Malaysia

Nur Ain Nasuha Anuar, School of Humanities, Universiti Sains Malaysia, Malaysia

Nurfarah Hadira Abdul Hadi, School of Humanities, Universiti Sains Malaysia, Malaysia

Thasnim Humida, Dept. of Mass Communication and Journalism, Begum Rokeya University, Rangpur, Bangladesh

The objective of this chapter is to conduct a sentiment analysis of the Harry Potter novel series written by British author J.K. Rowling. The text of the series is collected from GitHub as an R package provided by Bradley Boehmke. The chapter analyzed the text by R programming to explore dominant sentiments using a lexicon approach of natural language processing (NLP). The results revealed that Professor Slughorn scored the most positive sentiment among the main characters that have heroic qualities; Death Eaters had the most negative sentiment among the anti-hero characters; negative sentiment in the text around the anti-hero characters increased significantly, while the positive sentiment around the hero characters remained constant as the story progressed throughout the series; among the series of novels, The Deathly Hallows contained the most negative sentiment; among all the houses of Hogwarts School of Witchcraft and Wizardry, Hufflepuff had the most positive sentiment; and each book of the series appeared negative until the final chapter, which always ended with a positive sentiment.

Section 3
Opinion Mining and Social Media

Marilyn Minicucci Ibañez, National Institute of Space Research, Brazil & Federal Institute of São Paulo, Brazil

Reinaldo Roberto Rosa, National Institute for Space Research, Brazil

Lamartine Nogueira Frutuoso Guimarães, Institute for Advanced Studies, Brazil & Instituto Tecnológico de Aeronáutica, Brazil & National Institute for Space Research, Brazil

In recent decades, the internet access growth has generated a substantial increase in the information circulation in social media. Within the information variety circulating on the internet, extreme social events such as armed conflicts have become areas of great public interest because of their direct influence on society. The study of such data from social media is useful in understanding an event's evolution, in particular how threats over time can generate an endogenous evolution resulting in an extreme event. This chapter uses the technique of sentiment analysis to identify the threat degree of news about armed conflicts distributed in social media. This analysis generates an endogenous threat time series that is used to predict the future threat variation of the analyzed extreme social events. In the prediction of the endogenous time series, the authors apply the deep learning technique in a structure that uses the long short-term memory (LSTM) neural network.

Chapter 13

Haseeb Ahmad, National Textile University, Pakistan
Faiza Nasir, National Textile University, Pakistan
C. M. Nadeem Faisal, National Textile University, Pakistan
Shahbaz Ahmad, National Textile University, Pakistan

Depression is considered among the most common mental disorders impacting the daily lives of people around the globe. Online social media has provided individuals the platforms to share their emotions and feelings; therefore, the depressive individuals may also be identified by processing the content. The advancements of natural language processing have provided the methods for depression detection from the content. This chapter intends to highlight the mainstream contributions for depression detection from the text contents shared on online social media. More precisely, hierarchical-based segregation is adopted for detailing the research contributions in the underlying domain. The top hierarchy depicts early detection and generic studies, followed by method, online social media, and community-based segregation. The subsequent hierarchy contains machine learning, deep learning, and hybrid studies in the context of method, Facebook, Twitter, and Reddit in terms of online social media, and general, literary, and geography as subhierarchies of community.

Chapter 14

Elise Noga-Hartmann, ETIS UMR 8051, CY Cergy Paris University, France
Dimitris Kotzinos, ETIS UMR 8051, CY Cergy Paris University, France

This chapter proposes and explores all features of a model capable of capturing trends within large corpora of texts. Not only are trends assessed through a numerical index, but they are displayed alongside rhetorical and attitudinal information on all topics concerned for all relevant epochs. This way, trend evolutions can be analyzed in the light of wordings and thinking evolutions, thus allowing for a co-evolutionary approach to trend assessing. Each and every step is methodologically explained, as well as the interactions between them. Variations and adaptations are also discussed for a greater adaptability of the model to all use cases.

Chapter 15

Doğan Küçük, Gazi University, Turkey
Nursal Arıcı, Gazi University, Turkey

Public health surveillance has gained more importance recently due the global COVID-19 pandemic. It is important to track public opinions and positions on social media automatically, so that this information can be used to improve public health. Sentiment analysis and stance detection are two social media analysis methods that can be applied to health-related social media posts for this purpose. In this chapter, the authors perform sentiment analysis and stance detection in Turkish tweets about COVID-19 vaccination. A sentiment- and stance-annotated Turkish tweet dataset about COVID-19 vaccination is created. Different machine learning approaches (SVM and Random Forest) are applied on this dataset, and the results are compared. Widespread COVID-19 vaccination is claimed to be useful in order to cope with this pandemic. Therefore, results of automatic sentiment and stance analysis on Twitter posts on COVID-19 vaccination can help public health professionals during their decision-making processes.

Chapter 16
Rigoberto García-Contreras, Autonomous University of the State of Mexico, Mexico
J. Patricia Muñoz-Chávez, Technological University of the Metropolitan Area of the Valley
     of Mexico, Mexico
David Valle-Cruz, Autonomous University of the State of Mexico, Mexico
Asdrúbal López-Chau, Autonomous University of the State of Mexico, Mexico

The COVID-19 pandemic has become a critical and disruptive event that has substantially changed the way people live and work. Although several studies have examined the effects of remote work on organizational outcomes and behaviors, only a few have inquired into how its opportune implementation impacts aggregate emotions over time. This chapter aims to conduct a sentiment analysis with public reactions on Twitter about telework during the pandemic period. The results showed fluctuations in emotional polarity, starting with a higher positive charge in the early pandemic scenarios that became weaker, and the negative polarity of emotions increased. Fear, sadness, and anger were the emotions that increased the most during the pandemic. Knowledge about people's sentiments about telework is important to complement organizational research and to complement the framework for the development of efficient telework implementation strategies.

Preface

Over the past few decades, scholars of various disciplines have growingly acknowledged the importance of readers' responses and reactions both in giving meaning to a text and in its commercial success or disaster. Previous studies have shown that readers' emotions and responses to literary texts are of increasing interest to publishers and booksellers for marketing purposes and to sponsoring organizations in granting awards. Over the past two decades, the rapid advancements in information technologies and the emergence of different social media platforms have provided unprecedented opportunities for readers across the globe to interact with each other and express their thoughts and feelings about literary writings. Literary enthusiasts around the world increasingly use digital platforms such as Twitter, Goodreads, Facebook, among many others, to share their thoughts on their favorite novels, stories, plays, characters, scenes, and themes. As a result, the digital space has become a potential gold mine of readers' responses and public reactions for individuals, companies and organizations who are interested in understanding growing trends. That said, it is noteworthy that the impartiality of readers' responses to creative writings has long been a matter of critical debate. Public and critical analyses of creative works are often charged with biased and inaccurate understanding of the works. This particular problem is rooted in the traditional methods of manual data collection and analysis that fail to provide analytical precision and accuracy, especially when it comes to the analysis of representations and expressions of sentiments in relation to the underlying themes of a work of art.

In recent years, advancements in computer sciences and information technologies have benefited various disciplines in academia including the field of literary studies. Nowadays, literary scholars enjoy the opportunity to adopt computerized analytical methods to analyze a text or to examine the interconnection between its content and a reader's response. Opinion Mining, Text Analytics methods such Topic Modelling and Sentiment Analysis are among the most popular methods and techniques that researchers employ to carry out studies on themes, characterizations, reader's responses, sentiments, and viewpoints. A primary goal of this book is to explore recent developments and applications within this field.

Opinion mining is considered as a Natural Language Processing (NLP) technique for determining the emotional tone of a body of text. The information obtained from such analysis may be used for a variety of purposes. Therefore, an in-depth examination of how opinion mining and text analytics contribute to studies on literary works and social media is of timely significance. In this regard, this book aims to introduce advancements in applications of artificial intelligence and data analytics techniques that can be used to apply opinion mining and text analytics on literary works and social media. This book focuses on reviews, techniques, models, and approaches of data science that can be applied for analyzing texts from literary books and social media.

Figure 1. Opinion mining and text analytics on literary works and social media

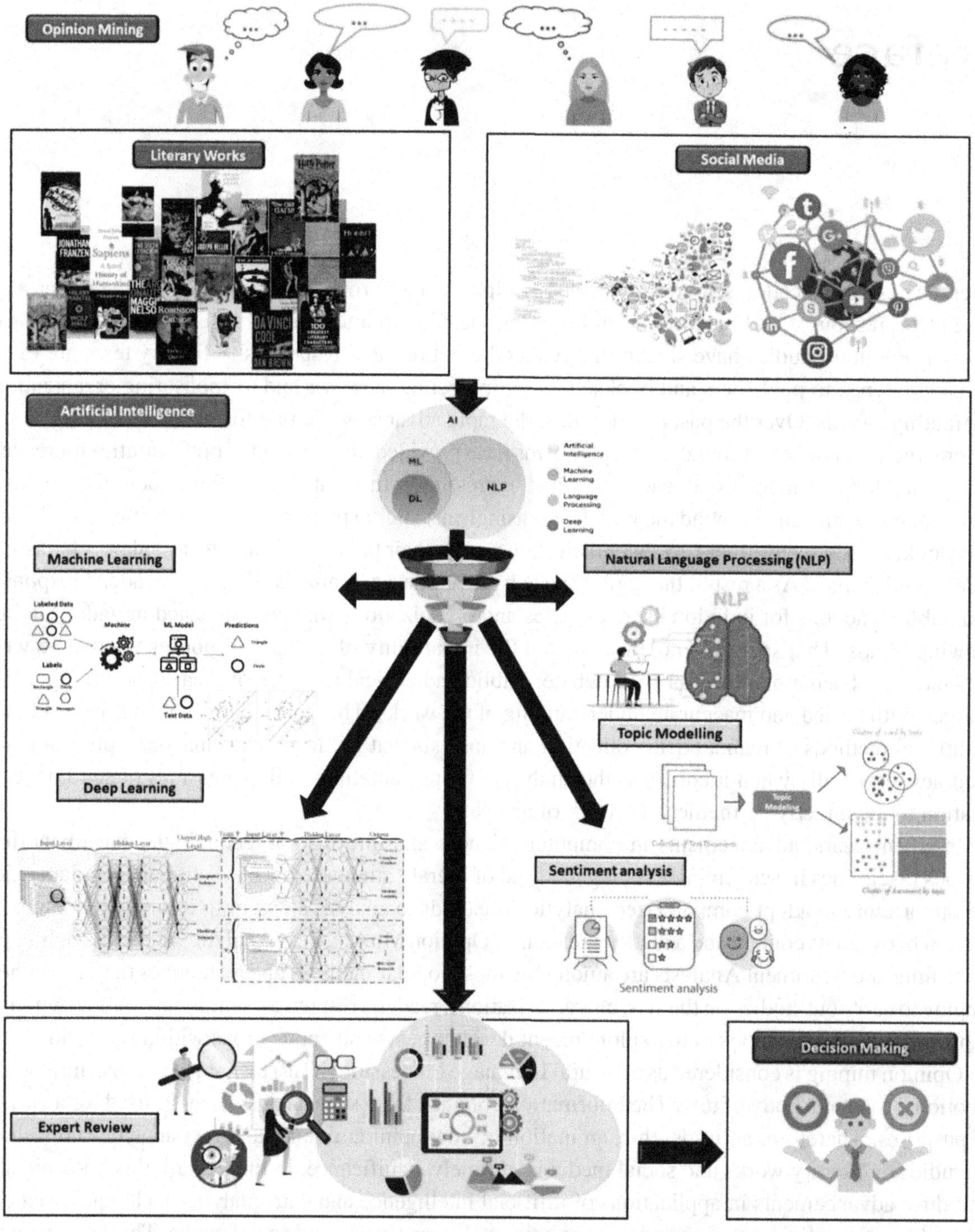

Figure 1 illustrates a general overview of the present volume in which opinion mining is the central approach adopted for various purposes. Different datasets from literary works such as life writings, novels, romance writings, readers' comments in online platforms, as well as texts from social media such as tweets, newspaper articles, Facebook posts, magazines, and book reviews are used for the purpose of analyses. After data pre-processing and data cleaning steps, various artificial intelligence techniques such as Natural Language Processing (NLP)—in particular topic modelling and sentiment analysis—machine learning, and deep learning are utilized to analyze the texts, create visualization, and generate meaningful information for assisting experts in making better conclusions. In this process, expert researchers review the results, validate them, and interpret them accordingly. The final results can be used by literary scholars, politicians, sociologists, publishing companies, news agencies, social media networks, for better decision making.

The present book is an interdisciplinary project that engages various disciplines such as literary studies, computer sciences, data sciences, communication and social media studies. It covers a wide range of topics such as opinion mining, sentiment analysis, and stance detection. Therefore, the book would be of great interest and importance to academicians, companies, agencies and organizations. In academia, the publication will benefit researchers, lecturers, and students by providing them with new insights into different fields such as digital humanities, digital transformation, digital literature, social science, and data science. The book is also beneficial for publishing companies by offering them new techniques and methods to study public reactions and interests. Moreover, the present volume can be helpful to sponsoring agencies and organizations who are seeking for computerized methods to detect current trends and identify popular books or publications to grant awards and prizes. And finally, the project is useful to policy makers and decision-making organizations that need to find a meaningful pattern in both public and critical responses in order to make large scale decisions.

ORGANIZATION OF THE BOOK

This book consists of three main sections that together are comprised of 16 chapters. Section 1 is entitled "Reviews, Techniques, and Models" and includes the following six chapters:

Chapter 1: Review on the Application of Lexicon-based Political Sentiment Analysis in Social Media
David Valle-Cruz, Asdrúbal López-Chau, Rodrigo Sandoval-Almazán

This chapter presented an analysis of the application of lexicon-based political sentiment analysis in social media. The aim is to identify the most frequently used lexicons in political sentiment analysis, their results, similarities, and differences. For this, the authors conducted a systematic literature review based on PRISMA methodology. Afinn, NRC, and SenticNet lexicons are tested and combined for data analysis from the 2020 U.S. presidential campaign. Findings show that political sentiment analysis is a new field studied for only ten years. Political sentiment analysis could generate benefits in understanding problems such as political polarization, discourse analysis, politician influence, candidate profiling, and improving government-citizen interaction, among other problems in the public sphere, enhanced by the combination of lexicons and multimodal analysis. The authors conclude that polarity was one of the critical dimensions identified for finding variations in the behavior and polarity of sentiments. Limitations and future work are also presented.

Chapter 2: Text Mining and Pre-Processing Methods for Social Media Data Extraction and Analytics

Santoshi Kumari

Huge amount of unstructured data is generated from social media platforms like Twitter. Volume of tweets, the velocity with which they are generating, on various topics presents extensive challenges in data analytics and processing techniques. Linguistic flexibility for writing tweet presents many challenges in preprocessing and natural language processing tasks. Addressing these challenges this paper aims to select, modify and apply information retrieval and preprocessing steps for retrieving, storing, and organizing, and cleaning real-time large scale unstructured Twitter data. This study focuses on reviewing the previous research and applying suitable preprocessing methods to improve the quality of data by removing unessential data. It is observed that using tweeter APIs and access tokens provides easy access to real-time tweets. Preprocessing methods are fundamental steps of text analytics and NLP tasks to process unstructured data. Analyzing suitable preprocessing methods like tokenization, removal of stop word, stemming, lemmatization and applied to normalize the extracted Twitter data.

Chapter 3: A Review of Text Analytics Using Machine Learning

Ajaypradeep Natarajsivam, Sasikala R.

In recent years, data analysis has been widely applied in many different domains. Especially text data plays an important role in prediction of various insights. The data produced in the form of user reviews, satisfactory forms, movie reviews, after sales product reviews and similar kind of representations serves as input for textual data analysis. In previous years, however, companies relied on paper-based satisfactory surveys, agent reports, etc. for business development or product outreach development purposes. As these methods involve human intervention, there is always a very high chance of false inputs. Hence, the development of computational intelligence-based strategies such as textual and sentimental analysis have been of enormous help for such companies. Automated tools and software have helped various business organizations and firms to develop their business, find their faults, bugs and relieve themselves from their limitations. This chapter discusses the basics of textual analysis, approaches for textual analysis, as well as the tools, solutions, and some limitations of applying textual analysis.

Chapter 4: Improving Comparative Opinion Mining Through Detection of Support Sentences

Teck Keat Yeow, Keng Hoon Gan

Comparative opinion contains contrasting views of products e.g., which aspect of product is better or worse. Most existing works for comparative opinion mining focus on single comparative sentences but have yet explored the benefits of additional comparative details in neighbouring sentences of a comparative sentence. Motivated by the needs to exploit these supporting details, this chapter proposes an approach to identify the link between a comparative sentence and its neighbouring sentences. As contextual similarity between comparative sentence and neighbouring sentence is crucial to determine their relatedness, contextual features of these two sentences are exploited to measure the similarity between them. Then, linear-chain Conditional Random Field (CRF) is used to identify neighbouring sentence that is related to comparative sentence. Detection of supporting neighbouring sentence using linear-chain CRF with optimized contextual features (cosine similarity, Wordnet similarity and comparative keywords) outperforms sentence similarity baseline by 4% in accuracy and 0.06 in F-score.

Chapter 5: Features of Semantic Similarity Assessment – Content- and Model-Based Perspectives
Vijayarani J., Geetha T. V.

Semantic similarity is a fundamental concept in computational linguistics. The models used for the representation of text have a major role in similarity computation. The text with multilingual and multimodal components insists the need for computing similarity based on different characteristics of text. This chapter studies various aspects of semantic similarity of linguistic units, cross-level similarity, semantic models and similarity measures. One of the main motivations of this chapter is to analyze semantic similarity models such as geometric models, feature-based models, graph-based models, vector space models and formal concept analysis models. In addition, a composite summary score based on words and hashtags is applied for the tweet summarization task which is effective when compared with other measures.

Chapter 6: A Topic Modeling-guided Framework for Aspect-Oriented Sentiment Analysis on Social Media
Nikhil Chandran, Anoop V. S., Asharaf S.

Social media platforms have incorporated more than half of the world's population, making it one of the most data-rich domains recently. The sentiments expressed by social media users hold great significance for various reasons, such as the identification of public opinion on a product or towards a governmental policy, to name a few. There are different domains where companies use social media sentiments to gather feedback from customers to provide them with better products and services. Only a few attempts have been reported on aspect-based sentiment analysis in the literature on sentiment analysis and opinion mining. This chapter proposes a framework for aspect-based sentiment analysis for social media using a topic modeling-powered approach. The experiments conducted on real-world datasets show that the proposed framework outperforms some existing works on aspect-oriented sentiment analysis.

Section 2 is entitled "Opinion Mining and Literary Studies." It includes the following five chapters:

Chapter 7: What Is Love? Text Analytics on the Romance Literature From the Perspective of Authors
Chuu Htet Naing, Xian Zhao, Keng Hoon Gan, Nur-Hana Samsudin

Descriptions of love can be found in a wide range of literature. The meaning of love that a reader grasps from reading a literary work is mostly the result of self-understanding and is very likely different from the one that the author tried to express. Therefore, it is interesting to explore what love is from the authors' perspective to help readers have a deeper understanding of the meaning of love written by the author. The goal of this study is to build a text analysis framework to identify common words or phrases describing love in romance literature. The proposed analysis is divided into three types, namely i. text classification and sentiment analysis, ii. key phrase extraction and iii. topic modeling. The evaluation is performed on ten romance books. The results of each analysis method are measured using performance metrics as well as presented using visuals like word cloud and histogram.

Chapter 8: Text Analytics Model to Identify the Connection Between Theme and Sentiment in Literary Works – A Case Study of Iraqi Life Writings
Nurul Najiha Jafery, Pantea Keikhosrokiani, Moussa Pourya Asl

The rapid advancements in data science techniques and approaches have influenced disciplines, such as literary studies, that are particularly engaged in qualitative text analysis. This chapter aims to apply Natural Language Preprocessing (NLP) to identify the connection between theme and sentiment in a corpus of six life writings by or about Iraqi people. To do so, the study uses Latent Dirichlet Allocation (LDA) from topic modeling and the two models of Gensim and Mallet. It also implements TextBlob dictionary to calculate the polarity and subjectivity scores to measure the sentiment for detected themes. Nine topics are extracted from both models. The extracted themes point to the prevalence of traumatic events that the authors have personally endured. Gensim works better than Mallet as it has high coherence score and relevant terms. In sentiment analysis, most of the themes appeared as positive. The application of LDA using Gensim also revealed that the selected life writings are shaped and influenced by the authors' personal feelings. It is hoped that the analytical models can encourage future studies to improve existing qualitative methods in literary studies.

Chapter 9: Opinion Mining and Text Analytics of Literary Readers' Responses – A Case Study of Reader Response to KL Noir Volumes in Goodreads Using Sentiment Analysis and Topic
Nikmatul Husna Binti Suhendra, Pantea Keikhosrokiani, Moussa Pourya Asl, Xian Zhao

Text mining is an important field of study that has proved beneficial for scholars of various disciplines. Literary scholars use text mining to examine the data produced by creative writers, literary readers, publishers and distributing companies. The produced data are generally in unstructured form that cannot be used to extract useful information. Text mining can discover the unstructured data and convert it to interesting information through several processes. This paper proposes a text mining technique by using topic modelling and sentiment analysis to retrieve information about the attitude of the user-readers toward the four volumes of KL Noir books in Goodreads website. The main significance of this approach is to gain the trends by analyzing the book reviews written in Goodreads websites.

Chapter 10: Opinion Mining and Text Analytics of Reader Reviews of Yoko Ogawa's *The Housekeeper and the Professor* in Goodreads
Nurfatin Binti Sofian, Pantea Keikhosrokiani, Moussa Pourya Asl

With the development of online social network platforms and social cataloging applications, large amounts of datasets are being generated daily in the form of users' reviews, evaluations, and instant messages. Readers of literary books from around the world now use social media to express their thoughts and feelings about literary works. Collecting and analyzing textual data to gain insight about the readers' interest poses a huge challenge to literary scholars and publishing industries. In this study, we aim to apply text analytics methods to analyze and interpret reader responses in the form of book reviews. To this end, we focus on readers' responses and reviews to Yōko Ogawa's *The Housekeeper and the Professor* (2003) as documented in Goodreads, a social cataloging website that allows readers across the globe to interact with each other about books. The collected data are preprocessed and explored and visualized to gain insight on public opinion about the novel. Finally, we analyze the collected data on Goodreads platform by using topic modelling and sentiment analysis in this paper.

Chapter 11: Sentiment Analysis of Harry Potter Series Using Lexicon-Based Approach
Md Habib Al Mamun, Pantea Keikhosrokiani, Moussa Pourya Asl, Nur Ain Nasuha Anuar, Nurfarah Hadira Abdul Hadi, Thasnim Humida

The objective of this paper is to conduct a sentiment analysis of Harry Potter novel series written by British Author J.K. Rowling. The text of the series is collected from GitHub as an R package provided by Bradley Boehmke. The paper analyzed the text by R programming to explore dominant sentiments using a lexicon approach of Natural Language Processing (NLP). The results revealed that Professor Slughorn scored the most positive sentiment among the main characters that have heroic qualities; Death

Eaters had the most negative sentiment among the anti-hero characters; negative sentiment in the text around the anti-hero characters increased significantly, while the positive sentiment around the hero characters remained constant as the story progressed throughout the series; among the series of novel the Deathly Hallows contained the most negative sentiment; among all the houses of Hogwarts School of Witchcraft and Wizardry, Hufflepuff had the most positive sentiment; and each book of the series appeared negative until the final chapter which always ended with a positive sentiment.

The third section is entitled "Opinion Mining and Social Media," which comprises of the following five chapters:

Chapter 12: Threat Emotion Analysis in the Social Medias, Considering Armed Conflict as Social Extreme Events

Marilyn Ibañez, Reinaldo Rosa, Lamartine Guimarães

In recent decades, the Internet access growth has generated a substantial increase in the information circulation in the social medias. Within the information variety circulating on the internet, extreme social events such as armed conflicts have become areas of great public interest because of their direct influence on society. The study of such data from social media is useful in understanding an event's evolution, in particular how threats over time can generate an endogenous evolution resulting in an extreme event. This chapter uses the technique of sentiment analysis to identify the threat degree of news about armed conflicts distributed in social media. This analysis generates an endogenous threat time series that are used to predict the future threat variation of the analyzed extreme social events. In the prediction of the endogenous time series applies the Deep Learning technique in a structure that uses the Long-Short Term Memory-LSTM neural network.

Chapter 13: Depression Detection in Online Social Media Users Using Natural Language Processing Techniques

Haseeb Ahmad, Faiza Nasir, C. M. Nadeem Faisal, Shahbaz Ahmad

Depression is considered among the most common mental disorders impacting the daily lives of people around the globe. Online social media has provided individuals the platforms to share their emotions and feelings, therefore, the depressive individuals may also be identified by processing the content. The advancements of natural language processing have provided the methods for depression detection from the content. This chapter intends to highlight the mainstream contributions for depression detection from the text contents shared on online social media. More precisely, hierarchical-based segregation is adopted for detailing the research contributions in the underlying domain. The top hierarchy depicts early detection and generic studies, followed by method, online social media, and community-based segregation. The subsequent hierarchy contains machine learning, deep learning, and hybrid studies in the context of method, facebook, twitter, and reddit in terms of online social media, and general, literary, and geography as subhierarchies of community.

Chapter 14: Assessing Together the Trends in Newspaper's Topics and User Opinions – A Co-Evolutionary Approach

Elise Noga-Hartmann, Dimitris Kotzinos

This chapter proposes and explores all features of a model capable of capturing trends within large corpora of texts. Not only are trends assessed through a numerical index, but they are displayed alongside rhetorical and attitudinal information on all topics concerned for all relevant epochs. This way, trend's evolutions can be analyzed in the light of wordings and thinking evolutions, thus allowing for a co-evolutionary approach to trend assessing. Each and every step is methodologically explained, as well as the interactions in-between them. Variations and adaptations are also discussed for a greater adaptability of the model to all use cases.

Chapter 15: Sentiment Analysis and Stance Detection in Turkish Tweets About COVID-19 Vaccination

Doğan Küçük, Nursal Arıcı

Public health surveillance has gained more importance recently due the global COVID-19 pandemic. It is important to track public opinions and positions on social media automatically, so that this information can be used to improve general public health. Sentiment analysis and stance detection are two social media analysis methods that can be applied to health related social media posts for this purpose. In this book chapter, the authors perform sentiment analysis and stance detection in Turkish tweets about COVID-19 vaccination. A sentiment- and stance-annotated Turkish tweet dataset about COVID-19 vaccination is created. Different machine learning approaches (SVM and Random Forest) are applied on this dataset and the results are compared. Widespread COVID-19 vaccination is claimed to be useful in order to cope with this pandemic. Therefore, results of automatic sentiment and stance analysis on Twitter posts on COVID-19 vaccination can help public health professionals during their decision making processes.

Chapter 16: Teleworkers' Experiences in #COVID-19 – Insights Through Sentiment Analysis in Social Media

Rigoberto García-Contreras, J. Patricia Muñoz-Chávez, David Valle-Cruz, Asdrúbal López-Chau

The COVID-19 pandemic has become a critical and disruptive event that has substantially changed the way of people live and work. Although several studies have examined the effects of remote work on organizational outcomes and behaviors, only a few have inquired into how its opportune implementation impacts aggregate emotions over time. This chapter aims to conduct a sentiment analysis with public reactions on Twitter about telework during the pandemic period. The results showed fluctuations in emotional polarity, starting with a higher positive charge in the early pandemic scenarios that became weaker, and the negative polarity of emotions increased. Fear, sadness, and anger were the emotions that increased the most during the pandemic. Knowledge about people's sentiments about telework is important to complement organizational research and to complement the framework for the development of efficient telework implementation strategies.

Finally, we would like to thank all the contributors and reviewers for their high-quality and intellectual works.

Section 1
Reviews, Techniques, and Approaches

Chapter 1
Review on the Application of Lexicon-Based Political Sentiment Analysis in Social Media

David Valle-Cruz
Autonomous University of the State of Mexico, Mexico

Asdrúbal López-Chau
Autonomous University of the State of Mexico, Mexico

Rodrigo Sandoval-Almazán
ⓘ https://orcid.org/0000-0002-7864-6464
Autonomous University of the State of Mexico, Mexico

ABSTRACT

This chapter presented an analysis of the application of lexicon-based political sentiment analysis in social media. The aim is to identify the most frequently used lexicons in political sentiment analysis, their results, similarities, and differences. For this, the authors conducted a systematic literature review based on PRISMA methodology. Afinn, NRC, and SenticNet lexicons are tested and combined for data analysis from the 2020 U.S. presidential campaign. Findings show that political sentiment analysis is a new field studied for only 10 years. Political sentiment analysis could generate benefits in understanding problems such as political polarization, discourse analysis, politician influence, candidate profiling, and improving government-citizen interaction, among other problems in the public sphere, enhanced by the combination of lexicons and multimodal analysis. The authors conclude that polarity was one of the critical dimensions identified for finding variations in the behavior and polarity of sentiments. Limitations and future work also are presented.

DOI: 10.4018/978-1-7998-9594-7.ch001

INTRODUCTION

Opinion mining and sentiment analysis has been applied to different areas of knowledge such as marketing, business, finance, and political contexts (Bing et al., 2012; Charalabidis et al., 2015; Valle-Cruz, Lopez-Chau, et al., 2021; Vinodhini & Chandrasekaran, 2012; Wang et al., 2020). Sentiment analysis allows identifying polarity in social media posts, inherent emotions in texts, images, videos, facial, and body expressions. Specifically, in social networks such as Twitter and Facebook, the analysis of polarity has been widely studied. However, some other classifications and models allow a multimodal analysis to determine different dimensions of emotional charges (Cambria et al., 2020; Valle-Cruz, Lopez-Chau, et al., 2021). Sentiment analysis, a neuralgic technique in natural language processing (Bing, 2012), is useful for social media analysis in different kinds of applications. These applications include prediction, profiling, emotion, sentiment analysis, polarity, and preference detection (Chau et al., 2021; López-Chau et al., 2020; Sandoval-Almazan & Valle-Cruz, 2020; Valle-Cruz, Fernandez-Cortez, et al., 2021), among others. Regarding the political context studies, from different perspectives, such as public policy, public administration, political campaigns, political communication, and discourse ideology; the analysis of conviction, polarization, as well as the emotions and biases generated are vital to understanding the phenomenon under study and its possible consequences (Rhodes, 2014; Riggs, 1965). In recent decades, the debate generated in social media around the political sphere has gained importance. Throughout the world, candidates use social networks to interact with citizens, express their ideology and promote their campaign promises. Although it is still necessary to campaign in the traditional way - not only virtually - but it has also become relevant to monitor the users' behavior towards the events that happen in the political scene. Political sentiment analysis makes it possible to identify the moods, sentiments, emotions, preferences, and impressions of potential voters in an electoral campaign (Anwar et al., 2021; Sandoval-Almazan & Valle-Cruz, 2020; Valle-Cruz, Lopez-Chau, et al., 2021).

Citizens' sentiments during political campaigns mediate between indifference, distrust, disinterest, hopelessness, anger, empathy, and joy. It is necessary to understand how these sentiments are dealt with, how they emerge, before which realities they are established, in which situations, and how they affect people. Sentiments move people to moral life and not reason. Decision-making and morals are expressions of the pleasure and joy that the pursuit of human happiness brings. Moral and political actions do not depend on reason but depend on the desires, passions, and affections of human beings. This does not mean following Hume's postulates (2004), that we cannot reason about the passions. Citizens acquire a sense of the public when reject -indignation- all those selfish actions that lead to sadness and feel happiness for those actions that bring about a greater good (Hume, 1989). Concern for the common good is a sign of the search for a good and dignified life. Sentiments express the vulnerability and rejection people feel in the face of any situation that shows moral harm. In other words, the preferences, approbations even the indifference of human beings in the face of misfortunes or the violation of rights erode or exalt the sentiments. Sentiments such as irritation and anger are closely related to situations of vulnerability in which people recognize the harm experienced. Sentiments express beliefs and generate reactions, finding a communicative and performative character (Nussbaum, 2006). For this reason, to create fear, a politician must convince the audience that bad things will happen and that such events cannot be prevented. Furthermore, if he/she seeks to generate anger, he must convince the audience that they have caused harm voluntarily and unjustly. The adoption of social media in the political context created a megaphone for political expression and communication, leading to the citizens' emotional exaltation and polarization, as well as the dissemination of subjective information.

Opinion mining allows subjective information extraction through analytical methods (Ying et al., 2020). Opinion analysis of the public sphere is a complex process, which is inevitably structured as a partial view. Social media does not replace the public square; however, it could magnify the perception of democracy and advance in terms of citizen participation (Criado et al., 2013). Social media users generate meaning and emotions to content related to the public sector, reacting emotionally. Consequently, much of the world is immersed in a virtual networked society, where citizens participate and comment instantly, in addition to replying with content that provokes the reaction of more users: the approval or disapproval of public content and public decisions go viral (Goncalves et al., 2015; Valle-Cruz, 2019). One way to understand the phenomena such as political polarization, electoral preferences, approval/disapproval of government decisions, public policies, and citizen satisfaction is with the political sentiment analysis in social media (Elghazaly et al., 2016). Since the analysis of the generated content on social platforms has the potential to work as a radar or sensor to understand the perception and emotions of citizens.

However, a problem when analyzing emotions and sentiment in the social media discourse is the implicit and derived bias from the communication strategy or objective. In addition to the different meanings that words have depending on the context, temporality, and situation. In this manner, a particular problem that arises when analyzing sentiments in social media is the accuracy in detecting polarity; this increases when applying multimodal models to find out multiple emotions (e,g. joy, sadness, anger, fear, surprise, and disgust) (Ekman, 1999). As can be seen, some algorithms detect emotions in social media, and by using a lexicon approach, the detection of emotions and polarity in texts can be performed. Some of the most widely used lexicons are Vader, NLTK, Sentiment 140, Bing Liu, NRC, Affin, and Sentic Net (Anwar et al., 2021; Aslam et al., 2020; Bing, 2012; Cambria et al., 2020; Keshavarz & Abadeh, 2017; Kiritchenko et al., 2014). Although these lexicons have been applied to different phenomena and areas, there is a lack of studies focusing on the political arena. In particular, the analysis of emotional charges in the political sphere is called political sentiment analysis (Dorle & Pise, 2018; Elghazaly et al., 2016; Kermanidis & Maragoudakis, 2013; Nandi & Agrawal, 2016).

Political sentiment analysis seeks to analyze polarity and emotions in political texts. Currently, it is being carried out using two main approaches: a) the use of lexicons and b) machine learning techniques (Cambria et al., 2017; Hussein, 2018; Valle-Cruz et al., 2020). In the first type of approach, the following are used as key elements, a lexicon (a list of entries -words- with their corresponding polarity values) and a strategy for weighting the entries found in the texts. Both elements are combined to calculate the polarity of a complete text. For the second, various features are extracted from documents, and predictive models are generated using previously analyzed and labeled texts. These models can then be applied to new documents to compute their polarities (Calefato et al., 2018; López-Chau et al., 2020; Valle-Cruz, Fernandez-Cortez, et al., 2021; Valle-Cruz, Lopez-Chau, et al., 2021). In this regard, this chapter aims to provide an overview of the application of lexicons in political contexts on Twitter. To achieve this, the authors found out the most frequently used lexicons (MFUL) in the social media political context. Moreover, the authors describe their main characteristics, the processing applied to these lexicons, and their scope, developing an analysis of Twitter posts using some trending topics of the U. S. 2020 political campaign. In addition, three lexicons are compared and combined: Affin, NRC, and SenticNet.

Three research questions guide this chapter, focused on research on the use of lexicons in social media in the political context:

- RQ1: What are the most frequently used lexicons (MFUL) in social media in the political context?
- RQ2: What conclusions or results have been reached by applying the most frequently used lexicons (MFUL)?
- RQ3: What are the similarities and differences between the results obtained with the application of the most frequently used lexicons (MFUL) to the political texts? i.e., Do the results converge or diverge? How similar or different are these results?

The structure of the chapter is as follows. The first section shows the state of the art on political sentiment analysis in social media, based on lexicons. The aim here is to further our understanding of the potential use of lexicons in sentiment analysis, answering research questions one and two. The second section describes the methodology of data analysis on Twitter and the description of each lexicon. The authors use a data collection of Tweets obtained during the U.S. presidential campaign of 2020. Section two and three answer research question 3, and the third section presents the comparative analysis of the lexicons. The final section presents the conclusions, limitations, and future work.

STATE OF THE ART

The purpose of a systematic literature review is to answer one or more research questions. This section is twofold. In the first subsection, the authors explore political sentiment analysis based on the MFUL in social media in the political context. In the second subsection, the authors show the findings of the systematic literature review, based on the PRISMA methodology. In this regard, the second subsection presents the state-of-the-art MFUL in the political context. To achieve this, the authors conducted a systematic literature review in Science Direct, IEEE Xplore, ACM Digital Library, Springer Link, IGI Global, and Google Scholar using the PRISMA methodology.

Systematic Literature Review Based on PRISMA

This section contributes to finding studies of the application of lexicons in political contexts (political sentiment analysis). The paper identification process consisted of 4 steps (See Figure 1).

Step 1: Identification

In the first stage, a logical paper search was performed in Google Scholar, Science Direct, IEEE Xplore, ACM Digital Library, Springer Link, and IGI Global to identify literature related to the application of lexicons in political contexts. In this step, were found 253 papers by performing the logical search "lexicon" AND "political" in the titles, abstracts, and keywords.

Step 2: Screening

In the second stage, 214 repeated papers and non-scientific texts were excluded. A large number of the documents were found in Google Scholar, for this reason, several documents that were not scientific or relevant to the research were discarded. In addition, there were several repeated papers on platforms such as Science Direct, IEEE Xplore, ACM Digital Library, Springer Link, and Google Scholar. Here, 39 papers related to the application of lexicons in political contexts remained.

Figure 1 Flow chart based on PRISMA. The authors identified 18 documents related to the application of lexicons in political campaigns
Source: Created by the authors

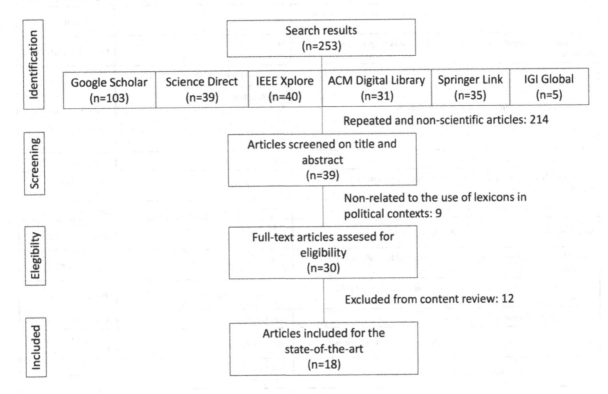

Step 3: Eligibility

In the third stage, titles and abstracts were screened. Nine papers that were not related to the application of lexicons in political contexts were omitted, resulting in 30 papers that were downloaded for in-depth analysis.

Step 4: Included

After analyzing the downloaded papers, 12 papers were discarded because of not been related to the central theme of this research or did not clarify what type of lexicons were used for sentiment analysis. For this reason, the state of the art of the lexicons application in political contexts consists of 18 papers that use or propose sentiment analysis through lexicons (See Table 1).

According to the systematic literature review, were identified 22 lexicons used in political sentiment analysis. Some of them, such as Bing Liu, SenticNet, AFFIN, NRC, and Plutchnik, have been widely used in different contexts. Other lexicons have been adapted to each language (such as Greek), combined with artificial intelligence techniques (such as convolutional neural networks), or blended to obtain better results. Listed below are the most used lexicons (MFUL) in social media in the political context:

1. Bing Liu
2. SentiWordNet
3. SenticNet
4. SentiStrength

Table 1. Lexicons used for political sentiment analysis

Title	Lexicons	Authors
Political Arabic Articles Orientation Using Rough Set Theory with Sentiment Lexicon	Bing Liu	(Alwan et al., 2011)
Opinionetit: Understanding the opinions-people network for politically controversial topics	OpinioNetIt Bing Liu	(Awadallah et al., 2011)
Comparing and combining sentiment analysis methods	Linguistic Inquiry and Word Count (LIWC) SentiStrength SentiWordNet SenticNet SASA Happines Index PANAS-t	(Gonçalves et al., 2013)
Political Opinion Mining from Twitter	SentiWordNet	(Sharma et al., 2016)
Prediction of election result by enhanced sentiment analysis on twitter data using classifier ensemble approach	SentiWordNet	(Jose & Chooralil, 2016)
Identifying political topics in social media messages: A lexicon-based approach	WordNet	(Jackson et al., 2017)
Sentiment analysis of tweets for the 2016 US presidential election	OpinionFinder Bing Liu	(Joyce & Deng, 2017)
Political sentiment mining: A new age intelligence tool for business strategy formulatio	WordNet Hindi SentiWord	(Bele et al., 2017)
A subword-based deep learning approach for sentiment analysis of political tweets	Bing Liu combined with CNN	(Pota et al., 2018)
Predicting political tendency of posts on Facebook	SentiWordNet	(Chiu & Hsu, 2018)
Sentiment Classification-How to Quantify Public Emotions Using Twitter	NRC lexicon	(Mahajan & Rana, 2018)
Stance classification towards political figures on blog writing	Sentiment Lexicon Orthography	(Jannati et al., 2018)
A hybrid method for sentiment analysis of election related tweets	Tsakalidis et al. manually annotated Greek lexicon Bing Liu	(Beleveslis et al., 2019)
Impact for whom? Mapping the users of public research with lexicon-based text mining	Bing Liu	(Bonaccorsi et al., 2021)
How much do Twitter posts affect voters? Analysis of the multi-emotional charge with affective computing in political campaigns	SenticNet	(Valle-Cruz, Lopez-Chau, et al., 2021)
Public sentiment on political campaign using Twitter data in 2017 Jakarta's governor election	SentiStrength	(Mihardi & Budi, 2018)
Emotion analysis of Portuguese Political Parties Communication over the Covid-19 Pandemic	Plutchnik	(Aparicio et al., 2021)
Sentiment Analysis of Political Tweets From the 2019 Spanish Elections	AFINN JAEN Linguakit SBU newLEX	(Rodríguez-Ibáñez et al., 2021)

Source: Created by the authors

5. WordNet
6. AFINN
7. Happines Index
8. Hindi SentiWord
9. JAEN
10. Linguakit

11. Linguistic Inquiry and Word Count
12. newLEX
13. NRC lexicon
14. OpinioNetIt
15. OpinionFinder
16. Orthography
17. PANAS-t
18. Plutchnik
19. SASA
20. SBU
21. Sentiment Lexicon
22. Tsakalidis et al (manually annotated Greek lexicon)

The following subsection presents the state-of-the-art main conclusions or results reached by applying the MFUL in the political context.

Most Frequently Used Lexicons in the Political Context

Sentiment analysis on Twitter has the potential to assess the opinions disseminated through this social media platform. The large volumes of text require tools capable of automatically processing a large amount of data without losing reliability. Sentiment analysis has been a widely used technique in business, marketing, economics, finance, and politics (Valle-Cruz, Fernandez-Cortez, et al., 2021). In the lexicon-based method, unigrams found in the lexicon, are assigned a polarity score. The overall text polarity score is calculated as the sum of the polarities of the unigrams. A lexicon can detect polarities, but some can perceive emotional levels such as joy, anger, or sadness.

This section presents the state-of-the-art findings on lexicon application in the political context. According to our systematic literature review, sentiment analysis in the political context through lexicons begins in 2011 with the research conducted by Awadallah et al. (2011) proposing a Lexicon called OpinioNetIt to automatically generate an opinion-person network map from news and other web documents, obtaining high accuracy in 30000 person-opinion-topic triples. Furthermore, Alwan et al. (2011) proposed a model for detecting politically oriented articles in the Arabic language by applying the Rough Set (RS) theory to increase the accuracy of the models in article orientation recognition. Their findings show an accuracy of 85.48% in assessing the orientation of Arabic political datasets, compared to 72.58% and 64.52% for Support Vector Machines and Naïve Bayes methods, respectively. Gonçalves and colleagues (2013) compared eight sentiment analysis methods, apart from combining them to provide the best coverage and competitive agreement results. In addition, they proposed a free web service called iFeel to access and compare the different sentiment methods results from a given text.

From 2016, there is a renewed interest in political sentiment analysis. Jose and Chooralil (2016) use a machine learning approach with lexicons to classify in real-time the political sentiment, determining the positivity or negativity of each tweet by the majority voting principle. They also use the concepts of negation and word sense disambiguation to achieve high accuracy. Sharma, Mittal, and Garg (2016) analyzed changes in people's political opinions over time to develop a tweet classification tool and a specialized phonetic dictionary for jargon and abbreviations. A year later, Bele, Panigrahi, and Srivastava (2017) analyzed the document-level political sentiment of Hindi blogs by extracting opinions on one of India's most famous leaders in the 2014 national elections. For achieving this, they proposed a lexicon and machine learning to classify sentiment, finding efficiency in combining the two perspectives. Meanwhile, Jackson and colleagues (2017) proposed a lexicon-based method to identify political themes in campaign messages generated by candidates on Facebook and Twitter in the 2016 U.S. presidential election. The authors found that this approach provides reliable results for eight out of nine categories of political themes. Besides, Joyce and Deng (2017) correlated sentiment generated in the 2016 U.S. presidential debates with preference poll data, finding a correlation of up to 94% with poll data using a moving average smoothing technique.

In 2018, Jannati and colleagues (2018) proposed an application for stance detection in the political domain to determine whether the writer of a blog post is up to support a political figure to compete and win in a general election event, e.g., a candidate for presidential elections. They conducted experiments with five different cases and examined three machine learning models using a combination of Ngrams, sentiment lexicon, orthography, and word embedding features. The highest average F1 scored was obtained by the model trained with the Support Vector Machine classifier using a combination of word2vec and unigram features, being 63.54%. Furthermore, Pota et al. (2018) studied the propagation of positive and negative opinions through Twitter and how important events influence public opinion. To achieve this, they used an approach based on convolutional neural networks to learn how to classify tweets based on sentiment based on an available labeled dataset. They found that the neural network approach represents an improvement over the lexicon-based ones to categorize positive/negative phrases.

In this year, there was a boom in applying sentiment analysis in the political context. The research of Mahajan and Rana (2018) presents a sentiment classification approach that employs an emotion detection technique based on the NRC lexicon. The proposed method is tested on Twitter datasets on government policies and reforms. Polarity components are applied and classify tweets into eight predefined emotions, obtaining good classification results. Chiu and Hsu (2018) analyzed Facebook posts to predict left-wing or right-wing politics. The results show that the F1 score can be as high as 0.95 when using TF-IDF with a decision tree, finding that sentiment analysis is sensitive to some classification algorithms. Mihardi and Budi (2018) analyzed public sentiment in the political campaign for governor and deputy governor of Jakarta in 2017. To achieve this, they used sentiStrength, classifying each tweet into three classes: positive, negative, and neutral. The results show that positive sentiments dominate negative sentiments for each gubernatorial and deputy gubernatorial candidate. Furthermore, they argue that positive sentiments for all peers have the same sequence as election results. Additionally, in 2019 Beleveslis et al. (2019) designed a sentiment analysis model to study European election-related tweets written in Greek. They rely on a hybrid perspective in conjunction with Greek lexicons and classification methods, showing how public sentiment was affected by specific events during the pre-election period.

For the year 2021 and in the context of the COVID-19 pandemic, Aparicio, de Sequeira, and Costa (2021) explored the use of emotions in the communication of Portuguese political parties during the pandemic. Using a standard lexicon, they classified emotions in different tweets to identify positivity and negativity over time. Their findings found different approaches to social media engagement according to diverse strategies rather than political ideology. Similarly, Bonaccorsi, Chiarello, and Fantoni (2021) developed a user lexicon with 76,857 entries, which saturates the semantic field of social user groups and allows their normalization. They used a lexicon to filter the textual structures of the 6,637 impact case studies collected in the UK Research Excellence Framework to construct visual maps of science, further exploring the properties of this new type of maps in which science is viewed from the perspective of research users. Similarly, Rodríguez-Ibáñez and colleagues (2021) analyzed thousands of tweets mentioning political parties and their leaders several weeks before and after the 2019 Spanish elections, identifying entropy, mutual information, and the Composite Aggregate Positivity Index. The results show that the metrics performed to provide an informative characterization of the sentiment dynamics throughout the electoral period, finding measurable variations in the behavior and polarity of sentiment between political parties and their leaders. According to the parties' position in the political spectrum, the authors found different dynamics, their presence at the regional or national level, and their nationalist or globalist aspirations.

Finally, Valle-Cruz, Lopez-Chau, and Sandoval-Almazan (2021) propose an analysis of emotional charges for the 2020 U.S. presidential election based on a hybrid approach combining affective computing and classical statistical analysis. Through this analysis, it is possible to determine the degree of affinity between candidates and voters. Political sentiment analysis has been studied for ten years, representing a new field to understand problems such as political polarization, discourse analysis, the influence of politicians, candidate profiling, and the improvement of government-citizen interaction, among other applications in the public sphere.

METHODS

This section aims to present the methods to Twitter data analyzed and compare the different lexicons useful for political sentiment analysis. For experimentation, the authors analyzed a data collection of Tweets obtained during the U.S. presidential campaign of 2020 and based on the trending topic that emerged during Trump and Biden's 2020 presidential debate. Methods consist of four steps. 1) Description of the data analyzed. 2) Comparison of the three lexicons chosen for the analysis. 3) Description of the process to analyze tweets using lexicons. 4) Process to compare the results of the three selected lexicons.

Twitter Data Description

The analyzed data consisted of the Twitter trending topics that emerged during the days surrounding the presidential debate between Joe Biden and Donald Trump. To identify the trending topics, it was necessary to follow the events generated around the 2020 U.S presidential debate between Joe Biden and Donald Trump. Ultimately, 10,000 tweets were downloaded from each trending topic, with the twitteR library. The total number of tweets analyzed was 170,000. Table 2 shows the list of identified trending topics useful for the political sentiment analysis.

Table 2. Analyzed tending topics during the 2020 U.S. political campaign

Trending topic	Tweets analyzed
#Biden	10000
#Clown	10000
#Debates2020	10000
#PrayForTrump	10000
#Trump	10000
#TrumpHasCovid	10000
#TrumpIsACoward	10000
#VoteHimOut	10000
Chris Wallace	10000
Joe Rogan	10000
Moderator	10000
Philadelphia	10000
Proud Boys	10000
The American	10000
Trump	10000
White Supremacists	10000
White Supremacy	10000
TOTAL	**170000**

Lexicons' Comparison

Sentiment analysis with lexicons results in three types of values. 1) Polarity, measuring the degree of positivity or negativity in emotions. 2) Basic emotional levels, such as fear, anger, surprise, and sadness. And 3) Complementary emotional levels, such as temper, attitude, and calmness. Some lexicons only focus on identifying polarity, while others detect polarity and basic emotions. There are even some types of lexicons that provide results on polarity, basic and complementary emotions. For this reason, the authors decided to use three lexicons, one of each type for experimentation.

The lexicons used are AFINN, NRC, and SenticNet lexicons on Twitter posts from the 2020 U.S presidential campaign for experimentation. First, were used AFFIN to measure sentiment polarity, with negative and positive values. Second, NRC calculates sentiment polarity and basic emotional charge based on eight emotion scales (fear, anger, anticipation, trust, surprise, sadness, disgust, and joy). Finally, were used SenticNet to calculate emotional polarity and basic emotional charge (anger, disgust, fear, joy, and sadness) as well as complementary emotion in Twitter posts: temper, attitude, calmness, and sensitivity. With the results, the authors were able to compare polarity in each lexicon, basic emotional charge between NRC and SenticNet, and complementary emotional scales calculations to detect the total emotional charge during the 2020 U.S. political campaign. Table 3 shows a comparison of these three lexicons.

Table 3. Summary of Lexicons used for the comparative

Lexicon	Brief description	Terms	Sentiments	Scoring
Afinn	It is a list of words rated for valence with an integer between minus five (negative) and plus five (positive).	3,382	Numeric	Integer between -5 to +5
NRC or Emolex	It is a list of English words manually associated by crowdsourcing with eight basic emotions. Used for general domain.	14,182	Positive Negative Anger Anticipation Disgust Fear Joy Sadness Surprise Trust	Real-valued
SenticNet	It is a framework for sentiment analysis. SenticNet provides a set of semantics, sentics, and polarity associated with 200,000 natural language concepts	200,000	Polarity Anger Disgust Fear Joy Sadness Attitude Calmness Eagerness Introspection Pleasantness Sensitivity Temper	Real-valued

Analysis of Tweets

Because each lexicon generates a different scale of values. A process of data cleaning, identification of polarities and emotions, as well as standardization was carried out, which is described below. Here, the process applied for the analysis of tweets:

1. Data cleaning. It consisted of the following steps:

    a. Punctuation symbols, numbers, Unicode characters, emoticons, mentions, multiple spaces, newlines, and URLs were removed from tweets.
    b. All letters were changed to lowercase.
    c. Stopwords were identified and got-rid-off of tweets.

Because preliminary tests showed that stemming techniques to the words in tweets does not influence the results, we did not apply them.

2. Identification of polarities. The tweet´s texts were separated into words, then polarity in the lexicons from each word was searched. The Afinn lexicon restores the polarity of a word as a positive or negative integer value. The NRC lexicon returns the relative frequency for each feeling related to the searched word. SenticNet computes much more information than the other lexicons: to each word it restores its polarity (which can be positive or negative), the values of introspection, temper, attitude, sensitivity in a range between zero and one; and related sentiments.

Because each lexicon uses a different scale, it was needed to normalize the values to a range between 0 and 1. This transformation makes it easier to compare results. The following equations summarize how to perform this normalization. With the eq. (1) the average of the polarities of each tweet is calculated, with the eq. (2) each polarity average is transformed into a value between a minimum of zero and a maximum of one.

$$P\left(t_i\right) = \frac{1}{T_i} \sum_{j=1}^{T_i} L\left(w_i^j\right) \tag{1}$$

Where:

t_i: the i-th tweeet

$P(t_i)$: the polarity of t_i

$L\left(w_i^j\right)$: polarity returned by lexicon L for w_i^j

w_i^j: the j-th word of i-th tweet

T_i: total of words in tweet t_i that are in lexicon L

$$P_n\left(t_i\right) = \frac{\left|min\left(P\right)\right| + P\left(t_i\right)}{\left|max\left(\left|min\left(P\right)\right| + P\left(t_i\right)\right)\right|} \tag{2}$$

With:

$P_n\left(t_i\right)$: normalize polarity of i-th tweet

P: the polarities in corpus (polarities of all tweets)

min(P): the minimum value of polarity

max(P): the maximum value of polarity

$\left|min\left(x\right)\right|$: absolute value of a value x

Comparison of Analysis Results with Lexicons

Comparing the results of the three selected lexicons consisted of four stages. 1) The authors joined all data sets (trending topics) to measure the overall sentiment during the political campaign. 2) To a better comparison of results, all values were normalized from 0 to 1. For polarity, the values closer to zero have negative sentiment and values closer to 1 have a higher positive sentiment. 3) The authors calculated averages and standard deviations for polarities, basic emotional charges, and SenticNet-specific complementary emotions. 4) Finally, were performed a results' comparison based on three phases: a) Comparison of polarity between the three lexicons. b) Comparison of common affective charges between NRC and SenticNet. c) Description of complementary emotions of NRC and SenticNet.

RESULTS

After performing the experiments, we found that the Affin lexicon only calculates the polarity of the tweets. Affin lexicon places N/A values where it cannot calculate polarity; for comparison purposes, all N/A values were replaced by zero. NRC lexicon calculates several dimensions of emotional charge to zero and it is not possible to determine the polarity of emotional values in each tweet, as in some Twitter posts they are assumed to be null. SenticNet calculates fewer values equal to zero and provides variety in complementary emotions such as calmness, eagerness, introspection, pleasantness, sensitivity, and temper (see Table 4).

Table 4. Results' comparison between lexicons

Dimension	Average	Standard Deviation
Affin lexicon		
Polarity	0.47928	0.04254
NRC lexicon		
Polarity	0.50047	0.04681
Anger	0.00683	0.03942
Disgust	0.01022	0.06037
Fear	0.00618	0.03566
Joy	0.00623	0.05603
Sadness	0.01223	0.07011
Surprise	0.00310	0.03892
Anticipation	0.02535	0.13614
Trust	0.00617	0.05038
SenticNet lexicon		
Polarity	0.42063	0.04135
Anger	0.00387	0.03925
Disgust	0.00423	0.03922
Fear	0.00928	0.05620
Joy	0.00888	0.05714
Sadness	0.01153	0.06518
Attitude	0.43956	0.03354
Calmness	0.00342	0.03004
Eagerness	0.00942	0.05681
Introspection	0.46350	0.04120
Pleasantness	0.00478	0.04149
Sensitivity	0.55867	0.03981
Temper	0.52011	0.03430

The polarities of the three lexicons are similar. However, SenticNet had the lowest polarity, while NRC had the highest. In this regard, NRC had a higher standard deviation in the results. Practically, there is a big difference between the polarity calculated by NRC and SenticNet. The emotions that NRC and SenticNet have in common are anger, disgust, fear, joy, and sadness, concerning emotional charge. When comparing both lexicons, a higher level of anger and disgust was identified in NRC in comparison with SenticNet. In addition to higher levels of fear and joy in SenticNet compared to NRC. The levels of sadness detected by both lexicons were similar.

According to the results of the three lexicons, the political campaign presented average levels of polarity (Affin = 0.47928, NRC = 0.50047, and SenticNet = 0.42063). According to the SenticNet results, the political contest showed levels of sensitivity, temper, introspection, and attitude. While the NRC lexicon detected a low but significant level of anticipation. SenticNet showed virtually zero levels of calmness, anger, disgust, and pleasantness. Concerning Gonçalves et al. (2013) research to the total emotional charge. 1) The average result of the three lexicons for polarity. 2) The average of NRC and SenticNet for anger, disgust, fear, joy, and sadness. 3) In addition to including the individual NRC scores for anticipation and trust, as well as the SenticNet scores for attitude, calmness, eagerness, introspection, pleasantness, sensitivity, and temper (see Table 5).

Table 5. Total emotional charge during the 2020 U.S. political campaign

Dimension			Average
		Polarity	0.46679
Emotional charge	Basic	Anger	0.00535
		Disgust	0.00723
		Fear	0.00773
		Joy	0.00756
		Sadness	0.01188
		Surprise	0.00310
	Complementary	Anticipation	0.02535
		Attitude	0.43956
		Calmness	0.00342
		Eagerness	0.00942
		Introspection	0.46350
		Pleasantness	0.00478
		Sensitivity	0.55867
		Temper	0.52011
		Trust	0.00617

CONCLUSION, LIMITATIONS, AND FUTURE WORK

This chapter presented an analysis of the application of lexicon-based political sentiment analysis in social media and is handle by three closely linked research questions: RQ1: What are the most frequently used lexicons (MFUL) in social media in the political context? RQ2: What conclusions or results have been reached by applying the most commonly used lexicons (MFUL)? RQ3: What are the similarities and differences between the results obtained with the application of the most frequently used lexicons (MFUL) to the political texts? i.e., Do the results converge or diverge? How much similar or different are these results? To answer the research questions, a systematic literature review on lexicons and political contexts was conducted in Science Direct, IEEE Xplore, ACM Digital Library, Springer Link, IGI Global, and Google Scholar using the PRISMA methodology. In addition, sentiment analysis was implemented on Twitter posts during the 2020 U.S. political campaign, comparing and combining three lexicons: Affin, NRC, and SenticNet.

Unimodal sentiment analysis is prevalent in the literature reviewed, where only the polarity from the negative to positive values is determined. This type of analysis provides accurate results in sentiment analysis. However, multimodal sentiment analysis has the potential to understand different emotions, where the emotional charge is estimated. In this chapter, the authors compared three lexicons that are widely used: Afinn, NRC, and Sentic Net. The similarities of both lexicons predominate in the calculation of polarity. For this reason, similar results are obtained with any of them. NRC and SenticNet have several similar emotions but change the calculations in each of them due to the number of terms used in each lexicon. In addition, there are some complementary emotions that only NRC calculates and others that are unique to SenticNet. Combining different lexicons has the potential to improve or extend sentiment analysis. First, because the results of each emotional dimension can be averaged, and second, the dimensions of analysis can be increased, providing more emotional levels: this is called multimodal sentiment analysis.

Also, this investigation provides only a comparison of different lexicons in the same data collection. The authors do not have data that could support barriers, errors, or drivers for improving the lexicons. With the analysis performed in this research, it is not possible to know the polarization of Biden or Trump. Much less to know who the winner of the political campaign would be. This type of analysis is more complex and depends on different factors or other types of analysis. As a result of our experience in this field, we can infer the following ideas that should test in future research. 1. Each campaign has different discourses, diverse needs, concepts, and ideas are built according to the needs of the voters at that moment. 2. Lexicons are limited to the use of words before and during the electoral campaign or of social media. 3. Lexicons are a tool in constant development and are expected to cover more concepts and their measurements. 4) Multi-modal sentiment analysis allows us to understand a broader spectrum of emotions and, therefore, be more detailed in inferring what voters perceive at that specific moment. It can serve as raw material to complement other analyses or use other statistical techniques and artificial intelligence tools. In sum, our findings can support that 1. The combination of lexicons substantially improves the analysis of political issues. 2. Multi-modal sentiment analysis allows for a more detailed and accurate study of social network usage, at least on Twitter. 3. The basic emotional loadings can measure the impact of political polarization, discourse analysis, and all others.

According to our findings, political sentiment analysis is a new field studied for only ten years. Political sentiment analysis, enhanced by the combination of lexicons and multimodal analysis, can generate benefits in understanding problems such as political polarization, discourse analysis, politician influence, candidate profiling, and improving government-citizen interaction, among other applications in the public sphere. All of this, because personal information is obtained from Twitter posts, which allow understanding citizens' sentiment towards political events. This kind of information is valuable to understand the needs and satisfaction in society. Our findings also showed that the combination of lexicons could improve sentiment analysis results in the political context. Some generate null results or have a dimension that only shows polarity in social media posts. Also, the lexicons analyzed in this research present similar levels of polarity but different levels in the basic emotional charges related to anger, disgust, fear, and joy. In addition, the authors found that the SenticNet lexicon calculates complementary emotions that allow for a more robust analysis.

Our analysis using the combined lexicons on the 2020 U.S. political campaign on Twitter found that polarity was one of the critical dimensions identified, supporting the previous research from Rodríguez-Ibáñez and colleagues (2021) in Spain, finding variations in the behavior and polarity of sentiments. Furthermore, our multimodal sentiment analysis found that the most predominant basic emotions were sadness and fear. In contrast, the one that showed the lowest level was the emotion surprise. This confirms previous research Valle-Cruz, Lopez-Chau, and Sandoval-Almazan (2021). The sentiment analysis of the 2020 U.S. political campaign on Twitter showed considerable levels of sensitivity and temper. Polarity was an essential dimension identified in the data analyzed.

Furthermore, the most predominant basic emotions were sadness and fear. The emotion that showed the lowest level was surprise. It is necessary to be aware that the political campaign was during the COVID-19 pandemic, which may have affected the results.

Finally, this research has some significant limitations to consider. The first one only uses Twitter data; other social media data could change or complement our findings. The second limitation is that we think lexicons are only supported by scholarly research and literature, as shown in the PRISMA methodology literature review. These days, many other lexicons are used to research social media and politics that are not listed here because they are not reported with rigorous research but can provide different results. The case of the political campaign in the U.S. using the Twitter platform is abnormal, in any case, because of the profiles of the candidates and, also, for the context conditions – COVID-19 pandemic – maybe the results could be different in another context. Unfortunately, our results did not measure other political outcomes – political discourse, political parties' online activities, candidate profiling or polarization. We should include them in the future search area. Another promising research is using artificial intelligence to complement the sentiment analysis technique using different tools such as machine learning which can expand and improve the understanding of this kind of political phenomenon.

REFERENCES

Alwan, J. K., Hussain, A. J., Abd, D. H., Sadiq, A. T., Khalaf, M., & Liatsis, P. (2011). Political Arabic Articles Orientation Using Rough Set Theory with Sentiment Lexicon. *IEEE Access: Practical Innovations, Open Solutions*, 9, 24475–24484. doi:10.1109/ACCESS.2021.3054919

Anwar, A., Ilyas, H., Yaqub, U., & Zaman, S. (2021). Analyzing QAnon on Twitter in Context of US Elections 2020: Analysis of User Messages and Profiles Using VADER and BERT Topic modeling. *DG.O2021: The 22nd Annual International Conference on Digital Government Research*, 82–88.

Aparicio, J. T., de Sequeira, J. S., & Costa, C. J. (2021). Emotion analysis of Portuguese Political Parties Communication over the covid-19 Pandemic. *2021 16th Iberian Conference on Information Systems and Technologies (CISTI)*, 1–6.

Aslam, F., Awan, T. M., Syed, J. H., Kashif, A., & Parveen, M. (2020). Sentiments and emotions evoked by news headlines of coronavirus disease (COVID-19) outbreak. *Humanities and Social Sciences Communications, 7*(1), 1–9. doi:10.105741599-020-0523-3

Awadallah, R., Ramanath, M., & Weikum, G. (2011). Opinionetit: Understanding the opinions-people network for politically controversial topics. *Proceedings of the 20th ACM International Conference on Information and Knowledge Management*, 2481–2484. 10.1145/2063576.2063997

Bele, N., Panigrahi, P. K., & Srivastava, S. K. (2017). Political sentiment mining: A new age intelligence tool for business strategy formulation. *International Journal of Business Intelligence Research, 8*(1), 55–70. doi:10.4018/IJBIR.2017010104

Beleveslis, D., Tjortjis, C., Psaradelis, D., & Nikoglou, D. (2019). A hybrid method for sentiment analysis of election related tweets. *2019 4th South-East Europe Design Automation, Computer Engineering, Computer Networks and Social Media Conference (SEEDA-CECNSM)*, 1–6.

Bing, L. (2012). *Sentiment Analysis and Opinion Mining (Synthesis Lectures on Human Language Technologies)*. University of Illinois.

Bing, L., Liu, B., & Zhang, L. (2012). A survey of opinion mining and sentiment analysis. *Mining Text Data*, 415–463.

Bonaccorsi, A., Chiarello, F., & Fantoni, G. (2021). Impact for whom? Mapping the users of public research with lexicon-based text mining. *Scientometrics, 126*(2), 1745–1774. doi:10.100711192-020-03803-z

Calefato, F., Lanubile, F., Maiorano, F., & Novielli, N. (2018). Sentiment polarity detection for software development. *Empirical Software Engineering, 23*(3), 1352–1382. doi:10.100710664-017-9546-9

Cambria, E., Das, D., Bandyopadhyay, S., Feraco, A., & ... (2017). *A practical guide to sentiment analysis*. Springer. doi:10.1007/978-3-319-55394-8

Cambria, E., Li, Y., Xing, F. Z., Poria, S., & Kwok, K. (2020). SenticNet 6: Ensemble application of symbolic and subsymbolic AI for sentiment analysis. *Proceedings of the 29th ACM International Conference on Information & Knowledge Management*, 105–114. 10.1145/3340531.3412003

Charalabidis, Y., Maragoudakis, M., & Loukis, E. (2015). Opinion Mining and Sentiment Analysis in Policy Formulation Initiatives: The EU-Community Approach. In E. Tambouris, P. Panagiotopoulos, Ø. Sæbø, K. Tarabanis, M. A. Wimmer, M. Milano, & T. Pardo (Eds.), *Electronic Participation: Proceedings of the 7th IFIP 8.5 International Conference on Electronic Participation (ePart 2015)* (pp. 147–160). Springer International Publishing.

Chau, A. L., Valle-Cruz, D., & Sandoval-Almazán, R. (2021). Sentiment Analysis in Crisis Situations for Better Connected Government: Case of Mexico Earthquake in 2017. In Web 2.0 and Cloud Technologies for Implementing Connected Government (pp. 162–181). IGI Global.

Chiu, S.-I., & Hsu, K.-W. (2018). Predicting political tendency of posts on Facebook. *Proceedings of the 2018 7th International Conference on Software and Computer Applications*, 110–114. 10.1145/3185089.3185094

Criado, J. I., Sandoval-Almazan, R., & Gil-Garcia, J. R. (2013). Government innovation through social media. *Government Information Quarterly, 30*(4), 319–326. doi:10.1016/j.giq.2013.10.003

Dorle, S., & Pise, N. (2018). Political sentiment analysis through social media. *2018 Second International Conference on Computing Methodologies and Communication (ICCMC)*, 869–873. 10.1109/ICCMC.2018.8487879

Ekman, P. (1999). Basic emotions. Handbook of Cognition and Emotion, 98(45–60), 16. doi:10.1002/0470013494.ch3

Elghazaly, T., Mahmoud, A., & Hefny, H. A. (2016). Political sentiment analysis using twitter data. *Proceedings of the International Conference on Internet of Things and Cloud Computing*, 1–5.

Goncalves, J., Liu, Y., Xiao, B., Chaudhry, S., Hosio, S., & Kostakos, V. (2015). Increasing the reach of government social media: A case study in modeling government-citizen interaction on Facebook. *Policy & Internet, 7*(1), 80–102.

Gonçalves, P., Araújo, M., Benevenuto, F., & Cha, M. (2013). Comparing and Combining Sentiment Analysis Methods. *Proceedings of the First ACM Conference on Online Social Networks*, 27–38. 10.1145/2512938.2512951

Hume, D. (2004). *Disertación sobre las pasiones y otros ensayos morales* (Vol. 5). Anthropos Editorial.

Hussein, D. M. E.-D. M. (2018). A survey on sentiment analysis challenges. *Journal of King Saud University-Engineering Sciences, 30*(4), 330–338. doi:10.1016/j.jksues.2016.04.002

Jackson, S., Zhang, F., Boichak, O., Bryant, L., Li, Y., Hemsley, J., Stromer-Galley, J., Semaan, B., & McCracken, N. (2017). Identifying political topics in social media messages: A lexicon-based approach. *Proceedings of the 8th International Conference on Social Media & Society*, 1–10. 10.1145/3097286.3097298

Jannati, R., Mahendra, R., Wardhana, C. W., & Adriani, M. (2018). Stance classification towards political figures on blog writing. *2018 International Conference on Asian Language Processing (IALP)*, 96–101. 10.1109/IALP.2018.8629144

Jose, R., & Chooralil, V. S. (2016). Prediction of election result by enhanced sentiment analysis on twitter data using classifier ensemble Approach. *2016 International Conference on Data Mining and Advanced Computing (SAPIENCE)*, 64–67. 10.1109/SAPIENCE.2016.7684133

Joyce, B., & Deng, J. (2017). Sentiment analysis of tweets for the 2016 US presidential election. *2017 Ieee Mit Undergraduate Research Technology Conference (Urtc)*, 1–4. 10.1109/URTC.2017.8284176

Kermanidis, K. L., & Maragoudakis, M. (2013). Political sentiment analysis of tweets before and after the Greek elections of May 2012. *International Journal of Social Network Mining, 1*(3–4), 298–317. doi:10.1504/IJSNM.2013.059090

Keshavarz, H., & Abadeh, M. S. (2017). ALGA: Adaptive lexicon learning using genetic algorithm for sentiment analysis of microblogs. *Knowledge-Based Systems, 122*, 1–16. doi:10.1016/j.knosys.2017.01.028

Kiritchenko, S., Zhu, X., & Mohammad, S. M. (2014). Sentiment analysis of short informal texts. *Journal of Artificial Intelligence Research, 50*, 723–762. doi:10.1613/jair.4272

López-Chau, A., Valle-Cruz, D., & Sandoval-Almazán, R. (2020). Sentiment Analysis of Twitter Data Through Machine Learning Techniques. In Software Engineering in the Era of Cloud Computing (pp. 185–209). Springer. doi:10.1007/978-3-030-33624-0_8

Mahajan, P., & Rana, A. (2018). Sentiment Classification-How to Quantify Public Emotions Using Twitter. *International Journal of Sociotechnology and Knowledge Development, 10*(1), 57–71. doi:10.4018/IJSKD.2018010104

Mihardi, M., & Budi, I. (2018). Public sentiment on political campaign using Twitter data in 2017 Jakarta's governor election. *2018 International Conference on Applied Information Technology and Innovation (ICAITI)*, 67–72. 10.1109/ICAITI.2018.8686740

Nandi, V., & Agrawal, S. (2016). Political sentiment analysis using hybrid approach. *International Research Journal of Engineering and Technology, 3*(5), 1621–1627.

Nussbaum, M. C. (2006). *El ocultamiento de lo humano: repugnancia, vergüenza y ley* (Vol. 77). Katz editores.

Pota, M., Esposito, M., Palomino, M. A., & Masala, G. L. (2018). A subword-based deep learning approach for sentiment analysis of political tweets. *2018 32nd International Conference on Advanced Information Networking and Applications Workshops (WAINA)*, 651–656.

Rhodes, R. A. W. (2014). Public administration. In The Oxford Handbook of Political Leadership. OUP.

Riggs, F. W. (1965). Relearning an old lesson: The political context of development administration. *Public Administration Review, 25*(1), 70–79. doi:10.2307/974009

Rodríguez-Ibáñez, M., Gimeno-Blanes, F.-J., Cuenca-Jiménez, P. M., Soguero-Ruiz, C., & Rojo-Álvarez, J. L. (2021). Sentiment Analysis of Political Tweets From the 2019 Spanish Elections. *IEEE Access: Practical Innovations, Open Solutions, 9*, 101847–101862. doi:10.1109/ACCESS.2021.3097492

Sandoval-Almazan, R., & Valle-Cruz, D. (2020). Sentiment Analysis of Facebook Users Reacting to Political Campaign Posts. *Digital Government: Research and Practice, 1*(2), 1–13. doi:10.1145/3382735

Sharma, Y., Mittal, E., & Garg, M. (2016). Political Opinion Mining from Twitter. *International Journal of Information Systems in the Service Sector, 8*(4), 47–56. doi:10.4018/IJISSS.2016100104

Valle-Cruz, D. (2019). Public value of e-government services through emerging technologies. *International Journal of Public Sector Management, 32*(5), 530–545. doi:10.1108/IJPSM-03-2018-0072

Valle-Cruz, D., Fernandez-Cortez, V., López-Chau, A., & Sandoval-Almazán, R. (2021). Does Twitter Affect Stock Market Decisions? Financial Sentiment Analysis During Pandemics: A Comparative Study of the H1N1 and the COVID-19 Periods. *Cognitive Computation*, 1–16. PMID:33520006

Valle-Cruz, D., López-Chau, A., & Sandoval-Almazán, R. (2020). Impression analysis of trending topics in Twitter with classification algorithms. *Proceedings of the 13th International Conference on Theory and Practice of Electronic Governance*, 430–441. 10.1145/3428502.3428570

Valle-Cruz, D., Lopez-Chau, A., & Sandoval-Almazan, R. (2021). How much do Twitter posts affect voters? Analysis of the multi-emotional charge with affective computing in political campaigns. *DG. O2021: The 22nd Annual International Conference on Digital Government Research*, 1–14.

Vinodhini, G., & Chandrasekaran, R. M. (2012). Sentiment analysis and opinion mining: A survey. *International Journal (Toronto, Ont.), 2*(6), 282–292.

Wang, Z., Ho, S.-B., & Cambria, E. (2020). A review of emotion sensing: Categorization models and algorithms. *Multimedia Tools and Applications*, *79*(47-48), 1–30. doi:10.100711042-019-08328-z

Ying, S. Y., Keikhosrokiani, P., & Asl, M. P. (2020). Comparison of data analytic techniques for a spatial opinion mining in literary works: A review paper. *International Conference of Reliable Information and Communication Technology*, 523–535.

ADDITIONAL READING

Cervantes, J., Garcia-Lamont, F., Rodríguez-Mazahua, L., & Lopez, A. (2020). A comprehensive survey on support vector machine classification: Applications, challenges and trends. *Neurocomputing*, *408*, 189–215. doi:10.1016/j.neucom.2019.10.118

Chau, A. L., Valle-Cruz, D., & Sandoval-Almazán, R. (2021). Sentiment Analysis in Crisis Situations for Better Connected Government: Case of Mexico Earthquake in 2017. In Web 2.0 and Cloud Technologies for Implementing Connected Government (pp. 162-181). IGI Global.

López-Chau, A., Valle-Cruz, D., & Sandoval-Almazán, R. (2020). Sentiment analysis of Twitter data through machine learning techniques. In *Software Engineering in the Era of Cloud Computing* (pp. 185–209). Springer. doi:10.1007/978-3-030-33624-0_8

Sandoval-Almazan, R., & Valle-Cruz, D. (2020). Sentiment Analysis of Facebook Users Reacting to Political Campaign Posts. *Digital Government: Research and Practice*, *1*(2), 1–13. doi:10.1145/3382735

Sandoval-Almazan, R., & Valle-Cruz, D. (2021). Social media use in government health agencies: The COVID-19 impact. *Information Polity*, (Preprint), 459 – 475.

Valle-Cruz, D. (2019). Public value of e-government services through emerging technologies. *International Journal of Public Sector Management*, *32*(5), 530–545. doi:10.1108/IJPSM-03-2018-0072

Valle-Cruz, D., Criado, J. I., Sandoval-Almazán, R., & Ruvalcaba-Gomez, E. A. (2020). Assessing the public policy-cycle framework in the age of artificial intelligence: From agenda-setting to policy evaluation. *Government Information Quarterly*, *37*(4), 101509. doi:10.1016/j.giq.2020.101509

Valle-Cruz, D., Fernandez-Cortez, V., & Gil-Garcia, J. R. (2021). From E-budgeting to smart budgeting: Exploring the potential of artificial intelligence in government decision-making for resource allocation. *Government Information Quarterly*, 101644. doi:10.1016/j.giq.2021.101644

Valle-Cruz, D., Fernandez-Cortez, V., López-Chau, A., & Sandoval-Almazán, R. (2021). Does twitter affect stock market decisions? Financial sentiment analysis during pandemics: A comparative study of the h1n1 and the covid-19 periods. *Cognitive Computation*, 1–16. PMID:33520006

Valle-Cruz, D., Sandoval-Almazan, R., & Gil-Garcia, J. R. (2016). Citizens' perceptions of the impact of information technology use on transparency, efficiency and corruption in local governments. *Information Polity*, *21*(3), 321–334. doi:10.3233/IP-160393

KEY TERMS AND DEFINITIONS

Emotion: Intense feeling of joy, sadness, anger (among others) produced by an event, an idea, or a memory. Lexicon-based sentiment analysis allows approaching the measurement of emotions.

Lexicon: Vocabulary of a person, language, or branch of knowledge. Lexicon-based sentiment analysis is based on a set of words labeled as positive, negative, and neutral sentiments.

MFUL: The most frequently used lexicons for sentiment analysis.

Polarity: Value assigned to a word or phrase, resulting from lexicon-based sentiment analysis. The assigned values can be negative and positive, or the absolute value of negativity or positivity.

Political Sentiment Analysis: Detection of polarity and emotions in political content. The content can be text, images, or videos.

Social Media: Online communication platforms where content is created by the users themselves using Web 2.0, such as blogs, social networks, instant messaging, and wikis.

Social Networks: Tools used to disseminate information and interact with people virtually. Some examples are Twitter, Facebook, Instagram, and Tik Tok.

Chapter 2
Text Mining and Pre-Processing Methods for Social Media Data Extraction and Processing

Santoshi Kumari
RUAS, India

ABSTRACT

A huge amount of unstructured data is generated from social media platforms like Twitter. Volume of tweets and the velocity with which they are generated on various topics presents extensive challenges in data analytics and processing techniques. Linguistic flexibility for writing tweets presents many challenges in preprocessing and natural language processing tasks. Addressing these challenges, this chapter aims to select, modify, and apply information retrieval and preprocessing steps for retrieving, storing, organizing, and cleaning real-time large-scale unstructured Twitter data. The work focuses on reviewing the previous research and applying suitable preprocessing methods to improve the quality of data by removing unessential data. It is also observed that using tweeter APIs and access tokens provides easy access to real-time tweets. Preprocessing methods are fundamental steps of text analytics and NLP tasks to process unstructured data. Analyzing suitable preprocessing methods like tokenization, removal of stop word, stemming, and lemmatization are applied to normalize the extracted Twitter data.

INTRODUCTION

Real-time sentiment analysis of continuously generating social media data aims to understand people's attitude and behavior on various topics discussed at present situations. The analysis on the current data for particular location helps to identify and understand the sentiments and opinion of the people on a critical event such as terrorism, fire alarm, tsunami, critical incidents, elections, political parties and natural hazards.

Main goal of this work is to identify a platform that provides large scale real time social media data. Correspondingly, it identifies suitable techniques and tools to extract real time social media data and build suitable preprocessing methods to improve the quality of the data to represent it easily into feature

DOI: 10.4018/978-1-7998-9594-7.ch002

vector for further analysis. This research work identifies one of the top social networking platform twitter on which people interact with each other known as tweets. It provides huge data source for academic and industrial social media researcher according to (Ahmed & Graduate 2018). The study proposed by Ahmed (2018) also explained about the top resources, platforms, methods and practical tools to retrieve, store and analyze social media data for conducting research on social media. According to Ahmed (2018), "The popularity of using Twitter for social media research, both in academia and in industry, remains high; no other platform has attracted as much attention from academics". There is no other social media platforms with an infrastructure like twitter to provide 100% of its data through Application Programming Interface known as APIs. It provides technologies to extract tweets at real time which is useful for analyzing data in various applications such as crisis communication and identifying emergency situation, natural disasters, e-governance and elections.

Bruns & Liang (2012) explained the importance of twitter for capturing information at real time in emergency situations. They also identified a method for extracting tweets related to natural disaster in real time, for the development of suitable research infrastructure, for tracking and analyzing large-scale tweets at nearly real time.

To perform real time text analytical research, some techniques such as machine learning and sentiment analysis are used to extract and analyze data from twitter, which is a platform with huge social media posts on various topics. There are various advance data analytical tools (Ahmed, 2018) such as R, Weka, KNIME that can be used to analyze the social media data.

Tweets are expressed in informal and cryptic form containing emoticons, special characters, URLs and short forms. Applying data analytical method to these unstructured tweets is difficult, it requires cleaning and removing unnecessary information to improve quality of the data for further machine learning and data analysis.

To improve the quality of extracted tweets, prepossessing methods are very essential. Preprocessing methods acts as basic fundamental step for all data analytical and NLP tasks to reduce complexity and improve quality of data. It is also foremost part of information retrieval processes to remove unwanted data and improve the quality of text.

Applying preprocessing methods like removal of special characters, URLs, Hashtags, stop words, numbers, punctuations from theses unstructured tweets and filtering unessential data is challenging task. Structured texts are extracted and represented in the form of individual tokens by applying suitable preprocessing methods like Bag of word, Term Document Matrix (TDM), Document Term Matrix(DTM), and Term Frequency-Inverse Document Frequency. Preprocessing step is necessary to extract meaningful and quality data from the corpus of tweets and building the feature vector for further analysis. In previous work, most of the miss classification and confusion caused in machine learning due to 40% of the unwanted data present in dataset (Fayyad et al., 2003) that need to be identified and preprocessed. Therefore, preprocessing is a major step of data analytics as it improves the quality of data for machine learning, reduces data size, enhance computational speed and accuracy.

The rest of this chapter is structured as follows. Section 2 contains a review of the related literature. Section 3 presents methods for data extraction and pre-processing of unstructured social media data. Section 4 describes the experimental setup. Results and analysis are discussed in Section 5. Section 6 presents a conclusions and future work.

LITERATURE REVIEW

The preprocessing methods plays significant role in sentiment analysis and opinion mining of social media data especially in microblog data such as tweets. Many previous research studies demonstrated different text mining and preprocessing methods and their effects on classification of various kinds of data. Various studies by Agarwal et al. (2011) and Mohammad et al. (2015) also presented the importance of applying preprocessing methods before feature selection, machine learning, and classification methods in sentiment analysis.

Most of the missclassification and confusion caused in machine learning due to 40% of the unwanted data presented in the datasets provided by Fayyad et al. (2003) that need to be identified and preprocessed.

Literature survey carried out on most of the previous research related to social media analytical and preprocessing methods such as text mining, web mining, information retrieval, social media structure, social media data preprocessing and analysis. Most of the previous works focused on machine learning based classification of social media data and analytical methods are applied on historical datasets. However, this will not be suitable social media data analysis as it is generating real time unstructured data continuously on various trending topics. These current trending topics on social media will not be trending on the next day or month.

The effect of preprocessing methods for sentiment classification on twitter data discussed in a study proposed by Singh & Kumari (2016), in which they intended to remove unessential URLs, hashtags, stop words, numbers. In addition, they presented importance of slang words and correction of spelling mistakes, and they used SVM (Support Vector Machine) for sentiment classification of twitter data.

In (Haddi & Liu 2013) author presented a role of preprocessing in movie reviews classification. They applied basic preprocessing methods such as stop word removal, stemming, negation handling with addition of 'Not' in the beginning and abbreviation extension. Used SVM algorithm for classification and correlated with the number of features for accuracy.

In a study proposed by Uysal & Gunal, (2014), preprocessing methods such as stemming, lowercase conversion, removal of stop word was applied to e-mail and news datasets. SVM classifier with micro-F1 score model was also used for final evaluation. They applied preprocessing method on two different languages and presented that "There is no unique combination of preprocessing method to improve the accuracy of classification model in different domain". However, it is also essential for researchers to analyze best possible combination of preprocessing methods suitable for classification of particular dataset in particular domain and language.

In (Xue et al. n.d.2008) this paper author has identified the drawbacks of bag of words and introduced new technique to check distribution of words in each documents to identify the importance of word in that document. Assigned a value to each word called distribution feature to identify first occurring of the word, Impact of that word in that document based on TF-IDF matrix and ensemble methods. Result shows distribution of features useful for text categorization and useful for long documents and casual writing style.

Raghavan, (1997) presented challenges of the algorithms used for data retrieval processes specially in automated search process in digital library and also explained the steps for writing the algorithm used for data retrieval process. The article by Sun et al. (2014) demonstrates practical results of NLP techniques for data preprocessing such as tokenization, Splitting, Stemming.

Rajman and Besançon (1998) explained the steps for data retrieval and knowledge discovery process for unstructured text data. The author designed a method for automatic extraction of information from text using probabilistic association of keywords. Presented NLP tool is necessary for extraction of information from the data. A method is proposed by Zhao et al. (2011) to identify topics and interesting keyword in large scale twitter data. This study developed a context sensitive topical PageRank method for ranking keyword. He also implemented probabilistic scoring function to identify related and interested keywords for the topics in large scale twitter data. Paper (Ferrara et al. 2014) explains various types of web data extraction methods. Also explained methods for social data extraction especially for large scale real time data extraction. It presented a method to identify and analyze human behavior and communication network of users in social media. Dueñas-Fernández et al. (Dueñas-Fernández et al. n.d. 2014) developed a model for trend detection and topic modeling on web using opinion mining. Model is developed in 4 steps as: Crawling web based on some predefined sources, Extract topics from retrieved documents, Retrieve opinioned document for each topic, extract sentiment from the data. Applied these methods to data collected for 8 moth from 20 sources and obtained F-score of 0.58 for related event detection After going through previous studies, the following points are identified:

- Examined various combination of preprocessing method and their effects on classification
- Preprocessing will improves the quality of data, hence improving the accuracy of machine learning and classification.
- Preprocessing has significance effect on improving the accuracy of feature selection, sentiment analysis and machine learning.
- Necessary to analyze best possible combination of preprocessing method suitable for classification of particular dataset in particular domain and language.
- There is no unique combination of preprocessing method to improve the accuracy of classification model in different domain.
- However researcher has to analyze best possible combination of preprocessing method suitable for classification of particular dataset in particular domain and language.

The aim of this work is to collect, modify and apply preprocessing methods obtained from previous study to improve the quality of unstructured social media data by removing unessential data.

DATA EXTRACTION AND PREPROCESSING METHODS FOR SOCIAL MEDIA DATA

Social media became a part of daily life, it has huge impact on business, market growth and people sentiment and changing trends. Various existing text mining and preprocessing methods are described for web data analytics, text analytics. But it is required to modify and apply for real time social media analytics. As real time social media data has much impact on business growth, current trends, people opinions and emotion towards product, government, economic and lifestyle.

Existing systems and previous research works are focused on historical data and batch processing methods. Several social media analytical research works are based on supervised machine learning method or unsupervised lexicon methods. But each of this method have its own drawbacks. Such as supervised machine learning method requires time to train manually hence not suitable for real time analysis. However unsupervised lexicon suitable for real time analytics but it reduces accuracy as it contains set of unigram or bigram lexicon word dictionary.

Hence this work motivates researcher to conduct research on real time data analytics such as machine learning and sentiment analysis of tweets. Twitter is a platform with huge social media posts on various topics. Correspondingly identify a methods and tools to extract real time social media data and build suitable preprocessing method to improve the quality of the data to represent it easily into feature vector for hybrid machine learning and sentiment analysis.

Social Media Analytics

Social media over internet has given new direction for sharing information in short text messages. Which provides huge source of information for sentiment analysis of people opinion and interests toward trending topics. Real time analysis of large scale social media to identify people sentiment has got significant impotence in current data science research area.

Social media analytics has become new research trend (Lazer et al. n.d. 2009) (Gandomi et al. 2015) (Cioffi-Revilla 2010) in computational social science that comprises of Machine Learning, Artificial Intelligence, Natural Language Processing, big data and data mining. This leads to development of many data analytical and service tools and platforms such as R, python, Hadoop, spark, mango DB, APIs from twitter, Facebook and Wikipedia.

Data form social media can be accessed through in three ways. Firstly, Data base available free containing historical data. Secondly, Data can be accessed through tool. Lastly, the data can be accessed through APIs provided by social media platform.

Figure 1. Social media data analytics

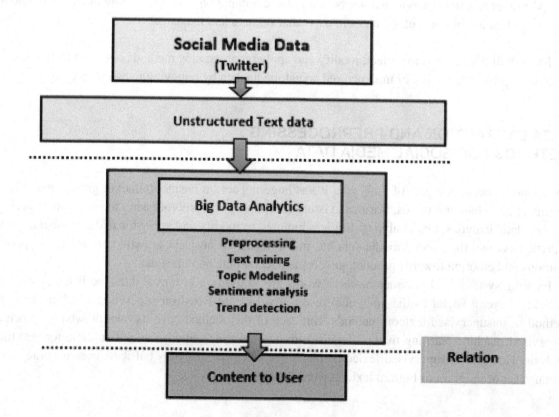

Social media platforms like twitter generates large amount of structured network data and unstructured text data as shown in Figure 3.1 Applying a social network analytics on social network data we can predict the link and communication between users, locations of users hence identifying the relations between the users. However this research work focuses on real time sentiment analysis of unstructured social media text data that is nothing but tweets. Big data analytical techniques need to be identified and applied to this data as shown in Figure 1 to process and extract relation between users to content. To extract and analyze unstructured text data from social media various text mining and NLP methods are applied, topic modeling, opinion mining and sentiment analysis methods are developed and applied to social media data.

Information Retrieval in Social Media

Social media platforms like twitter, Facebook generates huge amount of unstructured data every minute, every second of the day. It provides a great source of information for information retrieval research such as real time data extraction, social network analysis, sentiment analysis. Social media analytical research has got significant popularity due to huge amount of unstructured data generated can be used for analytics.

This work focuses on real time retrieval of unstructured twitter social media data and applying text mining and pre-processing methods to remove unessential content from it and preform feature extraction to extract important features from the data set. Finally to identify the impact of text mining and pre-processing on tweets for feature selection and machine learning for sentiment classification in future work.

A main characteristic of Twitter is its real-time environment and easy data availability. Tweeter has got more popularity in data analytical research and business activities compare to other social media platform due to easily available real time information by web based application programing interface(APIs) provided by twitter. This leads to vast advancement in data analysis tools and methods especially in big data analytics research area. Data analytical research area taking rapidly changes due to new tools, trends, events and information's available over the internet especially on social media has impact on daily life activities like news, marketing, opinion on product, people emotions, sharing new ideas. The paper (Batrinca & Treleaven 2014) provides a survey on various tools and technologies available for real time social media data extraction and preprocessing.

Twitter Data Retrieval: Social media like twitter provides powerful Application Programing Interface (APIs) to access and quick retrieve to social media data compare to other social platforms. Using APIs of twitter it is easy to retrieve data along with required contents like user information, location, followers, following count, friends group, retweets at real time. Based on research objective and analysis it is necessary to identify the requirement for twitter data such as: number of tweets, current or past tweets and event or topic on which research to be conducted. There are four means of retrieving twitter data based on intent and analysis as follows:

1. Using Twitter API
2. Using existing past twitter dataset
3. Buy from Twitter.
4. Access from service provider of twitter

In current days social media data can be easily accessed using APIs (Ferrara et al. 2014) according to Ferrara. In this work various web data extraction methods and applications are surveyed (Ferrara et al.

2014) . According to literature review, twitter APIs are the best possible method to retrieve large scale social data at real time. A method for crawling whole twitter platform is presented in the paper (Kwak et al. n.d. 2009) by accessing user profiles of 41.7 million people and 1.47 billion social relation. This work uses twitter API to retrieve maximum number of tweets related to top trending event after every 5 minutes. Such as real time retrieved data and preprocessed document contains 106 million tweets and 4262 trending topic.

Figure 2. Block diagram for Tweets data extraction and storage

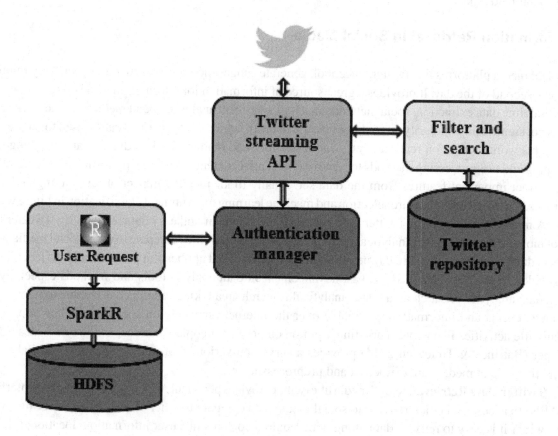

Twitter has powerful APIs to crawl entire social network of users compared to other social platform like Facebook. In this work twitter API used to integrate with R tool on spark framework as shown in Figure 3.2 to retrieve, process and store real time social media data.

Huge unstructured information generated form social media cannot be processed directly by machines. It is necessary to clean and remove unwanted information and make it in useful pattern. Such that it reduces time, and complexity in feature selection and machine learning. Therefor it is essential to apply preprocessing methods and algorithms to extract useful information form large scale unstructured data. Text mining and preprocessing is a part of various interdisciplinary fields like machine learning, natural language processing, data mining. Now it has taken a new route in web data analytics especially in social media analytics. Where many new challenges arise for text mining such as real time data extraction, large scale unstructured data storage and preprocessing, processing short text messages containing linguistic, numbers, URLs, images, emoticons, punctuation etc.

As we know information shared by user in social media contains informal natural language text. To apply ML and data analytical methods to this information is not directly appropriate. Hence information extraction and preprocessing need to be applied which plays a major role for extraction of information form these short messages.

Preprocessing Methods for Tweets

To mine knowledge and important features from unstructured tweets it is essential to apply various text mining and preprocessing method. As we know tweets are very linguistic, contains informal natural messages such as emoticons, URLs, punctuations, stop words and numbers. These information's are tokenized onto set of words know as corpus. Unessential information from this corpus is cleaned by applying suitable preprocessing methods as they carries least or no sentiments and opinions. Hence reduce in the data size, processing and ML training time. After cleaning unwanted information a plaintext is represented a set of words known as Bag of Word to identify the importance of word the document. Later represented in the form of vector to calculate numeric value for each word.

Let us consider set of extracted tweets as a set documents D consist of set of terms $T = \{t1.....; tm\}$ occurring in different document(tweet) d . The absolute frequency of term $t \in T$ in document $d \in D$ is given by $tf(d, t)$. Hence term vector t_d defined as follows:

$$\vec{td} = \left(tf\left(d, t1\right) ...., tf\left(d, tm\right) \right).$$

1. **Filtering**: main aim of filtering is to remove the words which carries least or no sentiments. Stop words like is, the, and, that, at are filtered using stop words library and removed from the corpus. Other content like articles, conjunctions and prepositions are removed. To further reduce the words in the corpus indexing or topic modeling methods are be used.

2. **Stemming:** To make word into its basic form by removing the strip from plural 's' from nouns, the 'ing' from verbs, or other affixes. Rule based stemming algorithm has been proposed by Porter (Porter 1980). He defined a set of production rules to transform English words into their stems iteratively.

Figure 3.

Rule			Example		
SSES	$\rightarrow$	SS	caresses	$\rightarrow$	caress
IES	$\rightarrow$	I	ponies	$\rightarrow$	poni
SS	$\rightarrow$	SS	caress	$\rightarrow$	caress
S	$\rightarrow$		cats	$\rightarrow$	cat

It is a process of transferring the words to it root word. It requires linguistic knowledge based on language dependency. Main idea behind stemming is that words with same root words carry same meaning or describes relative concepts. Example: computer, computerized stemmed to root word compute (User, used, using to root USE). Two types of errors arise in stemming process. One is over stemming happens when words of different roots are stemmed to same root. Next is under stemming happens when words with same root meaning stemmed to different root. Over stemming causes false positive and under stemming is false negative.

3. Lemmatization:

It is a process of identifying the lemma of the word. i.e finding the root meaning of the word. It is step in part of speech process (POS) to find proper meaning by analyzing morphological structure and vocabulary of the word. It returns the word in dictionary form to get root meaning of the word.

Lemmatization usually refers to doing things properly with the use of a vocabulary and morphological analysis of words, normally aiming to remove inflectional endings only and to return the base or dictionary form of a word, which is known as the lemma.

Difference between stemming and lemmatization is stemmer process words individually without considering the meaning of the word. Whereas lemmatization correctly determines the intended meaning of the word. Stemming is easy and runs fast compared to lemmatization which improves the accuracy of query recall in information retrieval process but it matters if it require to process and analyze some critical data. However it reduces true negative (precision) rate of the system

Preprocessing steps improves the quality and representations of corpus. Sequence of preprocessing steps are represented in the algorithm 1. Preprocessing unstructured tweets. Hence reduces the overall computational complexity and processing and training power and time of the model (Kuamri, S. and Babu, C.N., 2017) (Uysal & Gunal 2014). Hence improvising overall performance and efficiency of the system.

```
INPUT: SetOfDoc D_{i{i=1..N}} =Corpus(tweets(text))
OUTPUT: D_{i{i∈N}}
for all SetOfDoc do
    SetOfDoc = removePunctuation(SetOfDoc)
    SetOfDoc = removeNumbers (SetOfDoc)
    SetOfDoc = ConvertTotolower (SetOfDoc)
    SetOfDoc = removeStopWOrds(SetOfDoc)
    SetOfDoc = removeWhiteSpaces(SetOfDoc)
    Mylibrary = C(owns set of words)
    SetOfDoc = removeword(SetOfDoc, Mylibrary)
    SetOfDoc = stemDocument(SetOfDoc)
    SetOfDoc = Lemmatize(SetOfDoc)
        End for
```

Algorithm 1. Preprocessing Corpus of Tweets

4. Indexing:
In this method index terms or keywords are selected to describe the document. It is used to further reduce the size of the corpus by selecting indexing terms by applying keyword selection

algorithm (Deerwester et al. 1990). Simple method is entropy based keyword selection. For each word t in the vocabulary the entropy is computed (Lochbaum et al. n.d.) as follows:

$$W(t) = 1 + \frac{1}{\log_2 |D|} \sum_{d \in D} P(d,t) \log_2 P(d,t) \text{ with } P(d,t) = \frac{\text{tf}(d,t)}{\sum_{l=1}^{n} \text{tf}(d_l,t)}$$

5.   5. **Vector space model**: It is efficient method for analysis of large collection of documents by projecting down the document in low dimensional space. It is obtained by singular value decomposition of term document matrix. This results in saving the memory and query time according to (Berry et al. 1995) In this vector space model each word w in the set of document D is represented by feature vector $w(d)$ of m dimensional space. Aim of vector space model is to identify appropriate encoding for feature vector $w(d)$. It is used in many text mining research work for document retrieval and analysis. Binary vector is used most commonly to represent vector representation of document.

$$w(d) = \begin{cases} 0 & \textit{if word is not present in document d} \\ 1 & \textit{if word w is present in the document d} \end{cases}$$

The size of the vector is = total number of words (w=1) in the document D

Matrix representation of documents and related terms is as shows bellow. Different approaches for representation of terms and documents from the corpus into matrix are: (a) Document Term Matrix, (b) Term list and (c)Inverted Term Index matrix.

Table 1.

	t_1	t_2	t_3	t_4	t_5
d_1	0	0	1	1	0
d_2	0	1	0	1	0
d_3	1	1	0	1	1

Table 2.

Doc	terms
d_1	t_3, t_4
d_2	t_2, t_4
d_3	t_1, t_2, t_5

Table 3.

terms	doc
t_1	d_3
t_2	d_2, d_3
t_3	d_1
t_4	d_1, d_2
t_5	d_3

6.   6. **Term frequency-inverse document frequency**: it is most know method to calculate the occurrence of word in the document as well as it importance in the whole document set. i.e term frequency describes intra cluster similarity whereas inverse document frequency describes inter cluster similarity. It is represented as in equation (1)

$$tf\_idf_{(t,d)} = tf_{(t,d)} * idf_{(t,d)} \tag{1}$$

tf = importance of word t in the document d

idf = importance of document d containing word t within whole set of document D

Where *inverse document frequency* is represented as in equation (2):

$$idf_t = \log \frac{N}{df_t} \tag{2}$$

N: size of the document

D: collection of document contains term t

$w(d) = (w(d; t1); \cdots ; w(d; tm))$: vector of term weights in document d.

Two document d1, d2 similarity is represented by S (d1, d2) in equation 3 and calculated by inner product of the vectors

$$S(d_1, d_2) = \sum_{k=1}^{m} w(d_1, t_k) * w(d_2, t_k) \tag{3}$$

i.e cosine distance between two documents is given by: $\cos\theta = \dfrac{\vec{x}\vec{y}}{|\vec{x}| * |\vec{y}|} = 1 - \dfrac{1}{2}d^2\left(\dfrac{\vec{x}}{|\vec{x}|}, \dfrac{\vec{y}}{|\vec{y}|}\right)$ (4)

TF: It is used to determine the number of times word occurring in the document. i. e importance of the word in the document. If we consider only tem importance it lose document importance in the corpus. So it is necessary to consider term along with document frequency together for determining their importance in the corpus analysis. IDF is used to identify the importance of document in the corpus. The above equations 1 and 2 are reintern in terms of terms and documents as shown in bellow equation 5, 6 and 7.

$$TF(t,d) = \frac{Number\ of\ times\ term\ \boldsymbol{t}\ appears\ in\ a\ document\ \boldsymbol{d}}{Total\ number\ of\ terms\ in\ the\ document} \quad (5)$$

$$IDF(t,d,D) = log\_e\ \frac{Total\ number\ of\ documents\ \boldsymbol{D}\ \ .}{Number\ of\ documents\ \boldsymbol{d}\ with\ term\ \boldsymbol{t}\ in\ it} \quad (6)$$

$$TF - IDF(t,d,D) = TF(t,d) * IDF(t,d,D) \quad (7)$$

The value of IDF will be equals to, or greater than zero if log value inside the ratio value is one. More number of document containing the word TF-IDF will be closer to zero

7. Dimensionality Reduction

To identify and remove these least important words and documents from the corpus the algorithm 2 is designed to set the threshold. That eliminates words and document which are less than set threshold value. Hence reducing the overall dimensions of word vector, reduces overall computational complexity without losing essential information from the corpus.

Table 4. Algorithm 2. Removing Sparse terms from DTM using TF-IDF Weighting Scheme

INTPUT: (Corpus of documents D, Term Frequency **TF**, Inverse Document Frequency **IDF**)
Calculate **TF** = Term Document Matrix (term t_i є **T**, document d_i є **D**, T * D)
for all term t_i in document d_i **do**
$t_i = t_i + 1$
if t_i < threshold_Th **then**
remove **di**
else
calculate **IDF**
if IDF » 0 **then**
remove t_i from the **D**,
remove corresponding **TF**
else
calculate **TF*IDF**
if TF-IDF » 0 **then**
keep document d_i from **D**
else
remove document d_i from **D**
end

EXPERIMENTAL SETUP

Twitter has powerful APIs to crawl entire social network of users compare to other social platform like face book, Instagram. In this work twitter APIs is integrated with R tool on spark framework as shown in figure 4.1 to retrieve, process and store real time social media data.

Real Time R Connection to Twitter using Twitter API:

To establish connection between R tool with twitter for real time data extraction, following standard packages are used:

1. **TwitteR:** It is used to interface R studio to twitter APIs
2. **ROAuth:** It allows user to authenticate tweeter connection using OAuth specification to access tweets at real-time. ROAuth give third party access to twitter data.

Spark provides special feature called RDDs for in-memory computation. Hence allowing faster processing i.e 100x faster than Hadoop. Hence it is suitable for real time data processing. It also provides set of machine learning library called MLlib to analyze the data at application level and transferring complexity at application level.

Spark and R indivisibly having their own advantages and disadvantages. Spark is open source distributed parallel data processing framework suitable for large scale data processing. It offers RDDs for in-memory computation and hence 100x faster than Hadoop hence suitable for real time and stream data processing. But it is difficult to code and visualize and interpret the results at application level. To overcome this drawback R tool is deployed on spark and use it on application level.

R tool: It is open source contains more than 9000+ public packers for data analytics and statistics. It is easy to code and visualize the result on R studio. But it is limited to single core and single thread processing of data. It supports all in memory (RAM) sequential processing. Hence no support for parallel and distributed processing of data across several computers.

Considering the advantages and disadvantages of Spark and R, they are joined together as shown in figure 4.1 to scale R for distributed parallel processing of data on several computers (HDFS) and deploying it on spark framework to support multicore and multithread processing of streaming data over single computer hence increasing the processing capacity, easy coding and interpretation of results.

Figure 4. Generalized Spark + R framework for real time twitter data processing

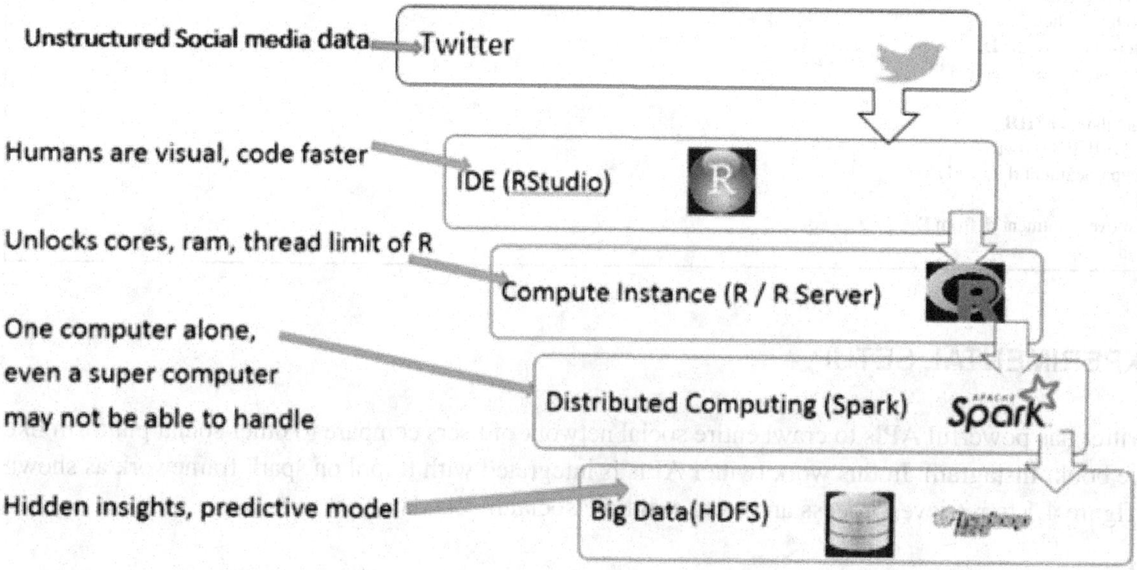

To access the tweets from twitter: It offers three types of APIs, they are as follows:

1. **Search APIs**: These APIs are available in twitteR package and used to search tweets at real time based on given search string. Search APIs allows to retrieve tweets using specific keyword, hashtag and specific user. But it will not give access to all the tweets. It gives access to only authorized tweets based on search string.

2. **REST APIs**: It allows to access basic tweet information such as status information, user data, timeline updates. Primarily used to get profile details, follower, following details of user. Secondly to get tweets and retweets.

3. **Streaming APIs**: These APIs provides real time streaming access to tweeter data. Compare to above two APIs it provides access to all public tweeter data in large scale. It offers many features to filter the tweets based on language, location, along with extraction of large scale keywords, hashtags and retweets.

Streaming APIs are used in this work to retrieve the tweets form twitter, as it is suitable for real time accesses to tweets in large scale with time stamp and location. 'streamR' package provides these APIs to access streaming data at real time.

-   *Twitter Data Extraction Using Streaming API:* Establishing connection between SaprkR and twitter, the data is extracted and filtered at real time using streaming API by giving input as keyword or hashtag with several options like time period, location, retweets based on interested topic for analysis. For this research work only English tweets are used and extracted from the particular location related to different events happening at real time. Data is stored on database system for preprocessing, feature section, machine learning and real time analysis.

-   *Preprocessing:* To apply data analytical method to these unstructured tweets is difficult, it requires cleaning and removing unnecessary information to improve quality of the data for machine learning and data analysis.

To improve the quality of extracted tweets, prepossessing methods are very essential. Twitter data prepossessing is carried out in sequence of steps as follows shown in figure 5

Figure 5. Twitter data preprocessing

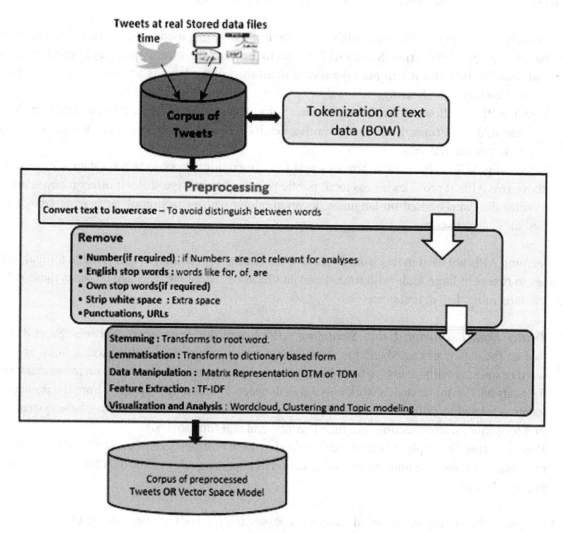

Steps of preprocessing from Figure 4.2 classifieds mainly in 4 steps.

1. Tokenization
2. Filtering
3. Indexing
4. Dimension reduction

Tokenization is the process of breaking a stream of text into words, phrases, symbols, or other meaningful elements. The aim of the tokenization is the exploration of the words in a sentence. The list of tokens becomes input for further processing such as parsing or text mining. It contains sequence of characters to parse the document as it contains words, punctuations, special characters, URL need to be filtered in subsequent steps.

Challenges: Tokenization is challenging based on language and slangs. In English, words in document are delimited by white spaces. Where in slangs, typographical structures in social communication language like (OMG: oh my god, LOL: laugh out loudly, plz: please, atfn: afternoon) requires additional lexical parsing and structure analysis.

Lowercase letters: All the data in the corpus is converted into lower case letters to maintain the uniformity in the document processing.

2. *Filtering or Removal of unwanted data:*

   a. *Remove numbers*: Numbers removal is an optional based on topic and data analysis because most of the cases numbers will not provide any sentiments.

   b. *Removal of stop words(English):* Sentences Witten in English contains frequent use of stop words like "is, the, that, this, of, to". English language contains around 400 to 500 stop word. Which are least essential in data analysis and information processing tasks as it doesn't carry any sentiment or opinion. Most of these stop words are identified and removed by matching it to stop word library from 'tm' text mining package. Remaining stop words requires lexical parsing of the document. Around 25% to 30% of English text document contains stop word. By removing these stop word reduces the computational complexity, processing and training power and time of the model (Uysal & Gunal 2014). Hence improvising overall performance of the system.

   c. *Remove white spaces, special characters and URLs*: In social media, style of writing tweets differs from person to person compare to normal writing style in English. People use extra white space to provide style and different look to their tweet. They also use special characters, emoticons URL or HTTP links to show their emotion like (party @..... 7pm ☺, plz follow URL https://www.google.co.in/search?q=palce+grond+banglor for venue). Hence removing extra white space and special catheter is challenging task for social media analysis. Most of the extra white space and special catheters are identified and removed using 'tm' text mining package. Reaming *white spaces, special characters and URLs* requires lexical parsing the document.

   d. *Remove punctuations*: Similar to stop word, punctuations also doesn't carry any opinion or sentiment and sometime people use extra punctuations to give style and different look to their tweet. These are also removed to reduce the computational complexity and processing and training power of the model.

   e. **Stemming**: It is a process of transferring the words to it root word. It requires linguistic knowledge based on language dependency. Main idea behind stemming is that words with same root words carry same meaning or describes relative concepts. Example: computer, computerized stemmed to root word compute (User, used, using to root USE). This work uses Dr. Martin Porter's stemming algorithm (Porter 1980) for stemming the twitter document(https://tartarus. org/martin/PorterStemmer/index.html)

   f. **Lemmatization**: It is used to make nouns and infinite tense to singular form. It is done using suitable dictionary and morphological analysis. Main aim of lemmatization is used to reduce the size of corpus by identifying inflected words and transforming them into dictionary or root form known as lemma.

3. **Data Manipulation and Indexing using Vector space model**

After removing unwanted data from the corpus next step is to index the corpus in the form of corpus of word vector i.e nothing but matrix of document and vector representation of words to identify the type of word and number of times word present in the document. It is essential to determine frequency of words in the document and count of document containing that word and overall weight to know importance of word and document to the topic and subsequent step of data analytics.

In this work Term Frequency-Inverse Document Frequency (TF-IDF) is used for indexing and determining the importance of word in the document and relative importance of document (tweet) in whole set of corpus of documents. TF-IDF is most commonly used mathematical model for text mining task to determine the importance of term and document in the corpus. It is represented in the form equation 7.

4. ***Dimensionality Reduction:*** Once calculating TF-IDF, less frequent and more frequent words are identified and removed by setting threshold value. To identify and remove these least important words and documents from the corpus the algorithm 3 is designed to set the threshold. That eliminates words and document which are less than set threshold value. Hence reducing the overall dimensions of word vector, reduces overall computational complexity without losing essential information from the corpus.

RESULT AND ANALYSIS

In this section results are analyzed for data extraction, preprocessing and vector representation and data reduction. The fraction of terms or documents resulting after preprocessing are significant to the topics is known as precision. Whereas recall is returning all terms or documents after preprocessing, that leads to poor precision. Most of the previous experimental evidence identified that there is a tradeoff between precision and recall for dynamic change of data.

Data Extraction and Representation

Real time extraction of social media data, twitter developer account is created and connection is established between R and twitter account. Tweets related to data science and machine learning is searched, in that conditions are given as 15000 tweets and language is specified English to extract english tweets for analysis. However search resulted with 10403 English tweets. Extracted data is saved in the form of data frame for further manipulation of twitter data. Twitter data frame contains 10403 rows (tweets or documents) and 17 attributes (columns). In that only text column is extracted for sentiment analysis as shown in following syntax.

Extracted text data from data frame is used to build the corpus and specified the source to be character vectors as shown in following syntax. Following preprocessing and text mining methods are applied to corpus of the document for cleaning and removing unessential information and framing into proper structure for further manipulation such as feature extraction, selection, machine learning and sentiment analysis.

Data Preprocessing and Cleaning

Following suitable text mining methods are identified and implemented to clean and preprocess the twitter data as shown in Table 5.

Table 5. Data preprocessing methods and results

Preprocessing Method	Resulted Document(tweets)
Convert To Lower Cases	[3] how data center infrastructure management (dcim) response to ai and machine learning? #datascience #ai… https://t.co/fk1ebycvtj [4] rt @calonsofdez: our paper "applications of data science to game learning analytics data: a systematic literature review" (computers & educ… [10] rt @odsc: phd candidates often work on some fascinating data science projects. here are 10 standout machine learning dissertations that may…
Remove Punctuation	[3] how data center infrastructure management dcim response to ai and machine learning datascience ai… httpstcofk1ebycvtj [4] rt calonsofdez our paper applications of data science to game learning analytics data a systematic literature review computers amp educ… [10] rt odsc phd candidates often work on some fascinating data science projects here are 10 standout machine learning dissertations that may…
Filter Stop Words	[3] data center infrastructure management dcim response ai machine learning datascience ai… httpstcofk1ebycvtj [4] rt calonsofdez paper applications data science game learning analytics data systematic literature review computers amp educ… [10] rt odsc phd candidates often work fascinating data science projects 10 standout machine learning dissertations may…
User-Defined Stop Words To Be Filtered Out	[3] data center infrastructure management dcim response ai machine learning datascience ai… [4] rt calonsofdez paper applications data science game learning analytics data systematic literature review computers educ… [10] rt odsc phd candidates often work fascinating data science projects 10 standout machine learning dissertations may…
Remove Numbers	[3] data center infrastructure management dcim response ai machine learning datascience ai… [4] rt calonsofdez paper applications data science game learning analytics data systematic literature review computers educ… [10] rt odsc phd candidates often work fascinating data science projects standout machine learning dissertations may…
Remove White Space In Text	3] data center infrastructure management dcim response ai machine learning datascience ai… [4] rt calonsofdez paper applications data science game learning analytics data systematic literature review computers educ… [10] rt odsc phd candidates often work fascinating data science projects standout machine learning dissertations may…
Stemming	[3] data center infrastructur manag dcim respons ai machin learn datasci ai… [4] calonsofdez paper applic data scienc game learn analyt data systemat literatur review comput educ… [10] odsc phd candid often work fascin data scienc project standout machin learn dissert may…

1. Data Manipulation and Indexing

To check the number of tokens (words) and unique tokens present in the corpus after preprocessing and before preprocessing a function is implanted. This function finds number of token that has word length minimum two as we know word of length less than or equals to two such as "to", "on", "rt", "u", "i" holds no or least sentiment. Before preprocessing corpus contains 224361 tokens out of which 16162 are unique tokens. After preprocessing corpus holds 126174tokens out of which 10067are unique tokens as shown in bellow syntax.

Applying preprocessing methods most of the unessential data is removed from corpus. To perform further analysis and extraction of important feature, the corpus is represented in the form of term document matrix (TDM) as shown in figure 5.1 or document term matrix (DTM) as shown in figure 5.2. TDM and DTM shows 9116 terms after stemming, 9850 terms before stemming in 10403 documents. Maximum length of word is 107. Due to over fitting and under fitting error of stemming method, it is not used in this research work.

TERM DOCUMENT MATRIX

Document Term Matrix

DTM and TDM matrix are repressed in matrix form as shown in figure 5.3 for further manipulations such as calculating frequency of word, important features identification, correlation and association between word, clustering related topics and topic modeling using LDA (Monish, P., Kumari, S. and Babu, C.N., 2018)

Figure 6. Term frequency in TDM

```
<<DocumentTermMatrix (documents: 10403, terms: 9850)>>
Non-/sparse entries: 110270/102359280
Sparsity            : 100%
Maximal term length: 107
Weighting           : term frequency (tf)
Sample              :
```

Docs	analytics	big	can	data	datascience	learning	machine	machinelearning	python	science
1156	0	0	0	2	0	1	1	0	0	0
5345	0	1	0	3	0	0	1	0	0	0
7069	0	1	0	1	0	1	1	0	0	0
7343	0	1	0	1	0	1	1	0	0	0
7636	0	1	0	1	0	1	1	0	0	0
7727	0	1	0	1	0	1	1	0	0	0
7729	0	1	0	1	0	1	1	0	0	0
7748	0	1	0	1	0	1	1	0	0	0
8013	0	0	0	1	0	1	1	0	0	0
951	0	0	0	1	0	1	1	0	0	0

In DTM or TDM most of the cells are with 0's and less frequent terms, they are identified and removed by applying TF (Term Frequency) weighting method to reduce computational complexity. After removing 0.02% and 0.01% sparsity DTM obtained contains only 55,133 most frequent terms respectively in 10403 documents. Following figure 5.3, figure 5.4, shows the word frequency in Term Document Matrix and word frequency after removing sparse terms in TDM.

Figure 7. Term frequency after removing sparse terms

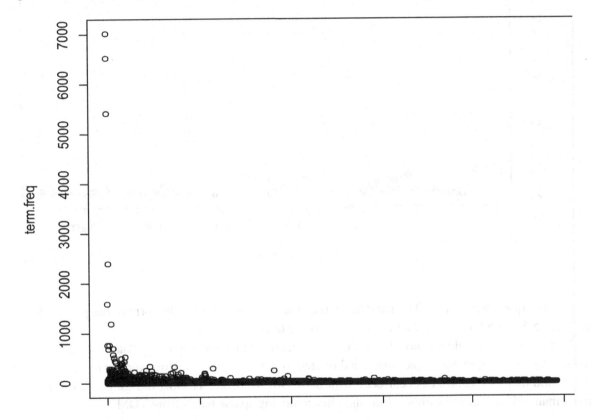

Figure 8. Most frequent words in TDM

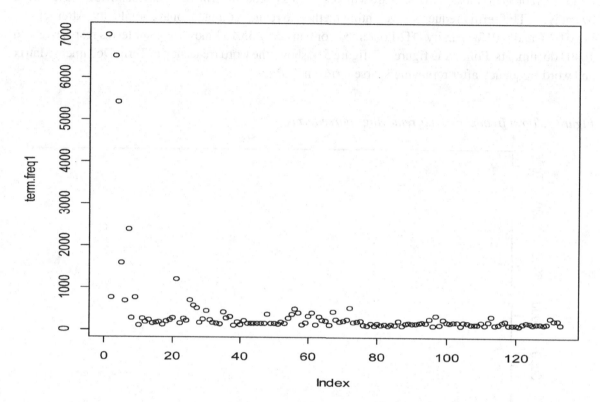

Most frequent terms in the TDM and their frequency is represented in the form of bar plot as shown in figure 5.5 and 5.6 before and after removing sparse terms respectively.

Using association rule the most frequent words occurring in association with "data", "machine" are recognized. That represents topics discussed related to these two words. However the most associated words and their percentage of occurrence with these two words are as show in figure 5.7. It represent more than 10% associated words before and after removing sparse terms from TDM.

Figure 9. Most frequent words in TDM after removing sparse terms

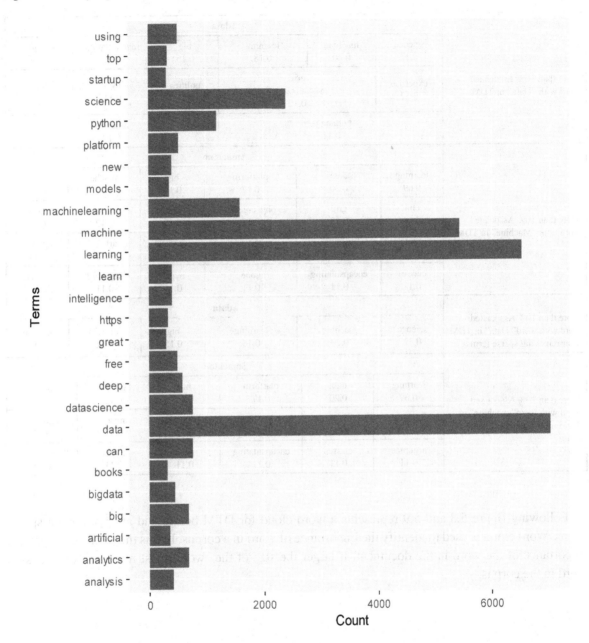

Table 6.

More than 10% Associated word with "Data" in TDM	**$data**					
	science 0.37	machine 0.20	learning 0.18	big 0.15	manipulation 0.13	scientist 0.12
	expertise 0.12	eric visualization 0.12		politics 0.11	loeb 0.11	sha 0.11
	bellanaija 0.11			analysis 0.10		
More than 10% Associated word with "Machine" in TDM	**$machine**					
	learning 0.69	data 0.20	platform 0.17	big 0.14	launches 0.13	clacical 0.13
	cml 0.13	gml 0.13	physorgcom 0.13	scientist 0.12	intersect 0.12	labs 0.12
	corporate 0.12	parsing 0.12	raises 0.12	sensitive 0.12	artific 0.12	argumen 0.11
	classes 0.11	encapsulating 0.11	gone 0.11	hyper 0.11	keyword 0.11	models 0.11
More than 10% Associated word with word" Data" in TDM after removing sparse terms	**$data**					
	science 0.37	machine 0.20	learning 0.18	big 0.15	scientist 0.12	analysis 0
More than 10% Associated word with word" machine" in TDM after removing sparse terms	**$machine**					
	learning 0.69	data 0.20	platform 0.17	big 0.14	launches 0.13	scientist 0.12
	intersect 0.12	labs 0.12	corporate 0.12	parsing 0.12	raises 0.12	sensitive 0.12
	argumen 0.11	classes 0.11	encapsulating 0.11	gone 0.11	hyper 0.11	keyword 0.11

Following figure 5.8 and 5.9 represents a word cloud for DTM before and after removing sparse terms. Word cloud is used to identify the importance of word in a corpus. In this the word size represent importance of the word in the document. If larger the size of the sword, most relevant and discussed word in the corpus.

Figure 10. Words associated with terms "data" and "machine" in TDM before and after removal of sparse terms

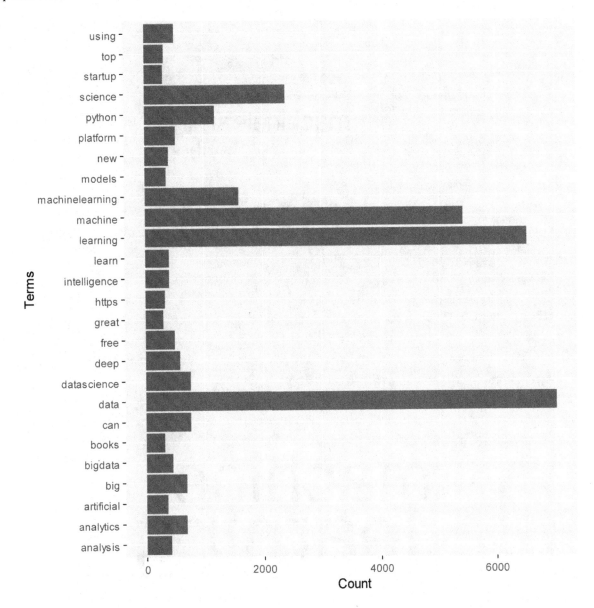

Figure 11. World cloud for most frequent terms in DTM

Figure 12. World cloud for most frequent terms in DTM after removing sparse terms

2. Clustering

Clustering identifies important words in the TDM which are grouped into clusters using hierarchical clustering method. The corpus of most frequent words are grouped into 8 clusters to identify the most correlated topics discussed in the collection of tweets related to term "data science". Hierarchical cluster are created before and after removing sparse terms as shown in Figure 13 and 14.

Figure 13. Hierarchical clusters for TDM most frequent terms

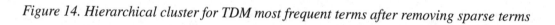

Figure 14. Hierarchical cluster for TDM most frequent terms after removing sparse terms

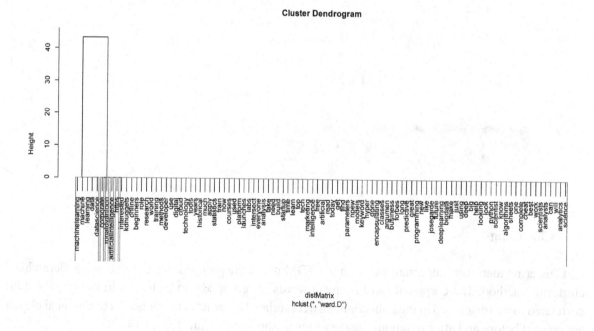

3.   Topic Modeling

Topic modeling is applied to discover hidden topics in the set of tweets (Monish, P., Kumari, S. and Babu, C.N., 2018). Using Latent Dirichlet Allocation (LDA) topic modeling method 8 abstract topics are discovered in the corpus of tweets and the relative 20 words are also recognized as shown in figure 5.12. The following syntax represents implementation of LDA method to discover hidden topics in the corpus.

Table 7.

Topic 1
"data, learning, datascience, machinelearning, machine, using, free, read, science, ronaldvanloon, mustread, bigdata, can, scientists, stats, mitcsail, startup, models, program, magic"
Topic 2
"learning, science, data, machine, machinelearning, bigdata, analytics, intelligence, big, future, datascience, https, forbes, great, best, startup, need, scientists, sheets, models"
Topic 3
"data, learning, machine, science, machinelearning, using, intelligence, platform, new, https, python, learn, deep, looking, bigdata, artificial, free, build, books, online"
Topic 4
"machine, data, learning, science, python, analytics, top, deep, platform, machinelearning, get, analysis, big, argumen, can, sentiment, great, corporate, years, keyword"
Topic 5
"data, machine, learning, science, platform, analytics, free, everyone, long, analysis, completely, https, models, startup, books, using, scientist, gone, parameters, intersect"
Topic 6
"learning, can, machinelearning, science, machine, learn, data, datascience, python, deep, artificial, will, sources, kdnuggets, datasets, volume, scientist, new, four, deeplearning"
Topic 7
"machine, python, learning, big, data, deep, new, can, top, science, help, best, will, analytics, tensorflow, one, work, free, machinelearning, mining"
Topic 8
"data, machine, machinelearning, learning, can, deep, python, large, datascience, analysis, stpiindia, multiple, programming, significant, training, historical, help, play, scientist, make"

Figure 15. Eight topics related to data science discovered using LDA Topic modeling

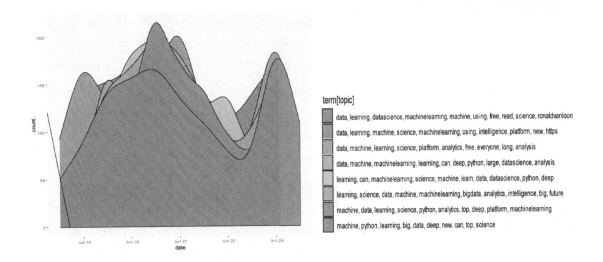

4.　　Dimensionality Reduction

After removing sparse terms from TDM through identifying less frequent and most frequent terms and document by applying TF-IDF model TDM resulting frequency of words is represented in figure 15 identified important features and compared the results with TDM.

Figure 16. Results of word frequency by applying TF-IDF

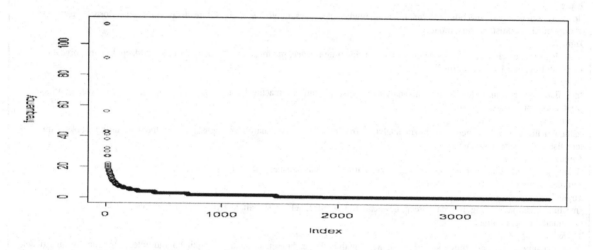

Most frequent terms obtained by applying customized TF-IDF method to TDM and top 10 most frequent words are represented in following figure 16.

The fraction of terms or documents resulting after preprocessing are significant to the topics is known as precision. Whereas recall is returning all terms or documents after preprocessing, that leads to poor precision. Most of the previous experimental evidence identified that there is a tradeoff between precision and recall for dynamic change of data.

Figure 17. Top 10 terms and their relative frequency by applying customized TF-IDF

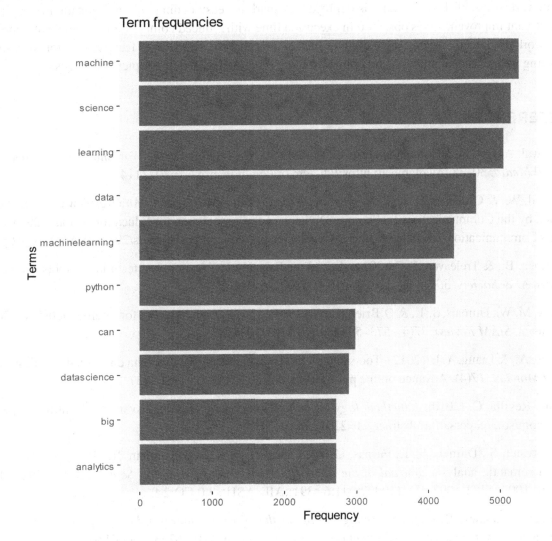

CONCLUSION

Social media platforms generates data in various format, languages and speed hence presents many challenges in advance data analytics and computing area to discover new value and extract knowledge. Huge amount of unstructured data generated from social media such as twitter. Thousands of tweets generated every second on various topics and issues. In this work several information retrieval and text mining methods are analyzed and customized for retrieving, storing, organizing and preprocessing real time large scale twitter data. It has analyzed that preprocessing methods improves the quality of data and remove the unessential data. It is also observed that using tweeter APIs and access tokens easy to retrieve twitter data at real time. Preprocessing and dimensionality reduction are fundamental step in data analytics and NLP tasks to process unstructured data into structured data. Suitable preprocessing method like tokenization, removal of stop word, stemming, lemmatization are customized and applied to normalize the social media data and improve the quality of data for machine learning. On the other hand to address the scalability issues such as real time analysis of large scale social media data spark framework is established. R studio is deployed on spark for easy coding and interpretation of results. Significant improvements is observed in execution time with reduced computational complexity. In future work preprocessed data can be used for further data analysis step such as feature selection, machine learning and sentiment analysis and opinion mining on real time trending topics and issues.

REFERENCES

Agarwal, A. (2011). Sentiment analysis of Twitter data. *Proceedings of the Workshop on Languages in Social Media*, 30–38. Available at: https://dl.acm.org/citation.cfm?id=2021114

Ahmed, W., & Graduate, D. (n.d.). *Using Social Media Data for Research: An Overview of Tools* Published by the Communication Technology Division of the Association for Education in Journalism and Mass Communication. Available at: http://www.joctec.org/wp-content/uploads/2018/04/A6_WA_v2.pdf

Batrinca, B., & Treleaven, P. C. (2014). Social media analytics: A survey of techniques, tools and platforms. *AI & Society*, *30*(1), 89–116. doi:10.100700146-014-0549-4

Berry, M. W., Dumais, S. T., & O'Brien, G. W. (1995). Using Linear Algebra for Intelligent Information Retrieval. *SIAM Review*, *37*(4), 573–595. doi:10.1137/1037127

Bruns, A., & Liang, Y. E. (2012). Tools and methods for capturing Twitter data during natural disasters. *First Monday*, *17*(4). Advance online publication. doi:10.5210/fm.v17i4.3937

Cioffi-Revilla, C. (2010). *A methodology for complex social simulations*. Available at: https://papers.ssrn.com/sol3/papers.cfm?abstract_id=2291156

Deerwester, S., Dumais, S. T., Furnas, G. W., Landauer, T. K., & Harshman, R. (1990). Indexing by latent semantic analysis. *Journal of the American Society for Information Science*, *41*(6), 391–407. doi:10.1002/(SICI)1097-4571(199009)41:6<391::AID-ASI1>3.0.CO;2-9

Dueñas-Fernández, R. (n.d.). *Detecting trends on the Web: A multidisciplinary approach*. Elsevier. Available at: https://www.sciencedirect.com/science/article/pii/S1566253514000116

Fayyad, U. M. (n.d.). *Summary from the KDD-03 Panel-Data Mining: The Next 10 Years*. Available at: www.DMXgroup.comwww.Kdnuggets.comwww.gm.com

Ferrara, E. (2014). *Web Data Extraction, Applications and Techniques: A Survey*. Available at: https://arxiv.org/pdf/1207.0246.pdf

Gandomi, A., & Haider, M. (2015). Beyond the hype: Big data concepts, methods, and analytics. *International Journal of Information Management*, *35*(2), 137–144. doi:10.1016/j.ijinfomgt.2014.10.007

Haddi, E., Liu, X., & Shi, Y. (2013). The Role of Text Pre-processing in Sentiment Analysis. *Procedia Computer Science*, *17*, 26–32. doi:10.1016/j.procs.2013.05.005

Kwak, H. (n.d.). *What is Twitter, a Social Network or a News Media?* Available at: http://bit.ly

Lazer, D. (n.d.). *Computational social science*. Available at: https://science.sciencemag.org/content/323/5915/721.short

Lochbaum, K., & Management, L. S.-I. P. (1989). *Comparing and combining the effectiveness of latent semantic indexing and the ordinary vector space model for information retrieval.* Elsevier. Available at: https://www.sciencedirect.com/science/article/pii/0306457389901003

Mohammad, S. M., Zhu, X., Kiritchenko, S., & Martin, J. (2015). Sentiment, emotion, purpose, and style in electoral tweets. *Information Processing & Management, 51*(4), 480–499. doi:10.1016/j.ipm.2014.09.003

Porter, M. F. (1980). An algorithm for suffix stripping. *Program, 14*(3), 130–137. Available at: http://www.emeraldinsight.com/doi/10.1108/eb046814

Rajman, M. (1998). *Text mining-knowledge extraction from unstructured textual data.* Springer. Available at: https://link.springer.com/chapter/10.1007/978-3-642-72253-0_64

Salton, G., Wong, A., & Yang, C. S. (1975). A vector space model for automatic indexing. *Communications of the ACM, 18*(11), 613–620. doi:10.1145/361219.361220

Singh, T., & Kumari, M. (2016). Role of Text Pre-processing in Twitter Sentiment Analysis. *Procedia Computer Science, 89,* 549–554. doi:10.1016/j.procs.2016.06.095

Sun, X. (n.d.). *Empirical studies on the nlp techniques for source code data preprocessing*. Available at: https://dl.acm.org/citation.cfm?id=2627514

Uysal, A. K., & Gunal, S. (2014). The impact of preprocessing on text classification. *Information Processing & Management, 50*(1), 104–112. doi:10.1016/j.ipm.2013.08.006

Webster, J. J., & Kit, C. (1992). Tokenization as the initial phase in NLP. In *Proceedings of the 14th conference on Computational linguistics* (p. 1106). Association for Computational Linguistics. doi:10.3115/992424.992434

Xue, X. (2008). *Distributional features for text categorization*. https://ieeexplore.ieee.org/abstract/document/4589210/

Zhao, W. (n.d.). *Topical keyphrase extraction from twitter*. Available at: https://dl.acm.org/citation.cfm?id=2002521

Chapter 3
A Review of Text Analytics Using Machine Learning

Ajaypradeep Natarajsivam
Vellore Institute of Technology, India

Sasikala R.
Vellore Institute of Technology, India

ABSTRACT

In recent years, data analysis has been widely applied in many different domains. Text data plays an important role in prediction of various insights. The data produced in the form of user reviews, satisfactory forms, movie reviews, after sales product reviews, and similar kinds of representations serve as inputs for textual data analysis. In previous years, however, companies relied on paper-based satisfactory surveys, agent reports, etc. for business development or product outreach development purposes. As these methods involve human intervention, there is always a very high chance of false inputs. Hence, the development of computational intelligence-based strategies such as textual and sentimental analysis have been of enormous help for such companies. Automated tools and software have helped various business organizations and firms to develop their business, find their faults and bugs, and relieve themselves from their limitations. This chapter discusses the basics of textual analysis, approaches for textual analysis, as well as the tools, solutions, and some limitations of applying textual analysis.

INTRODUCTION

Text mining or analysis generally refers to the extraction of data or information from large volume of texts. Indeed, the extracted information will possess quality content which can be used for different purposes. Text mining or text analysis can be applied where there is a large volume of text content. It is noteworthy that text does not only mean books, manuscripts, and theses. Text in all forms that appear in various platforms such as internet, social media, messengers, mails etc. can also be used for text mining and analytics. In recent years, different organizations, firms, industries, and even small-scale business units have felt the growing need to collect and analyze customers' feedback in order to improve their

DOI: 10.4018/978-1-7998-9594-7.ch003

services and productions. These kinds of inputs or data fed by the end user or customer offer genuine insights as they are given from users' perspective. Before the advancement in computational intelligence, the data on customer satisfaction or feedback were obtained in a paper format. As anyone could fill those forms, authenticity of the collected data was always a major constraint for the organizations to ensure the quality of the product/services. In some cases, based on customer's thinking the interest towards products are distinguished. For instance, when a person is happy and he/she searches for a product and if he/she finds a suitable one, he/she would opt for purchasing the product. Under the same scenario in a mixed mindset, he/she would search for reviews, dialup friends or relatives who own a similar product and ask for their experience using that product. Under the same scenario if a person is under depression or sad, even though the product is good and excellent in the market, he/she would not opt for purchasing it. Thus, everything is based on the situation and emotions of the end user which makes them to decide what to do next, whether to purchase or not. Thus customer's emotional incidence and customer feedback are very important for various decisions in business intelligence and product marketing. As customers decision may suddenly change for no reason, it is difficult to predict the exact outcome of a product based on surveys (Pang & Lee, 2008). Textual analysis gathers information from unstructured sources for the further perusal. User given input information plays a very important role in such textual analysis. In the current decade, people utilize 'internet' to express their thoughts and feelings. Various talk forums, social media hubs, blogspot(s), groups, etc. serve as platform for this purpose (Liu, 2010). This can be considered as general discussion forums where they share their opinions and feelings about a particular topic or a current happening. In the same way when it comes into a product or application, the inputs given by public impacts the real time sales of a 'product' or 'application'. In e-commerce platforms or commodity selling sites, people search with 'keywords' pertaining to the product they look for. For instance, name of the 'brand', 'capacity', 'manufacturer', 'warranty' etc are the common keywords in terms of 'product'. 'Vendor', 'version', 'validity' etc can be 'keywords' for an application. On searching with the keyword people will be shown search results of various brands, of various varieties and capacities. People's first noticeable constraint will be the 'reviews' of such product. In the world of e-commerce websites, previous customers' 'reviews' of a product play an important role in its sales. While negative reviews may discourage potential customers' from purchasing the product, positive reviews may have the opposite effect. Thus, the textual analysis plays a very important role in business analytics and sales prediction strategies. In this chapter, textual analysis will be carried out in 3 broader steps: The 'Document level', the 'sentence level' and the 'feature level'. The 'document' and 'sentence' levels of analysis perform the sentimental opinion about the products. The third level performs the process of 'features' based on the product. In the process of evaluation or analysis, each review or comment is considered to be a 'document' (Godara & Kumar, 2019). There are various open-source tools that are used for text analytics which predict and perform genuine response detection from the text inputs from various end users. These tools work on the basis of machine learning, deep learning-based algorithms and extensions and they reflect as the genuine source of extracting customer's sentiments and satisfaction measures. The Artificial Intelligence powered tools provide a broad space for analytics of data fed as input. This chapter discusses various such tools and their functionality as a review and further narrates how machine learning based systems have implications on text and emotional analytics and its future extensions.

This chapter reviews various tools and techniques which possess ML based strategies for text analytics in real time systems. The core functionality of such tools is based on advanced artificial intelligence strategies and thus the employability of manpower or hindrance of human is reduced considerably by availing these tools. Figure 1. Illustrates the extensive applications of textual data in real time.

Figure 1. Applications of textual data

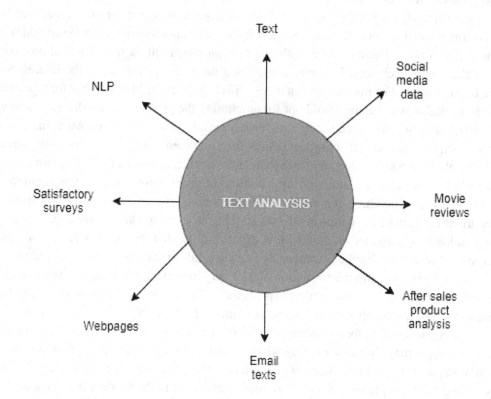

TEXT DATA - A BRIEF CYCLE

The application of text data is undoubtedly unavoidable in everyday life. Nowadays, nearly everything is online. After the COVID-19 pandemic, even teaching and learning have been moved to the category of 'online'. People spend more time on interacting with digital gadgets, laptops, AI devices etc. than other individuals. This means that large-scale datasets are being generated every moment. A few decades ago, people used 'postal communication' for festival seasons and other events. Then, fax machines, pagers, and mobile phones appeared. Now is the era of smart phones. With these advancements, the version of text has also changed from handwriting to digital version. Even though, we still use text.

Over the past two decades, text analytics and sentimental analysis have achieved tremendous growth in real time applications. The foresaid is not only applied for common analysis but also in sensitive research areas such as healthcare and medicine too. This outreach is a real success, and the research in the same are will lead to a great era in near future. The diagram specifies the brief life cycle of text in 'written' and 'digital' forms. The figure 2 illustrates the cycle of text analytics. As the approach of digital means of text analytics is considered to be as faster and better approach as the tools involved in the approach is automated and has advanced features and data visualization as embedded feature, the same analysis can be performed by traditional methods too. As traditional methods involve more 'paper' based work and have a lot of human interventions, the computational intelligence powered textual or sentimental analysis is much preferred. However, in cases like countable instance of values where there is very less amount of data, manual analysis can be performed, and the values can be cross-checked with digital means.

Figure 2. Cycle of text data analytics

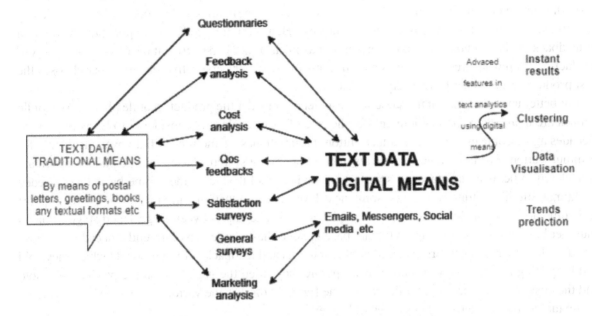

Real Need for Text Data Analysis

Machine learning and deep learning-based applications are being used in all domains and fields. All the tasks or applications which are performed computationally with the help of ML/DL algorithms can be conducted by traditional methods too. But the constraint is, it will be time consuming and may involve in human made errors. Rather in some cases like text mining the human made analysis may be useless and not efficient when compared with computational analysis. Thus, there exists a real need for application of computational based applications which is considered to be supreme and trust worthier.

Text mining and analysis extends an extensive method to evaluate large volumes of text data available in various sources such as internet. When it comes to a product or even a movie review, people search with the concerned 'keyword' relative to their search of interest. People may learn from the inputs, suggestions and review comments fed by various sources such as general public, end product consumers, commoners, opinion experts etc. (Bandorski et al., 2016; Liu et al., 2012). Thus, the methodology of text analysis plays an important role in sentimental analysis. The application of sentimental analysis or textual analysis is not only an important constraint in terms of enterprise perspective, but also it plays an important role in terms of customer perspective. Consider a product or an application for instance, the marketing of the concerned product or application is important in terms of the manufacturer or developer. The maximum outreach of the concerned product is achieved by marketing and various sources of advertising. As this process is maximized up to a massive extent, the product reaches public of all sorts and thus the 'success rate' or 'outreach' of a product can be classified. On the other side of customer perspective, a customer is spending a particular amount either its of less value or more value, he/she needs some input to validate the quality or effectiveness of the product or an application before he/she tends to purchase it. Interestingly decades ago, there wasn't a method for finding the effective quality of a product or application. The user must tend to buy the concerned product or application and should check for the possible results, and this may end in either positive or negative outcome. In the same scenario the customer may find some aspects of the product or application to be good and some to be bad as a mixed outcome (this happens in many instances). Hence for any product or application the opinion or feedback analysis tends to be an important part as in customer perspective it paves way to 'improved product development' free from flaws and in terms of customer perspective the customer chooses the best product or app as per his/her requirement.

For better understanding of the same scenario, let us consider the product 'mobile phone'. As mobile phones are unavoidable part of human life, the role of tasks it plays is considered to be as important. Decades ago, people use to have 'number button' based phones, as mobiles initially were used only for communication. The next stage was 'java/symbian' operating systems based mobile phones which are considered to be as initial stages of smart phones where mobiles performed some basic tasks needed for human life like setting reminders, some next level game collections, in built music player support and some advanced mobiles included video players too. The gap between stage 1 and stage 2 that is 'number button' phones and 'java/symbian' based phones has a large gap of around 2 decades. In those two decades the manufacturers gathered public opinions and feedbacks of the products which they sold and by getting massive input responses from public they filled the gap between the product they sold and the customer's expectation for the same. The figure 3. discuss the various aspects to be considered for textual analysis in terms of customer and seller.

Figure 3. Textual analysis in customer and seller aspect

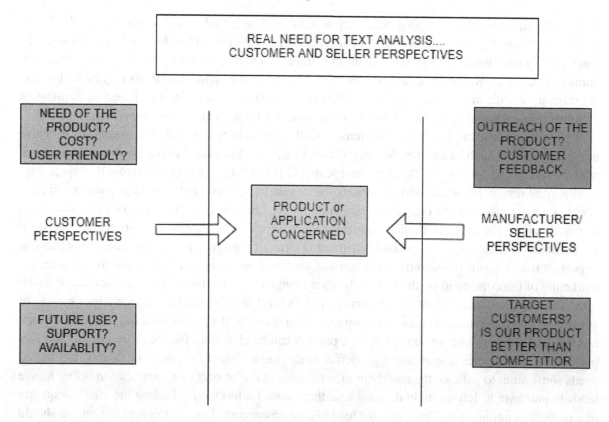

'Information' is considered to be as a rich assort. Information or data in all forms such as surveys, questionnaires, forms, satisfactory analysis reports etc. serves to be as forms as information in their respective fields and criteria in which they are collected. Such information which serves as input to sentimental or textual analysis can be further trained and fitted with computational intelligence-based machine learning or deep learning algorithms. Based on these various predictions can be designated. For instance, consider a movie review. Based on comments provided by various anonymous or registered users, text analysis can be made and the features which are trust worthier can be selected and used for training the model. Thus, input from various sources can be trained. This chapter is discussed machine learning systems, related studies, 'Bag-of-words' approach for text classification, tools for text analysis in brief, pros/cons of text data analysis and thereby describing various aspects related to text analysis.

MACHINE LEARNING SYSTEMS

Machine learning as an extension of application of AI is applied diversely in various domains extensively. The functionality of machine learning works on the basis of how data and algorithms work together, by which systems tend to attain human intelligence by repeated process. As human learn and improvise them gradually (say a child or student), machines too can be trained and gradually improved in terms of their performance (IBM Cloud Education, 2020).

In usual programming paradigm the user will feed data and programming code to the system, on analysis or processing the system will generate a solution or output. Similarly in machine learning based

Figure 4. Machine learning and usual programming strategy: differentiation

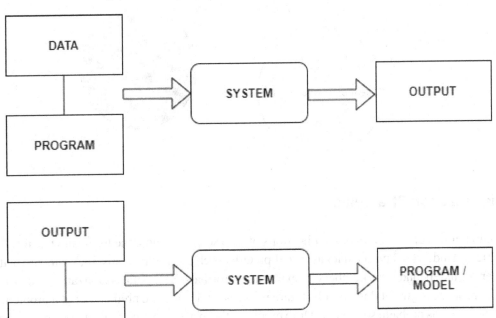

programming model, the user will feed the machine/ system with output and data, the machine will generate a model which will be the output. The model is unlike from traditional programming as it can predict, analyze, and generate results when a new data is fed. The figure 4. represents how the machine learning programming differs from the usual programming.

Machine Learning has 3 types of learning systems, namely:

1) Supervised Learning – (Given Labeled data with outputs)
2) Unsupervised Learning – (Given Unlabeled data)
3) Semi supervised Learning – (Given data with a few outputs) (Gupta, 2019). Figure 5. Illustrates various machine learning models.

Figure 5. Various machine learning models

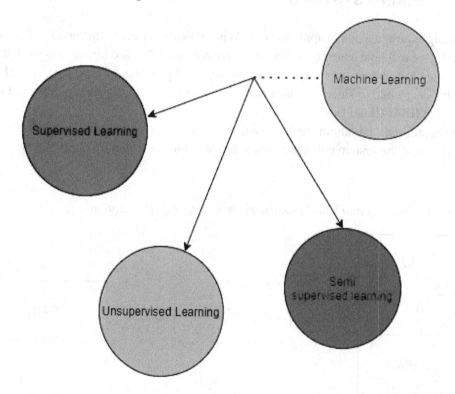

Data Visualization Strategies

Data visualization is one of the major applications of data science, where the user can visualize the data (Brush, 2020). Understanding the data as visual patterns such as graphs, maps, plots etc. are better and very easier to understand than numbers or exploratory formats. The data visualization patterns allow users to get proper insights of data, trends, future patterns, and elaborate predictions of a problem which is considered to be as problem statement. More precisely the exact application of such data visualizations can be applied to very large and extra ordinarily large datasets.

The more common way of explicating a data is in the form of 'table; or 'chart'. Various machine learning based packages visualize data patterns. 'Histogram' based plots is one of the common plotting techniques in practice and other than this there are various methods. Some of them are 'line charts', 'time series charts', 'scatter plots', 'tree maps' etc. (Brush, 2020). The major applications where data visualization-based techniques are applied are 'health care', 'financial analysis', 'stock market predictions', 'social media analysis' etc.

Related Studies

In the literature, several studies illustrate the applicability of machine learning and artificial intelligence-based methods for various real-world problems. Social media data analytics, movie review analysis, web search-based analysis and music player user search-based analysis are some of the common text and user sentimental analysis tasks carried out in current research. These tasks in turn reflect the exact scenario how the user is responding or will respond for a designated task.

Zhang et al. made a study on text mining on tweets based on covid 19. The authors applied 'NRC' and 'vader' methodsand evaluated the sentiment intensity scores for various time periods during the pandemic. On having keywords of 'mask', 'vaccine' and 'lockdown' the authors carried out the calculation of sentiment intensity scores. After the process the authors employed convergence mapping and found people had positive attitude towards 'mask' and negative towards 'vaccine' and 'lockdown'. The authors claim causal integrations influence people mindsets and based on this the outcomes are generated (Zhang et al., 2021).

Sejung et al. made a study on analysis of textual mining using machine learning based methods for finding the effect of social media on general public. The authors examined the methodology by employing 'youtube' API to collect data from the channel called 'video mug' which was claimed to be as korea's most viewed 'youtube' channel. The authors validated 23774 comments and from the evaluation the end results claimed that data from such human reaction evaluations are enough to classify human interest towards media and general news coverage. The analysis involved finding and evaluation of both 'positive' and 'negative' emotions. The authors finally claimed that around 59.55% of 'positive' emotional scores, 31.41% negative emotional scores and 9.03% of neutral scores were validated (Park et al., 2021).

Franciele et al. conducted a study on sentimental analysis in tourism-based research and authors collected various research articles from 'Scopus' database with the keywords of 'tourism' and 'sentimental analytics. From the collected articles the authors clustered the contents into respective field of studies. As results the authors found the united states and China are the nations which pay more attention for studies related to tourism (Manosso & Ruiz, 2021).

Tripathy et al. performed as study on grouping film reviews using advanced machine learning strategies. The authors employed traditional ML algorithms such as naivebayes, stochastic gradient descent, and support vector machine on 'IMDB' benchmark dataset and they found that SVM classifier was able to attain maximum accuracy of 88.9% by applying feature selection methods such as unigram and bigram (Tripathy et al., 2016).

Suresh et al. conducted a study on sentimental analysis on "twitter" for an end product and the authors fitted various traditional ML algorithms. The algorithms included SVM, naïve bayes, J48 decision tree. On the analysis the authors found that the J48 based prediction performed well and was able to generated output of 92% accuracy (Suresh & Raj, 2015). Wawre et al. differentiated two Machine Learning algorithms (naïve bayes and support vector machines) for prediction of sentimental analysis on 'IMDB' movie review dataset. The authors found that naïve bayes classifier was able to predict outputs with 65.57% accuracy (Liu, 2010).

ANALYSIS OF TEXT DATA FROM SOCIAL MEDIA OR WEB

This section discusses a sample text mining example and illustrates how the process happens in real time. "Bag of words" approach is used extensively in the literature as part of various studies for feature extraction from textual sources. The extracted features are used in training of models based on machine learning. The approach of bag-of-words will create a thesaurus list of all words occurring in a text file or source.

For understanding consider a small text source stated as 'C' of 'D'. 'C' refers to the text source and 'D' refers to the documents here.

We have 3 documents, for instance

Document 1: He is a cool person. He is calm.
Document 2: Shiva is an active person.
Document 3: Saraswathi is a jovial person.

From the three document sources, we tend to identify and segregate occurrence of important words conveying major information to the source. The important words are counted as 'N'. For the above example

['He', 'cool', 'person', 'calm','shiva','active','saraswathi','jovial']

are the important words.

Thus, for the above example, D=3 and N=8,

Table 1. depicts the training features from each document or text source. This methodology identifies the number of instances of a word and the number if documents. Hence it is coined as 'Bag-of-words' approach

Table 1. Bag-of-words approach

	He	Cool	Person	Calm	Shiva	Active	Saraswathi	Jovial
Doc 1	1	1	1	1	0	0	0	0
Doc 2	0	0	1	0	1	1	0	0
Doc 3	0	0	1	0	0	0	1	1

By extracting the important constraints from the table, we can deploy methods such as 'count vectorizer' to further evaluate the training set and further data visualization techniques that are readily available in python can be applied to visualize the dataset which helps the end-user or consumer to understand the dataset easily (Das, 2019) .

TOOLS FOR TEXT ANALYSIS

As various real time textual sources can be applied with sentimental or textual analysis, there is a very wide range of sources as input. As discussed, social media texts and web pages contribute more to be as source of input. This section discusses various tools for textual analysis. In general, open-source tools are considered to be as easily accessible be any kind of entity as they are almost free to download and use. Various open-source tools also offer equivalent or more features when compared to 'paid' or 'subscription' oriented tools or software(s). In textual analysis various tools provide customer with 'semi' access, means that free upto a certain limit and a nominal charge will be levied on the customer.

'Google Natural Language processing API', 'Apache Open NLP', 'Visual text', 'QDA miner'is some of the common tools used by textual data enthusiasts and data scientists. This section further discusses the features and setup of Google cloud API and the functionality of the tool 'Apache open NLP' in brief.

'Google Cloud Natural Language- API'

Google cloud natural language API is considered to be as top open-source tool for handling textual data. As Google based tools are easily accessible and almost all Google tools are free to use, it has a wide outreach. Google charges a nominal cost for the service when a limit exceeds. This coverage further discuss the setup and starting with Google NLP (Google, 2021).

'Google cloud natural language API' provides various embedded environments with user friendly aspects which will make analysis easier and will reduce the ease of the user. The API has 3 inbuilt environments which provide 'AutoML', 'NLP' and 'Healthcare NLP' access separately. Based on the user perspective he/she may choose an environment based on their nature of work. Since Google based services are known to be secure, the data involved in analytics will be safe and secure (Google, 2021).

IBM Watson

"IBM Watson" is a renowned tool that is being used in large scale for text analytics. Watson provides a broader environment for creating AI based applications and predictions. Watson ensures that the usage of software can be extended to both research-oriented applications and problems as well as business solutions for solving a specific task. On employing tools such as "IBM watson", more complex tasks may be evaluated and respective solutions can be delivered with less ease of the analyst thereby solving client needs with the speculated time (IBM, n.d.).

Apache Open NLP

'Apache Open NLP' is an 'open source' java powered tool for processing various natural language processing-based applications and tasks. Almost all natural language processing tasks are supported by apache open NLP. As it is an open-source application it has a wide range of target audience and users availing apache open NLP. 'The Apache open NLP' has various in-built library functions which has the capability to process and analyze various text-based datasets using machine learning based processing. Very large datasets, books, email texts and other common text inputs such as 'comments', 'reviews' etc can be processed using 'Apache Open NLP' similar to other tools. Some components of the 'Apache open NLP' library include 'sentence detector', 'tokenizer', 'parser', 'co reference resolution', 'document categorizer', 'name finder' etc. The end user will be able to access and avail all of the above stated features and various other embedded features in order to process his/her natural language processing-based tasks.

'Apache open NLP' provides two methods to access the application, one is the 'application program interface' (API) and the 'command line interface' (CLI). Based on the user's convenience he/she may opt to use any API (*Apache OPEN NLP Documentation*, 2017).

Real Time Applications of Text Analysis

The text analytics is applied vastly in various fields and domains as discussed. Described below are some of the domains where text analytics in applied especially in the current decade. Why current decade? Readers may wonder why this decade. The reason is as computational excellence increases, the chance for intervention and attacks also increases and without any debate, it is accepted by everyone. Though there are security methods, there is chance for attacks. Hence machine learning based strategies are widely applied for detection of various fraudulent activities and even categorizing emails and messages as safe and harmful. This section briefly discusses various real-time applications of text analysis subjected to current trend and decade.

Security and Automated Systems

Extensive application of text analytics in current trend and research focus on various security threats that prevail. The data security and genuineness are a challenging aspect when it comes in storing and retrieving large volumes of data. Though data stored and retrieved for analytics in 'big data clouds' are considered to be as secure enough, still there arises a question of data security. Text analytics formulated by automated systems are found to be as genuine. It is also stated that 'software reliability' and 'quality' also increases when automated analytics is made (Enck & Xie, 2014). Other aspect pertaining to same domain of security is the 'fraud detection'. As the technological outreach increases, various fraudulent activities too increase causing a serious threat for the further enhancement of the technology concerned. This is a big flaw that needs to be addressed.

Day to day new technologies and solutions arise as part of various human needs. As this development occurs in one side, on the other side the attackers or spammers targeting such new technologies also develop rapidly. This keeps on continuing in all levels of software, applications and tools for specific purposes etc. For better understanding of the application consider the scenario of an insurance company. The insurance vendor has certain constraints and rules to possess the insurance claim to the end users. Fraudsters and intruders in the past have targeted such firms and there is history of various such fraud activity occurrences in the past. Especially in developing counties these types of activities were common in the past. After the application of advance computation intelligence-based strategies such as machine learning and deep learning in such domains of insurance, vendors formulate textual analytics in their firms and scrutinize the persons who apply for such polices in the entry level itself. As textual analysis is known to deliver secure results, the fraudsters and defaulters can be found in the entry stage and can be avoided. This extends the ability of such companies to fasten the process of approving claims to genuine users in less period of time. Thus, application of textual analysis plays an important role in terms of security for current decade and trend.

Customer Service and Chat Bots

Whatever service we use, right from banking, mobile network service providers, Direct to Home connection providers, OTT's etc. The service providers have a dedicated application designed for mobile phones. Now in the current decade the market is ruled by 'android' smart phones. As every user of smart phones have any of the listed subscriptions, he/she can download the dedicated app for the same and can keep track of their usage, subscriptions, and manipulation too in some apps. This is common over the past decade from the rise of smart phones. After the advanced reach of computational intelligence powered textual analysis, these applications are enhanced to a great extent with 'chatbot' support. These chatbots collect inputs from users and provide necessary solutions based on the trained inputs as well as the 'similar case' of instances that occurred in the past.

For instance, when a person is approaching a 'mobile network service provider's' chatbot. The user inputs a query as I cannot access internet. The 'chatbot' will provide necessary solutions pertaining to the query for instance, such as signal strength, data balance, etc. On again selecting a particular option from the next level menu, the user will be directed to a solution which satisfy his/ her requirement. Thus, human intervention for solving user needs and queries is replaced by employing artificial intelligence based 'chatbots'.

Social Media Text Analytics

Social media-based text analytics is considered to be as the important and broader umbrella where textual analysis is made by a large scale of firms and companies in real time. This is because they gain large insights on their current product and can improvise themselves by continuous product developmental activities. If a question is aroused, "are you in social media?" people may laugh at the person who arouses such a question. May be decades back this question can be made into consideration, but in current trend right from 10+ children, senior citizens up to 80+ have accounts and spend more time in social media. This massive outreach of social media not only develops the tech giants who provide social media platforms, but also commoners who make use of such social media for advertisement and sponsored feeds. This results in a healthy environment where users of social media will get profited by using it. For instance, consider a 'product vendor' having a 'business account' in a famous social media site. The end users who make use of that 'product' follow a particular page. The page is used by the product vendor for outreach and the customers to contact the vendor easily than 'email' or telephones as the access is comparatively easy. The 'digital marketing' strategy employed by firms and companies reach numerous target audience and this enormously reduces the advertising cost spent by the respective firms.

The customers can avail the benefit of accessing the social handle page of the product firm and may share their consent on the foresaid product. If they are happy with the product, they find flaws or bugs that needs to be solved etc. Any kind of input can be shared and the same will be used by the firms for text analysis and future improvements of the product. The customer may use the page to check whether the product is genuine or bad with various inputs provided by the users who make use of the product already. This is similar as a product description page which has 'reviews' provided in an 'e-commerce' website. People generally search for a product with 3.5 to 4+ stars in average on a five-point ranking scale. Similar to 'search engine' optimization textual analytics can be helpful for social media-based text data. Thus, the application of social media text analysis works in a unique way such that both the seller and customer get profited by employing text analytics.

These kinds of analytics can be extended to large scale systems in near future and there will be a situation such that when the entire world moves into internet, there will be room only for 'digital marketing' which puts an end to traditional marketing and advertising systems.

DISCUSSION

The literature review showed that various works have claimed the importance of employing textual analysis in real time datasets as they have a great extent of analytics features and will result in identifying good insights too. It is to be noted that the roots of textual and sentimental analysis have extended to almost all domains which are as part of day-to-day human life. The usage of text-based inputs is unavoidable in human life and so, the root of applying textual analysis extends to various domains. The textual analysis is very much helpful in complex and sensitive domains such as medical or healthcare-based applications too. Zhang et al. made a study on analysis of 'covid 19' based tweets. In the current pandemic situation all over the world, people are supposed to be indoors and the day-to-day routines have changed a lot. In such a scenario, the authors worked to collect the exact reflection of human thoughts towards 'mask', 'vaccine' etc and correlated positive and negative trends for the same (Zhang et al., 2021). This work can be stated as a perfect example of how textual analysis or sentimental analysis can be claimed for complex situations and sensitive areas of research and analytics. Sejung et al. study portrays how the impact of social media and general entertainment is among the general public. The authors considered around 23000+ input data from 'youtube' based inputs from anonymous users. The authors claim that the human reactions are far enough to classify their interest towards a certain criterion (Park et al., 2021). The study performed by Franciele et al. focused on tourism development the study reflected which regions of the universe paved more attention to tourism based activities and entertainments (Manosso & Ruiz, 2021). Tripathy et al. focused on movie rating based on 'IMDB' based benchmark dataset. In the study authors focused on applying various machine learning algorithms and made prediction, ranking (Tripathy et al., 2016). Thus, the application of textual analysis is applied almost in all fields and domains where human expertise doesn't work. The discussed studies fall under health care, general entertainment, tourism etc. Thus, it can be noted that the application of textual analysis can play a vital role in analysis and prediction of various trends. Trends found as result of textual data analytics can be interpreted as plots and graphs using various 'data visualization strategies' provided by machine learning packages.

Pros and Cons of Textual Analysis

Pros

By applying textual analysis or sentimental analysis, there are various benefits and merits. Some of them are:

- The users will be able to find a solution for their problem statement (or find the exact issue that needs to be fixed for a problem)
- Stakeholders can improvise their products and applications from the wide range of inputs and comments rendered as feedbacks and satisfaction surveys from the end users and customers.
- The end users or customers will be able to find and fix their product of interest with less ease as they can select the 'best product or application; of their interest which is validated by computational intelligence means.
- Any kind of data that is of text form can be made to undergo textual or sentimental analysis.
- 'Burning issues' can be categorized and given high priority. This formulates which subject needs to be analyzed first and how they can be given ranking.

Cons

Though there are various advantages of applying textual or sentimental analysis, there are certain limitations of applying the method in various cases. Some of them are:

- In some test cases the rule created can be applied only to a particular form of datasets or particular kind. The same can't be applied to other pro forma's. The rule is set by an expert and his/her advice has to be availed when a newer kind of data/dataset is considered.
- The learning capability of the model is less until it is trained from a wide range of available sources. Finally, without a tool the process is not possible from a local 'IDE' or machine.
- The user has to be at least novice level user to handle the tool and have some insights on how it works. Thus, some of the disadvantages possessed by textual analysis needs to be fixed or overcome in the future by extensive development of new technologies and software(s).

Limitations

As there are various advantages of applying real time textual analysis, there are various drawbacks and limitations for applying the same. The 'pros and cons' briefed the either side of text analysis. The major requirement of building the gap between the user and the system needs to focus elaborately. As there are such tools, users should equip themselves to work with the tools and data. Another limitation that needs to be discussed is the data copyright. In many cases the data which is fed as input is not copyrighted. But in some cases, the data needs to undergo copyright claims as no other person can claim that the researcher or entity made use of his/her data for research or testing without his/her perusal. Another issue is the 'system requirements'. Though the discussed tools such as 'Google cloud natural language API' and 'Apache open NLP; will work along all sorts of systems, large, very large and extra ordinarily large datasets involve application of 'Graphical Processing Unit (GPU)' enabled systems to work around with data. GPU enabled systems; workstations have capability of processing larger tasks. Though an individual tester or researcher is not affordable to purchase a GPU enabled device or workstation setups, necessary help from various funding sources and agencies can be availed to address the same. Addressing these issues analysts or researchers can have a fruitful experience of collaborating text analytics in real time.

CONCLUSION

The chapter discussed the basics of textual analysis, its implications in real time business setups and firms. It also discussed the approaches and tools for textual and sentimental analysis. People often wonder what can be extracted from text, and whether a piece of text or sentence is enough to validate and extract information from data. These questions are answered with data analytics of textual data, which is now a massive research domain that is expanded every day, being embedded with novel strategies, advancements, and technologies. There is a growing need for development in resources and applications to cater user needs. In this context, textual analysis and sentimental analysis prove to be an unavoidable paradigm for analyzing user data. Data collection and analysis is harder in general perspective. But when it comes into text analysis, the source of data is easier to attain. The real implication is making the gathered data usable for business or developmental analysis and thereby benefiting from it. Thus, sentimental analysis with various other enhancements can be applied to any form of text data and the extracted features can be used for future analysis. The complex part is scrutinizing the important parameters or constraints. Another challenging task is that the user himself/herself should have certain understanding of the dataset and tools used for analysis. The understanding of tools tends to be a very basic requirement and in near future all users (who aren't analysts too) will require the need to understand and work around such tools for real time analytics of data. The tools play an important role in such analysis and the users are supposed to have basic knowledge in coding and handling the tools for data analysis. The tools do not only streamline the functionality but also reduce the human ease of working with data. The application of textual analysis does not work as standalone but is embedded with other machine learning and deep learning-based applications and strategies such as data visualization. The ease of the analyst or user is reduced considerably and thereby intervention of human and manpower in analytics is reduced considerably. Automation should not remove manpower as this may affect the employment of human. But in case of Artificial Intelligence based systems the human intervention is reduced and still the functionality of humans in terms of devising 'test cases' plays a mandatory part. This states that artificial intelligence does not replace humans, but help us to predict, decide and move ahead with various advanced embedded tools and strategies. The users or analysts should make use of the tools up to a maximum extent. Light weight tools named as 'lite' which are already in existence for various application(s) and software(s) should be devised for future systems. Such applications should possess the capability of executing large volume datasets at least in 'command line interface' in order to cater the analyst or user needs. The application of textual analysis should be extended to other domains too as the process is easier and provides users with great insights. Thus, if textual analysis is applied in a proper way and method, undoubtedly in near future the era of computational intelligence will be remarkable.

REFERENCES

Tripathy, A., Agrawal, A., & Rath, S. K. (2016). Classification of sentiment reviews using n-gram machine learning approach. *Expert Systems with Applications*, *57*, 117–126. doi:10.1016/j.eswa.2016.03.028

Apache OPEN NLP Documentation. (2017). https://opennlp.apache.org/docs/

Bandorski, D., Kurniawan, N., Baltes, P., Hoeltgen, R., Hecker, M., Stunder, D., & Keuchel, M. (2016). Contraindications for video capsule endoscopy. *World Journal of Gastroenterology*, *22*(45), 9898–9908. doi:10.3748/wjg.v22.i45.9898 PMID:28018097

Brush, K. (2020). *Data Visualization.* https://searchbusinessanalytics.techtarget.com/definition/data-visualization

Das, D. (2019). *Social Media Sentiment Analysis using Machine Learning : Part — II.* https://towards-datascience.com/social-media-sentiment-analysis-part-ii-bcacca5aaa39

Enck, W., & Xie, T. (2014). Tutorial: Text analytics for security. *Proceedings of the ACM Conference on Computer and Communications Security*, *1*, 1540–1541. 10.1145/2660267.2660576

Google. (2021). *Cloud Natural Language.* https://cloud.google.com/natural-language/docs/quickstart

Gupta, M. (2019). *ML | What is Machine Learning?* https://www.geeksforgeeks.org/ml-machine-learning/

IBM. (n.d.). *IBM Watson.* https://www.ibm.com/watson/about

IBM Cloud Education. (2020). *Machine learning.* https://www.ibm.com/in-en/cloud/learn/machine-learning

L, H. J. V. (2019). Opinion Mining using Machine Learning Techniques. *International Journal of Engineering and Advanced Technology*, *9*(2), 4287–4292. doi:10.35940/ijeat.B4108.129219

Liu, B. (2010). Sentiment analysis and subjectivity. Handbook of Natural Language Processing, Second Edition, 627–666.

Liu, C. L., Hsaio, W. H., Lee, C. H., Lu, G. C., & Jou, E. (2012). Movie rating and review summarization in mobile environment. *IEEE Transactions on Systems, Man and Cybernetics. Part C, Applications and Reviews*, *42*(3), 397–407. doi:10.1109/TSMCC.2011.2136334

Manosso, F. C. (2021). *Using sentiment analysis in tourism research : A systematic, bibliometric, and integrative review.* Academic Press.

Park, S., Bier, L. M., & Park, H. W. (2021). The effects of infotainment on public reaction to North Korea using hybrid text mining: Content analysis, machine learning-based sentiment analysis, and co-word analysis. *El Profesional de la Información*, *30*(3), 300306. doi:10.3145/epi.2021.may.06

Suresh, H., & Raj, D. G. (2015). Analysis of Machine Learning Techniques for Opinion Mining. *Advances in Research*, *3*(12), 375–381.

Zhang, Q., Yi, G. Y., Chen, L.-P., & He, W. (2021). *Text mining and sentiment analysis of COVID-19 tweets.* https://arxiv.org/abs/2106.15354

Chapter 4
Improving Comparative Opinion Mining Through Detection of Support Sentences

Teck Keat Yeow

School of Computer Sciences, Universiti Sains Malaysia, Malaysia

Keng Hoon Gan

School of Computer Sciences, Universiti Sains Malaysia, Malaysia

ABSTRACT

Comparative opinion contains contrasting views of products (e.g., which aspect of a product is better or worse). Most existing works for comparative opinion mining focus on single comparative sentences but have yet explored the benefits of additional comparative details in neighbouring sentences of a comparative sentence. Motivated by the needs to exploit these supporting details, this chapter proposes an approach to identify the link between a comparative sentence and its neighbouring sentences. As contextual similarity between comparative sentence and neighbouring sentence is crucial to determine their relatedness, contextual features of these two sentences are exploited to measure the similarity between them. Then, linear-chain conditional random field (CRF) is used to identify neighbouring sentence that is related to comparative sentence. Detection of supporting neighbouring sentence using linear-chain CRF with optimized contextual features (cosine similarity, Wordnet similarity, and comparative keywords) outperforms sentence similarity baseline by 4% in accuracy and 0.06 in F-score.

INTRODUCTION

Growing number of online review websites such as Trip Advisor, Eopinions, Amazon, CNet etc. enables people to express their opinions about services and products. As a result, huge number of opinion-based texts were generated from these platforms. These resources are very useful for both service providers and end users as they can offer clues towards various aspects of the services or products. However, time and effort are needed for both parties to read and digest these opinionated resources, e.g., scanning through

DOI: 10.4018/978-1-7998-9594-7.ch004

the sentences that carry opinions, filter and summarize them into simple conclusion like pros and cons, comparing between multiple features or attributes discussed, comparing between two (or more) different products or services and so forth.

To address such needs, research in opinion mining aims to make the opinions more explicit by summarizing the opinion using indicators like positive or negative. Combining both computational linguistics and text mining methods, opinion mining enables the detection of sentiment value expressed in textual form, which can be used as indicator of public responses on services, products or events (Hu & Liu, 2004). For example, in service industry like restaurant, feedback such as "The waiter is very friendly" can be classified as "positive" since the sentence contains positive sentiment word "friendly". On the other hand, comment on product like "New IPhone is a lousy phone" reflects "negativity" with the presence of "lousy" as negative word (Pang & Lee, 2008).

Within the field of opinion mining, comparative opinion mining is an emerging sub area that gained attention in opinion mining research lately (Jindal & Liu, 2006; Jindal & Liu, 2006b; Khan et al, 2020; Xu et al, 2011, Yang & Ko, 2011; Younis et al, 2020). A recent review by Varathan et al, 2017 has also shown the increasing of research works in this area. Instead of dealing with opinions of sentence, which is either positive or negative opinionated, this sub area of opinion mining research looks into sentence that makes comparison between different entities with respect to a common feature for e.g., IPhone 8 has better camera compared to Samsung S8". The sentence contains comparison relation, i.e., between IPhone 8 as first entity and Samsung S8 as second entity with regard to the common feature which is camera. In terms of opinion's sentiment, "better" indicate IPhone 8 is more superior compared to Samsung S8 in camera feature. Looking at the example, it is obvious that this type of opinion is useful for decision making in terms of comparative analysis. Hence, in this work, we are motivated to explore research in the direction of comparative opinion mining.

In opinion mining, customer reviews often contain opinions that make comparison between two products or services with respect to some common features. This type of opinion usually provides contrasting views of different products. Sometimes, it could be making similar remarks, such as, "Mi Note is as good as Iphone.". This type of review is particularly useful in situations where a consumer is making a decision to choose between two or more similar products.

From business point of view, comparative texts are important for companies to analyse and discover their competitors' products as well as to learn their relative weaknesses and strengths of their products. Conventionally, such information is available through analyst reports and expert reviews, which mostly contain opinions based on personal experiences of the expert. Also, product press release could be biased as it is written by the product's company.

In comparative opinion, sentiment analysis is normally based on the thought that relates some common features of two or more product entities. It goes beyond finding the polarity of the feature of an entity, but involves measuring the relation between the entities based on the sentiment keyword used. Considering a non-comparative sentence, "The camera is very expensive", the polarity at sentence level can be determined by simply summing positive and negative sentiment keyword. In this case, the polarity is negative since there is only one keyword, "expensive" which has a negative sentiment score. For aspect level, similar analysis of sentiment keywords applies, but the keywords need to be linked to aspect/feature rather than sentence in general. For example, the word "expensive" is linked to "price" feature before the sentiment analysis takes place. In this case, sentiment for "price" feature will be negative.

Different from non-comparative opinions, the goal of opinion mining for comparative opinion is to find positivity or negativity arisen from the relationship type of sentiment, for example, which entity is better or worse than the other entity. Various comparative relationships have been grouped into types like non-equal gradable, equal gradable, superlative and non-gradable (Singla and Singh, 2016). Take for example a comparative opinion, "camera X is very expensive compared to camera Y"; the first entity is 'camera X' and compared to the second entity 'camera Y', the comparative relation is 'very expensive'.

Prior research in comparative opinion mining focus on two main tasks. First, the focus is on identifying comparative sentence from text; The second focus is to extract comparative relations from the comparative sentences identified.

Basic processes in comparative opinion analysis range from tracking common keywords reflecting comparative relations, e.g., terms ending with "er" like faster, smoother, cheaper etc., and superlative keywords like fastest, cheapest etc. Other hints like additive transition (e.g., similarly, likewise etc.) or adversative transition (e.g., whereas, even more, yet etc.) may also be useful. These keywords can also include special terms like exceed, outperform, beat, etc. A total of 83 comparative keywords has been identified by Jindal and Liu (2006).

Another technique to identify comparative opinion is to parse and identify the opinion text based on part of speech (POS) tags. For example, POS tag JJR which is equivalent to adjective, POS tag RBR which is equivalent to adverb comparative, POS tag JJS which is adjective superlative or POS tags RBS which is equivalent to adverb superlative serve as good indicators to identify sentence containing comparative clues (Jindal and Liu 2006).

Likewise, manually annotated POS tag sequence with class information of comparative or non-comparative can be used to generate class sequential rules (CSR) (Jindal and Liu 2006a). For example, [camera/NN has /VBZ significantly/RB **more/JJR [KEYWORD]** noise/NN at/IN iso/NN → Comparative]. In Jindal and Liu (2006b), the author introduced label sequential rules (LSR) which is used as a model to extract comparative entities, comparative relations and comparative aspect that were previously not identified by CSR from Jindal and Liu (2006a).

Problem Statement

The approach of comparative opinion mining presented in previous section can identify single comparative sentence and its components i.e., entity mentioned, aspect involved in comparison and comparative relation. In research by Lee et al. (2008), the author found that online comments with sufficient level of detail are more persuasive than online comments with irrelevant or less details. Similar persuasive texts are common in comparative opinion in order to provide sufficient level of detail and support for the comparison made. As such, consumer commonly write comments in multiple sentences that are relatively linked. Nevertheless, current comparative opinion mining approach that only focuses on a single sentence is limited in capturing the supporting content portion of the opinion stated.

Below are two example scenarios of comparative opinion to illustrate the problem statement.

Scenario 1: G12 is better compared to LX5.
Scenario 2: G12 is better compared to LX5. G12 has great camera lense, long battery life and cheaper price.

In scenario 1, comparison is provided in one sentence, whereas in scenario 2, comparison is described with a few sentences. We can also interpret scenario 1 as only the main comparison sentence is considered in the analysis, whereas for scenario 2, additional sentences related to the comparison are considered. In

Jindal and Liu (2006), their method for comparative opinion mining employs sequential rules algorithm which tags each word in a sentence with POS tags and stores sequence of labelled comparative sentence. The method gives "G12" as first comparative entity, "LX5" as second comparative entity and "better" as comparative relation.

In scenario 1, approach from Jindal and Liu (2016b) is able to accurately extract the entities and comparative relation expressing "G12 is better compared to LX5".

In scenario 2, an additional sentence (one sentence after the comparative sentence) was included for comparative opinion mining. As this sentence contains explanation that supports the prior sentence (in this case, a list of features were mentioned in positive manner); analyzing it together with its prior sentence will offer better understanding to justify why G12 is more superior than LX5. Hence, it is clear that there is advantage in analyzing the neighbouring sentence of comparative sentence as it could possibly contain information that supports the comparative sentence.

For comparative opinion in scenario 2, existing methods from Jindal and Liu (2006) and Xu et al. (2011) do not handle the detection and extraction of the additional information from neighbouring sentence as their scope of works focus on single comparative sentence.

Figure 1. Example of useful information from neighbouring sentence for justifying the reason G12 is better

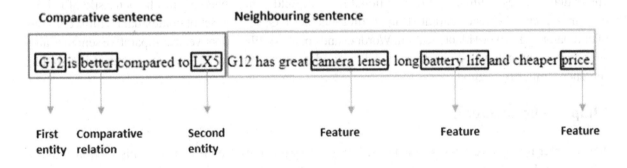

Ultimately, our goal is to obtain useful description through inclusion of related neighbouring sentences. Figure 1 shows how related neighbouring sentence is able to help improve the richness of information in comparative opinion mining. It is obvious that better justification on how certain comparison is concluded can be obtained when neighbouring sentence is included as part of comparative opinion mining. Hence, a more detailed output can be obtained, i.e., first comparative entity = 'G12', second comparative entity = 'LX5', comparative feature = 'great camera lense, long battery life, cheaper price' and comparative relation = 'better'.

From the discussions of the above scenarios, this leads to us to the main research question. Since the neighbouring sentence may or may not contain information that is related to the comparative sentence, how to determine whether the neighbouring sentences (before and after) of a comparative sentence is relevant, i.e. contain information that can be used to support the comparative sentence? These research questions are formulated based on our best knowledge as there is no prior research that includes neighbouring sentence in comparative opinion mining. Current research work focus on comparative opinion mining on single sentence to identify comparative entities, comparative feature and comparative relations.

Research Objectives

Our research aims to enhance comparative opinion mining by providing richer information for comparative sentence with information by identifying the impact of neighbouring sentences. Specifically, our research objectives are as follow:

- To incorporate contextual features in Conditional Random Field for supporting sentence identification.
- To identify supporting sentence for comparative opinion mining using an optimized set of contextual features in Conditional Random Field method.

Research Contribution

Comparative opinion mining in (Jindal and Liu, 2006, Jindal and Liu 2006b, Xu et al 2011) have focused on single sentence comparative opinion mining, in some cases comparative opinion is spread across neighbouring sentence (supporting sentence). Current comparative opinion mining algorithms assume neighbouring sentences did not carry impact to the comparative opinion made and hence ignores neighbouring sentence as part of comparative opinion mining. In this work, we incorporate optimized contextual features in linear-chain conditional random field which leverage the characteristic of neighbouring sentence in identification of supporting sentences. Optimized set of contextual features consists of comparative keyword identification, Wordnet and cosine similarity between comparative sentence and supporting sentence was shows to work better on identifying supporting sentence compared to simple sentence similarity method.

Chapter Organization

This chapter is organized into six sections. Introductory contents are presented in this section. This is followed by Literature Review in second section in which related works covering techniques of comparative mining, background of conditional random field and issues of support sentence identification are highlighted. The Methodology covers details of data preparation and proposed framework. The chapter then presents the Evaluation which comprises of the performance metric and baselines. In the Findings section, experiments on contextual features and support sentence identification are presented. This chapter wraps up with Conclusion as the last section.

BACKGROUND

Comparative opinion mining is a subarea of opinion mining that deals with opinions in comparative form, e.g., "Camera X is more expensive than camera Y". The key difference is that a comparative opinion has a reference point when the comment is made. Referring to the same example, camera Y can be a reference point of camera X, or vice versa. Comparative opinion mining involves two main tasks. First, comparative sentences identification from text sentences. Second, comparative relation extraction between comparative entities with respect to a common aspect.

Comparative sentence identification determines whether an opinionated sentence is a comparative type or otherwise. For example, for "Mercedes Benz generally is faster than BMW", comparative word "faster" indicates that the sentence potentially is a comparative sentence. In this identification process, the basic idea lies in the linguistic analysis of comparative words which are derived from comparative relations. For example, term ends with "er" like faster, smoother, cheaper etc. and superlative keywords like fastest, cheapest etc. Besides, other hints like additive transition (e.g., similarly, likewise etc.) or adversative transition (e.g. whereas, even more, yet, etc.) have also been identified as comparative word cues. Such comparative words are used establishing orderings of superiority, inferiority, and equality. Other indicative words like beat, exceed, outperform etc. was identified as a list of commonly used comparative keyword (Jindal and Liu, 2006).

Once the candidate comparative sentence has been identified, the second task of comparative opinion mining involves extraction of comparative relation and related entities from the sentence. Four types of comparatives relations were introduced by Jindal, N. and Liu, B (2006). Three of the relations are gradable comparatives (non-equal gradable, equative and superlative) and one is non-gradable comparative. Gradable comparatives contain relation hints as follows.

1. **Non-equal gradable:** Comparative type where one entity is more superior or more inferior than the other with respect to common feature. e.g., *Xiao Mi is cheaper than IPhone in price*.
2. **Equative:** Comparative type where the entity involved in comparison is equivalent with respect to common feature. e.g., *Xiao Mi camera as good as Iphone*.
3. **Superlative:** Comparative type where single entity is most superior or most inferior with respect to common feature. e.g., *Samsung S7 is lightest in weight*.

For non-gradable comparative opinion, entities in comparison cannot be graded as the opinion is made on different features e.g., *Iphone 7 has dual-camera, Huawei has feature long-range camera*.

Techniques in Comparative Opinion Mining

Lexicon-Based Approach

The earliest work on comparative opinion mining focused on comparative sentence identification from text. In Jindal and Liu (2006)'s research work, comparative sentence identification is carried out through a compiled list of 83 comparative keywords. In their research, 69 keywords were compiled through analysis on commonly use comparative keywords, then expanded using Wordnet to include their synonyms, and finally pruned manually to select related comparative keyword. Additional 9 keywords have been identified from usage in non-gradable comparison such as whereas, on the other hand etc.

Lastly, remaining comparative keywords were identified through their Part of Speech (POS) tags, i.e., JJR (adjective, comparative), RBR (adverb, comparative), JJS (adjective, superlative) and RBS (adverb, superlative). Each of these POS tags was treated as a single comparative keyword for identification (Santorini, 1990). Nevertheless, they found out the precision is rather low at 32% when using comparative keyword for comparative sentence identification, as many sentences which consists of comparative keyword is not a comparative sentence e.g. "The doctor will do their best to help out", whereby 'best' in this sentence does not indicate a comparative meaning.

Sequential Rule Based Approach

Class sequential rules (CSR) was introduced to overcome low precision issue in comparative opinion mining that used lexicon-based approach and label sequential rules (LSR) was introduced by Jindal and Liu (2006) for extraction of comparative element from comparative sentence. In CSR, opinion sentence with at least one comparative keyword was identified and then words within the radius of three from the comparative keyword were extracted for sequence construction. The extracted words were tagged with POS tags. Manual labelling was performed on each POS tagged sequence to indicate the sequence as either comparative or non-comparative class. LSR on the other hand was introduced for extraction on comparative element in identified comparative sentence. Jindal and Liu (2006b) in the same year presented another work on LSR for extraction of comparative element on sentence that was previously identified through CSR.

To illustrate how class sequential rule works, consider a sentence with comparative keyword, "This camera has significantly more noise at iso 100 than the Nikon 4500". In this sentence, comparative keyword "more" was found, and it is used as the pivot; words within the radius of three from the pivoted keyword were extracted for POS tagging. The resultant comparative sentence with POS tags were "camera/NN has /VBZ significantly/RB **more/JJR [KEYWORD]** noise/NN at/IN iso/NN". Manual inspection was conducted and then extracted sequences were labelled as either comparative class or non-comparative class., For this case it was classified as comparative class. With this, future sentence sequence of POS tags with "**NN VBZ RB KEYWORD NN IN NN**" will be classified as comparative class.

A simple illustration of how CSR is used to identify whether an input text is comparative or non-comparative is shown below.

Given class sequential rules as

$X \rightarrow Y$,

where X is a sequence and Y is the class label of either comparative or non-comparative.

An input sentence is said to satisfy a CSR if X is a subset of the sequence of an identified rule.

Consider five sequences shown in Table 1 with each of the data sequence classified to either C_{Comp} (comparative class) and C_{NComp} (non-comparative class) (in the example numerical representation is used for data sequence). Given the association rule that associates data sequence of {1}{3}{7,8} and class C_{Comp}, we are able to calculate the minimum support and minimum confidence for these association rules. The author found minimum support of 20% and minimum confidence of 40% as the best threshold from their experiments.

Table 1. Example of data sequence for class sequential rules

Rule No.	Data Sequence	Class
A	{1}{3}{5}{7,8,9}	C_{Comp}
B	{1}{3}{6}{7,8}	C_{Comp}
C	{1,6}{9}	C_{NComp}
D	{3}{5,6}	C_{NComp}
E	{1}{3}{4}{7,8}	C_{NComp}

In Table 1, rule B satisfies the association rule $\{1\}\{3\}\{7,8\} \to C_{Comp}$ where left side consists of sequence $\{1\}\{3\}\{7,8\}$ and right side is associated to class C_{Comp}. Rule A consists of a subset of data sequence $\{1\}\{3\}\{7,8\}$ and similarly the class is labelled as C_{comp}; therefore 2 out of 5 rules satisfy the condition.

On the right side of association rules, 2 rules in the Table 1 appear as C_{Comp} class out of 3 rules (rule A, B and E) containing sub-sequence of $\{1\}\{3\}\{7,8\}$; therefore confidence is 2 over 3 because sub-sequence $\{1\}\{3\}\{7,8\}$ matches the data sequence in rule A, rule B and rule E. This means that out of three rules, only rule A and rule B data sequences were associated as comparative class C_{Comp} while rule E was associated as non-comparative class C_{Comp}. Using CSR technique, rule with the highest confidence will be used to classify the input sentence as either comparative or non-comparative.

Identification using class sequential rules was further developed to become label sequential rules in Jindal and Liu (2006) where several findings and assumptions were made below:

1. Entity and feature often appeared in nouns form (i.e. nouns, plural nouns, proper nouns and pronouns).
2. In single comparative sentence, there exists only one comparative relation.
3. Sequence is created to predict and extract item that represent entity or features. Four labels were created, i.e. $ES1 as the first entity, $ES2 as the second entity and $FT as the feature. $NEF is created to handle non-entity feature in the case where nouns are assumed to be entities and features.
4. For every label identified, separate sequence was created with optimal radius of four within the identified label.

LSR algorithm works as below:

1) Highest confidence LSR rules will be selected to replace the matched item in the sentence with one of the three labels ($ES1, $ES2 and $FT).
2) After replacement of matched item with labels, selected rules will be removed and confidence for each remaining rule will be calculated.
3) Step 1 and step 2 go through iteration until no rule is left.

An illustration of the mentioned steps for LSR approach is shown in the following example from Jindal and Liu (2006).

Given the tagged and labelled sentence:

<{iPhone,NN} {is,VBZ} {preferred,JJ} {because,IN} {the,DT} {screen,NN} {is,VBZ} {better,JJR} {than,IN} {Samsung, NN}>

Assume rule 1, rule 2 and rule 3 match the comparative sentence with respective confidence.

Rule 1: < {*,NN} { VBZ} > → <{$ES1,NN} {VBZ}>; confidence 80%

Rule 2:< {DT} {*,NN} → < {DT} {$FT,NN}>; confidence 90%

Rule 3: <{$FT} {VBZ} {JJR} {than,IN} {*,NN}> → < {$FT} {VBZ} {JJR} {than,IN} {$ES2,NN}>; confidence 70%

Rule with the highest confidence 90% for in LSR is chosen which is rule 2. The sequence is replaced label $FT. Let us apply rule 2 into the comparative sentence.

Hence, we obtain,

< {iPhone,NN} {is,VBZ} {preferred,JJ} {because,IN} {the,DT} **{$FT}** {is,VBZ} {better,JJR} {than,IN} {Samsung,NN}>

After replacement of $FT, reiterates to calculate the confidence. Since $FT now appears in rule 3, hence rule 3 will have the highest confidence and $ES2 is found.

<{iPhone, NN} {is,VBZ} {preferred,JJ} {because,IN} {the,DT} {$FT} {is,VBZ} {better,JJR} {than,IN} **{$ES2,NN}**>

Lastly, apply rule 1 as last remaining rule to replace iPhone with $ES1.

<**{$ES1,NN}**{is,VBZ} {preferred,JJ} {because,IN} {the,DT} {$FT} {is,VBZ} {better,JJR} {than,IN} {$ES2,NN}>

Thus, LSR at the end replaces four comparative information, i.e. iPhone with $ES1, Samsung with $ES2, screen with $FT and relation word which is **"better"** in the example.

Although LSR was claimed to achieve high precision (97% precision) and high recall (91% recall), there are few gaps that were not addressed by LSR as follows.

1. LSR assumes that comparative sentences only have two comparative entities, thus comparative sentences that have more than two entities may not work accurately in LSR. In the case when the comparative sentence contains more than two comparative relations and these relations are interdependent, e.g. "Samsung S7 has better reception than Xiao Mi 4 and iPhone 6".

Existing approach will have difficulty generating two different comparative relations, which is first, between Samsung S7 and Xiao Mi 4 and second, between Samsung S7 and iPhone 6.

2. When the comparative relation between two entities is extracted through comparative keyword, the direction of comparative relation is not considered. For example, "Compared with Samsung, iPhone has a better camera" will not work in LSR as the outcome will be ($ES1=Samsung, $ES2=iPhone, $FT=camera, relation word=better). The direction of comparison needs to be improved to find the entity that is "better.

Supervised Learning-Based Approach

In Xu et al (2011), linear-chain CRF was used to identify the comparative relation direction (which entity is more superior, or inferior compared to the other). Consider the example below:

"IPhone is better than Samsung but worse than Huawei"

In the example sentence, the comparative relation direction is "Iphone is more superior than Samsung however it is more inferior compared to Huawei." To model the relations between all three entities the dependencies between each of the relation word is critical, in this case to correctly determine the comparative relation between IPhone and Huawei, conjunction word "but" is critical to model the dependencies between all three entities. Besides the dependencies between comparative relationship word was modelled, in Xu et al (2011) work, arrangement of entity and comparative relation word is critical for e.g, "Iphone is better than Samsung" where we have entity appeared (Iphone) in the first position, comparative relation appeared (better) secondly and lastly is second entity (Samsung). Neighbouring word plays a crucial role in accurately determined the comparative relation direction correctly as shown in the example above from Xu et al (2011).

A later work by Khan et al (2020) and Younis et al (2020) on comparative opinion attempts to classify the comparative sentence by different classes, such as Pos-Pos, Pos-Neg, Pos-Neu and so forth, to indicate the sentiment for the first and second entities. Different classifiers were evaluated using self-acquired comparative reviews from YouTube on different products: iOS - Android, Facebook - Twitter and Microsoft - Google.

Conditional Random Field

In Lafferty et al (2011), author demonstrates the difference of conditional random field (CRF) compared to classifier like hidden markov model (HMM) in name-entity recognition problem, where in HMM relies on only single feature like word's entity however CRF can take neighbouring feature into account on its label prediction. In many cases of name-entity recognition research specifically like proper names that is not in the training set results in using word entity alone have limited usage. In order to identify proper name that have not appear in current training set, a set of features can be defined to help in identifying unseen words, features such as word capitalization, the neighbouring words. word prefixes and suffixes, identify the word from a compiled list of people and locations, etc.

One of the key features in this list which is neighbouring words is useful in application like named entity recognition (NER). Consider these two examples from Pathak et al (2013) below:

1st Sentence: the patient has diabetes.
2nd Sentence: The patient was given diabetes education.

The objective is to identify what is the role of the word "diabetes" in the sentence. In the first sentence diabetes is a disease in the sentence. In the second sentence diabetes education is a finding. From this example we notice that the neighbouring word is significant in deciding what role "diabetes" word appeared in the sentence.

Neighbouring word shown to have significant impact in named-entity recognition as shown in Pathak et al (2013). Linear-chain CRF is the most popular and basic form of CRF that can take transition feature (neighbouring feature) into account, which in HMM model transition feature ignores.

For example, in Figure 2 HMM model only considered local features which are X to determine the final label Y, however in Figure 3 shows the linear-chain CRF model that can take neighbouring feature and local features to determine the final label for Y. To have a better illustration, consider there are three label in cascading sequence as y_1, y_2, y_3, for each label of y it consists of local features which is x directly connect from its y label. In HMM graphical model from Figure 2 label y_1 is determined by its direct connected features x_{11}, x_{12} and x_{13}. In linear-chain CRF graphical from Figure 3 label y_2 is connected by local feature x_{21}, x_{22} and x_{23} and its previous feature x_{11}, x_{12} and x_{13} and this is illustrated in the diagram through connected edges between the features.

Figure 2. HMM graphical model that mimic linear-chain CRF
(Sutton & McCallum, 2006)

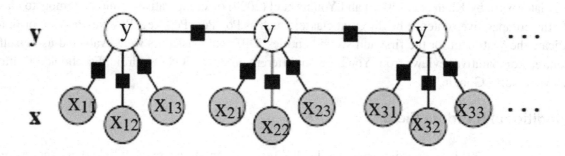

Figure 3. Linear-chain CRF graphical model which taken into account of transition features
(Sutton & McCallum, 2006)

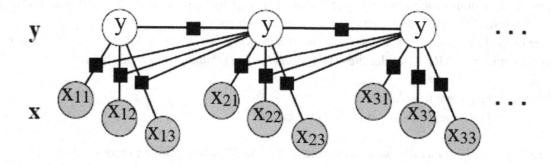

In Kunpeng et al (2014), accuracy of sentiment identification using CRF was improved in comparison to other methods (Compositional Semantic Rule – CSR, Support Vector Machine – SVM, Logistic Regression – LR and Hidden Markov Model – MM). The motivation of Kunpeng et al (2014) work was to address the limitation of rule-based method to improve sentiment identification where analysis on sentiment in longer documents was needed. One of the remarks from Kunpeng et al (2014) findings is that sentiment identification was improved when sentence feature before current sentence and sentence feature after were considered. In their finding, in a document, when sentences are treated as a group of sequences, current sentence more likely to carry positive sentiment when the sentence before and sentence after are positive.

In this work, to identify supporting sentence that is providing information to comparative sentence technique, we adapt similar approach of predicting the sentence label as either comparative sentence with supporting sentence or comparative sentence with non-supporting sentence through current sentence features and neighbouring sentence features. For example, consider this example "Iphone is more expensive compared to Samsung. New Iphone price is starting from RM4000 !!", HMM model illustrated in Figure 2 that only considers local feature is insufficient to model the linkage between between current sentence label and previous sentence label as each sentence label will be determined through their local feature such as detecting comparative keyword existence. HMM can identify comparative sentence using comparative keyword existence however without neighbouring sentence such as context similarity detection, HMM is unable to identify the linkage between these two sentences.

In linear-chain CRF model in Figure 3, due to their capability of taking neighbouring feature into account, we can model the linkage between the two sample sentences through context similarity e.g., expensive is mentioned in the first sentence and price is mentioned in the second sentence. Linear-chain CRF demonstrated the capability to achieve the research objectives on identifying supporting sentence in this research.

Issues

Research work discussed in the previous section focuses on identification of comparative sentence and comparative element such as entities, features and relations within the sentence. Two important works in this area, i.e., comparative opinion mining works from Jindal and Liu (2006) and Xu et al (2011) have covered the mining of comparative elements that occurs in single comparative sentence.

However, in reality, user comparative comments, i.e., comparative elements and their related details are elaborated using more than one sentence. This means the neighbouring sentences that is written either before or after a comparative sentence could possibly contain details about the comparative elements. In previous research (Jindal and Liu, 2006, Jindal and Liu, 200b, Yang and Ko, 2011 and Xu et al 2011), the authors assume all comparative elements are expressed within single sentence. This results in limitation on the extraction of comparative element and inaccurate interpretation of comparative sentiment when user comments spread across more than one sentence.

Supporting Sentence Identification

Approaches introduced by Jindal and Liu (2006), Jindal and Liu (2006b) and Xu et al (2011) only focus on single sentence comparative opinion mining. Cases where comparative elements that were spread across the neighbouring sentence will result in incomplete mining of crucial information about comparative element. Hence, identification of supporting sentence from neighbouring sentence is important to improve comparative opinion mining. Let us consider a review segment below from Amazon.com to understand the importance of neighbouring sentence for comparative opinion mining.

The selected example consists of three sentences. The first sentence is a neighbouring sentence that comes before comparative sentence. The second sentence the comparative sentence itself and the third sentence is a neighbouring sentence that comes after the comparative sentence.
Example of comparative opinion segment:

My wife, who has never used a camera before, picked it up and soon got the hang of the fact that if you don't like what you have created you just delete and try again. The photos she took are better than the results i got from my nikon slr and range of lenses. This is a big plus for those who a shifting to digital and the Canon G3 is large mobile screen helps with this.

Using the approach from existing research work where comparative elements only exists within individual sentence, (neighbouring sentences are not considered), the comparative sentence that will be analysed by the state-of-art algorithm will be:

Single Comparative Sentence: *"the photos she took are better than the results i got from my nikon slr and range of lenses!"*

Several shortcomings like missing information and ambiguity occur when the mining is limited to single sentence, as follows.

1. In this comparative sentence, only one entity (Nikon slr) is found. Comparative keyword 'better' enables us to know that this is a non-equal gradable sentence, in which comparative word 'better' is normally used to state that one entity is better than the other entity. In non-equal gradable sentence, it should contain at least two entities for comparison.
2. This sentence is full of ambiguity we are unable to know what type of object "she" is using. "She" could be using a handphone instead of camera. If we are targeting a deeper analysis on the object, we are also unable to know the person "she" who handles the object.
3. The comparative comment that was made by user is unclear and hard to understand the reason user mentioned "the photos she took are better".

Considering the importance of neighbouring sentence of a comparative sentence, if neighbouring sentence before and after comparative sentence was taken into consideration, more reasonable comparative clues can be possibly found.

Next, let us reconsider the same review example, but this time with neighbouring sentences before and after comparative sentence involved and shown below.

Neighbouring Sentence Before Comparative Sentence: *my wife, who has never used a camera before, picked it up and soon got the hang of the fact that if you don't like what you have created you just delete and try again.*

Comparative Sentence: *the photos she took are better than the results i got from my nikon slr and range of lenses.*

Neighbouring Sentence After Comparative Sentence: *this is a big plus for those who a shifting to digital and the Canon G3 is large mobile screen helps with this.*

With these additional sentences, we present the discussions on how the current shortcomings can be addressed.

In the first issue mentioned, as the comparative sentence appeared as non-equal gradable comparative sentence, it should contain more than one entity in its comparison. However, from the previous case, only "nikon slr" was obtained. This issue can be resolved by analysing the neighbouring sentence that comes after the comparative sentence, whereby Canon G3 in the sentence can explains the missing entity for the previous non-equal gradable sentence.

In the second issue, the word "she" is ambiguous as to who is the person the comparative sentence is referring. In neighbouring sentence before comparative sentence "my wife" was mentioned and "she" was most likely referring to "my wife".

Lastly in the third issue, the reason of the comment stated "the photos she took are better" is not justified. To improve the reasoning, the neighbouring sentence that comes before comparative sentence mentioned "if you don't like what you have created you just delete and try again" could be used to clarify the point where "the photos she took are better" because of the action/functionality where the user can just delete and try again in order to get better picture in the camera.

As such, the approaches from previous works (Jindal and Liu, 2006 and Xu et al 2011) that do not take into accounts the details in the sentence before and after comparative sentence are likely to be insufficient for comparative element extraction in cases where users express their comparative comment across multiple sentences.

As mentioned in previous section, conditional random field was used in several works where neighbouring features shown to have significant impact in classification process when words or sentences are in sequences. In Kunpeng et al (2014), they incorporate conditional random field to improve sentiment identification where one of their contributions was using linear-chain CRF to identify current sentence sentiment and in their finding, they stated that current sentence most likely will be positive if neighbouring sentence is classified as positive.

In identification of comparative sentence with supporting sentence, we can leverage the neighbouring feature to predict current sentence label and linear-chain condition random field only consider previous neighbouring feature on label prediction is particularly useful for our work in identifying supporting sentence using a combination of current feature and neighbouring feature.

METHODOLOGY

Formal Definition

Given an opinionated text, comparative sentence, S_{com}, is a sentence that contains comparative elements, i.e., comparative entities, features and relation as defined by Jindal & Liu (2006). Figure 4 shows an example comparative sentence with its elements.

Figure 4. A sample comparative sentence, S_{com}, and its comparative elements by Jindal and Liu, (2006)

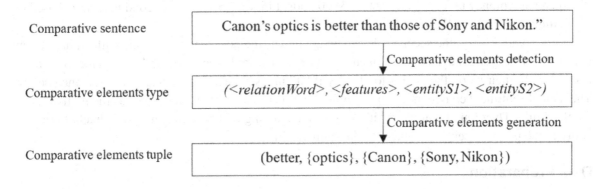

Comparative sentence	Canon's optics is better than those of Sony and Nikon."
	↓ Comparative elements detection
Comparative elements type	(<*relationWord*>, <*features*>, <*entityS1*>, <*entityS2*>)
	↓ Comparative elements generation
Comparative elements tuple	(better, {optics}, {Canon}, {Sony, Nikon})

Given a comparative sentence, S_{com}, there is a set of sentences that appears before (or after) it. These sentences are known as the neighbouring sentences for S_{com}. Since these sentences are connected with S_{com}, details or explanations that justify why certain comparisons are made in S_{com} may be found in the sentences.

However, not all neighbouring sentences are useful as well. Hence, before a neighbouring sentence can be used to enhance the understanding of comparative sentence; its relevancy needs to be identified.

A relevant neighbouring sentence is defined as below:

For a comparative sentence, S_{com}, a neighbouring sentence which is relevant to S_{com} is known as supporting sentence for comparative sentence. The supporting sentence is denoted as S_{supp}.

In this research, one sentence before and one sentence after comparative sentence, S_{com}, is shortlisted as supporting sentence candidate. A candidate supporting sentence needs to satisfy the following rules before it can be selected as a supporting sentence for comparative opinion mining.

1. There is similarity in the context between a comparative sentence and its prior/post candidate supporting sentence, i.e., both sentences contain semantic similarities.
2. There is a connectivity between a comparative sentence and its prior/post candidate supporting sentence, i.e., either one of the sentences has certain linguistic characteristics such as a sentence begins with "it has <noun phrase>", "this is <noun phrase>" etc.

Based on the two characteristics above, we are able to identify supporting sentence, S_{supp} from neighbouring sentence of a comparative sentence. Below is sequence of three sentences from Amazon.com that satisfies the characteristics mentioned, with the prior supporting sentence denoted as $<S_{supp\_pre}>$ and post supporting sentence denotes as $<S_{supp\_post}>$.

"$<S_{supp\_pre}>$ you can always spend more money to get a better one$</S_{supp\_pre}>$.
$<S_{com}>$ however, for a \$ 600 - \$ 800 budget, i think this camera is an best choice$</S_{com}>$.
$<S_{supp\_post}>$ it has a beautiful design, lots of features, very easy to use, very configurable and customizable, and the battery duration is amazing! $</S_{supp\_post}>$"

If we look at S_{com} and S_{supp_pre}, it is obvious that these two sentences contained similarity in context as both sentences talk about price. Identification of context can be carried out in different ways such as using physical word similarity (e.g. using string edit distance) or semantic similarity (e.g. using wordnet word distance). For example, although there is no similar word used in $<S_{supp\_pre}>$ and $<S_{com}>$, but terms like spend and money in S_{supp_pre} and \$600 - \$800 budget in $<S_{com}>$ can act as good indicators based on their similarity scores in Wordnet.

For S_{com} and S_{supp_post}, the second rule can be applied as the post sentence begins with "it has <noun phrase>". In Ding and Liu (2010), sentiment consistency was said to be particularly useful for coreference resolution. In their work, the goal is to identify if "it" in a sentence is referring to the sentence before. The idea of sentiment consistency can be applied in this research work and serves as the motivation of the third rule. They found that when "it" is used in beginning of a sentence, it is very likely to refer to entity in the previous sentence which is "this camera" in S_{com}.

Data Preparation

In this research, we adopted a publicly available comparative review dataset from Jindal and Liu (2006). This data set is suitable for our research as it contains a set of reviews with labelled comparative sentence, which can be used as the seed to further identify the supporting sentence from these comparative sentences.

Comparative Review Data Source

Table 2. Details of Jindal and Liu, 2006 comparative datasets

Comparative Dataset	
Sentence labeled	**Identified comparative sentence**
5890	905

In Jindal & Liu (2006) dataset, 5890 sentences were manually inspected by experts and 905 comparative review sentences were identified (see Table 2). The annotated dataset contains customer reviews collected from different sources such as Amazon.com, Eopinions.com and dcresource.com. In the annotated dataset by Jindal & Liu (2006), identified comparative sentences were grouped into four groups (non-equal gradable, equative, superlative and non-gradable).

Comparative-Supporting Sentences Data Annotation

Using the comparative data from Jindal & Liu (2006), two sets of annotated data are prepared with respect to the two subtasks mentioned. The example output of the annotated data are as follows.

1. **Annotated Comparative-Supporting Sentence**

The following output shows that both before and after sentences that connect to the comparative sentence is supporting sentence. For cases which are not supporting sentence, the sentence is annotated as *<before_is_not_supporting_sentence>* or *<after_is_not_supporting_sentence>*.

<comparative_review>
<before_is_supporting_sentence></ before_is_supporting_sentence>
<comparative_sentence></comparative_sentence>
*<after_is_supporting_sentence>< after*_is_supporting_sentence>
</comparative_review>
Example annotated data:
<comparative_review>
<before_is_not_supporting_sentence>
you can always spend more money to get a better one. </ before_is_not_supporting_sentence>
<comparative_sentence>
however, for a $ 600 - $ 800 budget, i think this camera is an excellent choice </comparative_sentence>
<after_is_supporting_sentence>
it has a beautiful design, lots of features, very easy to use, very configurable and customizable, and the battery duration is amazing!
</ after_is_supporting_sentence>
</comparative_review>

2.   Annotated Comparative-Supporting Elements

From the data set in i, the comparative review that consist of supporting sentence, i.e. has either <before_is_supporting_sentence> or <after_is_supporting_sentence> is further annotated at the element level. This annotation output consists of the comparative, the supporting sentence and two types of mappings, MAP_{EE} and MAP_{EA}.

<comparative_review>
<comparative_sentence></comparative_sentence>
<supporting_sentence type= "before/after"></supporting_sentence>
< map_ee>
<com_entity></com_entity>
<supp_entity></supp_entity>
</ map_ee>
< map_ea>
<com_entity></com_entity>
<supp_attribute></supp_attribute>
</ map_ea>
</comparative_review>
Example annotated data:
<comparative_review>
<comparative_sentence> however, for a \$ 600 - \$ 800 budget, i think this camera is an excellent choice
</comparative_sentence>
<supporting_sentence>it has a beautiful design, lots of features, very easy to use, very configurable and customizable, and the battery duration is amazing!
</supporting_sentence>
< map_ee>
<com_entity>this camera</com_entity>
<supp_entity>it</supp_entity>
</ map_ee>
< map_ea>
<com_entity>this camera</com_entity>
<supp_attribute>beautiful design</supp_attribute>
</ map_ea>
<map_ea>
<com_entity>this camera</com_entity>
<supp_attribute> Battery duration is amazing</supp_attribute>
</map_ea>
</comparative_review>

Figure 5. Sample of Jindal and Liu (2006) comparative review dataset for supporting sentence annotation

you can always spend more money to get a better one.	**(Sentence before S**com**)**
<cs-3>	
however, for a $ 600 - $ 800 budget, i think this camera is an excellent choice	**(S**com**)**
</cs-3>	
it has a beautiful design, lots of features, very easy to use, very configurable and customizable, and the battery duration is amazing!	**(Sentence after S**com**)**

Before annotation is conducted, preprocessing is performed on Jindal & Liu (2006) dataset to extract only their annotated comparative sentences, and its neighbouring sentences. In Figure 5, the sample dataset from Jindal & Liu (2006) contained one comparative sentence (S$_{com}$), hence for this comparative sentence, the preprocessing step will extract one neighbouring sentence before and one neighbouring sentence after this comparative sentence. In the preprocessing phase, three sentences will be obtained per each comparative sentence.

According to the Jindal & Liu dataset, special tags are used identify comparative sentence from normal sentences. Four types of tags are used, <cs-1> (for non-equal gradable comparative sentence), <cs-2> (for equative comparative sentence), <cs-3> (for superlative comparative sentence) and <cs-4> (for non-gradable comparative sentence). The extraction process was automated using Python script to identify the comparative sentence for all these four tags, followed by extraction of the sentence set.

Figure 6. Supporting sentence annotation interface

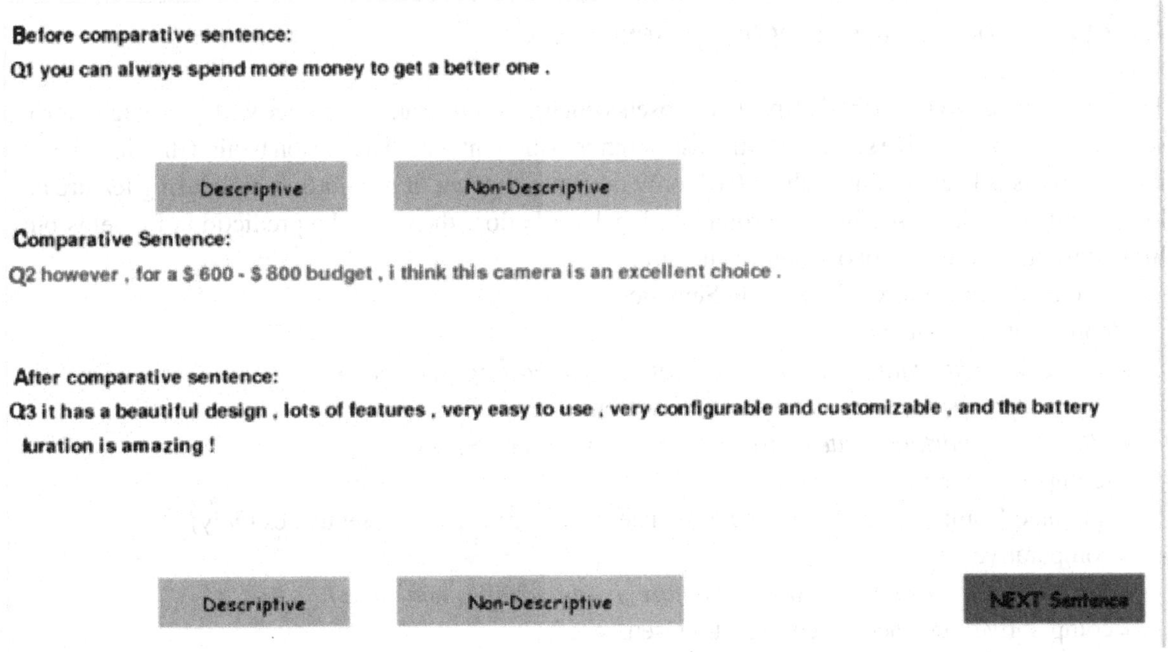

Before comparative sentence:

Q1 you can always spend more money to get a better one .

Descriptive	Non-Descriptive

Comparative Sentence:

Q2 however , for a $ 600 - $ 800 budget , i think this camera is an excellent choice .

After comparative sentence:

Q3 it has a beautiful design , lots of features , very easy to use , very configurable and customizable , and the battery duration is amazing !

Descriptive	Non-Descriptive	NEXT Sentence

Once the comparative review (consisting of three sentences per review) are prepared, the data is ready to be annotated by three selected experts. In Jindal & Liu (2006) reviews, since there are several domains of products involved for e.g., Camera, Processor, MP3 player, etc., the expert annotators selected are well-versed in English language and they are familiar with online products purchase.
Each annotator is given instruction to use the application (Figure 6).

1. First, the annotator is briefed on the functionalities of the application, e.g., functions of buttons and page navigation.
2. Second, the annotator is briefed on the task which is to identify the sentence by the following criteria.
    a. If the neighbouring sentence before comparative sentence is elaborating, explaining, or providing additional information with regards to the comparative sentence, then select the descriptive button, otherwise, select the non-descriptive button.
    b. If the neighbouring sentence after comparative sentence is elaborating, explaining or providing additional information with regards to the comparative sentence, then select the descriptive button, otherwise, select the non-descriptive button.
3. Proceed to next comparative review after completing the current task.

Annotators' Agreement

In the case where three sets of annotated review have disagreement on the labels, majority selected label was used as the final label for e.g., if annotator A and annotator B have stated that neighbouring sentence X as supporting sentence, but annotator C annotated the same sentence as non-supporting sentence, the final label for the neighbouring sentence will be annotated as supporting sentence since two out of the three annotators voted as supporting sentence.

Annotated Comparative-Supporting Review Data

The annotated data will be divided into two subsets which are comparative sentence with pre-neighbouring sentence and comparative sentence with post-neighbouring sentence. The reason behind dividing dataset into two parts is because linear-chain CRF only take into account of previous neighbouring feature and local features as discussed in Background on label prediction, therefore the prediction of label is only limited to the distance of two sentences feature.
Annotated Comparative-Supporting Sentence
<comparative_review>
<before_is_supporting_sentence></ before_is_supporting_sentence>
*<after_is_supporting_sentence>< after_*is_supporting_sentence>
</comparative_review>
Annotated Comparative-Supporting Sentence (Comparative + Pre Sentences Only)
<comparative_review>
<before_is_supporting_sentence></ before_is_supporting_sentence>/
</comparative_review>
Annotated Comparative-Supporting Sentence (Comparative + Post Sentences Only)

<comparative_review>
*<after_is_supporting_sentence>< after_*is_supporting_sentence>
</comparative_review>

Note: For cases which are not supporting sentence, the sentence is annotated as *<before_is_not_supporting_sentence>* or *<after_is_not_supporting_sentence>*.

Figure 7. Sample of annotated data on comparative sentence and its pre-neighbouring sentence

```
1   <before-is-supporting-sentence>
2   it 's very sleek looking with a very good front panel button layout , and it has a great feature set .
3   </before-is-supporting-sentence>
4   < Comparative sentence >
5   Apex fast-forward and rewind work much more smoothly and consistently than those of other models i 've had .
6   </Comparative sentence >
7   <before-is-not-supporting-sentence>
8   the body construction - buttons , casing , etc , are too plastic .
9   </before-is-not-supporting-sentence>
10  < Comparative sentence >
11  the G2 was better in this respect .
12  </Comparative sentence>
```

Figure 8. Sample of annotated data on comparative sentence and its post-neighbouring sentence

```
1   < Comparative sentence >
2   Apex fast-forward and rewind work much more smoothly and consistently than those of other models i 've had .
3   </Comparative sentence >
4   <after-is-not-supporting-sentence>
5   it plays alternate video formats ( vcds , svcds , cvds ) very well .
6   </after-is-not-supporting-sentence>
7   < Comparative sentence >
8   the G2 was better in this respect .
9   </Comparative sentence>
10  <after-is-supporting-sentence>
11  it had a heavier and more sturdy casing .
12  </after-is-supporting-sentence>
```

In Figure 7 shows output of two annotated comparative reviews that consist of comparative sentence and its pre-neighbouring sentence (before comparative sentence) and Figure 8 shows the output of two annotated comparative reviews data consists of comparative sentence and its post-neighbouring sentence (after comparative sentence).

Table 3. Number of annotated comparative sentence with supporting sentence

Annotated Comparative Review	Comparative sentence with post-supporting sentence	Comparative sentence with pre-supporting sentence	Comparative sentence with pre and post supporting sentence
400	65	63	13

From 905 comparative sentences from Jindal & Liu (2006), 400 were annotated. Table 3 shows the distribution of supporting sentence identified from 400 annotated comparative review where 65 comparative sentences contained post-supporting sentence, 63 of the comparative sentences with pre-supporting sentence and only 13 comparative sentence which have both pre and post-supporting sentence.

For supporting element annotation, it is done through direct mapping by ourselves. Golden standard for entity tuple list which is mapping between comparative entity and supporting entity (MAP_{EE}) and golden standard for supporting attribute tuple list mapping between comparative entity and supporting attribute (MAP_{EA}) are created through our manual inspection.

Framework

Figure 9. Proposed framework for identification of supporting sentence

Model Training

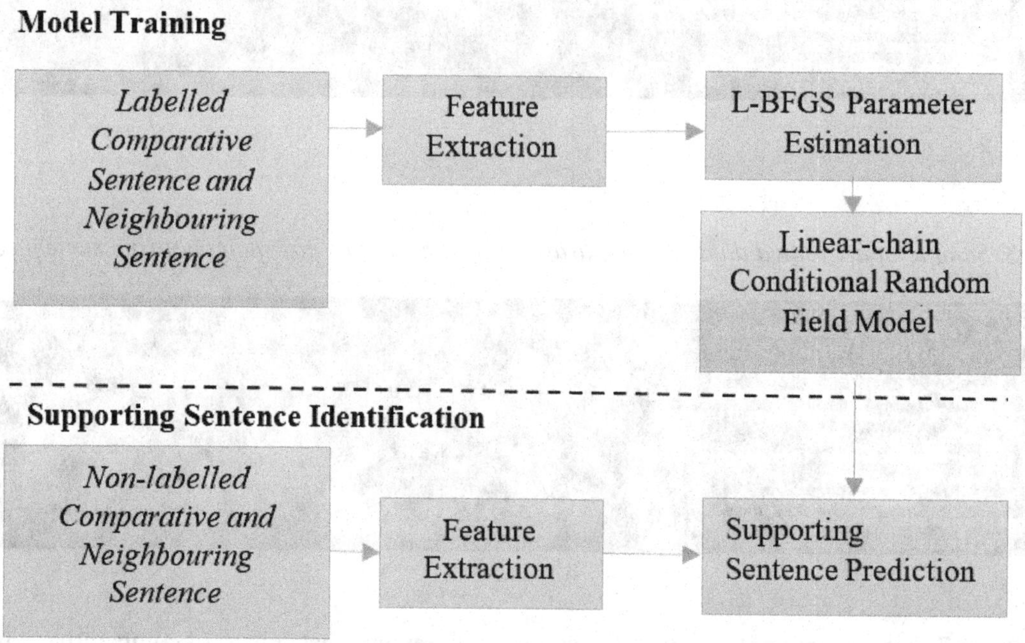

In this section, we present the overall framework for this study on identifying supporting sentence (see Figure 9). The input will be comparative sentence S_{com} and its supporting sentence, S_{supp_pre} for sentence before comparative sentence and S_{supp_post} for sentence after comparative sentence that were defined in the Definition section.

In the process to identify supporting sentence, linear-chain conditional random field classifier will be used to identify the neighbouring sentence as either supporting sentence that is related to the comparative sentence or is neighbouring sentence that is not related to comparative sentence.

Model Training

We use linear-chain conditional random field for identification process. Fifty percent (200 out of 400) of the annotated comparative sentences with its neighbouring sentences were used as training data for linear chain CRF. To create the trained model for linear-chain CRF for our experiment, feature function extraction from labelled comparative sentences and neighbouring sentence is required. Features extracted basically go through parameter estimation where linear-chain CRF to learn the weight for each feature function and a trained linear-CRF model is created and in prediction phase this trained model is used to predict each comparative sentence and its neighbouring sentence label.

For feature function extraction, two main feature function categories which are semantic features and part-of feature and details for each feature function and implementation is in the following section.

1. Feature Extraction

Semantic features generally are feature category consists of feature that use to detect the context similarity between sentences for e.g., cosine similarity, comparative keyword detection, wordnet similarity and semantic similarity. For cosine similarity, which was used to measure the similarity of word used between two sentences (neighbouring sentence and comparative sentence). Comparative keyword occurrence is detection of commonly used comparative keywords in the sentence from (Jindal & Liu 2006).

For comparative keywords occurrence, a compiled list of comparative features is used as follows by Jindal and Liu (2006).

- Comparative adjectives (JJR)
- Comparative adverbs (RBR),
- Superlative adjectives (JJS),
- Superlative adverbs (RBS),
- 69 indicator keywords list through identifying frequently used comparative keyword like "win", "defeat", "compared to" etc.
- Comparative structural pattern ("as <adj/adv> as", "same as", "identical to" etc.)

Latent semantic indexing that was introduced by Deerwester et al (1990) is a commonly used singular value decomposition technique to capture semantic similarity. Basically, this feature uses all the sentences in the dataset to create a term frequency – inverse document frequency vectors in order to produce a matrix which contains commonly used word from the dataset.

Wordnet (Fellbaum, 1998) is lexical database that was built to identify cognitive synonyms, simple example like the word 'ship' and the word 'boat is categorized under the same group and hence their Wordnet similarity score will be high 0.91 out 1.0. In our experiment Wordnet similarity score is on the sentence level rather than word level and this is one of the key features to measure similarity between sentence that was mentioned in Canhasi (2013).

Part-of feature is the second feature category. In this category, three features are introduced i.e., is-between feature, has-a feature and it-has-a feature. For is-between feature basically detect in the sentence whether consist of word such as is, are, was and were between two nouns for example "G12 is a good camera" where the word "G12" is a proper noun, and the word "camera" is noun. For has-a feature, it is similar as is-between features. Instead of is, are, was and were it check for has, have, and had between two nouns. For it-has feature is checking on the sentence where contains the word "it" before has which was commonly appear at the beginning of the sentence. For example, "it has better menu".

2.   L-BFGS Parameter Estimation & Linear-chain Conditional Random Field

For identification process of training and testing on linear-chain CRF, CRF++ toolkit (Taku910. github.io, 2017) that is publicly available is used in this work. In the training phase, each feature extracted from the sentence will go through parameter estimation which basically adjust appropriate weightage for each feature using a fast-training method called a quasi-Newton method using Broyden-Fletcher-Goldfarb-Shannon algorithm (L-BFGS) to deal with slow-convergence issue. Each annotated comparative sentence and its neighbouring sentence label which was obtained from three annotators is included as linear-chain CRF. A trained linear-chain CRF model will be created with the weight of each feature through model training phase.

Supporting Sentence Identification

A linear-chain CRF model is trained and in prediction phase using the remaining 200 of the annotated comparative sentences with its neighbouring sentence. In testing phase, annotated label is served as the ground truth for evaluation on the trained linear-chain CRF model. The remaining 200 out of 400 annotated comparative sentences were used as unlabeled data for the trained model, prediction results are compared with the benchmark label for evaluation of our model.

In prediction phase, each comparative sentence and its neighbouring sentence go through same feature extraction process e.g., semantics feature and part-of feature extraction on each of the sentences. Using the weight that was assigned for each feature function in the trained model, linear-chain CRF will make the prediction on whether the sentence is a comparative sentence with supporting sentence or a comparative sentence without supporting sentence. At the end of the prediction phase, predicted result by the trained model of linear-chain CRF is compared to the benchmark data for evaluation on the CRF classifier.

EVALUATION

Performance Metric

Four metrics are introduced in our evaluation for performance in our experiment which are accuracy, recall, precision and F-score.

Recall is the relevant instance that is correctly predicted by the classifier among all the relevant instances that was annotated by annotator while precision is percent of relevant instances is correctly predicted by classifier among all instances that was predicted by classifier as relevant instance. F-score is the common measure for classifier evaluation where it takes the harmonic mean for precision and recall. To calculate precision, recall and F-score involves four different measurements on the predicted label they are true positive, false positive, true negative and false negative. True positive is when the classifier predicts the test data to be positive and the condition is true, true negative is when the classifier predict the test data to be positive and the condition is false. For false positive is when the classifier predicts the test data to be negative and the condition is true and lastly false negative is when the classifier predict the test data to be negative and the condition is false.

Calculation of Accuracy

Calculation of accuracy is done by counting the correctly predicted label compared to manually actual labels.

$$Accuracy = \frac{True\,Positive + False\,Positive}{True\,Positive + False\,Positive + True\,Negative + False\,Negative},$$

Calculation of Recall

Recall is calculated to identify the label that is correctly predicted (true positive) from the overall predicted label (true positive + false negative). Recall formula is as follow:

$$Recall = \frac{True\,Positive}{True\,Positive + False\,Negative},$$

Calculation of Precision

Precision is calculated to identify the label that is correctly predicted (true positive) from the overall predicted label (true positive + true negative).

$$Precision = \frac{True\,Positive}{True\,Positive + False\,Positive},$$

Calculation of F-score

F-Score is calculated from recall and precision value. It is acting as a mean calculation of classifier to determine overall how well a classifier is. F-score is calculated with the formula as follows:

$$F-score = 2 * \frac{recall * precision}{recall + precision}$$

Baseline for Identification of Supporting Sentence

To our best knowledge, this is the first work on improving comparative opinion mining through identification of supporting sentence, hence, in our experiment, we adopt a baseline with the nearest research objective, which is the sentence similarity measure using word distance method as our evaluation reference. Leveshtein distance method is one of the popular methods used in measuring sentence similarity. In the work of Takagi & Naoko (2015), they used Levenshtein distance as one of the key features for sentence similarity. In our work, this baseline is used as sentence similarity is an important feature to identify supporting sentence. For sentences that contain high similarity, they are most likely to be related to each other. Levenshtein distance is calculated according to the distance required to transform the source sentence to become the target sentence using action such as deletions, insertions or substitution.

For the baseline experiment, to detect supporting sentence using sentence similarity, in this baseline Levenshtein distance score is used. For Levenshtein distance score, the lower the score the more similar between two sentences, since our work is a binary classification (classified to either contained supporting sentence or no supporting sentence), median of all the annotated test datas were used as the threshold to decide on the classification. In our experiment, median of Levenshtein distance score of 80 was obtained as the threshold where any value below 80 is classified as high similarity hence contained supporting sentence and any value above 80 is classified as low similarity hence does not contain supporting sentence.

Table 4 shows the evaluation results of identifying supporting sentence using Levenshtein distance method.

Table 4. Baseline result using Levenshtein distance to identify supporting sentence

Performance Metric / Supporting sentence	Accuracy	Precision	Recall	F-score
Comparative sentence with pre-supporting sentence	0.43	0.65	0.14	0.23
Comparative sentence with post-supporting sentence	0.64	0.27	0.64	0.37

FINDINGS

Contextual Feature for Linear-Chain CRF

Selection of good similarity features are critical during the training of linear-chain CRF model. Incorrect selection of features can cause "confusion" to the CRF model and will affect the accuracy during sentence label prediction process.

In our experiment, we create an optimized feature list through the feature selection process to identify the best features combination. Subset of features is selected through elimination of worst performance feature, and through evaluation of different combinations, most optimized features are obtained to create the model for identification of supporting sentence.

Feature Selection Process for Post-supporting Sentence Results

Table 5. Combination of features for post-supporting sentence results for feature selection

Accuracy	Precision	Recall	F-Score	Detection of comparative keyword in current sentence	Detection of comparative keyword in previous sentence	Latent Sematic Indexing	Cosine Similarity	Wordnet Similarity	Part-of Feature
0.61	0.48	0.46	0.47	✓	✓		✓	✓	
0.53	0.39	0.42	0.41	✓	✓		✓	✓	✓
0.56	0.33	0.42	0.37	✓	✓		✓	✓	✓
0.61	0.30	0.37	0.33	✓	✓		✓	✓	✓
0.54	0.24	0.29	0.26	✓	✓		✓	✓	✓
0.62	0.27	0.25	0.26	✓			✓	✓	
0.52	0.21	0.26	0.23	✓			✓	✓	
0.53	0.18	0.21	0.20	✓	✓		✓		
0.51	0.15	0.13	0.14				✓	✓	
0.51	0.09	0.085	0.09			✓	✓		

Table 5 shows the subset of features used (mark with a tick) in the feature selection process. In the feature selection process, Latent Semantic Indexing (LSI) feature (between sentences) gives a low precision and recall. All the sentences in the dataset are used to create a term frequency – inverse document frequency vectors in order to produce a matrix which contains commonly used word from the dataset. Original dataset from Jindal and Liu (2006) includes 11 different products from different domains i.e., camera, processor, handphone, dvd player, etc. LSI generally works well on a single targeted domain where similar word is mentioned frequently in the domain, that helps in deriving useful LSI score that can be used in determining the similarity in context between two sentences. Feature combination with LSI results in only 3 out of 33 comparative-supporting sentences paired being identified correctly.

At the initial stage of the research, part-of feature was mentioned to be a potential good feature in building linear-chain CRF. Part-of feature commonly appeared in neighbouring sentence as mentioned in the Methodology section. In our work part-of feature potentially exists in post-supporting sentence as commonly post-supporting sentence will further provide information on the comparative sentence made. In the annotated dataset, instead of post-supporting sentence contained this feature, comparative sentence contained such feature as well. Therefore, using this feature for our annotated dataset causes lower accuracy during evaluation phase.

From the features subset, the optimized features for post-supporting sentence identification consists of existence of comparative keyword from current and previous sentence, cosine similarity feature and Wordnet similarity feature between comparative sentence and neighbouring sentence.

Detection of comparative keyword feature is used to identify the position of comparative sentence. The position of comparative sentence is important as supporting sentence exists either before or after the comparative sentence, since in linear-chain CRF we want to know the sequence of the sentence therefore by knowing the position of the comparative sentence we can find the neighbouring sentence that can potentially classify as supporting sentence. For example, if in the current sentence there is comparative keyword detected therefore it is a comparative sentence, the sentence appeared before and after current sentence is potentially pre and post supporting sentence.

Cosine similarity and Wordnet similarity features is important in detecting supporting sentence however in our experiment where the best feature combination which yield 0.47 F-score. 18 out of 33 comparative-supporting sentences pairs were wrongly predicted, 12 out of 18 wrongly predicted comparative-supporting sentence were due pair to long sentences (word count of the sentence above 25 words) on either comparative sentence or supporting sentence.

In cosine similarity and wordnet similarity feature, similarity score between sentence are depends on the identical word appeared in sentence for cosine similarity and total of context identical word for Wordnet similarity. In long supporting sentence or comparative sentence, every word in the sentence that is not identical in terms of context or word will contribute to lower similarity score.

Remaining 6 post-supporting sentences that were wrongly labeled as non-supporting sentence is due to no similar word or related context found in both comparative sentence and supporting sentence. Comparative sentences that do not have any context or word similarity with supporting description is another short-coming of our linear-chain CRF model. For example, one of the supporting sentences that was predicted wrongly by the model has comparative sentence *"it took them twice as long to get to my unit as they said"* and post-supporting sentence *"moreover, they want total of $107 to repair it"*.

Feature Selection Process for Pre-supporting Sentence Results

Table 6. Combination of feature for pre-supporting sentence results for feature selection

Accuracy	Precision	Recall	F-Score	Detection of comparative keyword in current sentence	Detection of comparative keyword in previous sentence	Cosine Similarity	Wordnet Similarity	Part-of Feature
0.53	0.31	0.23	0.26	✓	✓	✓	✓	✓
0.56	0.27	0.19	0.22	✓		✓	✓	✓
0.52	0.27	0.19	0.22	✓	✓	✓	✓	
0.53	0.18	0.21	0.20	✓	✓	✓		
0.51	0.15	0.13	0.14			✓	✓	

Table 6 shows the outcome of pre-supporting sentence identification using different features subset. In the evaluation for pre-supporting sentence, latent semantic indexing was not included for feature selection process as in post-supporting sentence. This feature is omitted since we have found out that LSI feature is not appropriate since the training dataset contains products from different domains which yields rather poor results when LSI was included.

The results on accuracy and F-score for pre-supporting sentence are lower than post-supporting sentence where the best feature subset combination obtained only 53% accuracy with F-score of 0.26. The same features subset that we used for post supporting sentence does not react well for pre-supporting sentence due to the characteristic of pre-supporting sentences which appeared to have less sentence similarity or context similarity with comparative sentences compared to post-supporting sentence. For example, pre-supporting sentence identified by annotator is **"however, using the lcd seems to eliminate this minor problem."** and the comparative sentence is **"overall it is the best camera on the market.".** Also, it is rather difficult to get good results with either cosine similarity or Wordnet similarity when most of the pre-supporting sentence consists of short and contained implicit meaning between comparative sentence and pre-supporting sentence.

As pre-supporting sentences did not give a satisfactory outcome, it is still possible to look into other sentences aspect in the future.

Supporting Sentence Identification Using Linear-Chain CRF

Table 7 shows the evaluation results of linear-chain CRF model for post-supporting sentence and pre-supporting sentence identification in comparison with its baseline which uses Levenshtein distance to identify similarity between two sentences.

Results shows that for pre-supporting sentence identification, Levenshtein distance has higher precision 0.65 compared to identification of pre-supporting sentence through linear-chain CRF which is 0.31. However, Levenshtein distance method suffers low recall which leads to lower F-score of 0.23 (Levenshtein distance) and 0.26 (linear-chain CRF). Lower accuracy has also been recorded for baseline at 43% while linear-chain CRF records 53%.

Table 7. Evaluation results of supporting sentence identification using linear-chain CRF and baseline method

Identification of supporting sentence/ Performance metrics	Baseline: Pre-supporting sentence identification through Levenshtein distance	Pre-supporting sentence identification through linear-chain CRF	Baseline: Post-supporting sentence identification through Levenshtein distance	Post-supporting sentence identification through linear-chain CRF	Mean baseline performance metrics	Mean linear-chain CRF performance metrics
Accuracy	43%	**53%**	**64%**	61%	53.5%	**57%**
Precision	**0.65**	0.31	0.27	**0.48**	**0.46**	0.395
Recall	0.14	**0.23**	**0.64**	0.44	**0.39**	0.335
F-score	0.23	**0.26**	0.375	**0.46**	0.30	**0.36**

For pre-supporting sentence identification, the baseline sentence similarity (Levenshtein distance) does not perform well. For pre-supporting sentence, baseline sentence similarity yields 43% accuracy and F-score of 0.23 compared to post-supporting sentence 64% accuracy and F-score of 0.46. This is similar to Section 4.3.2's findings where pre-supporting sentence generally does not contain word similarity or context similarity with its comparative sentence.

For post-supporting sentence, Levenshtein distance method produced better accuracy 64% and recall 0.64 compared to linear-chain CRF. However, using Levenshtein distance in post-supporting sentence produced lower precision 0.27 compared to linear-chain CRF which obtained 0.48 precision. Sentence similarity and context similarity work well for post-supporting sentence, using Levenshtein distance alone can achieve high accuracy but suffered in precision. Linear-chain CRF outperform Levenshtein distance method in terms of precision where linear-chain CRF yields 0.48 compared to Levenshtein distance method which yields 0.24.

Generally, linear-chain CRF with optimized features perform better in identifying supporting sentence compared to the baseline which used Levenshtein distance method. The optimized features that we use for this experiment perform better in identification of post-supporting sentence compared to pre-supporting sentence due to features that we use for our model focuses on detecting word similarity and semantic similarity between comparative-supporting sentence pairs.

As from our finding, comparative with pre-supporting sentence contained very little to no similar word mentioned compared to post-supporting sentence where usually contained similar words or similar semantic that was mentioned. We evaluated the accuracy and F-score of baseline and linear-chain CRF model that was created in terms of their average performance on pre and post supporting sentence, linear-chain CRF outperform baseline model in accuracy by 4% and F-score by 0.06.

Discussions

In evaluation phase, supporting sentence is divided into post-supporting sentence and pre-supporting sentence. Through feature selection process, optimized feature combination was found and incorporating optimized feature combination into linear-chain CRF yields the best result of 61% accuracy and 0.47 F-score in post-supporting sentence.

The optimized feature combinations consist of detection of comparative keyword existence, cosine and wordnet similarity between comparative sentence and post supporting sentence. However, there is certain limitation of the features implemented where long sentences in post-supporting sentence and comparative sentence lower the accuracy of word similarity score (cosine similarity) and context similarity score (wordnet similarity) in linear-chain CRF prediction.

For pre-supporting sentence, using the optimized feature combination produced worse result compared to post-supporting sentence. Incorporating comparative keyword existence feature, cosine similarity feature, wordnet similarity feature and part-of feature yield the best results of 53% accuracy and 0.26 F-score.

The feature combination we used in our experiments shows better accuracy and F-score in post-supporting sentence compared to pre-supporting sentence. The reason behind this is that post-supporting sentences often contain similar word or context mentioned between comparative sentence and post-supporting sentence. However, in pre-supporting sentence identification, word similarity and context similarity features accuracy is worse as many of the identified pre-supporting sentences did not contain similar word appear between comparative sentence and post-supporting sentence.

Linear-chain CRF using optimized contextual features generally outperforms the baseline where Levensthein distance method was used on both pre-supporting and post supporting sentences identification. Incorporating neighbouring features is one of the main reason linear-chain CRF was selected in this work; and neighbouring features such as cosine similarity and wordnet similarity help in identifying supporting sentence better than using Levensthein distance method which only calculate word distance similarity between two sentences.

CONCLUSION

In this work, we are motivated to improve comparative opinion mining through identification of supporting sentences. Single sentence comparative opinion mining is insufficient when users provide their comparative opinion across multiple sentences. Incorporating linear-chain conditional random field using optimized contextual feature i.e., comparative keyword existence, cosine similarity between sentences and Wordnet similarity between sentences achieved 61% accuracy and F-score of 0.47 in comparative sentence that contained post-supporting sentence and 53% accuracy and F-score of 0.27 for comparative sentence that contained pre-supporting sentence. Linear-chain CRF shown to outperform baseline model which uses simple sentence similarity matching method in identifying supporting sentence. Hence, the research objective on incorporating optimized contextual feature to identify supporting sentence is achieved.

Limitation

In most of the previous comparative opinion mining research, single comparative sentence is considered without considering the impact of neighbouring sentence and this results in most of the annotated dataset during annotation of data remove all neighbouring sentence that is not required in their work. Building a new ground truth will consume significant effort and time.

In our research we used Jindal and Liu (2006) dataset which contained neighbouring sentences. However in some cases neighbouring sentence seem to be disconnected as in their dataset there is no separation between data that was collected from different section.

In our work, linear-chain CRF model was trained on relatively small imbalanced dataset (only 33 percent of the dataset consists of comparative sentence with supporting sentence). Limited comparative sentence with supporting sentence could results in less accurate learning of linear-chain CRF on identification of supporting sentence.

FUTURE RESEARCH DIRECTIONS

For future work, using higher number of raw sentences from online reviews and annotation dataset by expert from each different domain in dataset preparation can be built. Higher number of quality annotated dataset sets can help in better analysis of feature to incorporate into linear-chain conditional random field.

Supporting sentences without word or context similarity was hard to identify. Future work can exploit feature that can identify supporting sentence without context similarity. Lastly, to develop extraction on supporting element which appeared in certain action. For example, "Iphone is better compared to Samsung. Most of the people use iphone when they are running" where supporting sentence provide supporting attribute in verb form, in this case is "running".

REFERENCES

Bach, N. X., Van, P. D., Tai, N. D., & Phuong, T. M. (2015). Mining vietnamese comparative sentences for sentiment analysis. In *Proceedings of Seventh International Conference on Knowledge and Systems Engineering* (pp. 162-167). IEEE. 10.1109/KSE.2015.36

Canhasi, E. (2013). Measuring the sentence level similarity. In *Proceedings of 2ⁿᵈ International Symposium of Computing in Informatics and Mathematics* (pp. 35-42). Academic Press.

Deerwester, S., Dumais, S. T., Furnas, G. W., Landauer, T. K., & Harshman, R. (1990). Indexing by latent semantic analysis. *Journal of the American Society for Information Science, 41*(6), 39–407. doi:10.1002/(SICI)1097-4571(199009)41:6<391::AID-ASI1>3.0.CO;2-9

Ding, S., Cong, G., Lin, C. Y., & Zhu, X. (2008). Using conditional random fields to extract contexts and answers of questions from online forums. In *Proceedings of ACL-08: HLT* (vol. 8, pp. 710-718). Association for Computational Linguistics.

Ding, X., & Liu, B. (2010). Resolving object and attribute coreference in opinion mining. In *Proceedings of the 23rd International Conference on Computational Linguistics* (pp. 268-276). Association for Computational Linguistics.

Ding, X., Liu, B., & Yu, P. S. (2008). A holistic lexicon-based approach to opinion mining. In *Proceedings of the 2008 International Conference on Web Search and Data Mining* (pp. 231-240). ACM. 10.1145/1341531.1341561

Fellbaum, C. (1998). *WordNet*. John Wiley & Sons, Inc. doi:10.7551/mitpress/7287.001.0001

Galley, M. (2006). A skip-chain conditional random field for ranking meeting utterances by importance. In *Proceedings of the 2006 Conference on Empirical Methods in Natural Language Processing* (pp. 364-372). Association for Computational Linguistics. 10.3115/1610075.1610126

Ganapathibhotla, M., & Liu, B. (2008). Mining opinions in comparative sentences. In *Proceedings of the 22nd International Conference on Computational Linguistics* (vol. 1, pp. 241-248). Association for Computational Linguistics.

Hu, M., & Liu, B. (2004). Mining and summarizing customer reviews. In *Proceedings of the tenth ACM SIGKDD International Conference on Knowledge Discovery and Data Mining* (pp. 168-177). ACM.

Hu, M., & Liu, B. (2006). Opinion feature extraction using class sequential rules. In *AAAI Spring Symposium: Computational Approaches to Analyzing Weblogs* (pp. 61-66). American Association for Artificial Intelligence.

Jindal, N., & Liu, B. (2006). Identifying comparative sentences in text documents. In *Proceedings of the 29th Annual International ACM SIGIR Conference on Research and Development in Information Retrieval* (pp. 244-251). ACM.

Jindal, N., & Liu, B. (2006b). Mining comparative sentences and relations. In *Proceedings of the 21st International Conference on Artificial Intelligence* (vol. 22, pp. 1331-1336).

Khan, A., Younis, U., Kundi, A. S., Asghar, M. Z., Ullah, I., Aslam, N., & Ahmed, I. (2020). Sentiment classification of user reviews using supervised learning techniques with comparative opinion mining perspective. In *Proceedings of Advances in Computer Vision* (Vol. 944, pp. 23–29). Springer.

Lafferty, J., McCallum, A., & Pereira, F. (2001) Conditional random fields: Probabilistic models for segmenting and labeling sequence data. In *Proceedings of the 8th International Conference on Machine Learning* (vol. 1, pp. 282-289). doi:10.1007/978-3-030-17798-0_3

Lee, J., Park, D. H., & Han, I. (2008). The effect of negative online consumer reviews on product attitude: An information processing view. *Electronic Commerce Research and Applications, 7*(3), 341–352. doi:10.1016/j.elerap.2007.05.004

Liu, B. (2012). Sentiment analysis and opinion mining. *Synthesis Lectures on Human Language Technologies, 5*(1), 1–167. doi:10.2200/S00416ED1V01Y201204HLT016

Liu, J., Huang, M., & Zhu, X. (2010). Recognizing biomedical named entities using skip-chain conditional random fields. In *Proceedings of the 2010 Workshop on Biomedical Natural Language Processing* (pp. 10-18). Association for Computational Linguistics.

Loper, E., & Bird, S. (2002). NLTK: The natural language toolkit. In *Proceedings of the ACL-02 Workshop on Effective Tools and Methodologies for Teaching Natural Language Processing and Computational Linguistics* (vol. 1, pp. 63-70). Association for Computational Linguistics.

Miller, G. A. (1995). WordNet: A lexical database for English. *Communications of the ACM, 38*(11), 39–41. doi:10.1145/219717.219748

Pang, B., & Lee, L. (2008). Opinion mining and sentiment analysis. *Foundations and Trends in Information Retrieval, 2*(1-2), 1–135. doi:10.1561/1500000011

Pang, B., Lee, L., & Vaithyanathan, S. (2002). Thumbs up?: sentiment classification using machine learning techniques. In *Proceedings of the ACL-02 Conference on Empirical Methods in Natural Language Processing* (vol. 10, pp. 79-86). Association for Computational Linguistics. 10.3115/1118693.1118704

Pathak, P., Goswami, R., Joshi, G., Patel, P., & Patel, A. (2013). CRF-based clinical named entity recognition using clinical NLP. *Proceedings of the 10th International Conference on Natural Language Processing.*

Roger, L., & Manning, C. D. (2004). Deep dependencies from context-free statistical parsers: correcting the surface dependency approximation. In *Proceedings of the 42nd Annual Meeting of the Association for Computational Linguistics (ACL-04)* (pp. 327–334). Academic Press.

Santorini, B. (1990). *Part-of-speech Tagging Guidelines for the Penn Treebank Project (3rd revision).* Academic Press.

Sutton, C., & McCallum, A. (2006). An introduction to conditional random fields for relational learning. *Introduction to Statistical Relational Learning, 2*, 93–128.

Takagi, N. M. T. (2015). WSL: Sentence similarity using semantic distance between words. In *Proceedings of the 9th International Workshop on Semantic Evaluation* (pp.128-131). Academic Press.

Taku910.github.io. (2017). *CRF++: Yet Another CRF toolkit.* https://taku910.github.io/crfpp/

Titov, I., & McDonald, R. A joint model of text and aspect ratings for sentiment summarization. In *Proceedings of ACL-08: HLT* (pp. 308-316). Association for Computational Linguistics.

Varathan, K. D., Giachanou, A., & Crestani, F. (2017). Comparative opinion mining: A review. *Journal of the Association for Information Science and Technology, 68*(4), 811–829. doi:10.1002/asi.23716

Wilson, T., Wiebe, J., & Hoffmann, P. (2005). Recognizing contextual polarity in phrase-level sentiment analysis. In *Proceedings of the Conference on Human Language Technology and Empirical Methods in Natural Language Processing* (pp. 347-354). Association for Computational Linguistics. 10.3115/1220575.1220619

Xu, K., Liao, S. S., Li, J., & Song, Y. (2011). Mining comparative opinions from customer reviews for competitive intelligence. *Decision Support Systems*, *50*(4), 743–754. doi:10.1016/j.dss.2010.08.021

Yang, S., & Ko, Y. (2011). Extracting comparative entities and predicates from texts using comparative type classification. In *Proceedings of the 49th Annual Meeting of the Association for Computational Linguistics* (pp. 1636–1644). Academic Press.

Younis, U., Asghar, M. Z., Khan, A., Khan, A., Igbal, J., & Jilani, N. (2020). Applying machine learning techniques for performing comparative opinion mining. *Open Computer Science*, *10*(1), 461–477. doi:10.1515/comp-2020-0148

Zhang, K., Xie, Y., Yang, Y., Sun, A., Liu, H., & Choudhary, A. (2014). Incorporating conditional random fields and active learning to improve sentiment identification. *Neural Networks*, *58*, 60–67. doi:10.1016/j.neunet.2014.04.005 PMID:24856246

Zhang, L., & Liu, B. (2014). Aspect and entity extraction for opinion mining. In *Proceedings of Data Mining and Knowledge Discovery for Big Data* (pp. 1–40). Springer Berlin Heidelberg. doi:10.1007/978-3-642-40837-3_1

Chapter 5
Features of Semantic Similarity Assessment:
Content- and Model-Based Perspectives

Vijayarani J.
Anna University, Chennai, India

Geetha T. V.
Anna University, Chennai, India

ABSTRACT

Semantic similarity is a fundamental concept in computational linguistics. The models used for the representation of text have a major role in similarity computation. The text with multilingual and multimodal components shows the need for computing similarity based on different characteristics of text. This chapter studies various aspects of semantic similarity of linguistic units, cross-level similarity, semantic models, and similarity measures. One of the main motivations of this chapter is to analyze semantic similarity models such as geometric models, feature-based models, graph-based models, vector space models, and formal concept analysis models. In addition, a composite summary score based on words and hashtags is applied for the tweet summarization task which is effective when compared with other measures.

INTRODUCTION

Computing semantic similarity is a necessary process in natural language processing and information retrieval. Semantic similarity has different aspects, such as proximity, closure and continuity, in addition to similar meaning. Semantic relations and attributes are intrinsically connected, where relations are more global than attributes (Goldstone *et al.*, 1991). Semantic relatedness is more general than similarity. It covers all possible semantic relations (Zhu & Iglesias, 2017) and has a broad range of applications. Semantic relations such as hypernym or hyponym ('is-a-kind-of'), meronym ('is-a part-of', 'is an ex-

DOI: 10.4018/978-1-7998-9594-7.ch005

ample of') and antonym ('is-opposite-of') show the diversity of relatedness (Mohammad & Hirst, 2005). 'Teacher' and 'professor' are semantically similar, but 'teacher' and 'student' are semantically related.

Attributional, relational and functional similarities determine the most relevant meaning. The attributional similarity shows the correspondence between the attributes of two objects (Bollegala *et al.*, 2011). 'Hot' and 'cold' have similar attributes such as 'temperature' and are considered related even though they are antonyms. Similarly, 'winter' and 'summer' share seasonal attributes. 'Dog' and 'cat' share relational attributes, and the pairs (Dog: bark) and (Cat: meow) describe a relational similarity. (Wheel, rotate) and (Birds, fly) are related to functional similarity. Words that are hierarchically related, such as (Furniture, table) and (Flowers, rose), have taxonomical similarity.

Additional research has been carried out on the similarity among words, sentences and documents (Ahsaee *et al.*, 2014; Deguchi & Ishii 2021; Lopez-Gazpio *et al.*, 2019; Sultan *et al.*, 2015; Vigneshvaran *et al.*, 2013). Word similarity is analyzed with features such as cooccurrence, context and sense. The similarity may vary over time due to inter- or intralinguistic factors causing semantic variations such as broadening, narrowing, metaphoric and metonymic (Tang *et al.*, 2016). Concept similarity is derived from the information content of concepts based on a knowledge graph (Zhu & Iglesias, 2017). Ontology-based similarity measures rely on the 'is-a' hierarchy or taxonomical features (Sanchez *et al.*, 2012). Word and context similarities provide concept mapping between ontologies (Zhen *et al.*, 2008).

Sultan *et al.* (2015) used word alignment and semantic vector composition to analyze the similarity of sentences. Document similarity is examined in parts of the document, such as words, phrases, and sentences, and then the similarities are aggregated into a single unit. Cross-level similarities require that the complexity of similarity computation should be extended with the multilingual (Khakimova *et al.*, 2020) and multimodal (Diao *et al.*, 2020) contents of the text. Semantic models define the ways of projecting the text onto the semantic space and provide a mapping between the text and semantic space. They are categorized as geometric (Demaine *et al.*, 2021), feature, graph, vector space, formal concept analysis (FCA) (Belohlavek & Mikula, 2020) and hybrid models. Similarity measures are categorized as corpus- and knowledge-based (Gomaa & Fahmy, 2013; Gupta *et al.*, 2017) or path-, 'information content'- and feature-based (Abdelrahman & Kayed 2015; Elavarasi *et al.*, 2014).

The rest of this chapter is organized as follows: Section 2 gives the background of research on semantic similarity. Section 3 reviews the textual content-based perspectives, presents a detailed explanation of model-based perspectives for similarity assessment and explains the use of path-, 'information content'- and feature-based similarity measures. The tweet summarization application explained in section 4, implements linguistic unit-based perspective and applies a composite summary score. The key concepts recognized, issues identified and comparison of models is discussed in section 5. Finally, conclusion and implications are included in section 6.

BACKGROUND

The majority of the work on text similarity has covered similarity of the word or sentence or document and not all types simultaneously. Semantic models that describe different ways of representing text have not been studied in detail.

Hatzivassiloglou *et al.*, (1999) integrated primitive features (morphological, syntactic, and semantic) into a composite feature and proposed a composite similarity metric for text summarization. Ghosh and Mitra (2008) applied a linear combination of structure and the content kernel to yield a composite support vector machine (SVM) kernel for classifying semi-structured XML documents. They used simple measures for structure and content and then combined those using composite kernels. Bar *et al.* (2012, 2015) investigated text characteristics from content, structure and style perspectives and framed a new composite similarity measure for text reuse detection. However, cross-lingual and cross-modal similarities were not the focus. Wang and Dong (2020) systematically analyzed text similarity assessment based on text distance and text representation. However, the use of hybrid models was not discussed.

Gomaa and Fahmy (2013) analyzed text similarity measures based on characters, terms, corpus and knowledge. Similarity measures are either 'path-based', such as the lowest common subsume (LCS), depth and shortest path (Castillo, 2011; Gupta & Yadav, 2014; Meng *et al.*, 2013), or 'information content-based', which depends on the corpus or taxonomy in the knowledge base (Islam & Inkpen, 2008; Mihalcea *et al.*, 2006; Saruladha *et al.*, 2010; Zhu & Iglesias, 2017), or feature-based, which is related to the common and distinctive features among the concepts (Liu *et al.*, 2015; Tversky & Gati, 1978; Ma *et al.*, 2015). The choice of measure depends on the type of semantic model used, and the measures may be hybrid (Hu & Cho, 2015). Chandrasekaran and Mago (2021) discussed about knowledge-based, corpus-based, deep neural network-based methods and hybrid methods. However, the link between the various models and measures was not focused.

Most of the approaches used for the text similarity are suitable for structured or semi-structured text and not for unstructured text. Challenges with unstructured text representation and the use of appropriate semantic models have not been discussed. To resolve these issues, this chapter focuses on content-based features, from linguistic unit-level features to cross-level features, and the relation between semantic models and measures.

MAIN FOCUS OF THE CHAPTER

Semantic Similarity Assessment

Text similarity computation requires analysis of various perspectives based on the contents in the text, models used for the representation of the text and the choice of similarity measures (Figure 1).

Figure 1. Text similarity computation

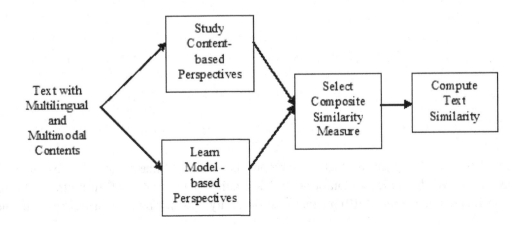

The content-based and model-based perspectives for similarity assessment are described below.

Content-Based Perspective: Linguistic Unit-Level Similarity

Similarity is measured between two linguistic or conceptual units, such as words, word pairs, concepts, sentences, short texts and documents.

Word Similarity

A word has many syntactic features, such as whether it is a noun or a verb or singular or plural. Context-dependent information plays a major role in determining word meaning. Word similarity in a thesaurus is determined using edge-counting methods that utilize semantic links and corpus-based approaches that combine corpus statistics with taxonomic distance (Amasyah, 2006). It may be determined from multiple information resources, such as lexical knowledge bases and corpus statistics. WordNet is a large-scale semantic lexicon for English that contains more than 1,18,000 words organized with more than 90,000 different word senses (Miller, 1995). It combines the features of a dictionary and thesaurus. Using WordNet, semantic distance and depth can be used for measuring the similarity of words (Hao *et al.*, 2011). However, technical terms may not be present in WordNet, and not all types of semantically related terms can be quantified.

For example, 'tree' and 'shadow' are semantically related but not semantically similar. The sense hierarchies obtained from WordNet (Figure 2) for these semantically related words do not have any common terms.

Figure 2. Sense hierarchies of 'tree' and 'shadow'

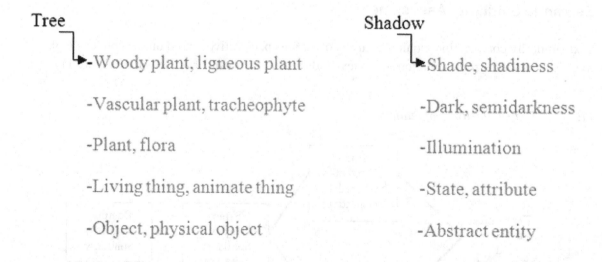

Context-based similarity ensures that similar words occur in the same context. For example, 'table' represents either 'wooden table' or 'data structure' depending on the context of 'furniture' or 'computer science'. Iosif and Potamianos (2010) obtained the similarity of words by comparing the contextual information of words and proved that context is a better feature for determining similarity than occurrence. The web search engine-based approach makes use of page counts and snippets. Snippets of words are extracted from a search engine, and then patterns having the same semantic relations are identified and clustered (Lavanya & Arya, 2012). The output obtained is a cluster of synonymous and non-synonymous words. The page count and snippets of web pages provide the maximum similarity among words based on pattern extraction and pattern clustering (Kumari & Ravishankar, 2013).

Word pairs are less frequent and less ambiguous than words. Both path length- and information content-based similarity for a word pair were obtained by Meng *et al.* (2013). The word pairs ('Teacher', 'teach') and ('Dancer', 'dance') are similar. However, the pairs ('Wonder', 'won') and ('Ponder', 'pond') are dissimilar. 'Back and forth', 'cup and saucer' and 'bride and groom' are semantically related cooccurring word pairs that are irreversible. 'Well aware', 'fast asleep' and 'wide awake' are unrelated word pairs. Hence, it cannot be inferred that all cooccurring word pairs are semantically related. Ontologies and dictionaries play an important role in concept similarity. Similarity between concepts is described as a 'similar degree' based on relations, properties and instances of concepts (Li *et al.*, 2010). The information content (IC) of a concept is given as the negative log likelihood of the probability of the concept (Resnik, 1999). Two concepts c_1 and c_2 are similar if IC (LCS(c_1, c_2)) is nearly equal to IC(c_1) and IC(c_2).

Sentence Similarity

The segmented semantic comparison approach (Liu & Liang, 2013) divides a sentence into a trunk and segments. The trunk is assigned some weight, but the segments are further divided into shorter segments that have been assigned different weights. The grammatical and semantic structure of the sentence is analyzed to find the similarity of the trunk as well as the whole sentence. Roostaee *et al.* (2014) proposed approaches such as decision trees, decision rule classifiers, multilayer perceptrons, naive Bayes classifiers, k nearest neighbors classifiers, SVMs and logistic regression for constructing classification models for the similarity of short sentences. Guo and Diab (2012) suggested a 'weighted textual matrix factorization' model for handling missing words in sentences. An alignment was obtained between words in two sentences, and the sum of the similarity of the aligned word pairs gave the sentence similarity. Words in two sentences are aligned (Sultan *et al.*, 2015) based on their similarity and local semantic context. Alternatively, aligning pairs of word n-grams of variable length improves the similarity computation (Lopez-Gazpio *et al.*, 2019).
Sample sentences follow:

- Ram is **play**ing the keyboard
- Ram is **play**ing cricket
- Ram is watching the **play** in the theatre
- **Tears** lubricate the eyes
- He **tears** the paper

The first three sentences have different meanings even though most of the words are similar. The word 'tears' has different meanings as a verb and adjective due to its homonymy. The issues are due to polysemy and homonymy, which give different senses to a sentence.

Short Text Similarity

Finding the similarity of short texts is not trivial due to their limited information. Zhang *et al.* (2013) introduced a two-stage method based on topic models and rough sets that can measure the similarity of short texts directly. Shirakawa *et al.* (2015) proposed an extended naive Bayes algorithm to obtain the similarity of noisy short text. Short text features combined with hidden topics obtained from latent Dirichlet allocation improve the measure for short text similarity (Chen *et al.*, 2017). The issues related to short texts are due to their semi-structured, heterogeneous and time-varying nature. Hence, it is essential to extract features other than term frequency.

Document Similarity

Most studies on document similarity have been performed based on the syntactic and semantic structure of documents (Madylova & Oguducu, 2009; Shibata *et al.*, 2010; Vigneshvaran *et al.*, 2013). Shibata *et al.* (2010) classified academic papers and patents into clusters based on their topological structures and found the similarity between clusters. Madylova and Oguducu (2009) extracted words with IS-A relations from documents and computed the cosine similarity of the concept vectors of documents. Vigneshvaran *et al.* (2013) identified synonyms of co-occurring words in a document from WordNet and computed the mean squared deviation of documents as a similarity measure. Pairwise document similarity is possible (Elsayed *et al.*, 2008) using the 'map reduce' framework for large document collections. Document similarity computation can be enhanced by clustering the words using semantic distances, which in turn reduces the dimension of document vectors into the number of word-clusters (Deguchi & Ishii, 2021). However, computing the similarity between documents containing both text and images is a difficult task.

Content-Based Perspective: Cross-Level Similarity

The similarity between multilingual words depends on their translation-equivalent, morphological and semantic representations. Bilingual corpora and bilingual semantic networks are good resources of information. Medical and scientific documents have cross-ontology similarity, whereas social media texts are semi-structured and have cross-language and cross-modal similarities.

Cross-Language Similarity

Similarity computation among bilingual documents is possible if the conversion between the languages of the documents is performed with the help of a translator. The representation of individual languages or the unified representation of multiple languages can be learned. Huang *et al.* (2008) and Huang and Kuo (2010) used sense-based representation and measured the similarity of abstract concepts in documents using 'Tversky's notion' and the 'F-measure'.

Translation between two languages is performed by creating a bilingual corpus using WordNet as a lexicon resource. Muhic *et al.* (2012) applied an alignment of correspondences of document vectors of multilingual documents to obtain the similarity among documents. The k-means algorithm was used to find the centroid of document vectors for document alignment. Artetxe *et al.* (2017) proposed a self-learning iterative framework for learning bilingual word embeddings, even from small dictionaries. Bilingual dictionaries are not available for many languages. Semantic similarity of multilingual texts can be measured on the basis of cross-lingual semantic implicit links between the documents (Khakimova *et al.*, 2020). In the case of cross-lingual information retrieval and machine translation, the key issue is the word sense disambiguation of polysemous words. Hence, language-independent and sense-level representation is the solution for cross-language similarity.

Cross-Ontology Similarity

Ontology is a knowledge base that is described as a hierarchy of concepts. It is represented by the resource description framework (RDF) and ontology web language (OWL). Ontology describes knowledge about a specific domain, such as a unified medical language system and medical subject headings, by providing a vocabulary related to that domain. The similarity between overlapping concepts or entities in different ontologies collectively determines the cross-ontology similarity. Knowledge is dispersed more in one ontology and less in another ontology either taxonomically or non-taxonomically. If ontologies are considered as geometric models, the relative distance between concepts in the ontological structure gives the inter concept similarity. Batet *et al.* (2013) obtained the similarity among multiple ontologies by finding the union of the super concepts of a given pair of concepts in all ontologies. Rodriguez and Egenhofer (2003) introduced a matching process that used synonym sets, distinguished features and semantic relations of entity classes to model the similarity between ontologies by creating associations across ontologies. Representing and mapping multilingual, multidomain ontologies for evaluating the semantic relatedness of concepts is an important issue.

Cross-Modal Similarity

Estimating the similarity between cross-modal concepts is a complex issue. To obtain the similarity between words and images, the concepts invoked by both must be compared.

Word-Image Similarity

The similarity between a word and image depends on how the word describes the image or the image represents the word and the interaction between the word and image. The captions of images are not sufficient, and images must be annotated with labels. If the word or image is ambiguous, a large image database, such as ImageNet is required for disambiguation. ImageNet[1] is an ontology of images that extends the hierarchical structure of WordNet by attaching relevant images to each synonym set. However, there are some words that cannot be represented with their equivalent images. Verma and Jawahar (2014) proposed a 'novel structural SVM' for searching an image from the set of unannotated images for the given word and for finding the relevant word from the corpus for the given image. Bruni *et al.* (2014) built a multimodal distributional model to represent an image as a bag of visual words based on which the similarity between a word and the image was computed. Li *et al.* (2015) integrated feature-extraction methods for text and images with deep neural networks using restricted Boltzmann machines to find the bimodal similarity. Kurach *et al.* (2017) described a multimodal model for incorporating visual information into text representation. Diao *et al.* (2020) introduced a graph convolutional neural network to infer relation aware similarities with both the local and global alignments for image-text matching. The key issues for this task are related to mapping an image to a polysemous word, choosing the size of the dataset used for training and deciding how frequently it is updated.

Denotation-Image Similarity

Young *et al.* (2014) computed denotation similarities by constructing a 'denotation graph' based on a corpus of images with their captions and estimating the 'denotation probability' of expressions. Devereux *et al.* (2013) performed representational analysis independent of the input modality by employing 'word visual', 'object visual' and semantic category models. Li *et al.* (2015) analyzed the similarity of complex systems with multimodal data containing text and images and proposed a bimodal deep architecture by combining deep neural networks and neural autoencoders. Xie *et al.* (2015) proposed a 'cross-modal semantic generation model' for finding the 'semantic correlation' at a high level of abstraction closer to human understanding. The joint probability of the features of the image and text was used to estimate the similarity.

Model-Based Perspective: Semantic Similarity Models

Semantic similarity models describe a way of projecting the text onto a semantic space. New semantic models with complex structures and hybrid natures are becoming more popular. The choice of model depends on the nature of the application and the features used. The feature representation, measures and challenges of different semantic models are compared in Table 1.

Table 1. Semantic models

Model	Representation	Measures	Challenges
Geometric	Multidimensional Scaling (Hout *et al.*, 2016)	Distance measures (Minkowski, city-block)	No partial matches; Not suitable for structural similarity
Feature	Features as set theory (Ma *et al.*, 2015; Tversky & Gati, 1978)	Tversky, Pirro	Not suitable for structural similarity
Graph	Features as a network or tree (Rajagopal *et al.* 2013)	Shortest path, depth (Wu Palmer, Leacock)	Sparse and under-specified
Vector Space	Matrices (Turney & Pantel, 2010)	Distance measures	Ignores semantic relationships among features; Sparse matrices
Formal Concept Analysis	Concept Lattice (Codocedo *et al.*, 2014)	Information content (Resnik, Lin) (Meng *et al.*, 2013)	Finding an efficient mapping to identify meaningful concepts

Semantic similarity assessment is purely based on the kind of model, category of data, complexity of the background computational logic and issues related to each model. The semantic similarity models are categorized in the next sections.

Geometric Model

In the geometric model, concepts are denoted as points in two-dimensional or multidimensional space using multidimensional scaling (MDS). A matrix is computed as the scalar products between points and factored into eigenvalues and vectors (Shepard, 1980). Each dimension is a property of the concept, and the range of dimensions represents all possible values of the property. The similarity between concepts is calculated by applying spatial distance measures such as Euclidean distance. MDS is the most relevant method of implementing the geometric model for predicting similarity or dissimilarity in terms of distance measures (Demaine *et al.*, 2021). It is applied as a measure to quantify similarity (Hout *et al.* 2016). The choice of dimension in MDS is an issue and is resolved by using the 'stress' measure. It is calculated (Shepard, 1980) as

$$\text{Stress} = \sqrt{\frac{\sum(d1_{ij} - d2_{ij})^2}{\sum d1_{ij}^2}} \tag{1}$$

where $d1_{ij}$ is the actual distance and $d2_{ij}$ is the predicted distance.

Text represented as a distance matrix is plotted with 2D and 3D scaling (Figures 3a and 3b). This shows that as the dimension increases, similar terms are grouped together according to the decrease in stress values and the increase in goodness of fit. With 3D scaling, similar words are closer together as well as at the same height. MDS differs from the vector space in the sense that it is based on similarity, dissimilarity and proximity measures such as Euclidean and string-edit distance by relating objects perceptually. Scaling can be performed on multiple distance matrices for data with diverse domains and for heterogeneous representations (Bai *et al.* 2017). Despite these merits, geometric models are not capable of distinguishing semantically related terms as synonyms or hyponyms and are not scalable with large datasets.

(a) 2D Scaling (Stress - 27.30969) (b) 3D Scaling (Stress - 5.074948)

Figure 3. Multidimensional scaling

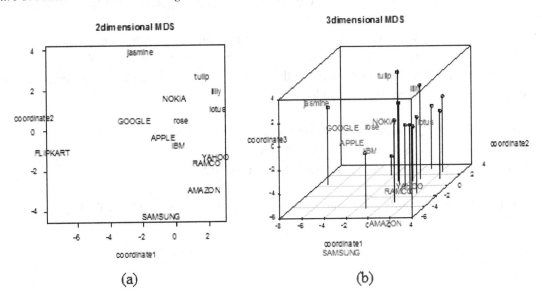

(a) (b)

Feature Model

Feature models are specified using set theory, where the property values of a concept are represented as elements in the feature set. Feature-based similarity models are used in recommender systems (Elbadrawy & Karypis, 2014) to find items of interest for different users. Ma *et al.* (2015) suggested a similarity metric based on multifeature fusion and utilized alignment-based word sense disambiguation. They extracted multiple features from the input, represented them using usual Tf-idf vectors and employed unsupervised learning of Wikipedia tags to compute the similarity.

The similarity of the concepts x and y is defined as a feature-matching function 'f' of their joint $(x \cap y)$ and unique $(x - y, y - x)$ features (Tversky & Gati, 1978):

$S(x, y) = f(x \cap y, x - y, y - x)$ (2)

Pirro and Euzenat (2010) proposed feature-based models called the 'contrast model', with normalized similarity values, and the 'ratio model', without normalization. They applied the extended information content (eIC) to obtain the information shared by two concepts in the ontological structure. The similarity computation with the contrast model (3) and ratio model (4) is performed by taking into account both common and distinct features at the scale 'f' in the feature space (Pirro & Euzenat, 2010; Tversky & Gati, 1978).

$$S(x,y) = \theta f(x \cap y) - \alpha f(x - y) - \beta f(y - x) \ \theta, \alpha, \beta \geq 0 \tag{3}$$

$$S(x,y) = \frac{f(x \cap y)}{f(x \cap y) + \alpha f(x - y) + \beta f(y - x)} \ \alpha, \beta \geq 0 \tag{4}$$

In feature-based models, two concepts are defined using set theory as domain 'S_1' and domain 'S_2', given by

S_1: $\{a_1, a_2, a_3, ...\}$ where a_i is the image of 'a_i' in S_1 or the value of S_1 at 'a_i', $a_i \epsilon S_1$.

S_2: $\{b_1, b_2, b_3, ...\}$ where b_i is the image of 'b_i' in S_2 or the value of S_2 at 'b_i', $b_i \epsilon S_2$.

The similarity between concepts is higher if there are more common features between them. There are three possibilities when relating S_1 and S_2.

- Case i) If $S_1 \subseteq S_2$, S_1 is semantically related to S_2
- Case ii) If $S_2 \subseteq S_1$, S_2 is semantically related to S_1
- Case iii) If $S_1 \subseteq S_2$ and $S_2 \subseteq S_1$, $S_1 = S_2$ and S_1 is similar to S_2

A collection of features of birds and flight is represented as two sets S_1 and S_2 in Table 2.

Table 2. Set of features

Set	Size	Features
S$_1$ (Birds)	10	fly, walk, move, run, eggs, tail, feathers, wings, legs, beak
S$_2$ (Flight)	10	fly, move, wings, wheels, engine, cockpit, tail, nose, land, cabin
S$_1$ ∩ S$_2$	4	fly, move, wings, tail
S$_1$ - S$_2$	6	walk, run, eggs, legs, feathers, beak
S$_2$ - S$_1$	6	wheels, engine, cockpit, nose, land, cabin

There are 40% common features between S$_1$ and S$_2$. Hence, they are not closely related to each other. The elements of a set are related by exact lexical match, and linguistic issues such as polysemy and homonymy should be handled with additional complexity. However, distinguishing between similar and related features is an issue.

Graph Model

In the graph model, concepts are represented as nodes that are connected through semantic relations as edges. Any multiword expression can be schematically drawn as a network or tree structure by adding entities as leaf nodes. The hierarchical relationship of the tree gives the measure of similarity. Rajagopal *et al.* (2013) studied concept extraction by exploiting a 'parse graph' to map all multiword expressions in a knowledge base and found syntactically and semantically related concepts (Figure 4).

Figure 4. Parse graph

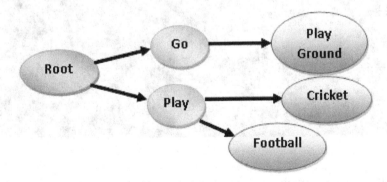

Hajian and White (2011) constructed semantic multi-trees with concepts as nodes and semantic relations obtained from Wikipedia as edges. The similarity weight was calculated using a recursive function and propagated from the leaf nodes to the root. Multiple trees of two concepts were combined to obtain a new tree, and the weights were updated. The weight of the root of the combined tree was used as the similarity score between concepts. A new measure, a 'random walk' for triples, such as <summer-hot-square> represented as a semantic network graph (De Deyne *et al.*, 2012), shows that 'summer' is more semantically related to 'hot' than to 'square'. Minkov and Cohen (2012) proposed a 'path constrained graph walk' algorithm to find meaningful paths of interrelated nodes for assessing the similarity of different word types.

The transition probabilities of nodes in the WordNet graph (Singh *et al.*, 2013) are used to find the similarity of concepts. Schuhmacher and Ponzetto (2014) devised a semantic model based on graphs to represent concepts from documents extracted using the DBpedia spotlight and obtained the document similarity using graph edit distance. The complete network representation (Figure 5) shows that the flower names closer together at the top left are more similar.

Figure 5. Network model

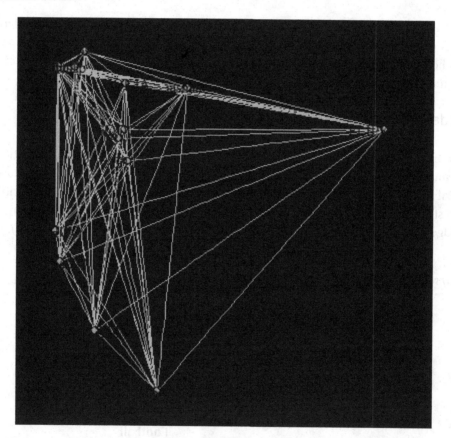

Compared to other models, graph-based models better identify weakly related concepts from nodes at different levels and similar concepts from nodes at the same level.

Vector Space Model

The vector space model is an algebraic model used for representing text documents as vectors and for finding similarity using distance measures (Aurora *et al.*, 2020). These may be term-document, word-context, pair-pattern or triple-pattern vectors (Turney & Pantel, 2010). The vector space is of more than

20,000 dimensions, and some similar documents may not be close. Hence, dimensionality reduction is required for analyzing similarity and relatedness with lower complexity. It is performed using singular value decomposition (SVD) or principal component analysis (PCA) (Turney & Pantel, 2010), which maps the term-document space into a lower-dimensional subspace to bring terms closer together without loss of meaning. SVD is useful for mapping text along singular values. PCA can be computed using SVD by aligning text along one of the best principal components.

Kernel PCA of 'crude' data with the 'Laplacian' kernel function (Figure 6b) finds the principal components in a different space to obtain a better representative direction than PCA (Figure 6a), especially in nonlinear form.

Figure 6. Dimensionality reduction

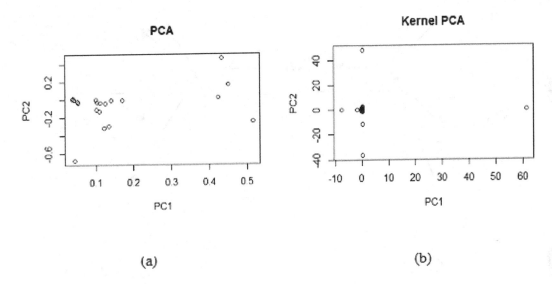

(a)   (b)

'Word embedding' is a combination of language modeling and feature learning techniques used for mapping words or phrases from a vocabulary to a continuous-valued vector of fixed dimension and for capturing syntactic and semantic regularities in language (Mikolov *et al.*, 2013a). 'Word2Vec' is useful for analogies and similarity metrics (Church, 2017) because it learns word embeddings. The continuous bag-of-words (CBOW) model predicts the target word for the given context words, whereas the skipgram model predicts the context words for the given word (Figure 7). The objective of CBOW is to maximize the average log probability of a word given context words from vocabulary V (Mikolov *et al.*, 2013b).

$$\frac{1}{V}\sum_{i=1}^{V}\sum_{-c \le j \le < c} logp(w_i \mid w_{i+j}) \tag{5}$$

Similarly, the skipgram model is written as

$$\frac{1}{V}\sum_{i=1}^{V}\sum_{-c\leq j\leq<c} logp(w_{i+j} \mid w_i)$$
(6)

Figure 7. Word2vec model

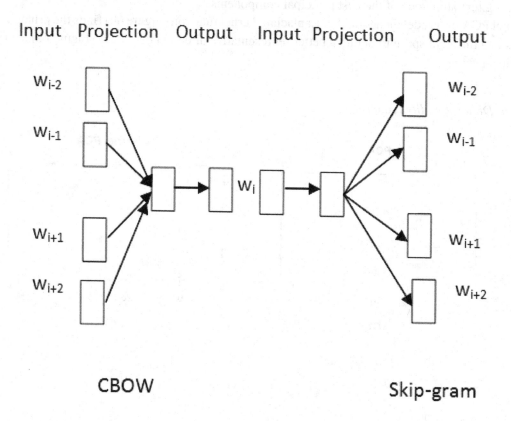

The same word has different vector representations as a word and as context. Gao and Ichise (2017) achieved better cosine similarity between synonyms by fine-tuning the word2vec model using autoencoders. The word2vec model (vocabulary = 816, alpha = 0.025, window = 5) is trained with bibliographic data (Table 3). With CBOW and skipgram models, the cosine similarity of a given word pair either increases or decreases when the word embedding dimension is increased from 20 to 200.

Table 3. Word embedding dimension vs. similarity

Words	Dimension	CBOW	Skipgram
Agenda, Review	20	-0.36817613	0.4614236
	50	-0.15751304	0.4422469
	100	-0.07914327	0.5537749
	200	-0.026748635	0.5665424
Society, Organizations	20	0.35702175	0.90514165
	50	0.17869955	0.876866
	100	0.08378598	0.8617826
	200	0.057166096	0.84720045
Agency, Business	20	-0.19869982	0.71319884
	50	-0.17327487	0.7506675
	100	-0.14941813	0.8095486
	200	-0.08918856	0.8152274
Stress, Crisis	20	0.3074752	0.74359536
	50	0.2794845	0.6627233
	100	0.06531049	0.6460146
	200	0.03122731	0.6082015

The similarity values increase with the dimension for (agenda, review) and (agency, business), and decrease for the pairs (society, organizations) and (stress, crisis). However, the variation in similarity is not significant in skipgram model compared to the variation in CBOW model. Hence, skipgram model is more suitable for analysing text similarity than CBOW model.

Sent2vec is modeled for composing the sentence embeddings (Pagliardini *et al.*, 2017) using word vectors and n-gram embeddings. The extension of 'word2vec' is 'topic2vec' (Niu *et al.*, 2015), where topics and words are represented in the same topical embedding space and words belonging to more similar topics are brought closer together. Elekes *et al.* (2017) studied how the distribution of similarity values changes with different word embedding algorithms and parameters. Finding vectors of words that are not present in the vocabulary and evaluating word embeddings are the issues to be resolved.

Formal Concept Analysis Model (FCA)

A concept is constituted by its 'extension' and 'intension'. The extension comprises all objects belonging to the concept, and the intension includes all attributes that apply to all objects of the extension (Wille, 2005). The concept is represented as a basic data type such as a table called 'formal context'. FCA uses the 'formal context' as input and produces a 'concept lattice' and attributes implications as output. The concept lattice[2] gives the hierarchy of concepts, and the attribute implication gives the valid data dependency. It is a collective representation of all formal concepts for a given 'formal context'. Information content-based similarity measures are suitable for this model.

FCA is applicable to the hierarchical organization of web search results, data analysis and data mining (Belohlavek, 2008; Belohlavek & Mikula, 2020). Cimiano *et al.* (2005) suggested an approach for the automatic acquisition of concept hierarchies from text corpora using FCA and derived implicit relationships between objects. Tang and Cai (2010) studied the role of FCA in ontology construction. Codocedo *et al.* (2014) used the 'concept lattice' as the 'semantic index' to organize documents for information retrieval. In the FCA model, the implied relation between concepts 'a' and 'b' is that every concept having all attributes of concept 'a' also has all attributes of concept 'b' if 'a' and 'b' are similar. Table 4 describes the formal context of objects {Dog, Cat, Hen, Car, Auto} with attributes {has legs, lives on land, has wheels, can move, needs fuel}.

Table 4. Formal context

Objects	Attributes				
	Has legs	Lives on land	Has wheels	Can move	Needs fuel
Dog	x	x		x	
Cat	x	x		x	
Hen	x	x		x	
Car			x	x	x

The corresponding concept lattice (Figure 8) shows the subconcept-superconcept relation between concepts.

Figure 8. Concept lattice

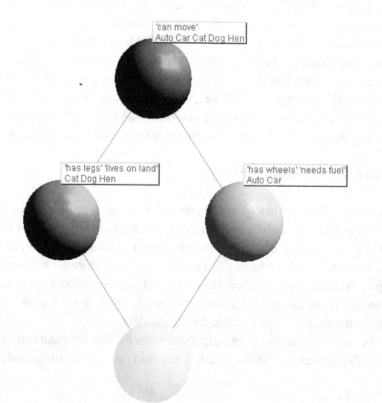

The association rules for the above context with minimum support 50% and minimum confidence 50% are written as

- {can move} => {has legs, lives on land}
- {has legs} => {can move, lives on land}
- {lives on land} => {can move, has legs}
- {has wheels} => {needs fuel}
- {needs fuel} => {has wheels}

The intensity of a lattice node depends on the object count at each node. The concept lattice (Figure 7) clearly shows that similar objects are grouped as (dog, cat, hen) and (car, auto) based on their context. FCA provides better concept hierarchies with hypernym and hyponym relations for semantic relatedness and functional similarity in ontology. The problem is that there will be an increase in complexity with the size of the lattice.

Hybrid Model

A combination of any set of models such as graph, feature and geometric models, leads to a hybrid model. Only limited work has been carried out on the hybrid model. A blend of network and feature or geometric models used by Schwering (2005) provides a structured knowledge representation. Aletras and Stevenson (2015) pooled knowledge-based and distributional semantic models. The synset vectors of words were created using WordNet and then enhanced by applying the graph-based technique to obtain good word sense disambiguation. The hybrid model is required for cross-language and cross-modal similarities.

Semantic Similarity Measures

The size of a linguistic item and the type of model determine the choice of the similarity measures used. It may be based on path or 'information content' or features. The shortest path, depth, edge count and lowest common subsumer (LCS) are suitable features for graph representation (Castillo, 2011). Knowledge-based measures such as those of Wu-Palmer, Lesk, Resnik, Leacock & Chodorow (Jiang & Conrath, 1997) and Lin (Meng *et al.*, 2013) use the 'information content' and LCS of concepts in knowledge sources such as WordNet, whereas web-based measures utilize page counts and snippets. Saruladha *et al.* (2010) analyzed the 'information content' using edge-and node-counting approaches for ontology-based information retrieval. Pirro and Euzenat (2010) used the number of links between concepts in ontology as a feature. Liu *et al.* (2015) categorized semantic similarity features as WordNet-based (path, LCS), corpus-based (tf/idf, LSA), word2vec-based (Word2vec, Sentence2vec, Text2vec), alignment-based (word alignment) and literal-based (sentiment, length, digit overlap). LDA groups words based on topical features and improves the similarity of short texts (Chen *et al.*, 2017).

Islam and Inkpen (2008) combined string measures (normalized LCS, maximal consecutive LCS) and corpus-based measures (second order co-occurrence PMI) to improve the similarity score. Gupta and Yadav (2014) analyzed similarity measures based on distance, 'information content', features and hybrid characteristics. Hu and Cho (2015) proposed a graph- and vector-based hybrid measure using gene ontology by representing the magnitude of the common induced subgraph of two graphs as a vector.

Based on the discussion in the previous sections, now the tweet summarization task can be performed by considering the linguistic unit levels, such as tweet, words and hashtags. In addition, there is a need for a composite measure to summarize the tweets.

SOLUTIONS AND RECOMMENDATIONS

Application - Tweet Summarization

The information generated by users on social media networks such as Twitter has tremendously increased recently (Cossu *et al.*, 2020). Tweets contain cross lingual and cross modal components. Due to lack of gold dataset for tweet summarization, existing dataset like UK geolocated Twitter data[3] has been used and tweet summarization is evaluated using the manually created reference summaries. For convenience, the dataset is split (Table 5) into two time slices from (14-04-16 to 17-04-16) and (18-04-17 to 21-04-16) for summarization task. Pre-processing is done for removing urls, mentions and redundant tweets.

Table 5. Twitter dataset

Dataset	No. of Tweets	No. of Preprocessed Tweets
Ukgeo1 (14-04-16 to 17-04-16)	97,138	34,769
Ukgeo2 (15-04-16 to 21-04-16)	71,895	27,339

Topics from the dataset are identified as rain, wind, London, humidity and barometer. Reference summaries (Table 6) of maximum 150 characters have been created manually by two persons based on the five topics.

Table 6. Reference summaries (Ukgeo1)

Topic	Reference Summary1	Reference Summary2
Rain	Pressure is rising slowly and rain today	Falling temperature and rain today
Wind	More wind and temperature is falling	Wind is 1.6 mph and pressure value increases
London	London bridge and #JerseyBoys Theatre	London Theatre and Jersey Boys
Humidity	Humidity ukweather weather	Humidity #ukweather #weather
Barometer	Barometer value shows Pressure is rising slowly	Wind is 1.6 mph and Barometer value is rising

Automated summaries (Table 7) are created from the data in two ways. In the first method only words have been taken into account, whereas in the second method both words and hashtags) from the Twitter dataset using a composite summary score based on similarity from Word2vec model. The Skipgram-based Word2vec model is trained with the Twitter dataset to obtain 200 dimension vectors and cosine is used for similarity computation.

Table 7. Automated summaries (Ukgeo1)

Topic	Words	Words and hashtags
Rain	Pressure and temperature rising slowly rain today	#ukweather temperature rising #rain showers today
Wind	Light rain and little wind	White cloud and little wind #weather
London	Want to work in London England	#hiring in #London #Jobs #CareerArc
Humidity	Humidity Weather is pretty vile	Humidity fairly fine improving #UKWeather #iwn
Barometer	Barometer rising Forecast fine weather	Barometer rising slowly #ukweather #connemara

A standard metric for evaluating text summarization is ROUGE-N (Cossu *et al.*, 2020; Lin, 2004; Lin & Hovy, 2003).

$$\text{ROUGE-N} = \frac{\sum_{s \in RS} \sum_{ngrams \in s} match\left(ngrams\right)}{\sum_{s \in RS} \sum_{ngrams \in s} count\left(ngrams\right)} . \tag{7}$$

where s is the summary, RS - reference summaries, n - ngram length, count(ngram) represents the number of ngrams in the reference summary, and match(ngram) denotes the number of cooccurring ngrams between the reference (RS) and automated summaries (AS).

Equation 7 is modified to compute precision, recall and Fmeasure of ROUGE-1 for composite summary score (Equations 8, 9).

$$\text{Precision} = p = \text{ROUGE-1} = \frac{\sum_{s \in RS} \sum_{ugram_{wh} \in s} match\left(ugram_{wh}\right)}{\# RS \sum_{ugram_{wh} \in AS} count\left(ugram_{wh}\right)} . \tag{8}$$

$$\text{Recall} = r = \text{ROUGE-1} = \frac{\sum_{s \in RS} \sum_{ugram_{wh} \in s} match\left(ugram_{wh}\right)}{\sum_{s \in RS} \sum_{ugram_{wh} \in s} count\left(ugram_{wh}\right)} . \tag{9}$$

where, match ($ugram_{wh}$. denotes the number of cooccurring unigrams of words and hashtags in reference summaries and count ($ugram_{wh}$. represents the number of unigrams of words and hashtags in reference summaries.

$$\text{Fmeasure} = \frac{2pr}{\left(p + r\right)} \tag{10}$$

ROUGE-1 measures for the reference summaries (Table 8) are computed by comparing the summary refsum1 with refsum2 and vice versa. For evaluation, automated summaries have been compared against the reference summaries. The procedure is repeated for the second set of tweets Ukgeo2.

Table 8. ROUGE1 for reference and automated summaries

UK-Geolocated Data	Method	Level	ROUGE-1		
			Precision	Recall	F measure
Ukgeo1	RefSum1 RefSum2 Average	Tweet Tweet	0.25 0.232 0.241	0.258 0.224 0.241	0.2539 0.2279 0.2409
	Automated Summary Composite Summary	Words Words & Hashtags	0.232 **0.267**	0.224 **0.258**	0.227 **0.262**
Ukgeo2	RefSum1 RefSum2 Average	Tweet Tweet	0.32 0.31 0.315	0.331 0.304 0.3175	0.3254 0.3069 0.316
	Automated Summary Composite Summary	Words Words & Hashtags	0.32 **0.347**	0.332 **0.338**	0.3258 **0.3424**

Boldface indicates that higher ROUGE1 values are obtained for the composite summary

Table 8 shows that for automated summaries with only words, precision and recall measures of the ROUGE-1 metric are nearly same as that of the reference summary values. The score values have been improved by combining both words and hashtags. It proves the effectiveness of the composite summary score as well as a composite similarity measure for tweet summarization. Opinion mining can be combined with summarization for extracting sentiments from the user-generated contents (Ramón-Hernandez *et al.*, 2020). Summarized tweets can be utilized for detecting user's attitudes and emotions in an effective manner.

DISCUSSION

A similarity computation procedure can be derived by combining content and model features based on the nature of the text. Based on the review performed in the previous sections, the following concepts and issues have been identified.

- Structured texts such as database tables have semantic relationships with linguistic units. Hence, linguistic unit-based similarity model represented with VSM or graph-based models and IC or path-based measures is applicable.
- For semi-structured text, linguistic unit-level similarity combined with a feature, FCA or hybrid model is a good choice.

- Cross-level similarity with hybrid models and hybrid measures is the best choice for unstructured text.
- Issues with word-level similarity associated with polysemous words can be resolved with multiple synsets from WordNet.
- Many new words come into usage every day, and some words (such as 'floppy disk') have disappeared. The meanings of existing words are subjected to changes such as broadening ('cell' coming to mean a mobile phone in addition to a biological unit), narrowing (the meaning of 'meat' changing from any food to flesh) or shifting (the meaning of 'tablet' changing from drugs to computers). Meaning is purely context-dependent, and estimating the similarity of such words is challenging.
- Finding the similarity of two sentences with different grammatical structures and different words with similar meanings is difficult.
- Dealing with social media text comprising hashtags, mentions and internet slang words (such as lol) is a difficult task. Lexical normalization can be performed to resolve such issues.
- Conceptual and ontological similarities are connected with hierarchical relationships and should be implemented with the FCA model.
- A hybrid model requires a hybrid form of path-, IC- and feature-based measures.
- The multidimensional views of linguistic unit-level similarity, cross-level similarity and semantic similarity models are interrelated.

Comparison of Semantic Similarity Models

To select a semantic model for exploring the changes in the usage of a word or group of words, the existing models are to be evaluated for text similarity computation. Hence, the similarity evaluation is performed by comparing the word, sentence and document similarities with the standard datasets (MSRvid[4], SMTeur[4], STS2017en-en[4], and Tweets[5]) and using different measures (Table 9). MSRvid data comprise 1500 sentence pairs of video description snippets. SMTeur consists of 1293 pairs of sentences. STS2017en-en-track5 includes 250 pairs of sentences. Twitter trial data have 50 pairs of tweets that were tokenized, split into sentences and labeled for the same meaning (true, score-1) or not (false, score-0).

Table 9. Similarity evaluation

Level	Semantic Similarity Model	Feature/ Measure	Dataset			
			MSRvid	SMTeur	STS2017 en-en	Tweets
Word	Feature	Ngram Overlap	0.731780	0.797681	0.355685	0.2477368
	Feature	Longest Common Substring	0.77336	0.687742	0.570219	0.2796013
	Feature	Optimal String Alignment	0.526192	0.428175	0.514263	0.2599485
	Feature	Pairwise-compare /Jaccard	0.651328	0.332364	0.562296	-0.07406496
	Word2vec	Cosine	0.792	**0.79984**	0.6844	**0.4226**
Sentence	Vector Space	Sentence Vector /Cosine	0.74	0.73	0.54	0.069409
	Feature	Optimal Matching	0.77	0.33	0.341	0.347
	Sent2vec	Cosine	**0.812**	0.787	**0.735**	0.421
Document	Vector Space	Cosine	0.808	0.5273	0.7191	0.387
	Vector Space	Latent Semantic Analysis	0.7574	0.105	0.7033	0.393
	Geometric	Multi Dimensional Scaling	0.5432	0.4999	0.3735	0.269
	Doc2vec	Cosine	0.802	0.781	0.723	0.418

Boldface indicates that higher correlation values are obtained for the embedding models

Higher Pearson correlation of similarity values is obtained for the Word2vec and Sent2vec models. Hence, word embedding models are more suitable for measuring the similarity and changes in the similarity.

FUTURE RESEARCH DIRECTIONS

In future the characteristics of multilingual text similarity can be explored. Cross-modal similarity has a wide scope of research under the category of cross-level similarities. Hybrid models and composite similarity measures adapted to a broad range of contexts can be studied. The relationship between the evolving use of text and the similarity of text can be examined.

CONCLUSION

This chapter gives an overview of various aspects of similarity assessment. The word, sentence, short text and document similarities discussed in this chapter, provide an outline of the similarity of linguistic units. Semantic similarity models described in this chapter provide a clear understanding of different methods of projecting the text onto a semantic space. Hybrid models that are specifically defined for an application domain can provide an effective method of computing similarity. The analysis performed provides complete background knowledge on the structure of models and features of similarity. Path-, 'information content'- and feature-based measures show the availability of diverse measures. However, the impact of the evolving use of words and the historical nature of text on similarity has not been analyzed. To conclude, (i) comprehensive knowledge about the computational aspects of semantic similarity assessment based on content has been discussed, which will be useful for new researchers; (ii) semantic models have been studied extensively in detail; (iii) among the various models discussed, the WE model has achieved higher correlation for similarity values; (iv) WE models can be chosen for investigating semantic similarity based on the cooccurrence context; (v) tweet summarization can be performed in an effective manner with higher ROUGE1 values, using a composite summary measure and (vi) opinion mining can be combined with tweet summarization.

REFERENCES

Abdelrahman, A. M., & Kayed, A. (2015). A survey on semantic similarity measures between concepts in health domain. *American Journal of Computational Mathematics*, 5(02), 204–214. doi:10.4236/ajcm.2015.52017

Ahsaee, M. G., Naghibzadeh, M., & Naeini, S. E. Y. (2014). Semantic similarity assessment of words using weighted WordNet. *International Journal of Machine Learning and Cybernetics*, 5(3), 479–490. doi:10.100713042-012-0135-3

Aletras, N., & Stevenson, M. (2015). A Hybrid Distributional and Knowledge-based Model of Lexical Semantics. SEM@ NAACL-HLT, 20-29. doi:10.18653/v1/S15-1003

Amasyah, M. F. (2006). *An Approach for Word Categorization Based on Semantic Similarity Measure Obtained from Search Engines. 2006 IEEE 14th Signal Processing and Communications Applications.*

Artetxe, M., Labaka, G., & Agirre, E. (2017). Learning bilingual word embeddings with (almost) no bilingual data. *Proceedings of the 55th Annual Meeting of the Association for Computational Linguistics*, 1, 451-462. 10.18653/v1/P17-1042

Bai, S., Bai, X., Latecki, L. J., & Tian, Q. (2017). Multidimensional Scaling on Multiple Input Distance Matrices. AAAI, 1281-1287.

Bar, D., Zesch, T., & Gurevych, I. (2012). Text reuse detection using a composition of text similarity measures. *Proceedings of COLING, 2012*, 167–184.

Bar, D., Zesch, T., & Gurevych, I. (2015). *Composing Measures for Computing Text Similarity*. Academic Press.

Batet, M., Sanchez, D., Valls, A., & Gibert, K. (2013). Semantic similarity estimation from multiple ontologies. *Applied Intelligence*, 38(1), 29–44. doi:10.100710489-012-0355-y

Belohlavek, R. (2008). *Introduction to formal concept analysis*. Palacky University, Department of Computer Science.

Belohlavek, R., & Mikula, T. (2020). Typicality in Conceptual Structures Within the Framework of Formal Concept Analysis. CLA, 33-45.

Bollegala, D., Matsuo, Y., & Ishizuka, M. (2011). A web search engine-based approach to measure semantic similarity between words. *IEEE Transactions on Knowledge and Data Engineering*, 23(7), 977–990. doi:10.1109/TKDE.2010.172

Bruni, E., Tran, N. K., & Baroni, M. (2014). Multimodal distributional semantics. *Journal of Artificial Intelligence Research, 49*, 1–47. doi:10.1613/jair.4135

Castillo, J. J. (2011). A WordNet-based semantic approach to textual entailment and cross-lingual textual entailment. *International Journal of Machine Learning and Cybernetics, 2*(3), 177–189. doi:10.100713042-011-0026-z

Chandrasekaran, D., & Mago, V. (2021). Evolution of Semantic Similarity—A Survey. [CSUR]. *ACM Computing Surveys, 54*(2), 1–37. doi:10.1145/3440755

Chen, H. C., Guo, X. H., Liu, L. Q., & Zhu, X. H. (2017). A Short Text Similarity Measure Based on Hidden Topics. *Computer Science and Technology: Proceedings of the International Conference (CST2016)*, 1101-1108. 10.1142/9789813146426_0124

Church, K. W. (2017). Word2Vec. *Natural Language Engineering, 23*(1), 155–162. doi:10.1017/S1351324916000334

Cimiano, P., Hotho, A., & Staab, S. (2005). Learning concept hierarchies from text corpora using formal concept analysis. *Journal of Artificial Intelligence Research, 24*, 305–339. doi:10.1613/jair.1648

Codocedo, V., Lykourentzou, I., & Napoli, A. (2014). A semantic approach to concept lattice-based information retrieval. *Annals of Mathematics and Artificial Intelligence, 72*(1-2), 169–195. doi:10.100710472-014-9403-0

Cossu, J. V., Torres-Moreno, J. M., SanJuan, E., & El-Bèze, M. (2020). *Intweetive Text Summarization.* arXiv preprint arXiv:2001,11382.

De Deyne, S., Navarro, D. J., Perfors, A., & Storms, G. (2012). *Strong structure in weak semantic similarity: A graph based account.* Cognitive Science Society.

Deguchi, T., & Ishii, N. (2021). Document Similarity by Word Clustering with Semantic Distance. *International Conference on Hybrid Artificial Intelligence Systems*, 3-14. 10.1007/978-3-030-86271-8_1

Demaine, E., Hesterberg, A., Koehler, F., Lynch, J., & Urschel, J. (2021). Multidimensional scaling: Approximation and complexity. *International Conference on Machine Learning*, 2568-2578.

Devereux, B. J., Clarke, A., Marouchos, A., & Tyler, L. K. (2013). Representational similarity analysis reveals commonalities and differences in the semantic processing of words and objects. *The Journal of Neuroscience: The Official Journal of the Society for Neuroscience, 33*(48), 18906–18916. doi:10.1523/JNEUROSCI.3809-13.2013 PMID:24285896

Diao, H., Zhang, Y., Ma, L. & Lu, H., (2021). *Similarity Reasoning and Filtration for Image-Text Matching.* Technical Report.

Elavarasi, S. A., Akilandeswari, J., & Menaga, K. (2014). A survey on semantic similarity measure. *International Journal of Research in Advent Technology, 2*, 389–398.

Elbadrawy, A., & Karypis, G. (2014). *Feature-based similarity models for top-n recommendation of new items. Department of Computer Science, University of Minnesota.* Tech. Rep.

Elekes, A., Schaler, M., & Bohm, K. (2017). On the Various Semantics of Similarity in Word Embedding Models. *Digital Libraries (JCDL), 2017 ACM/IEEE Joint Conference on,* 1-10. 10.1109/JCDL.2017.7991568

Elsayed, T., Lin, J., & Oard, D. W. (2008). Pairwise document similarity in large collections with MapReduce. In *Proceedings of the 46th Annual Meeting of the Association for Computational Linguistics on Human Language Technologies: Short Papers.* Association for Computational Linguistics. 10.3115/1557690.1557767

Gao, X., & Ichise, R. (2017). Adjusting Word Embeddings by Deep Neural Networks. ICAART, (2), 398-406. doi:10.5220/0006120003980406

Ghosh, S., & Mitra, P. (2008). Combining content and structure similarity for XML document classification using composite SVM kernels. *Pattern Recognition, 2008. ICPR 2008. 19th International Conference on,* 1-4. 10.1109/ICPR.2008.4761539

Goldstone, R. L., Medin, D. L., & Gentner, D. (1991). Relational similarity and the nonindependence of features in similarity judgments. *Cognitive Psychology, 23*(2), 222–262. doi:10.1016/0010-0285(91)90010-L PMID:2055001

Gomaa, W. H., & Fahmy, A. A. (2013). A survey of text similarity approaches. *International Journal of Computers and Applications, 68,* 13–18. doi:10.5120/11638-7118

Guo, W., & Diab, M. (2012). A simple unsupervised latent semantics based approach for sentence similarity. In *Proceedings of the Sixth International Workshop on Semantic Evaluation.* Association for Computational Linguistics.

Gupta, A., Kumar, M. A., & Gautam, J. (2017). A Survey on Semantic Similarity Measures. *IJIRST-International Journal for Innovative Research in Science & Technology, 3,* 12.

Gupta, A., & Yadav, K. (2014). Semantic similarity measure using information content approach with depth for similarity calculation. *International Journal of Scientific & Technology Research, 3,* 165–169.

Hajian, B., & White, T. (2011). Measuring semantic similarity using a multi-tree model. CEUR Workshop Proceedings, 756.

Hao, D., Zuo, W., Peng, T., & He, F. (2011). An approach for calculating semantic similarity between words using WordNet. *Digital Manufacturing and Automation (ICDMA), 2011 Second International Conference on,* 177-180. 10.1109/ICDMA.2011.50

Hatzivassiloglou, V., Klavans, J. L., & Eskin, E. (1999). Detecting text similarity over short passages: Exploring linguistic feature combinations via machine learning. *Proceedings of the 1999 joint sigdat conference on empirical methods in natural language processing and very large corpora,* 203-212.

Hout, M. C., Godwin, H. J., Fitzsimmons, G., Robbins, A., Menneer, T., & Goldinger, S. D. (2016). Using multidimensional scaling to quantify similarity in visual search and beyond. *Attention, Perception & Psychophysics, 78*(1), 3–20. doi:10.375813414-015-1010-6 PMID:26494381

Hu, Q., & Cho, Y. R. (2015). An integrative measure of graph-and vector-based semantic similarity using information content distance. *Bioinformatics and Biomedicine (BIBM), 2015 IEEE International Conference on,* 517-522.

Huang, H. H., Yang, H. C., & Kuo, Y. H. 2008, November. A Sense Based Similarity Measure for Cross-Lingual Documents. *Intelligent Systems Design and Applications, 2008.ISDA'08.Eighth International Conference on, 1,* 9-13. 10.1109/ISDA.2008.284

Huang, H. H., & Kuo, Y. H. (2010). Cross-lingual document representation and semantic similarity measure: A fuzzy set and rough set based approach. *IEEE Transactions on Fuzzy Systems, 18*(6), 1098–1111. doi:10.1109/TFUZZ.2010.2065811

Iosif, E., & Potamianos, A. (2010). Unsupervised semantic similarity computation between terms using web documents. *IEEE Transactions on Knowledge and Data Engineering, 22*(11), 1637–1647. doi:10.1109/TKDE.2009.193

Islam, A., & Inkpen, D. (2008). Semantic text similarity using corpus-based word similarity and string similarity. *ACM Transactions on Knowledge Discovery from Data, 2*(2), 10. doi:10.1145/1376815.1376819

Jiang, J. J., & Conrath, D. W. (1997). *Semantic similarity based on corpus statistics and lexical taxonomy.* arXiv preprint cmp-lg/9709008.

Khakimova, A.K., Charnine, M.M., Klokov, A.A. & Sokolov, E.G. (2020). *Approaches to assessing the semantic similarity of texts in a multilingual space.* Academic Press.

Kurach, K., Gelly, S., & Jastrzebski, M. (2017). *Better Text Understanding Through Image-To-Text Transfer.* arXiv preprint arXiv:1705.08386.

Lavanya, S., & Arya, S. S. (2012). An approach for measuring semantic similarity between words using SVM and LS-SVM. *Computer Communication and Informatics (ICCCI), 2012 International Conference on,* 1-4. 10.1109/ICCCI.2012.6158835

Li, W., Zheng, S., Liu, D., & Jiao, S. (2010). A novel computational approach to concept semantic similarity. *Computer, Mechatronics, Control and Electronic Engineering (CMCE), 2010 International Conference on, 1,* 89-92. 10.1109/CMCE.2010.5610535

Li, R., Feng, F., Wang, X., Lu, P., & Li, B. (2015). Obtaining cross modal similarity metric with deep neural architecture. *Mathematical Problems in Engineering, 2015,* 2015. doi:10.1155/2015/293176

Liu, Y., & Liang, Y. (2013). A Sentence Semantic Similarity Calculating Method based on Segmented Semantic Comparison. *Journal of Theoretical and Applied Information Technology, 48,* 231–235.

Liu, Y., Sun, C., Lin, L., Wang, X., & Zhao, Y. (2015). Computing Semantic Text Similarity Using Rich Features. PACLIC.

Lopez-Gazpio, I., Maritxalar, M., Lapata, M., & Agirre, E. (2019). Word n-gram attention models for sentence similarity and inference. *Expert Systems with Applications, 132,* 1–11. doi:10.1016/j.eswa.2019.04.054

Ma, B., Yang, Y., Zhao, F., Dong, R., & Zhou, X. (2015). Semantic Similarity Computation Based on Multi-Features Fusion. *International Journal of Hybrid Information Technology*, *8*(5), 31–40. doi:10.14257/ijhit.2015.8.5.04

Madylova, A., & Oguducu, S. G. (2009), September. A taxonomy based semantic similarity of documents using the cosine measure. *Computer and Information Sciences, 2009.ISCIS 2009. 24th International Symposium on*, 129-134.

Meng, L., Huang, R., & Gu, J. (2013). *An Effective Algorithm for Semantic Similarity Metric of Word Pairs*. Academic Press.

Mihalcea, R., Corley, C., & Strapparava, C. (2006). Corpus-based and knowledge-based measures of text semantic similarity. AAAI, 6, 775-780.

Mikolov, T., Yih, W. T., & Zweig, G. (2013a). Linguistic regularities in continuous space word representations. *Proceedings of the 2013 Conference of the North American Chapter of the Association for Computational Linguistics: Human Language Technologies*, 746-751.

Mikolov, T., Sutskever, I., Chen, K., Corrado, G. S., & Dean, J. 2013b. Distributed representations of words and phrases and their compositionality. Advances in Neural Information Processing Systems, 3111-3119.

Miller, G. A. (1995). WordNet: A lexical database for English. *Communications of the ACM*, *38*(11), 39–41. doi:10.1145/219717.219748

Minkov, E., & Cohen, W. W. (2012). Graph based similarity measures for synonym extraction from parsed text. *Workshop Proceedings of TextGraphs-7 on Graph-based Methods for Natural Language Processing, Association for Computational Linguistics*, 20-24.

Mohammad, S., & Hirst, G. (2005). *Distributional measures as proxies for semantic relatedness*. Academic Press.

Muhic, A., Rupnik, J., & Skraba, P. (2012). Cross-lingual document similarity. *Information Technology Interfaces (ITI), Proceedings of the ITI 2012 34th International Conference on*, 387-392.

Niu, L., Dai, X., Zhang, J., & Chen, J. (2015). Topic2Vec: learning distributed representations of topics. *Asian Language Processing (IALP), 2015 International Conference on*, 193-196.

Pagliardini, M., Gupta, P., & Jaggi, M. (2017). *Unsupervised learning of sentence embeddings using compositional n-gram features*. arXiv preprint arXiv:1703.02507.

Pirro, G., & Euzenat, J. (2010). A feature and information theoretic framework for semantic similarity and relatedness. *The Semantic Web–ISWC, 2010*, 615–630. doi:10.1007/978-3-642-17746-0_39

Prathvi Kumari, R. K. (2013). Measuring Semantic Similarity between Words using Page-Count and Pattern Clustering Methods. *International Journal of Innovative Technology and Exploring Engineering*.

Rajagopal, D., Cambria, E., Olsher, D., & Kwok, K. (2013). A graph-based approach to commonsense concept extraction and semantic similarity detection. *Proceedings of the 22nd International Conference on World Wide Web*, 565-570. 10.1145/2487788.2487995

Ramón-Hernández, A., Simón-Cuevas, A., Lorenzo, M. M. G., Arco, L., & Serrano-Guerrero, J. (2020). Towards Context-Aware Opinion Summarization for Monitoring Social Impact of News. *Information (Basel)*, *11*(11), 535. doi:10.3390/info11110535

Resnik, P. (1999). Semantic similarity in a taxonomy: An information-based measure and its application to problems of ambiguity in natural language. *Journal of Artificial Intelligence Research*, *11*, 95–130. doi:10.1613/jair.514

Rodriguez, M. A., & Egenhofer, M. J. (2003). Determining semantic similarity among entity classes from different ontologies. *IEEE Transactions on Knowledge and Data Engineering*, *15*(2), 442–456. doi:10.1109/TKDE.2003.1185844

Roostaee, M., Fakhrahmad, S. M., Sadreddini, M. H., & Khalili, A. (2014). Efficient calculation of sentence semantic similarity: A proposed scheme based on machine learning approaches and NLP techniques. *Scientific Journal of Review*, *3*, 94–106.

Sanchez, D., Batet, M., Isern, D., & Valls, A. (2012). Ontology-based semantic similarity: A new feature-based approach. *Expert Systems with Applications*, *39*(9), 7718–7728. doi:10.1016/j.eswa.2012.01.082

Saruladha, K., Aghila, G., & Raj, S. (2010). A survey of semantic similarity methods for ontology based information retrieval. *2010 Second International Conference on Machine Learning and Computing*, 297-301. 10.1109/ICMLC.2010.63

Schuhmacher, M., & Ponzetto, S. P. (2014). Knowledge-based graph document modeling. *Proceedings of the 7th ACM international conference on Web search and data mining*, 543-552. 10.1145/2556195.2556250

Schwering, A. (2005). Hybrid model for semantic similarity measurement. *On the Move to Meaningful Internet Systems 2005: CoopIS, DOA, and ODBASE*, 1449-1465.

Shepard, R. N. (1980). Multidimensional scaling, tree-fitting, and clustering. *Science*, *210*(4468), 390–398. doi:10.1126cience.210.4468.390 PMID:17837406

Shibata, N., Kajikawa, Y., & Sakata, I. (2010). How to measure the semantic similarities between scientific papers and patents in order to discover uncommercialized research fronts: A case study of solar cells. *Technology Management for Global Economic Growth (PICMET), 2010 Proceedings of PICMET'10*, 1-6.

Shirakawa, M., Nakayama, K., Hara, T., & Nishio, S. (2015). Wikipedia-based semantic similarity measurements for noisy short texts using extended naive bayes. *IEEE Transactions on Emerging Topics in Computing*, *3*(2), 205–219. doi:10.1109/TETC.2015.2418716

Singh, J., Saini, M., & Siddiqi, S. (2013). Graph Based Computational Model for Computing Semantic Similarity. *Emerging Research in Computing, Information, Communication and Applications, ERCICA*, *2013*, 501–507.

Sultan, M. A., Bethard, S., & Sumner, T. (2015). DLS @ CU: Sentence Similarity from Word Alignment and Semantic Vector Composition. *SemEval@ NAACL-HLT*, 148-153.

Tang, S., & Cai, Z. (2010). Tourism domain ontology construction from the unstructured text documents. *Cognitive Informatics (ICCI), 2010 9th IEEE International Conference on*, 297-301. 10.1109/COGINF.2010.5599723

Tang, X., Qu, W., & Chen, X. (2016). Semantic change computation: A successive approach. *World Wide Web (Bussum)*, *19*(3), 375–415. doi:10.100711280-014-0316-y

Turney, P. D., & Pantel, P. (2010). From frequency to meaning: Vector space models of semantics. *Journal of Artificial Intelligence Research*, *37*, 141–188. doi:10.1613/jair.2934

Tversky, A., & Gati, I. (1978). Studies of similarity. *Cognition and Categorization*, *1*, 79-98.

Verma, Y., & Jawahar, C. V. (2014). Im2Text and Text2Im: Associating Images and Texts for Cross-Modal Retrieval. BMVC, 1, 2.

Vigneshvaran, P., Jayabalan, E., & Vijaya, K. (2013). A predominant statistical approach to identify semantic similarity of textual documents. *Pattern Recognition, Informatics and Mobile Engineering (PRIME), 2013 International Conference on*, 496-499. 10.1109/ICPRIME.2013.6496721

Wang, J., & Dong, Y. (2020). Measurement of text similarity: A survey. *Information (Basel)*, *11*(9), 421. doi:10.3390/info11090421

Wille, R. (2005). Formal concept analysis as mathematical theory of concepts and concept hierarchies. *Formal Concept Analysis*, *3626*, 1-33.

Xie, L., Pan, P., & Lu, Y. (2015). Analyzing semantic correlation for cross-modal retrieval. *Multimedia Systems*, *21*(6), 525–539. doi:10.100700530-014-0397-6

Young, P., Lai, A., Hodosh, M., & Hockenmaier, J. (2014). From image descriptions to visual denotations: New similarity metrics for semantic inference over event descriptions. *Transactions of the Association for Computational Linguistics*, *2*, 67–78. doi:10.1162/tacl_a_00166

Zhang, Z., Miao, D., & Yue, X. (2013). *Similarity measure for short texts using topic models and rough sets*. Academic Press.

Zhen, Z., Shen, J., & Lu, S. (2008). WCONS: An ontology mapping approach based on word and context similarity. *Proceedings of the 2008 IEEE/WIC/ACM International Conference on Web Intelligence and Intelligent Agent Technology, IEEE Computers & Society*, *3*, 334–338.

Zhu, G., & Iglesias, C. A. (2017). Computing semantic similarity of concepts in knowledge graphs. *IEEE Transactions on Knowledge and Data Engineering*, *29*(1), 72–85. doi:10.1109/TKDE.2016.2610428

ENDNOTES

[1]   http://www.image-net.org/
[2]   Lattice Miner is a data mining prototype for exploring concept lattices https://lattice-miner.soft112.com/
[3]   http://www.followthehashtag.com/datasets/170000-uk-geolocated-tweets-free-twitter-dataset/
[4]   http://ixa2.si.ehu.es/stswiki/index.php/STSbenchmark
[5]   https://alt.qcri.org/semeval2015/task1/data/uploads/tp_trial_data.txt

Chapter 6
A Topic Modeling–Guided Framework for Aspect-Oriented Sentiment Analysis on Social Media

Nikhil V. Chandran
Kerala University of Digital Sciences, Innovation, and Technology, India

Anoop V. S.
Kerala University of Digital Sciences, Innovation, and Technology, India

Asharaf S.
Kerala University of Digital Sciences, Innovation, and Technology, India

ABSTRACT

Social media platforms have incorporated more than half of the world's population, making it one of the most data-rich domains recently. The sentiments expressed by social media users hold great significance for various reasons, such as the identification of public opinion on a product or towards a governmental policy, to name a few. There are different domains where companies use social media sentiments to gather feedback from customers to provide them with better products and services. Only a few attempts have been reported on aspect-based sentiment analysis literature on sentiment analysis and opinion mining. This chapter proposes a framework for aspect-based sentiment analysis for social media using a topic modeling-powered approach. The experiments conducted on real-world datasets show that the proposed framework outperforms some existing works on aspect-oriented sentiment analysis.

INTRODUCTION

Sentiment analysis techniques are now being used in business and social domains to identify and understand human behaviour. The need to identify the sentiments from social media platforms such as social

DOI: 10.4018/978-1-7998-9594-7.ch006

networks and discussion forums is also increasing. Sentiment analysis attempts to identify the opinion or view over a topic or event using natural language processing. These opinions are subjective expressions of people and are not facts. Text sentiment analysis has recently focussed on the vast amount of unstructured social media data available through online platforms. The application areas of sentiment analysis include product reviews, political opinions, law-making, and psychology (Alessia et al., 2015). For instance, product review data is now available on almost all e-commerce sites and enables a better user experience for customers by providing feedback on the available products. Companies' continuous opinion tracking on products can help them get real-time feedback on their market performance. This feedback can thus help companies plan their product and brand improvements. Sentiment analysis can help companies access actionable facts and figures, essential for improving their online image. Organizations in the e-commerce space compete to offer better customer experiences as there is an enormous growth in the online purchase of products. These sites provide innovative solutions like product recommendations and a comparison of products.

The data mined from social media platforms such as Twitter can provide valuable insights into global events like the Covid-19 pandemic (Boon-Itt & Skunkan, 2020). Moreover, these platforms enable feedback regarding the user experience and opinions. Product level feedback may not provide accurate opinions on individual product features due to the diverse nature of the review. Aspect level sentiment analysis can be used in this scenario and focuses on analyzing the sentiments at individual aspect levels (Pontiki et al., 2016). Twitter data can be used to track healthcare-related issues such as the spread of diseases and the general public's awareness regarding health advisories. Topic Modeling and sentiment analysis of tweets can be used to identify common discussion themes related to the pandemic. There can be various classification levels such as word, sentence, document, or aspect. Specific terms and phrases can be considered polarity keywords to identify the sentiment they convey. Data-driven methods can be used to find the keywords, finding the relationship between words and reviews. Sentiment analysis on social media like Twitter is usually done to understand the polarity of the users' various topics. For example, analysis of a current trending topic such as a newly released movie or album can be helpful to understand the overall sentiment towards it (Yue et al., 2019).

Similarly, the sentiment or opinion about a product or company can be mined from Twitter data. Some previous works have attempted to perform sentiment analysis on tweets obtained by refining Twitter API queries. A tweet dataset is created by filtering out tweets containing particular hashtags or user profiles in such works (Agarwal et al., 2011). The challenge with raw tweets is that the data must be pre-processed before inputting to a sentiment analysis module. The raw tweets are character-limited by Twitter to 280 characters as of 2021 and usually contain emojis and URLs which need to be removed. A difficult task is identifying the semantics and extracting opinions from such short texts. Ambiguity is another issue while dealing with short tweets and affects the performance of the sentiment analysis model (Saif et al., 2012). Few tweet datasets are publicly available, and they were annotated by crowdsourcing. Contributors were given the raw tweets and then made to classify tweets as positive, negative, or neutral. Such sentiment-labelled tweet datasets can be used for supervised models.

Topic modeling approaches identify hidden topic clusters from an unstructured corpus. Latent Dirichlet Allocation (LDA) is a generative model for discrete data such as text corpora (Blei et al., 2003). It is the most common and simplistic model which generates a probabilistic distribution of topics. In the context of sentiment analysis, topic modeling can be performed to create a condensed representation of the documents. Individual word-level polarity classification contains mixed opinions and cannot be used for sentiment analysis. People express their subjective opinions in ambiguous ways, posing a significant challenge in sentiment analysis. In most topic modeling approaches, the topics are modeled as word unigrams, and then the aspects are extracted using topic modeling. There have been few attempts performing topic modeling-based sentiment analysis. After performing a topic modeling algorithm such as Latent Dirichlet Allocation (LDA), the output is topics represented as probabilistically weighted lists of words. These topic clusters are not labelled with a topic label. Traditionally this topic labelling is done manually, and in very few cases, the use of machine learning techniques was attempted (Cano Basave et al., 2014). Identifying the aspects and mapping the topic to an aspect is challenging. In specialized areas such as healthcare, this process requires domain expertise. Creating an automated framework for performing this topic-aspect mapping with high precision is a difficult task in NLP. If such a general-purpose domain-independent framework is developed for this task, it will benefit a variety of use-cases and domains. The work further described in this chapter is an initial attempt towards a domain-independent automated framework for aspect-based sentiment analysis using topic modeling and deep learning techniques.

In the present-day social media scenario, emotions are represented compactly as smileys, and emotion recognition is used to find the expressed sentiment. The sentiment of a product might be influenced by the sentiment towards different features or aspects of the product. Consider an example of user reviews of a mobile phone; various mobile device features might influence the overall sentiment towards the product. The mobile phone manufacturer might be interested in knowing which of the product's features are taken positively by the consumers and which are not. Thus, aspect-based sentiment analysis is done by extracting various aspects of a product (Thet et al., 2010). Aspects are traditionally identified manually, but recently there have been automated approaches for aspect identification. Deep learning-based approaches have recently become popular, and many such models have produced state-of-the-art results in NLP. Pre-trained Transformer based embedding models are used extensively for sentiment analysis tasks. A few works have attempted to perform sentiment analysis using Bidirectional Encoding Representations from Transformer (BERT) models. Although topic modeling approaches have been used in sentiment analysis models, there is no common framework for aspect-based sentiment analysis. This chapter focuses on building an automated framework for aspect-based sentiment analysis for social media using a topic modeling-powered approach.

Contributions of this chapter: The significant contributions of this chapter can be summarized as follows:

- This chapter discusses some of the recent and prominent approaches to aspect-oriented sentiment analysis.
- Outlines the details of Latent Dirichlet Allocation (LDA), which is one of the most popular topic modeling algorithms.
- This work proposes a framework using deep learning techniques and topic modeling for aspect-oriented sentiment analysis.
- Compare and discuss the advantages of the proposed framework with some of the already existing methods.

Organization of the chapter: The remainder of this chapter is organized as follows: The background section discusses the recent advancements in sentiment analysis, topic modeling and how it works. The following section discusses the proposed framework. The solutions section discusses the experimental details, results, and discussions. The authors conclude the chapter in the final section and give some future research dimensions.

BACKGROUND

Topic modeling is a statistical technique used to identify topics from a collection of documents. It is used for the discovery of hidden semantic structures from a corpus. The main objective of sentiment analysis is to identify the polarity of a given text, whether the text under consideration is positive, negative, or neutral. Aspect-based sentiment analysis aims to classify the given text based on the different features or aspects that are identified. The attempts to identify public opinions began in the early 20th Century and utilized various computational linguistic methods. The major revolution in opinion mining started with the arrival of the world-wide-web as data availability became abundant. Classification of human emotions or opinions on events, movies, or products based on the availability of digital data has become a popular research area. Sentiment analysis can be broadly classified into document, sentence, and aspect levels. This work is based on aspect-level sentiment analysis guided by topic modeling approaches. Let us look at some of the recent works that have shaped this domain in the following sections.

SemEval is a series of evaluations of computational semantic analysis systems. The SemEval task of 2016, (Pontiki et al., 2016) provided 19 training and 20 testing datasets for eight languages and seven domains and a standard evaluation procedure. One of the first works combined the word embeddings from neural language models and learning on weakly supervised data. A new model was described (Severyn & Moschitti, 2015) for initializing the parameter weights of the convolutional neural network learning model for sentiment analysis of tweets. This is required for reducing the number of features while maintaining the model's accuracy. The sentiment analysis of tweets was performed for predicting polarities at both the sentence and phrase levels. Social media analysis of Twitter data produced helpful information about the trends in discussion on the Covid-19 pandemic (Boon-Itt & Skunkan, 2020). Their results indicate that analyzing Twitter data is very important to understand public perception of current trends in the health domain. Another study analyzed 16 million tweets to examine the relationship between public sentiment revolving around Brexit with stock prices and the British pound sterling (Ilyas et al., 2020). They used topic modeling to find whether the topics being discussed on Twitter are representative of the events. Studies like these help the government better interpret public perception and build better forecasting models for the economy.

Sentiment polarity categorization is one of the fundamental problems of sentiment analysis. Several works have (Fang & Zhan, 2015) aimed to tackle this problem by performing sentence-level and review-level categorization. Product reviews from online e-commerce sites were used for this study. There are various levels of sentiment classification like document level, sentence level, and aspect level (Lin et al., 2016). The broad document level classifies the polarity of a document, while the sentence level is concerned with the sentence's sentiment categorization. The aspect level sentiment analysis focuses on people's opinions about specific aspects of a product or service. For example, a product review like a personal computer would include battery life, camera quality, screen resolution, price, and battery. The reviews can associate a polarity or sentiment for each of these aspects. This kind of analysis can be helpful for companies to improve their products or services.

A cascaded framework of feature selection and classifier ensemble using particle swarm optimization for aspect-based sentiment analysis was found to be effective (Akhtar et al., 2017). This work is composed of aspect term extraction and sentiment classification. Another approach using SentiWordNet lexical resource (Shelke et al., 2017) uses an unsupervised method for domain-independent feature-specific sentiment analysis. An ontology-based method (Salas-Zárate et al., 2017) to detect aspects concerning diabetes in tweets was proposed in the English language. Latent Dirichlet allocation (LDA) topic modeling was used for aspect-based sentiment analysis of e-commerce data (Anoop & Asharaf, 2020). Extracted topic words are then mapped with aspects, and sentiment analysis gives promising results. A novel pre-processing scheme (Yadav et al., 2021) enabled the conversion of ABSA inputs to binary form with limited information loss. This learning architecture allowed human-level interpretable results with reasonable accuracy.

Recently, many studies have focused on deep learning for aspect-based sentiment analysis (Tul et al., 2017). Deep learning models such as Convolutional Neural Networks (CNNs), Recurrent Neural Networks(RNNs), Deep Belief Nets, and the recent transformer models are being studied for sentiment analysis and opinion mining applications. Investigating the language used in reviews is a challenging task that requires an expert understanding of the language. The sentiment analysis of short texts is a difficult task. They extract characters to sentence-level features using convolutional neural networks for sentiment analysis to obtain better results (Dos Santos & Gatti, 2014). The sentiment polarity is highly related to the concerned aspect, and some works (Wang et al., 2016) have attempted to model aspect sentiment analysis with attention mechanisms. A variant of Latent Dirichlet Allocation (LDA) is used (Ozyurt & Akcayol, 2021). Another work attempts to label the best word from a topic based on features (Lau et al., 2010); this was an early attempt at automated topic labelling. The process of assigning a descriptive phrase to represent a topic cluster after topic modeling is known as topic labelling. Automatic topic labelling attempts to automate the process via machine learning techniques. There are two main steps for generating topic labels. The first step is to create possible candidate labels, known as candidate label generation. Candidate label ranking ranks the generated labels based on semantic relevance scoring methods. The above work (Lau et al., 2010) attempts to label topic clusters with one of the words present in that cluster. This method uses different ranking mechanisms such as pointwise mutual information and conditional probabilities. When the topics are coherent, this method works well, but this method does not perform well for complex and ambiguous topic clusters. To accurately identify the meaning of each topic is a difficult task due to the lack of ontological information.

Topic models can automatically extract exciting topics in the form of multinomial distributions from the text. Probabilistic methods were proposed to label topic models with meaningful phrases (Mei et al., 2007). This proposed approach was defined as an optimization problem involving minimizing the Kullback-Leibler divergence between word distributions and maximizing word distributions between a label and a topic model. The workflow involved extracting a set of candidate labels from a reference collection and finding a good relevance scoring function. Next, the score is used to rank candidate labels for each topic model. Finally, to label the corresponding topic, they select the top-ranked labels. Associating a topic with an image was attempted (Aletras & Stevenson, 2013), denoting the central theme or subject. Since images are language-independent, this method has advantages over labelling topics with texts. For candidate labels, the top five topic terms are used to query Google to retrieve the top twenty images used as candidates for each topic. The images retrieved are featured with textual information and visual information. The textual information is the concatenated web page title with the image file name which is obtained as the metadata retrieved by the above search. The visual information is extracted using low-level image keypoint descriptors called Scale-Invariant Feature Transform (SIFT). This gives a Bag-of-Visual word (BOVW). The graph is constructed where each node represents a candidate image, and each edge denotes similarity scores between two images using the two features of each image. Then, they used Personalized PageRank (PPR), a modified PageRank algorithm that emphasizes specific nodes in the graph to make PPR prefer images with information like the topic terms. Three different metrics for weighting graph edges were used: Pointwise Mutual Information (PMI) between images with co-occurrence count strained over Wikipedia with sliding window 20, Explicit Semantic Analysis (ESA) which is a knowledge-based similarity measure, and visual features extracted from the images where visual words (BOVW described above) are used to compute the cosine similarity between a pair of images. Following the ranking method, the image with a top PPR score is a representative image label for each topic.

The most generic approach to automatic labelling has been to use as primitive labels the top n words in a topic distribution learned by a topic model such as LDA (Cano Basave et al., 2014). Such top terms are usually ranked using the marginal probabilities $P(w_i|t_j)$ associated with each word w_i for a given topic t_j. Given K topics over the document collection D, the topic labelling task consists of discovering a sequence of words for each topic $k \in K$. This work proposes to generate topic label candidates by summarising topic relevant documents. Such documents can be derived using the observed data from corpus D and the inferred topic model variables. They investigate lexical features by comparing three well-known multi-document summarization algorithms against the top-n topic terms baseline. These algorithms include Sum Basic (SB), a frequency-based summarization algorithm that weights each sentence with an average probability of words, then picks the most probable word from the most probable sentence. Hybrid TF-IDF is a TF-IDF-based summarization algorithm. Maximal Marginal Relevance (MMR) is a relevance-based ranking algorithm that avoids redundancy in the collection by measuring the dissimilarity between given documents and previously selected words in the ranked list. Text Rank is a graph-based summarization algorithm where each vertex denotes each word in the collection and uses the PageRank algorithm to weigh each node. For Candidate Label Ranking, Candidates are ranked based on the weight calculated in the above summarization algorithms, and top labels are retrieved based on their scores. Top-ranked terms in each algorithm are used to represent each topic, similar to top-10 terms are used to describe each topic in the LDA model.

Recently, attempts to label the topics with neural embedding were successful (Bhatia et al., 2016). This work describes a label generation approach based on combined word and document embeddings, which is considerably simpler and empirically superior to the state-of-the-art generation method. A simple label ranking approach that exploits character and lexical information is superior to the state-of-the-art ranking approach. They also released an open-source implementation of their method, including a new topic label ranking evaluation dataset. Wikipedia article titles retrieved by the two search engines in the above work are used as potential labels. By greedily parsing each Wikipedia article, they generate their word2vec and doc2vec models. This is made possible as the traditional word2vec model produces word vectors for unigrams. Representing the potential labels as vectors, the cosine similarity between top-10 topic terms and their average scores are calculated to assign the score for each label. This is done for both word2vec and doc2vec models. Both models are equally weighted to produce top candidate labels considered in the ranking method. After generating the candidate labels based on neural embeddings, they re-rank them on a supervised learn-to-rank model with a few features. The letter Trigram feature measures a character level similarity consisting of tri-letter grams. The Letter Trigram feature measures the association between labels and each top topic term. PageRank scores for each label are calculated and fed into the model as a feature, since all candidate labels are valid Wikipedia articles with pages. The number of words in each label is denoted as the NumWords feature. Topic Overlap represents the lexical overlap between the candidate label and the top-10 topic terms. The supervised model is trained against the gold standard labels from human annotators using a support vector regression model (SVR) over these four features. After training the SVM model, each label with extracted features is fed into the SVM model, and the model outputs the ranking of the candidate labels.

The potential of using contextual word embeddings from pre-trained language model Bidirectional Encoder Representations from Transformers (Devlin et al., 2018) was explored by some studies (Hoang & Rouces, 2019). BERT was found to perform well on different NLP tasks due to many training text data. Aspect Extraction (AE) and Aspect Sentiment Classification (ASC) tasks are solved using two modules named Parallel Aggregation and Hierarchical aggregation over the BERT model (Karimi et al., 2020). These two modules utilizing the hidden representation of the BERT language model produced deeper semantic representations of the input sequence. Additional post-training on review text for ABSA has further improved the performance of BERT (Xu et al., 2019). This post-training work assigned a machine reading comprehension technique called review reading comprehension and formulated the ABSA task as a question answering problem. Constructing an auxiliary sentence from the aspect and converting ABSA to a sentence pair classification task have improved performance on benchmarks (Sun et al., 2018). This fine-tuned and pre-trained model from BERT achieved better results using the sentence pair method on the SentiHood and SemEval Task 4 dataset. Word sequences that form the input for BERT cannot provide contextual information. To solve this problem, the input texts are fed into BERT and context-aware embeddings independently (Li et al., 2020). Next, a gating mechanism controls the transmission of sentiment features from BERT output with context-aware embeddings. Depending on the context, fine-grained inferences about sentiment can be extracted using Targeted Aspect Based Sentiment Analysis (TABSA). Context-Guided BERT learns to distribute attention under different contexts by adapting a context-aware transformer (Wu & Ong, 2020). This work provides proof for adding context-dependencies to pre-trained attention-based language models.

Topic Modeling Using Latent Dirichlet Allocation

Vast quantities of unstructured and unlabeled data can be analyzed using topic modeling techniques. Topic modeling algorithms are used to find hidden representations from a collection of documents. Traditionally statistical Topic modeling approaches were based on Latent Semantic Analysis (LSA) and Latent Dirichlet Allocation (LDA). Latent Semantic Analysis (Dumais et al., 1988) is one of the earliest works in statistical topic modeling. LSA utilizes Singular Value Decomposition (SVD) to find the similarities among the entities in a reduced dimensional space. Probabilistic Latent Semantic Analysis finds a probabilistic model with latent topics to generate the data observed in our term-document matrix (Hofmann, 1999). Latent Dirichlet Allocation (Blei et al., 2003) uses Dirichlet priors for document-topic and word-topic distributions. This can be considered as a 'distribution over distributions' and achieves better generalization of topics.

The basic unit of discrete data in LDA is represented as a word, which is defined to be an item from a vocabulary indexed in the range $\{1...V\}$. Let the document be a sequence of N words, $\mathbf{w} = (\mathbf{w}_1, ...\mathbf{w}_n)$ where $\mathbf{w}_n$ is the nth word in the sequence, and a corpus is a collection of "M" documents denoted by $\mathbf{D} = \mathbf{W}_1 ... \mathbf{W}_m$. The generative process for each

1.   Choose $\mathbf{N} \sim$ Poisson (ξ)
2.   Choose $\boldsymbol{\theta} \sim$ Dir $(\boldsymbol{\alpha})$

3. For each n-words W_n:
    a. Choose a topic $z_n \sim$ Multinomial(θ)
    b. Choose a word w_n from $p(w_n \mid z_n, \beta)$, a multinomial probability conditioned on the topic z_n

A k-dimensional Dirichlet random variable can take values in the **(k-1)** simplex, and a **k**-vector θ lies in the **(k-1)** simplex if $\theta \geq 0, \sum_{i=1}^{k} \theta_i = 0$ and has the following density on this simplex:

$$P(\theta \mid a) = \frac{\Gamma(\sum_{i=1}^{k} a_i)}{\prod_{i=1}^{k} \Gamma(a_i)} \theta_1^{a_1} \dots \theta_1^{a_k - 1}$$

The parameter $\boldsymbol{\alpha}$ is a k-**vector** with components $\alpha i > 0$, and where $\Gamma(x)$ is the $\boldsymbol{\gamma}$ function. Given the parameters $\boldsymbol{\alpha}$ and $\boldsymbol{\beta}$, the joint distribution of a topic mixture, a set of *n* topics z and a set of *n* words w, is given by

$$P(\theta, z, w \mid a, \beta) = P(\theta \mid a) \prod_{n=1}^{N} \sum_{Z_n} P(z_n \mid \theta) + P(w_n \mid Z_{n,\beta})$$

Where $P(Z_n \mid \theta)$ is simply θ_i for the unique **i** such $Z_n = 1$, integrating over $\boldsymbol{\theta}$ and summing over z, obtain the marginal distribution of a document as follows:

$$P(w \mid a, \beta) = \int P(\theta \mid a) \left(\prod_{n=1}^{N} \sum_{Z_n} P(Z_n \mid \theta) + P(w_n \mid Z_n, \beta) d\theta \right)$$

Lastly, taking the product of the marginal probabilities of single documents obtains the probability of the corpus as:

$$(D \mid a, \beta) = \prod_{d=1}^{M} \int P(\theta_d \mid a) \left(\prod_{n=1}^{N} d \sum_{z_{dn}} P(z_{dn} \theta_d) + P(W_{dn} \mid Z_{dn}, \beta) d\theta_d \right)$$

PROPOSED WORK

This section discusses the proposed framework for topic modeling guided aspect-oriented sentiment analysis. The overall workflow of the proposed framework is shown in Figure 1, and as shown in the figure, the proposed approach consists of six steps for the sentiment classification process. The process starts with collecting and pre-processing the dataset. For this experiment, this work uses the data collected from Twitter - one of the world's most popular microblogging and social network services. The collected data will be pre-processed for removing unwanted noises such as figures, special symbols, emojis, URLs, and other irrelevant characters. Other pre-processing such as stopword removal and lemmatization will be performed on the collected data. Then topic modeling will be done on the pre-processed corpus to gather the topics where topics are collections of co-occurring words according to some probability distributions. Topic modeling is a suite of text understanding algorithms in natural language processing. It uses statistical modeling to discover the latent or abstract "topics" that occur in a collection of documents. The third step in the proposed framework deals with aspect identification from the text. The data collected from Twitter is about electronic gadgets, specifically mobile phones and accessories. This experiment manually identified the aspects related to mobile phones, such as the battery, display, sound, and price. The next step in the proposed approach is to map the aspects with the topics, and for this process, the probability of words is taken and assigned with an aspect label. For example, if a topic contains sound, quality, loud, noise, hear, etc., the aspect label sound is assigned for that particular topic. Similarly, aspect labels were given to all the topics generated for this experiment.

This work has used a pre-trained model called BERT (Bidirectional Encoder Representations from Transformers) designed to pre-train deep bidirectional representations from unlabeled text data. BERT is used in this experiment for feature engineering and contextualizing the text. Once the output is collected from the embedding, BERT will train the classifier to classify the sentiment into either positive, negative, or neutral. This framework uses different models such as the MALLET implementation, Top2Vec - an algorithm used to map the word level and document level embeddings jointly, and Lda2vec - obtained for the topic modeling by modifying the skip-gram word2vec variant. While Top2Vec and Lda2Vec give the vectorized topics that can be directly used for the classification tasks, some manual processes were done for the MALLET.

For sentiment classification, this experiment has used different deep learning models such as Long Short Term Memory (LSTM), Bi-Directional Long Short Term Memory (BiLSTM), Convolutional Neural Network (CNN), and Gated Recurrent Unit (GRU). The Bi-Directional LSTM (BiLSTM) network captures the sequence data structure forward and backward, whereas Long Short Term Memory can do this only in the forward direction in a looped form. Many machine learning and natural language processing applications such as sequence labelling and language modeling use this advantage of Bi-directional Long Short Term Memory. Convolutional Neural Network: One famous neural network architecture initially proposed for image processing got significant attention and application in the text. Convolution can be seen as a simple application that applies a filter to an input that results in activation. CNN is a multi-layer neural network containing at least two hidden layers. The hidden layers are responsible for the tasks such as convolution and pooling. Gated Recurrent Unit: Gated recurrent unit (GRU), on the other hand, uses a simple gating function compared to Long Short Term Memory and contains two types of gates for its operation - an update gate and a reset gate. The reset gate takes input from the previous hidden state and current input, and a sigmoid activation function is calculated.

Figure 1. The overall workflow of the proposed approach

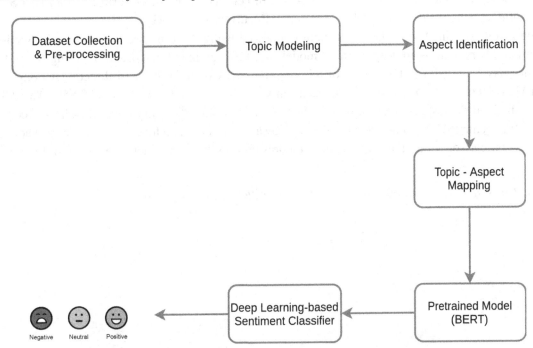

EXPERIMENTS AND RESULTS

This section details the experiment conducted to implement the framework and the results obtained from the experiment. The proposed approach uses tweets on mobile phone reviews and descriptions collected from tweets generated by users on Twitter. This work has used the APIs provided by Twitter for collecting the data. For this experiment, a total of 12753 tweets were collected for one week. A total of 826 duplicate tweets were removed from the dataset, and the pre-processing was done as mentioned in the proposed work section. The emojis were extracted using the emoji Python library, publicly available at https://pypi.org/project/demoji/. This process removed 24 emoji tweets from the dataset.

For this experiment, only the tweets in the English language were considered, and the 1276 messages tweeted in other languages were removed. The above was done with the help of the *langdetect* library available at https://pypi.org/project/langdetect/. Thus, the final tweet count in the pre-processed dataset was 10627. We have also expanded the contractions where Contractions are words or combinations of words that are shortened by dropping letters and replacing them with an apostrophe. For example, "might've" should be replaced with "might have", "we've" should be replaced with "we have", and so on. This contraction expansion has been applied to all the datasets and collected common contractions replacement details available for English. A total of 10627 tweets have been tokenized using Keras (https://keras.io/) tokenizer module. Stopwords were removed during the pre-processing stage, and lemmatization of the words was done using the Natural Language Toolkit (NLTK) library available in Python. This work uses the BERT pre-trained language model to create the feature vector and train the deep neural networks. Then Keras embedding module is used for creating the word embedding layer for the deep neural network. Then all the deep neural architectures were trained, as discussed in Section 3, such as the Long Short Term Memory (LSTM), Bi-directional Long Short Term Memory (BiLSTM), Convolutional Neural Networks (CNN), and Gated Recurrent Unit (GRU).

The results obtained from the experiment conducted using the framework discussed in Section 4 are outlined here. Out of all deep learning models used for sentiment classification, Long Short Term Memory has recorded a test accuracy of 87.76% and test loss of 28.70%. Bi-directional Long Short Term Memory (BiLSTM) has recorded a test accuracy of 87.93% and a test loss of 29.55%. The (CNN) model obtained the test accuracy of 81.14% and test loss of 45.68%, and finally, the Gated Recurrent Unit (GRU) achieved 89.82% test accuracy and 63.09 as the test loss, all for 30 epochs. The test accuracy and loss comparison for all the deep learning models used in this experiment are shown in Figure 2.

Figure 2. Test accuracy and test loss comparison of different deep learning models

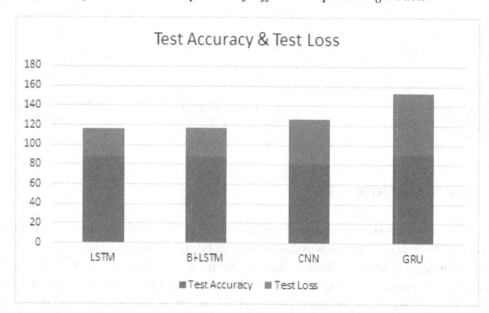

So out of all the four deep learning models, Gated Recurrent Unit (GRU) performed better but with a higher test loss. The close competitor was BiLSTM, with an accuracy of 87.93%. As this was an early attempt to check the topic modeling-based sentiment classification on microblogging data, the authors plan to conduct this experiment on a larger dataset with modified parameters to enhance the accuracy.

FUTURE RESEARCH DIRECTIONS

Various automated approaches are being attempted for topic labelling after topic modeling. In the proposed framework, topic modeling was done using the Latent Dirichlet allocation (LDA) to obtain the topic distributions. Then the topic clusters were labelled with the corresponding topic labels. A potential improvement over the current framework would be to perform this labelling using an automated method. After this step, topic-aspect mapping was performed using probabilistic criteria. This topic to aspect mapping can be done using a machine learning technique. This step can be simplified by incorporating the aspect extraction functionality into the base LDA algorithm. Modifying the LDA algorithm to include aspect extraction is a potential future opportunity. The pre-trained BERT model is then used to create a contextual embedding for the sentences. In the future, a modified form of BERT can be used to automatically assign a sentiment polarity to the sentences based on the detected aspects. Future works will simplify this framework by combining and modifying the existing framework components.

CONCLUSION

This chapter proposed a novel framework for aspect-based sentiment analysis using topic modeling and deep learning techniques. Initially, the corpus was pre-processed by removing stopwords, emojis, URLs, and other unwanted characters. Then the stemming, lemmatization and normalization of the corpus were done. This pre-processed corpus was input to the Latent Dirichlet Allocation (LDA) algorithm. The resulting topic clusters and associated probabilities reduce the computational complexity of the sentiment analysis on the full dataset. The sentiment analysis was performed using a deep learning classifier (BERT). Out of the four deep learning models trained, GRU performed better but with a higher test loss. There are various steps in this pipeline, and some of these stages can be simplified in the future.

ACKNOWLEDGMENT

The authors would like to thank all the research scholars and staff of the Data Engineering Lab and Kerala Blockchain Academy at Kerala University of Digital Sciences, Innovation, and Technology for their invaluable support for carrying out this research. The authors also thank the staff of the Kerala University of Digital Sciences, Innovation, and Technology for providing us with the infrastructure support for carrying out research work of this scale.

REFERENCES

Agarwal, A., Xie, B., Vovsha, I., Rambow, O., & Passonneau, R. J. (2011, June). Sentiment analysis of twitter data. In *Proceedings of the workshop on language in social media (LSM 2011)* (pp. 30-38). Academic Press.

Ain, Q. T., Ali, M., Riaz, A., Noureen, A., Kamran, M., Hayat, B., & Rehman, A. (2017). Sentiment analysis using deep learning techniques: A review. *International Journal of Advanced Computer Science and Applications*, *8*(6), 424.

Akhtar, M. S., Gupta, D., Ekbal, A., & Bhattacharyya, P. (2017). Feature selection and ensemble construction: A two-step method for aspect based sentiment analysis. *Knowledge-Based Systems*, *125*, 116–135. doi:10.1016/j.knosys.2017.03.020

Alessia, D., Ferri, F., Grifoni, P., & Guzzo, T. (2015). Approaches, tools and applications for sentiment analysis implementation. *International Journal of Computers and Applications*, *125*(3).

Aletras, N., & Stevenson, M. (2013, June). Representing topics using images. In *Proceedings of the 2013 Conference of the North American Chapter of the Association for Computational Linguistics: Human Language Technologies* (pp. 158-167). Academic Press.

Anoop, V. S., & Asharaf, S. (2020). Aspect-Oriented Sentiment Analysis: A Topic Modeling-Powered Approach. *Journal of Intelligent Systems, 29*(1), 1166–1178. doi:10.1515/jisys-2018-0299

Basave, A. E. C., He, Y., & Xu, R. (2014, June). Automatic labelling of topic models learned from twitter by summarisation. In *Proceedings of the 52nd Annual Meeting of the Association for Computational Linguistics (*Volume 2*: Short Papers)* (pp. 618-624). Academic Press.

Bhatia, S., Lau, J. H., & Baldwin, T. (2016). *Automatic labelling of topics with neural embeddings.* arXiv preprint arXiv:1612.05340.

Blei, D. M., Ng, A. Y., & Jordan, M. I. (2003). Latent dirichlet allocation. *The Journal of Machine Learning Research, 3*, 993-1022.

Boon-Itt, S., & Skunkan, Y. (2020). Public perception of the COVID-19 pandemic on Twitter: Sentiment analysis and topic modeling study. *JMIR Public Health and Surveillance, 6*(4), e21978. doi:10.2196/21978 PMID:33108310

Devlin, J., Chang, M. W., Lee, K., & Toutanova, K. (2018). *Bert: Pre-training of deep bidirectional transformers for language understanding.* arXiv preprint arXiv:1810.04805.

Dos Santos, C., & Gatti, M. (2014, August). Deep convolutional neural networks for sentiment analysis of short texts. In *Proceedings of COLING 2014, the 25th International Conference on Computational Linguistics: Technical Papers* (pp. 69-78). Academic Press.

Dumais, S. T., Furnas, G. W., Landauer, T. K., Deerwester, S., & Harshman, R. (1988, May). Using latent semantic analysis to improve access to textual information. In *Proceedings of the SIGCHI conference on Human factors in computing systems* (pp. 281-285). 10.1145/57167.57214

Fang, X., & Zhan, J. (2015). Sentiment analysis using product review data. *Journal of Big Data, 2*(1), 1–14. doi:10.118640537-015-0015-2

Hoang, M., Bihorac, O. A., & Rouces, J. (2019). Aspect-based sentiment analysis using bert. In *Proceedings of the 22nd Nordic Conference on Computational Linguistics* (pp. 187-196). Academic Press.

Hoffman, T. (1999). Probabilistic latent semantic analysis. *Proc. of the 15th Conference on Uncertainty in AI.*

Ilyas, S. H. W., Soomro, Z. T., Anwar, A., Shahzad, H., & Yaqub, U. (2020, June). Analyzing Brexit's impact using sentiment analysis and topic modeling on Twitter discussion. In *The 21st Annual International Conference on Digital Government Research* (pp. 1-6). 10.1145/3396956.3396973

Karimi, A., Rossi, L., & Prati, A. (2020). *Improving BERT Performance for Aspect-Based Sentiment Analysis.* arXiv preprint arXiv:2010.11731.

Lau, J. H., Newman, D., Karimi, S., & Baldwin, T. (2010, August). Best topic word selection for topic labelling. In *Coling 2010* (pp. 605–613). Posters.

Li, X., Fu, X., Xu, G., Yang, Y., Wang, J., Jin, L., ... Xiang, T. (2020). Enhancing BERT representation with context-aware embedding for aspect-based sentiment analysis. *IEEE Access : Practical Innovations, Open Solutions*, *8*, 46868–46876.

Liu, B. (2012). Sentiment analysis and opinion mining. *Synthesis Lectures on Human Language Technologies*, *5*(1), 1–167.

Mei, Q., Shen, X., & Zhai, C. (2007, August). Automatic labeling of multinomial topic models. In *Proceedings of the 13th ACM SIGKDD international conference on Knowledge discovery and data mining* (pp. 490-499). 10.1145/1281192.1281246

Ozyurt, B., & Akcayol, M. A. (2021). A new topic modeling based approach for aspect extraction in aspect based sentiment analysis: SS-LDA. *Expert Systems with Applications*, *168*, 114231. doi:10.1016/j.eswa.2020.114231

Pontiki, M., Galanis, D., Papageorgiou, H., Androutsopoulos, I., Manandhar, S., Al-Smadi, M., ... Eryiğit, G. (2016, January). Semeval-2016 task 5: Aspect based sentiment analysis. In *International workshop on semantic evaluation* (pp. 19-30). 10.18653/v1/S16-1002

Saif, H., He, Y., & Alani, H. (2012, November). Semantic sentiment analysis of twitter. In *International semantic web conference* (pp. 508-524). Springer. 10.1007/978-3-642-35176-1_32

Salas-Zárate, M. D. P., Medina-Moreira, J., Lagos-Ortiz, K., Luna-Aveiga, H., Rodriguez-Garcia, M. A., & Valencia-Garcia, R. (2017). Sentiment analysis on tweets about diabetes: An aspect-level approach. *Computational and Mathematical Methods in Medicine*, *2017*, 2017. doi:10.1155/2017/5140631 PMID:28316638

Severyn, A., & Moschitti, A. (2015, August). Twitter sentiment analysis with deep convolutional neural networks. In *Proceedings of the 38th international ACM SIGIR conference on research and development in information retrieval* (pp. 959-962). 10.1145/2766462.2767830

Shelke, N., Deshpande, S., & Thakare, V. (2017). Domain independent approach for aspect oriented sentiment analysis for product reviews. In *Proceedings of the 5th international conference on frontiers in intelligent computing: Theory and applications* (pp. 651-659). Springer. 10.1007/978-981-10-3156-4_69

Sun, C., Huang, L., & Qiu, X. (2019). *Utilizing BERT for aspect-based sentiment analysis via constructing auxiliary sentence.* arXiv preprint arXiv:1903.09588.

Thet, T. T., Na, J. C., & Khoo, C. S. (2010). Aspect-based sentiment analysis of movie reviews on discussion boards. *Journal of Information Science*, *36*(6), 823–848. doi:10.1177/0165551510388123

Wang, Y., Huang, M., Zhu, X., & Zhao, L. (2016, November). Attention-based LSTM for aspect-level sentiment classification. In *Proceedings of the 2016 conference on empirical methods in natural language processing* (pp. 606-615). 10.18653/v1/D16-1058

Wu, Z., & Ong, D. C. (2020). Context-guided bert for targeted aspect-based sentiment analysis. Association for the Advancement of Artificial Intelligence, 1-9.

Xu, H., Liu, B., Shu, L., & Yu, P. S. (2019). *BERT post-training for review reading comprehension and aspect-based sentiment analysis.* arXiv preprint arXiv:1904.02232.

Yadav, R. K., Jiao, L., Granmo, O. C., & Goodwin, M. (2021, May). Human-level interpretable learning for aspect-based sentiment analysis. In *The Thirty-Fifth AAAI Conference on Artificial Intelligence (AAAI-21)*. AAAI.

Yue, L., Chen, W., Li, X., Zuo, W., & Yin, M. (2019). A survey of sentiment analysis in social media. *Knowledge and Information Systems*, *60*(2), 617–663. doi:10.100710115-018-1236-4

Section 2
Opinion Mining and Literary Studies

Chapter 7
What Is Love?
Text Analytics on Romance Literature From the Perspective of Authors

Chuu Htet Naing
School of Computer Sciences, Universiti Sains Malaysia, Malaysia

Xian Zhao
(iD) https://orcid.org/0000-0003-1794-6233
School of Computer Sciences, Universiti Sains Malaysia, Malaysia

Keng Hoon Gan
School of Computer Sciences, Universiti Sains Malaysia, Malaysia

Nur-Hana Samsudin
School of Computer Sciences, Universiti Sains Malaysia, Malaysia

ABSTRACT

Descriptions of love can be found in a wide range of literature. The meaning of love that a reader grasps from reading a literary work is mostly the result of self-understanding and is very likely different from the one that the author tried to express. Therefore, it is interesting to explore what love is from the authors' perspective to help readers have a deeper understanding of the meaning of love written by the author. The goal of this study is to build a text analysis framework to identify common words or phrases describing love in romance literature. The proposed analysis is divided into three types, namely 1) text classification and sentiment analysis, 2) key phrase extraction, and 3) topic modeling. The evaluation is performed on 10 romance books. The results of each analysis method are measured using performance metrics as well as presented using visuals like word cloud and histogram.

DOI: 10.4018/978-1-7998-9594-7.ch007

INTRODUCTION

The ability to perceive love is one of the important capabilities of everyone in the real world, and it may directly affect a person in establishing connections with others, and it will also have a decisive impact on the feelings of themselves and others. The characters in literary works often come from real life, and the text reflects the love in real society. It may express love directly, or it may be implicit words or phrases to express love. The latter requires us to discover and understand its deeper meaning. Therefore, it is very important to start from the source, that is, to analyze what is love from the authors' perspective, and to convey information about love to readers. In creative writing domain, a story always requires some clues to connect the past, present, and future plot. The plot development of the works and the character setting are based on the narrative thread and serve the main thread. The focus of love is one of the most important storylines because a lot of content in literary works portray characters where feelings and emotions evolved that lead to the embodiment of love. This is especially crucial in romantic literatures, where the focuses are more on describing the relationship and love between two people. Therefore, to understand love from literature, the most basic thing is to know which words describe love, which positively affect readers and authors. According to Ebaid (2018), adjectives are defined as an indispensable part of language structure, because it is the main component of describing, identifying and modifying nouns, so adjectives are widely used to express love. Nouns are equally important, in which is it usually used in endearment to create a sense of closeness between two people. Thus, one part in this research is to describe what embody love from this perspective.

In the field of natural language processing, sentiment analysis has emerged for mining public opinion, analyzing, and extracting knowledge from the subjective information published on the Internet, while machine learning (ML) algorithms are very common for analyzing sentiment. Up to now, sentiment analysis has been a hot research field in data mining and natural language processing (NLP) recently and has been used to do the process of automatically identifying whether user-generated text expresses a positive, negative, or neutral view of an object. To analyze these sentiments, various machine learning (ML) algorithms, and natural language processing-based approaches have been used in the past. Hussain & Cambria (2018) explored a novel semi-supervised learning model based on the combined use of random projection scaling as part of a vector space model, and support vector machines to perform reasoning on a knowledge base. Perikos et al. (2021) introduced Hidden Markov Models (HMMs) for sentiment analysis, in which HMMs has the ability to produce different probability to identify the most possible identification of the sentiment. They are also able to provide visualization on every probability of the decisions made, resulting the ability to show the way the sentiments change from the start to the end of the sentence.

Sentiment classification can be divided into three levels. The first is *aspect* or *feature* level, which identifies the sentiment from the datasets collected from the products features or reviews. The second is *sentence* level which classifies each sentence first as subjective or objective and identifies the class of positive, negative, or neutral. The third is *document* level which use the whole document as dataset or analysis object to classify the document sentiment into positive or negative class (Yousefpour et al., 2014). There are many approaches for sentiment analysis using Machine Learning (ML) approaches based on variety of machine learning algorithms to classify data. Lexicon based approach determines the sentiment polarity by using a dictionary which contains positive and negative words. Hybrid approaches combine the ML and lexicon approach to classify text Agarwal & Mittal, (2017). But in other research, the sentiment analysis combines text classification for build many classifiers to complete the analysis.

Deep learning-based methods are becoming very popular due to their high performance in recent times (Yadav & Vishwakarma, 2020). Deep neural network (DNN) models are being applied to sentiment analysis tasks and get some promising results, long short-term memory (LSTM) models and its variants such as gated recurrent unit (GRU), and (Basiri et al., 2021) propose an attention-based bidirectional CNN-RNN deep model for sentiment analysis. Related analysis techniques are developing rapidly and is constantly being applied to sentiment analysis.

This research focuses on an analysis and categorization on words based on ten romantic literatures to identify what constitute love from the perspective of the authors. Sentiment analysis techniques are applied to the textual content, in which text analysis process is conducted on the content of the creative writing to identify and extract subjective information in materials by using natural language processing, text mining, and computational linguistics. Realizing love is a more than just an analysis and probability of words, this research is focusing on the lexical representation of words that embody love.

In this chapter, we developed an analytics system built based on different solutions. The remaining part of this research is organized as follows: Section 2 will explain the research questions and objectives. Section 3 describes related works and the current trend in similar domain, Section 4 presents the methodology used, including i. text classification and sentiment analysis, ii. key phrase extraction, iii. topic modeling. In Section 5, the experiment and evaluation will be discussed, and Section 6 will conclude this chapter.

Research Questions and Objectives

In this research, the top 10 romantic literary works by O'Sullivan (2020) is selected for analysis, to explore the following questions:

1. Can the expression of loves from literary work be identified using different text analysis approaches, such as sentiment analysis, information extraction and topic modeling?
2. Can the text analysis approaches from 1) produce meaningful words and visualization to aid in better analytics outcome on what is associated with love?

Therefore, the objectives of this research are as follows:

1. Apply text classification and sentiment analysis to discover different emotions of the literature.
2. Apply one of the information extraction techniques called Key Phrase Extraction (KPE) to extract the main phrases from the books.
3. Use topic modeling to understand the underlying topics of the romantic literatures.
4. Use external representation to visualize different plots to understand the meaning of love from the indispensable part of language structure of romantic literatures.

BACKGROUND

Related Works on Text Classification and Sentiment Analysis

Text classification and sentiment analysis is a usual machine learning problem and is used in a lot of tasks like product predictions, music recommendations, etc. (Medhat et al., 2014). Sentiment analysis is also named opinion mining; it is a natural language processing technology that processes textual data likes opinions, attitudes, sentiments, emotions, and appraisals of people concerning products, movies, music, events, issues, topics and related features. There are different names for this area of study, such as: sentiment mining, review mining, text mining, opinion extraction, affect analysis, and emotion analysis (Yousefpour et al., 2014). Figure 1 shows a wide range of emotions that can be expressed by human.

Moreover, any supervised classification approach, including text classification, can be further divided into three types based on the number of categories involved, which are binary, multiclass, and multilabel classification respectively (Liu & Chen, 2015). If it has two class labels, it is called binary classification. If a problem of classifying instances into three or more classes, it's referred to as multiclass classification (Liu & Chen, 2015). It is applied widely in recent years, so a large amount of research has already been conducted in the field of sentiment analysis through a single classifier, however, also used multi- classifiers and their combinations (known as classifier ensemble in sentiment analysis) in some works. In this chapter, we will use and implement a wide range of classifiers.

Figure 1. Depiction of different emotions and feelings in human
(Source: Perikos et al., 2021), https://peacelearner.org/courses/edu-596-f2012/learning-modules/welcome-to-peace-pedagogy/1-5/)

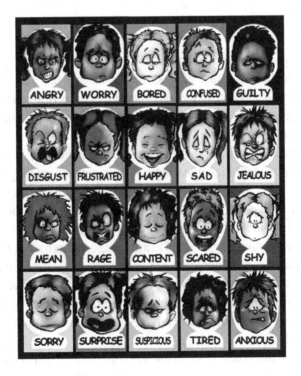

Scikit-Learn

Scikit-learn, also known as scikits.learn or sklearn, is a free and open-source machine learning library for the Python programming language. It is mainly written in Python and widely uses numpy for high-performance linear algebra and array operations. In addition, part of core algorithms are written in Cython for improving its performance. Scikit-learn can integrate well with many other Python libraries, such as matplotlib and plotly used for plotting, numpy used for array vectorization, pandas dataframes, scipy, and so on (Pedregosa et al., 2011).

Parametric Models

Parametric model is a learning model that use limited number of parameters to summarizes data and is independent of the number of training instances. And it won't change its demand about parameters it needs whether how much data you throw into a parametric model (Russell & Norvig, 2020). Logistic regression, despite the name, is a linear model for classification tasks rather than regression tasks. Logistic regression is also named as maximum-entropy classification (MaxEnt), logit regression or the log-linear classifier in the literature. In this model, a logistic function is used to model the probability that describes the possible outcomes of a single experiment (Pedregosa et al., 2011). Linear Discriminant Analysis (LDA) was proposed by R. Fischer in 1936. The analysis can find a projection hyperplane which can minimize the interclass variance and maximize the distance between the projected means of the classes. LDA is similar to PCA, these two goals can be solved via way of solving an eigenvalue problem with the corresponding eigenvector. The hyperplane is a powerful classification method and can be used for dimensionality reduction and interpretation of the importance of the given features (Xanthopoulos et al., 2013).

Nonparametric Models

Nonparametric algorithms are forms of algorithms which do not create strict assumptions concerning the form of the mapping function. Because of this, they can freely learn any functional form from the training data. A nonparametric model can't be characterized by a finite set of parameters. They are sensible when we have a great deal of data and no prior knowledge, and when we don't wish to fret too much about selecting just the right features (Russell & Norvig, 2020).

K-Nearest Neighbors classifier is a common technique. Neighbors-based classification is a kind of instance-based learning or non-generalizing learning. It does not construct a general internal model, but merely stores instances of the training data. Classification is computed using the simple majority vote of the nearest neighbors of each point, and the query point is assigned to the data class which has the most representatives within the nearest neighbors of this point (Pedregosa et al., 2011).

Naive Bayes methods are a family of supervised learning algorithms based on applying Bayes' theorem with the "naive" independence assumption between every pair of features given the value of the class variable (Pedregosa et al., 2011). The Naive Bayes model is also called Bayesian classifier (Russell & Norvig, 2020). It calculates and predicts the probability of each class such as the probability that given each input value belongs to a particular class. Naïve Bayes classifier assumes that all features are all independent (Brownlee, 2017).

Classification and Regression Trees (CART) are a non-parametric supervised learning method used for classification and regression tasks (Pedregosa et al., 2011). They constructed a binary tree from the training data. For minimizing the cost function, it chooses the split points via evaluating each attribute and its value in the training data (Brownlee, 2017). A decision tree (also called classification tree) is a predictive model which is a map of possible outcomes from observations about an item to conclusions about its target value (Bener et al., 2015).

Support Vector Machines (SVMs) are a family of supervised learning methods used for classification, regression and outliers detection (Bird et al., 2015). They seek a line to best separates to two classes to make a binary classification problem. Those data instances closest to this line that best separates the classes are called support vectors and affect the placement of the line. SVM has been extended to multi-classes problems (Brownlee, 2017). In scikit-learn, it performs binary and multi-class classification on a dataset by using SVC, NuSVC and LinearSVC. And SVC and NuSVC are similar methods but can use some different parameters and have different mathematical formulations. On the other hand, LinearSVC is much faster implementation of Support Vector Classification than SVC for the case of a linear kernel, especially the training set is very large (scikit learn, 2011b).

Ensemble Algorithms

Ensemble algorithms are powerful and more advanced type of machine learning algorithms. These techniques combine predictions from multiple models to provide more accurate predictions (Brownlee, 2017). The ensemble methods can combine the predictions of several base estimators constructed using a given machine learning algorithm to improve the generalizability and robustness of a single estimator. In the different ensemble methods, voting classifier is to combine conceptually different machine learning classifiers and use soft vote, that is, the average predicted probabilities or majority vote, to predict the class labels. The classifier is useful for a set of equally well performing model which can balance their individual weaknesses (scikit learn, 2011a).

Facebook's AI Research (FAIR)

FAIR Lab creates the library, fastText, for learning of word embeddings and text classification. Researchers can use the model to create an unsupervised learning or supervised learning algorithm for getting vector representations for words. Facebook makes available pre-trained models for 294 languages (fastText, 2020; Sabin, 2017). It is a library for efficient learning of word representations and sentence classification (fastText, 2016), and it uses a neural network for word embedding (fastText, 2020; Sabin, 2017).

Related Works on Information Extraction

Information extraction (IE) is to automatically retrieve specific information related to a specific topic from one or more text bodies. Information extraction tools make it possible to extract information from text documents, databases, websites or multiple sources which are unstructured, and/or semi-structured, and machine-readable text (Grishman, 2015). It is a process of acquiring knowledge by skimming texts and finding the appearance of objects of a specific object and the relationship between objects (Russell & Norvig, 2020).

Key Phase Extraction (KPE)

Automatic key phrase extraction is a basic textual information processing task. It automatically extracts key phrases from a document and its goal is that these phrases can summarize its content. In other words, these extracted key phrases provide a summarization for that given document (Grishman, 2015). Keyword and phrase extraction, as the name indicates, is the IE task concerned with extracting important words or phrases that capture the gist of the text from a given text document. It's useful for several downstream NLP tasks, such as search/information retrieval, automatic document tagging, recommendation systems, text summarization, etc. (Liu & Chen, 2015).

Named Entity Recognition (NER)

NER refers to the IE task of identifying the entities in a document. Entities are typically names of persons, locations, and organizations, and other specialized strings, such as money expressions, dates, products, names/numbers of laws or articles, and so on. NER is an important step in the pipeline of several NLP applications involving information extraction.

Topic Modeling

Topic modeling is one of the most common applications of NLP in industrial use cases (Liu & Chen, 2015) and powerful techniques in text mining especially for data mining, latent data discovery, and discovering relationships among data and text documents (Jelodar et al., 2019). It can be considered as a methodology for presenting a large volume of data generated technology companies and presenting the hidden concepts, important feature or latent variables according to the application context. Various topic modeling algorithms are provided to find hidden semantics in document collection and cluster the themes as topics. The distributional model can be used to derive word meaning representation based on the analysis of statistics such as vector space, Latent semantic analysis, Probabilistic Latent Semantic Model and Latent Dirichlet Allocation (Kherwa & Bansal, 2020). Actually, the technique that's most commonly used is LDA (Medhat et al., 2014).

LDA

Latent Dirichlet allocation (LDA) is an unsupervised generative probabilistic model of a corpus. The documents are represented as random mixtures of semantic topics and each topic is characterized by a distribution over words. LDA is a popular topic modeling method, first proposed by David M Blei, A. Y. Ng and Jordan in 2003 (Blei et al., 2003). LDA represents topics by word probabilities. Usually getting a good idea about the topic can be through the words with the highest probabilities in each topic. LDA is a common practical topic modeling method. It assumes that each document can be represented as a probabilistic distribution of latent topics, and that topic distributions in all documents have a common Dirichlet prior. Latent topics in the LDA model are also represented as word probabilistic distributions which have a common Dirichlet prior as well (Jelodar et al., 2019).

LSA

Latent semantic analysis (LSA) is a special TM method, also called LSI. It uses a multi-step process to approximate a corpus' structure by identifying terms and mathematically modeling the context(s). Conceptually, similar to traditional Exploratory Factor Analysis (EFA) which reduces the corpus to a series of eigenvectors that can be compared, it can use the following steps. First, develop a document-term matrix (DTM) which comprises word counts per paragraph. The LSA uses a mathematical method called singular value decomposition (SVD) to reduce the number of rows of the matrix. Then it is approximating the relative similarity by comparing the angular association in the vector space between two words' eigenvectors through SVD. Like EFA, LSA uses a factor rotation of the resulting eigenvectors to create a nonoverlapping fit for the model (Valdez et al., 2018).

METHODOLOGY

Overview of the Proposed Solution

In this chapter, the analytics system is built based on four separate solutions as shown in Figure 2. As mentioned before, top ten romance books is acquired from the 25 listed romance books by O'Sullivan (2020). However, since the books are in their eBook format, an external library is used to generate the corpus. That library is called Apache Tika, a toolkit that can detect and extract metadata and text from more than a thousand different file types (such as PPT, XLS, and PDF) (Apachae Software Foundation, 2021). For pre-processing, the NLTK (Natural Language Toolkit) is used, which also includes contain TweetTokenier, a twitter-aware tokenizer to tokenize and pre-process the external twitter dataset. Finally, the data is fed to separate analytics system in order to observe the perspective of the authors on words that embody love. Our experiment was implemented on "virtual machine" from google cloud. The virtual machine has 8vCPU, 64GB of RAM, 128GB SSD and 16Gbps network bandwidth.

Figure 2. Overview of the text analytics components

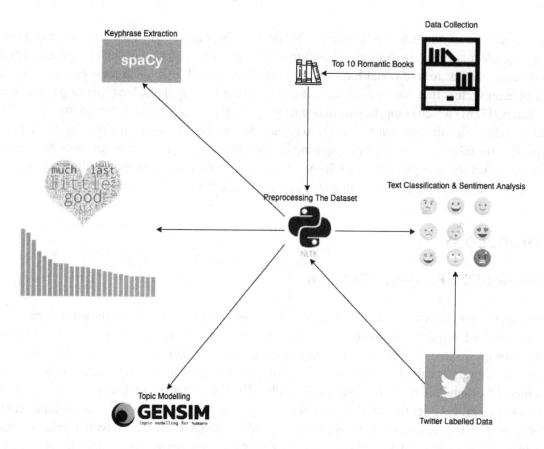

Text Classification and Sentiment Analysis

For text classification and sentiment analysis system, a machine learning system is implemented with the help of two popular libraries called scikit-learn (Pedregosa et al., 2011) and fastText (fastText, 2016). In scikit-learn, there is a wide range of algorithms to implement the classification system. Therefore, the algorithms are separated into linear models and non-linear models' categories, and the best algorithm from each category is obtained. As a result, it is found that linear regression and support vector classifier algorithms respectively from linear and non-linear models performed better than their peers. Furthermore, a technique called hyperparameter is applied to optimize both algorithms to be tuned for this research objectives. Finally, both classifiers are combined with the help of ensemble machine learning algorithm called Voting Classifier (scikit learn, 2011a). Additionally the fastText library is used from Facebook's AI Research (FAIR) Lab, which is easy to be used, and it uses neural network for word embedding (fastText, 2020; Sabin, 2017).

Figure 3. Three sub analytics components, (i) Text Classification and Sentiment Analysis (left), (ii) Key Phrase Extraction (middle) and (iii) Topic Modelling (right)

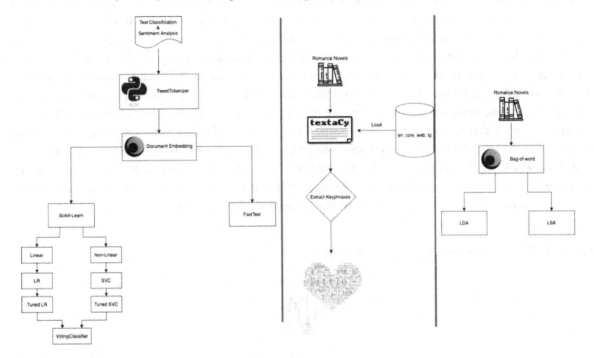

Key Phrase Extraction

The implementation on the Key Phrase Extraction (KPE) system is quite straightforward when compared with text classification and sentiment analytics system. The textacy library is used to build on the high-performance spaCy library (Burton, 2020). In textacy, the en_core_web_lg, an English multi-task CNN trained on OntoNotes is used, with GloVe vectors trained on Common Crawl, as the language's model data (spaCy, 2020). Finally, the top 500 key phrases are extracted and visualized with the word cloud and frequency histogram for further analysis.

Topic Modelling

Like the implementation of KPE system, topic modeling system is also used to compare to the text classification system. For extracting features from text, the bag-of-word in word embedding is used which is available as doc2bow function from the gensim library (Kite, 2018). For implementation, we two popular algorithms in topic modeling are used which are called Latent Dirichlet Allocation and Latent Semantic Analysis. Finally, the topic names related to the top ten topics generated from our LDA and LSA models are annotated and formulated.

Text Pre Processing

In text pre-processing the texts preparation need to be done prior to the analysis of components mentioned in Figure 3. Firstly, a series of text preprocessing (see Figure 4) is performed to clean the dataset used in order to obtain a better analysis result. Since this research is working on novels, it is important to note that several fictional character names created by the authors and the names usage are repeated in the whole novels. Moreover, there are huge number of stop words in all the novels since they are important to decorate the text for authors. However, in term of analysis, the occurrences can distort the results since lexically; the words do not carry meaning to conclude the analysis. Therefore, it is necessary to remove the names using NER system from spacy library (spaCy, 2018) and removing stop words with the using NLTK library (NLTK, 2021). Furthermore, NLTK library is used to perform stemming and lemmatization. In stemming, the affixes are removed and reduced a word to its base form. Thus, all variants of a word can be represented by the same form. For example, "cat" and "cats" are both reduced to "cat". On the other hand, lemmatization is the process of mapping all the different forms of a word to its base word, or lemma (Vajjala et al., 2020) where the words are converted into its base lemma. For example, bad, worse, worst are all forms of the word bad, therefore bad is the lemma of all these words. Finally, the word cloud and frequency histogram are used for further analysis.

Figure 4. Text pre-processing for literature texts

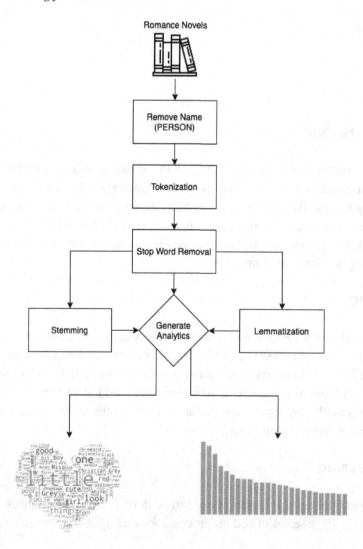

EXPERIMENT AND EVALUATION

Evaluation on Text Classification and Sentiment Analysis

For the text classification and sentiment analysis, experiments on linear models and non-linear models are conducted. Based on their performances on default hyperparameter, a comparison on Logistic Regression model and Linear Discriminant Analysis model are observed. Similarly, the K-Nearest Neighbors classifier model, Decision Tree Classifier model, Gaussian Naïve Bays model and Support Classifier model are compared from the non-linear models. According to two groups, the best model is chosen from each category where the Logistics Regression model from linear model and Support Vector Classifier model from non-linear model shown to have the highest accuracy as shown in Figure 5. Moreover, we performed the hyperparameter optimization on our selected Logistics Regression Model and Support Vector Classifier Model and the model accuracy is compared again with baseline models as shown in Figure 6. Finally, we use the optimized Logistics Regression model and Support Vector Classifier model to build the voting classifier ensemble model. The performance of the voting classifier model is shown in Figure 7.

However, in essence, accuracy is not a complete and holistic measure to evaluate a model on its classification performance. Specifically, when dealing with multiclass data where one class is inherently common than the other. In this case most of the data comes from the neutral class whereas the other classes like anger are significantly under- represented. This fact accounts for the overall low accuracy of the results. When dealing with such data, more attention should be paid on precision and recall rather than on accuracy alone. As shown in Table 1 we the classification report for voting ensemble model is used to explore the performance where the weighted average of precision and recall are 27% and 30% respectively. On the other hand, the experiment on the Facebook fastText library gives better results in terms of both precision and recall. According to Table 2 both P@1 and R@1 are reported to achieve 33%.

Figure 5. Performance comparison on linear and non-linear models

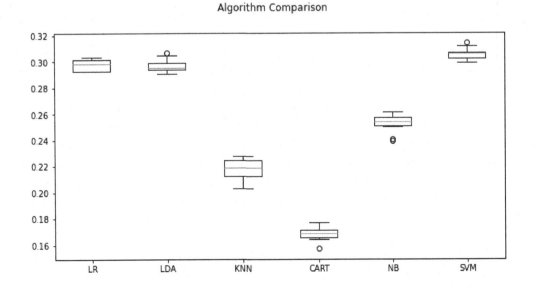

Figure 6. Performance comparison on default models and hyperparameter optimization

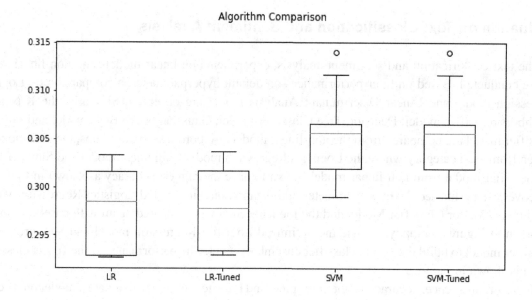

Figure 7. Accuracy evaluation on ensemble machine learning model

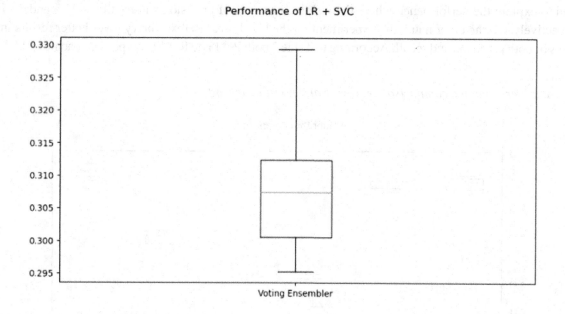

Table 2. Precision and recall using Facebook FastText

Number of Test Samples	Precision	Recall
Test Samples: 800	Precision@1: 33.0625	Recall@1: 33.0625
Test Samples: 800	Precision@2: 26.6375	Recall@2: 53.2750
Test Samples: 800	Precision@3: 22.1833	Recall@3: 66.5500
Test Samples: 800	Precision@4: 18.4344	Recall@4: 73.7375
Test Samples: 800	Precision@5: 15.8050	Recall@5: 79.0250

Evaluation on Topic Modeling System

For the evaluation of the topic modelling, the coherence score is used to determine the performance. The concept of topic coherence combines a number of measures into a framework to evaluate the coherence between topics inferred by a model. It measures score a single topic by measuring the degree of semantic similarity between high scoring words in the topic. Moreover, we used the number of topics to optimize the performance of our models. As shown in Figure 8, our LDA model has higher performance on less topics where we can see gradually decreasing performance with the higher number of topics. In contrast, LSI performance result from Figure 9 shows the stable performance across any number of topics less than 50.

Figure 8. Coherence score of the LDA model

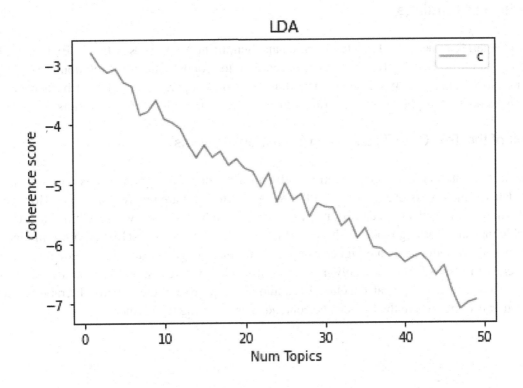

Figure 9. Coherence score of the LSI model

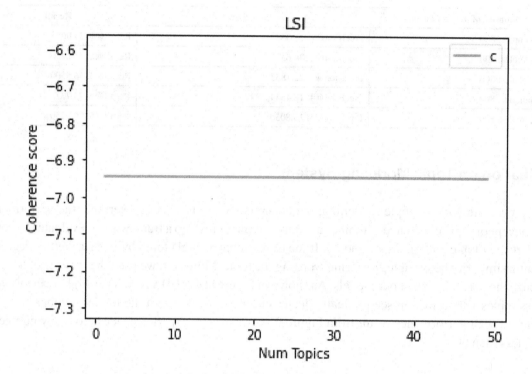

Results and Findings

In this chapter, four methods: Text classification and Sentiment Analysis, Key Phrase Extraction, Topic Modeling and Raw Text Analytics were used according to proposed analytics solution. The generated output is Histogram and/or WordCloud illustration. The words or phrases would describe "what is love". Sections below will display output of different methods and discussions of these results.

Result of the Text Classification and Sentiment Analysis

As the implementation of text classification and sentiment analysis component was done on an imbalanced dataset, the results of the model on the romance literature are not very accurate. However, the overall analysis of results is said to be able to perform from both models where VotingClassifier with ensemble machine learning model is shown in Figure 10 and Facebook fastText is shown in Figure 11. The 'neutral' on both results are higher where the ensemble is giving the highest count of 'neutral'. However, both results have reasonably high on 'worry' class where fastText has the highest count on 'worry' class. Therefore, we can conclude the authors' perspective of the romance literature on love is based on 'worrying' where the love can be concluded as worrying the partner.

Figure 10. Result of the ensemble machine learning model

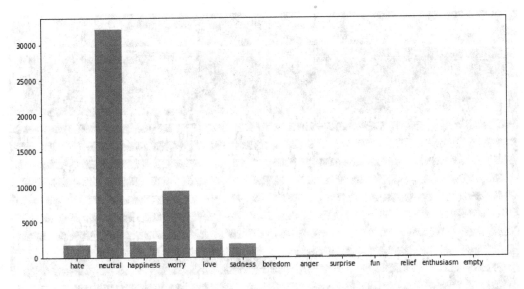

Figure 11. Result of the FastText model

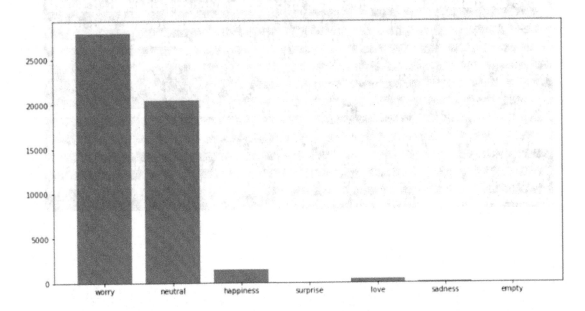

We also provide some examples of the classified sentences. The way the apache tika decodes the epub and pdf format books into raw text file is paragraph by paragraph by detecting the newline character in the original book. For example, the original text in epub format book from figure 12 has four new lines where the generated text file from Figure 13 also has four lines (line 266, line 268, line 270 and line 272) where each line represents each paragraph from original epub text.

Figure 12. Original text from epub format from Fifty Shades Trilogy novel

CHAPTER ONE

I scowl with frustration at myself in the mirror. Damn my hair—it just won't behave, and damn Katherine Kavanagh for being ill and subjecting me to this ordeal. I should be studying for my final exams, which are next week, yet here I am trying to brush my hair into submission. *I must not sleep with it wet. I must not sleep with it wet.* Reciting this mantra several times, I attempt, once more, to bring it under control with the brush. I roll my eyes in exasperation and gaze at the pale, brown-haired girl with blue eyes too big for her face staring back at me, and give up. My only option is to restrain my wayward hair in a ponytail and hope that I look semi-presentable.

Kate is my roommate, and she has chosen today of all days to succumb to the flu. Therefore, she cannot attend the interview she'd arranged to do, with some mega-industrialist tycoon I've never heard of, for the student newspaper. So I have been volunteered. I have final exams to cram for and one essay to finish, and I'm supposed to be working this afternoon, but no—today I have to drive 165 miles to downtown Seattle in order to meet the enigmatic CEO of Grey Enterprises Holdings, Inc. As an exceptional entrepreneur and major benefactor of our university, his time is extraordinarily precious—much more precious than mine—but he has granted Kate an interview. A real coup, she tells me. Damn her extracurricular activities.

Kate is huddled on the couch in the living room.

"Ana, I'm sorry. It took me nine months to get this interview. It will take another six to reschedule, and we'll both have graduated by then. As the editor, I can't blow this off. Please," Kate begs me in her rasping, sore throat voice. How does she do it? Even ill she looks gamine and gorgeous, strawberry blond hair in place and green eyes bright, although now red rimmed and runny. I ignore my pang of unwelcome sympathy.

Figure 13. Converted into ".txt" text file with apache tika from Fifty Shades Trilogy novel

266   I scowl with frustration at myself in the mirror. Damn my hair—it just won't behave, and damn Katherine Kavanagh for being ill and subjecting me to this ordeal. I should be studying for my final exams, which are next week, yet here I am trying to brush my hair into submission. I must not sleep with it wet. I must not sleep with it wet. Reciting this mantra several times, I attempt, once more, to bring it under control with the brush. I roll my eyes in exasperation and gaze at the pale, brown-haired girl with blue eyes too big for her face staring back at me, and give up. My only option is to restrain my wayward hair in a ponytail and hope that I look semi-presentable.

267

268   Kate is my roommate, and she has chosen today of all days to succumb to the flu. Therefore, she cannot attend the interview she'd arranged to do, with some mega-industrialist tycoon I've never heard of, for the student newspaper. So I have been volunteered. I have final exams to cram for and one essay to finish, and I'm supposed to be working this afternoon, but no—today I have to drive 165 miles to downtown Seattle in order to meet the enigmatic CEO of Grey Enterprises Holdings, Inc. As an exceptional entrepreneur and major benefactor of our university, his time is extraordinarily precious—much more precious than mine—but he has granted Kate an interview. A real coup, she tells me. Damn her extracurricular activities.

269

270   Kate is huddled on the couch in the living room.

271

272   "Ana, I'm sorry. It took me nine months to get this interview. It will take another six to reschedule, and we'll both have graduated by then. As the editor, I can't blow this off. Please," Kate begs me in her rasping, sore throat voice. How does she do it? Even ill she looks gamine and gorgeous, strawberry blond hair in place and green eyes bright, although now red rimmed and runny. I ignore my pang of unwelcome sympathy.

Figure 14. Converted into python array from the raw text of Fifty Shades Trilogy novel

```
[107]: combined_raw_books[:4]

[107]: ['I scowl with frustration at myself in the mirror. Damn my hair—it just won't behave, and damn Katherine
        Kavanagh for being ill and subjecting me to this ordeal. I should be studying for my final exams, which a
        re next week, yet here I am trying to brush my hair into submission. I must not sleep with it wet. I must
        not sleep with it wet. Reciting this mantra several times, I attempt, once more, to bring it under contro
        l with the brush. I roll my eyes in exasperation and gaze at the pale, brown-haired girl with blue eyes t
        oo big for her face staring back at me, and give up. My only option is to restrain my wayward hair in a p
        onytail and hope that I look semi-presentable.',
        'Kate is my roommate, and she has chosen today of all days to succumb to the flu. Therefore, she cannot
        attend the interview she'd arranged to do, with some mega-industrialist tycoon I've never heard of, for t
        he student newspaper. So I have been volunteered. I have final exams to cram for and one essay to finish,
        and I'm supposed to be working this afternoon, but no—today I have to drive 165 miles to downtown Seattle
        in order to meet the enigmatic CEO of Grey Enterprises Holdings, Inc. As an exceptional entrepreneur and
        major benefactor of our university, his time is extraordinarily precious—much more precious than mine—but
        he has granted Kate an interview. A real coup, she tells me. Damn her extracurricular activities.',
        'Kate is huddled on the couch in the living room.',
        '"Ana, I'm sorry. It took me nine months to get this interview. It will take another six to reschedule,
        and we'll both have graduated by then. As the editor, I can't blow this off. Please," Kate begs me in her
        rasping, sore throat voice. How does she do it? Even ill she looks gamine and gorgeous, strawberry blond
        hair in place and green eyes bright, although now red rimmed and runny. I ignore my pang of unwelcome sym
        pathy.']
```

In Figure 14, the raw text file is read line by line and converted into the python array. The python array will be used as a test data when predicting the classification of sentiment. So, the machine learning system will perform the sentiment analysis for each line of the python input array. The example results of classified four paragraphs are shown in the Figure 15.

Figure 15. The example results of sentiment analysis

```
[107]: combined_raw_books[:4]

[107]: ['I scowl with frustration at myself in the mirror. Damn my hair—it just won't behave, and damn Katherine
       Kavanagh for being ill and subjecting me to this ordeal. I should be studying for my final exams, which a
       re next week, yet here I am trying to brush my hair into submission. I must not sleep with it wet. I must
       not sleep with it wet. Reciting this mantra several times, I attempt, once more, to bring it under contro
       l with the brush. I roll my eyes in exasperation and gaze at the pale, brown-haired girl with blue eyes t
       oo big for her face staring back at me, and give up. My only option is to restrain my wayward hair in a p
       onytail and hope that I look semi-presentable.',
        'Kate is my roommate, and she has chosen today of all days to succumb to the flu. Therefore, she cannot
       attend the interview she'd arranged to do, with some mega-industrialist tycoon I've never heard of, for t
       he student newspaper. So I have been volunteered. I have final exams to cram for and one essay to finish,
       and I'm supposed to be working this afternoon, but no—today I have to drive 165 miles to downtown Seattle
       in order to meet the enigmatic CEO of Grey Enterprises Holdings, Inc. As an exceptional entrepreneur and
       major benefactor of our university, his time is extraordinarily precious—much more precious than mine—but
       he has granted Kate an interview. A real coup, she tells me. Damn her extracurricular activities.',
        'Kate is huddled on the couch in the living room.',
        '"Ana, I'm sorry. It took me nine months to get this interview. It will take another six to reschedule,
       and we'll both have graduated by then. As the editor, I can't blow this off. Please," Kate begs me in her
       rasping, sore throat voice. How does she do it? Even ill she looks gamine and gorgeous, strawberry blond
       hair in place and green eyes bright, although now red rimmed and runny. I ignore my pang of unwelcome sym
       pathy.']

[108]: my_prediction[0][:4]

[108]: [['__class__worry'],
        ['__class__worry'],
        ['__class__neutral'],
        ['__class__worry']]
```

Result of the Key Phrase Extraction System

The generated Word Cloud (Figure 16) and Histogram (Figure 17) contains more information than expected. As shown in Figure 16, the top words that represent the key phrases "Love" are 'good', 'cute', 'red', 'smile' 'miss'. This may be the relevant things that might associate with "Love", where the adjective 'good' is usually used for people or thing that one likes, 'cute' is used to describe the girls who are pleasant and very easy to be liked, 'red', the color of blood and fire, connected with meanings of love, passion, romance, sexuality, anger, danger and so on. Moreover, love is associated with 'red' alongside other emotions because love itself is also related to these emotions. Interestingly, the adjective word 'little' is showing as most frequent word and the occurrence of 'little' in key phrases is around 400 times where others are around only less than 20 times which can be clearly seen in Figure 17. Therefore, an analysis is performed on 'little' word with more detail information.

Figure 16. WordCloud of key phrase extraction result

Figure 17. Frequency histogram of key phrase extraction result

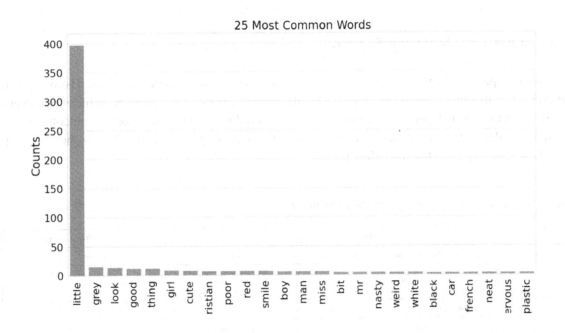

In Figure 18, it shows the top 15 extracted key phrases. As previously explained, the unbalanced usage of 'little' key word from Figure 17 can also be seen detail in given Figure 18. From the given information, we can analyze more on the appearance of 'little' word. According to the WordNet, the little word has three different part of speech as 'Noun', 'Adjective' and 'Adverb' (WordNet, 2005). However, it can be concluded that every usage of 'little' word in here are used as adjective. For example, it is used as adjective in 'soft little smile' and 'good little girl'. At the same time, the romantic usage of little and how it is used to describe love can be seen. Therefore, it is also possible to conclude the frequent occurrence of 'little' in key phrases is very meaningful and how the authors shape and portray the romance with the word 'little'.

Figure 18. Screenshot of key phrase extraction result

```
1. have
2. on
3. Carrick Grey Elliot Grey Christian Grey Dr. Grace Trevelyan Anastasia Steele Mia Grey Newspaper
4. Carrick Grey Dr. Grace Trevelyan Christian Grey Elliot Grey Mia Grey
5. little one
6. little small thing
7. cute little half smile
8. good little girl
9. soft little smile
10. little smile line
11. since,-a good little child
12. little thing cancer kid
13. like man
14. hard little thing
15. like calm date
```

Result of the Topic Modeling System

As a result of topic modelling, the following highest-ranking keywords from the LDA model is concluded. However, topic modelling needs the manual identification of the topic as appended at the end of every sentence with the square bracket, as shown in Table 3. According to the topic modelling outcome, it can be concluded that love is about marriage, body contact and meeting lover family. Below shows the top ten highest score topics as the modelling result.

Table 3. Highest-ranking topics from the LDA model

No.	Highest-ranking topics	Topic Annotation
1	henry never knew people house little every thought said elizabeth wedding good way time going many see know old say	[get married]
2	said know tell get drew say want go think time going wanted something right anything got sure need well long	[want something right]
3	door eyes turned back room white hand open take reached look black moved red tried front says blue face long	[scary]
4	head back hand hands hair bed arms face walked eyes arm clare side seemed put chest feel shoulder behind stopped	[body contact]
5	looked went love dad kitchen sorry eat laugh please little started says kept wrong something coffee came make took really	[dinner with lover dad]
6	felt look looking seen stood sitting face late room desk bed morning ever man person minutes window thanks looks ten	[accompany]
7	saw time without since school jane guess fine smiled opened friends beer either shall left friend year dinner future room	[met an old friend]
8	kissed mouth already body kiss exactly back true along dead fingers elevator mark want cup skin run lips hand birthday	[kiss in elevator]
9	pulled got miss may well tiny date girl found present come matter dress kids made baby kind olivia years point	[kid]
10	see told father real sister asked says called silence probably meant work happy tired family gotten wait laughing weeks answered	[approve from family]

Result of the Raw Text Analysis (Pre-Processing)

As a result of text analysis, Word Cloud and Histogram used to represent the result. Figure 19 shows the Word Cloud of Noun and the Adjective before lemmatization, and the followed Figure 20 and Figure 21 are the frequency histogram of Noun and Adjective words, respectively.

In romance literature, many descriptions about figures can be found, as shown in Figure 19 (left), including appearance, like 'hand', 'eye', 'head', 'face', and living environment, like 'room', 'house' and so on. Similarly, adjective words are also an important part of description of Love, such as 'good', 'great', 'soft', 'beautiful', etc., shown in the same figure (right). Therefore, it can be concluded that the authors' perspective on love are based on figures, and they mostly decorate it with adjectives such as little and good.

Figure 19. WordCloud of noun (left) and adjective (right)

Figure 20. Frequency histogram of noun words

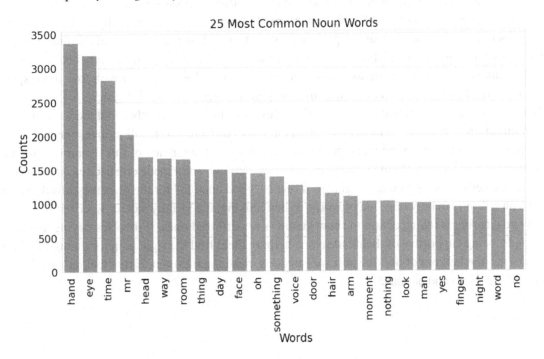

Figure 21. Frequency histogram of adjective words

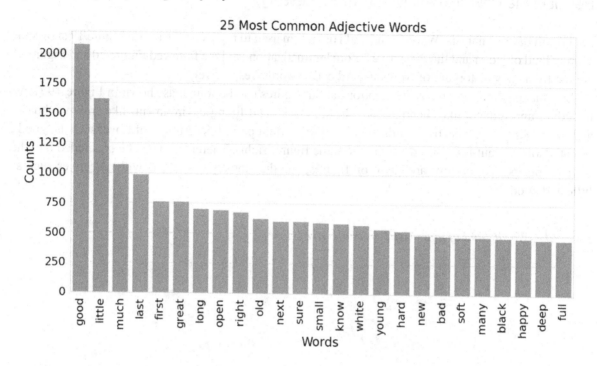

CONCLUSION

As a conclusion, this work has developed and applied the proposed framework to romance literatures to find what is love from the perspective of authors. From the results of extracted key words or phrases and topic modeling, we could conclude that the love is the content about marriage, body contact, meeting lover family, and detail information such as description of lovers' appearance: eye, hand, face, hair, cute, living surroundings: life, room, bed. This key information will make readers easily think of scenes and feelings about love. It is better that the proposed system should output more words or phrases closely related to love so thus reader can directly experience the scene or feelings of love from the text. Since the analysis results contain some commonly used words and cannot be associated with love in no specific situation, more classifiers are added to improve the performance of the entire system.

The classification system that has been proposed express the love is mostly about the worrying. It has the several different reasons, some healthy, others less so. At the time one fall in love, one worry about the loved ones' well-being. When it comes to love and worry, another side of this dynamic is worrying about oneself. The worries about own feelings and own actions, often made one become self-conscious and unsure whether one is "doing it right" or if one is "good enough" for the ones they loved. As far as a story can tell, it is mainly one side of worry. When looking at a healthy side of worry, it is caring. In other words, caring is taking action to show kindness to our loved ones. It involves paying attention to their needs, being supportive of their endeavors, helping them find the right path for themselves. When love "worries the hell out of us," the best we can do is make the most out of that feeling and channel it into healthy choices and actions.

REFERENCES

Agarwal, B., & Mittal, N. (2017). Machine Learning Approaches for Sentiment Analysis. *Artificial Intelligence: Concepts, Methodologies, Tools, and Applications, 3*, 1740–1756.

Apachae Software Foundation. (2021). *Apache Tika - A content analysis toolkit.* https://tika.apache.org/

Basiri, M. E., Nemati, S., Abdar, M., Cambria, E., & Acharya, U. R. (2021). ABCDM: An Attention-based Bidirectional CNN-RNN Deep Model for sentiment analysis. *Future Generation Computer Systems, 115*, 279–294. doi:10.1016/j.future.2020.08.005

Bener, A., Misirli, A. T., Caglayan, B., Kocaguneli, E., & Calikli, G. (2015). Lessons Learned from Software Analytics in Practice. In C. Bird, T. Menzies, & T. Zimmermann (Eds.), *The Art and Science of Analyzing Software Data* (pp. 453–489). Morgan Kaufmann. doi:10.1016/B978-0-12-411519-4.00016-1

Bird, C., Menzies, T., & Zimmermann, T. (2015). The Art and Science of Analyzing Software Data. In C. Bird, T. Menzies, & T. Zimmermann (Eds.), *The Art and Science of Analyzing Software Data.* Morgan Kaufmann. doi:10.1016/B978-0-12-411519-4.00001-X

Blei, D. M., Ng, A. Y., & Jordan, M. I. (2003). Latent dirichlet allocation. *Journal of Machine Learning Research, 3*, 993–1022.

Brownlee, J. (2017). *Machine Learning Mastery with Python: Understand Your Data, Create Accurate Models and Work Projects End-To-End.* Jason Brownlee.

Burton, D. (2020). *textacy: NLP, before and after spaCy.* https://github.com/Joiike/textacy

Ebaid, H. A. (2018). Adjectives as Persuasive Tools: The Case of Product Naming. *Open Journal of Modern Linguistics, 8*(6), 262–293. doi:10.4236/ojml.2018.86022

fastText. (2016). *What is fastText?* https://fasttext.cc/docs/en/support.html

fastText. (2020). *Wiki word vectors.* https://fasttext.cc/docs/en/pretrained-vectors.html

Grishman, R. (2015). Information Extraction. *IEEE Intelligent Systems, 30*(5), 8–15.

Hussain, A., & Cambria, E. (2018). Semi-supervised learning for big social data analysis. *Neurocomputing, 275*, 1662–1673.

Jelodar, H., Wang, Y., Yuan, C., Feng, X., Jiang, X., Li, Y., & Zhao, L. (2019). Latent Dirichlet allocation (LDA) and topic modeling: Models, applications, a survey. *Multimedia Tools and Applications, 78*(11), 15169–15211.

Kherwa, P., & Bansal, P. (2020). Topic modeling: A comprehensive review. *EAI Endorsed Transactions on Scalable Information Systems, 7*(24), 1–12.

Kite. (2018). *doc2bow.* https://www.kite.com/python/docs/gensim.corpora.Dictionary.doc2bow

Liu, S. M., & Chen, J. H. (2015). A multi-label classification based approach for sentiment classification. *Expert Systems with Applications, 42*(3), 1083–1093.

Medhat, W., Hassan, A., & Korashy, H. (2014). Sentiment analysis algorithms and applications: A survey. *Ain Shams Engineering Journal*, *5*(4), 1093–1113.

NLTK. (2021). *Natural Language Toolkit.* https://www.nltk.org/

O'Sullivan, K. (2020). *25 Best Romance Novels to Make You Believe in Love Again.* https://www.the-pioneerwoman.com/news-entertainment/g32157911/best-romance-novels/

Pedregosa, F., Varoquaux, G., Gramfort, A., Michel, V., Thirion, B., Grisel, O., Blondel, M., Prettenhofer, P., Weiss, R., Dubourg, V., Vanderplas, J., Passos, A., Cournapeau, D., Brucher, M., Perrot, M., & Duchesnay, É. (2011). Scikit-learn: Machine Learning in Python. *Journal of Machine Learning Research*, *12*(85), 2825–2830.

Perikos, I., Kardakis, S., & Hatzilygeroudis, I. (in press). Sentiment analysis using novel and interpretable architectures of Hidden Markov Models. *Knowledge-Based Systems.*

Russell, S., & Norvig, P. (2020). *Artificial Intelligence: A Modern Approach.* Pearson. http://aima.cs.berkeley.edu/global-index.html

Sabin, D. (2017). *Facebook Makes A.I. Program Available in 294 Languages.* https://www.inverse.com/article/31075-facebook-machine-learning-language-fasttext

scikit learn. (2011a). *Ensemble methods.* https://scikit-learn.org/stable/modules/ensemble.html#

scikit learn. (2011b). *Support Vector Machines.* https://scikit-learn.org/stable/modules/svm.html#svm

spaCy. (2018). *Industrial-strength Natural Language.* https://spacy.io/

spaCy. (2020). *Available trained pipelines for English.* https://spacy.io/models/en#en_core_web_lg

Vajjala, S., Gupta, A., Surana, H., & Majumder, B. (2020). *Practical Natural Language Processing: A Comprehensive Guide to Building Real-World NLP Systems.* O'Reilly Media Inc.

Valdez, D., Pickett, A. C., & Goodson, P. (2018). Topic modeling: Latent semantic analysis for the social sciences. *Social Science Quarterly*, *99*(5), 1665–1679.

WordNet. (2005). *WordNet Search - 3.1.* http://wordnetweb.princeton.edu/perl/webwn?s=cow

Xanthopoulos, P., Pardalos, P. M., & Trafalis, T. B. (2013). *Robust data mining.* Springer.

Yadav, A., & Vishwakarma, D. K. (2020). Sentiment analysis using deep learning architectures: A review. *Artificial Intelligence Review*, *53*(6), 4335–4385.

Yousefpour, A., Ibrahim, R., Hamed, H. N. A., & Hajmohammadi, M. S. (2014). A comparative study on sentiment analysis. *Advances in Environmental Biology*, *8*(13), 53–68.

Chapter 8
Text Analytics Model to Identify the Connection Between Theme and Sentiment in Literary Works:
A Case Study of Iraqi Life Writings

Nurul Najiha Jafery
Faculty of Electrical Engineering, Universiti Teknologi Mara, Malaysia

Pantea Keikhosrokiani
https://orcid.org/0000-0003-4705-2732
School of Computer Sciences, Universiti Sains Malaysia, Malaysia

Moussa Pourya Asl
https://orcid.org/0000-0002-8426-426X
School of Humanities, Universiti Sains Malaysia, Malaysia

ABSTRACT

The rapid advancements in data science techniques and approaches have influenced disciplines, such as literary studies, that are particularly engaged in qualitative text analysis. This chapter aims to apply natural language preprocessing (NLP) to identify the connection between theme and sentiment in a corpus of six life writings by or about Iraqi people. To do so, the study uses Latent Dirichlet Allocation (LDA) from topic modeling and the two models of Gensim and Mallet. It also implements TextBlob dictionary to calculate the polarity and subjectivity scores to measure the sentiment for detected themes. Nine topics are extracted from both models. The extracted themes point to the prevalence of traumatic events that the authors have personally endured. Gensim works better than Mallet as it has high coherence score and relevant terms. In sentiment analysis, most of the themes appeared as positive. The application of LDA using Gensim also revealed that the selected life writings are shaped and influenced by the authors' personal feelings. It is hoped that the analytical models can encourage future studies to improve existing qualitative methods in literary studies.

DOI: 10.4018/978-1-7998-9594-7.ch008

INTRODUCTION

Rapid sociopolitical developments in the twenty-first century, along with advances in computer science and digital technology, have pushed issues of space and spatiality to the forefront of literary and cultural studies (Tally, 2017). Recently, the study of Middle Eastern life literature has been marked by a shared concern in geographical issues of international migration as well as public opinion and sentiment (Asl, 2020). The area of life writing by/about Middle Eastern women has gone mostly unexplored: On the one hand, the existing body of critical readings do not match the enormous number of creative writings created by Middle Eastern women over the last three decades. On the other hand, existing critical analyses are frequently accused of being prejudiced and untruthful in their interpretations of the women's works as exclusively portraying a poor image of their birthplace and location. This issue stems from traditional manual data collection and analysis approaches that lack analytical precision and accuracy, particularly when it comes to analyzing representations of places and expressions of feelings in connection to underlying themes. Therefore, a computerized method that can objectively examine literary works in terms of themes, setting, and emotion is required. To this end, this chapter aims to identify the main topics or themes in a collection of life writings by or about Iraqi people using a computerized method called Latent Dirichlet Allocation (LDA). Specifically, we aim to explore the hidden patterns and dominant topics in the data and to understand the authors' interest through this modelling. Two different algorithms of Gensim and Mallet in LDA are used to find out the optimal number of topics. Both algorithms are tested and compared in order to see which one works better in extracting the topics. The polarity score of words in each topic is calculated too (Pollak, 2020). Furthermore, sentiment analysis using TextBlob is utilized to calculate the score for the word distribution in each topic. To analyze the sentiment, two measures of Polarity (talks about how positive or negative the opinion) and Subjectivity (talks about how subjective the opinion) are used.

This paper is structured as follow: Section 2 describes previous studies related to NLP, LDA and sentiment analysis. Sections 3 describes the methodology and implementation of LDA and sentiment analysis. In section 4, discussion revolves around the experimental results, as well as the evaluation of the model. The conclusion and future works are described in section 5.

RELATED WORK

Qualitative analysis approach is used to extract insights from a large volume of textual data specially in the field of literature and social sciences. Because of the large volume and complexity of the data, determining the patterns and trends from the text becomes more difficult. Due the vast volume of content, it is challenging for the readers to identify hidden opinions from the books. Finding relevant information, extracting it, reading it, summarizing it, organizing it into meaningful information, in a short amount of time without computerized method is problematic. Furthermore, human interpretation from the text might be biased and include controversy. Therefore, sentiment analysis and topic modelling attract researchers' attention to extract sentiment from the text and to find the hidden topics, themes, and opinion from the text automatically (Malik et al., 2021; Ying et al., 2021). There are several related works in the field of text analysis that used called Latent Dirichlet Allocation (LDA) LDA and sentiment analysis.

NLP is utilized for the present qualitative text analysis using LDA from topic modeling and TextBlob dictionary from sentiment analysis. TextBlob is a python library and offers a simple API to access methods and performs basic NLP task (Gujjar & HR, 2021). This algorithm is used in this chapter for identifying the theme, geography, and sentiment in a corpus of six life writings. The LDA algorithm performs well on long documents and large corpora. Guo and Wei (2021) proposed an improved LDA topic model based on partition (LDAP) for medium and long texts. LDAP not only preserves the benefits of the original LDA but also refines the modelled granularity from the document level to the semantic topic level, which is especially suitable for medium and long text topic modelling. LDA considers the co-occurrence pattern of a word in the document to be important.

Phang et al. (2021) proposed a new framework known as Malay-English social media text pre-processing for performing the steps of pre-processing the noisy mixed language (Malay-English language) of social media posts. Topic modelling is used to identify hidden topics within member-shared posts. Using Python, three different topic models are applied to the dataset with and without stemming: latent Dirichlet allocation (LDA) in GenSim, LDA in MALLET, and latent semantic analysis. In this chapter, we apply the LDA model using two different algorithms (Gensim and Mallet) which is an unsupervised text analytic for finding the group of words from a given document (Islam, 2019). Then, the word in each topic is calculated using TextBlob dictionary, and we reveal the relationship between the results that we gain through the discussion.

Natural Language Processing (NLP)

Natural Language Processing (NLP) is a set of theoretically motivated computer approaches for evaluating and modelling naturally occurring texts at one or more levels of linguistic analysis to achieve human-like language processing for a variety of activities and applications. It is also considered a discipline within Artificial Intelligence (AI) and concerned with giving computers the ability to understand text and spoken words in much the same way human beings can (Liddy, 2001; Chowdhury, 2003). AI based on natural language processing (NLP) techniques can have a practical application for understanding the semantic and emotional aspects, and for the retrieval of useful information from within the incel comments. (Jelodar & Frank, 2021).

Liu et al. (2021) take an input x, usually text, and predict an output y using a model $P(y|x;)$ in a standard supervised learning system for NLP. y could be a label, a text string, or any other type of output. They use a dataset with pairs of inputs and outputs to learn the parameters of this model, and then train a model to predict this conditional probability. They use two clichéd examples to demonstrate this. First, text classification predicts a label y from a fixed label set Y using an input text x. Sentiment analysis (Pang et al., 2002; Socher et al., 2013), for example, may take an input x="I adore this movie." and predict a label y = ++ from a label set Y = ++, +, -, —. Conditional text generation, on the other hand, accepts an input x and generates a new text y. Machine translation (Koehn, 2009) is one example, where the input is text in one language, such as "Hyva a huomenta." in Finnish, and the output is English y = "Good morning." in English.

Recently, a new fine-tuning methodology for equipping smaller language models (LMs) with few-shot capabilities has emerged: Using a cloze task to directly adapt the pre-trained LM as a predictor (Schick & Schutze, 2020; Gao et al., 2020; Liu et al., 2021) treat the downstream task as a (masked) language modeling problem. These prompts can be utilised in finetuning to convey additional task information to the classifier, particularly in the low-data regime. Notably, Scao and Rush (2021) discover that prompting can often compensate for hundreds of data points on average across multiple classification tasks. However, selecting appropriate prompts necessitates domain expertise, and handcrafting a high-performing prompt frequently necessitates impractically large validation sets (Perez et al., 2021). Recent research (Liu et al., 2021; Zhao et al., 2021) has found that the manual prompt format can be sub-optimal, resulting in accuracy ranging from random guess performance to state-of-the-art. As a result, previous approaches attempted to find discrete prompt tokens automatically. Obtaining an optimized prompt template and target label token for common classification tasks, on the other hand, is not trivial. Specific classification tasks, for example, relation extraction with the label of alternate name and country of birth, cannot be specified with a single label token in the vocabulary. A novel pluggable, extensible, and efficient approach named DifferentiAble pRompT (DART) (Zhang et al., 2021) can convert small language models into better few-shot learners without any prompt engineering.

Latent Dirichlet Allocation (LDA)

LDA has received a lot of attention in literary analyses for topic extraction (Blei et al., 2003; Malik et al., 2021; Ying et al., 2021, 2022). Topic modelling based on LDA method is a very popular technique for semantic exploration and inference of subjects. LDA considers each document as a collection of topics (k-topics) in a certain proportion and each topic as a collection of keywords in a certain proportion. We provide the optimal number of topics, and it rearranges the topics' distribution within topics to obtain a good composition of topic-keywords distribution. (Boussaadi et al., 2020; Islam, 2019).

LDA is ineffective on short texts without modification or adaptation due to a lack of co-occurrence patterns and a data sparsity problem. To overcome this problem, a novel method for ABSA and extracting product aspects from user reviews is introduced as SS-LDA which is a method based on LDA, the most well-known topic modelling algorithm (Ozyurt & Akcayol, 2021).

Researchers have started to apply machine learning to classify texts, because it can account for peculiarities of the texts under study. A machine learning algorithm is used to create a statistical model based on the trained data which is then used to create a statistical model to predict the sentiment of unlabeled texts. In state-of-the-art systems, machine learning algorithms generally outperform dictionaries, but their performance is highly dependent on the availability of sufficient training material. The use of dictionaries is more explicit and straightforward. When applied to a task or domain other than the one for which it was designed, however, all automated approaches will perform worse. This makes it difficult to predict which strategy is the most effective or how well it operates in advance. Ex-ante estimation is tough, which emphasizes the significance of verifying each approach for its specific objective. (Rosenthal et al., 2017; Van Atteveldt et al., 2021).

As Figure 1 shows, LDA is a model based on factorization of matrix. To learn a model, the process of inference of topics takes as input the matrix of co-occurrences (documents, term) which it decomposes into product of two matrixs of reduced dimesion: (topics, word) and (documents, topics) (Boussaadi et al., 2020).

Figure 1. Matrix decomposition for LDA

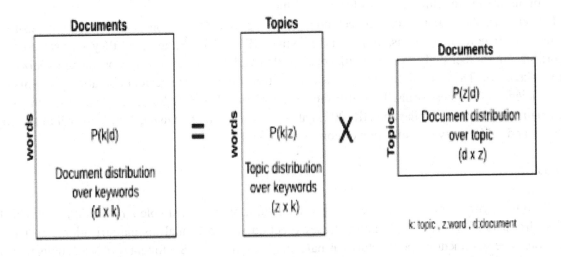

Gensim: Topic Modeling

Gensim is a python package based on numpy and scipy packages for unsupervised topic modeling and NLP using modern statistical machine learning. Gensim features are memory independent, meaning that there is no need for the whole training corpus to be on the RAM at any given time. Gensim introduces Simplistic implementations for tf-idf and Latent Semantic Analysis and Latent Dirichlet Allocation. It also allows writing simple similarity queries for documents in their semantic representation. Gensim is mainly based on the concepts of a corpus, vector, models, and sparse matrices (Akef et al., 2016; Boussaadi et al., 2020)

Mallet: Machine Learning for Language Toolkit

Mallet is a Java-based console application for language processing, document classification, clustering, topic modeling and other machine learning application. It uses Latent Allocation, Pachinko Allocation and Hierarchical Latent Dirichlet Allocation for topic modeling (Akef et al., 2016). There are several packages in Mallet topic modelling such as fast and highly scalable implementation of LDA through Gibbs Sampling, efficient method for document-topic hyperparameter optimization and tools for inferring topics for new documents given trained models (Boussaadi et al., 2020).

Sentiment Analysis (SA)

Sentiment analysis systems is closely related with NLP and is applied in almost every business and social domain, because opinions are central to almost all human activities and are key influencers of human behaviors (Liu, 2010; Ozyurt & Akcayol, 2021). Sentiment is often represented by two important properties of subjectivity and polarity. Subjectivity is the style of the sentence as either subjective or objective. Polarity is the general description of emotion as positive, negative, or neutral (Jagdale et al., 2016; Jockers, 2016). Sanders et al. (2021) use natural language processing, clustering, and sentiment analysis techniques to organise tweets about mask-wearing into high-level themes, then use automatic text summarization to relay narratives for each theme.

Pak and Paroubek (2010) proposed techniques for categorizing tweets on Twitter as neutral, positive, or negative. To collect the tweets, they used the Twitter API, and for the analyses, they used Nave-based algorithms. In another study, Praveen Gujjar et al. (2018) said that the purpose of a business organization is to make profit. The profitability analysis is done to throw light on the current operating performance and efficiency of business firms. They also showed how to use TextBlob for understanding sentiment of the email conversations. Gujjar and HR (2021) also proposed a method using TextBlob API to identify polarity and subjectivity for collection of comments or reviews.

TextBlob

TextBlob is a python library for processing textual data. It provides a simple API for diving into NLP task such as part-of-speech tagging, noun phrase extraction, sentiment analysis, classification, translation and more. The sentiment property returns as namedtuple of the form Sentiment (polarity, subjectivity). The polarity score is a float within the range [-1.0, 1.0]. the subjectivity is a float within the range [0.0, 1.0] where 0.0 is very objective and 1.0 is very subjective. (Loria, 2018). Sentiment analysis is a type of data mining that deals with opinion mining based on NLP, computational linguistics and text analysis. There are two approaches in sentiment analysis to classify the results as positive or negative which is lexicon-based approach and machine learning approach. Lexicon-based approach requires predefined lexicon while machine learning approach automatically classifies the text which requires training data. A lexicon is a stock of terms that belongs to a particular subject or language. This study uses lexicon-based approaches because we do not have a training data. Natural Language Toolkit (NLTK) is an open-source NLP platform for python, developed in conjunction with computational linguistics at university of Pennsylvania in 2001. It provides an easy-to-use interface over 50 corpora, lexicon resources such as SentiWordNet with a suit of text preprocessing libraries (Bonta & Janardhan, 2019; Bhadane, 2015).

MATERIALS AND METHODOLOGY

In this section, we explain the different stages of the modeling process as shown in Figure 2. We determine the number of topics, the tools and execution environment of two algorithms of LDA, and also how we calculate the sentiment score for each topic that is extracted.

Figure 2. Modeling process

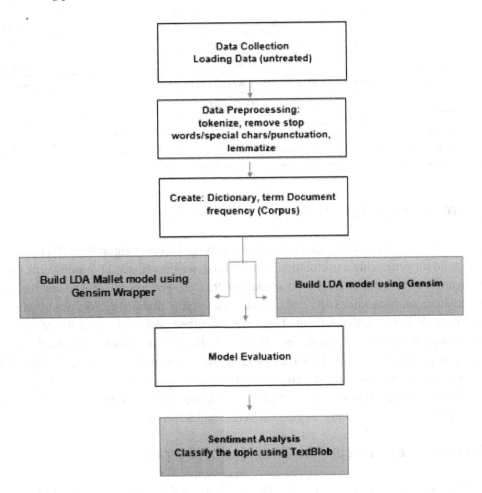

Data Collection and Data Extraction

The data used in this project is a corpus of 6 life writings written by diasporic women from Iraq in the present century. All the works provide non-fictional and auto-/biographical information about women's life in Iraq, an area that has attracted global attention after the US invasion of the country in 2003 (Asl, 2019, 2020). The data used here is unstructured data and the format of the data are in EPUB and PDF format. Table 1 provides information about the 6 books that are selected as dataset for this study. The information includes the title of the work, author's name, and date of publication. All the books are converted into text file format to load in the Python. We use Python libraries pandas for data manipulation.

Table 1. Dataset contains 6 books write by Iraq women writers

No	Title	Author, Year
1	The Beekeeper: Rescuing the Stolen Women of Iraq	(Mikhail, 2018)
2	Diary Of a Teenage Girl in Iraq	(Ross, 2009)
3	Betrayed: A Terrifying True Story of a Young Woman Dragged Back to Iraq	(Shears & Ali, 2009)
4	Rain Over Baghdad: A Novel of Iraq	(El Badry, 2014)
5	Mayada: Daughter of Iraq- Dutton Adult	(Sasson, 2003)
6	Between Two Worlds: Escape from Tyranny: Growing Up in The Shadow of Saddam	(Salbi & Becklund, 2006)

Data Pre-Processing (Topic Modeling)

Data pre-processing is one of the key components in many text mining algorithms (Islam, 2019). Data cleaning is crucial for generating a useful topic model. First, we downloaded the stopwords from NLTK (Natural Language Toolkit) and spacy's en model for text pre-processing. It is clear that the parsed full-text tweets have many newlines and extra spaces that is quite distracting. We used Python Regular Expression (re module) to eliminate them. Then, we tokenized each text into a list of words and removed punctuation and unnecessary characters. We used Python Gensim package for further processing. Gensim's simple_preprocess() is used for tokenization and removing punctuation. We used Gensim's Pharses model to build bigrams. Certain parts of English like conjunctions or the word are meaningless to a topic model that are called as stopwords are being removed from token list. We use spacy model for lemmatization to keep only the nouns, adjectives, verbs, and adverbs.

Create Dictionary and Document-Term Matrix (Corpus)

The result of the data cleaning stage is texts, a tokenized, stopped, and lemmatized list of words from a text. There are two main inputs to LDA topic model: the dictionary (id2word) and the document word matrix (Corpus) (Islam, 2019; Boussaadi et al., 2020).

Build LDA (Gensim and Mallet)

To build the LDA Gensim model, we must provide the number of subjects and adjust certain parameters to the dictionary and the corpus (Boussaadi et. al, 2020). For Mallet model, we must update the system environment variables and provide the path to Mallet file (Boussaadi et. al, 2020). Then, we build the model using Gensim Wrapper.

Optimal Number of Topics

LDA is an unsupervised learning, so the set of possible topics are unknown. To find out the optimal number of topics, we used compute_coherence_values() to train multiple LDA models and provide the model and their corresponding score (Prabhakaran, 2018).

Model Evaluation

After that, we selected the top three of the optimal number with the highest coherence score. Then, we built the model one by one. Afterwards, the coherence scores for Gensim and Mallet are compared once again. The coherence score and pyLDAvis's output are used to determine which model is the best.

Sentiment Analysis

We used the topics that have been extracted from the best LDA model for our further analysis. Based on the words in the topics, the dominant themes are detected, and the polarity score and subjectivity score is calculated using TextBlob. Several packages and codes have been implemented in Python to calculate polarity and subjectivity such as "Import NLTK", "From Textblob Import Textblob", "Text = Textblob("Text1")" and "Print (Format (Text1.Sentiment)). Polarity can take value between -1 to +1. Here, 0 indicates neutral, -1 indicates highly negative sentiment and +1 indicates highly positive sentiment. Subjectivity, on the other hand, has a value ranging from 0 to +1. In this case, 0 indicates that the statement is highly objective, while +1 indicates that it is highly subjective (Gujjar & HR, 2021).

RESULT AND DISCUSSION

Our experimental approach yields the following results.

Optimal Number of Topic and Coherence Score

To find out the optimal number of topic, we used compute_coherence_values() to train multiple LDA models and provide the model and their corresponding score (Prabhakaran, 2018). Figure 3 shows that the coherence score keeps increasing but is also fluctuating.

Figure 3. Graph of number of topic vs. coherence score

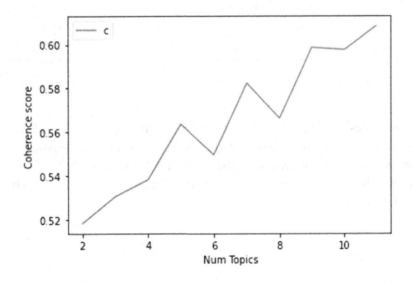

Table 2 shows more clear details with values of coherence score and number of topics. It is clear that when the number of topics is odd, the coherence increases, but when the number of topics is even the coherence score decreases with little values. The highest coherence score is 0.5986 when the number of topic equal to 9 and the lowest coherence score is 0.518 when the number of topics equals to 2.

Table 2. Number of topic vs. coherence score for train models

Number of Topics	2	3	4	5	6	7	8	9	10
Coherence Score	0.5182	0.5305	0.5382	0.5636	0.5496	**0.5823**	0.5662	**0.5986**	**0.5975**

For further analysis, we chose the top three with the highest coherence score which means the number of topics that equals to 7, 9 and 10. Then we built Gensim and Mallet model with three different number of topics (7,9,10), and we compared the results again. Table 3 shows the coherence score between Gensim and Mallet. Gensim and Mallet show the same results: the highest coherence score is the number of topics that equals to 9 with 0.6314 and 0.5914, respectively. The shortest time taken to build the Gensim and Mallet model is the number of topics that equal to 7 with 93.7093 and 61.7857, respectively. The lowest coherence score for Gensim and Mallet is when the number equals to 10 with 0.5944 and 61.7814, respectively. When comparing the results from table 2 (LDA train model) with table 3, we can see there is an increase in coherence score when the model is built separately. In Table 2, the number of topics equal to 7 have the lowest coherence score, whereas in Table 3, the lowest of coherence score is when the number of topics equal to 10.

Table 3. Coherence score and time taken of Gensim and Mallet model for selected number of topics

Number of Topics	Gensim	Mallet
7	Coherence Score: 0.6139 Time taken (seconds): 93.7093	Coherence Score: 0.5757 Time taken (seconds):61.7857
9	Coherence Score: **0.6314** Time taken (seconds):115.9256	Coherence Score: **0.5914** Time taken (seconds): 64.8648
10	Coherence Score: 0.5944 Time taken (seconds): 103.3286	Coherence Score: 0.5895 Time taken (seconds): 61.7814

Coherence scores assesses the quality of the topics by examining the degree of semantic similarity between each topic's top words. The higher the score, the better the model (Boussaadi et. al, 2020). According to coherence score, we can say that Gensim model is better than Mallet. Even though in some related studies Mallet gives a high coherence score than Gensim, Gensim works much better than Mallet for the dataset in the present study.

Visualization

This study used pyLDAvis, which is a web-based interactive visualization of topics as estimated by LDA. Gensim's pyLDAvis is the most used visualization tool to visualize the information contained in a topic model. As shown in Figure 4, each bubble on the left-hand side plot represents a topic. The larger the bubble, the more prevalent is that topic. A good topic model has big, non-overlapping bubbles scattered throughout the chart instead of being clustered in one quadrant. A model with too many topics typically has many overlapping, small sized bubbles clustered in one region of the chart. In right hand side, the words represent the salient keywords. Based on the model in Figure 4, we can say that Mallet is a much better model than Gensim. This is because mallet has bigger bubbles, and only two of them are overlapping.

Figure 4. Intertopic distance map of LDA model for k=9

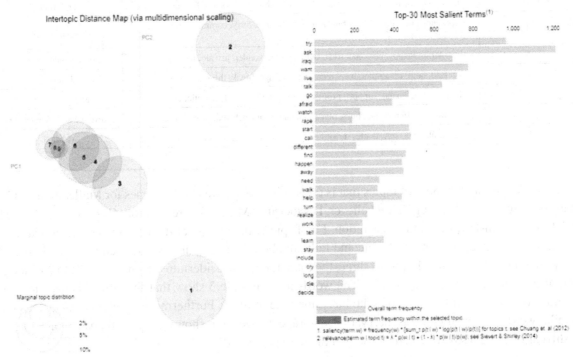

Topic Frequency Distribution

Table 4 and Table 5 contain the list of top 10 most relevant terms that have been extracted from LDA model with Gensim and Mallet. In this study, we chose only 10 relevant terms that have been frequently used by authors, as detected by Gensim and Mallet, to determine the suitable themes. For example, based on the words in topic 1, the authors frequently use words related to the theme of motivation. The writer wants to tell how she keeps strong, continues to live, talk, learn, and start a new life in another country after a long time of suffering. In addition, topic 4 tells us what kind of sexual abuse Iraqi woman have faced. Some of them have become rape victims or divorcees. This has generated a negative experience in them. As they have difficulty in facing public censure and reaction, they end up feeling dirty and lonely. Topic 4 can be considered as the causing factor of topic 6 as Iraqi woman feeling cause hatred because of all the traumatic events and negative transformations that they have endured. Gensim model shows nine different themes are discussed by authors such as motivation, peace and gratitude, tradition, sexual abuse, personal character, hatred, migrant crisis, revenge, and vengeance, and marriage. From all the topic obtained from Gensim, one can conclude that all topics are correlated to each other, and this is the reason why the bubble in pyLDAvis is so close to one another.

Table 4. List of top 10 most relevant terms with themes (gensim)

Topic	Top 10 most relevant terms	Themes
1	Live, talk, start, happen, learn, cry, wrong, international, strong, suffer, return	Motivation
2	Long, decide, free, grateful, dance, barely, manage, pray, public, past	Peace and Gratitude
3	Traditional, dress, resist, red, original, abayas, shine, design, confiscate, horrific	Tradition
4	Rape, enormous, difficult, publicly, lonely, divorce, dirty, comment, experience, massive	Sexual Abuse
5	Afraid, happy, personal, trust, laugh, good, wonder, private, feel, nice	Personal character
6	find, help, remember, love, recognize, change, break, think, hate, force	Hatred
7	Iraqi, realize, social, support, promise, worried, release, flee, smile, emotional	Migrant Crisis
8	watch, different, die, bury, reveal, punish, apart, beloved, prove, young	Revenge and Vengeance
9	try, walk, turn, stay, come, surround, special, listen, marry, treat, move, speak	Married

Since the optimal number of topics that is chosen is 9, there are also 9 themes for Mallet model. The themes include child learning, faith/ believer, Desiderium, Misery and repression, Oppression, Memoir, Misfortune, Iran-Iraq war, and Expectation. For Topic 1, the dominant theme seems to be on learning because words like listen, read, Arabic and talk are about learning, and words such as play, short and easy are related to children. For topic three, the main theme is desiderium which means feeling of longing or grief for something that is lost. The words used in topic 3 show that the author is showing her feelings of longing for her husband who has joined the military. Furthermore, Mallet has also detected similar words as Gensim such as marry, flee, and rape. However, it shows different themes which makes it difficult to find a suitable theme based on the extracted words.

Table 5. List of top 10 most relevant terms with themes (Mallet)

Topic	Top 10 most relevant terms	Themes
1	talk, gather, short, listen, read, fast, play, sound, Arabic, easy	Child Learning
2	find, walk, leave, Egyptian, notice, promise, flee, worried, religious, accept	Faith/ believer
3	strong, remember, feel, marry, shout, military, run, sad, discover, disappear	Desiderium
4	change, poor, carry, long, arrest, remain, save, young, serve, share	Misery and repression
5	cry, return, wait, Kurdish, free, suffer, Arab, red, head, hot	Oppression
6	happen, work, love, afraid, travel, write, whisper, surprised, plan, wrong	Memoir
7	move, pray, refuse, rape, hold, lie, forward, fear, simply, unable	Misfortune
8	Iraqi, force, order, personal, secret, dress, release, Iranian, normal, tired	Iran-Iraq War
9	watch, reach, place, white, stand, expect, study, eat, quietly, green	General (noise)

Sentiment Analysis

We implemented a set of techniques for aspect classification and polarity score using TextBlob. As Figure 5 shows, our experiment found that 16421 sentences are neutral, 10360 sentences are positive, and only 6007 sentences are negative. The polarity score for all books is 0.046, which means that most of the sentence that are used have positive associations.

Figure 5. Bar graph of polarity score

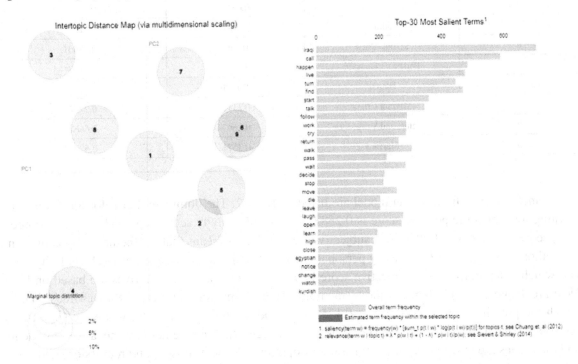

For sentiment analysis, we used TextBlob to calculate the score for the word distribution in each topic. To analyze the sentiment, two measures of Polarity (talks about how positive or negative the opinion) and Subjectivity (talks about how subjective the opinion) are used. Only top 10 relevant words are included to make sure we can detect a correlation between theme and sentiment. Polarity range is between -1 to 1; and subjective range is between 0-1(0 being very objective and 1 being very subjective).

As shown in Table 6, the main theme for topic 1 is motivation. Here, polarity score is 0.0174, and subjectivity score is o.5333. In topic 5 (personal character), polarity is 0.2571 and subjectivity is 0.6107. For topic 8 (revenge and vengeance), polarity is 0.2667 and subjectivity is 0.6667. Topic 9 (married) has polarity of 0.3571 and subjectivity score of 0.5714. This means that the dominant themes are attached with positive sentiments, and the authors writings are influences by their personal feelings. For topic 2 (peace and gratitude) and topic 7 (migrant crisis), the polarity scores are 0.03 and 0.1111, while subjectivity scores are 0.3233 and 0.2722. This also suggests that the theme is positive, and the authors' writings are based on facts. Topic 3 (tradition) has a polarity of -0.1563 and subjectivity of 0.6250, meaning that the theme is negative sentiment, and the authors writings are influenced by personal feelings or opinions. Topic 4 (sexual abuse) and Topic 6 (hatred) have polarity scores of -0.24 and -0.15, and subjectivity scores of 0.88 and 0.75. The scores show that the themes are negative and subjective as the narratives are affected by authors' personal feelings.

Table 6. List of topics, themes, polarity score and subjectivity (Gensim)

Topic	Themes	Polarity	Subjectivity
1	Motivation	0.0174	0.5333
2	Peace and Gratitude	0.0300	0.3233
3	Tradition	-0.1563	0.6250
4	Sexual Abuse	-0.2400	0.8800
5	Personal character	0.2571	0.6107
6	Hatred	-0.1500	0.75
7	Migrant Crisis	0.1111	0.2722
8	Revenge and Vengeance	0.2667	0.6667
9	Married	0.3571	0.5714

Themes obtained from Mallet model are listed in Table 7. The dominant theme for topic 1 is child learning for which the polarity score is 0.2583 and the subjectivity score is o.5333. Topic 5 (oppression) scores a polarity of 0.267 and a subjectivity of 0.55. This means that the themes are positive, and the authors' writing are influences by personal feelings. For Topic 2 (faith/believer), the polarity score is 0 which is neutral, and the subjective score is 0.25, which means the narratives are based on facts. Next are Topic 3 (desiderium), Topic 6 (memoir), Topic 7 (misfortune), Topic 8 (Iran-Iraq war), for which the polarity scores are -0.0556, -0.125, -0.50 and -0.1625 respectively; while the subjectivity scores are 0.6111, 0.825, 0.5 and 0.5875. The scores suggest that the themes have negative sentiments, and the stories are affected by personal feeling or opinions. Topic 4 (misery and repression) and Topic 9 (general (noise)) themes have the same polarity score of -0.1. They also have the subjectivity scores of 0.35 and 0.15. The scores show that the themes are negative and objective, meaning that the authors have written based on facts.

Table 7. List of topics, themes, polarity score and subjectivity (Mallet)

Topic	Themes	Polarity	Subjectivity
1	Child Learning	0.2583	0.5333
2	Faith/ believer	0.0	0.2500
3	Desiderium	-0.0556	0.6111
4	Misery and repression	-0.1000	0.3500
5	Oppression	0.267	0.5500
6	Memoir	-0.1250	0.8250
7	Misfortune	-0.5000	0.5000
8	Iran-Iraq War	-0.1625	0.5875
9	General (noise)	-0.1000	0.1500

CONCLUSION

LDA-based topic modeling is a very effective and powerful technique in topic modeling for topic extraction. In our study, we have built an LDA model using Gensim and Mallet. The optimal number of topics for our dataset is k=9. Both models have given good results which makes it difficult to choose one over the other. When comparing based on coherence score, Gensim has the highest coherence score than Mallet. But when we compare using pyLDAvis, Mallet proves to be a better model because the cluster is well distributed, and the extracted topics do not overlap. Comparing based on the identified top 10 relevant terms, Gensim is shown to perform better than Mallet. This is because the words extracted from Mallet are too general which makes it difficult to find a suitable theme that is related to the terms. For the sentiment analysis part, all the 6 books are analyzed. The results show that the sentence used by authors are predominantly neutral or positive. Lastly, textblob was used to calculate both the polarity score and the subjective score. It is concluded that the themes generated by Gensim are mostly positive, and the narratives are affected by authors' personal feelings. Whereas, themes generate by Mallet are mainly negative, and the stories are likewise shown to be affected by the writers' personal feelings. Overall, Gensim have given us better results than Mallet. It is noteworthy that TextBlob only describes the polarity and subjectivity, and hence, TextBlob may not give the accurate analysis for certain biased sentences. In future, more experiment on sentiment analysis using different dictionary and approaches can be conducted. Supervised and unsupervised learning can also be used to address the limitations of the present study.

REFERENCES

Akef, I., Arango, J. S. M., & Xu, X. (2016). Mallet vs GenSim: Topic modeling for 20 news groups report. *Univ. Ark. Little Rock Law J.*

Ali, L., & Shears, R. (2009). Betrayed: A terrifying true story of a young woman dragged back to Iraq (1st ed.). Academic Press.

Asl, M. P. (2019). Foucauldian rituals of justice and conduct in Zainab Salbi's Between Two Worlds. *Journal of Contemporary Iraq & the Arab World, 13*(2-3), 227–242. doi:10.1386/jciaw_00010_1

Asl, M. P. (2020). Micro-Physics of discipline: Spaces of the self in Middle Eastern women life writings. *International Journal of Arabic-English Studies, 20*(2), 223–240. doi:10.33806/ijaes2000.20.2.12

Bhadane, C., Dalal, H., & Doshi, H. (2015). Sentiment analysis: Measuring opinions. *Procedia Computer Science, 45*, 808–814. doi:10.1016/j.procs.2015.03.159

Blei, D. M., Ng, A. Y., & Jordan, M. I. (2003). Latent dirichlet allocation. *Journal of Machine Learning Research, 3*, 993–1022.

Bonta, V., & Janardhan, N. K. N. (2019). A comprehensive study on lexicon based approaches for sentiment analysis. *Asian Journal of Computer Science and Technology, 8*(S2), 1–6. doi:10.51983/ajcst-2019.8.S2.2037

Boussaadi, S., Aliane, H., Cerist, A., & Abdeldjalil, P. O. (2020). *Modeling of scientists profiles based on LDA*. Academic Press.

Chowdhury, G. G. (2003). Natural language processing. *Annual Review of Information Science & Technology, 37*(1), 51–89. doi:10.1002/aris.1440370103

El Badry, H. (2014). Rain Over Baghdad: An Egyptian Novel (1st ed.). The American University in Cairo Press.

Gujjar, J. P., & HR, P. K. (2021). Sentiment Analysis: Textblob For Decision Making. *International Journal of Scientific Research & Engineering Trends*, (7), 1097–1099.

Gujjar, J. P., & Manjunatha, T. (2018). Profitability Analysis of Indian Information Technology Companies using DuPont Model. *Asian Journal of Management, 9*(3), 1105–1108. doi:10.5958/2321-5763.2018.00176.2

Guo, C., Lu, M., & Wei, W. (2021). An improved LDA topic modeling method based on partition for medium and long texts. *Annals of Data Science, 8*(2), 331–344. doi:10.100740745-019-00218-3

Islam, T. (2019). Yoga-veganism: Correlation mining of twitter health data. *8th KDD Workshop on Issues of Sentiment Discovery and Opinion Mining (WISDOM)*.

Jagdale, R. S., Shirsat, V. S., & Deshmukh, S. N. (2016). Sentiment analysis of events from Twitter using open source tool. *International Journal of Computer Science and Mobile Computing, 5*(4), 475–485.

Jelodar, H., & Frank, R. (2021). *Semantic Knowledge Discovery and Discussion Mining of Incel Online Community: Topic modeling*. arXiv preprint arXiv:2104.09586.

Jockers, M. L. (2016). The ancient world in nineteenth-century fiction; or, correlating theme, geography, and sentiment in the nineteenth century literary imagination. *DHQ: Digital Humanities Quarterly, 10*(2), 1–17.

Koehn, P. (2009). *Statistical machine translation.* Cambridge University Press. doi:10.1017/CBO9780511815829

Liddy, E. D. (2001). *Natural language processing.* Academic Press.

Liu, B. (2010). Sentiment analysis and subjectivity. In *Handbook of natural language processing* (2nd ed., pp. 627–666). Taylor and Francis Group.

Liu, P., Yuan, W., Fu, J., Jiang, Z., Hayashi, H., & Neubig, G. (2021). *Pre-train, prompt, and predict: A systematic survey of prompting methods in natural language processing.* arXiv preprint arXiv:2107.13586.

Loria, S. (2018). textblob Documentation. *Release 0.15, 2,* 269.

Malik, E. F., Keikhosrokiani, P., & Asl, M. P. (2021). Text mining life cycle for a spatial reading of Viet Thanh Nguyen's *The Refugees* (2017). *The 2021 International Congress of Advanced Technology and Engineering (ICOTEN).* 10.1109/ICOTEN52080.2021.9493520

Mikhail, D. (2018). *The beekeeper: Rescuing the stolen women of Iraq* (1st ed.). New Directions Publishing.

Ozyurt, B., & Akcayol, M. A. (2021). A new topic modeling based approach for aspect extraction in aspect based sentiment analysis: SS-LDA. *Expert Systems with Applications, 168,* 114231. doi:10.1016/j.eswa.2020.114231

Pak, A., & Paroubek, P. (2010, May). Twitter as a corpus for sentiment analysis and opinion mining. In LREc (Vol. 10, No. 2010, pp. 1320-1326). Academic Press.

Pang, B., Lee, L., & Vaithyanathan, S. (2002). *Thumbs up? Sentiment classification using machine learning techniques.* arXiv preprint cs/0205070.

Perez, E., Kiela, D., & Cho, K. (2021). *True Few-Shot Learning with Language Models.* arXiv preprint arXiv:2105.11447.

Phang, Y. C., Kassim, A. M., & Mangantig, E. (2021). Concerns of Thalassemia Patients, Carriers, and their Caregivers in Malaysia: Text Mining Information Shared on Social Media. *Healthcare Informatics Research, 27*(3), 200–213. doi:10.4258/hir.2021.27.3.200 PMID:34384202

Pollak, S., Martinc, M., & Poniz, K. M. (2020). Natural Language Processing for Literary Text Analysis: Word-Embeddings-Based Analysis of Zofka Kveder's Work. In DHandNLP@ PROPOR (pp. 33-42). Academic Press.

Prabhakaran, S. (2018). *Topic Modeling with Gensim (Python).* Machine Learning Plus.

Rosenthal, S., Farra, N., & Nakov, P. (2017, August). SemEval-2017 task 4: Sentiment analysis in twitter. In S. Bethard, M. Carpuat, M. Apidianaki, S. M. Mohammad, D. Cer, & D. Jurgens (Eds.), *Proceedings of the 11th international workshop on semantic evaluation (SemEval-2017)* (pp. 502–518). Association for Computational Linguistics. 10.18653/v1/S17-2088

Ross, J. (2009). *IraqiGirl: Diary of a teenage girl in Iraq.* Haymarket Books.

Salbi, Z., & Becklund, L. (2006). *Between two worlds: Escape from tyranny: Growing up in the shadow of Saddam.* Penguin.

Sanders, A. C., White, R. C., Severson, L. S., Ma, R., McQueen, R., Paulo, H. C. A., . . . Bennett, K. P. (2021). Unmasking the conversation on masks: Natural language processing for topical sentiment analysis of COVID-19 Twitter discourse. medRxiv, 2020-08.

Sasson, J. (2003). *Mayada, daughter of Iraq* (1st ed.). Dutton Adult.

Scao, T. L., & Rush, A. M. (2021). *How Many Data Points is a Prompt Worth?* arXiv preprint arXiv:2103.08493.

Schick, T., & Schütze, H. (2020). *Exploiting cloze questions for few shot text classification and natural language inference.* arXiv preprint arXiv:2001.07676.

Socher, R., Perelygin, A., Wu, J., Chuang, J., Manning, C. D., Ng, A. Y., & Potts, C. (2013, October). Recursive deep models for semantic compositionality over a sentiment treebank. In *Proceedings of the 2013 conference on empirical methods in natural language processing* (pp. 1631-1642). Academic Press.

van Atteveldt, W., van der Velden, M. A., & Boukes, M. (2021). The Validity of Sentiment Analysis: Comparing Manual Annotation, Crowd-Coding, Dictionary Approaches, and Machine Learning Algorithms. *Communication Methods and Measures, 15*(2), 121–140. doi:10.1080/19312458.2020.1869198

Tally, R. T. Jr., (Ed.). (2017). *The Routledge handbook of literature and space.* Taylor & Francis. doi:10.4324/9781315745978

Zhang, N., Li, L., Chen, X., Deng, S., Bi, Z., Tan, C., . . . Chen, H. (2021). *Differentiable prompt makes pre-trained language models better few-shot learners.* arXiv preprint arXiv:2108.13161.

Ying, S. Y., Keikhosrokiani, P., & Asl, M. P. (2021). Comparison of data analytic techniques for a spatial opinion mining in literary works: A review paper. In F. Saeed, F. Mohammed, & A. Al-Nahari (Eds.), *Innovative Systems for Intelligent Health Informatics* (pp. 523–535). Springer International Publishing. doi:10.1007/978-3-030-70713-2_49

Ying, S. Y., Keikhosrokiani, P., & Asl, M. P. (2022). Opinion mining on Viet Thanh Nguyen's The Sympathizer using topic modelling and sentiment analysis. *Journal of Information Technology Management, 14*(Special Issue), 163–183. doi:10.22059/jitm.2022.84895

Chapter 9

Opinion Mining and Text Analytics of Literary Reader Responses:
A Case Study of Reader Responses to KL Noir Volumes in Goodreads Using Sentiment Analysis and Topic

Nikmatul Husna Binti Suhendra

School of Computer Sciences, Universiti Sains Malaysia, Malaysia

Pantea Keikhosrokiani

https://orcid.org/0000-0003-4705-2732

School of Computer Sciences, Universiti Sains Malaysia, Malaysia

Moussa Pourya Asl

https://orcid.org/0000-0002-8426-426X

School of Humanities, Universiti Sains Malaysia, Malaysia

Xian Zhao

https://orcid.org/0000-0003-1794-6233

School of Computer Sciences, Universiti Sains Malaysia, Malaysia

ABSTRACT

Text mining is an important field of study that has proved beneficial for scholars of various disciplines. Literary scholars use text mining to examine the data produced by creative writers, literary readers, publishers, and distributing companies. The produced data are generally in unstructured form that cannot be used to extract useful information. Text mining can discover the unstructured data and convert it to interesting information through several processes. This chapter proposes a text mining technique by using topic modelling and sentiment analysis to retrieve information about the attitude of the user-readers toward the four volumes of KL Noir books on the Goodreads website. The main significance of this approach is to gain the trends by analyzing the book reviews written on Goodreads.

DOI: 10.4018/978-1-7998-9594-7.ch009

INTRODUCTION

Nowadays, large amounts of data are stored in intranets, internet, and databases. Some examples of electronic data that are available are the customer feedbacks and communications on social media platforms. As millions of users in social media platforms, or any other websites, are now able to share information, the amount of data produced daily is very large. The question is how this massive amount of data is handled and stored, as well as what medium or tools are being used. This is where text mining comes into light.

As the data quantity is rapidly increasing day by day, the amount of data that needs to be collected for many purposes has similarly increased. Using text mining to extract useful data from natural language texts is a new field that needs to be explored. Text mining is an important field of study that has proved beneficial for scholars of various disciplines. Literary scholars use text mining to examine the data produced by creative writers, literary readers, publishers and distributing companies (Ying et al., 2021). Text mining is a process of analyzing text in order to extract useful information for a specific purpose. Text is unstructured, ambiguous, and difficult to process when compared to the type of data stored in databases as text is also considered as one of the most suitable ways for the information changing (Kalra, 2013). Of this, the textual data is the data type that the text mining always deals with because analyzing the data with the text mining can identify the new insights. The goal of text mining is to discover new information that has not yet been found and written by anyone else. As the text mining is a relatively new field that aims to extract useful data from natural language text, numerous studies and research had been conducted (Malik et al., 2021; Ying et al., 2022). In recent years, social media has become a powerful data source in many ways such as an analytical platform to explore certain objectives.

To develop more understanding in social media mining, this paper aims to analyze the readers' responses in Goodreads website to discover the attitude of the users toward certain books by extracting the book's information such as their rates and reviews. Goodreads is a platform where users can use its database of books, annotations, quotes, and reviews to conduct searches. To achieve the aim of this paper, we will use the four volumes of *KL Noir* that has been assigned to gain the trends and analyze users' attitude towards the books. The books are anthologies that explore the darker side of Malaysian capital city, Kuala Lumpur. Cities and places have always intrigued literary writers, and in recent years, literary scholars have shown increasing interest in the study of settings and places in creative writings (Asl, 2021, 2022). By using text mining techniques, the aim of the first process is to recognize key phrases and relationships. It accomplishes this by searching for predefined text sequences, a process known as pattern matching. Next, key topics and words that appear in the same paragraphs or sentences are used to extract the main keywords. Then, using text mining techniques like topic modelling and others, the characteristics and frequency of the words are defined and analyzed. Sentiment analysis is also applied to measure the attitude of the users toward the review of the book which they describe in a text. Next, to scrap the reviews from Goodreads, we need to setup the Python environment in the Jupyter Notebook by installing required Python packages that we need to use such as pandas and selenium. Next, to gain insight, we will explore the text and study the frequent words using a bar chart and wordcloud. Prior to that, the text must be normalized and the process of tokenization, noise removal, stopwords removal and lemmatization will be done. After that, topic modelling model is developed. The goal is to investigate the major topics that have been discussed by the users toward the books. The topic modelling output is a series of keyword lists that have been classified with the coherence scores using Latent Dirichlet Allocation (LDA) (Jelodar et al., 2019) and Latent Semantic Indexing (LSI) (Adomavicius & Tuzhilin,

2005) algorithms. The next phase needs to contain the works of Vader algorithm and textblob from the sentiment analysis. There are many ways of classifying texts, using machine learning techniques. Sentiment analysis is one of the techniques where a system identifies whether the text being analyzed is positive, negative, or neutral based on its topics.

Therefore, the goals of this research are to analyze the collected data and results about the reviews of the users from each book of *KL Noir* by using text mining techniques and sentiment analysis, identify the patterns that appear most among the bag of words, then compare whether a sentence or fragment of the text falls into one of two categories which are positive or negative, finally summarize the reviews for better understanding.

BACKGROUND

Text Mining

As the data are largely produced by multiple data source, the data itself consist of structured and unstructured data. While extracting the value structured data is not a big issue, for the unstructured data, the data need to be transformed into information that machine can understand through text mining. Text mining is the automatic extraction of information from various written resources by a computer to discover new, previously unknown information (Gupta & Lehal, 2009). It is the process of analyzing text in order to extract information useful for a specific purpose. Text mining is not the same as what we are used to seeing in web searches. In most cases, when someone searches for something, they are looking for something that is already well-known and has been written by someone else. The issue is putting aside all of the material that is not currently relevant to your needs in order to find the information you need. The goal of text mining is to find previously unknown information that no one knows about and thus could not have been written down. The process of structuring the input text, deriving patterns within the structured data, and finally evaluating and interpreting the output is known as text mining.

There are four basic steps in the text mining which are retrieval, processing, extraction and analysis. Each step is crucial to ensure a smooth state transition for the project. The first step is retrieval. This step is involving the problem definition. This phase is about acquiring data from any source that is related to the project. Next is processing. This step will transform the acquired data into something that a machine can work with. In this step, we can use computational tool to perform basic and advanced Natural Language Processing (NLP) such as correct spelling, remove capitalization, classify words by grammatical category or disambiguate meaning by context. Next step is extraction, which is the process of acquiring specific information from the data which is relevant to the problem definition. In this stage, there are many methods that can be applied to the text. For example, metadata is added in the data to allows the search engine obtain the information and determine the relationship between them. Lastly, is an analysis. This step is about showing the outcomes, reach an insight, and answer to the problem definition.

Social Media Mining

Social media is defined as a group of the Internet based applications. Users can communicate with one another on an unprecedented scale thanks to social media. The popularity of social media continues to rise at a breakneck pace, resulting in the emergence of social networks, blogs, wikis, and others.

Social media mining is the process of representing, analyzing and extracting actionable patterns from social media data. It has been used for many ways in the industry as it can track what people are talking about online and having a method to discover trends for particular purposes. Data mining on social media sites such as Twitter, LinkedIn, Facebook, and others is used to discover secret patterns and trends. Machine learning, mathematics, and mathematical methods are commonly used to accomplish this.

Most social media data is created by users. The data on social media is massive, noisy, dispersed, unstructured, and constantly changing. These characteristics make developing new efficient techniques and algorithms for data mining tasks difficult. Data from social media platforms can be very noisy, depending on the platform (Gundecha & Liu, 2012). Before performing effective mining, it is necessary to remove the noise from the data. The first technique in social media mining is keyword extraction, key extraction is the procedure for extracting keywords from a text in order to summarize or categorize it based on the name implies. It also enables data visualizations such as idea clouds to aid data analysis. Second is Sentiment Analysis which is a common application of AI text analysis that involves analyzing keywords and phrases in a text to decide if it is positive, negative, or neutral. This is useful for analyzing social media messages and determining customer feedback patterns. Lastly is summary extraction. A text is condensed into a comprehensive synopsis using summary extraction. This can be done by constructing a description from key points in a document or by producing new sentences based on comprehension of the text's context. Machine learning algorithms must understand the language and message in each text in both cases. This is useful for creating newsletters and reviewing a large number of company documents.

Topic Modelling: Comparison Table of Different Algorithms

A model is a representation of data and relationship in a dataset that is abstract. While there is not enough quantitative data to use in a production situation, it does provide directional information by abstracting the credit score and interest rate relationship. Topic modelling offers us tools for arranging, comprehending, and summarizing vast volumes of textual data (Kherwa & Bansal, 2020). It aids in:

- Identifying secret topical trends that appear in the collection
- Annotating records with these subjects in mind
- Organizing, scanning, and summarizing documents, use these annotations.

Modelling is a technique for extracting a group of words such as a topic from a set of documents that best reflects the information in the set. It's also a form of text mining which is a technique for detecting recurring patterns of words in textual data. Table 1 shows the comparison of different topic modelling algorithms (Julia & David).

Table 1. Comparison of different topic modelling algorithms

Algorithm method	Concept	Advantages	Disadvantage
Latent Dirichlet allocation (LDA)	Represents documents as a mix of topics that spit out probabilistic terms. It is assumed that records will be produced in the following manner.	Priors and potentially lower-risk estimate.	For the smaller amounts of data, it cannot be well performed. The number of topics in the dataset are specified by the user
Latent semantic indexing (LSI)	Learns latent topics by performing matrix decomposition (SVD) on the term-document matrix.	LSI is used in conjunction with, and not instead of, common Boolean search weighting functions such as tf-idf.	Lower accuracy. LSI's decreased dependence on direct term matches allows for the extraction of hidden relationships among concepts.
Latent semantic analysis (LSA)	Principal component analysis applied to text data. It is a linear algebra method.	Performance: LSA is capable of assuring decent results much better than plain vector space model. It works well on dataset with diverse topics.	The latent topic dimension cannot be chosen to arbitrary numbers. It depends on the rank of the matrix, so can't go beyond that.

Sentiment Analysis Comparison Table of Different Algorithms

Sentiment Analysis is the method of using natural language processing, text analysis and statistics to assess customer sentiment. In social media, it is meant to figure out the sentiment by knowing what the feeling of the person is about a brand or a project as included in comments, mentions and shares. How much people talk about a brand and whether the sentiments are located on the positive or negative spectrum are important. To analyze sentiment data, Sentiment Analysis involves 5 different steps (Table 2) which are data collection, text preparation, sentiment detection, sentiment classification and presentation of output.

Table 2. Sentiment analysis steps

Steps	Explanation
Data collection	Gather data from user generated content on social media. These data are disorganized, expressed in variety way using a variety of vocabularies and slangs.
Text preparation	The process of cleaning the extracted data before analyzing it. Only textual content can be used for data analysis.
Sentiment detection	After cleaning, the content is examined. Sentences containing subjective expressions such as opinions, and views are kept, whereas sentences containing objective communication such as facts are discarded
Sentiment classification	Subjective sentences are categorized in this phase into positive, negative, good, and bad such as like, hate, but classification can be done with multiple points
Presentation of output	The main aim of sentiment analysis is to turn unstructured text into useful data. The text results are shown on graphs such as pie charts, bar charts, and line graphs until the analysis is completed. Time can also be analyzed and graphically displayed by creating a sentiment timeline over time with the chosen value (frequency, percentages, and averages).

Sentiment analysis consists of three approaches which are machine learning based, hybrid and lexical based (Medhat et al., 2014).

Machine Learning Based

The primary role of Machine Learning in sentiment analysis is to develop and automate sentiment analysis' low-level text analytics features, such as part of speech tagging (Agarwal & Mittal, 2017). Data scientists may, for example, train a machine learning model to recognise nouns by feeding it a large number of text documents with pre-tagged examples. The model will learn what nouns look like using supervised and unsupervised machine learning techniques such as neural networks and deep learning. If the model is complete, the same data scientist will use the same training methods to create new models to recognise different parts of expression. The result is a fast and efficient service. Speech tagging is a form of tagging which aids in the identification of text in a larger text analytics system.

Lexical Based

In several emotion classification activities, opinion terms are used (Yousefpour et al., 2014). Positive opinion words convey desired states, while negative opinion words express undesirable states. Opinion lexicon refers to the set of phrases and idioms that express one's point of view. There are three primary methods for compiling or collecting an opinion word list. The manual process is very time-consuming.

Hybrid Based

The combination of this Machine Learning and Lexicon-Based approaches in the hybrid approach has the potential to improve sentiment classification efficiency. Depending on the intent of the study, there are certain benefits and disadvantages to using these various methods. For polarity identification, the hybrid approach of Sentiment Analysis uses both statistical and knowledge-based approaches. It inherits high accuracy (statistical methods) and stability (lexicon-based approach) from Machine Learning. Table 3 shows the Sentiment Analysis approaches (D'Andrea et al., 2015).

Table 3. Sentiment analysis approach

Approaches	Technique	Advantages and limitations
Machine learning • Bayesian • Networks • Naive Bayes • Classification • Maximum Entropy • Neutral Networks • Support Vector Machine	Term presence and frequency Part of speech information Negations Opinion words and phrases	ADVANTAGES the ability to adapt and create trained models for specific purposes and contexts LIMITATIONS the low applicability to new data because it is necessary the availability of labeled data that could be costly or even prohibitive
Lexical based • Dictionary based approach • Novel Machine • Learning Approach • Corpus based approach • Ensemble Approaches	Manual construction, Corpus-based Dictionary-based	Advantages wider term coverage Limitations finite number of words in the lexicons and the assignation of a fixed sentiment orientation and score to words
Hybrid based • Machine learning • Lexicon based	Sentiment lexicon constructed using public resources for initial sentiment detection Sentiment words as features in machine learning method	Advantages Lexicon/learning symbiosis, the detection and measurement of sentiment at the concept level And the lesser sensitivity to changes in topic domain

DATA SCIENCE LIFE CYCLE

Figure 1 shows the data science life cycle that we used in this project. There are six phases in the cycle which are business understanding, data understanding, data preparation, modelling, evaluation, and deployment. The data used for this study has been collected from the Goodreads reviews on the four volumes of *KL Noir*. Then, data preprocessing and cleaning is done using stopword removal, tokenization, lemmatization. For the modelling step, there are wo process that need to be complete which are Topic Modelling and Sentiment Analysis. In Topic Modelling, the algorithms we used are Latent Dirichlet Allocation (LDA) and Latent Semantic Indexing (LSI) algorithms while for the Sentiment Analysis, Vader and Textblob algorithms have been used. The output of the results will be evaluated and discussed to determine which algorithm is the best.

Figure 1. Data science life cycle

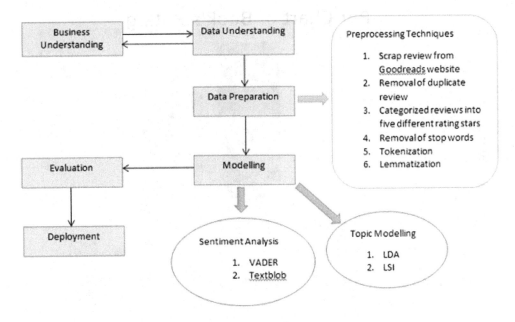

RESULTS

This part will discuss about the series of the book's results from the data that has been collected from the Goodreads. First, the processed data will be undergoing several processes which are text normalization, text visualization, topic modelling and sentiment analysis. All the results are recorded as below. The following four volumes are:

KL NOIR: RED (2013) (68 Review)

Text Normalization and Visualization

Figure 2 presents information about the total number of ratings that the book received from 68 reviews. The ratings are from 1, 2, 3, 4 and 5. It can be seen that the highest rate of KL NOIR: RED is 3 by having 28 users. The difference between the number 4 and 2 rates are relatively huge which are differences by 14 users. The lowest number of user rate for this book is 1 by having only 1 rate. However, the total user from the data is 68 users while the total ratings that have been counted are 67. For this book, there is one user who did not give the rate. To conclude this bar chart, the most common rating that is given by the viewers toward this book is 3, followed by 4, 3, 5 and 1.

Figure 2. KL NOIR: RED rating bar chart

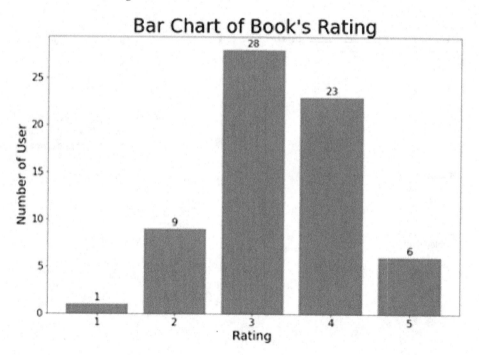

Figure 3 illustrates the count of the top 10 common words that have been used for the KL NOIR: RED. The most used word is 'good' with 40 counts. The word 'good' and 'noir' are slightly different with 1 count and comparison for the next two words which are 'short' and 'dark' shows difference with a count at 35 and 34 respectively. The total count is decreasing from the word 'anthology' and 'long'. Meanwhile, there are two pairs of words having the same counts which are words 'way' and 'collection' for 18 counts and 'side' and 'flower' for 16 counts. In conclusion, the bar chart shows the most word that are frequently used by users and the most used word for this chart is 'good''.

Figure 3. KL NOIR: RED top common word bar chart

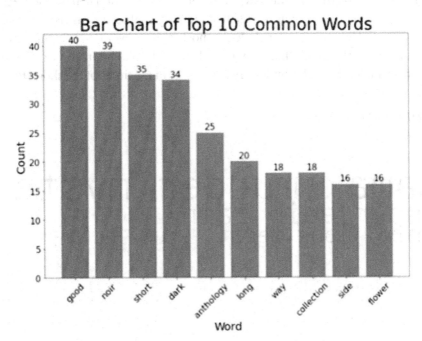

The bigram for KL NOIR: RED is shown in Figure 4. The frequency of two terms that appear repeatedly in user reviews is depicted in a bigram. As the frequency of two words rises, the size of terms on the diagram rises as well. The bigram shows the popular tittle of the short stories in the book from the words 'gift flower', 'mamak murder' and 'chasing butterfly'. To summarize, A Gift of Flower story had the highest frequency occurrence in this bigram.

Figure 4. KL NOIR: RED bigram

The trigram for KL NOIR: RED is illustrated in Figure 5. The trigram depicts the frequency of three words that appear repeatedly in user reviews. As the frequency of three words rises, the size of terms on the diagram rises as well. Here, we can conclude the most frequent words are 'mamak murder mystery' followed by 'chasing butterfly night', 'butterfly night kris' and 'mud brain gomez'. To summarize, the most frequent words which is Mamak Murder Mystery is one of the tittles of the short stories in the book.

Figure 5. KL NOIR: RED trigram

Topic Modelling

Figure 6 shows the results of the top 30 words for whole topics and the bubbles in first volume of KL Noir. This book results contain two bubbles which are far from each other thus making it more different and easier to figure. The highest frequent word used for this book is 'good' followed by 'noir', 'short', 'way' and 'collection' describing the review of the users to this book.

Figure 6. Top 30 words for whole topics

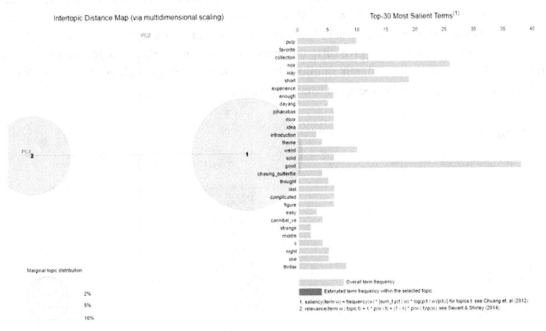

Topic 1 which has largest bubble with 67.2% of tokens contains the most frequent words that being used in the topic (Figure 7). From this figure, it is shown that the most frequent term for the topic has the longest red bar. The highest relevant terms indicated by the red bars and the most used words in this book are 'good' followed by 'dark', 'noir' and 'anthology'. For the certain words which are 'dark', 'thriller', 'mystery', and 'adventure' seems to be about the theme of the book which is about the dark side of the city. In conclusion, topic 1 is describing the genre for the short stories in the book.

Figure 7. Top 30 words for topic 1

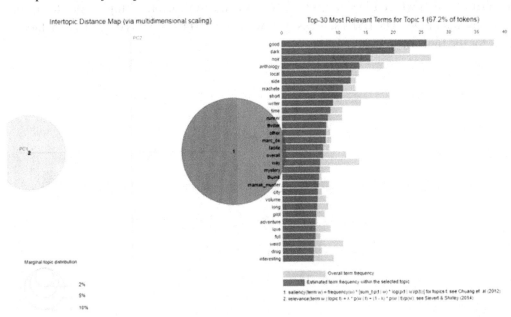

As shown in Figure 8, topic 2 consists of a bubble that is smaller than bubble in topic 1. The score of the top 30 most relevant terms is 32.8%. In this topic, the most relevant terms are about the reaction of the users for examples the words 'good', 'favorite', 'weird' and 'interesting'. This book contains 15 distinct stories thus each story will give different reaction to each user. Based on the frequent word in the figure, different users write different opinions based on their thinking such as interesting or weird. As a result, topic 2 appears to be about the users' reactions.

Figure 8. Top 30 words for topic 2

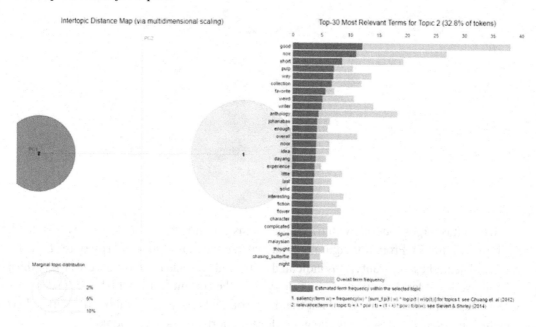

Figure 9 shows the graph of coherence score between two algorithms. These algorithms generate different number of topics where LDA generates 2 topics and LSI generates 4 topics. For the result, LSI's score is highest than LDA. The LSI's score is 0.49 while the LDA's score is 0.42. To conclude, the best algorithms for the topic modelling is LSI.

Figure 9. Coherence Score of LDA and LSI

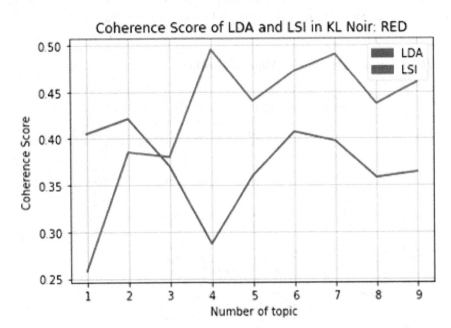

Sentiment Analysis

To illustrate the result, we used a lexicon and rule-based sentiment analysis tool which is named VADER. Vader algorithm produces a sentiment score ranging from -1 to 1, with -1 being the most negative and 1 being the most positive. In VADER, the score is differentiated into 4 categories which are compound, negative, neutral, and positive. The compound score is made up of positive, negative, and neutral scores which are then normalized between -1 and +1. The closer the compound score is to +1, the more positive the text is. To get the score of the sentence, VADER incorporates the impact of each sub-text on the perceived intensity of sentiment in sentence-level text using a set of rules which contain punctuation, capitalization, booster words and many more.

Textblob is a library for python that analyzes text and returns sentiments score. The polarity and subjectivity of a sentence are returned by Textblob. Sentiment is calculated based on the number of positive or negative emotions in a paragraph and character level sentiment. All sentences with positive sentiment are assigned to 1 and all sentences with negative sentiment are assigned to -1. In Textblob, the score is differentiated into 2 categories which are polarity and subjectivity. Polarity is a float that ranges from -1 to 1, with -1 denoting negative sentiment and +1 denoting positive sentiment. Subjectivity is also a float with value between 0 and 1. Personal opinion, emotion and judgment are all examples of subjective sentences.

Figure 10 shows the top 10 positive sentences from the 68 reviews for the first volume of the KL Noir. The reviews have been sorted in descending order based on the compound score. The first line of the figure which is line 52 has the highest compound score which is 0.9988 as the rules say the closer the compound score to 1, the higher the positivity of the sentence. Next, for example in line 65, "overall a mixed bag but that's what you have to…" with the positive score of 0.143 used the word 'but' as the conjunction in a sentence makes the positive score of the sentence decreased.

Figure 10. Top 10 positive sentences using Vader algorithm

```
The top 10 positive sentences are:
     Score Compound  Score Negative  Score Neutral  Score Positive  \
52          0.9988          0.060          0.769           0.171
43          0.9982          0.102          0.760           0.138
65          0.9954          0.076          0.780           0.143
31          0.9883          0.008          0.781           0.211
27          0.9840          0.026          0.785           0.189
50          0.9705          0.068          0.745           0.187
34          0.9665          0.040          0.837           0.123
29          0.9638          0.055          0.710           0.235
25          0.9624          0.025          0.811           0.164
57          0.9597          0.028          0.742           0.230

                                                           Sentence
52  I have a soft spot in my heart for short story...
43  KL Noir Red is the first of a planned series o...
65  Overall a mixed bag but thats what you have to...
31  I bought this book for fun And fun it is until...
27  I was really excited when I found this book si...
50  I havent read too many english anthologies but...
34  KL Noir is a compilation of short stories that...
29  Every city has a dark side The Mamak Murder My...
25  Every city has a dark side Damn right This boo...
57  I love reading anthologies  the variety of sto...
```

Figure 11 shows the top 10 negative sentences from the 68 reviews for the first volume of the KL Noir. The reviews have been sorted in ascending order based on the compound score. The first line of the figure which is line 40 has the lowest compound score. The sentence of line 40 "THIS BOOK IS FUCKEP UP AND IT TURNS ME ON…" has the cursing words that plays an important role and makes the sentences has the highest negative score.

Figure 11. Top 10 negative sentences using Vader algorithm

```
The top 10 negative sentences are:
     Score Compound  Score Negative  Score Neutral  Score Positive  \
40         -0.6597          0.328          0.672           0.000
30         -0.5321          0.133          0.746           0.121
55         -0.4753          0.106          0.894           0.000
4          -0.4019          0.128          0.790           0.082
33         -0.1761          0.133          0.867           0.000
19         -0.1531          0.060          0.903           0.038
24          0.0000          0.000          1.000           0.000
46          0.0000          0.000          1.000           0.000
54          0.0000          0.000          1.000           0.000
58          0.0000          0.000          1.000           0.000

                                                           Sentence
40         THIS BOOK IS FUCKED UP AND IT TURNS ME ON
30  Wait an anthology The last time Ive ever read ...
55  It had such an intriguing introduction on what...
4   Some of the stories that captured my interest ...
33  Some of the short story in this book really sc...
19  My first book that belongs to the Noir genre I...
24  The Highlights1 The Runner2 Asian Angel3 Vanis...
46                                            35 stars
54  by far my favourite KL Noir book out of the se...
58                                                   I
```

Figure 12 shows the top 10 positive sentences from the 68 reviews for the first volume of the KL Noir. The reviews are sorted in descending order based on the polarity float. The first line of the figure which is line 59 has the highest polarity float with 1.00000, which means that the statement is positive, and 1.00000 subjectivity means that the sentence is mostly personal opinion and not factual information. The second line sentence which had the word 'good' play the important role in the sentence to give the review the positive sentiments.

Figure 12. Top 10 positive sentences using Textblob

```
The top 10 positive sentences are:
     Polarity  Subjectivity                                    Sentence
59   1.000000      1.000000   A couple of impressive stories in a compilatio...
45   0.700000      0.600000   The start and ending parts are good but those ...
6    0.502500      0.660000   25 Not all the stories here are my cup of te...
38   0.500000      0.600000       Fully agree oh the book I love it I dont care
8    0.400000      0.533333   I found some stories interesting but some didn...
39   0.386111      0.638889   A good try to make our own Malaysian version o...
63   0.357143      0.523810   Not much to say Thankfully KL Noir did not dis...
35   0.350000      0.450000   I dont usually do short stories but these were...
26   0.344444      0.516667   I only like three out of fifteen short stories...
0    0.337500      0.697500   Most of the stories was nice and only 12 was a...
```

Figure 13 shows the top 10 negative sentences from the 68 reviews for the first volume of the KL Noir. The reviews have been sorted in ascending order based on the polarity float. The first line of the figure which is line 40 has the lowest polarity with -0.600000, which means that the statement is negative, and 0.700000 subjectivity suggests that mostly the sentence is a personal opinion as there is some word like 'fucked up' and 'turns me on' which is classified to the user's emotion.

Figure 13. Top 10 negative sentences using Textblob

```
The top 10 negative sentences are:
     Polarity  Subjectivity                                    Sentence
40   -0.600000     0.700000        THIS BOOK IS FUCKED UP AND IT TURNS ME ON
47   -0.173333     0.373333   25 stars There were a few boring stories whic...
29   -0.091667     0.283333   Every city has a dark side The Mamak Murder My...
49   -0.025000     0.562500   Such a pleasure to know there are local voices...
5    -0.002917     0.588333   This book told about the dark side of the KL w...
4    0.000000      0.000000   Some of the stories that captured my interest ...
24   0.000000      0.000000   The Highlights1 The Runner2 Asian Angel3 Vanis...
46   0.000000      0.000000                                           35 stars
58   0.000000      0.000000                                                  I
66   0.000000      0.000000   I bought and read this book because fadzlishah...
```

Table 4 shows the score comparison between the Vader and Textblob algorithm based on 68 reviews. Overall, there are only slightest differences between the algorithms such as for neutral and negative scores, there difference is only by one while for the positive score the difference is only by two. However, when comparing between the algorithms, VADER performed the best because its produce accurate result for the score. This was primarily due to its ability to accurately assign sentiment to words used.

Table 4. Total score of VADER and Textblob algorithms

Sentiment Analysis Model	Positive	Neutral	Negative
VADER	56	6	6
TextBlob	58	5	5

KL NOIR: WHITE (KL NOIR #2) (2013) (51 reviews)

Text Normalization and Visualization

The bar chart illustrated in Figure 14 shows the number of user rating for KL NOIR. WHITE. This book consists of 51 reviews. It is clear that the highest rate of this book is 4. The rate of 4 has 21 users. The difference between the second's highest is 3 users which is rate of 3, at 18 users. There are 6 users give the rating for 5 and it is slightly difference from rate 2 which are having 4 users. From the chart, the lowest rate of this book is 1, having 1 user respectively. The total of users who rate the book is 50. Thus, there is a single user who did not rate the book. Overall, the figures shown that the highest rate of the book is 4, followed by 3, 5, 2, and 1.

Figure 14. KL NOIR. WHITE rating bar chart

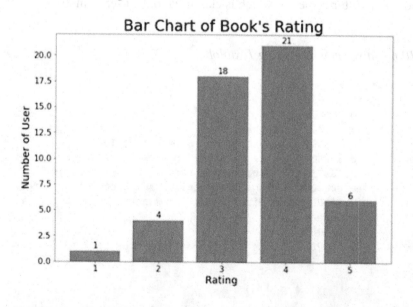

Figure 15 shows the most frequent common words that has been count in the KL NOIR: WHITE. The word 'short' is the most frequent that has been used. The total count of the word is 22. As we can see, the next three word which are 'short', 'noir' and 'time' also a slight difference with a total of one difference on each word at 22, 21 and 20. The word 'good' and 'dark' are having the same number of counts at 18. Next, following words after 'dark' are decrease by a count starting from 'side' which has 15 counts, the word 'red' and 'white' having the same total count, which is 14, the word 'man' with 13 counts and lastly 'anthology' with 12 counts.

Figure 15. KL NOIR: WHITE top common word bar chart

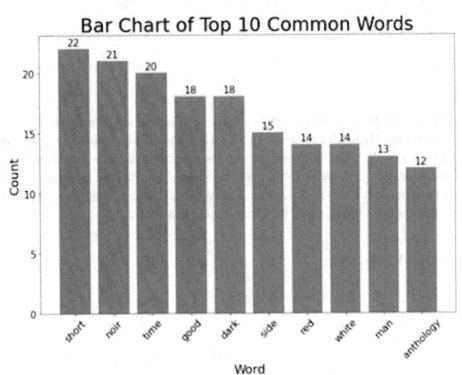

The bigram for KL NOIR: WHITE is shown in Figure 16. The frequency of two terms that appear repeatedly in user reviews is depicted in a bigram. As the frequency of two words rises, the size of terms on the diagram rises as well. From the bigram, we can conclude that most of the words in bigram is describing the tittle of the short stories in the book. From the words 'time agent' and 'father hero', the words are describing the short stories in the book. To sum up, short story titled Time Agents by Lim Li Anne had the highest frequency occurrence in this bigram.

Figure 16. KL NOIR: WHITE bigram

The trigram for KL NOIR: WHITE is shown in Figure 17. The trigram depicts the frequency of three words that appear repeatedly in user reviews. As the frequency of three words rises, the size of terms on the diagram rises as well. From the figure, we can see that the most frequency word that been used is 'aviator titanic nightmare' followed by, 'bertha stone justice', and 'titanic nightmare Christmas'. To summarize, the most frequent words are describing The Aviator, Titanic & a Nightmare before Christmas by Raja Faisal which is one of the tittle of the short stories in the book.

Figure 17. KL NOIR: WHITE trigram

Topic Modelling

Figure 18 shows the overall results, which include the bubbles and the most prominent terms that users frequently use. For the second volume of the books, a total of four bubbles were produced. Here, we can see that the bublels are not collided with each other. In this book, the most frequent words that are used are 'anthology', 'good', 'dark', 'twist' and 'red' are describing the plot of the stories.

Figure 18. Top 30 words for whole topics

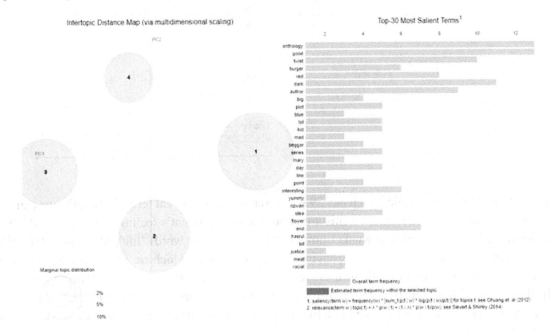

Figure 19 shows the topic 1 which is the dominant in the term of size of the bubble and the percentage of the relevant terms for the topics. In topic 1, most of the relevant terms for this topic are about 'twist', 'dark' and 'good'. These words are having frequently repeated by the users thus make it has the longest red bars. Most frequent terms for topic 4 are 'rizwan' and 'hasrul' which are one of the contributors in this book. This author created the story about the leading role that have the desire of man to improve his male genitals which is shown by the word 'penis'. In conclusion, topic 1 is about the stories about desire and passion of the role in achieving the things they want.

Figure 19. Top 30 words for topic 1

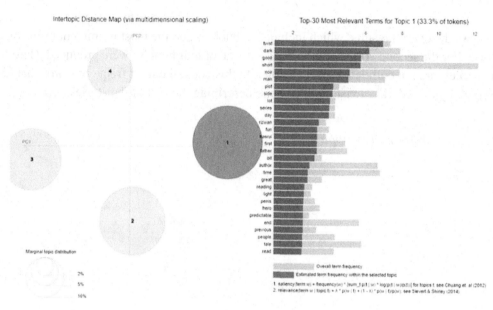

Figure 20 illustrates that topic 2 includes 29.4% of the most of relevant term. Generally, we can see that most of the words in the relevant terms are about the environment's feeling of the story which is having unfiltered story occurring at Kuala Lumpur. This because the words 'life', 'dark' and 'bad' and 'tale' are about describing the surrounding environment in each story which are commonly discussed by the users. On the term of 'interesting', the users review this book because the stories are about to exploring the dark side and light side that only existing in the fantasy. To conclude, topic 2 is about the feeling of the surrounding that have been describe in the stories which are attracting the users to frequently use the terms to reviews this series.

Figure 20. Top 30 words for topic 2

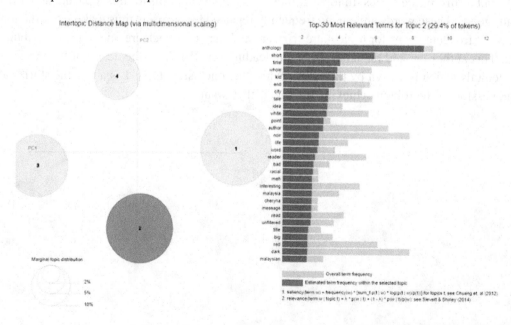

As shown in Figure 21, topic 3 has 23.9% of the top 30 most relevant terms. Here, we can see that majority of the words shown are describing one of the stories. The highest terms for topic 3 are 'burger', 'interesting' and 'guy'. It is because the words for topic 3 are describing one of the stories in this series which is Burger without Sides. The words 'tale', 'pin' and 'dirty' from the figure is related to the stories where the main role whose name is Pin is working at the burger stalls set the rules to his customers when eating there. In conclusion, most of the words in topic 5 are about the quaint story about the main role handling the dystopian society.

Figure 21. Top 30 words for topic 3

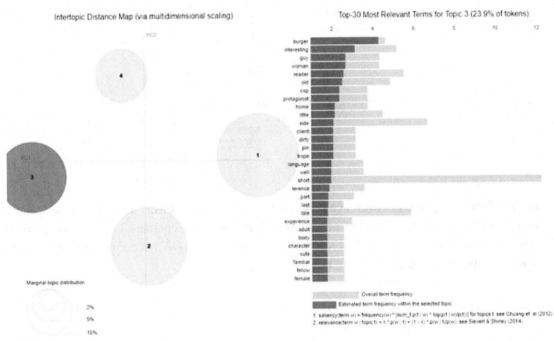

Figure 22 shows the results of topic 4 which has 13.5% of tokens from the top 30 most relevant terms and the bubble of topic 4 is not collided with any bubble. In this topic, a few words need to be highlighted such as 'violence', 'savage' and 'justice'. These words are described about the emotion of the role in the stories. Next, the word 'beggar' and 'mary' are described about the role whose having misfortune in their life. Hence, this topic is about the users reviews the emotion of the lead in this story whose are having unlucky fate in their lives.

Figure 22. Top 30 words for topic 4

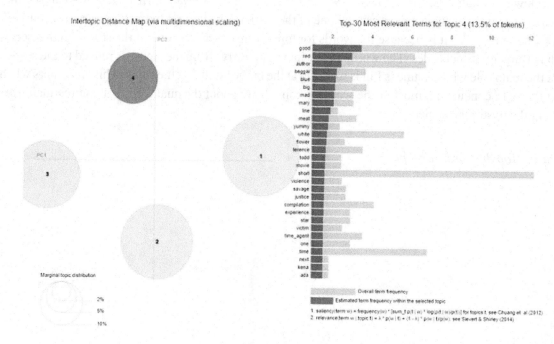

Figure 23 shows the graph of coherence score between two algorithms. These algorithms generate different number of topic where the LDA generates 4 topics and LSI generates 2 topics. For the result, LSI's score is highest than LDA. The LSI's score is 0.50 while the LDA's score is 0.34. To conclude, the best algorithms for the topic modelling is LSI.

Figure 23. Coherence score of LDA and LSI

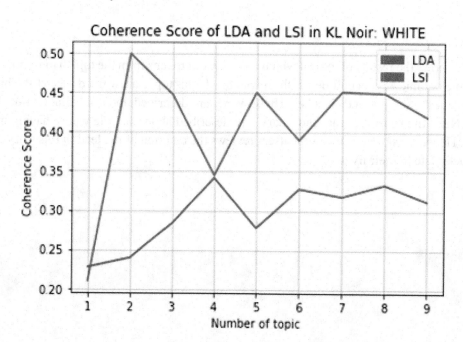

Sentiment Analysis

Figure 24 illustrates the top 10 positive sentences from the 51 reviews for the second volume of the KL Noir. The reviews have been sort in descending order based on the compound score. The first line of the figure which is line 34 has the highest compound score which is 0.9982 as the rules say the closer the compound score to 1, the higher the positivity of the sentence. Besides, in line 18, "Personally I enjoyed KL Noir White more than K…." with the positive score 0.718 has the booster word 'more' that make an impact of the intensity of the sentence is increase more towards the positive.

Figure 24. Top 10 positive sentences using Vader algorithm

```
The top 10 positive sentences are:
     Score Compound  Score Negative   Score Neutral   Score Positive  \
34       0.9982          0.110           0.739            0.152
25       0.9981          0.054           0.706            0.240
47       0.9844          0.000           0.528            0.472
1        0.9530          0.015           0.836            0.149
18       0.9492          0.093           0.718            0.188
14       0.9484          0.113           0.711            0.176
43       0.9451          0.000           0.497            0.503
40       0.9294          0.056           0.740            0.204
28       0.9092          0.053           0.700            0.247
3        0.8971          0.000           0.648            0.352

                                                        Sentence
34  KL Noir White has 18 unfiltered stories  hence...
25  so much genitals of the supernatural male geni...
47  I liked Red much better but White is still a w...
1   To be honest its not that i dislike the book b...
18  Personally I enjoyed KL Noir White more than K...
14  Loved it Its incredible how this book managed ...
43  I dont have much to say read review but I grea...
40  18 UNFLITERED STORIESEdited by Amir Hafizi I t...
28  The first half was ok The second half was bett...
3   I love RED more than WHITEMy favorite shorties...
```

Figure 25 shows the top 10 negative sentences from the 51 reviews for the second volume of the KL Noir. The reviews have been sort in ascending order based on the compound score. The first line of the figure which is line 31 has the lowest compound score with -0.9654. In review line 45, the sentences "18 unfiltered stories it braggedMore like 18 t…" has the highest negative score with 0.311, 0.631 neutral score and 0.059 positive score. This sentence has the highest negative score because the sentence consists negative word such as 'gross'.

Figure 25. Top 10 negative sentences using Vader algorithm

```
The top 10 negative sentences are:
      Score Compound  Score Negative  Score Neutral  Score Positive  \
32       -0.9654          0.138          0.811           0.050
45       -0.9617          0.311          0.631           0.059
20       -0.9022          0.157          0.773           0.070
19       -0.8282          0.144          0.777           0.079
27       -0.7964          0.122          0.809           0.068
11       -0.3400          0.246          0.560           0.194
6        -0.3291          0.134          0.768           0.097
17       -0.1791          0.099          0.812           0.089
0         0.0000          0.000          1.000           0.000
8         0.0000          0.000          1.000           0.000

                                                        Sentence
32   When a book mainly highlights the dark underto...
45   18 unfiltered stories it braggedMore like 18 t...
20   Lets go beyond the portrayal of KL from touris...
19   Gah Im not sure where to start I like the fact...
27   KL Noir White has 18 unfiltered stories  hence...
11   White is preferable Stories I liked savages ma...
6    Only one actually memorable short a whole lott...
17   This book is a bit plain maybe because it is w...
0    finished in one daypredictable plot twistsI ex...
8              read Burgers Without Sides first or last
```

Figure 26 depicts top 10 positive sentences from the 51 reviews for the second volume of the KL Noir. The reviews have been sort in descending order based on the polarity float. The first line of the figure which is line 30 has the highest polarity float with 0.65000, which means that the statement is positive, and 0.644444 subjectivity refers that the sentence contains opinion of the reviewer by the word 'impress'.

Figure 26. Top 10 positive sentences using Textblob

```
The top 10 positive sentences are:
     Polarity  Subjectivity                                        Sentence
30   0.650000    0.644444   Like the first instalment this offering is als...
50   0.600000    1.000000   its a compilation youve to read and experience...
37   0.533333    0.600000   great short stories from great authorsjoysadho...
0    0.500000    0.500000   finished in one daypredictable plot twistsI ex...
29   0.500000    0.500000   I gave this book 4 stars because of these stor...
2    0.440000    0.540000   I like this one better than KL NOIR REDThe sto...
46   0.437500    0.458333   The first five had plots that were plausible a...
14   0.331481    0.603148   Loved it Its incredible how this book managed ...
40   0.329167    0.561458   18 UNFLITERED STORIESEdited by Amir Hafizi I t...
47   0.327273    0.436364   I liked Red much better but White is still a w...
```

Figure 27 shows the top 10 positive sentences from the 51 reviews for the second volume of the KL Noir. The reviews have been sort in ascending order based on the polarity float. The first line of the figure which is line 13 has the lowest polarity with -0.100000, which means that the statement is negative and 0.400000 subjectivity. The highest subjectivity float is in line 15 by the sentence "You want gory tale You want twisted stuff You…" that mostly the sentence is about personal opinion of the users.

Figure 27. Top 10 negative sentences using Textblob

```
The top 10 negative sentences are:
      Polarity  Subjectivity                                          Sentence
13  -0.100000    0.400000  KL Noir is a collection of short stories akin ...
15  -0.066667    0.806481  You want gory tale You want twisted stuff You ...
44  -0.056250    0.710417  Wow i didnt think this book can be as clear an...
9   -0.018519    0.546296  The 2nd instalment of KL Noir does not disappo...
11  -0.006250    0.450000  White is preferable Stories I liked savages ma...
45  -0.006250    0.300000  18 unfiltered stories it braggedMore like 18 t...
34  -0.002381    0.326190  This book is a bit plain maybe because it is w...
39   0.000000    0.000000                too explicit but what should i expect
41   0.000000    0.000000                                                  RED
48   0.000000    0.000000  never ask someone to describe this for you do ...
```

Table 5 shows the score comparison between the Vader and Textblob algorithm based on 51 reviews. Here we can compare the score like for the positive score Textblob has the higher score than VADER where the Textblob score is 41 and VADER score is 37. For Neutral score, the difference between the score is 3 where VADER consist score of 6 and Textblob consist score of 3. Next, for negative score, there is only a difference between the score where VADER has 8 score and Textblob has 7 score. However, when comparing between the algorithms, VADER performed the best because its produce accurate result for the score. This was primarily due to its ability to accurately assign sentiment to words used.

Table 5. Total score of VADER and Textblob algorithms

Sentiment Analysis Model	Positive	Neutral	Negative
VADER	37	6	8
TextBlob	41	3	7

KL NOIR: BLUE (KL NOIR #3) (2014) (32 reviews)

Text Normalization and Visualization

The chart illustrated in Figure 28 indicates the number of users give the rating for the KL NOIR: BLUE. It can see that the book has 32 reviews. The rate of 4 represents the highest value for the rate followed by 3, 5 and 2. The rate of 4 has the highest number of users at 16 whereas the rate of 3 has 8 users. The rate of 5 and 2 are having the same number of users and they made up 8 users of the total figure. The rate of 4 is clearly shown the highest value for the total figure compared to other rates.

Figure 28. KL NOIR: BLUE rating bar chart

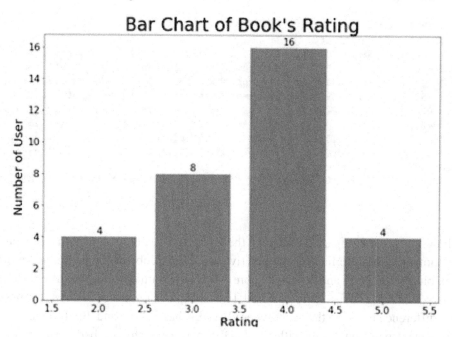

Figure 29 illustrates the total of common words that are always used in KL NOIR: BLUE. The word 'noir' is the most frequent word in this book with 16 counts and followed by the word of 'piece' with 13 counts, 'good' with 12 counts and 'bag' with 11 counts. The word 'saint', 'writer' and 'monster' are having the same number of counts with 10 while the word 'woman', 'blue' and 'sinful' is the least frequent with 8 counts.

Figure 29. KL NOIR: BLUE top common word bar chart

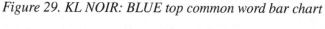

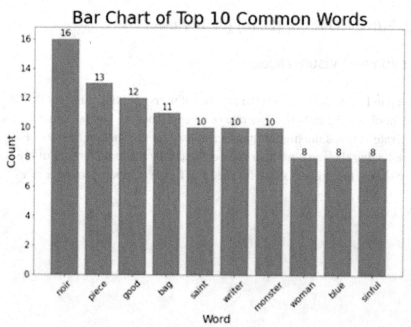

The bigram for KL NOIR: BLUE is shown in Figure 30. The frequency of two terms that appear repeatedly in user reviews is depicted in a bigram. As the frequency of two words rises, the size of terms on the diagram rises as well. From the bigram, we can conclude that most of the words in bigram is describing the tittle of the short stories in the book. From the words 'sinful saint' followed by 'bathroom wall', 'woman place' and 'unwanted utopia', these words are describing the short stories in the book. To sum up, short stories tittle Sinful Saints by Iqbal Abu Bakar had the highest frequency occurrence in this bigram.

Figure 30. KL NOIR: BLUE bigram

Figure 31 shows the trigram for KL NOIR: BLUE. The trigram depicts the frequency of three words that appear repeatedly in user reviews. As the frequency of three words rises, the size of terms on the diagram rises as well. From the figure, we can see that the most frequency word that been used is 'utopia ii deviant' followed by 'unwanted utopia ii', 'iqbal abu bakar' and 'saint iqbal abu'. To summarize, the most frequent words are describing *Unwanted Utopia II: Deviant by* Joelyn Alexandra and which is one of the tittles of the short stories in the book.

Figure 31. KL NOIR: BLUE trigram

Topic Modelling

Figure 32 shows the overall results which contain the bubbles and the most salient terms that are frequently used by the users. The third book consists of five bubbles which are far from each other. For the top 30 most salient terms in the user reviews such are 'good', 'kl_noir', 'fixi' and 'blue' are describing about the interest of the users towards this book.

Figure 32. Top 30 words for whole topics

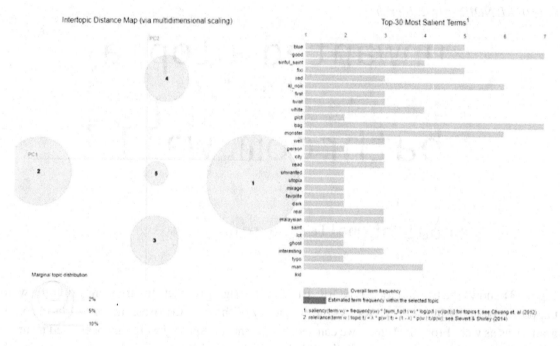

Based on Figure 33, topic 1 bubble is the largest topic. Topic 1 consists of 48.5% for the 30 most relevant terms of the topic. For the most frequent terms used by the reviewers are 'writer', 'rozlan', 'karina' and 'zedeck'. All these terms are about the contributors of this book who are the Goodreads author. There are also some words like 'entertaining' and 'great' that describe the reviews of the users about the story in the book. It can conclude for the topic 1 is about the author of the Goodreads.

Figure 33. Top 30 words for topic 1

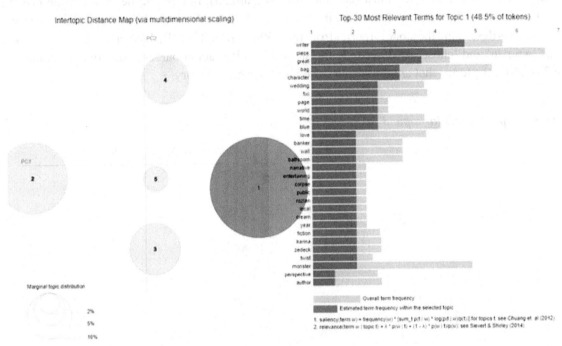

As shown in Figure 34, topic 2 score is 24.5% of the most relevant terms. Topic 2 is biut describing the character personality in the book where there is word like 'man', 'ballerina' and 'woman' that are describing the character with their personality which are described by the words 'monster', 'gangster' and 'sinful_saint'. To conclude, this topic is about the personality that the character has in the story.

Figure 34. Top 30 words for topic 2

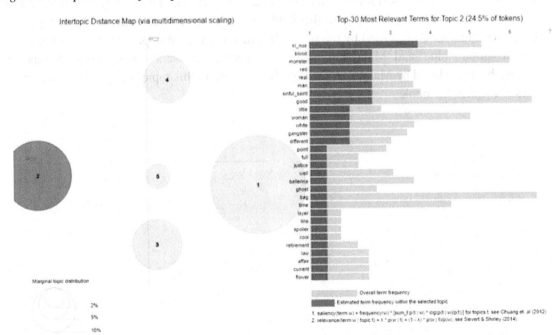

Topic 3 score is 12.9% of the most relevant terms (Figure 35). In topic 3, the bubble is describing about one of short story which is A Woman in Five Pieces because from the word 'reprint', we can say that the word is describing the story is reprint from the "Whose Blood Was It, Anyway?". The other words such as 'woman' and 'ghost' are describing the story which it is about paranormal story. To conclude, topic 3 is about the terms that are the reviews used to describe this story.

Figure 35. Top 30 words for topic 3

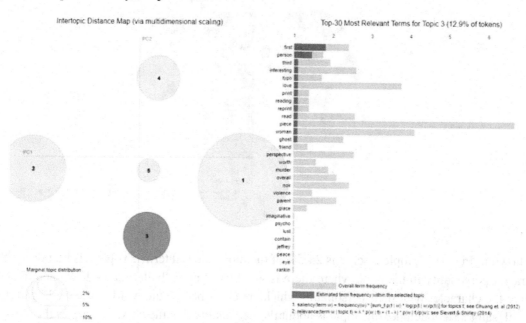

In topic 4, the score for the most relevant terms is 11.2% (Figure 36). The bubble of this topic also did not collide with others, thus, the topic for this bubble is different from the others. In this topic, the most related terms that have been used by the reviewers are about their compliment towards the book. From the word 'good', 'blue', and 'Malaysian', we can say that the reviewers want to praise this series of book that have been produced by Malaysian's author. In conclusion, this topic is about the compliment of the users to towards the book.

Figure 36. Top 30 words for topic 4

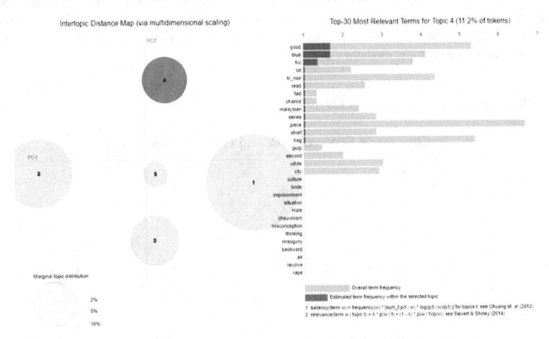

As shown in Figure 37, topic 5 is the smallest topic and having the least number of percentages which is only 3%. Although this topic is the smallest, the bubble of this topic is located at the center and did not collide with any bubble.

Figure 37. Top 30 words for topic 5

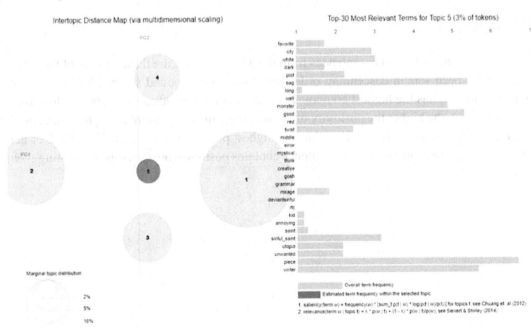

Figure 38 is about the graph of coherence score between two algorithms. These algorithms generate different number of topic where the LDA generates 5 topics and LSI generates 8 topics. For the result, LSI's score is highest than LDA. The LSI's score is 0.65 while the LDA's score is 0.47. To conclude, the best algorithms for the topic modelling is LSI.

Figure 38. Coherence Score of LDA and LSI

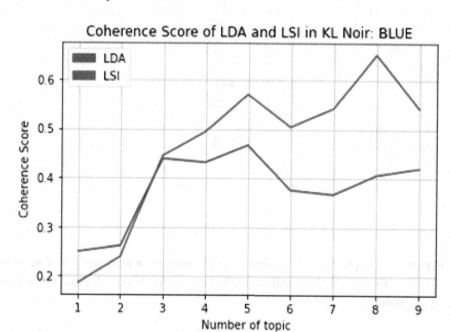

Sentiment Analysis

Figure 39 shows the top 10 positive sentences from the 32 reviews for the third volume of the KL Noir. The reviews have been sort in descending order based on the compound score. The first line of the figure which is line 10 has the highest compound score which is 0.9990 as the rules say the closer the compound score to 1, the higher the positivity of the sentence. In review number 28, the sentence "This felt like a bit of a mixed bag although I ..." has the highest positive score with 0.272, 0.632 of neutral score and 0.096 negative score because the sentence contains positive words such as 'interesting', 'enjoy' and 'satisfying'.

Figure 39. Top 10 positive sentences using Vader algorithm

```
The top 10 positive sentences are:
     Score Compound   Score Negative   Score Neutral   Score Positive  \
10      0.9990           0.053            0.789           0.158
5       0.9930           0.065            0.775           0.160
22      0.9923           0.104            0.687           0.208
26      0.9584           0.020            0.775           0.206
12      0.9473           0.078            0.760           0.162
28      0.9424           0.096            0.632           0.272
14      0.9287           0.000            0.853           0.147
7       0.9030           0.000            0.795           0.205
6       0.8727           0.156            0.602           0.242
0       0.8622           0.050            0.714           0.235

                                              Sentence
10   Amir Muhammad has probably made more money fro...
5    I thought the first story Ballerina in Pink Ro...
22   Murkier blue Love the diversity of ideas I lik...
26   I really enjoyed this one despite of my on and...
12   firstly the cover it is interesting to note th...
28   This felt like a bit of a mixed bag although I...
14   KL Noir Blue was the second book that I read a...
7    This is the second KL Noir book Ive read after...
6    I must say that this book is better than White...
0    Lots of nice stories  some were average Still ...
```

Figure 40 illustrates the top 10 negative sentences from the 32 reviews for the third volume of the KL Noir. The reviews have been sort in ascending order based on the compound score. The first line of the figure which is line 18 has the lowest compound score with -0.8815. In review line 4, the sentences "The first half of this book of short stories is…" has the negative score with 0.255, 0.745 neutral score and 0.000 positive score. This sentence has word 'boring' thus make the sentence is negative sentiment.

Figure 40. Top 10 negative sentences using Vader algorithm

```
The top 10 negative sentences are:
     Score Compound   Score Negative   Score Neutral   Score Positive  \
18     -0.8815          0.099            0.813           0.088
2      -0.6855          0.145            0.745           0.110
4      -0.5859          0.255            0.745           0.000
21     -0.4767          0.137            0.728           0.135
9      -0.3612          0.112            0.828           0.060
11     -0.1901          0.163            0.662           0.175
31     -0.1531          0.265            0.515           0.221
3       0.0000          0.000            1.000           0.000
19      0.0000          0.000            1.000           0.000
27      0.0000          0.000            1.000           0.000

                                              Sentence
18   I already knew what to say about KL Noir No Ar...
2    There are some stories that felt too draggy an...
4    The first half of this book of short stories i...
21   Better than Yellow or White thats for sure The...
9    I find this one a tad depressing Maybe because...
11   its okay  some stories are so cool but no way ...
31      My favorite is Sinful Saints by Iqbal Abu Bakar
3                                               RTC
19   These two deserve 5 Unwanted Utopia II  Devian...
27       It gives a different perspective of the city
```

Figure 41 shows the top 10 positive sentences from the 32 reviews for the third volume of the KL Noir. The reviews have been sort in descending order based on the polarity float. The first line of the figure which is line 20 has the highest polarity float with 0.550000, which means that the statement is positive, and 0.650000 subjectivity refers that the sentence contains emotion of the reviewer by the word 'like'.

Figure 41. Top 10 positive sentences using Textblob

```
The top 10 positive sentences are:
      Polarity  Subjectivity                                            Sentence
20   0.550000     0.650000   Another good KL Noir book I like most of the s...
 1   0.500000     0.500000   I dont quite understand what happen in monster...
31   0.500000     1.000000    My favorite is Sinful Saints by Iqbal Abu Bakar
11   0.425000     0.575000   its okay  some stories are so cool but no way ...
17   0.400000     0.533333   A collection of short stories which revolve ar...
 8   0.375000     0.850000                     Funny I quite enjoyed this book
16   0.333333     0.100000   1 Ballerina in Pink2 Whose Blood Was It Anyway...
29   0.330000     0.580000   Worth reading some of the story is quite good ...
23   0.312500     0.500000   I enjoy reading most of the stories because it...
21   0.281250     0.392361   Better than Yellow or White thats for sure The...
```

Figure 42 illustrates the top 10 positive sentences from the 32 reviews for the third volume of the KL Noir. The reviews have been sort in ascending order based on the polarity float. The first line of the figure which is line 4 has the lowest polarity with -0.183333, which means that the statement is negative and 0.360000 subjectivity. The highest subjectivity float is in line 15 by the sentence "Better stories Sadly couldn't find it anymore h…" that mostly the sentence is about personal opinion and emotions of the users by the words of 'better stories' and 'sadly'.

Figure 42. Top 10 negative sentences using Textblob

```
The top 10 negative sentences are:
      Polarity  Subjectivity                                            Sentence
 4  -0.183333     0.360000   The first half of this book of short stories i...
 3   0.000000     0.000000                                                 RTC
13   0.000000     0.000000   My favorites areMonstersSinful saintsBathroom ...
15   0.000000     0.750000   Better stories Sadly couldnt find it anymore h...
19   0.000000     0.000000   These two deserve 5 Unwanted Utopia II  Devian...
27   0.000000     0.600000       It gives a different perspective of the city
 6   0.030000     0.430000   I must say that this book is better than White...
 9   0.060000     0.400000   I find this one a tad depressing Maybe because...
 2   0.083333     0.641667   There are some stories that felt too draggy an...
26   0.100000     0.361364   I really enjoyed this one despite of my on and...
```

Table 6 shows the score comparison between the Vader and Textblob algorithm based on 32 reviews. Here we can compare the score like for the positive score Textblob has the higher score than VADER where the Textblob score is 26 and VADER score is 22. For Neutral score, the difference between the score is 2 where VADER consist score of 3 and Textblob consist score of 5. Next, for negative score, there is 6 score difference between the score where VADER has 7 score and Textblob has 1 score. However, when comparing between the algorithms, VADER performed the best because its produce accurate result for the score. This was primarily due to its ability to accurately assign sentiment to words used.

Table 6. Total score of VADER and Textblob algorithms

Sentiment Analysis Model	Positive	Neutral	Negative
VADER	22	3	7
TextBlob	26	5	1

KL NOIR: YELLOW (KL NOIR #4) (2014) (30 reviews)

Text Normalization and Visualization

The graph in Figure 43 shows the book's rating for KL NOIR: YELLOW which consists of 30 reviews. Nearly, majority of viewers give the rating of the book are 4 and 3, with just 3 viewers different between the two. Rate of 5 had dropped to 2 reviews of the total and rate of 1 is continuing dropped to 1 review. To summarize, the graph shows that each user had rate the book, the most rating by the users is 4 followed by 3, 5 and 2.

Figure 43. KL NOIR: YELLOW rating bar chart

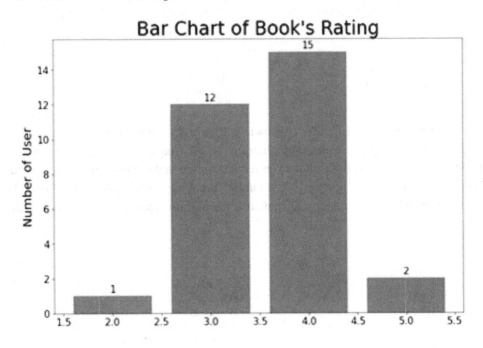

The chart in Figure 44 indicates total top common words that have been used for KL NOIR: YELLOW. It is clear that 'noir' is the most popular word with 40 counts. the next word, which is 'good' fell to 24 counts and having a small difference with the next two words which are 'series' and 'fry' at 18 and 16. Next, there are two pairs of the word having the same total counts at 15 and 12. The first pair are 'collection', 'french' and 'point' and the second are 'short' and 'writer'.

Figure 44. KL NOIR: YELLOW top common word bar chart

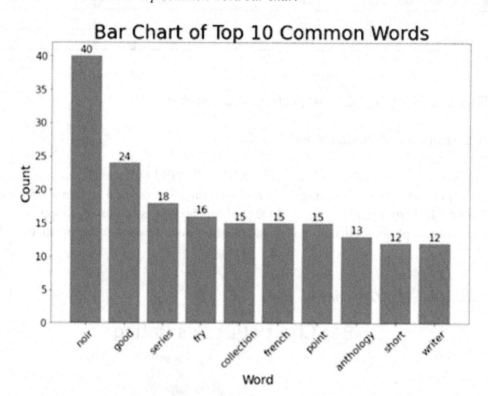

The bigram for KL NOIR: YELLOW is shown in Figure 45. The frequency of two terms that appear repeatedly in user reviews is depicted in a bigram. As the frequency of two words rises, the size of terms on the diagram rises as well. From the figure, we can see that the most frequency word that been used is 'french fry' followed by 'noir series', 'kl noir', 'breaking point' and 'noir yellow'. To sum up, short stories tittle French Fries for Aunty Kamala had the highest frequency occurrence in this bigram.

Figure 45. KL NOIR: YELLOW bigram

The trigram for KL NOIR: YELLOW is illustrated in Figure 46. The trigram depicts the frequency of three words that appear repeatedly in user reviews. As the frequency of three words rises, the size of terms on the diagram rises as well. From the figure, we can see that the most frequency word that been used is 'kl noir series' followed by 'timothy nakayama ambrosia', 'favourite french fry', 'noir yellow bit' and 'pilgrim happy family'. To summarize, the most frequent words are describing about this series as this is the last series of the KL Noir.

Figure 46. KL NOIR: YELLOW trigram

Topic Modelling

For the fourth volumes of KL Noir, Figure 47 shows the overall results, which include the bubbles and the most frequently used terms by users. For this book, there are six bubbles produced. The first and fifth bubbles are touching each other while others not. The most salient terms in this book are 'noir' which consist of the longest blue bar followed by 'series' and 'collection' describing the latest and last series of collection KL Noir.

Figure 47. Top 30 words for whole topics

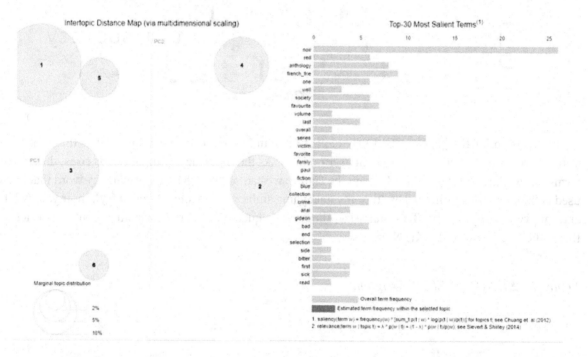

Figure 48 illustrates topic 1 which is dominantly in term of size of the bubble and percentage which is 34.3%. The most used term in topic 1 is 'good' which occupying half of the blue bar with the red bar. Some of the relevant terms for topic 1 were taken from the title of the short stories such as words 'french_frie', 'ambrosia' and 'anai'. These words are frequently reviewed by the users because their similarity storyline is about murder and get the most intention than others short stories. To conclude, topic 1 is about the crime title which are frequently discussed by the reviewers.

Figure 48. Top 30 words for topic 1

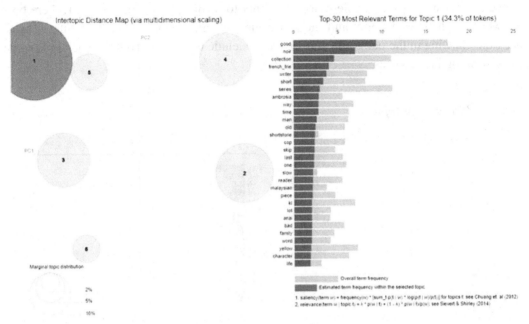

Figure 49 shows the results of topic 2. The bubble of the topic 2 is mostly distant from the other topics. The most frequent word that has been used in this topic is 'noir', 'anthology', 'red' and 'fiction'. Here we can see that the terms that has pick the users eye is about their short stories in this series. From the words 'crime', 'series' and 'collection' we can conclude that the reviewers are discussing about the collections because it has the most strongest and twisted stories.

Figure 49. Top 30 words for topic 2

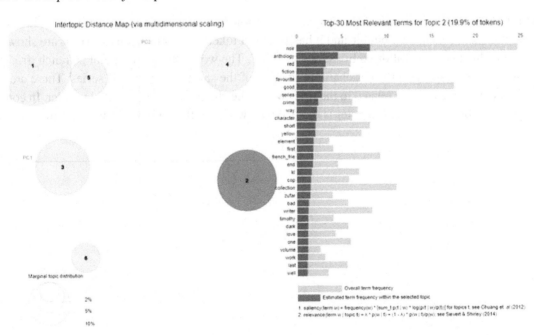

The results of topic 3 are shown in Figure 50. Topic 3 is having 17% from the top 30 most relevant terms. Since the distance of the bubble in topic 3 is not to further than bubble topic 1, there be some repetitive words such as 'collection' and 'noir'. Besides, there are words 'voice', 'young', 'man' and 'girl' that were showing in the bar graph that we can conclude topic 3 is about the social life of people that were describing in the series.

Figure 50. Top 30 words for topic 3

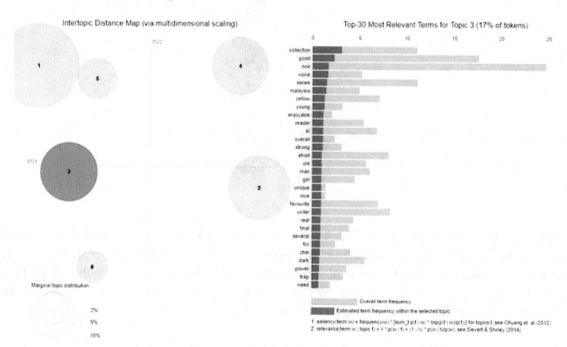

Figure 51 shows the intertopic distance map and the top 30 words that appeared in topic 4. Bubble in topic 4 is not collided with any bubble and it has 16.2% of tokens. The highest used words are shown by the red bars which is 'noir' followed by 'series' and 'kl'. The words 'breaking_point', 'french_frie' and 'ambrosia' that are gain from the bar chart are the title of the short stories in this series. There are also word 'character' which can be related to the titles where the character is the potential murder. In conclusion, topic 4 is about to tell the character is the one who will give the reviewers shocked from the titles.

Figure 51. Top 30 words for topic 4

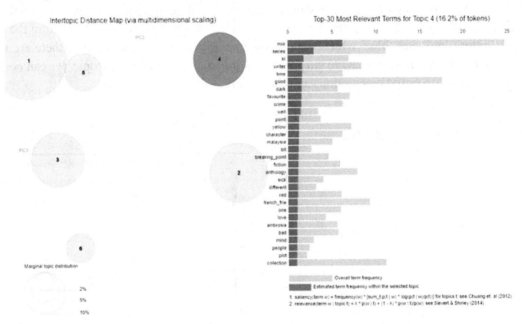

Figure 52 shows the results of the topic 5 in the fourth volume of KL Noir books. The bubble for topic 5 is collided with the bubble from topic 1 thus it makes some of the words from both topics are similar. For example, the words 'noir' which is highest frequent terms in this topic is also repeated in topic 1. From the most top 30 relevant terms for topic 5, certain words on this topic can be categorize to social life such as 'victim', 'family' and 'man'. There are also words such as 'dark', 'crime' and 'trap' that describing the anthology in the series. To conclude this, topic 5 is about the social life which is potential to be stuck with the dark side.

Figure 52. Top 30 words for topic 5

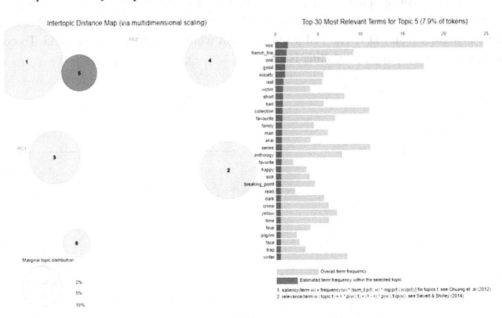

Topic 6 consist of the smallest size of bubble and percentage of the most relevant terms from other topics (Figure 53). From the bar graph, we can see that the size of the red bars in topic 6 was really short comparing to other topics. In this topic, some words can be categorized as an emotion from the words 'twisted', 'bitter', 'red' and 'blue' which were symbolize as passion and calm. Also, there are maybe related words to the emotions which are purposed to word 'society'. As for this topic, we can conclude that topic 6 is mainly focused on emotions and the society.

Figure 53. Top 30 words for topic 6

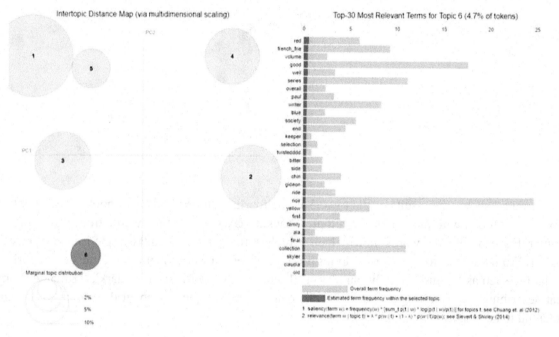

Figure 54 illustrates the graph of coherence score between two algorithms. These algorithms generate different number of topic where the LDA generates 6 topics and LSI generates 2 topics. For the result, LSI's score is highest than LDA. The LSI's score is 0.68 while the LDA's score is 0.35. To conclude, the best algorithms for the topic modelling is LSI.

Figure 54. Coherence Score of LDA and LSI

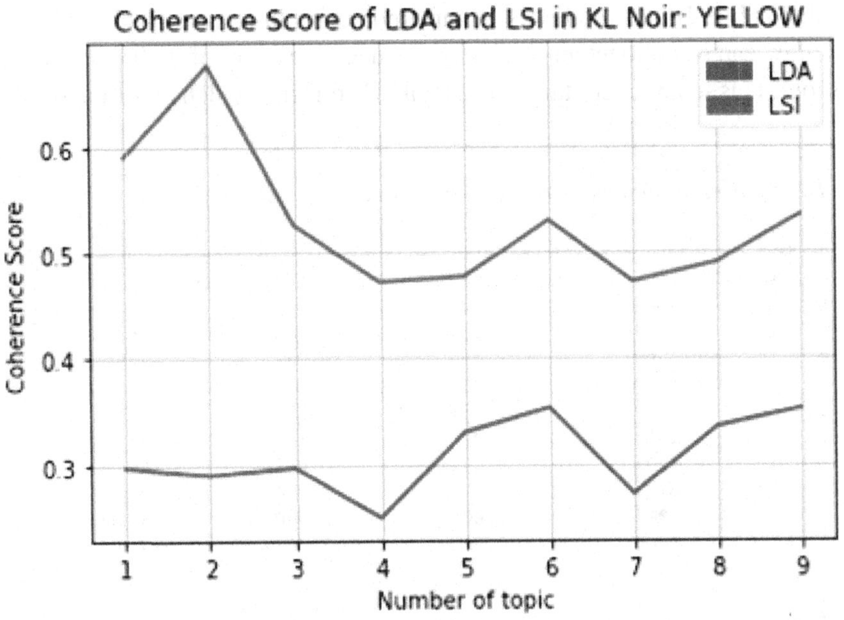

Sentiment Analysis

Figure 55 shows the top 10 positive sentences from the 30 reviews for the fourth volume of the KL Noir. The reviews have been sort in descending order based on the compound score. The first line of the figure which is line 1 has the highest compound score which is 0.0.9960 as the rules say the closer the compound score to 1, the higher the positivity of the sentence. Next, for example in line 0, "Feels like Malaysian some were actually good s..." with the positive score of 0.461 used the word 'like' and 'good' which represent positive sentiments.

Figure 55. Top 10 positive sentences using Vader algorithm

```
The top 10 positive sentences are:
     Score Compound  Score Negative  Score Neutral  Score Positive  \
1          0.9960          0.106          0.733          0.161
13         0.9957          0.010          0.757          0.232
17         0.9826          0.081          0.802          0.118
24         0.8922          0.074          0.707          0.219
0          0.8779          0.000          0.539          0.461
14         0.8176          0.043          0.772          0.185
16         0.7745          0.072          0.841          0.087
22         0.7030          0.000          0.654          0.346
20         0.6652          0.000          0.611          0.389
19         0.5859          0.178          0.541          0.281

                                           Sentence
1    I rate anthologies for the sum of their parts ...
13   My second KL NOIR series read was indeed much ...
17   Disclaimer  Fixi Novo is the publisher of my c...
24   The darkest among the series Provoking as usua...
0    Feels like Malaysian some were actually good s...
14   My favorites are Paul GnanaSelvams The Ride Ti...
16   I have no idea that this is the last book of t...
22   Last anthologies KL Noir which wasnt disappoin...
20    My least favourite but still enjoyed few stories
19   Saya suka cerita Anai walaupun ia sangat distu...
```

Figure 56 illustrates the top 10 negative sentences from the 30 reviews for the fourth volume of the KL Noir. The reviews have been sort in ascending order based on the compound score. The first line of the figure which is line 18 has the lowest compound score. In review number 23, the sentence "To the bitter end Yellow can stand together si..." with the negative score of 0.103, 0.855 neutral score and 0.042 positive score. This sentence contains words 'bitter' and 'cry' which represent negative sentiments.

Figure 56. Top 10 negative sentences using Vader algorithm

```
The top 10 negative sentences are:
     Score Compound   Score Negative   Score Neutral   Score Positive  \
18       -0.9804          0.107           0.817           0.076
3        -0.9104          0.178           0.704           0.118
10       -0.8708          0.094           0.845           0.061
5        -0.8360          0.112           0.846           0.042
26       -0.6509          0.136           0.726           0.138
21       -0.6458          0.097           0.842           0.062
23       -0.4939          0.103           0.855           0.042
27       -0.0781          0.182           0.664           0.155
11        0.0000          0.000           1.000           0.000
29        0.0000          0.000           1.000           0.000

                                                      Sentence
18  The last book in the KL Noir series I found Ye...
3   the cover makes me hungry trap mindblowing a g...
10  Guess Ill just come right out and say it I do ...
5   I read this book after Ive finished my SPM Tri...
26  Fixis popular KL Noir series is completed this...
21  Finally I have to say that this last part of K...
23  To the bitter end Yellow can stand together si...
27  I really liked French Fries for Aunty Kamalam ...
11                                          TWISTEDDDD
29  Finished the whole Noir series and Id have to ...
```

Figure 57 shows the top 10 positive sentences from the 30 reviews for the fourth volume of the KL Noir. The reviews have been sort in descending order based on the polarity float. The first line of the figure which is line 14 has the highest polarity float with 0.500000, which means that the statement is positive and 0.712500 subjectivity floats. In review number 6, the sentence "1 Trap2 French Fries for Aunty Kamalam3 the Ki..." has 0.750000 of subjectivity float. The sentence is a personal opinion of the reviewers of the book.

Figure 57. Top 10 positive sentences using Textblob

```
The top 10 positive sentences are:
     Polarity  Subjectivity                                         Sentence
14   0.500000   0.712500   My favorites are Paul GnanaSelvams The Ride Ti...
6    0.450000   0.750000   1 Trap2 French Fries For Aunty Kamalam3 The Ki...
0    0.435000   0.640000   Feels like Malaysian some were actually good s...
25   0.275000   0.575000   KL NOIR TO THE BITTER END Edited by Kris Willi...
28   0.200000   0.532143   some of the shortstories are being too cliche ...
13   0.188029   0.438503   My second KL NOIR series read was indeed much ...
3    0.158780   0.444048   the cover makes me hungry trap mindblowing a g...
12   0.147727   0.527273   Ive made an unbelievable slow progress on this...
17   0.146493   0.427344   Disclaimer  Fixi Novo is the publisher of my c...
1    0.121806   0.482209   I rate anthologies for the sum of their parts ...
```

Figure 58 shows the top 10 negative sentences from the 30 reviews for the fourth volume of the KL Noir. The reviews have been sort in ascending order based on the polarity float. The first line of the figure which is line 21 has the lowest polarity with -0.071528, which means that the statement is negative and 0.364583 subjectivity.

Figure 58. Top 10 negative sentences using Textblob

```
The top 10 negative sentences are:
     Polarity  Subjectivity                                         Sentence
21  -0.071528   0.364583   Finally I have to say that this last part of K...
22  -0.066667   0.422222   Last anthologies KL Noir which wasnt disappoin...
18  -0.015691   0.497428   The last book in the KL Noir series I found Ye...
2    0.000000   0.000000   Like the editor said it comes with fries And y...
4    0.000000   0.000000   My favorites areAnaiThe rideBreaking pointNeve...
11   0.000000   0.000000                                         TWISTEDDDD
20   0.000000   0.400000    My least favourite but still enjoyed few stories
9    0.008073   0.578125   Frankly this is my least favorite of the serie...
19   0.017143   0.621429   Saya suka cerita Anai walaupun ia sangat distu...
10   0.026885   0.475066   Guess Ill just come right out and say it I do ...
```

Table 7 shows the score comparison between the Vader and Textblob algorithm based on 30 reviews. Here we can compare the score like for the positive score Textblob has the higher score than VADER where the Textblob score is 23 and VADER score is 19. For Neutral score, the difference between the score is 1 where VADER consist score of 3 and Textblob consist score of 4. Next, for negative score, there is 5 score difference between the score where VADER has 8 score and Textblob has 3 score. However, when comparing between the algorithms, VADER performed the best because its produce accurate result for the score. This was primarily due to its ability to accurately assign sentiment to words used.

Table 7. Total score of VADER and Textblob algorithms

Sentiment Analysis Model	Positive	Neutral	Negative
VADER	19	3	8
TextBlob	23	4	3

TEXT VISUALIZATION

Comparison of the Four Volumes of KL NOIR

From the pie chart (Figure 59), it is clear that the majority of the users are more likely to read KL NOIR: RED which has the highest percentage at 37.6%, with just 9.4% differences between the KL NOIR: WHITE at 28.2% followed by KL NOIR: BLUE (17.7%) and KL NOIR: YELLOW (16.6%).

Figure 59. Percentage of four volumes of KL NOIR

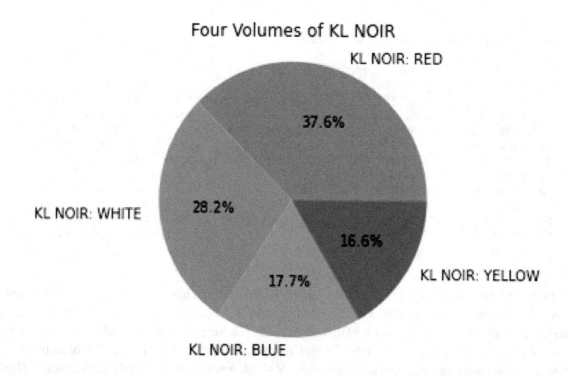

Figure 60 presents the overall rating for the volume of KL NOIR books. Y-axis is represented as the number of users who give the reviews and X-axis is used to show the rating each book gets. Four lines are used to differentiate each other. In this figure, we can conclude the most popular books from the volume are KL NOIR: RED.

Figure 60. Overall rating for the books

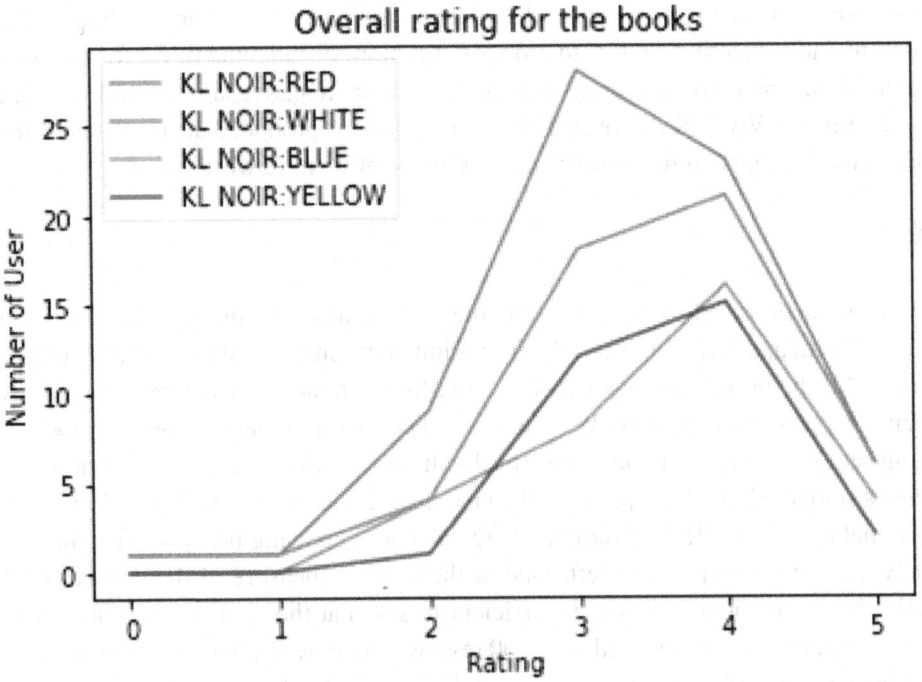

DISCUSSION AND CONCLUSION

To study the process of text mining, we used the data collected from the books which are the four volumes of *KL Noir* from the Goodreads website. As the project is about to extract the information based on reader-users' review, we performed the process of text mining on each book to get different views for each book. From the results above, we can conclude that text mining can help the users to analyze the words that have always been used to describe the books and summarize the users' feedback. Also, from the results that we gain, we conclude that our objective of this project has been achieved.

First, to extract the data from the books in the Goodreads, we used the scrapping method for each book. Then, we discovered the rate and the top topic that the users used to review the books by doing text visualization. Text visualizations gives us faster understanding to the most important keywords in a text, summarizes the content, and reveals patterns and trends. The visuals that we had on this project are bar chart, pie chart, graph chart and bigram and trigram.

To describe topics within the data, Topic Modelling entails counting words and grouping similar word patterns. In this project, we used 2 algorithms which are Latent Dirichlet Allocation (LDA) and Latent semantic indexing (LSI). These algorithms show 10 major topics with the coherence score in the graph and the highest coherence score means that the topic is the best topic among the users. In LDA, the important part is that we use visualisations to analyse the clusters created by LDA where each bubble in the results represent the topics. However, when we compare the coherence scores between the two algorithms, the results show that LSI coherence score is higher than LDA. To conclude, the best algorithms for the topic modelling is LSI.

As for sentiment evaluation, we used Vader and textblob algorithm. In Vader algorithm, we detected whether the sentence is positive, negative, or neutral sentiment while in textblob, we used polarity and subjectivity where the polarity is determined to detect whether the sentence is positive, negative, or neutral sentiment and subjectivity refers to emotion, opinion, or judgement. As for the results we got, we compare the results based on the scores which are positive, negative, and neutral. To conclude what we got from the results, VADER performed the best because it produced accurate result for the score. This was primarily due to its ability to accurately assign sentiment to words used.

Limitation

The limitation we encountered in this project is the code ethics. Writing a code that a computer can understand is different and difficult. Next, the limitation is the small number of the reviews that are left after scrapping. All the books have plenty of review; for example, first volume contains 205 reviews but after been scrapped, the reviews only 68 are left. The second volume originally had 154 reviews, but after being scrapped only 51 are left. The third volume initially contained 97 reviews out of which only 32 reviews remained after scrapping. Likewise, in the fourth volume only 30 reviews were left out of the original number of 91. The number of reviews is decreasing because after the data had been scrapped, only the unique reviews are left. Due to the smaller measure of the number of the reviews for each book, the results obtained were insufficient to say that the results were the best because the numbers of reviews are not even succeeded to 100 reviews. Also, when the data processed, the data that we extracted from Goodreads needed to be broken down to make the computer understand the data, a process that was very time consuming.

CONCLUSION AND FUTURE WORK

Finally, we can say that text mining refers to the process of extracting interesting and non-trivial information and knowledge from unstructured text in general. In this project, we have applied all the processes needed—that is, text normalization, text visualization, topic modeling and sentiment analysis—to successfully achieve the objective results. This project identified and explored patterns and trends using data from the Goodreads website. The results listed in this paper represent a small fraction of the potential for this approach in social media mining. In future, we hope that the limitations in this project can be overcome to prevent unwanted results. We also hope that the development on this research become deeper as more functions are being added to Machine Learning and Natural Language Processing, and old functions are being revised to support more processes.

REFERENCES

Adomavicius, G., & Tuzhilin, A. (2005). Toward the next generation of recommender systems: a survey of the state-of-the-art and possible extensions. *Transactions on Knowledge and Data Engineering, 17*(6), 734–749. https://ieeexplore.ieee.org/abstract/document/1423975/

Agarwal, B., & Mittal, N. (2017). Machine Learning Approaches for Sentiment Analysis. In *Artificial Intelligence, Concepts, Methodologies, Tools, and Applications*. doi:10.4018/978-1-5225-1759-7.ch070

Asl, M. P. (2021). Gender, space and counter-conduct: Iranian women's heterotopic imaginations in Ramita Navai's City of Lies. *Gender, Place and Culture*, 1–21. Advance online publication. doi:10.10 80/0966369X.2021.1975100

Asl, M. P. (2022). Truth, space, and resistance: Iranian women's practices of freedom in Ramita Navai's City of Lies. *Women's Studies*. Advance online publication. doi:10.1080/00497878.2022.2030342

D'Andrea, A., Ferri, F., Grifoni, P., & Guzzo, T. (2015). Approaches, Tools and Applications for Sentiment Analysis Implementation. *International Journal of Computers and Applications*, *125*(3), 26–33. doi:10.5120/ijca2015905866

Gundecha, P., & Liu, H. (2012). Mining Social Media: A Brief Introduction. *2012 TutORials in Operations Research, Dmml*, 1–17. doi:10.1287/educ.1120.0105

Gupta, V., & Lehal, G. (2009). A Survey of Text Mining Techniques and Applications. *Journal of Emerging Technologies in Web Intelligence*, *1*(1). Advance online publication. doi:10.4304/jetwi.1.1.60-76

Jelodar, H., Wang, Y., Yuan, C., Feng, X., Jiang, X., Li, Y., & Zhao, L. (2019). Latent Dirichlet allocation (LDA) and topic modeling: Models, applications, a survey. *Multimedia Tools and Applications*, *78*(11), 15169–15211. doi:10.100711042-018-6894-4

Julia, S., & David, R. (n.d.). *6 Topic modeling | Text Mining with R*. Retrieved January 1, 2022, from https://www.tidytextmining.com/topicmodeling.html

Kalra, P. (2013). Text mining: Concepts, process and applications. *Journal of Global Research in Computer Science*, *4*, 36–39.

Kherwa, P., & Bansal, P. (2020). Topic modeling: a comprehensive review. *EAI Endorsed Transactions on Scalable Information Systems*, *7*(24).

Malik, E. F., Keikhosrokiani, P., & Asl, M. P. (2021). Text mining life cycle for a spatial reading of Viet Thanh Nguyen's *The Refugees* (2017). In *The 2021 International Congress of Advanced Technology and Engineering (ICOTEN)*. 10.1109/ICOTEN52080.2021.9493520

Medhat, W., Hassan, A., & Korashy, H. (2014). Sentiment analysis algorithms and applications: A survey. *Ain Shams Engineering Journal*, *5*(4), 1093–1113. doi:10.1016/j.asej.2014.04.011

Ying, S. Y., Keikhosrokiani, P., & Asl, M. P. (2021). Comparison of data analytic techniques for a spatial opinion mining in literary works: A review paper. In F. Saeed, F. Mohammed, & A. Al-Nahari (Eds.), *Innovative Systems for Intelligent Health Informatics* (pp. 523–535). Springer International Publishing. doi:10.1007/978-3-030-70713-2_49

Ying, S. Y., Keikhosrokiani, P., & Asl, M. P. (2022). Opinion mining on Viet Thanh Nguyen's The Sympathizer using topic modelling and sentiment analysis. *Journal of Information Technology Management*, *14*(Special Issue), 163–183. doi:10.22059/jitm.2022.84895

Yousefpour, A., Ibrahim, R., Hamed, H. N. A., & Hajmohammadi, M. S. (2014). A comparative study on sentiment analysis. *Advances in Environmental Biology*, *8*(13), 53–68.

Chapter 10
Opinion Mining and Text Analytics of Reader Reviews of Yoko Ogawa's The Housekeeper and the Professor in Goodreads

Nurfatin Binti Sofian

School of Computer Sciences, Universiti Sains Malaysia, Malaysia

Pantea Keikhosrokiani

(iD) https://orcid.org/0000-0003-4705-2732

School of Computer Sciences, Universiti Sains Malaysia, Malaysia

Moussa Pourya Asl

(iD) https://orcid.org/0000-0002-8426-426X

School of Humanities, Universiti Sains Malaysia, Malaysia

ABSTRACT

With the development of online social network platforms and social cataloging applications, large amounts of datasets are being generated daily in the form of users' reviews, evaluations, and instant messages. Readers of literary books from around the world now use social media to express their thoughts and feelings about literary works. Collecting and analyzing textual data to gain insight about the readers' interest poses a huge challenge to literary scholars and publishing industries. In this study, the authors aim to apply text analytics methods to analyze and interpret reader responses in the form of book reviews. To this end, they focus on readers' responses and reviews to Yōko Ogawa's The Housekeeper and the Professor (2003) as documented in Goodreads, a social cataloging website that allows readers across the globe to interact with each other about books. The collected data are preprocessed and explored and visualized to gain insight on public opinion about the novel. Finally, the authors analyze the collected data on Goodreads platform by using topic modelling and sentiment analysis in this chapter.

DOI: 10.4018/978-1-7998-9594-7.ch010

INTRODUCTION

Text mining technology is now widely applicable to a wide range of industries, markets, social media, research and business needs (Rejito et al., 2021). Industries may use text mining to analyze a process and track relevant information to their daily activities. Text mining is an artificial intelligence (AI) technology that uses Natural Language Processing (NLP) to transform the free (unstructured) text in the documents and databases into normalized, structured data that can be analyzed to drive machine learning algorithms. Text mining identifies facts, relationships and assertions that would otherwise stay hidden in the mass of big data. Once extracted, the information is translated to a structured form that can be further analyzed or directly used for clustering or classification (NLP) (Malik et al., 2021; Rejito et al., 2021; Tan, 1999; Ying et al., 2021, 2022).

Text mining is also known as text data mining which is similar to text analytics. It is the process of extracting some important information from unstructured text documents such as books, websites, emails, reviews and articles (Rejito et al., 2021). Text mining is different from other available methods utilized for web searches. It is a more complex task than data mining as it involves dealing with the text data that are permanently unstructured and fuzzy (Rejito et al., 2021; Tan, 1999). Typically, text mining task includes information retrieval, text analysis, information extraction, text clustering, text categorization, visualization and data mining. The purpose of text mining is to discover a piece of unknown information or something that no one knows and could not have yet written down. A most common example of data mining in marketing and sales is banks that use data mining to analyze the use of credit card usage for the customers to purchase something. When certain outliers perform certain transactions, it also analyses fraud detection.

This study examines the Goodreads platform, an online book cataloguing website to extract some important information such as reader reviews and ratings from certain topics. Goodreads is a popular social book reading platform that allows people to rate books, post reviews, and their opinion with others. Numeous research has been conducted to examine and analyze the textual data on Goodreads. This paper seeks to analyze book readers' reviews on Goodreads platform. In this paper, we aim to study the different methods of Natural Learning Processing (NLP) algorithms such as Topic Modelling and Sentiment Analysis. NLP is making a lot of progress in doing small subtasks in text analysis. In the present study, we use NLP to extract data of the readers' reviews of the novel Yōko Ogawa's *The Housekeeper and the Professor* (2003) from Goodreads platform (Lin & Horng, 2010). Then, the collected data is explored, normalized, and visualized to gain insight on public opinion about Yōko Ogawa's *The Housekeeper and the Professor* (2003). The data is analyzed by using Topic Modelling and Sentiment Analysis.

LITERATURE REVIEW

Social Media Mining

Social media mining is the process of representing, analyzing, and extracting meaningful patterns from social media data, resulting from social interactions (Barbier & Liu, 2011; Correia et al., 2020; Du et al., 2020; Pickell, 2019). It is used to uncover hidden patterns and trends from social media platforms such as Twitter, LinkedIn, Facebook and Instagram. It also uses basic concepts from computer science, data mining, machine learning, statistics and algorithms that are suitable for investigating massive social media data. Social media mining means collecting data from social media users and analyzing it to draw conclusions. This includes trend analysis which analyzes topics, mentions and important keywords that are currently trending in social media (Barbier & Liu, 2011; Du et al., 2020; Pickell, 2019). Twitter uses a tool called Twitter Streaming Application Programming Interface (API) which allows users to pull tweets off of Twitter according to certain keywords. There is also event detection from Twitter streams that aims to utilize social media monitoring by detecting a new event in real-time. There are also attempts to analyze signals in the frequency domain (Barbier & Liu, 2011; Correia et al., 2020; Du et al., 2020; Pickell, 2019). An example of this is social spam detection such as in Twitter where spammers and bots are very popular. Bots often find gaps on Twitter to spam users with annoying and useless content. It takes some time to detect the bots. With social media mining, the platforms are getting better at spam detection (Barbier & Liu, 2011; Correia et al., 2020; Du et al., 2020; Pickell, 2019).

Topic Modelling

Topic Modelling is a Machine Learning that is capable of scanning a series of documents, detecting words and phrase patterns and automatically clustering word groups that best represent the information in the collection. It provides methods to organize, understand and summarize large collections of information (Hong & Davison, 2010; Vayansky & Kumar, 2020). It is frequently used as text mining tool for discovering hidden patterns that are present across a collection, annotating documents according to the topics, and using the annotations to organize, search and summarize texts. There are some techniques/methods that can be used to obtain topic models as shown below:

Latent Semantic Analysis (LSA)

Latent Semantic Analysis(LSA) is used to analyze large amounts of raw text data by changing them into words and separating them into meaningful sentences or paragraphs. LSA computes how frequently words occur in the documents and the whole corpus and it uses standard methods which is the term frequency-inverse document frequency(tf-idf). It also can generate a vector-based representation for texts by using Singular Value Decomposition (SVD) that captures the maximum variance across the corpus and calculates all dimensions of vector space (Albalawi et al., 2020; Hong & Davison, 2010; Vayansky & Kumar, 2020).

Latent Dirichlet Allocation (LDA)

Latent Dirichlet Allocation (LDA) uses sampling from Dirichlet distribution to generate text with a specific topic where text is usually composed of some latent topics (Albalawi et al., 2020; Hong & Davison, 2010; Liu, 2013; Luo et al., 2020; Vayansky & Kumar, 2020). Then, the topics are sampled repeatedly to generate each word from the document. Thus, the latent topics can be seen as the probability distribution of the words in the LDA model and each document is expressed as the random mixture according to specific proportion. Corpus is organized as a random mixture of latent topics in LDA model. There are three main parameter of model which are the number of topics, the number of words per topic, and the number of topics per document (Liu, 2017; Luo et al., 2020).

Non-Negative Matrix Factorization (NMF)

Non-negative Matrix Factorization (NMF) is an unsupervised matric factorization which can perform dimension reduction and clustering simultaneously (Albalawi et al., 2020). It is a group of linear algebra algorithms for identifying the latent structure in data as non-negative matrix. This method can extract relevant information about the topics without any previous insight into the original data. It provides useful results in several areas such as in text analysis, and it can handle the decomposition of non-understandable data like videos.

Principal Component Analysis (PCA)

Principal Component Analysis (PCA), known as Karhunen-Loeve expansion, is an extraction features and data representation techniques in the area of pattern recognition and computer vision such as face recognition. This method is commonly used for dimensionality reduction by projecting each data onto the first principal components to obtain lower-dimensional data. When the variable in the data highly correlate, correlation is required which has redundancy in the set of data. it also reduces the original variables into a smaller number of new variables (Albalawi et al., 2020; Karamizadeh et al., 2013). Table 1 shows the comparison among various topic modeling methods.

Table 1. Comparison methods of topic modelling

Criteria Method	Advantage	Disadvantage
Latent Semantic Analysis (LSA)	• It is quick and efficient method • It is the most frequent topic modelling analysis method • Reduce the dimensionality of tf-idf frequencies by using Singular Value Decomposition (SVD)	• Lack of interpretable embedding • It requires for really large set of documents and vocabulary to get accurate results • Less efficient for representation
Latent Dirichlet Allocation (LDA)	• The size of LDA model parameter space has nothing to do with the number of training data. • Most suitable for handling long-scale corpus • Handle mixed-length documents • Efficient probability inference algorithms to calculate model parameters • It can predict topics for new unseen documents • It provides more semantic interpret data and perform well if there no time constraint	• Lots of fine-tuning is required • It needs human interpretation which it needs a human to label them in order to present the results to non-expert's people • Slow process algorithm
Non-negative Matrix Factorization (NMF)	• Able to extract meaningful topics without advance information or knowledge in the original data • Suitable for handling long-scale corpus	• Sometimes provide semantic incorrect results • Lack of uniqueness • Lack of iterative algorithms
Principal Component Analysis (PCA)	• Reduce the dimensionality of the data by removing the noise and redundancy in the data • Used in finding patterns in data of high dimension in the field of finance, and data mining • Works on moderately low-dimensional data and best possible estimate	• Expensive to compute for high-dimensional text datasets • Even the simplest invariance could not be captured unless the training data directly provides this information

Sentiment Analysis

Sentiment Analysis known as opinion mining that is a Natural Language Processing algorithm that gives a general idea about positive, neutral and negative sentiment of texts. In the Sentiment Analysis, there are three main classification levels such as document-level, sentence-level and aspect-level (Devika et al., 2016). In document-level, it classifies an opinion document as expressing a positive or negative opinion or sentiment. The purpose of sentence-level is to classify sentiment expression in each sentence in the texts which is to identify whether it is subjective or objective (Devika et al., 2016). Then, it will determine the opinion. Meanwhile, aspect-level aims to classify sentiment with respect to the specific aspect of entities. Sentiment Analysis is divided into three approaches which are machine learning approach, lexicon based approach and rule based approach.

Machine Learning Approach

Machine learning strategies work by training a dataset of algorithms before applying it to the actual data set. It trains an algorithm with some specific inputs with known outputs so that the new unknown data can be used later. There are some algorithms used to command and train machines to perform sentiment analysis as listed in Table 2.

Table 2. Comparison methods of machine learning approach

Method	Concept	Advantage	Disadvantage
Naïve Bayes Method (Hossain et al., 2021; Wongkar & Angdresey, 2019)	It is a simple probabilistic (mathematical) algorithm that assigns a probability that a given word or phrase should be positive or negative.	• Simple and intuitive algorithms • It combines efficiency with reasonable accuracy	• Used when the size of training set is less • Assumes independence among linguistic features
Support Vector Machine (SVM) (Bourequat & Mourad, 2021; Khanday et al., 2021; Syahputra, 2021)	It used the algorithms to train and classify text within sentiment polarity model. It can make use of the concept of decision planes that define boundaries. A decision plane is one that separates between set of object having different class membership. By using SVM, the more complex the data, the more accurate the predictor will become.	• High-dimensional input space • Few irrelevant features • More accurate machine learning	• Large amount of training set is required • Data collection is tedious
K-NN and weighted K-NN method (Al-Ghadir et al., 2021; Isnain et al.)	K-NN is based on the fact of the classification that similar to the vector space nearby. In weighted K-NN, certain element in the training set will be calculate the sentiment of text in word by word.	• It easier to implement • No training set is required • New data can be added seamlessly	• Required large storage space • Sensitive to noise in dataset • Testing is slow • Does not work well with high dimensions

Lexicon Based Approach

The Lexicon-Based approach involves calculating sentiment polarity for a review using the semantic orientation of words or sentence in the text (Devika et al., 2016). The semantic orientation is a measure of subjectivity and opinion in the text (Benlahbib, 2021; Collomb et al., 2014). It is like using dictionary-matching approach. This method uses dictionaries of words with the semantic orientation that need to be analyzed whether the text sentiment label is positive, negative or neutral. In other words, to capture the text opinion, sentiment or attitude within its content (Benlahbib, 2021; Collomb et al., 2014; Devika et al., 2016).

Rule Based Approach

Rule Based Approach is used by define the various rules for getting the opinion words in a text and then classifies it based on the number of positive and negative words (Benlahbib, 2021; Collomb et al., 2014). There are different rules for classification such as dictionary polarity, idioms, emoticons, and mixed opinions. Different sentiment analysis methods are compared in Table 3.

Table 3. Comparison methods of sentiment analysis

Approach	Advantage	Disadvantage
Machine Learning Approach	• Dictionary is not necessary • Demonstrate the high accuracy of classification • Most popular method because it fits on data learning representations	• Does not work with classifier training on dataset in one domain
Lexicon Based Approach	• Dictionary is necessary • Labelled data and the procedure of learning is not required • Not require any training data	• Large number of words and expressions are not included • Require powerful linguistics resources
Rule Based Approach	• Training data is not required • High precision	• Difficult and tedious to list all the rules

METHODOLOGY

There are several tools that we used to perform this project namely, Anaconda Individual Edition, Python 3.9 and Jupyter notebook application. This is because Python is a suitable programming language to perform text analytics and has simple syntax. To do text mining, we used NLP algorithms such as topic modelling and sentiment analysis.

In topic modelling method, it is machine learning that automatically analyses text data to determine cluster words from a set of topics which is known as 'unsupervised' machine learning method. There are some techniques that are used for topic modelling which are Latent Dirichlet Allocation(LDA) and Latent Semantic Analysis(LSA). Thus, in this paper, we used LDA to visualize the results from the topics.

Moreover, sentiment analysis is a technique of determining the emotional value of a given expression in natural language where the given input text or data is classified into positive, neutral or negative sentiment. In sentiment analysis, we aim to measure the attitude, sentiments, evaluations, and emotions of a users' reviews based on subjectivity in a text. The different methods that we use to do sentiment analysis are shown as below:

VADER Algorithm

VADER (Valence Aware Dictionary for Sentiment Reasoning) is a model used for text sentiment analysis that is sensitive to both polarity (positive/ negative) and intensity (strength) of emotion. VADER uses a combination of a sentiment lexicon which is lexical features such as words known as sentiment score. The sentiment score of a text can be obtained by summing up the intensity of each word in the text.

Textblob Algorithm

Textblob sentiment analyze returns a sentiment object which is two properties for a given input sentence as shown below:

- Polarity is a float that lies between [-1,1], -1 is indicates a negative sentiment and +1 indicates positive sentiments.
- Subjectivity is also a float which is lies in the range of [0,1]. Subjective sentences generally refer to personal opinion, emotion or judgement.

Data Science Lifecycle

The methodology adopted for this project is based on the Cross Industry Process for Data Mining (CRISP-DM) that comprised of six stages for Data Science Lifecycle, which includes business understanding, data understanding, data preparation, modelling, evaluation, and deployment. Figure 1 shows the proposed framework of data science lifecycle that is implemented in this project. In this project, the data was collected from Goodreads platform from users' reviews on Yōko Ogawa's novel *The Housekeeper and the Professor* (2003). Then data cleaning and preprocessing was applied which includes tokenization, removal of noise, removal of punctuation, removal of special characters, removal of stopwords, and lemmatization were utilized. Nevertheless, we focused more on modelling. For topic modelling, LDA and LSA model were utilized, and the results are compared. As for sentiment analysis, VADER and Textblob algorithm were used and compared (see Figure 1).

Figure 1. The proposed framework of data science lifecycle

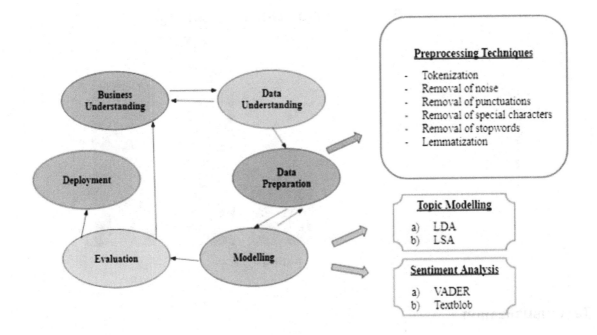

RESULTS AND ANALYSIS

In this project, the data is collected from Goodreads platform from users' reviews on Yōko Ogawa's novel *The Housekeeper and the Professor* (2003). Before we do the topic modelling and sentiment analysis, we implemented data cleaning and tokenization to split the text into sentences, and removed punctuation and all stopwords. We also carried out lemmatization to reduce the number of unique words in the topics. After that, the extracted data went through text normalization and visualization to gain the outcomes.

Text Normalization

After extracting the users' reviews from Goodreads data, we explore the text and study the frequent words by constructing different methods of charts such as bar chart, pie chart and word cloud to visualize the collected data to obtain the accuracy of the collected data.

Text normalization captures all the users' reviews with the ratings from the specific topic. The figure above shows the number of the user's rating of the book The Housekeeper and the Professor (2003) by Yōko Ogawa. The extracted data shows that there was a total of 496 users' reviews. However, only 486 users' review are shown in the bar chart above as 10 users did not rate the book. Figure 2 shows the results number of the users against rating. It can be seen that the highest rating of this book is 4 which is 227 number of users' review followed by 180 number of users' review in rating 5 and the least rating is 1 which is rated by only 3 users.

Figure 2. Bar chart of book's rating

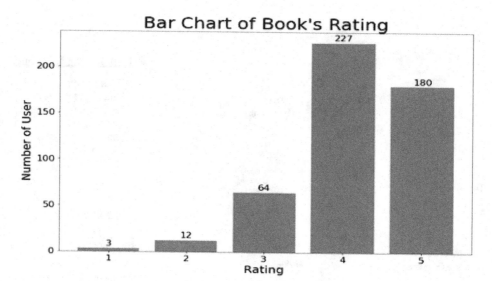

Text Visualization

Furthermore, visualization is produced after text normalization. There are a few methods that have been added to visualize the collected data such as Bigram WordCloud, Trigram WordCloud and Pie Chart. Figure 3 shows the top 10 common words that are used by the users from the extracted reviews. The bar chart is already sorted from the highest common words count to the lowest. We can see that the most common words are the 'professor,' which is the highest of 937 words count followed by the common words 'housekeeper' which is 659 words count, 'math' (499), 'number' (427), 'memory' (400), 'son' (331), 'baseball' (258), 'root' (255), 'mathematic' (252) and 'minute' (241) words count. From the graph above, it is clear that there is a huge difference between the highest common words of 'professor' words count and the lowest common words of 'minute' words count.

Figure 3. Bar chart of top-10 common words

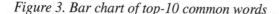

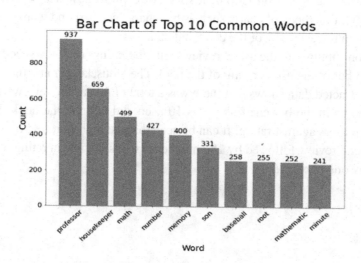

Figure 4. Most frequently occurring Bigram Wordcloud

Figure 4 shows the word bigrams that consists of two words that frequently appear in the users' reviews. As we can see, the most frequently the words are used, the larger and bolder it is displayed. From the graph, it can be seen that the 'housekeeper son' is the most frequent in the bigram which is the highest frequency, followed by 'housekeeper professor', 'memory minute', 'year old' and 'yoko ogawa'. It can be concluded that the words in the bigrams appear as it is a result that produced from collection of 100 frequent words from the reviews.

Figure 5. Most frequently occurring Trigram Wordcloud

Figure 5 shows the trigrams word figure where it contains the three words most frequently used by users in the reviews. It is similar to the bigram words diagram. The biggest word in the word cloud is the most frequent in the review. As we can see, the 'short term memory' is the biggest that appears in the diagram which indicates that it is the most frequently used word in the reviews, followed by the 'year old son', 'housekeeper year old', 'professor housekeeper son' and 'housekeeper son professor'.

Figure 6 shows the most frequently occurring bigrams in the reviews. The pie chart shows the 10 most frequently appears in the reviews that are used by the users. As we can see, the words 'housekeeper son' is the highest percentage which is 17.1%, followed by 'housekeeper professor' words with 14.7%, 'memory minute' words with 10% while the 'son professor' words with 7.2% which is the least percentage used by the users. We can conclude that 'housekeeper son' words the most frequently occurring bigrams and 'son professor' words are the least appears in the book.

Figure 6. Pie chart of most frequently occurring Bigram

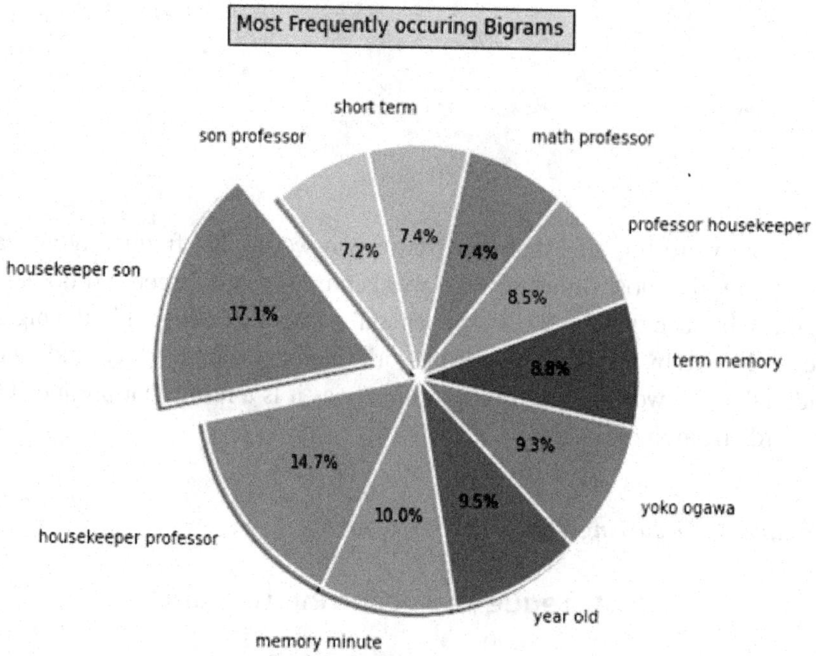

Topic Modelling Results

Topic modelling is machine learning method that automatically analyses text data to determine cluster words for a set of topics which is known as 'unsupervised' machine learning method. There are some techniques that are used for topic modelling which are Latent Dirichlet Allocation (LDA) and Latent Semantic Analysis (LSA). As a result of the topic modelling below, we used pyLDAvis output to visualize the modelled results.

As shown in Figure 7, it can be seen that the keywords for each topic and the weightage (importance) of each keyword using best_topics = best_model.print_topics(). It can be said that there are 5 total topics that appear in the Goodreads reviews on Yōko Ogawa's *The Housekeeper and the Professor* (2003).

Figure 7. The keyword in the 5 topics

```
[(0,
  '0.030*"professor" + 0.015*"housekeeper" + 0.014*"love" + 0.014*"number" + '
  '0.011*"memory" + 0.010*"math" + 0.009*"read" + 0.008*"son" + '
  '0.008*"baseball" + 0.007*"character"'),
 (1,
  '0.026*"professor" + 0.019*"housekeeper" + 0.016*"math" + 0.012*"number" + '
  '0.010*"love" + 0.010*"read" + 0.010*"memory" + 0.008*"son" + '
  '0.008*"mathematic" + 0.007*"root"'),
 (2,
  '0.024*"professor" + 0.022*"housekeeper" + 0.014*"math" + 0.011*"number" + '
  '0.010*"love" + 0.009*"son" + 0.009*"read" + 0.008*"baseball" + '
  '0.008*"memory" + 0.007*"time"'),
 (3,
  '0.027*"professor" + 0.020*"housekeeper" + 0.012*"math" + 0.011*"number" + '
  '0.011*"read" + 0.010*"memory" + 0.009*"love" + 0.008*"son" + '
  '0.007*"mathematic" + 0.007*"baseball"'),
 (4,
  '0.023*"professor" + 0.015*"math" + 0.015*"housekeeper" + 0.014*"memory" + '
  '0.011*"love" + 0.011*"son" + 0.010*"number" + 0.009*"read" + '
  '0.008*"mathematic" + 0.007*"character"')]
```

For example, we can interpret that Topic 0 is represented as *('0.030*"professor" + 0.015*"house-keeper" + 0.014*"love" + 0.014*"number" + '0.011*"memory" + 0.010*"math" + 0.009*"read" + 0.008*"son" + ''0.008*"baseball" + 0.007*"character"').* It means the top 10 keywords that contribute to this topic are: 'professor', 'housekeeper', 'love', 'number', 'memory', 'math', 'read', 'son', 'baseball', 'character' and the weight of 'professor' on topic 0 is 0.030. This is because the weights reflect that how important each keyword is to that topic.

Figure 8 shows the top-30 keywords that appear in the users' reviews. As we can see, there are 5 bubbles each of which represents a topic. The larger the bubble, the higher the percentage of the number of appears that reviewed by the users in the corpus is about the topic. As we can see that blue bars represent that overall frequency of each word in the corpus.

Figure 8. The top-30 most salient terms

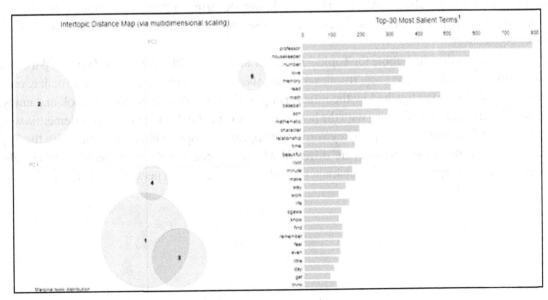

Figure 9 shows Topic 1 is the biggest bubble among the other topics which means it is the most importance topic that reviewed by the users. As we can see from figure 8, there are about almost 800 times of the word 'professor', and this term is used about almost 400 times within the Topic 1. The word with the longest red bar is the word that is used most in the users' reviews and appears belonging to the topic. From that, the red bars are given the estimated number of times a specific term was generated by a given topic. The top 10 words that mostly salient in Topic 1 are 'professor', 'housekeeper', 'math', 'number', 'love', 'read', 'memory', 'son', 'mathematic', and 'root'.

Figure 9. The top-30 keywords for topic 1

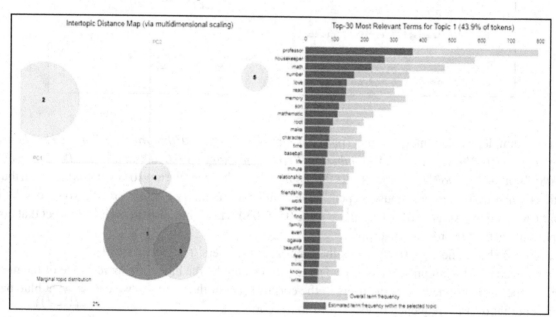

From the top 30 keywords, the top 10 words have related to the title of the book which is a brilliant math Professor with a peculiar problem that lived with short-term memory and there have an astute young Housekeeper with her son calls Root. Therefore, it exists the cast of a charming story of mathematics and love connection.

Figure 10 shows that the bubble for Topic 2 is further and non-overlapping from Topic 1. We can say that the further the bubbles are away from each other, the more different they are. For instance, one of the reviewers said she was touched by the relationship of the three characters in this book and enjoyed trying to solve the math proofs along with the housekeeper and hoped that the professor's dementia would improve and he love math. The top 30 keywords that appears in Topic 2 have similarity with the Topic 1 and there are some of the keywords are different which are 'character' and 'baseball'. Nevertheless, 'professor', 'housekeeper', 'son' and 'character' can be categorized as a person in this book.

Figure 10. The top-30 keywords for topic 2

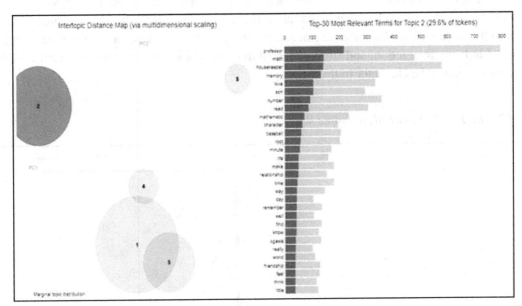

Figure 11shows similarity in Topic 1, which means there are some keywords from the top 30 words that appear in the Topic 3. There are some different words such as 'baseball', and 'time'. For instance, one of the reviewer said the professor starts fresh every 80 minutes, the present becomes of utmost importance and the housekeeper, her son and the professor create a beautiful time together. In this case, it showed that the emotion of his deep love for numbers. As we can conclude, 'number', 'math' and 'time' can be categorized as mathematics which is most relevant that have related with this book.

Figure 11. The top-30 keywords for topic 3

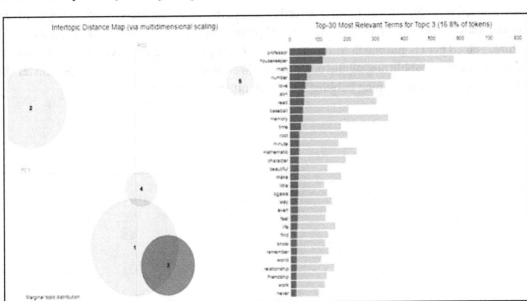

Based on Figure 12, there are no huge differences between Topic 4 and Topic 1. They are overlapping on each other, and there are a few words that are different such as 'baseball' and 'minute'. As we can relate from the book within 80-minute segments, the three characters create a life together with full of emotional, kindness, interaction, and strong friendship to each other. It can be categorized as personal relationships between the character in this book.

Figure 12. The Top-30 Keywords for topic 4

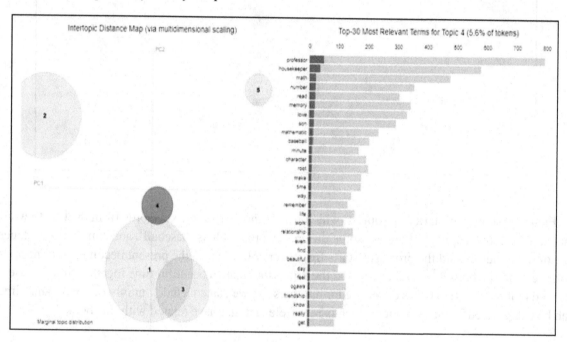

As we can see from Figure 13, Topic 5 is further away from other topics. Out of 30 keywords found in the figure above, there are a few words that have higher counts highlighted in blue color such as 'go', 'get', 'think', etc. There is not much to discuss about this topic among the reviewers. This is because Topic 5 is the smallest bubble among the other topics. We can conclude that a good topic model should be the big one and non-overlapping bubbles with each other in the chart.

Figure 13. The top-30 keywords for topic 5

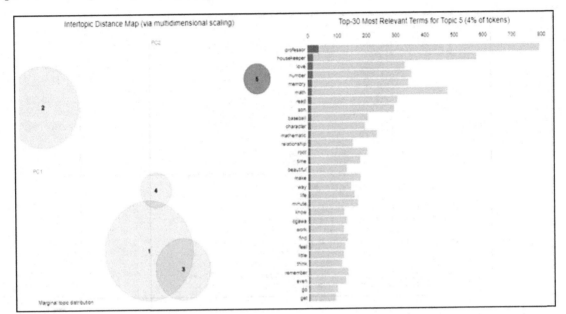

Sentiment Analysis Results

Sentiment analysis is a technique of identifying the emotional value of a given expression in natural language in which the input text or data is categorized as positive, neutral or negative sentiment. Sentiment analysis focuses on measuring the attitude, emotions, opinions and evaluations of a user's reviewers based on subjectivity in a text. In addition, we use different methods to do sentiment analysis such as VADER Algorithm and Textblob Algorithm.

VADER Algorithm

It returns a dictionary of scores in each four categories which are Score Compound (computed by normalizing the scores above), Score Negative, Score Neutral and Score Positive. The Score Compound is a metric that calculates the sum of all the lexicon ratings which have been normalized between -1 (most extreme negative) and +1 (most extreme positive). The more the Score Compound is closer to +1, the higher the positivity of the text. Hence, it is closer to -1 or 0 (neutral).

Figure 14 shows that the Top-10 of positive sentences found from 495 reviews extracted from the reviews on *The Housekeeper and the Professor (2003) by Yōko Ogawa*. It has been scored based on the sentiment by using VADER algorithm and we can see that all 10 sentences mostly effective towards to positive compared to negative (see Figure 14).

Figure 14. The top-10 of positive sentences using VADER algorithm

```
The top 10 positive sentences are:

        Score Compound  Score Negative  Score Neutral  Score Positive  \
377          0.9993          0.027          0.786          0.187
357          0.9992          0.078          0.665          0.258
376          0.9992          0.009          0.711          0.280
402          0.9991          0.050          0.678          0.272
321          0.9990          0.050          0.774          0.177
152          0.9988          0.071          0.743          0.186
335          0.9988          0.047          0.819          0.134
343          0.9988          0.045          0.776          0.179
404          0.9987          0.067          0.693          0.240
320          0.9985          0.060          0.825          0.115

                                                           Sentence
377    I remember learning in my interpersonal commun...
357    Audiobook performed by Cassandra Campbell5 and...
376    Some books stay with you They make you pause t...
402    The Housekeeper and the Professor by Yōko Ogaw...
321    Happy Cubs opening day 2018 has not been the r...
152    When I picked up this book I was intrigued by ...
335    A highly polished smooth shining surface of a ...
343    This book is truly original not your normal ru...
404    The Professor is a brilliant mathematician who...
320    Life by the NumbersNumbers are everywhere  Rea...
```

For example, the sentence in review number 376, "Some books stay with you They make you pause t..." has a positive score with 0.280 and a negative score with 0.078. Based on the sentence, "stay" gave affect to the emotional of the reviewers toward of this book.

Figure 15 shows the top-10 negative sentences found from 495 reviews that are extracted from this book. We can see that all 10 sentences are generally towards to negative sentiment with score compound -0.8360. The positive score is not found in the 4 sentences which are in the review number 379, 27, 257 and 226. From all 10 sentences, there is one sentence with the highest score positive of 0.182 which is the review number 265 with "liked" word that brought to positive sentiment. Although, it gave the negative score of 0.436 with sentence, "Liked it but didn't love it". For instance, the sentences "wtf I literally hate this genre so much..." in the review number 27, has the highest negative score from all 10 sentences which is 0.556. As we can relate from this sentence, negative sentiment measured with "literally" and "hate" word. It shows the reviewer gave negative expression towards this book and that the reviewer dislikes their choice.

Figure 15. The top-10 of negative sentences using VADER algorithm

```
The top 10 negative sentences are:

      Score Compound  Score Negative  Score Neutral  Score Positive  \
379       -0.8360          0.111          0.889          0.000
27        -0.8176          0.556          0.444          0.000
442       -0.7722          0.253          0.616          0.131
480       -0.6550          0.105          0.809          0.086
265       -0.5650          0.436          0.383          0.182
316       -0.4939          0.191          0.694          0.115
134       -0.4409          0.082          0.828          0.090
257       -0.4199          0.085          0.915          0.000
14        -0.4019          0.069          0.897          0.034
226       -0.4019          0.088          0.912          0.000

                                                      Sentence
379    The Professor is an expert in Mathematics Afte...
27                 wtf i literally hate this genre so much
442    Mathematics baseball brain trauma tenderness O...
480    Once again Im in the minority with my review I...
265                       Liked it but didnt love it
316    I read it in the original Japanese Petty and f...
134    Yoko Ogawa is one of the best writers Ive read...
257    The premise  a math professor who has 88 minut...
14     Simple and poignant Also a little bit stiffly ...
226    This is a very intimate book If you have ever ...
```

Figure 16 shows the top-10 positive sentences using Textblob algorithm found from 495 reviews that are extracted about this book. It can be seen that 3 of 10 sentences from above designated mostly to positive sentiments of polarity and subjectivity which are review number of 85, 97 and 187. For instance, "wonderful" and "superb" words found from the sentence, "Is a wonderful story", "superb novel" and "Wonderful story weaved around 3 people The pro…" brought strong positivity from the reviewers to this book. It concludes that the reviewers show the positive expression to this book.

Figure 16. The top-10 of positive sentences using Textblob algorithm

```
The top 10 positive sentences are:

      Polarity  Subjectivity                                    Sentence
85      1.0000         1.00                          Is a wonderful story
97      1.0000         1.00                                  Superb novel
187     1.0000         1.00   Wonderful story weaved around 3 people The pro...
145     0.9375         0.55     I loved this book One of the best Ogawas works
186     0.8500         1.00   At its heart a rather beautiful story about th...
52      0.8000         0.80                          Loved loved loved this book
23      0.7750         0.90   Beautifully written Who knew that mathematics ...
174     0.7500         0.90                                       Amazing
111     0.7000         0.60   Good thing the professor didnt have the internet
31      0.6750         0.75   The most beautiful formula in mathematics ther...
```

Figure 17 shows the top-10 of negative sentences using Textblob algorithm found from 495 reviews that extracted from this book. We can see that the review number 27 has the highest negativity sentiment compared to others with -0.366667 polarity and 0.700000 subjectivity. In this case, the words "hate" found in the sentence, "wtf I literally hate this genre so much" brought a heavy negative sentiment. As a result, it shows that the reviewers do not like this book's story and the genre type of this book.

Figure 17. The top-10 of negative sentences using Textblob algorithm

```
The top 10 negative sentences are:

      Polarity  Subjectivity                                        Sentence
27   -0.366667     0.700000             wtf i literally hate this genre so much
442  -0.293056     0.463889  Mathematics baseball brain trauma tenderness O...
399  -0.250000     0.650000                   A short sad but heartwarming story
440  -0.250000     1.000000  With my preconceptions based on Hotel Iris and...
419  -0.218750     0.375000  A little gem of literature The plot is already...
264  -0.183333     0.783333  I read this in one sitting A sweet story I am ...
316  -0.156250     0.687500  I read it in the original Japanese Petty and f...
289  -0.100000     0.000000  355 Book Riots 2019 Read Harder Challenge  10 ...
457  -0.083100     0.622145  This book surprised me in a big wayThis book w...
14   -0.071591     0.421861  Simple and poignant Also a little bit stiffly ...
```

DISCUSSION

The results in previous sections show that topic modelling and sentiment analysis proves to be the suitable methods to perform text mining in the social cataloguing platforms especially in Goodreads platform. These two methods were chosen because they are providing with the methods to organize and summarize large collections of textual data. They also can determine the emotional attachment of expressions in Goodreads platform.

Comparison of Topic Modelling

As shown in Figure 18, we can see that the LDA's coherence score for each topic is different from the LSA's. The optimum number of topics for LDA is 5 with coherence score of 0.313974. Meanwhile, the optimum number of topics for LSA is 1 with coherence score of 0.309395. In terms of the score of each topic that produced, LDA model had the highest score compared to LSA model. In this case, LDA model is the best for topic modelling as it is used to address these issues and it can work better to generalize a new document easily.

Figure 18. Comparison of LDA and LSA model

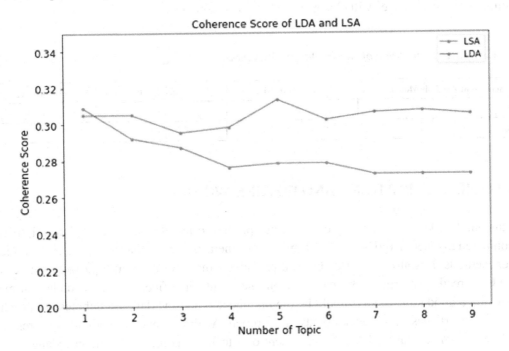

From the topic modelling results above, it builds a topic per document model and words per topic model, modelled as Dirichlet distributions. Thus, in topic modelling it showed that the different top-30 keywords most salient terms appear in each topics based on the users' reviews. However, in each topic, it has the highest probability to be part of the topic which is the accurate classification with the relevant keywords.

Comparison of Sentiment Analysis

As for sentiment analysis evaluation, VADER algorithm is used to detect how much of positive or negative expression of the text and also the intensity of the emotion in the Goodreads platform with the specific topic given. It showed that the top-10 of positive or negative sentences were found from the extracted data has been scored based on Score Compound in four categories which are score compound, score neutral, score negative and score positive. The comparison results obtained from both VADER and Textblob algorithm based on their total of positive, neutral and negative reviews from the book.

Table 4 shows the comparison of the scores of VADER and Textblob algorithm based on 495 users' reviews. There is a slight difference between two models for the positive and negative score. For positive score, VADER had recorded 453 users' reviews compared to Textblob which recorded 450 users' reviews with 3 differences. Furthermore, Textblob obtained 28 users' reviews of scores neutral compared to VADER which had 23 users' reviews of neutral score. Both models also had slight differences which VADER with 19 users' reviews of negative score and Textblob had 17 users' reviews. From the comparison above, we can say that VADER model is better for texts from social cataloguing. This is because it is based on lexicons of sentiments and each word in the lexicon is rated whether it is positive or negative. Therefore, when it comes to analyzing the comments or users' reviews from others platform, the sentiment of the sentences will change based on the emoticons.

Table 4. Comparison methods of sentiment analysis model

Sentiment Analysis Model	Score Positive	Score Neutral	Score Negative
VADER	453	23	19
Textblob	450	28	17

CONCLUSION, LIMITATIONS AND FUTURE WORK

In conclusion, the LDA method in topic modelling approach offers the best-educated descriptive topics when compared to other methods. The LDA approach generates a more coherent score in the topics than the other methods. It is also more flexible and provides a more meaningful topic with extracted data from the Goodreads platform. As we can see from the results, it defines the best and clearest meaning of a topic and a good topic model should be the big one and non-overlapping bubbles with each other in the chart. Nevertheless, different methods in Sentiment Analysis came out with different results. The VADER algorithm can easily detect he sentiment of a text that contains emoticons, slangs, conjunctions, and punctuations. The results from the VADER algorithm are not only remarkable but also very encouraging. The Textblob algorithm calculates subjectivity by looking at the intensity of the sentences from the extracted data on the Goodreads platform as it has one more parameter. Intensity discovers if have any word modifies in the next word. In consequence, the higher the subjectivity means that the sentence contains personal opinion rather than factual information. In topic modelling, the LDA method was slower, but it was more consistent and useful than simple word frequency. The findings of topic modelling should not be over-interpreted unless the number of topics in a particular corpus is known. Otherwise, a dataset is not suitable for topic modelling if the length of the document or text is too short. Topic modelling can easily be misused if they are misunderstood as an objective representation of a text's meaning. Furthermore, due to limitations of sentiment analysis, it may have difficulty recognizing unique texts or funny ones and may be hard to perceive them. There may not be enough context for reliable sentiment analysis with only a few phrases and a piece of text. Topic modelling is useful for future studies in developing a real-time social recommendation system that aims to analyze the users' recommendations. Moreover, when exploring new market research, sentiment analysis can determine when we can correlate sentiment with behavior more accurately and continue deeper on likes, and comments and help to be able to aim better serve the customers. In other words, there should be an expansion in the implementation of NLP techniques in the future.

REFERENCES

Al-Ghadir, A. I., Azmi, A. M., & Hussain, A. (2021). A novel approach to stance detection in social media tweets by fusing ranked lists and sentiments. *Information Fusion*, *67*, 29–40. doi:10.1016/j. inffus.2020.10.003

Albalawi, R., Yeap, T. H., & Benyoucef, M. (2020). Using Topic Modeling Methods for Short-Text Data: A Comparative Analysis. *Frontiers in Artificial Intelligence*, 3(42), 42. Advance online publication. doi:10.3389/frai.2020.00042 PMID:33733159

Barbier, G., & Liu, H. (2011). Data mining in social media. In C. C. Aggarwal (Ed.), *Social Network Data Analytics* (pp. 327–352). Springer US. doi:10.1007/978-1-4419-8462-3_12

Benlahbib, A., & Nfaoui, E. H. (2021). Mtvrep: A movie and tv show reputation system based on fine-grained sentiment and semantic analysis. *Iranian Journal of Electrical and Computer Engineering*, 11(2), 1613. doi:10.11591/ijece.v11i2.pp1613-1626

Bourequat, W., & Mourad, H. (2021). Sentiment Analysis Approach for Analyzing iPhone Release using Support Vector Machine. *International Journal of Advances in Data and Information Systems*, 2(1), 36–44. doi:10.25008/ijadis.v2i1.1216

Collomb, A., Costea, C., Joyeux, D., Hasan, O., & Brunie, L. (2014). A study and comparison of sentiment analysis methods for reputation evaluation. *Rapport de recherche RR-LIRIS-2014-002*.

Correia, R. B., Wood, I. B., Bollen, J., & Rocha, L. M. (2020). Mining Social Media Data for Biomedical Signals and Health-Related Behavior. *Annual Review of Biomedical Data Science*, 3(1), 433–458. doi:10.1146/annurev-biodatasci-030320-040844 PMID:32550337

Devika, M., Sunitha, C., & Ganesh, A. (2016). Sentiment analysis: A comparative study on different approaches. *Procedia Computer Science*, 87, 44–49. doi:10.1016/j.procs.2016.05.124

Du, X., Kowalski, M., Varde, A. S., Melo, G., & Taylor, R. W. (2020). Public opinion matters: Mining social media text for environmental management. *SIGWEB Newsl.*, (Autumn), 5. Advance online publication. doi:10.1145/3352683.3352688

Hong, L., & Davison, B. D. (2010). Empirical study of topic modeling in Twitter. *Proceedings of the First Workshop on Social Media Analytics*. 10.1145/1964858.1964870

Hossain, E., Sharif, O., & Hoque, M. M. (2021). Sentiment polarity detection on bengali book reviews using multinomial naive bayes. In *Progress in Advanced Computing and Intelligent Engineering* (pp. 281–292). Springer.

Isnain, A. R., Supriyanto, J., & Kharisma, M. P. (n.d.). Implementation of K-Nearest Neighbor (K-NN) Algorithm For Public Sentiment Analysis of Online Learning. *Indonesian Journal of Computing and Cybernetics Systems*, 15(2), 121-130. doi:10.1007/978-981-33-4299-6_23

Karamizadeh, S., Abdullah, S. M., Manaf, A. A., Zamani, M., & Hooman, A. (2013). An overview of principal component analysis. *Journal of Signal and Information Processing*, 4(03, 3B), 173–175. doi:10.4236/jsip.2013.43B031

Khanday, A. M. U. D., Khan, Q. R., & Rabani, S. T. (2021). SVMBPI: support vector machine-based propaganda identification. In Cognitive Informatics and Soft Computing (pp. 445-455). Springer. doi:10.1007/978-981-16-1056-1_35

Lin, F.-M., & Horng, W.-S. (2010). The housekeeper and the professor by Yoko Ogawa. *The Mathematical Intelligencer*, 2(32), 75–76. doi:10.100700283-009-9100-8

Liu, Y. H. (2017). *Python Machine Learning By Example*. Packt Publishing Ltd.

Liu, Z. (2013). *High performance latent dirichlet allocation for text mining*. Brunel University School of Engineering and Design PhD Theses.

Luo, J. M., Vu, H. Q., Li, G., & Law, R. (2020). Topic modelling for theme park online reviews: Analysis of Disneyland. *Journal of Travel & Tourism Marketing, 37*(2), 272–285. doi:10.1080/10548408.2020.1740138

Malik, E. F., Keikhosrokiani, P., & Asl, M. P. (2021). Text mining life cycle for a spatial reading of Viet Thanh Nguyen's *The Refugees* (2017). *2021 International Congress of Advanced Technology and Engineering (ICOTEN)*.

Pickell, D. (2019). *Social Media Data Mining – How it Works and Who's Using it*. G2 Company.

Rejito, J., Atthariq, A., & Abdullah, A. (2021). Application of text mining employing k-means algorithms for clustering tweets of Tokopedia. *Journal of Physics: Conference Series*.

Syahputra, H. (2021). Sentiment Analysis of Community Opinion on Online Store in Indonesia on Twitter using Support Vector Machine Algorithm (SVM). *Journal of Physics: Conference Series*.

Tan, A.-H. (1999). Text mining: The state of the art and the challenges. *Proceedings of the pakdd 1999 workshop on knowledge discovery from advanced databases*.

Vayansky, I., & Kumar, S. A. P. (2020). A review of topic modeling methods. *Information Systems, 94*, 101582.

Wongkar, M., & Angdresey, A. (2019). Sentiment analysis using Naive Bayes Algorithm of the data crawler: Twitter. *2019 Fourth International Conference on Informatics and Computing (ICIC)*.

Ying, S. Y., Keikhosrokiani, P., & Asl, M. P. (2021). Comparison of data analytic techniques for a spatial opinion mining in literary works: A review paper. In F. Saeed, F. Mohammed, & A. Al-Nahari (Eds.), *Innovative Systems for Intelligent Health Informatics* (pp. 523–535). Springer International Publishing., doi:10.1007/978-3-030-70713-2_49.

Ying, S. Y., Keikhosrokiani, P., & Asl, M. P. (2022). Opinion mining on Viet Thanh Nguyen's The Sympathizer using topic modelling and sentiment analysis. *Journal of Information Technology Management, 14*(Special Issue), 163–183. doi:10.22059/jitm.2022.84895

Chapter 11
Sentiment Analysis of the Harry Potter Series Using a Lexicon–Based Approach

Md Habib Al Mamun

School of Computer Sciences, Universiti Sains Malaysia, Malaysia

Pantea Keikhosrokiani

(iD) https://orcid.org/0000-0003-4705-2732

School of Computer Sciences, Universiti Sains Malaysia, Malaysia

Moussa Pourya Asl

(iD) https://orcid.org/0000-0002-8426-426X

School of Humanities, Universiti Sains Malaysia, Malaysia

Nur Ain Nasuha Anuar

School of Humanities, Universiti Sains Malaysia, Malaysia

Nurfarah Hadira Abdul Hadi

School of Humanities, Universiti Sains Malaysia, Malaysia

Thasnim Humida

Dept. of Mass Communication and Journalism, Begum Rokeya University, Rangpur, Bangladesh

ABSTRACT

The objective of this chapter is to conduct a sentiment analysis of the Harry Potter novel series written by British author J.K. Rowling. The text of the series is collected from GitHub as an R package provided by Bradley Boehmke. The chapter analyzed the text by R programming to explore dominant sentiments using a lexicon approach of natural language processing (NLP). The results revealed that Professor Slughorn scored the most positive sentiment among the main characters that have heroic qualities; Death Eaters had the most negative sentiment among the anti-hero characters; negative sentiment in the text around the anti-hero characters increased significantly, while the positive sentiment around the hero characters remained constant as the story progressed throughout the series; among the series of novels, The Deathly Hallows contained the most negative sentiment; among all the houses of Hogwarts School of Witchcraft and Wizardry, Hufflepuff had the most positive sentiment; and each book of the series appeared negative until the final chapter, which always ended with a positive sentiment.

DOI: 10.4018/978-1-7998-9594-7.ch011

INTRODUCTION

Computational analysis of literary works is still considered as a big challenge in the field of digital literary studies, computational linguistics, machine learning, and neurocognitive poetics (Jacobs, 2015; Nalisnick & Baird, 2013; Ying et al., 2021, 2022). Sentiment analysis is a flourishing area which intersects linguistics and computer science. Sentiment Analysis is used to discover the sentiment contained in a text that can be assessed as positive or negative (Malik et al., 2021; Taboada, 2016). Sentiment Analysis is the key challenge that can assess the emotional information encoded in a literary text. Although, over the last two decades, a remarkable progress has been shown in Sentiment Analysis (Liu, 2015). The progression has occurred mostly in social media for business purposes, but few research can be found in literary works. Arthur M. Jacobs studied on sentiment analysis of poetic texts such as Shakespeare's sonnets where he focused on predicting aesthetic emotions (Jacobs et al., 2017). He also carried out Sentiment Analysis of novels such as *Harry Potter* book series and computed emotional and personality profiles of the protagonists (Jacobs, 2019). However, this type of work is rarely seen in the research domain of Sentiment Analysis. The authors have chosen this research topic considering the lack of research of Sentiment Analysis in digital literary studies.

In general, two approaches have been found for extracting sentiment automatically; a) lexicon based approach that is unsupervised, and b) machine learning approach that is supervised (Taboada et al., 2011). Both approaches of Sentiment Analysis have their pros and cons. Lexicon-based approaches have a benefit over machine learning approach as they do not require labeled data for forecasting unseen instances (Sazzed & Jayarathna, 2021). Natural Language Processing (NLP) is a technique that uses lexicon based approach to classify the sentiment polarity from the text using a sentiment lexicon (Nasukawa & Yi, 2003). Machine learning approach entails constructing classifiers from the text which are usually labeled (Pang et al., 2002), while lexicon-based approach computes the orientation from words or phrases in a document (Turney, 2002).

The study employed lexicon-based approach for extracting sentiment from *Harry Potter* series. Although varieties of dictionaries exist to evaluate the sentiment or opinion from texts, the study uses three of them: AFINN, BING, and NRC. The text of the series was collected from GitHub as an R package provided by Bradley Boehmke. The study depicted three categories of character (Main character, Hero character and Villain Character) from the data set of *Harry Potter* book series for conducting the Sentiment Analysis. The study has proposed a framework which was adopted from knowledge discovery in databases (KDD) method. The study used R programming language for analyzing and preprocessing the texts of the *Harry Potter* dataset. As a fundamental requirement of text-mining, some tidy data tools have been used in this analysis.

The objective of this paper is to propose a framework to conduct a Sentiment Analysis of *Harry Potter* book series written by British author J.K. Rowling. The paper will extract sentiment from various contexts such as a) frequency of words in the *Harry Potter* series, b) frequency of characters, c) prominent characters in each book, d) frequency of Sentimental words, e) Sentiment Analysis for each book, f) character-based Sentiment Analysis, g) sentiment of Hogwarts Houses, h) sentiment of *Harry Potter* series by page.

LITERATURE REVIEW

Harry Potter

To this day, British author J. K. Rowling's most celebrated Harry Potter series remains a highly valued story to children and adults alike across the world, becoming a hallmark in itself since the beginning of the new millennium. The series chronicles the life of Harry Potter, an orphan boy living with his abusive relatives, Mr. and Mrs. Dursley whose world revolves around their spoiled, insolent child, Dudley Dursley. On Harry's 11th birthday, he received an admissions letter to the Hogwarts School of Witchcraft and Wizardry, where he learned of his wizarding parentage and his fate as the 'Boy Who Lived' as well as newfound friends, mentors and enemies. In the seven-book span with each presenting a year in the life of Harry, Rowling's Harry Potter has sold over 400 million copies, each book adapted into one of the biggest film-franchises of all time as well as translated into over 80 languages (Barton, 2017; Carly, 2020). Written as a children's literature, the success of the book chronology lies in Rowling's blend of attention and skill at retelling the familiar story of a boy in a traditional boarding school, a genre in trend at the time of late twentieth-century, in an original manner, highlighting the author's excellent control over a complex plot and a brilliant sense of pace that expanded across all different books.

Children adore Harry as an underdog hero seeking dependency metaphorically, from the way he gained independence under the abusive Dursley's household to how he conducted himself across threats and dangers of Lord Voldemort. Though predictable in the sense that the hero will always win, Rowling's exceptional understanding of a good children's story can be seen from her unique characterization. Harry's unassuming role as a hero is challenged when doubt seeds in himself during Hogwarts's traditional sorting ceremony, where students are sorted into different 'houses' according to their main attributes. Harry was given a choice whether to be sorted into the cunning Slytherin or the courageous Gryffindor, making him an interesting hero that is not inherently a conduit of 'goodness' (Martus, 2009). Readers who thus come under the spell of the young wizard are ultimately charmed by Rowling's magical touch in the weaving of the stories that grips both the young and old through the dramatization of Harry's adventure in all the seven series.

Established from the very first book Harry Potter and the Sorcerer's Stone (1997), Rowling centers the stories around Harry with Ron Weasley and Hermione Granger who make up the heroic trio, along with some other notable counterparts in Hogwarts. Harry, Ron, and Hermione are significant characters in that they each represent a wide spectrum of wizarding types in terms of birth and wealth, thus challenging the dogma that an inherited place in society is superior (Martus, 2009). Harry and Ron have a prominent lineage in their ancestry, albeit Harry being only a 'half-blood' due to his mother's muggle-born background, a wizarding term for an ordinary human; and Ron's family reputation that compassions over muggles but lacking in wealth thus making them a scorn subject to the hierarchical society. Hermione, on the other hand, is a first-generation wizard as she was born an ordinary human, positioning her as the lowest in the inclusive social stratum. However, her sense and intelligence are what pilot the trio of friends in the novels. Like most other Gryffindor's students, they are daring, nerve and chivalrous in their traits with Harry in particular being attributed to gallantry, bravery, and courage, which are typical main traits of a hero (Salim & Saad, 2016). In this way, Harry is the chief male character known for most positive attributes in the series. Additionally, another key character in the series is Albus Dumbledore, the headmaster of Hogwarts. Professor Dumbledore represents the fount of wisdom and has a long-lasting reputation for inner strength, judgement of character and goodness (Martus, 2009). Hogwarts becomes a safe territory so long as he is in control, and this is demonstrated by the end of the series when he was forced to retreat, exposing the students to imminent threats by forces of evil.

Children's stories are made more intriguing with the looming presence of anti-hero and the Harry Potter series has some of the most infamous antagonists. Different kinds of villainous characters are portrayed, ranging from the stereotypical and static arch-villain Lord Voldemort to school bully Draco Malfoy and vicious Potion's instructor Severus Snape. At the heart of the novels, Voldemort is referred to as "the greatest dark sorcerer of all time" as well as "the most powerful Dark wizard for a century (Rowling, 1998, 2000), making him the most threatening anti-hero figure in the book. He is chiefly associated with a sense of darkness, with death, immortality, and a hatred for love at the center of his traits (Hinterberger, 2020). His power and domination over the wizarding world are hinted at several times when no one dared to refer to Lord Voldemort by his name, opting instead to 'He Who Must Not Be Named'. Voldemort is a developing antagonist in the span of the seven books as readers are made aware of his past and the shift in identity from Tom Riddle, a once brilliant and stunning young wizard to Voldemort, a less-human-like being involved in the Dark Magic. He is ultimately the main villain with most negative traits associated in all the series.

Furthermore, another anti-hero character worth mentioning is the school bully, Draco Malfoy. Malfoy's dominant attributes are that of which were brought by the influence of his upbringing i.e., an obsession with true blood and antiquated rules of wizard behavior. He values his position as a pure blood and hides in himself layers of prejudice in his hierarchical view of the magical society (Martus, 2009). Due to this skewed preconception, Malfoy reveals a sustained effort at harmless violence against Harry and his friends, especially Hermione who is a capable wizard yet tainted by her birthright. Similarly, an antagonistic character that illustrates such unfairness is Professor Snape. Though Hogwarts as an institution appraises student's welfare and safety, promising undivided protection to its pupils, the contrast can be said towards Snape as he is much fueled by the obvious lack of fairness when it comes to Malfoy's dispute with Harry. Snape's lessons are always located in dark, gloomy dungeons, a reflection of his malign character that brings in suspicion and unease (Martus, 2009). However, he is not necessarily an all-evil figure as his position in the novels are made ambivalent, veiling a true purpose to his allegiance as a member of the Order of the Phoenix and saving Harry's life at several points. Therefore, apart from Voldemort, it is hard to identify a character as inherently evil as the novel chronology reveals enough details that places all characters, including Harry, in a gray area that is neither good nor evil.

Like most other books that are written as parts of a long series, one of the chief elements that maintains readers' interest and a good storytelling is character development. Character development can be understood as changes in characters' attributes, or "the evolution of the character(s)" (Nieminen, 2021). For this reason, The Harry Potter Series is a suitable example of Bildungsroman, a form of narrative "depicting the journey from youth to maturity" (Graham, 2019), which essentially highlights the challenges of growing up that involve character development. In this series, many characters go through major and minor changes throughout the course of the books as a result of internal and external forces at play. These changes can be observed in the protagonists, the minor characters, and the antagonists.

The first category is the protagonists, such as Harry Potter and Hermione Granger. At the beginning of the series, in 'Harry Potter and the Philosopher's Stone', Harry begins as a meek, bullied orphaned child who lives in the cupboard under the staircase of his Aunt Petunia's house. This misfortune, nevertheless, takes a change for the better after he discovers his parentage roots and goes to Hogwarts School of Witchcraft and Wizardry to study magic. Furthermore, he is also left with a fortune from his parents and a good status in the wizardry world. Besides the observable changes, across the seven volumes of the series, Harry also grows internally from a naive and ignorant child into a tactful, mature individual with knowledge and mastery (Tally, 2012). Another note-worthy protagonist in the series is Hermione Granger. In the case of Hermione Granger, she is introduced as a strait-laced student who values intelligence and school over other things. However, as the series progresses, she is seen to be continuously breaking the rules she has set for herself in helping her friends. Like Harry who grows mature, Hermione realizes that there are more important things she learns to value other than school, like her friends.

Besides the protagonists, minor characters such as Neville Longbottom can be noted for his changes from his first appearance in the book series until the latest instalment. Neville Longbottom is most convincingly the character who has gone through the most changes among all of the casts of the series. From a shy, forgetful, obedient, and insecure young boy (Alvanita, 2018), Neville seems to have developed a solid self-confidence and becomes a hero in the last book, which is a thoughtful and gradual development over time. He proves his courage and eagerness by being among the few who are willing to help Harry to face the Death Eaters in 'Harry Potter and the Deathly Hallows'. Although a minor character, he displays traits of a hero or a protagonist through his bravery and leadership when facing Voldemort, stripping his 'squib' status he has established in his youth into a courageous and righteous adolescent.

Similarly, an antagonist character, Draco Malfoy, has also changed significantly in the more recent novels in the series in comparison to the first book. He is characterized upon his introduction as a bully and self-important person. For instance, Draco Malfoy is continuously seen taunting Harry, Ron, and Hermione in the beginning, flaunting his family's 'pure' bloodline. Although he initially wishes to go along with his father's beliefs and his loyalty to Lord Voldemort, Draco is able to see the negative impact of his parents' beliefs when tasked with the impossible; that is to kill Albus Dumbledore to restore Voldemort's good grace on his family. Although his character development is implicit, at the end of the series, he becomes a better parent to his child, taking lessons from his own parents' failed upbringing.

Besides the character development, public reception of the novels is another important point to be discussed. In terms of public reception, like most children's books, the first novel of The Harry Potter Series, 'Harry Potter and the Philosopher's Stone' did not receive immediate attention upon its publication. Being a debuting author, Rowling also did not have an existing group of dedicated readers. In addition to that, children's books often receive less review and media coverage. Only a few reviewers came forward to give their thoughts on the first book of the series. Gradually, however, more critics took interest in the book following its winning of Gold Award in Nestles Smarties Book Prizes, a prestigious award voted by children all over the country.

'Harry Potter and the Philosopher's Stone' received much love, especially from children, after its publication. Most critics acknowledge that the book appeals to children due to Rowling's great story-telling strengths, imaginative capacity, quirkiness and sense of humor. In a review by The Glasgow Herald, the book is said to be attractive to children: 'I have yet to find a child who can put it down. Magic stuff (Martus, 2009). Some significant elements in the book that attract children are the gripping themes of bravery, magic, and love and friendship, in addition to the attention to details of the world building of a compelling fictional universe. Eccleshare (2002) states about the character Harry Potter that Rowling had managed to create as "a child character whose ability to take on adults by adult responsibilities while still remaining essentially child-like" (p. 11), which is in itself an engaging attribute given to the main character of a children's book.

Following this, it is only fitting that the book soon becomes popular. In the year 1998, 'Harry Potter and the Philosopher's Stone' swept all the major children's books awards selected by children, establishing its merit as the most famous and loved children's book by children of its time. Some of the awards won are Children's Book Award, Young Telegraph Paperback of the Year Award, Birmingham Cable's Children Book Award, and Sheffield Children's Book Award (Martus, 2009). As it gained more attention, the book received favorable feedback from adult audiences too. In the years following Rowling's debut with 'Harry Potter and the Philosopher's Stone', The Harry Potter Series continues to receive massive support and anticipation from children and older audiences. Whereas Rowling herself had become a major, well-known children's book author.

Sentiment Analysis

The term Sentiment Analysis (SA), first appeared in (Nasukawa & Yi, 2003), is also called Opinion Mining as it is a field that examines people's opinions, appraisal, attitudes, sentiments, and emotions towards entities which can be organizations, products, services, issues, topics, events or individuals whose attributes are expressed in a written text. Sentiment Analysis is a data mining approach that deals with people's opinions through Natural Language Processing, text analysis, and computational linguistics (Rupapara et al., 2021; Ying et al., 2021, 2022). A methodology provided by Sentiment Analysis is to computationally process unstructured data (Piryani et al., 2017). Unstructured text is not limited to an entire document but is also part of a sentence, with or without embedded metadata. It is stated that Sentiment Analysis process will normally involve texts that have been pre-processed through tokenization, stemming, lemmatization, part of speech tagging, entity extraction and relation extraction and followed by polarity detection which usually categorizes sentiment-based scale of rating 1 to 5. Essentially there are two approaches that can perform Sentiment Analysis, Lexicon-Based approaches, and Machine Learning approaches. The word lexicon renders insight of a picture as it requires a priori construction of a suitable lexicon to classify text into positive phrases or negative phrases. First, sentiment lexicon will be created by researchers through compiling sentiment word list, and then the degree of subjectivity of a text unit will be determined based on positive or negative indicators identified by the lexicon (Pang & Lee, 2004). There is no limited domain restriction on using lexicon-approaches to perform sentiment analysis as it is domain independence and is prone to be improved and extended. When an error occurs, one can correct some existing rules or add new rules to system's rule base. Unfortunately, texts are often considered as a collection of words without considering the relations between individual words (Boiy & Moens, 2009). Nevertheless, a lot of time is spent to build the initial knowledge based of lexicon, pattern and rules (Liu, 2012). Machine learning approaches will automatically perform classification. However, it needs training data sets. Algorithms will be constructed, and model will be built by selecting feature and by learning from labelled training datasets. Through optimization, learning algorithm can automatically adapt and learn from all kinds of features for classification. Machine learning can be categorized as supervised machine-learning and unsupervised machine-learning. The ways on how both machine-learning approaches used to learn about data make significant differences. Prior information about real value of outputs is needed for supervised machine-learning before algorithm are used to approximate the mapping function from the input to the output. Once the algorithm learned about the dataset on what is input what is output attached, when there is new input inserted, the model can make prediction on what will be output. Well-known methods including the support vector machine (SVM), Naïve Bayes, and the N-grams model which have been used for sentiment classification (Ye et al., 2009). Unsupervised machine-learning requires no prior information as it uses clustering concept to cluster sentiment based on the hidden structure from the given input. There is no right or wrong answer based on parameter turning and how well researchers understand the dataset. Most researchers will adopt supervised machine-learning as compared to unsupervised machine-learning. However supervised machine-learning technique requires manual annotation of sufficient and representative training data, which is often very costly and time consuming. Moreover, as it relies on training data, a sentiment classifier trained from the labelled data in one domain often does not work in another domain. Regardless of machine learning approaches or lexicon-based approaches, sentiment analysis can be conducted at three levels of document level, sentence level and aspect level.

Document-Level

As the name suggests, document-level sentiment analysis will be applied on document level to determine overall positive or negative sentiment of a text. Normally it is used in forum discussions, question-answering systems, online reviews, or blogs to identify and classify sentiment orientations or polarities within a whole opinion document (Pang & Lee, 2004).

Aspect-Level

Aspect-level sentiment analysis is used in case of availability of attributes inside post, entity, or input text. Instead of relying on language constructs such as paragraphs, sentences, and documents, aspect level analysis directly concentrates on opinion that aims to identify sentiment targets and assign sentiments to the targets (Hu & Liu, 2004). For example, a review on a tablet has the attribute of battery life, screen light, camera, and other attributes where each attribute has a different sentiment. Reviews as: "My tablet is really nice with high camera pixel and vivid screen but non lasting battery". The aspect here is tablet while the attributes are battery and camera where sentiment detection leads to the following results: (screen, positive), (battery, negative) and (camera, positive).

Sentence-Level

Only sentences are analyzed to determine sentiment polarities. Subjectivity classification is the main focus for sentence-level analysis which distinguishes sentences (i.e., objective sentences) that express factual information from sentences and expresses subjective views and opinions (i.e., subjective sentences). Unlike document-level analysis which often neglect the neutral sentiment, the neutral sentiment cannot be ignored in sentence-level classification because a document may contain many sentences that express neither positive nor negative sentiment.

MATERIALS AND METHODOLOGY

Dataset Description

The dataset of *Harry Potter* book series has been collected from GitHub. Bradley Boehmke who prepared an R package (harrypotter) that contains text from all seven books of the Harry Potter series. Each text is constituted in a character vector as a single element which forms a single chapter. Table 1 presents the elements that the package 'harrypotter' contains.

Table 1. Dataset elements

SL	Name of Book	Name of Package Elements
1	Harry Potter and the Sorcerer's Stone (1997)	philosophers_stone
2	Harry Potter and the Chamber of Secrets (1998)	chamber_of_secrets
3	Harry Potter and the Prisoner of Azkaban (1999)	prisoner_of_azkaban
4	Harry Potter and the Goblet of Fire (2000)	goblet_of_fire
5	Harry Potter and the Order of the Phoenix (2003)	order_of_the_phoenix
6	Harry Potter and the Half-Blood Prince (2005)	half_blood_prince
7	Harry Potter and the Deathly Hallows (2007)	deathly_hallows

The study depicted three categories of character from the data set of Harry Potter series for conducting the sentiment analysis. Table 1 presented the category of characters and incorporated member.

Table 2. Category of characters

Character	Number of Character	Name of Character
Main Character	3	Harry, Ron and Hermione
Hero Character	16	Lily, James, Hagrid, Dumbledore, Sirius, Lupin, Moody, Slughorn, Dobby, Cedric, Luna, Tonks, Mcgonagall, Ginny, Order of the phoenix, and Neville
Villain Character	19	Voldemort, Nagini, Snape, Draco, Lucius, Umbridge, Pettigrew, Dementor, Dementors, Greyback, Bellatrix, Quirrell, Riddle, Death eaters, Aragog, Basilisk, Dudley, Vernon, and Petunia

Sentiment Analysis Approaches

There are 2 main sentimental analysis approaches: (1) Lexicon-based approach and (2) machine learning approach as shown in Figure 1.

Figure 1. Summary of sentimental analysis approaches

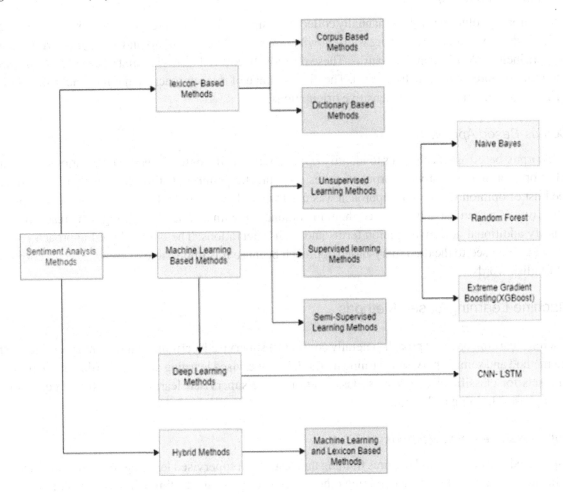

Lexicon Based Methods

This method makes use of lexicons or dictionaries. The semantic orientation or polarity of words or phrases in the text is used in this phase to calculate the orientation of a language. The lexicon-based approach does not necessitate the handling of a vast amount of data, as a machine learning approach does. It computes the orientation of a text using a lexicon or dictionaries. Semantic Orientation (SO) is a measure of textual subjectivity and judgment that captures the polarity and power of terms or phrases. The overall sentiment orientation of the text is determined by both of these terms. Opinion lexicons can be produced manually or automatically. The manual approach to developing the opinion lexicon can be time-consuming, so it must be combined with other automated approaches. This section defines two types of manual lexicons: general lexicons and category specific lexicons. The traditional lexicon consists of terms with the same sentiment meaning as the default sentiment, broken words, negation and blind negation words (D'Andrea et al., 2015; Manda, 2019).

Dictionary-Based Approach

The dictionary solution involves manually collecting a small collection of terms with known orientations, which is then expanded by scanning well-known corpora for their synonyms and antonyms. Well-known corpora include WordNet and thesaurus. These recently discovered words are first returned to the original list until no more words are discovered. The disadvantage of this approach is that it cannot find opinion terms with domain and context sensitive orientations.

Corpus-Based Approach

The corpus-based approach seeks to identify opinion terms with context-specific orientations. To locate other opinion words in a vast corpus, it relies on syntactic patterns that appear together, as well as a seed list of opinion words. This approach was used when they began with a limited number of opinion adjectives as a seed list and then used them in conjunction with a collection of linguistic restrictions to classify additional adjective opinion terms and their orientations. The corpus-based approach is inefficient as opposed to the dictionary-based approach because it is impossible to create a broad corpus of all English words.

Machine Learning Based Methods

Machine learning based approach generally consists of supervised learning method, unsupervised learning method and semi-supervised learning method. Unsupervised learning approaches do not use training data sets for classification, whereas classification using supervised learning algorithms requires two main phases: training and testing.

Supervised Learning Methods

Supervised learning method requires training and testing. In supervised learning method, a well-labeled collection is required to perform training otherwise the training and testing will be difficult to perform. There are two forms of supervised learning: regression and classification. In regression, labeled data sets are given that have been trained, and using the solutions available, they attempt to forecast and refine the model iteratively. Classification tries to assist us in locating the relevant class markers that can be used to forecast positive, negative, and neutral feelings. In supervised learning, a machine learning model is created that uses labeled data to train and interpret tweets and attempts to predict their sentiments. In supervised learning, several algorithms can be used; logical regressions, neural networks, support vector machines (SVM), decision trees, random forests, and Naive Bayes classifiers.

Unsupervised Learning Methods

Unsupervised learning method can either be based on machine learning or lexicon. In unsupervised learning methods there is no need for labeled model, because it is known as pattern discovery; such as clustering. A Sentiment Lexicon is typically used with an unsupervised approach to sentiment analysis. The semantic orientation technique is used for text classification, in which different algorithms extract phrases containing adjectives or adverbs to approximate a phrase's semantic orientation. The reviews are then classified using semantic orientation.

Semi-Supervised Learning

Semi-supervised learning acts as a middle learning method between supervised learning and unsupervised learning models which means labeled data and unlabeled data utilized in this method. The aim of this approach is to use a labeled information collection to identify some of the unlabeled data. This model is most often used in portfolio price analysis and is not useful in sentiment analysis of datasets. There are a few problems when estimating the sentiment of Twitter datasets, such as the size of the unlabeled dataset should be larger than labeled data, input-output proximity symmetry, easy labeling, and low dimension.

Hybrid Methods

The Hybrid approach consists of machine learning and lexicon-based methods. Classifiers in this technique are used in a cascade fashion, but when one fails, the next one classifies, and so forth before the document or text is classified.

Applied Sentiment Analysis Approach

The study applied lexicon-based approach for extracting subjectivity and polarity of sentiments from texts of Harry Potter. The study used mainly three external dictionaries to classify the given dataset into two classes: positive and negative. Although there are varieties of dictionaries to evaluate the sentiment or opinion from texts, the study uses three of them:

AFINN

The dictionary is developed by Finn Årup Nielsen. AFINN uses a wordlist-based approach for sentiment analysis which contains over 3,300 English words with a polarity score associated with each word. The words are manually rated for valence with an integer from minus five (negative) to plus five (positive) and the dictionary formed a data frame with one row for each term.

BING

The dictionary is developed by Bing Liu and collaborators. Bing is a general-purpose English sentiment lexicon that categorizes words in a binary fashion, either positive or negative and the dictionary formed a data frame with 6,786 rows and 2 variables.

NRC

The dictionary is developed jointly by Saif Mohammad and Peter Turney. NRC sentiment lexicon is a list of English words and their associations with eight basic emotions (anger, fear, anticipation, trust, surprise, sadness, joy, and disgust) and two sentiments (negative and positive). The annotations were manually done by crowdsourcing.

Proposed Framework for Sentiment Analysis

The study has proposed a framework for sentiment analysis of the Harry Potter series as demonstrated in Figure 2. The framework is adopted from knowledge discovery in databases (KDD) method which is used for extracting valuable and non-trivial information from large databases. KDD is a kind of data mining method that follows five stages to extract knowledge – data selection, preprocessing, transformation, data mining and evaluation or interpretation (Fayyad et al., 1996). The proposed framework also works by following five stages. The first stage is data collection that focuses on the dataset and its subset. In second stage, data cleaning and preprocess take place to get the reliable data. In third stage, text analysis extracts the insight from unstructured text. In fourth stage, external lexicons are used to score the sentiment of the given dataset. Finally, the positive and the negative sentiment polarity is reported in the last stage.

Figure 2. Proposed framework

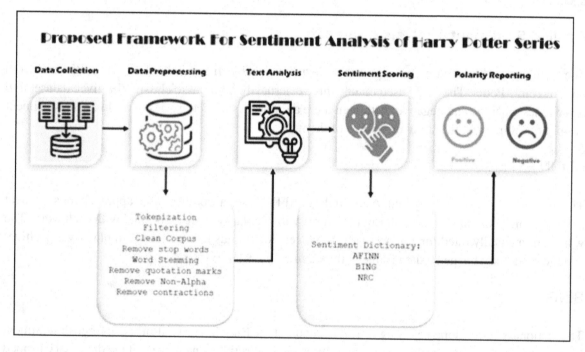

Data Analysis and Preprocessing

The study uses R programming language for analyzing and preprocessing the texts of the Harry Potter dataset. As a fundamental requirement of text-mining, some tidy data tools have been used in this analysis. Figure 3 shows how tidy data tools have been used in sentiment analysis.

Figure 3. Sentiment Analysis using Tidy data tools

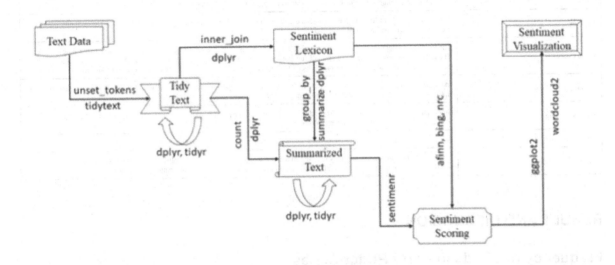

Table 3 explains the tidy tools that have been used in this study.

Table 3. Tidy tools for sentiment analysis

Name of Tools/Package	Tools Description
TIDYTEXT	'tidytext' is a text-mining tool or package which provides functions and supporting data sets to allow conversion of text to and from tidy formats, and to switch seamlessly between tidy tools and existing text mining packages.
DPLYR	'dplyr' is another tidy tool that is considered as a grammar of data manipulation. It provides a set of verbs that used to solve various data manipulation challenge such as mutate, select, filter, summarize, and arrange.
TIDYR	'tidyr' is a R package which helps to create tidy data, where each column is a variable, each row is an observation, and each cell contains a single value. The tool also used for pivoting, nesting, un-nesting of a dataset. It also handles missing values.
SENTIMENTR	'Sentimentr' is designed to quickly calculate text polarity sentiment in the English language at the sentence level and optionally aggregate by rows or grouping variable(s). It follows dictionary lookup approach.
WORDCLOUD2	'wordcloud2' is a fast visualization tool for creating wordcloud. It is a JavaScript library to create wordle presentation on 2D canvas or HTML.
GGPLOT2	'ggplot2' is data visualization package. It is called "The Grammar of Graphics". The tools were used to generate various kind of chart and plots.

In data analysis stage, the study used several preprocessing techniques to prepare the data for achieving high quality mining result. Table 4 described the data-preprocessing techniques applied in this study.

Table 4. Data processing techniques

Preprocess Step	Step Description
Tokenization	Tokenization is a technique that breaks up the text into individual words and counts how many times each word appears in the text. In text analysis, token is a word, phrase, sentence, a paragraph, even a whole chapter. In tidy text framework, text has split into individual tokens for transforming it to a tidy data structure by using 'unset_tokens ()'function.
Filtering	The study used 'dplyr filter' function to subset a data frame, retaining all rows that satisfy the preset conditions.The technique has applied to both grouped and ungrouped data.
Clean Corpus	The foundational steps involve loading the text file into an R Corpus, then cleaning and stemming the data before performing analysis. The technique has applied a series of cleaning functions to it in order, then returns the updated corpus. The text has been set to lower case, fix apostrophe and remove constraction by custom function associated with 'gsub()' function. Finally, it converted to tidy format.
Remove stop words	In the stage of preprocess, the techniques remove the uninformative stop-words such as "the", "and", "of" etc. The tidy format allows to make use of the dplyr grammar and snowball stemming library for removing stopwords.
Word Stemming	Stemming is another useful preprocessing technique that is used in the preprocessing stage. The stemming technique reduced words across the document by 'stemDocument()' function.
Remove quotation marks	A custom function has been built to remove quotation mark from the text for data preprocessing.
Remove Non-Alpha	In this stage of preprocessing, the study removed all non-alphanumeric (punctuation, numbers, and other no-characters) symbols from and then put into a string. The study used 'gsub()' function to replace all the matches of a pattern from a string.

RESULT AND DISCUSSION

Frequency of Words in Harry Potter Series

Figure 4 shows frequency of top ten words used in Harry Potter text. The analysis depicts three words- 'Harry', 'Ron' and 'Hermione' as the most frequent in all Harry Potter series. The word 'Harry' is used over sixteen thousand times which secures the highest word frequency. The other words 'Ron' and 'Hermione' followed Harry with relatively fewer score, 5750 and 4912 respectively.

Figure 4. Frequency of words of all seven books

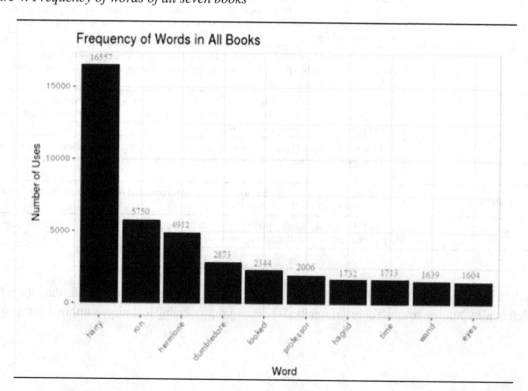

Figure 5 exhibits the word frequency of all books individually. The result shows that three words-'Harry', 'Ron' and 'Hermione' are used most frequently except in- Book 1: philosophers_stone and 'Book 6: half_blood_prince' where the two words of 'Hagrid' and 'Dumbledore' came in top three.

Figure 5.

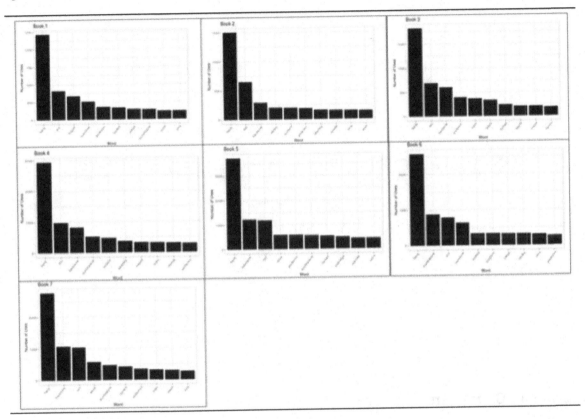

Frequency of Characters

Figure 6 shows a combination of wordcloud and chart which presents the frequency of characters in the whole Harry Potter series. The results show that the main characters 'Harry', 'Ron' and 'Hermione' scored the highest frequency in terms of the used first-name. On the other hand, as per last name, the characters 'Dumbledore', 'Hagrid', and 'Snape' came at top three position among ten.

Figure 6. Frequency of characters in all books

Frequency of Characters in All Books

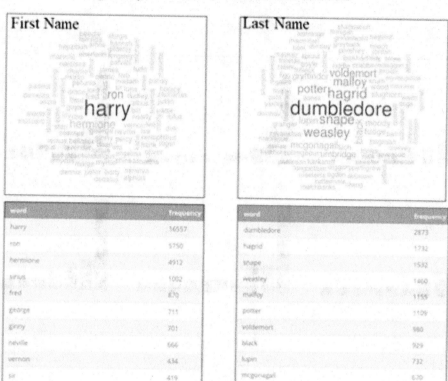

Prominent Characters per Book

Figure 7 exhibits that Professor Dolores Jane Umbridge appeared as the most popular character in all of the books. Professor Remus John Lupin ranked second throughout but highest in the 'Prisonar of Azaban'. Professor Horace E. F. Slughorn appeared as the least prominent, scoring the lowest score in the list.

Figure 7. Prominent Character per Book by TF-IDF Scoring

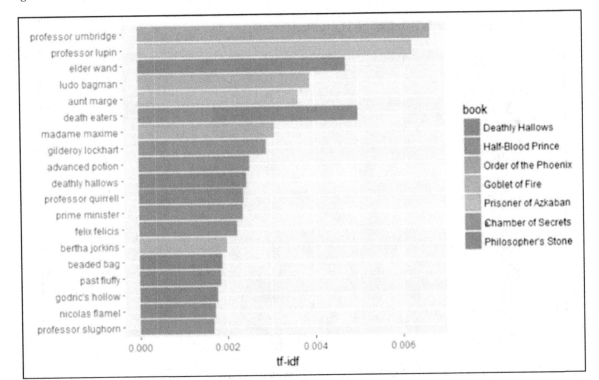

Frequency of Sentimental Words

Figure 8 shows the frequency of sentimental words based on the Bing dictionary. The figure visualizes the frequency of top ten sentimental words that scored either positive or negative in the entire series. The result shows that three sentimental words among ten – 'like', 'well', and 'right' scored over 1.5K as positive. On the other hand, 'dark', 'death' and 'hard' indicated as negative which scored relatively lower.

Figure 8. Frequency of sentimental words

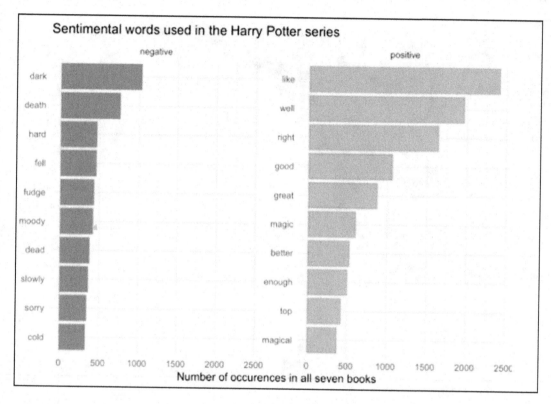

Figure 9 shows positive words used in each book of the Harry Potter series. The graph reveals that 'like', 'right' and 'well' are used most frequently in every Harry Potter book.

Figure 9. Positive words per book by Bing Dictionary

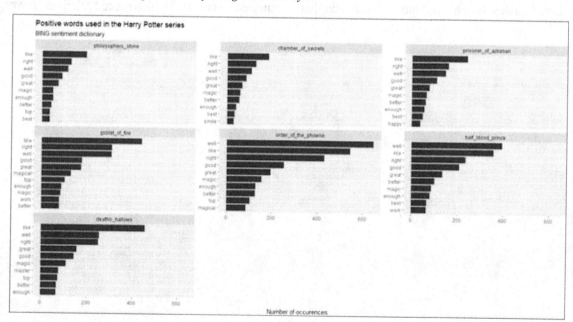

Figure 10 represents the frequency of negative word in each Harry Potter book. The bar graph shows that the negative word 'dark' scored as the most frequent in four books among seven. The word 'death' also came at top three position in four books. The frequency of 'death' scored highest in book 7 of Deathly Hallows. The word 'Moody' scored significantly in the book 4 of Goblet of Fire.

Figure 10. Negative words per book by Bing dictionary

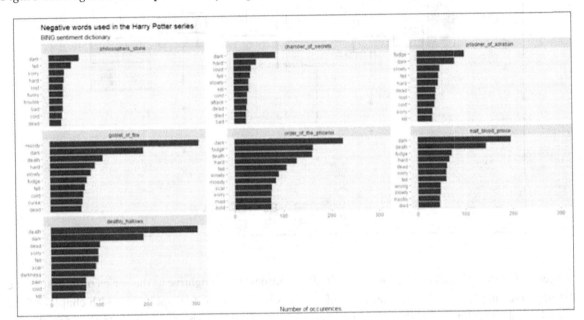

Sentiment Analysis per Book

Figure 11 was generated by Sentiment Analysis package and converted into binary response by giving 1 value for positive word and minus 1 for negative words. The result shows that the sixth book 'Half Blood Prince' has the most positive average sentiment and the last book has the lowest average sentiment.

Figure 11. Sentiment analysis by book

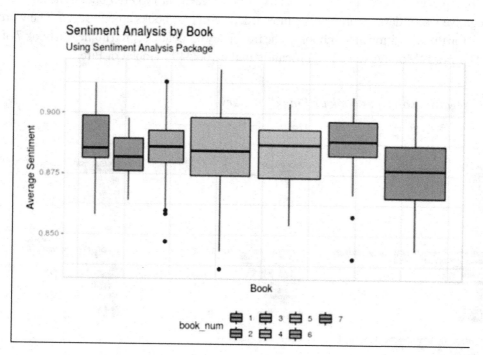

Figure 12 presented that the sentiment gradually becomes more negative as the series progresses. The most negative chapter is the 93rd chapter in all of the series, which corresponds to 34th chapter of the 4th book 'Goblet of Fire'. The most positive chapter is the 74th, which corresponds to the 15th chapter of the 4th book 'Goblet of Fire'.

Figure 12. Progress of sentiment by book

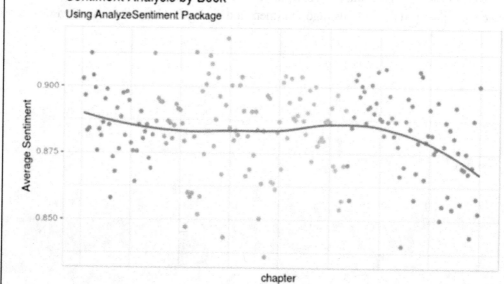

Figure 13 presents the positive/negative sentiment for each book over time using the AFINN diction-ary. The plot determines score how positive or negative a word according to AFINN dictionary by as-signing the values to each word of the series. The series looks to get darker as it progresses. The pattern appeared almost similar in the plot as in the previous sentiment analysis.

Figure 13. Sentiment analysis by book using AFINN dictionary

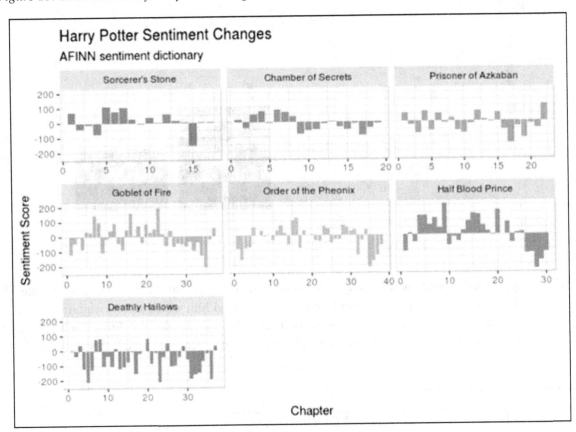

Character Based Sentiment Analysis

Figure 14 presents the sentiment of the main character of Harry Potter series. The main trio are Harry Potter, Ron Weasley and Hermione Granger. The result shows that Harry Potter has less positive senti-ment in the text around him than Ron Weasley and Hermione Granger. Harry scored less than the average score of sentiment, whereas Ron and Hermione scored around ten which was much more than Harry.

Figure 14. Sentiment of main characters

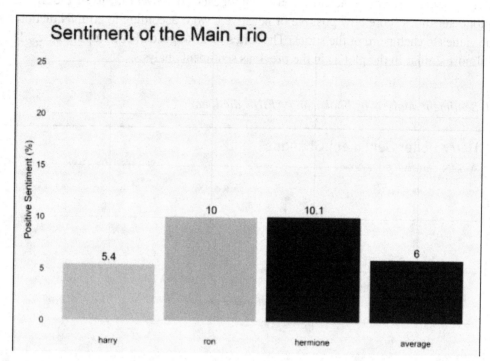

For the analysis of sentiment, the study enlisted sixteen characters for the hero category. Figure 15 shows that Professor Slughorn has the most positive text around him which is very significant. Luna Lovegood has the second most positive text around her. The plot also revealed that Professor Moody had the most negative sentiment. The second most negative sentiment appeared around Harry's mother, Lily.

Figure 15. Sentiment of hero characters

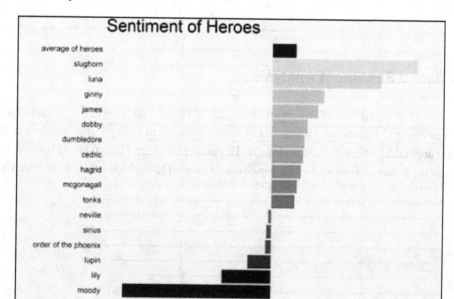

The study categorized 19 villainous characters for the Sentiment Analysis. Figure 16 shows that Tom Riddle, Professor Quirrell, and Professor Snape contain more positive text than negative text. On the other hand, Professor Umbridge, surprisingly, has the most positive sentiment. Unsurprisingly, the werewolf, ancient snake, and giant spider all have extremely negative sentiments.

Figure 16. Sentiment of villain characters

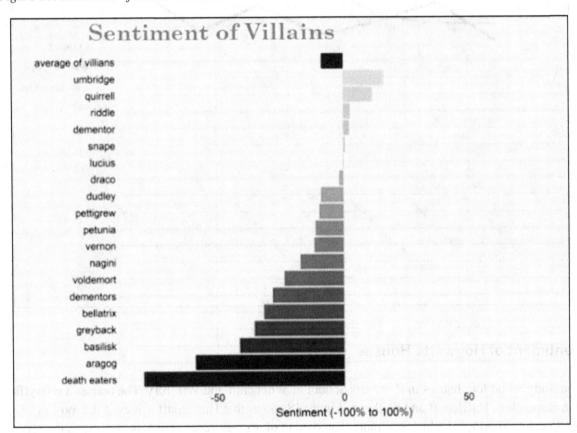

Figure 17 shows how the sentiments of these main trio, heroes and villains change across each book. The chart shows that the average sentiment for the main trio, heroes, and villains progress gradually from first book to the last. The study shows that the negative sentiment in the text around the villains grows significantly. Negative sentiment appeared more balanced for the main trio and the heroes. Largest difference found in the 'Goblet of Fire' between the sentiment around the villain and sentiment around the main trio and heroes. In 'Chamber of Secrets', text mentioning the main trio and heroes were more negative than villains. The book 'Deathly Hallows' (Book 7) appeared featuring the most negative sentiment.

Figure 17. Sentiment of heroes, villains, main trio across books

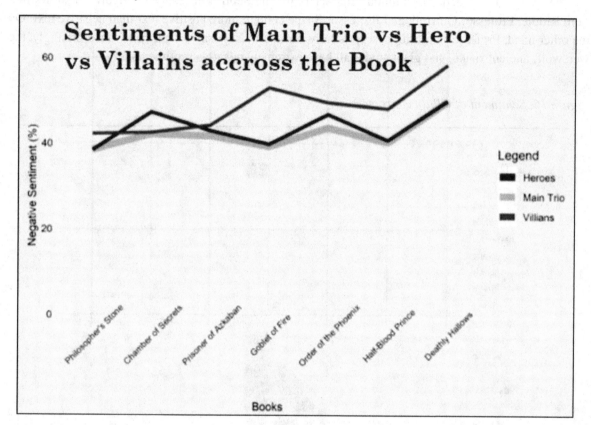

Sentiment of Hogwarts Houses

The study found four houses in Hogwarts School of Witchcraft and Wizardry. The houses are Gryffindor, Ravenclaw, Hufflepuff and Slytherin. Figure 18 shows that Hufflepuff achieved the most positive sentiment by scoring 47 which was more than double of average score. The Ravenclaw has the second highest sentiment score, whereas Slytherin has the lowest in the list.

Figure 18. Sentiment of houses

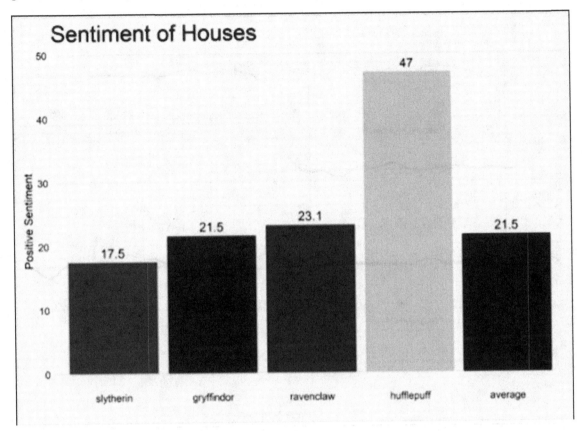

Sentiment of Harry Potter Series by page

Figure 19 presents the sentiment per page of each book. The plot shows that in 'Prisoner of Azkaban', a significant negative slop is found in the final third. 'Goblet of Fire' has very happy middle. 'Deathly Hallows' carries mostly negative sentiment throughout the book. On the other hand, 'Half-Blood Prince' is surprisingly positive until to the end. A significant trend is that every book appeared as negative sentiment until the final chapter. Another common trend is that each chapter ends with a challenging and positive note where heroes get victory with the help of main trio.

Figure 19. Sentiment of Harry Potter series by page

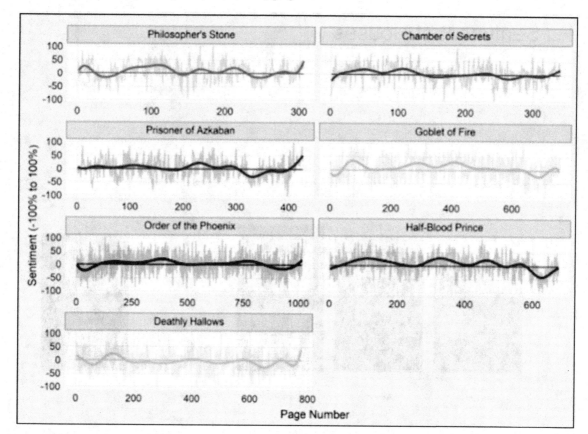

CONCLUSION

The objective of this study was to evaluate a Sentiment Analysis of *Harry Potter* novel series written by British author J.K. Rowling. A lexicon approach of Natural Language Processing (NLP) technique and a proposed framework are applied in this study. The text-data of the book series was sourced from GitHub since an R package is already provided by Bradley Boehmke. The study used R programming along with 'tidy' data tools and dictionaries for analyzing the sentiment and representing in an appropriate visualization. The results showed that Professor Slughorn scored the most positive sentiment among the hero characters, while Death Eaters had the most negative sentiment among the anti-hero characters. The results also revealed that negative sentiment in the text around the anti-hero characters increased significantly, while the positive sentiment around the hero characters remained constant as the story progressed. Besides, it was revealed that among the series of novel the *Deathly Hallows* contained the most negative sentiment. Finally, the results revealed that among all the houses of Hogwarts School of Witchcraft and Wizardry, Hufflepuff had the most positive sentiment, and each book of the series appeared negative until the final chapter which always ended with a positive sentiment. The authors hope that the proposed framework and methodology can work as a reference for future research to analyze literary works for extracting the sentiments.

REFERENCES

Alvanita, A. (2018). The Character Development of Neville Longbottom in the Harry Potter Series. *Lexicon*, *1*(3). Advance online publication. doi:10.22146/lexicon.v1i3.42080

Barton, G. (2017). *Harry Potter and the translator's nightmare.* VOX. https://www.vox.com/culture/2016/10/18/13316332/harry-potter-translations

Boiy, E., & Moens, M. F. (2009). A machine learning approach to sentiment analysis in multilingual web texts. *Information Retrieval*, *12*(5), 526–558. doi:10.100710791-008-9070-z

Carly. (2020). The Big Six Translations of Harry Potter. *The Rowling Magazine.* https://www.therowlinglibrary.com/2020/07/22/the-six-translations-of-harry-potter/

D'Andrea, A., Ferri, F., Grifoni, P., & Guzzo, T. (2015). Approaches, Tools and Applications for Sentiment Analysis Implementation. *International Journal of Computers and Applications*, *125*(3), 26–33. doi:10.5120/ijca2015905866

Fayyad, U., Piatetsky-Shapiro, G., & Smyth, P. (1996). From Data Mining to Knowledge Discovery in Databases. *AI Magazine*, *17*(3), 37–37. doi:10.1609/AIMAG.V17I3.1230

Graham, S. (2019). *A history of the bildungsroman.* Cambridge University Press. doi:10.1017/9781316479926

Hinterberger, K. (2020). *The portrayal of villains in J.K. Rowling's "Harry Potter."* doi:10.25365/thesis.62071

Hu, M., & Liu, B. (2004). Mining and summarizing customer reviews. *KDD-2004 - Proceedings of the Tenth ACM SIGKDD International Conference on Knowledge Discovery and Data Mining*, 168–177. 10.1145/1014052.1014073

Jacobs, A. M. (2015). Neurocognitive poetics: Methods and models for investigating the neuronal and cognitive-affective bases of literature reception. *Frontiers in Human Neuroscience*, *9*(APR), 1–22. doi:10.3389/fnhum.2015.00186 PMID:25932010

Jacobs, A. M. (2019). Sentiment Analysis for Words and Fiction Characters From the Perspective of Computational (Neuro-)Poetics. *Frontiers in Robotics and AI*, *6*, 53. doi:10.3389/frobt.2019.00053 PMID:33501068

Jacobs, A. M., Schuster, S., Xue, S., & Lüdtke, J. (2017). What's in the brain that ink may character.... *Scientific Study of Literature*, *7*(1), 4–51. doi:10.1075sol.7.1.02jac

Liu, B. (2012). Sentiment Analysis and Opinion Mining. In Synthesis Lectures on Human Language Technologies (Vol. 5). doi:10.2200/S00416ED1V01Y201204HLT016

Liu, B. (2015). Sentiment analysis: Mining opinions, sentiments, and emotions. *Sentiment Analysis: Mining Opinions, Sentiments, and Emotions*, 1–367. doi:10.1017/CBO9781139084789

Malik, E. F., Keikhosrokiani, P., & Asl, M. P. (2021). Text mining life cycle for a spatial reading of Viet Thanh Nguyen's *The Refugees* (2017). In *The 2021 International Congress of Advanced Technology and Engineering (ICOTEN).* 10.1109/ICOTEN52080.2021.9493520

Manda, K. R. (2019). Sentiment Analysis of Twitter Data Using Machine Learning and Deep Learning Methods. In *Blekinge Institute of Technology*. Faculty of Computing, Department of Computer Science.

Martus, T. (2009). A Guide to the Harry Potter Novels. *Children's Literature Association Quarterly*, *27*(4), 233–234. doi:10.1353/chq.0.1431

Nalisnick, E. T., & Baird, H. S. (2013). Character-to-Character Sentiment Analysis in Shakespeare's Plays. *ACL*, 479–483. http://www.ibiblio.org/xml/examples/shakespeare/

Nasukawa, T., & Yi, J. (2003). Sentiment analysis: Capturing favorability using natural language processing. *Proceedings of the 2nd International Conference on Knowledge Capture, K-CAP 2003*, 70–77. 10.1145/945645.945658

Nieminen, E. (2021). *The Character Development of Neville Longbottom in J.K. Rowling's Harry Potter Novel Series*. https://trepo.tuni.fi/handle/10024/124797

Pang, B., & Lee, L. (2004). A Sentimental Education: Sentiment Analysis Using Subjectivity Summarization Based on Minimum Cuts. *Computing Research Repository - CORR*, 271–278. doi:10.3115/1218955.1218990

Pang, B., Lee, L., & Vaithyanathan, S. (2002). Thumbs up? Sentiment Classification using Machine Learning Techniques. *Proceedings of the Conference on Empirical Methods in Natural Language Processing (NLP)*, 79–86. 10.3115/1118693.1118704

Piryani, R., Madhavi, D., & Singh, V. K. (2017). Analytical mapping of opinion mining and sentiment analysis research during 2000–2015. *Information Processing & Management*, *53*(1), 122–150. doi:10.1016/j.ipm.2016.07.001

Rowling, J. K. (1998). *Harry Potter and the chamber of secrets*. Bloomsbury Pub.

Rowling, J. K. (2000). *Harry Potter and the Goblet of Fire*. Bloomsbury.

Rupapara, V., Rustam, F., Amaar, A., Washington, P. B., Lee, E., & Ashraf, I. (2021). Deepfake tweets classification using stacked Bi-LSTM and words embedding. *PeerJ. Computer Science*, *7*, e745. doi:10.7717/peerj-cs.745 PMID:34805502

Salim, H., & Saad, N. N. (2016). Portraying the Protagonists: A Study of the Use of Adjectives in Harry Potter and the Deathly Hallows. *Undefined*, *5*(6), 259–264. doi:10.7575/aiac.ijalel.v.5n.6p.259

Sazzed, S., & Jayarathna, S. (2021). SSentiA: A Self-supervised Sentiment Analyzer for classification from unlabeled data. *Machine Learning with Applications*, *4*, 100026. doi:10.1016/j.mlwa.2021.100026

Taboada, M. (2016). Sentiment Analysis: An Overview from Linguistics. *Annual Review of Linguistics*, *2*(1), 325–347. doi:10.1146/annurev-linguistics-011415-040518

Taboada, M., Brooke, J., Tofiloski, M., Voll, K., & Stede, M. (2011). Lexicon-Based Methods for Sentiment Analysis. *Computational Linguistics*, *37*(2), 267–307. doi:10.1162/COLI_a_00049

Tally, R. T. (2012). The Way of the Wizarding World: Harry Potter and the Magical Bildungsroman. In *J. K. Rowling: Harry Potter*. Macmillan Education UK. doi:10.1007/978-1-137-28492-1_4

Turney, P. D. (2002). Thumbs Up or Thumbs Down? Semantic Orientation Applied to Unsupervised Classification of Reviews. *Proceedings of 40th Meeting of the Association for Computational Linguistics*, 417. 10.3115/1073083.1073153

Ye, Q., Zhang, Z., & Law, R. (2009). Sentiment classification of online reviews to travel destinations by supervised machine learning approaches. *Expert Systems with Applications, 36*(3), 6527–6535. doi:10.1016/j.eswa.2008.07.035

Ying, S. Y., Keikhosrokiani, P., & Asl, M. P. (2021). Comparison of data analytic techniques for a spatial opinion mining in literary works: A review paper. In F. Saeed, F. Mohammed, & A. Al-Nahari (Eds.), *Innovative Systems for Intelligent Health Informatics* (pp. 523–535). Springer International Publishing. doi:10.1007/978-3-030-70713-2_49

Ying, S. Y., Keikhosrokiani, P., & Asl, M. P. (2022). Opinion mining on Viet Thanh Nguyen's The Sympathizer using topic modelling and sentiment analysis. *Journal of Information Technology Management, 14*(Special Issue), 163–183. doi:10.22059/jitm.2022.84895

Section 3
Opinion Mining and Social Media

Chapter 12
Threat Emotion Analysis in Social Media:
Considering Armed Conflicts as Social Extreme Events

Marilyn Minicucci Ibañez

National Institute of Space Research, Brazil & Federal Institute of São Paulo, Brazil

Reinaldo Roberto Rosa

National Institute for Space Research, Brazil

Lamartine Nogueira Frutuoso Guimarães

Institute for Advanced Studies, Brazil & Instituto Tecnológico de Aeronáutica, Brazil & National Institute for Space Research, Brazil

ABSTRACT

In recent decades, the internet access growth has generated a substantial increase in the information circulation in social media. Within the information variety circulating on the internet, extreme social events such as armed conflicts have become areas of great public interest because of their direct influence on society. The study of such data from social media is useful in understanding an event's evolution, in particular how threats over time can generate an endogenous evolution resulting in an extreme event. This chapter uses the technique of sentiment analysis to identify the threat degree of news about armed conflicts distributed in social media. This analysis generates an endogenous threat time series that is used to predict the future threat variation of the analyzed extreme social events. In the prediction of the endogenous time series, the authors apply the deep learning technique in a structure that uses the long short-term memory (LSTM) neural network.

DOI: 10.4018/978-1-7998-9594-7.ch012

INTRODUCTION

The evolution of the internet has enabled the advent of the social media as one of the main means of circulation of personal, political, and publicity information. As such, there is a need for the use of modern techniques such as machine learning and sentiment analysis to assist in the accurate verification of specific information among these enormous volumes of data. One such area of the society that calls for a more profound analysis of its causes and consequences are social extreme events, such as armed conflicts. An extreme event is a sequence of small events generated by human emotions or some reaction of nature that can evolve into a major event and even a catastrophic event. Armed conflicts are social extreme events that are part of the history of the human development (Sornette, 2006). Within this context, an armed conflict refers to a sequence of threats that eventually lead to physical conflict or war. Due to the problems generated by armed conflicts, it is important to find a solution that can help the analysis, prediction, and recognition of such events in order to minimize their damaging effects. This project studies two models of armed conflicts as case studies of social extreme events: the armed conflict between Syria and the USA, and the armed conflict between Iran and the USA.

The study of the dynamics of the process of triggering an armed conflict is an area that has been analyzed for decades in many ways. One of the great scholars in this area, Lewis Richardson, has several approaches to the analysis of armed conflicts that cover different models: game-theoretic models, evolutionary games and agent-based models (ABMs), differential equations (DEQ) models, and statistical analyses of time-structured data (Gleditsch, 2020; Richardson, 1960). Thus, this chapter uses sentiment analysis and machine learning to examine the emotions contained in social media texts as a possible source of the beginning of armed conflicts. More specifically, it examines the emotions contained in the threats uttered by heads of states who are involved in the conflicts.

For data collection, the chapter uses web search engine Google (Google LLC, 1998) and chatbot (Lateral GmbH, 2019) to find the related news to social and political threats. Each collected news story is stored and grouped based on the ascending order of its publication date.

The information is collected from the world reference social media, such as Reuters (2019), CNN (2020), and The Guardian (2020). To process the news collected from social media the technique of sentiment analysis, which allows the identification of human emotions present in a text document, is used. Sentiment analysis makes it possible to identify how similar a text is to a given context, using a base text with words referring to a domain (Bird, Klein, & Loper, 2009). In this case, the domain is the threat of these extreme events (Ibañez, Rosa, & Guimarães, 2020). Thus, the aim is to determine the percentage of threat existing in each news story.

The result of this collection is a portfolio of threats with time series, with the threat level referring to these extreme events. A P-model algorithm (Meneveau & Sreenivasan, 1987) is applied to the data of this portfolio to generate a time series with endogenous characteristics. This model of time series considers only the elements that exert some internal influence on the domain under study (Sornette, 2006). The generated endogenous series is used as input for a system developed with machine learning to create a model for predicting social extreme events. The social media data allows the application of the deep learning technique due to its automatically extracting features as well as the nonlinear correlations existing in the data (Goodfellow, Benbio, & Courville, 2016). For applying the concepts of Deep learning, a recursive neural network, Long Short-Term Memory (LSTM), is developed in a system that uses deep learning API TensorFlow Kera's (Chollet, 2015). LSTMs are suitable for classifying, processing, and predicting time series due to the lengthy delays of some series (Hochreiter & Schmidhuber, 1997).

Based on the results, this chapter aims to present a methodology that uses the technique of sentiment analysis to identify the degree of threat emotion in each news item. Also, based on threat variation of these endogenous social and natural extreme events, the study aims to be able to identify the possibility of future occurrence of these phenomena. In this way, the proposed methodology can be applied to data from diverse areas in future.

BACKGROUND

This section presents the study of works related to sentiment analysis and prediction of extreme social events considering the armed conflict, intending to show the state of the art of these areas.

Papers Related to Sentiment Analysis

Article, entitled A Model for Sentiment Analysis Based on Ontology and Cases (Ceci, Gonçalves, & Webe, 2016) presented a work using the Case-Based Reasoning technique with the use of ontology to assist in the classification process in sentiment analysis. The model proposes that the stores to reasoning already developed to be used in future classification. The project used Amazon's information about cameras and movies as a database, and used the ratings posted by users as a star rating. The paper presented as a result the comparison of the developed model with Naive Bayes (NB) and Support Vector Machine (SVM) techniques. For the movie domain, the model had an accuracy of 85.0% while the NB and SVM techniques had 78.7% and 78.6%, respectively. For the camera domain, the model had an accuracy of 91.0%, while both the NB and SVM techniques had 84.5%.

Google has released an API of the JAVA language (Google LLC, 2016) about natural language in the cloud, this new service offers developers access to Google's sentiment, entity recognition, and syntax analysis from Google. The part of the sentiment analysis of the API shows the following functionalities:

1. Checking the structure and meaning of text, offering powerful machine learning models in an easy to use.
2. Extraction of information about people, places, events and more, mentioned in text documents, news articles or blog post.
3. Understanding the sentiment about the product in social media.
4. Analyzing the intent of conversations with customers in a call center or messaging application.
5. Analyzing the text sent in a request or integration with or integration with Google Cloud Storage.

The book titled Sentiment Analysis in Social Networks has reviewed the published works on sentiment analysis. In each chapter, a topic related the technique of sentiment analysis is presented. Chapter six, titled Sentiment Analysis in Social Network: A Machine Learning Perspective, presents the studies conducted using supervised and unsupervised machine learning, biased and supervised machine learning, and polarized and non-polarized classification.

The article titled Social Media Sentiment Analysis: Lexicon versus Machine Learning compared the lexical analysis-based approach with the machine learning approach to address three research questions:

1. Are these two existing sentiment analysis techniques appropriate for the analysis of social media conversations?
2. To what extent do the results of the two approaches differ when used in social network conversations?
3. Does a combined approach improve the overall accuracy of the classification of sentiment of social media conversations?

To answer these questions, data is collected from Facebook. The data is analyzed using the RText-Tools, which is a machine learning package in R for automatic text classification, and the LIWC2015 text mining tool, which is used to conduct a sentiment analysis based on lexical analysis of the data sample. Results reveal that both approaches achieved higher accuracy in classifying positive sentiment than negative.

Article Understanding #worldenvironmentday user opinions in twitter: A topic based in the approach of sentiment analysis identified the social, economic, environmental, and cultural factors related to sustainable care for the environment and public health that most concern Twitter users. To identify the factors related to sustainable care for the environment and public health, downloaded n = 5.873 tweet that used the hashtag #WorldEnvironmentDay on the respective day. A neural network Support Vector Machine (SVM) was used for sentiment classification and uses to the NVivo Pro tool to classify the sentiments into positive, neutral, and negative. As results, we identified the main factors that concern the global population regarding the planet's sustainable development of the planet, public health, and the environment. Determined to the importance of these results by the relevance of the analysis of public opinion in social networks about the environment in social networks.

Article named Topic modeling and sentiment analysis of global climate change tweets (DAHAL et al., 2019) addressed the use of social network data for the verification of climate change in each location. In the work, used to data from the social network Twitter with geotags that made it possible to identify the location, date, and time of the messages. To perform the data classification, it was used Natural Language Processing techniques such as sentiment analysis and Latent Dirichlet Allocation (LDA). As a result, observed to that sentiment analysis shows that the general discussion is negative, especially when users are reacting to extreme political or weather events. The topic shows that the discussions on climate change are diverse, but some topics are more prevalent than others.

Papers Related with Extreme Events – Armed Conflict

In comparing random forest with logistic regression for predicting class-imbalanced civil war onset data (Muchlinski, Siroky, He, & Kocher, M). This paper shows a comparison of the performance of the Random Forest technique with three versions of logistic regression (classical logistic regression, rare event logistic regression, and L1 regularized L1). This comparison founds to that the algorithmic approach provides significantly more accurate predictions of the onset of the civil war on sample data than any of the logistic regression models. The paper further discusses these results and the ways in which algorithmic statistical methods such as Random Forest may be useful for more accurately predicting rare events in conflict data.

The study entitled Predicting armed conflict: Time to adjust our expectations? (Cederman & Weidmann, 2017) presented a review of several papers on prediction of armed conflict. The review shows the use of simple neural network techniques and the problems each have, mainly related to obtaining realistic information about the social and realistic information of the social and political conditions of the region in conflict. Finally, the author suggests the use of more current machine learning techniques for the analysis and prediction of armed conflicts due to the diverse characteristics of its data.

Project Views: A political violence early-warning system (Hegre, et al., 2018) presented an early-warning system on political violence that seeks to be maximally transparent, publicly available, and uniformly covered. O project described the methodological innovations needed to achieve these goals. ViEWS still produces national and subnational monthly forecasts for 36 months into the future and all three types of violence organized by UCDP: conflict state-based conflict, non-state conflict, and unilateral violence in Africa. The project uses data from UCDP and ACLED, as well as logit modeling (a generalized linear model), dynamic simulation, and Random Forest techniques.

Subsequently, the project Improving armed conflict prediction using machine learning: Views+ (Helle, Negus, & Nyberg, 2018) expanded the functional age of the software Violew Early Warning System (ViEWS), which uses numerous variables to perform forecasting. The project goal would be to perform variable selection automatically and thus improve the efficiency, speed, and accuracy of the forecasts compared to the previous version of the tool. This project used the techniques of Random Forest and the Python Scikit-learn API.

Paper Trends and fluctuations in the severity of interstate wars (Clauset, Trends and fluctuations in the severity of interstate wars, 2018) presented a data-based analysis of the general evidence for trends in the sizes and years between interstate wars around the world. It also shows the use of the resulting models to characterize the plausibility of a trend toward peace since the World War II end. Captures to the underlying variability in these data using an ensemble approach, that specifies a stationary process by which to distinguish trends from fluctuations in the time of onset of war, the severity of wars, and the joint attacks and severity distribution.

Chapter Modeling social and geopolitical disasters as extreme events: a case study considering the complex dynamics of international armed; conflicts (Rosa, Neelakshi, Pinheiro, Barchi, & Shiguemori, 2019) from the book Towards Mathematics, Computers, and Environment: A Disasters Perspective, presented how the turbulent dynamics of international armed conflicts relates to with the framework of complex multiagent systems. The analysis explicitly considers the properties of the inhomogeneous multiplicative cascade, where endogeny and exogeny are key points in the phenomenon mathematical model. As result, the study presented a prototype cellular automaton that allows characterizing regimes of extreme armed conflicts, such as the September terrorist attacks and the great world wars.

Article The global conflict risk index: A quantitative tool for policy support on conflict prevention (Halkia, Ferri, Schiellens, & Papazoglou, 2020) presented, validated, and discussed the Global Conflict Risk Index Conflict Risk Index (GCRI), the quantitative starting point of the Global Conflict Early Warning European Union's Conflict Early Warning System. Using logistic regression, the GCRI calculates the probability of national and sub-national conflict risk. Despite its standard and simple methodology, the model predicts better than six others published quantitative conflict published quantitative conflict early warning systems for ten out of twelve reported performance metrics. As such, the paper aims to contribute to a cross-fertilization of academic and governmental efforts in quantitative conflict risk modeling.

Papers Related the Predicting of Times Series Using Deep Learning

The article Time-series forecasting with deep learning: a survey (Lim & Zohren, 2021), presents a review of several papers that use data modeling using time series applied to topics such as climate modeling, life sciences, medicine, business decisions, and finance. The paper also presents a review of how the deep learning technique perform to the prediction of these series applying machine learning concepts such as nonlinear layers, convolutional neural network (CNN), recurrent neural network (RNN) with LSTM – Long Short-Term Memory, probabilistic hybrid models, non-probabilistic hybrid models, multivariate hybrid models. As a conclusion, the article shows that despite the various models used to learn how to predict time series, there are still some limitations such as in data sets with random intervals and improved performance in multivariate models.

The article DeepAR: probabilistic forecasting with autoregressive recurrent networks (Salinas, Flunkert, & Gasthaus, 2018), proposes a methodology for producing accurate probabilistic forecasts, based on training an auto-regressive recurrent network model on numerous related time series. The DeepAR show numerous key advantages compared to classical approaches and other global methods:

1. As the model learns seasonal behavior and dependencies on given covariates across time series, minimal manual feature engineering is needed to capture complex, group-dependent behavior.
2. DeepAR makes probabilistic forecasts in the form of Monte Carlo samples that can be used to compute consistent quantile estimates for all sub-ranges in the prediction horizon.
3. By learning from similar items, our method can provide forecasts for items with little or no history at all, a case where traditional single-item forecasting method fail.
4. Our approach does not assume Gaussian noise, but can incorporate a wide range of likelihood functions, allowing the user to choose one that is appropriate for the statistical properties of the data.

In the result, the paper show through extensive empirical evaluation on several real-world forecasting data sets accuracy improvements of around 15% compared to state-of-the-art methods.

The article Deep state space models for time series forecasting (Rangapuram, et al., 2018), presents a novel approach to probabilistic time series forecasting that combines state space models (SSM) with deep learning. The method scales gracefully from regimes where little training data is available to regimes where data from large collection of time series can be leveraged to learn accurate models. In this paper, proposes to bridge the gap between these two approaches by fusing SSMs with deep (recurrent) neural networks. Presents to, a forecasting method that parametrizes a particular linear SSM using a recurrent neural network (RNN). In the conclusion, the paper presents that under regimes of limited data the method clearly outperforms the other methods by explicitly modelling seasonal structure.

The state-of-the-art literature review within the topic and techniques addressed in the chapter demonstrates the innovation of the multidisciplinary methodology used. This methodology applies the techniques of sentiment analysis, endogenous time series and deep learning with LTSM networks with the data model on extreme social events considering armed conflicts.

MAIN FOCUS OF THE CHAPTER

Newspaper and Magazines as Source Information on the Social Medias

The concept of social media emerged in the mid-1979s with the development of the on-line posting system known as Usenet by Tom Truscott and Jim Ellis of the Duke University in North Carolina, USA. For many years, used to the concept was for any means of communication such as magazines, newspapers, and radio. This media model has the characteristic of single-handed means of communication, in which there is little interaction with the user. With the emergence of the social networks, blogs, wikis, and sharing sites, the concept of social media also include user interaction applications. Today, defines to social media as a set of applications that are based on the Internet and that are founded on the ideological and technological of Web 2.0, allowing the creation and exchange of user-generated content (Moyer & Kaplan, 2020). The following shows a resume of the concepts about social media used in this chapter.

1. Social Media in the begin of 1979: Single-handed means of communication with little iteration with the user (magazines, newspapers, radio).
2. Social Media currently: Set of applications that are based on Web 2.0 and allow for creation and exchange of content by the user (magazines, newspapers, radios, wikis, blogs, social networks).
3. Social Media in this chapter: Single-handed means of communication (magazines and newspapers),

In this chapter applies to the concept of social media as the Single-handed means of communication: newspapers and magazines.

Armed Conflict as Social Extreme Events

According to (Department of Peace and Conflict Research at Uppsala University, 1980), armed conflict characterizes to by a disagreement between governments and territories, in which there is the use of armed force by one of the governments of one of the states. For to characterize as armed conflict, an event extreme needs to generate of at least 25 battle-related deaths in a calendar year.

According to (Clauset, 2018), an extreme event is a human or natural action that can lead to some extreme event or even a catastrophe. Thus, for (Sornette, 2006) the extreme events are part of the evolution of Society and can designate social, political, and natural events in an endogenous system due to their self-organizing characteristics. So, can consider the armed conflicts as a social extreme event. An endogenous system characterizes by events that suffer action only inside its domain, (Sornette, 2006).

For the analysis of endogenous social extreme events, the armed conflicts, collects to data of newspapers and magazines with large global circulation ((CNN, 2020), (Reuters, 2019), (The Guardian, 2020), etc.). Moreover, considers to data that has relation with some form of verbal threats or offenses between heads of state of countries that might suggest the outbreak of an armed conflict. For this analysis considers to as case study the news about two conflicts models, as presented following.

1. Syrian and USA in the period from January 1, 2016, to April 5, 2017. The end date of this conflict coincides with the day before the launch of the Tomahawk missiles, considered medium-range and invisible to radars, by two USA ships in the Mediterranean Sea to the air base of Bashar Al-Assad's regime (UOL, 2017).
2. Iran and USA in the period from January 16, 2019, to January 7, 2020. The end date of the Iran and USA conflict coincides with the attack by jihadist group on USA base in Iraq.

To carry out this process, one initially collects news stories that present evidence of threats related to the analyzed extreme events. Next, it is verified if this threat can lead to a sequence of minor events, and finally, it is verified if the result of the minor events can lead to an endogenous extreme event. Figure 1 illustrates the reflection of this process.

Figure 1. Reflection for social media news gathering

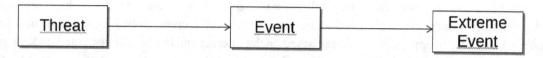

The idea of the analysis of armed conflicts, considering the reflection presented in Figure 1, characterize to as presents Table 1.

Table 1. Characterization of the terms threat, event, and extreme event for social extreme events

Concept	Characterization
Threat	any form of verbal offense
Event	attack occasioned by threat
Extreme Event	armed conflict generated by verbal offense and attack

In news-gathering, uses to internet search and automated search with chatbots (Lateral GmbH, 2019), considering the words like present in Table 2.

Table 2. Sample of some words about armed conflicts used in the news collect by search internet and by the chatbot

arms	attack	force
threat	weapons	tanks
conflict	armed	war

For each an of the news-gathering pull out date and URL information and store to in a .csv file, that presents the structure show in Table 3.

Table 3. Example of the organization of news about extreme social events stored in the ".csv" file

Data	URL
03/06/17	cnn.com/trump-travel-ban
03/07/17	cnn.com/save-the-children
03/09/17	cnn.com/jon-huntsman
03/10/17	cnn.com/russia-turk
03/10/17	cnn.com/syria-aleppo

Sentiment Analysis on Social Media Mining Datasets

Data Science is the orderly study of data and information pertinent to business and all the inferences that may involve a given topic. It is a science that studies information, its process of capture, transformation, generation and, later, data analysis. Data science involves several disciplines: computing, statistics, mathematics, and business knowledge (ZAFARANI et al, 2014). Figure 2 illustrate this concept of data science.

Figure 2. Illustration of the data mining concept
Source: *(Zafarani, Abbasi, & Liu, 2014)*

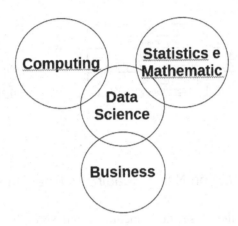

Applies to data science, in this research, using the concept of social media mining. This concept is an emerging discipline that performs the process of representation, analysis, and extraction of actionable patterns from social media data (Zafarani, Abbasi, & Liu, 2014).

To discover patterns of the data collected from social media, this chapter used a process called Knowledge Discovery in Database (KDD). The utilization of the basic phases of the KDD in this research is shown in Figure 3.

Figure 3. Using of the basic phases of the KDD
Source: *(Zafarani, Abbasi, & Liu, 2014)*

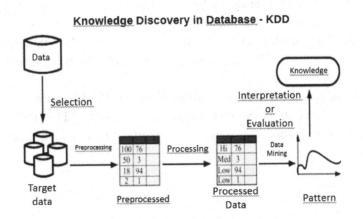

The Figure 4 shows the sample of the application of the KDD process in the social media data collected from the research. Applies to, in this chapter, the KDD to organizer the data in increase order of date.

Figure 4. Application of the basic phase of the KDD in this study

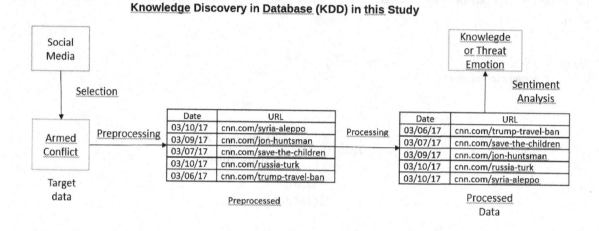

Knowledge Discovery in **Database** (KDD) in **this** Study

Natural Language Processing on News Reading in Real Time

After the KDD process, starts to the phase of treatment and analysis of the collected news texts. Performs to the reading of this news in real time, directly in the source of the information on the Internet. This process allows the extraction of the texts contained between the tags *<p> </p>* in the .html file of each of the news. For the treatment of the news applies the Natural Language Processing (NLP) concepts. NLP is a subfield of artificial intelligence and enables the development of systems that allow the interaction between computer and human (Jackson & Mouliner, 2002) using natural human language either by text or by speech (Oliveira, 1990). Second (Jackson & Mouliner, 2002), NLP can be divided in the phases the description presents following about each phase of the Natural Language Processing.

1. **Text:** News of the Social Media.
2. **Tokenization:** It is used, in this research, for the elimination of characters with no meaning for the text such as the symbols !, ?, #, @, http,::, etc. In this way, in the tokenization process, considers to the approach Languages Delimited by Spaces - like the European languages, only indicates to word boundaries by the insertion of blank spaces.
3. **Lexical Analysis:** Performs text analysis at the level of the word. In this analysis of natural language, logical analysis dismantles the words of a sentence in its grammatical components (noun, adjective, pronoun, etc.).
4. **Syntactic Analysis:** It is the task of recognizing a sentence and assigning it a syntactic structure. Attributes to the syntactic structures by Context Free Grammar (CFG), that generates a representation in a tree structure. These trees analyze an important intermediate state of representation for semantic analysis.

5. **Semantic Analysis:** Attributes these representations of intermediate meanings to phrases based on the knowledge acquired with the logical and grammatical phases. Thus, uses to this type of analysis in the understanding of the meaning of a sentence. It is also widely used for elimination of ambiguities.

6. **Pragmatic Analysis:** In this phase elaborates to the meaning based on contextual knowledge and logical form. Moreover, uses to this type of analysis to validate the semantic analysis. In this analysis, it considers to those words can be associated by meanings (water, swimming) or subject proximity (water, well).

7. **Text Knowloged:** In this research obtains to as knowledge of text, the threat emotion.

In this work, used to the tokenization phase of the NLP process to eliminate symbols and characters, !, ?, $, &, etc, that have no meaning representation for analysis. Applies to the tokenization using the NLTK (Natural Language toolKit (Bird, Klein, & Loper, 2009) in the Python and Embedded Language of Keras Tensorflow APIs (Chollet, 2015).

Sentiment Analysis for Times Series Generation by Extraction Threats Emotion

The area of Sentiment Analysis refers to the tasks of analysis, identification and classification of all information that is characterized emotionally, subjectively or opinion-generating, whether the information is in the format of text, image, or sound (Cuadrado & Gómez-Navarro, 2011). To perform these tasks of sentiment characterization, it is, usually, used the techniques of Natural Language Processing, statistics, and machine learning methods. According to (Cuadrado & Gómez-Navarro, 2011), these tasks can be divided as shown in the Table 4.

Table 4. Sentiment analysis tasks classification

Classification	Definition
Subjectivity	Deals with the identification of parts of the texts that demonstrate a feeling of subjectivity.
Polarity	Classifies to the texts into positive or negative feelings.
Intensity	Works with the emotional intensity expressed in the text. This approach divides to into the classes: strongly positive, positive, strongly negative or neutral.
Sentiment analysis based on topics or features	model of analysis basis to on the verification of existing characteristics related to feelings about the subject.
Sentiment Mining	Retrievals information from a query. Thus, it is possible to query a specific topic and classify it into a certain category.

In this work, uses to the task classification of the sentiment analysis based on topics or features to analysis the texts collected from social media. In this phase of news analysis, applies to the concepts of sentiment analysis using the SpaCy (Industrial-Strength Natural Language) library (SpaCy, 2019). SpaCy is a free, open-source library for advanced natural language processing in Python. SpaCy was designed specifically for production use and helps create applications that process and understand large volumes of text. It can be used to build systems for information extraction or natural language understanding, or to pre-process text for deep learning. In this process of information extraction, initially defines, empirically and considering the knowledge of the people in this study about the subject, the concept of the threat emotion that one would like to identify, creating to a base text. Thus, considers to that base text represents 100% the threat emotion. The Table 5 shows the excerpts from the base texts for the armed conflict between Syria and USA, and Table 6 shows the excerpts from the base texts for the armed conflict between Iran and USA.

Table 5. Excerpt from the base text for the theme armed conflict between Syria and USA

The jihadist organization Jabhat al-Nusra, involved in Síria civil war since 2012, announced in a video that it is formally detaching itself from al-Qaeda. The move, which had been negotiated for well over a year, was confirmed on July 28. Renamed as Jabhat Fatah al-Sham, Nusra will try to bring other rebel factions into a unified body, liberating their lands, giving victory to their faith and upholding their testimony of faith. Some US-based observers quickly reacted with suspicion and derision. Thomas Joscelyn in the Long War Journal dismissed the statement as propaganda with no substance: Even if Joulani did say that his group had really split from al-Qaeda. White House spokesman Josh Earnest commented: There continues to be increasing concern about Nusra Fronts growing capacity for external operations that could threaten both the United States and Europe.

Table 6. Excerpt from the base text for the theme armed conflict between Iran and USA

The United States Army has released a bleak assessment of its 2003 invasion of Iraq and subsequent attempts to defeat a Sunni Muslim insurgency until a 2011 withdrawal claiming that neighboring Iran was the only true winner of the operation the decision to attack was a preemptive response to accusations that Iraqi President Saddam Hussein possessed weapons of mass destruction and offered tacit support to the AlQaeda militant group that conducted the attacks of 2001 US President Donald Trump's view that a conflict with Iran would be a short war was an illusion and that his threat of obliteration amounted to threatening genocide Citing a number of troubling and escalatory indications from Iran Bolton said the US was deploying warships to the Middle East to send a clear and unmistakable message that it would meet any Iranian attacks on US interests with unrelenting force United Kingdom Russia France China Germany and the European Union failed to protect Iran oil and banking industries from US sanctions

After the generated base text, identifies to the similarity percentage of the news by processing it with the base text through the SpaCy library. The result of this process is the threat similarity degree (TSD) that each news item represents relating to the extreme event analyzed. Stores to this threat degree for each news story in the TSD field of the .csv file.

The processing of the information, contained in the texts collected from social media, is performed using the concepts of natural language processing using the tokenization step. After the base text creation, identifies to the similarity percentage of the next news by processing it with the base text using the SpaCy library. The result of this process is the degree of threat similarity (DTS) that each news item represents relating to the extreme event analyzed. Figure 5 presents a representative scheme of the steps described for the application of sentiment analysis.

Figure 5. Steps following in this study for application of the concepts of the sentiment analysis

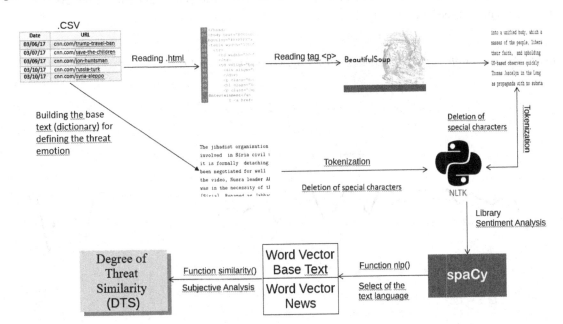

In this chapter, applies to the DTS values to generate the time series that represent the variation of threat in the period analyzed.

Time Series to Representation of the Threat Variation

In the generation of the time series of the threats, organizes to date of DTS values in ascending order. The time series calculation process generated as a result a threat portfolio that contains the information on date, URL, threat degree, and threat for each event model analyzed. The Table 7 presents the excerpt from the threat's portfolio of the armed conflict of the Syrian and USA.

Table 7. Excerpt from the threat´s portfolio of the armed conflict of the Syrian and USA

Date	URL	Degree of Threats Similarity (DTS)
12/01/2016	https://time.com/4180526/what-obama-gets-wrong-about-conflict-in-the-middle-east/	0.941640414401327
29/02/2016	https://qz.com/625389/us-backed-rebel-groups-are-ready-to-turn-on-each-other-in-syria/	0.895609868593785
04/05/2016	https://mepc.org/commentary/who-blame-syria	0.946603316792111
03/06/2016	https://www.washingtonpost.com/graphics/national/obama-legacy/intervention-libya-and-syrian-crisis.html	0.952931143190229
07/10/2016	https://www.euractiv.com/section/global-europe/interview/middle-east-expert-syrian-war-is-only-going-to-get-bloodier-no-end-in-sight/	0.869353843401692
16/11/2016	https://www.dw.com/en/donald-trumps-vision-for-syria/a-36412242	0.939145174720283
21/12/2016	https://time.com/4611414/donald-trump-middle-east-policy/	0.947719027093682
25/01/2017	https://blog.cei.iscte-iul.pt/obamas-military-legacy-iii-the-wars-in-libya-and-syria/	0.956159081557196
21/02/2017	https://www.forbes.com/sites/dougbandow/2017/02/21/u-s-troops-dont-belong-in-syria-america-should-stay-out-of-another-middle-eastern-ground-war/?sh=11c11aaf40c8	0.939912987021703
14/03/2017	https://www.thelancet.com/journals/lancet/article/PIIS0140-6736(17)30758-4/fulltext	0.750967102048839
05/04/2017	https://www.vox.com/world/2017/4/5/15189820/trump-response-atrocity-syria-blame-obama	0.935767353592602

The date and URL information from the threat´s portfolio allowed to generate a threats time serie with 47 elements, as seen in the Figure 6.

Figure 6. Threat´s time series of armed conflict between Syrian and USA

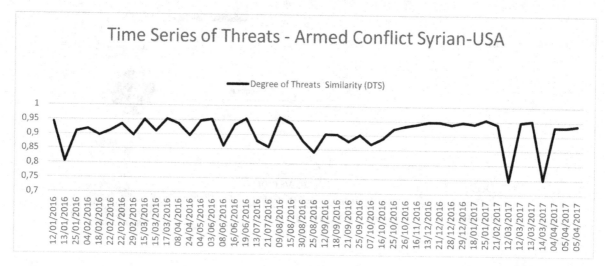

For the case study of the Iran-US armed conflict, applies to the same process for the creation of the portfolio and consequent time series. The Table 8 show an excerpt from the threat´s portfolio of the armed conflict of the Iran and USA.

Table 8. Excerpt from the threat´s portfolio of the armed conflict of the Iran and USA

Date	URL	Degree of Threats Similarity (DTS)
15/01/2019	https://smallwarsjournal.com/jrnl/art/americas-strategic-options-middle-east	0,929298929
21/01/2019	https://www.jpost.com/arab-israeli-conflict/defense-site-iran-has-a-stronger-military-than-israel-578131	0,71554728
29/01/2019	https://iranprimer.usip.org/blog/2019/jan/29/us-intelligence-community-iran	0,961092571
04/02/2019	https://edition.cnn.com/interactive/2019/02/middleeast/yemen-lost-us-arms/	0,95993139
04/02/2019	https://www.aljazeera.com/news/2019/2/4/us-needs-military-base-in-iraq-to-watch-iran-trump-says	0,942323328
05/02/2019	https://www.trtworld.com/opinion/iraq-is-more-than-just-a-watchtower-for-the-us-over-iran-23897	0,970754268
05/01/2019	https://qz.com/1779727/attack-on-irans-soleimani-fits-a-long-history-of-us-military-actions/	0,941168922
05/01/2020	https://www.reuters.com/article/us-iraq-security-iran-usa/u-s-lacks-courage-for-military-confrontation-with-iran-iran-army-chief-idUSKBN1Z407W	0,781198346
06/01/2020	https://edition.cnn.com/2020/01/05/opinions/us-iran-history-ware-intl/index.html	0,789359923
06/01/2020	https://www.marketwatch.com/story/what-stock-market-investors-need-to-know-about-intensifying-us-iran-tensions-2020-01-04	0,948445074
07/01/2020	https://www.reuters.com/article/us-iraq-security/trump-softens-rhetoric-after-iranian-missile-attacks-says-tehran-appears-to-be-standing-down-idUSKBN1Z60NL	0,852567888

The threat´s portfolio information of the armed conflict between Iran and USA generated a time series of threats with 58 elements. The representation of this time series can be visualized in the Figure 7.

Figure 7. Threat's time series of armed conflict between Iran and USA

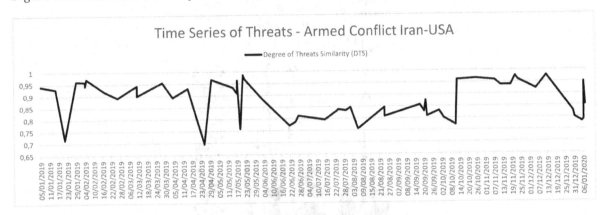

Applies to the threat´s time series data in the generation of endogenous threat´s time series, as presents in the next section.

Endogenous Characteristics in the Threat´s Time Series

In the time series creation with endogenous characteristics applies to the P-Model algorithm (Meneveau & Sreenivasan, 1987) (Halsey, Jensen, Kadanoff, Procaccia, & Shraiman, 1987). This algorithm, in (Rosa, Neelakshi, Pinheiro, Barchi, & Shiguemori, 2019), create a non-homogeneous cascade compatible with the fluctuations observed in the stochastic time series. According to (Rosa, Neelakshi, Pinheiro, Barchi, & Shiguemori, 2019), this non-homogeneous cascade is compatible with the energy dissipated by extreme events up to the moment of their apex, where one has the maximum energy dissipation. Figure 8 presents an example of this energy dissipation for extreme events referring to armed conflicts.

Figure 8. Multiplicative cascade for armed conflict. (a) Scale hierarchy for armed conflict; (b) Respective density expected of energy spectrum pattern showing the transition from the inertial range to extreme event, response to high dissipative regime

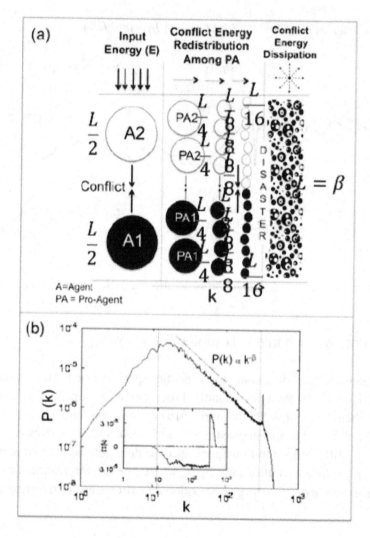

The multiplicative cascade of the P-Model is represented by Equation 1, and is defined in (Halsey, Jensen, Kadanoff, Procaccia, & Shraiman, 1987).

Equation 1: Equations to represent multiplicative cascade of the P-Model

$$a = \frac{\log_2 p_1 + (w-1)\log_2 p_2}{\log_2 l_1 + (w-1)\log_2 l_2}$$

$$f(a) = \frac{(w-1)\log_2(w-1) - w\log_2 w}{\log_2 l_1 + (w-1)\log_2 l_2}$$

where,

α- singularity strength

p_i - probability that some event occurs in the i-th fraction, for i = 1, 2

w - multiplication weight given by 1 - (1 - 2p)

l_i - i - ith fraction of an eddy of size L, for i = 1, 2

f() - describes how densely distributed the singularities are

In (Rosa, Neelakshi, Pinheiro, Barchi, & Shiguemori, 2019), in generalized form, the P-Model presents a classical view of the eddy cascade before the inertial interval of the fully developed turbulence, in which the energy flux (EK), as presented in Figure 8 (a), dissipates over the Kolmogorov scale length (Keylock, 2017) into eddies of size L. Subsequently, each eddy of size L is divided into two equal parts, being represented as $L / 2$, l_1 and l_2. Distributed to, in this way, at each step of the cascade, the energy flow as a probability, unequally in fraction of p_1 and p_2 $1 - p_1$, where $p_1 + p_2 = 1$. Iterated to, this process over fixed p_1 until each eddy reaches the Kolmogorov scale (Keylock, 2017). Starting with a non-homogeneous energy distribution, transferred to a fraction $f(\ )$ of the multifractal mass from one half to the other in the randomly chosen direction. This is equivalent to multiplying the originally uniform density field on both sides by factors. Repeated to the same procedure M times, recursively at smaller and smaller scales, using fractions that varying from in segments of length L_{2n}, in which the multiplicative weight w is parameterized as $1 - (1 - 2p)$, resulting in the discrete matrix $C(m)$ where m counts as time steps. This procedure of the P-Model algorithm, given by Venema (Bonn, 2019), can produce time series in which the variance is finite if you extrapolate their power spectrum to infinitely large scales (Rosa, Neelakshi, Pinheiro, Barchi, & Shiguemori, 2019).

The time series,, with, representing the extreme inhomogeneous, generated to the turbulent event using Venema's algorithm, in which the inputs are: the size of the time series in number of points, the power spectrum, and the value of, with the cascading fractional energy distribution being similar to inhomogeneous turbulence . Recovered to the homogeneous dissipative process near thermodynamic equilibrium when. Exacerbated to the deviations from the homogeneous cascade by abrupt changes in the frequency and magnitude of social conflict. Called to these changes, extreme events (XE) and their cause may be due to internal rather than external factors. When the level of conflict increases significantly due to internal interactions due to internal interactions, called to the extreme event endogenous (XEendo). When external energy transfer or abrupt dissipation is the main cause of XE, it is called an exogenous extreme event (XEexo). In the power law domain, XEendo and XEexo events belong to different universality classes (ROSA et al., 2019). The typical endogenous and exogenous processes, combining the P-Model and SDGA (Sornette-Deschtres-Gilbert-Ageo) algorithm, are obtained for and, respectively. Figure 9 shows the XE time series for different combinations of p and PSD. Defined to the cumulative energy of the process in the time domain as normalized mean where is a chosen window time interval along the signal. According to Rosa et al. (2019), typical cumulative energy trends are nonlinear, being logarithmic for XEendo (Figure 9 (c)) and exponential for XEexo (Figure 9 (d)).

Figure 9. Two typical time series shaved from the PModel algorithm by fixing p=0.25 and varying the value of β. (a) Pattern XEendo of $\beta = 0.39$. (b) XEexo pattern of $\beta = 0.72$. Figures (c) and (d) show the respective cumulative energy, endogeny (log) and exogeny (exp)

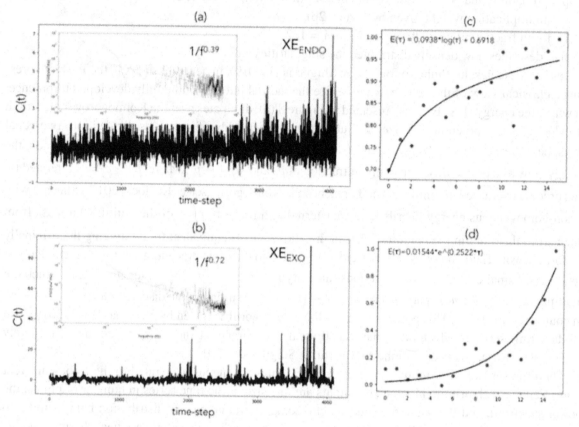

In this chapter, uses to endogenous series and the following parameters as input to the P-Model algorithm

1. $M = 2^{14} = 16384$ points: amount of data of the endogenous series with better representation, according (Ibañez, Rosa, & Guimarães, Análise de emoções em mídias sociais utilizando aprendizado de máquina e séries temporais considerando informações de eventos extremos sociais e naturais, 2021)

2. $p = 0.60$ (Rosa, Neelakshi, Pinheiro, Barchi, & Shiguemori, 2019): parameter for the definition of endogenous series

3. β: spectral index, named *slope* and calculated using the concept of DFA (Detrended Fluctuation Analysis) (University of Harvard, 2019). In this chapter, performs to the calculation of DFA using the function DFA () from the nops library of the programming language Python 3.7. The input of the function is the threat´s series, generated by applying the technique of sentiment analysis on the data collected from social media.

In the Figure 10 shows to a schematic representation of the use of the P-Model in the generation of the endogenous threat´s time series.

Figure 10. Schematic representation of the application the P-Model algorithm to generate the threat´s endogenous time series

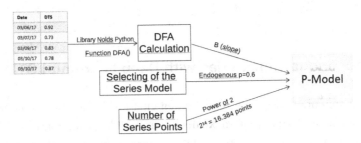

Table 9 shows the data input of the P-Model algorithm for each armed conflict analyzed in this study.

Table 9. Input values used in the P-Model algorithm for the creation of the endogenous time series of the armed conflicts between Syria and the USA, and Iran and USA

Armed Conflict	Amount of Data of the Endogenous Series (M)	p	β (slope)
Syrian and USA	2^{14}=16384	-0.60	0.5606194965951611
Iran and USA	2^{14}=16384	-0.60	0.9132939832232201

The Figure 11 shows the endogenous time series generated, with values of the Table 9, for armed conflict between Syrian and USA and Figure 12 shows the endogenous time series generated, with values of the Table 9, for armed conflict between Iran and USA.

Figure 11. Endogenous threat´s time series of the Syria-USA armed conflict

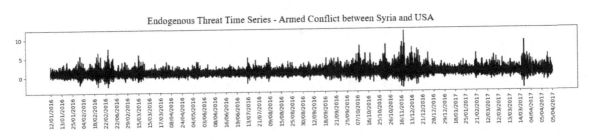

Figure 12. Endogenous threat´s time series of the Iran-USA armed conflict

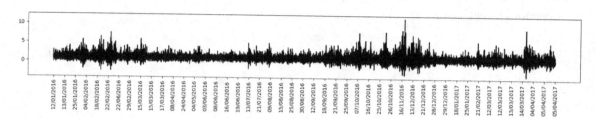

Forecasting Endogenous Time Series with Deep Learning-LSTM

Deep Learning is a subarea of artificial intelligence that enables the creation of neural network models with large dimensions that can be taught to make decisions with high accuracy based on data characteristics (Goodfellow, Benbio, & Courville, 2016). This technique has a good performance in extracting features from large volumes of data (Emmert-Strib, Yang, Feng, Tripathi, & Dehmer, 2018). Various network architectures can be used to build these models. In this chapter, a recursive neural network known as Long Short-Term Memory - LSTM.

Long Short-Term Memory networks are a recurrent neural network model capable of learning order dependence in sequence prediction problems (Brownlee, 2017). The LSTM consists of a cell, an input gate, an output gate, and a forget gate. The cell remembers values for arbitrary time intervals, and the three gates regulate the flow of information in and out of the cell. The gates control the interactions between neighboring memory cells and the memory cell itself. O input gate adds useful information to the current state of the cell. On the other hand, the output gate extracts useful information from the current state of the cell to pass to the next cell. In addition, the forget gate deletes information that does not contribute to the current state of the cell (Bao, Yue, & Rao, 2017). Figure 13 shows an example of this network architecture.

Figure 13. LSTM neural network architecture representation

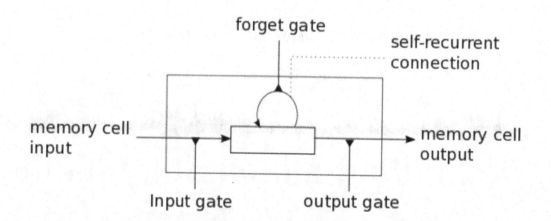

For the elaboration of the model Deep Learning-LSTM, the deep learning Keras (Chollet, 2015) is used from the language Python 3.7. This architecture using the LSTM network was applied to perform the prediction of the social extreme events, the armed conflicts analyzed with the technique of sentiment analysis. The representation of each layer of the neural network architecture, built with the deep learning API Keras, is shown in Figure 14.

Figure 14. Architecture of the neural network deep learning - LSTM built with API Keras

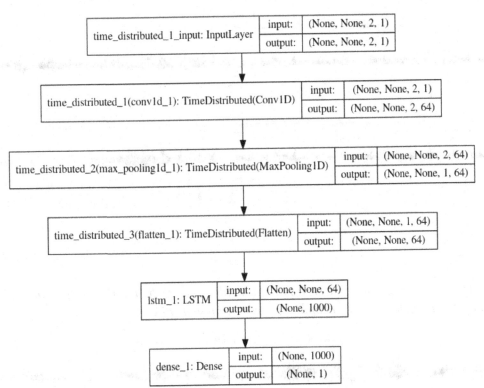

The main objective of this chapter is to predict the threat variation of social extreme events, considering the data of armed conflicts stored in threat portfolios. The prediction of the endogenous time series uses to a 20% fraction of the endogenous data for comparison with the remaining data in the series, and the prediction of the future of that series, which generates new data of threat variation. Selects to the 20% fraction based on the suggested split of training, validation, and testing data of 60%, 20%, 20%, suggested in (Haykin, 2008). Divides to this prediction into two phases: in the first phase performs to the prediction of a fraction of the endogenous time series, and in the second phase performs to the prediction of the future of the analyzed threat data.

First Phase: Prediction of a Fraction of the Endogenous Time Series

After the creation of the endogenous time series of threats, we performed the application of the deep learning architecture with the LSTM neural to predict a fraction of this endogenous time series for the application of the developed methodology. Figure 15 and Figure 16 show two endogenous time series for armed conflicts between Syria-USA and Iran-USA, respectively: the first is the original P-Model's time series, which is all in black, and the second is the series with prediction of 3276 points in gray, of the original time series.

Figure 15. Original endogenous time series in black color and prediction time series with 3276 points in gray color, referring to the armed conflict between Syria and USA

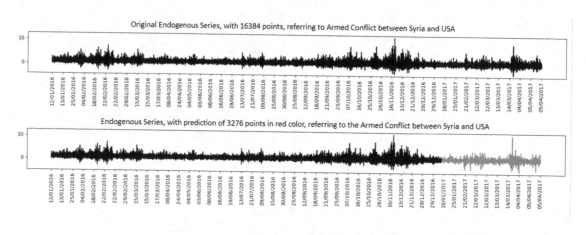

Figure 16. Original endogenous time series in black color and prediction time series with 3276 points in gray color, referring to the armed conflict between Iran and USA

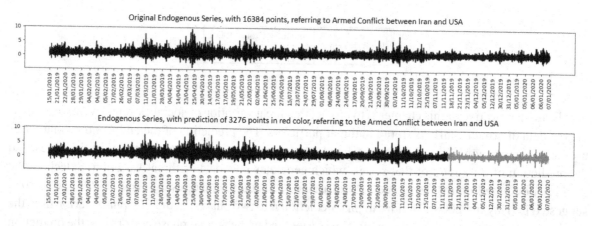

To verify the accuracy of the result presented in Figure 15 and Figure 16, generates to an overlay plot of the predicted data with the original series data. In addition to this overlap, calculates to the similarity between the two series, using the Dynamic Time Warping - DTW concept. The DTW is used to calculate the dissimilarity between two time series of the same dimension (Giusti & Batista, 2013), that represents the degree of difference between the two parts of the series. In this chapter, uses to the DTW through the package tslearn.metrics.dtw (Tavenard, et al., 2020) in Python 3.7. The Equation 2 presents the math representation of the Dynamic Time Warping concept.

Equation 2: Mathematic representation of the DTW concept

$$DTW(\text{x}, \text{y}) = \sqrt{\sum_{i.j \in \pi}(X_i - Y_j)^2}$$

where,

X and Y — represent the series to be compared

i and j — represent the positions i, j in a matrix of each element of the series

pi — represents the set of paths between the series

The graph in Figure 17, with the overlapping of the time series for the armed conflict Syria-USA, shows the DTW value subtracted from 100, to obtain the value of similarity between the excerpts of the analyzed series.

Figure 17. Overlap of the prediction with the original part of the series together with similarity value for armed conflict between Syria and USA

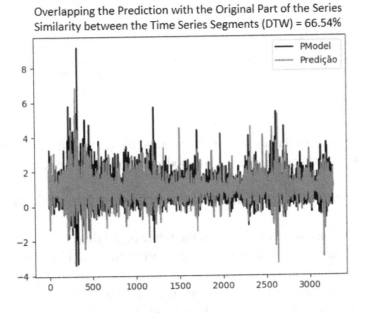

Figure 17 presents a similarity of about 66.54% between the parts of the analyzed time series. This similarity value also represents the prediction accuracy, of this endogenous series, by the deep learning architecture with LSTM network developed in the methodology. This value also demonstrates a good performance for the developed prediction model.

Considering the same concepts of DTW employed for the armed conflict between Syria and the USA, the graph in Figure 16, also overlapping of the time's series for the armed conflict Iran-USA. This graph also shows the DTW value subtracted from 100, to obtain the value of similarity between the excerpts of the analyzed series.

Figure 18. Overlap of the prediction with the original part of the series together with similarity value for the armed conflict between Iran and USA

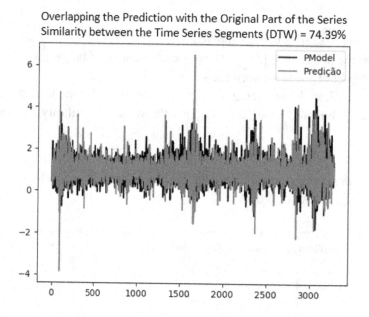

Observes to in the Figure 18 that the similarity between the parts of the analyzed time series is of 74.39%. This value of similarity demonstrate again a good performance for the developed prediction model.

Second Phase: Prediction of the Future of the Analyzed Threat Data

In the second phase, performs to the prediction of the future of the time series of threats of armed conflicts between Syria and the USA and armed conflict between Iran and USA. In this prediction phase, uses to the same deep learning architecture used in the prediction of the endogenous series fraction of the prediction in the first phase. The difference consists in the application of a repetition structure that, for each new set of predicted values, feeds back the network. Repeats to this process until the prediction of 3276 elements, that represents 20% of the total number of data points of the input series. This number of points represents an approximate period of 3 months. Figure 17 shows the result, in gray color, of the prediction of the future of about 3 months, for armed conflict Syria-USA.

Figure 19. Prediction of the future of 3 months, in the gray color, of the threats of the armed conflict between Syria and USA

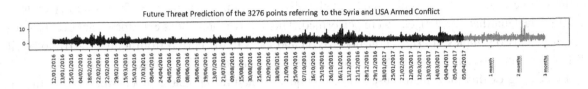

Figure 19 shows that the variations of future threats continue at the same in the same intensity over the predicted period. Considering that the armed conflict between Syria and the USA had a continuity in threats (Dejevsky, 2017), which lasts until now, the result suggests that the architecture of deep learning made a good representation of the future of this conflict.

For the armed conflict between Iran and USA, applies to the same technique used in the results of the Figure 19. These results can be visualized in the Figure 20.

Figure 20. Prediction of the future of 3 months, in the gray color, of the threats of the armed conflict between Iran and USA

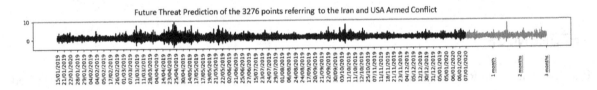

Observes to in the Figure 20 that the variations of future threats continue in the same intensity over the predicted period. Whereas the threats between the heads of state of these countries continued after the analyzed period (Marcus, 2020) there is a good response of the methodology and architecture of architecture for predicting the future of this conflict.

FUTURE RESEARCH DIRECTIONS

The use of sentiment analysis for the study and identification of emotions in the most diverse form of information is an area still with a lot of growth potential. Thus, as a continuation of this work, it would be the analysis of texts through the identification of emotions such as sarcasm and irony, and the use of image data.

CONCLUSION

In this chapter, analysis of data collected from globally circulating social media ((CNN, 2020), (Reuters, 2019), (The Guardian, 2020)), etc. were performed. This information about extreme social events, considering the two samples of armed conflicts: Syria and USA in the period from January 2016 to April 2017 USA and between Iran and USA in the period from January 2019 to January 2020.

Processing of this information uses the techniques of natural language processing and sentiment analysis. This processing creates a threat portfolio, from which uses to the information to generate endogenous time series and predict future threats of these conflicts, applying Deep Learning and LSTM neural network techniques. The results achieved with the application of the neural network model developed, reached an accuracy of 65.12% for the conflict Syria and USA and 74.39% for the conflict Iran and USA.

So, these results suggest that the prediction of future threats of this extreme event, using the methodology of this study, presents a good representation of the continuity of this event.

ACKNOWLEDGMENT

I would like to thank the Federal Institute for Education, Science, and Technology of São Paulo - IFSP campus São José dos Campos, for the qualification license granted for the development of the studies.

REFERENCES

Bao, W., Yue, J., & Rao, Y. (2017). A deep learning framework for financial time series using stacked autoencoders and long-short term memory. *PLoS One*, *12*(7), 1–24. doi:10.1371/journal.pone.0180944 PMID:28708865

Bird, S., Klein, E., & Loper, E. (2009). *Natural language processing wiht python: analysing text with the natural language toolkit*. O'Reilly Media.

Bonn, U. (2019). *Venema P-Model algorithm*. Retrieved from https://www2.meteo.uni-bonn.de/staff/venema/themes/surrogates/

Brownlee, J. (2017, May 24). *A Gentle introduction to long short-term memory networks by the experts*. Retrieved from Machine Learning Mastery: https://machinelearningmastery.com/gentle-introduction-long-short-term-memory-networks-experts/

Ceci, F., Gonçalves, A. L., & Webe, R. (2016). A model for sentiment analysis based on ontology and cases. *IEEE Latin America Transactions*, *14*(11), 4560–4566. doi:10.1109/TLA.2016.7795829

Cederman, L., & Weidmann, N. (2017). Predicting armed conflict: Time to adjust our expectations? *Science*, *355*(6324), 474–476. doi:10.1126cience.aal4483 PMID:28154047

Chollet. (2015). *Keras: The Python deep learning library*. Retrieved from Keras: https://keras.io/

Clauset, A. (2018). Trends and fluctuations in the severity of interstate wars. *SciencesAdvances -. Social Sciences*, *4*(2), 1–10. doi:10.1126ciadv.aao3580 PMID:29507877

CNN. (2020). *CNN - breaking news, latest news and videos.* Retrieved from CNN: https://edition.cnn.com

Cuadrado, J. C., & Gómez-Navarro, D. P. (2011). *Un modelo lingüístico-semántico basado en emociones para la clasificación de textos según su polaridad e intensidad.* Facultad de Informática Universidad Complutense de Madrid, Departamento de Ingeniería del Software e Inteligencia Artificial . Madri: Facultad de Informática Universidad Complutense de Madrid.

Dejevsky, M. (2017, june). *As Syria's war enters its endgame, the risk of a US-Russia conflict escalates.* Retrieved from The Guardian: https://www.theguardian.com/commentisfree/2017/jun/21/syria-war-endgame-us-russia-conflict-washington-moscow-accidental-war

Department of Peace and Conflict Research at Uppsala University. (1980). *Uppsala Conflict Data.* Retrieved from Uppsala Conflict Data Program - UCDP: https://ucdp.uu.se/

Dhaoui, C., Webster, C., & Tan, L. (2017, August). Social media sentiment analysis: Lexicon versus machine learning. *Journal of Consumer Marketing, 34*(6), 480–488. Advance online publication. doi:10.1108/JCM-03-2017-2141

Emmert-Strib, F., Yang, Z., Feng, H., Tripathi, S., & Dehmer, M. (2018). An introductory review of deep learning for prediction models with big data. *Frontiers in Artificial Intelligence - Deep Learning in Computational Social Science, 27*, 16-32. doi:10.3389/frai.2020.00004

Giusti, R., & Batista, G. E. (2013, Oct 19). An empirical comparison of dissimilarity measures for time series classification. *Brazilian Conference on Intelligent System*, 82-88. 10.1109/BRACIS.2013.22

Gleditsch, N. P. (2020). *Lewis Fry Richardson: His Intellectual Legacy and Influence in the Social Sciences.* Springer. doi:10.1007/978-3-030-31589-4

Goodfellow, I., Benbio, Y., & Courville, A. (2016). *Deep learning – adaptive computation and machine learning series.* MIT Press.

Google, L. L. C. (1998, September 4). *Google.* Retrieved July 2016, from Google Search: www.google.com

Google, L. L. C. (2016). *API cloud natural language.* Retrieved February 25, 2017, from Google cloud: https://cloud.google.com/natural-language?hl=pt-br

Halkia, M., Ferri, S., Schiellens, M. K., & Papazoglou, M. (2020). The global conflict risk index: A quantitative tool for policy support on conflict prevention. *Progress in Disaster Science, 6*, 100069. Advance online publication. doi:10.1016/j.pdisas.2020.100069

Halsey, T. C., Jensen, M. H., Kadanoff, L. P., Procaccia, I., & Shraiman, B. I. (1987). Fractal measures and their singularities: The characterization of strange sets. *Nuclear Physics B - Proceedings Supplement, 2*, 501–511. doi:10.1016/0920-5632(87)90036-3

Haykin, S. O. (2008). *Neural networks and learning machines.* Pearson.

Hegre, H., Allansson, M., Basedau, M., Colaresi, M., Croicu, M., Fjelde, H., ... Schneider, G. (2018). Views: A political violence early-warning system. *Journal of Peace Research, 56*(2), 474–476. https://journals.sagepub.com/doi/full/10.1177/0022343319823860

Helle, V., Negus, A., & Nyberg, J. (2018). *Improving armed conflict prediction using machine learning: views+*. Retrieved from https://pdfs.semanticscholar.org/3008/beffb4496316bb1677253de89eb-4b2a695c3.pdf

Hochreiter, S., & Schmidhuber, J. (1997). Long short-term memory. *Neural Computation, 9*(8), 1735–1780. doi:10.1162/neco.1997.9.8.1735 PMID:9377276

Ibañez, M. M., Rosa, R. R., & Guimarães, L. N. (2020). Sentiment Analysis Applied to Analyze Society's Emotion in Two Different Context of Social Media Data. *Inteligencia Artificial*, 66-84. doi:10.4114/submission/intartif.vol23iss66pp66-84

Ibañez, M. M., Rosa, R. R., & Guimarães, L. N. (2021). *Análise de emoções em mídias sociais utilizando aprendizado de máquina e séries temporais considerando informações de eventos extremos sociais e naturais*. Instituto Nacional de Pesquisas Espaciais - INPE. Retrieved from http://urlib.net/rep/8JMKD3MGP3W34R/44H7S82

Jackson, P., & Mouliner, I. (2002). *Natural language processing for online applications: Text retrieval, extraction and categorization*. John Benjamins B.V. doi:10.1075/nlp.5(1st)

Keylock, C. J. (2017). Multifractal surrogate-data generation algorithm that preserves pointwise hölder regularity structure, with initial applications to turbulence. *Physical Review. E, 95*(3), 032123. doi:10.1103/PhysRevE.95.032123 PMID:28415176

Lateral Gmb, H. (2019). *NewsBot - Give me 5*. Retrieved March 2018, from Related news at the click of a button: https://getnewsbot.com/

Lim, B., & Zohren, S. (2021). *Time-series forecasting with deep learning: a survey*. The Royal Society Publishing. doi:10.1098/rsta.2020.0209

Marcus, J. (2020, April). *US-Iran war of words raises fresh fears of Gulf clash*. Retrieved from BBC News: https://www.bbc.com/news/world-middle-east-52399283

Meneveau, C., & Sreenivasan, K. R. (1987). Simple multifractal cascade model for fully developed turbulence. *Physical Review Letters, 59*(13), 1424–1427. doi:10.1103/PhysRevLett.59.1424 PMID:10035231

Moyer, J. D., & Kaplan, O. (2020, June 6). *Will the Coronavirus fuel conflict projections based on economic and development data show an increased*. Retrieved from Foreign Policy – the Global Magazine of News and Ideas: https://foreignpolicy.com/2020/07/06/coronavirus-pandemic-fuel-conflict-fragile-states-economy-food-prices/

Muchlinski, D., Siroky, D., He, J., & Kocher, M. (n.d.). Comparing random forest with logistic regression for predicting class-imbalanced civil war onset data. *Political Analysis, 24*(1), 87-103. Retrieved from https://www.jstor.org/stable/24573207

Oliveira, C. A. (1990). *IDEAL - uma interface dialógica em linguagem natural para sistemas especialistas*. São José dos Campos: Instituto Nacional de Pesquisas Espaciais (INPE). Retrieved from http://urlib.net/rep/6qtX3pFwXQZ3r59YCT/GUpqq

Pozzi, F. A., Fersini, E., Messina, E., & Liu, B. (2016). *Sentiment analysis in social networks*. Morgan Kaufmann.

Rangapuram, S. S., Seeger, M. W., Gasthaus, J., Stella, L., Wang, Y., & Januschowski, T. (2018). Deep State Space Models for Time Series Forecasting. In Advances in Neural Information Processing Systems. Curran Associates, Inc. Retrieved from https://proceedings.neurips.cc/paper/2018/file/5cf68969fb67a a6082363a6d4e6468e2-Paper.pdf

Reuters. (2019). *Reuters news agency: World's largest news agency*. Retrieved from Reuters: https://www.reuters.com/

Reyes-Menendez, A., Saura, J., & Alvarez-Alonso, C. (2018, November). Understanding #worldenvironmentday user opinions in twitter: A topic-based sentiment analysis approach. *International Journal of Environmental Research and Public Health, 15*(11), 2537. Advance online publication. doi:10.3390/ijerph15112537 PMID:30428520

Richardson, L. F. (1960). *Arms and Insecurity: A Mathematical Study of the Causes and*. Boxwood.

Rosa, R. R., Neelakshi, J., Pinheiro, G. A., Barchi, P. H., & Shiguemori, H. (2019). Modeling social and geopolitical disasters as extreme events: a case study considering the complex dynamics of international armed conflicts. In L. Santos, R. G. Negri, & T. J. Carvalho (Eds.), *Towards mathematics, computers and environment: a disasters perspective* (pp. 233–254). Springer. doi:10.1007/978-3-030-21205-6_12

Salinas, D., Flunkert, V., & Gasthaus, J. (2018). *DeepAR: Probabilistic Forecasting with Autoregressive Recurrent Networks*. Cornell University. arXiv:1704.04110

Sornette, D. (2006). Endogenous versus exogenous origins of crises. In S. Albeverio, V. Jentsch, & H. Kantz (Eds.), Extremes events in nature and society (pp. 107-131). Springer. doi:10.1007/3-540-28611-X_5

SpaCy. (2019). *Industrial-strength natural language processing*. Retrieved June 2018, from SpaCy: https://spacy.io/

Tavenard, R., Fouzi, J., Vandewiele, G., Divo, F., Androz, G., Holtz, C., ... Woods, E. (2020). Tslearn, a machine learning toolkit for time series data. *Journal of Machine Learning Research, 21*(118), 1–6. https://jmlr.org/papers/v21/20-091.html

The Guardian. (2020). *News, sport and opinion from the guardian's US edition*. Retrieved from The Guardian: https://www.theguardian.com/international

University of Harvard. (2019). *Detrended fluctuation analysis (DFA)*. Retrieved from University of Harvard: http://reylab.bidmc.harvard.edu/download/DFA/intro/

UOL. (2017). *EUA ataca síria com mais de 50 mísseis*. Retrieved from UOL: https://noticias.uol.com.br/ultimas-noticias/ansa/2017/04/06/

Zafarani, R., Abbasi, M. A., & Liu, H. (2014). *Social media mining - an introduction*. Cambridge University Press. doi:10.1017/CBO9781139088510

KEY TERMS AND DEFINITIONS

Data Science: Collection, preparation, and analysis of a great amount of data.

Endogenous Events: Event that generates reaction based only on the domain of the event itself.

Extreme Events: Natural or social events that generate large problems for society.

Interstate Conflict: Conflict that takes place between different countries.

Sentiment Analysis: Analysis to identify emotions in some kind data as text, video, sound, and image.

Social Conflict: Conflict generated by some social situation such as economic, political and health.

Social Media: Place where public information is made available that can be collected and analyzed to extract some value´s type.

Chapter 13
Depression Detection in Online Social Media Users Using Natural Language Processing Techniques

Haseeb Ahmad
National Textile University, Pakistan

Faiza Nasir
National Textile University, Pakistan

C. M. Nadeem Faisal
National Textile University, Pakistan

Shahbaz Ahmad
National Textile University, Pakistan

ABSTRACT

Depression is considered among the most common mental disorders impacting the daily lives of people around the globe. Online social media has provided individuals the platforms to share their emotions and feelings; therefore, the depressive individuals may also be identified by processing the content. The advancements of natural language processing have provided the methods for depression detection from the content. This chapter intends to highlight the mainstream contributions for depression detection from the text contents shared on online social media. More precisely, hierarchical-based segregation is adopted for detailing the research contributions in the underlying domain. The top hierarchy depicts early detection and generic studies, followed by method, online social media, and community-based segregation. The subsequent hierarchy contains machine learning, deep learning, and hybrid studies in the context of method, Facebook, Twitter, and Reddit in terms of online social media, and general, literary, and geography as subhierarchies of community.

DOI: 10.4018/978-1-7998-9594-7.ch013

INTRODUCTION

The proliferation of Online Social Media (OSM) has enabled individuals to communicate their interests, feelings, emotions, and observations. Such contents are being used for various scientific investigations, including behavioral intentions detection, personalization for recommendations, community detection, etc. In a behavioral and psychological context, such contents may also be used to reveal users' opinions, preferences, and sentiments towards some events. Moreover, the personality traits of individuals may also be extracted from such content. Such traits may be further used to detect users' current mental states and disorders and predict their future actions (Back et al., 2010). Among other disorders, major depressive disorder or simply depression is being widely detected by the scholastic Community. Since the "language of depression" can affect others in many ways, it can affect the people who read and follow depressive contents in case the writers have a huge fan following. Therefore, the depression detection problem aims to suggest treatments to the potential users so that extreme reactions may be avoided. As a result, the users may regain the joy of life, and other users may get positivity from such users. Moreover, research has shown promising early screening results as on-time treatment leads to higher working productivity and reduces absenteeism (Abboute et al., 2014).

Figure 1. Hierarchical segregation of sections

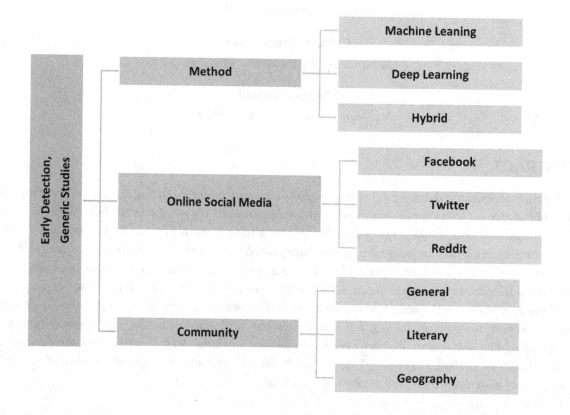

As per World Health Organization (WHO), around 264 million persons suffer from temporary to severe levels of depression around the globe. Mild depression causes the usual mood fluctuations, while the severe condition may also lead to committing suicide. As per estimations by WHO, around 0.8 million persons are committing suicide yearly. Suicide is the second leading cause of death for persons of age 15-29, and most of the users of this age use OSM for sharing their feelings, emotions, and observations ("WHO", 2021). Individuals share these contents in textual and multimedia forms. Different methods are used for depression detection. For instance, computer vision methods are being used for detecting depression from multimedia data. Moreover, psychiatric questionnaires and tests are used by the practitioners for detecting depression from the patients. Thanks to Natural Language Processing (NLP) tools for enabling the researchers and practitioners to detect the depression from textual data and mine opinion from contents as mentioned earlier shared on OSM. The contents shared in a depressive state of mind may contain unusual words having different polarity levels (Efron & Winget, 2010). For instance, it is researched that the depressive users use more stress-related negative emotions, especially negative adverbs, and adjectives, for example, "gloom," "lonely," "lost," "tired," "sad," "miserable." Moreover, the depressive users use more self-expressing pronouns like "I," "my," "me," "mine," "myself." These can be used as features or key points to identify depressive symptoms in OSM users. NLP approaches may classify the depressive and non-depressive contents using lexicon and polarity and other similar information (De Choudhury et al., 2013).

BACKGROUND

Depression is an emergent mood sickness. More than grief in life's struggles and obstacles. Depression may affect thinking, feeling, and functional activities. It may affect the ability to study, work, eat, sleep and appreciate life. Lack of courage and helpless feeling could be extreme and persistent, with diminutive or no relief. Some health specialists and psychologists define depression as "living in a black hole," feeling of future trouble, feelings of emptiness, and apathy. It can be different in genders, such as men may feel restless and anger most of the time. No matter how individual experiences this disease, it needs to be treated rightly; otherwise, it can become a severe health condition. Many powerful treatments can be taken to overcome depression to regain the joy of life. But before providing any treatment, we need to identify the person in depression (Higuera, 2021).

There is ongoing research on depression detection, in which numerous symptoms are discovered that may classify level of depression among individuals. Once the symptoms are known, identifying individuals having such symptoms becomes viable no matter which methods are applied. According to the American psychiatric association ("What Is Depression?", 2021), depression symptoms may include depressed mood, loss of pleasure, sleep disorders, loss of appetite, aimless increased physical activities, difficulty in making a decision, feelings of tiredness, worthless and suicidal thoughts. Another study by health online states that to diagnose depression, at least five of the following signs must be present for more than two weeks; depressed feeling, lack of pleasure in all activities, sleep disorder, weakness or lack of strength, feelings of guilt, lack of concentration or focus on important things, eating disorder, persistent thoughts of suicide ("Depression Tests and Diagnosis," 2021).

Table 1. Depression detection studies

Author	Features	Method	Social Media	Study
(Trotzek et al., 2020)	Parts of Speech	CNN, ERDE score as metric	Reddit (135 depressed users, 752 control group users)	Early detection of depression
(Ma et al., 2017)	Word embeddings, Word frequencies,	Similarity clustering	54-million tweets	Depression analysis
(Wongkoblap et al., 2018)	Demographic SWLS and CES-D scores Posting time Text Activities	SVM, Logistic Regression, NB, DT	Facebook	Depression analysis
(Zucco et al., 2017)	Facial expression, Speech Gestures, Movements	Sentiment analysis	Twitter	Early detection
(Yueh et al., 2020)	Multimodal features including image, text and behavior, Season, Timing, Weekday, Locations, Time interval	CNN, LSTM, GRU, BLSTM, SVM, RNN, RF, DT	Instagram	Depression analysis
(Yarkoni, 2010)	Personality, category by LIWC, word-based	Correlation	694 Blogs google posts	Depression analysis
	Emotional process, Temporal process, Linguistic style	DT, KNN, SVM	7145 Facebook posts	Depression analysis
(Hoffmannová & Ku, 2019)	Formal/informal positive/negative sentiment	Depression, Anxiety and Stress Scale (DASS-21).	Primary research (N = 172, 83 men, 89 women)	Depression analysis
(Park et al., 2018)	Themes	K-means algorithm	Reddit	Depression analysis
(Wu et al., 2020)	Depression Screening Test, The CES-D questionnaire Segmentation Word and content representation	LSTM, DL	1453 Facebook users	Depression analysis
(Stankevich et al., 2019)	TF IDF Bag-of-words Embedding Bigram models using the CLEF/ Erisk 2017 dataset	SVM, RF	887 Reddit users	Depression analysis
(Sokratous et al., 2013)	TF-IDF vectorization Sentiment polarization VADER Analysis	Logistic Regression, SVM, KNN, RF	Dataset built by Losada and Crestani	Early detection
(Park et al., 2018)	Collgram profiles	SVM, BERT	Facebook (78 entries), and Reddit (69 entries).	Depression analysis
(Hu et al., 2019)	Social media messages Keyword extraction, Word2vector	The DSM-5-based method	SM platform PTT in Taiwan 9000 posts	Depression analysis
(Zhou, 2018)	Picture analysis Color analysis Image analysis	Scorecard strategy	Social media	depressive symptoms
(Wolohan & Sayyed, 2018)	Depression Stigma Language usage	LIWC Analysis, NLP Classification	12,106 Reddit users	Depression analysis
(Katchapakirin & Wongpatikaseree, 2018)	Positive/negative sentiments, Self-harm, Day posts, Night posts	NLP techniques, WEKA with SVM	35 Facebook users	Depression analysis

Continued on following page

Table 1. Continued

Author	Features	Method	Social Media	Study
(Reece & Danforth, 2017)	Image analysis, Color analysis, Face detection	ML	Instagram 166 people 43,950 photos	The results predicted with 94% accuracy
(De Choudhury et al., 2014)	Social engagement Emotion Linguistic styles Ego network Mentions of antidepressant	NLP, Statistical classifier	Facebook 25000 posts	Depression measurement
(Abboute et al., 2014)	Keywords extraction	NLP algorithm, Information retrieval, NB	Twitter	Explored Twitter for suicide anticipation
(Alsagri & Ykhlef, 2020)	Personal pronoun, TFIDF Sentiment, Number of posts, Avg of posts a day, Time, Number of replies, synonyms	SVM with different kernels, DT, NB	3000 tweets	Depression analysis

According to mind health analysts, if the person has at least three to four of the following symptoms, he may have major (clinical) depression (Higuera, 2021).

- Crying invocations, empty feelings
- Inability to enjoy, avoiding social gatherings
- Major changes in sleep, appetite
- Tiredness, anger, irritability
- Anxiety
- Pessimism
- Loss of energy, fatigue
- Unexplained heartburns, pains
- Feelings of worthlessness, hopelessness, shame, or guilt
- Inability to make decisions or concentrate on life
- Excessive alcohol or drug use
- Recurrent death or suicidal thoughts

Table 1 presents the overview of the studies, including the author (First column), extracted features (Second column), methods used in these studies (Third column), and the social media used in each study (Fourth column).

MAIN FOCUS OF THE CHAPTER

This chapter focuses on presenting the evolution and recent advancements in depression detection by using NLP and other related tools used for textual data. More precisely, at the first hierarchy level (Figure 1), contributions of early depression detection are segregated from that of generic depression detection. The presented literature is classified in subsequent level w.r.t. incorporated Method, targeted OSM, and underlying Community. In detail, the Method Section discusses the ML, DL, and Hybrid approaches. The Section briefing the OSM discusses the traits and counts of users and reasons for selecting the OSM among Facebook, Twitter, and Reddit. Finally, the community section briefs about the user types, for instance, general users belonging to the specific Community such as literary writers, and the geographical locations, i.e., country or continents, etc.

SOLUTIONS AND RECOMMENDATIONS

To detect the depression and rescue such persons, researchers from diverse domains have come forward to reveal the effective features/symptoms in scientific ways. Moreover, contributions from NLP and ML also played a vital role for the progress in this direction. At first hierarchy level, the papers on depression detection are divided into two subsections: early detection studies and generic studies.

EARLY DEPRESSION STUDIES

Early depression detection observes and identifies the disease in childhood or young adulthood. According to a study, the earliest age is three, at which depression is identified (Luby M.D., 2017). In fact, depression is the second major cause of death in the age group between 15 to 29 years (Bonner, 2019). Moreover, a study revealed the major symptoms of depression in children and adults are similar, such as disturbed sleep and appetite, mood disorder, and sadness Garland & Solomons, 2021). Therefore, early depression can be more acute and inherently ascertained. It may also result in persistent depressive behavior, particularly any negative event in a depressive person's life that perpetuates the disease.

A recently published study by Harvard business school on mental health paints a black picture of depression among the young generation ("What causes depression? - Harvard Health", 2019). Depression is not only affecting the aged people, professionals, youngsters but even children are suffering. In such circumstances, the challenge is developing a depression detection framework so the patients can be detected, and treatment may be provided before they undergo danger. Fortunately, this disease is among the most curable of mental disorders if detected on time. OSM platforms can improve public health by facilitating timely identification and intervention of depression among individuals by analyzing their shared contents

A survey-based study across the United States college found that 53% of students had depression, with nine percent suicidal attempts (Rude et al., 2004). The American College Health Association study on 2- and 4-years students found that 38.2% of students stated feeling "so depressed that it was difficult to function." In addition, a study on Facebook profiles of students showed 25% depression and anxiety symptoms (Calvo et al., 2017).

Few studies have observed that early detection of depression may prevent the negative impact of the disorder (Arora & Arora, 2019). For instance, (Ophir et al., 2017) analyzed 190 Facebook posts of teenagers between 14 to 18 years who were at risk and received psychosocial therapy (e.g., youth with behavioral problems or low self-esteem, engaged in criminal activities, dropped out of school). The authors analyzed offline and online symptoms of depression and explored distinctive features. They presented 190 posts to 10 licensed psychologists. Each expert judge was asked to rate each status update to the following forms of stress: depression, peer victimization, anxiety. These experts rated the status separately on a 6-point scale; 0 not at all, 1 low, 2 somewhat, 3 moderates, 4 very, 5 high. The inter-rater reliability was significant for anxiety 0.78, for peer victimization 0.90, and high for depression 0.96. Initially, for each rated post, the expert computed mean depression scores and identified depressive status posts. Second, they contrasted the subject features of depressive and not depressive status posts. Next, they developed a numerical coding method by applying a verbal analysis method (Chi, 1997) to distinguish between the two classes. Finally, they used bottom-up multiple regression analysis on computed data to identify the features of depression. The study found 13 features, including depressive symptoms, depressive status posts, poetic content, and negative attitude, differentiating depressive and not depressive posts. Additionally, they applied multiple regression analysis that identified four features that forecast depression scores: (1) cognitive distortions, (2) DSM-5 depressive indicators including emotive and behavior, (3) poetic or dramatic content, and (4) feelings about others.

ML model and Convolutional Neural Network (CNN) have also been used to classify user's social media messages. Linguistic metadata is classified and compared to different word embeddings. These studies used popular early depression detection error (ERDE) score as a metric. These studies achieved notable results in early depression detection (Trotzek et al., 2020).

Another early detection research on the Reddit dataset used Bidirectional Long Short-term Memory (BLSTM) for the classification. Multiple features were considered, including Trainable Embed Features, Glove Embed features (every word in a vector of dimension 300), Word2Vec, metadata features. The best performance metric was achieved from Word2Vec+Meta features (Shah et al., 2020).

GENERIC STUDIES

Depression develops negative thoughts among sufferers that create hopelessness, decrease life activities, and increases suicide rates (Shah et al., 2020). This disease may present among all age groups, but it cannot be diagnosed unless the sufferer admits it and seeks mental help from a psychiatrist. Hence, many generic studies have been presented to discover depression at different stages and potential patients of different age groups.

In a study conducted by (Karmen et al., 2015), the authors developed an NLP method to identify depression and its frequency from the depression indicative words from Internet forums. The proposed Depression Symptom Detection (DepreSD) firstly creates dictionary files with depression terms and their synonyms. Secondly, it generates files with frequency terms in 4 classes always, never, often, sometimes. The next step uses NLP on texts to examine depression indicators, correlated frequencies, negation, personal pronouns, and finally, it generates depression scores.

(De Choudhury et al., 2013) identified some eccentric features linked with depression from posting activities, such as more negative sentiments, narcissistic attitude, less social contact, and use of depression-associated terms. Moreover, the authors proposed a ML method to classify depression using behavioral, content-based, and environmental data. This study attained 70% accuracy using a method that assessed the scores observed with BDI and the center of Epidemiologic Studies Depression Scale on linguistic indicators and action patterns of depression to develop a tool for evaluating depressive disorder in individuals.

A recent study (Yueh et al., 2020) proposed a novel CNN method, DeprNet, which analyzes the electroencephalogram test data to diagnose depression subjects. The competence of DeprNet is presented by two experiments, the record-wise and subject-wise split of data. They build multimodal architecture for text, image, and posting activities, including the number of likes, periods, seasons, etc. Such data can effectively contribute to an in-depth analysis of depression. A proficient neural network is used to extract the features from Instagram automatically. Furthermore, a CNN is used to extract image features. In addition, Word2vec (Mikolov et al., 2013) is espoused to understand vector illustrations of words to find text features. The proposed method outperformed with 0.9937 accuracy and AUC 0.999 with the record-wise split of data.

The study published in frontiers in psychology proposed a novel method in which the authors analyzed written text to obtain the relationships between linguistic properties and depression among the writers. More precisely, the writers were classified into depressive, and not depressive groups (men=83, women=89) based on the scores achieved in the DASS-21 test. The analysis was performed on an adult concerning age and education (Hoffmannová & Ku, 2019).

The study by Morales & Levitan is based on depression detection multimodal data obtained from phones and OSM. The proposed architecture has three layers. At first, the speed-time layer collects textual data, audio files, and images and presents real-time computations to identify individuals' moods. Second batch layer identifies offline mood computation. In the serving layer, the collective results are then processed to provide coherent information to the physicians (Morales & Levitan, 2016). (R. Islam et al., 2018) examined different linguistic signs to detect sentiment trigger events, positive sentiment, negative sentiment, sadness, anger and anxiety, a temporal method like the present, past, and future focus, linguistic words like prepositions, articles, auxiliary verbs, conjunctions, personal pronoun, impersonal pronouns, verbs, and negation. Lin et al. (2020) proposed deep textual visual multimodal learning approach. They identified multiple features set, including the activities, tweet counts, social interactions such as followers and following, profiles, visual, emotional, LIWC features, image features, valence, arousal, and dominance features, topic features obtained through Latent Dirichlet Allocation (LDA). Additionally, they made a lexicon of antidepressants from Wikipedia, and based on DSM-IV standard; they extracted depressive symptoms.

Recent studies have found an association between OSM and psychiatric disorders. One of such disorders is depression and anxiety (Pachouly et al., 2021).

METHOD

The scope of methods used to detect depression is broad, from data collection to feature extractions and model creation that may effectively segregate depressive patients. NLP methods are used to break the written text into its grammatical components. These methods convert the language into interpretable form for computer processes (Cortis & Davis, 2021). NLP methods allow the machine to automatically comprehend the content that people share on OSM to reveal writer's psychology. Moreover, NLP studies have shown that ML can effectively identify symptoms connected with depression by using lexical and logical analyses of text on OSM (Wolohan et al., 2018). Furthermore, linguistic inquiry and word count software are also used in many studies. In addition, ML, DL, and hybrid (ML, DL and NLP based) approaches have been implemented to present effective models based on NLP features (Dreisbach et al., 2019).

Machine Learning

This section explores the studies that used ML for depression detection. A total of 46 studies included in this chapter that used the ML methods including supervised and unsupervised algorithms. ML methods build a classifier using various features that may detect depression in the given content. Supervised machine learning uses structured data to learn and make future predictions, whereas Semi or Unsupervised machine learning without structured data and training are used for predictions. The first step towards ML includes data extraction and preprocessing of the unstructured data. The second phase is to explore the data and extract the constructive features. These features can then be used to analyze the sentiments in text, and classify the text into depressive or not depressive categories. The effective ML classifiers include Support Vector Machines (SVM), Naïve Bayes (NB), K-Nearest Neighbor (KNN), Decision Trees (DT) and Random Forest (RF) that are applied to classify and predict the results (Lee et al., 2018). Text classification relies on identifying the class label based on the features obtained from the text. On the other hand, feature engineering uses topic-based features to build classifiers (Stankevich et al., 2018). Other studies used LDA and Topic Modeling to classify depression from a hidden topic.

NB, SVM, DT, RF classifiers are widely used to classify depression in social media users. The NB classifier uses the Bayes hypothesis to calculate the conditional probability and divide the data into separate classes. KNN gets similarity among predefined groups and uses Euclidean distance to classify text. DT have been used in many depressions' detection studies. It determines the significance of an object varies based on numerous variables of the given input data. The RF classifier generates the forest as several trees. The accuracy of the classifier depends on the number of trees. The higher the trees, the greater the accuracy. SVM is a supervised machine learning method used for both regression and classification tasks. SVM divides linearly independent data into two classes, keeping the maximum class distance between both classes. Md. Rafqul Islam proposed an ML model for depressive post recognition. The model takes 21 psycholinguistic features obtained from LIWC as input. Moreover, this study only measures the Facebook posts, not the sufferers. The proposed model employed SVM, DT, KNN, and Ensemble classifiers and achieved 60 to 80% accuracy (R. Islam et al., 2018). (Reece & Danforth, 2017) built a supervised learning model to detect depression in Twitter posts. For this purpose, they probed few features, linguistic style, and perspective of tweets. The best results were obtained from RF classifier with 1200 trees and 0.866 precision. In another similar study, Multinomial Naive Bayes (MNB) achieved the best accuracy with an 83.29 F1 score (Arora & Arora, 2019). MNB and Support Vector Regression (SVR) classifier successfully implemented on 4,696 tweets to detect depression with 78% and 79.9% accuracy, respectively (Arora & Arora, 2019). Gradient boost tree is used in one study along with DT and RF. The algorithm performed best overall, with 98.32% accuracy (Marerngsit & Thammaboosadee, 2020). De Choudhury et al. explored different features, including social engagement behavior, emotional language, ego networks, mentions of antidepressant treatments, and linguistic styles. They developed an SVM classifier based on these attributes with 70% accuracy. One more study used the ML method to recorded EEG data of 28 subjects from 128 channels. In the ensemble method, a deep forest converted the initial features to the new feature set to improve the feature engineering. Moreover, SVM attained 89.02% accuracy (Zucco et al., 2017). Four studies adopted the ML model to utilize EEG data for depression detection tasks (William, 2013), (Morales, 2018), (Kim & Delen, 2018). Another study used SVR and MNB to classify 3754 Twitter posts for depression and anxiety recognition. The model achieved an accuracy of 79.7% with SVR and78% with MNB. SVR works similar to SVM except that it finds the hyperplane that increases the distance between two classes. It classifies text by utilizing the nearest neighbors method built on similarity (Arora & Arora, 2019).

Deep Learning

DL is the most advanced, complex, multipart approach to produce effective results. A total of 15 studies used the DL for depression detection task (L. Yang et al., 2017), (Wongkoblap et al., 2021), (Wu et al., 2020), (Geraci et al., 2017), (Shah et al., 2020), (Lin et al., 2020), (Yueh et al., 2020). DL is, in fact, is an extension of ML that uses an artificial neural network to classify depression. The neural network classifier takes the training dataset as input and grows until an adequate error is observed.

Different Deep Neural Networks (DNN) are shown to be more efficient in NLP tasks than traditional approaches (Deng and Yu 2014). One study used Multilayer Perceptron and Radial Basis Function Network (RBFN). RBFN is found to be more effective, with a classification accuracy of 84%. (Kumar et al., 2020a). Two studies on depression detection proposed DL and ensemble methods based on EEG features. In the DL approach, the authors used CNN to recognize the depression in EEG features. Another work incorporated DL method and achieved 0.99 accuracy (Seal et al., 2021). A subsequent work achieved 96.0% accuracy (Acharya et al., 2018). In addition, Recurrent Neural Networks (RNN) successfully observed the semantics of social media posts. RNN examines the important features and effectively incorporates the behavioral, surviving atmosphere, and content-based features to forecast depression (Orabi et al., 2018). Moreover, Long- Short-Term Memory (LSTM) is another artificial RNN applied in depression detection study, which got 70.89% accuracy with 50.24% precision and 70.89% recall. This study performed better than different state-of-the-art methods (Kholifah et al., 2020). The process starts by creating a lexicon of depression symptoms. The next step is extracting multiple features, including sentiment, personal pronouns, oppressor words, and negative emotions and words. The results show that a depressed personality is strongly connected to self-hopelessness, persistent sadness, suicidal ideas. The authors in (L. Yang et al., 2017) trained the Deep CNN model for social media audio, video, and text data. DCNN has many hidden layers which can extract more features and provides improved accuracy.

The novel models have also been developed by using word embedding and DNN. The Usr2Vec method converts text into embeddings. The Multinomial Logistic Regression was applied on embedding matrices to train a model and the DL model to represent chronological words in tweets. Moreover, this study also used one-dimensional CNN to predict depression. Another work for Twitter users introduced novel multiple instances learning Model MIL-SocNet. In this study, the authors introduced an anaphoric resolution that identifies the topic of the post. Along with this, LSTM layers with word embedding are applied to discover a chronological sequence of tweets words. The authors assessed the proposed model against formerly published DL methods. The study generates better results (Wongkoblap et al., 2021).

Hybrid

The hybrid approach is used as a combination of ML and DL algorithms. In general, the clustering is used at preprocessing stage and the supervised algorithm is then used as a classifier. Among selected works, seven studies mentioned the keyword hybrid in the title of the paper or the keyword list. (Kumar et al., 2020b) used hybrid technique for depression and anxiety detection model. The model is a fusion of Bayes Network, NB, K-Star, Multilayer Perceptron, Local Nearest Neighbor, RBFN, RF. In addition, K-Star, and RF method is also applied. The combination of these two algorithms increased the accuracy; however, these are time-consuming.

In subsequent work, three hybrid methods are considered for classifying depression among users. These methods merge ML with manual procedures. In the first approach, single-label multi-class classification with CRF and SVM classifier identifies 15 groups. In the second approach, separate binary classifiers with SVM and CRF are trained for all 15 groups and provide the classification union. Finally, in the third method, multi-class and binary classifiers with SVM and CRF are combined on different subcategories of the training dataset. All three approaches are assessed on 300 undetected posts. The model with the second approach yields the best results with a 45.6% F1 score (Liakata et al., 2012). Another hybrid model is generated on CollGram profiles and a DL algorithm BERT (Bidirectional Encoder Representations from Transformers). CollGram analysis identifies how text is composed with its attributes. In short, CollGram identifies the collocation intensity of each text. Moreover, CollGram, along with sentiment assessment, provides improved accuracy. CollGram analysis was first introduced in 2014 (Bestgen et al., 2014). It measures three values; t-score that measures familiar words collocations, Mutual Information factor (MI) that measures rare words collocations, and the number of individual components that produce the CollGram and percentages of bigrams that can be errors or creative groups (Christa., 2021).

Besides, a DL hybrid model used two Deep CNN and DNN to analyze the audio and video dataset. In addition, 5 DCNN-DNN models along with fusion DNN were used to analyze text data. The results obtained from these architectures are combined (L. Yang et al., 2017). (Lin et al., 2020) proposed CNN classifier and BERT to extract features from text and image. Subsequently, visual and textual features are used to analyze the users. More precisely, the authors classified depression and normal users through a Neural Network and compared the results with NB and Multi Social Networking learning (MSNL). MSNL is a multi-view learning model that analyzes data through a composite of informants. It predicts binary classification (Shen et al., 2017). Figure 2 provides an overview of the different features that are used to classify depression across research studies.

Figure 2. Different features explored in depression detection studies

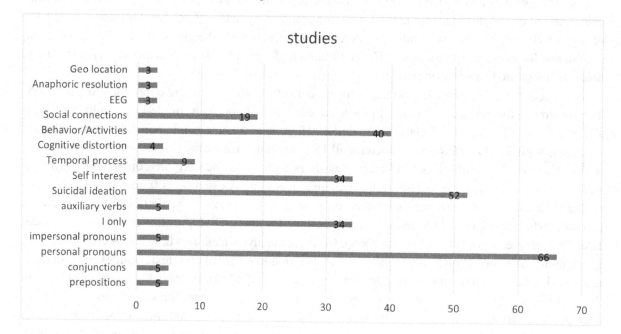

ONLINE SOCIAL MEDIA

Social media provides abundant social data to analyze deep emotions among users of different domains. Depression detection requires self-reporting of disease, and social media posts may be effectively trained as a competent model. Researchers have done experiments on different social media for both early depression and generic depression detection. The underlying section focuses on the OSM data used for depression detection. Recently, numerous works explored OSM to investigate the potential depressive patients (Nguyen 2017; Hu & Flaxman 2018). Recent studies provide evidence that OSM users post about their mental health condition and even the procured therapy on social media (Park et al., 2018). According to a study, approximately 3.8 billion profiles were registered on OSM in 2021, representing half of the worldwide (Giuntini et al., 2020). Individuals with depression are increasingly using mobile phones (Pizzagalli et al., 2020). Almost half of the psychiatric patients have social media profiles, especially younger people.

Facebook

Facebook has around one billion user profiles and these will grow with time. For underlying study, six works have considered Facebook data for depression detection. The reason could be the strict user privacy policies by Facebook, hence not allowing access to the users' data even though they record every type of personal data of individual users. Moreno et al. (2011) studied one year Facebook status updates of 200 students to determine the visible signs of depression. In general, 25% of profiles showed depression among students. Eichstaedt et al. (2018) investigated the Facebook profiles of 683 patients who visited an urban academic emergency department. Among these, 114 individuals were diagnosed with depression. Katchapakirin & Wongpatikaseree (2018) mined 35 Facebook users with a total of 1105 posts who agreed to share their data for the research. Among these, 22 were classified as depressed, and 13 were normal users.

M. R. Islam et al. (2018) mined various features from Facebook posts, including the emotional and temporal process and linguistic style to study depression. Among 7145 comments, around 58 percent were depressive, and 42 percent were non-depressive. Their dataset has five emotional measures: positive, negative, anger, sad, anxiety, 3 temporal measures including present, past and future focus, 9 linguistic attributes, e.g., articles, auxiliary verb, prepositions, adverbs, pronoun, conjunctions, verbs, and negations.

Besides one more study by De Choudhury et al. (2014) explored a novel dataset of 165 mothers who posted about their depression on Facebook. To inspect postpartum depression, the authors also measured several features, including the regularity of posts, shared media, likes, comments, linguistic style, and emotional language. The authors (Wu et al., 2020) investigated 1453 very active Facebook individuals who proposed the DL depression model with D3-HDS heterogeneous data sources. The authors investigated environment, behaviors, content in Facebook posts.

Twitter

According to a report, approximately six thousand tweets are sent on Twitter every second and around two hundred billion per year (Bonner, 2019). People regularly use Twitter to express their feelings and thoughts in written posts. Twitter posts are particularly important because these provide deep insights regarding individual's mood and activities. Hence, Twitter is an important OSM with 28 papers regarding depression detection studies. The authors (Deshpande & Rao, 2018) examined 10000 user tweets for depression detection. The authors collected the tweets randomly by employing a pre-generated wordlist for words signifying depression. These keyword-specific tweets are then combined with a common set of tweets in the form of JSON objects. Subsequently, the JSON objects are analyzed to obtain text data from a tweet. The activity and language change on OSM is always associated with depression studies. Linguistic features extracted from OSM posts are shown to signify depression (Hawn, 2009, Pachouly et al., 2021, Yazdavar et al., 2017). The authors have developed a trend analysis method, "TwitterMonitor" that recognizes recurrent geographical sources of trends on Twitter. (Mathioudakis & Koudas, 2010). The topic models have been developed to study twitter profiles of clinically analyzed patients (Guntuku et al., 2017, Oyebode & Orji, 2020). The topic model is designed through LDA to find 200 topics from text data to classify depressed profiles.

O'Dea et al. (2015) examined Twitter as the most researched platform for depression detection. Their collected dataset of 2,000 tweets for suicide ideation contains the statements like "tired of living." The dataset is manually labeled as "strongly concerning," "possibly concerning," and "safe to ignore." Another study on depression detection among Twitter users introduced Multiple Instance Learning (MIL) models. The authors introduced an anaphoric resolution that identifies the post topic (Wongkoblap et al., 2021). The classifiers developed comprise a tweet encoder, word attention, tweet classification, user encoder, anaphoric resolution encoder, tweet attention, and user classification layers. BLSTM layers were used to learn the sequence of words and order of tweets posted on a timeline. MIL-SocNet considered the following features from Twitter, word attention in the tweet, tweet encoder, tweet classification, tweet attention, user encoder, and user classification. They used LSTM and extended the MIL-SocNet as MILA-SocNet by adding anaphoric resolution. Overall, 2132 users with 5 million tweets in depression class and 2036 users with 4.2 million random tweets are examined.

Besides, a study used the same anaphoric resolution with two MIL models to explore depression among self-reported tweets containing 1983 users who declared themselves depressed and 1699 general tweets. The regular expressions are applied to extract 4892 tweets from 4545 tweeter users that wrote, "I was diagnosed with depression" (Wongkoblap et al., 2021). De Choudhury et al. extracted 2 million tweets from 476 individuals' profiles who were depression patients. (Reece & Danforth. 2017) collected Twitter data of 204 depressed users and applied CESD scores for the detection of depression among them. De Choudhury et al. (2013b) describe the SMDI method as a Social Media Depression Index (SMDI). These standard score tweets are geolocated to the state level. These scores attained 0.51 correspondence against ground truth built on the Centre for Disease Control (CDC) calculations. In (De Choudhury et al. 2013a), the authors trained and tested different ML algorithms on Twitter data to uncover depressive symptoms, including mood, loss of appetite, disrupted sleep, and exhaustion. Jamil et al. explored depressed users' tweets and self-diagnosis to keep or remove the user from the training dataset. In another study, the authors examined 37000 prepartum and 40000 postpartum tweets of 376 new mothers. They developed a training dataset with 33 features based on empirical tolerance. These features include the measures of linguistic style and social engagement and the changes between pre and postpartum periods. They built a classifier that predicted the depression in mothers from only prepartum data with 71% accuracy (Calvo et al., 2017). Another study on Twitter data collected 1,402 users with 292,564 posts and images with depression and 36,993 users with 35 million posts and images without depression. Precision, recall, and f-measures were applied as performance metrics (Lin et al., 2020).

(S & S. Raj, 2021) examined 2500 Twitter posts for the prediction of emotion. The proposed classification method with NB and SVM. Moreover, Geolocated Twitter data is studied to analyze the geographic movements associated with suicide. For instance, Sadilek et al., in 2013, extracted the data of 6237 Twitter users who allowed their current location. Several features were extracted, including the time and tweets number, social network, LIWC classifications. In another study, the data is collected from the public tweet and current location tags. Specifically, the users are those who tweet in English, have a minimum of 100 tweets in general, have a minimum of 30 geolocated tweets in the US and their 30 percent geolocated tweets are in one state. Syarif et al. (2019) collected usernames along with tags for depression from Twitter. They classified 8105 posts in "high," "moderate," and "low" levels of depression.

Reddit

Reddit is a public platform with specific communities, and the members can post content and vote on the other person's posted content. Every community has relevant content that is termed subreddits (Giuntini et al., 2020). This platform has gained the interest of researchers because there are many discussion groups about depression, its survivors, diagnosis, and treatments. A study researched bag-of-words, embeddings, and bigrams in Reddit users 'text messages with the CLEF/eRisk 2017 dataset. This publicly available dataset has Reddit comments and posts of 135 depressed 752 random users. In addition, stylometric and morphology features were computed as well. These additional features improved the classification (Trotzek et al., 2018). Another study conducted by Choudhury et al. examined Reddit users' posts who shared their depression publicly and spoke about suicidal ideation. They collected 22808 Reddit posts in which 9971 posts are collected from subreddit anxiety, panic party, health anxiety, and social anxiety. The remaining 12837 are general posts. The important features, i.e., self-interest, social engagement, anxiety and hopeless posts, and linguistic style, were considered for the depression detection task. To recognize depression among Reddit users, the dataset is formed on random messages containing various topics. The total number of depressions revealing posts is 1293 and standard posts are 548. Depression posts were collected from the depression support subreddit. Standard posts are collected from subreddit associated with friends and family (Tadesse et al., 2019). Apart from social media platforms, some other online data sources have also been explored in depression detection studies. These include online support forums, medically diagnosed patients' data, online blogging platforms, and publicly available datasets, e.g., CLEF/eRisk 2017 and suicidal notes.

COMMUNITY

This section focuses on the depression detection communities, which are explored in collected papers. Communities are individual social groups that share similar interests and attitudes. Most of the papers are produced on general social media users, i.e., social media text messages, status updates; however, few unique communities are found quite effective in obtaining useful features. Therefore, this section provides a brief overview of these communities.

SELF-REPORTED OR MEDICALLY DIAGNOSED USERS

The following papers are presented on previously diagnosed patients (Wolohan & Sayyed, 2018), (Sokratous et al., 2013), (He et al., 2017), (Syarif et al., 2019), (De Choudhury et al., 2014), (Park et al., 2018), (Yazdavar et al., 2017). Such users are already clinically diagnosed with depression and taking the treatment, or self-diagnosed users who shared their depression publicly on different online support platforms. They have posted their status updates with depression tags or depression support communities tags.

LITERARY DATA

The authors studied the literature and poetry communities as a tool to explore depression features. Apart from research, the new dataset publicly available datasets have also been utilized. For instance, the corpus of suicidal notes is used in 2 studies (Ghosh et al., 2021). In addition, researchers also used Poems of suicidal poets to extract etymological signs of depression, e.g., words more connected with self, first-person pronouns, lack of social involvement, and desires of death. In addition, one study investigated a dataset comprised of 300 poems of 9 writers and found first-person pronouns in the writings of depressive writers (Stirman & Pennebaker, 2001). Another study analyzed cognitive distortions in the work of 36 depressive and not depressive poets. The authors claimed significantly higher cognitive distortion presence in the literary pieces of depressive poets (Thomas & Duke, 2007).

GEOGRAPHICAL DATA

Location-based social media data can present rich insights into individuals' observations of space and its significance to public health. Unfortunately, we have found few papers in our compiled depression detection papers exploring social media data regarding GPS location. The first paper is presented by De

Choudhury et al., in 2013, in which the tweets with geolocation to state level are considered and scored on the SMDI method, which is a Social Media Depression Index. Moreover, the second paper examined geographic movements associated with suicide. Specifically, the users in this study have at least 30 geo-located tweets from the united states (Homan et al., 2011). Finally, Sadilek et al. (2013) extracted the data of 6237 Twitter users who allowed their current location. Several features were extracted, including the time and tweets number, social network, LIWC classifications.

Researchers found 14097 active patients with 14 clusters of depression in South Africa. The eastern and northern areas were in the most depressive cluster (Cuadros et al., 2019). (W. Yang & Mu, 2015) filtered the tweets posted in the US. They used the keywords "depress" and its related words to extract depressive content. Another study captured the depressive attitudes based on GPS locations in the UK (Breedvelt et al., 2018). (Müller et al., 2021) examined depression in 57 million spatial points among 57 regular students in the US.

A CASE STUDY

A case study is presented that reveals important feature extraction for classification of depressive content from normal text.

DATA ACQUISITION

The dataset for this case study is taken from Kaggle Poetry Foundation Poems Dataset. The dataset contains authors information in the first column and the poems in the second column. We used labeled dataset of 50 depressive and 50 normal poems for our training phase. For depression class we searched the hashtag "depression" and collected 50 poems and labelled them depressive. Similarly for the normal class we used keywords "lived", "happy", "nature", "beauty" and collected 50 poems in normal class. In Preprocessing phase, we removed noisy text including characters links, names, numerical values etc. Furthermore, all text is converted to lower case and sentences are divided into tokens. Subsequently, stop words are removed for further processing.

Figure 3. Sentiment supporting words in poem data

METHODOLOGY

The case study presents machine learning classification method to classify poems in depressive and not depressive classes. For feature extraction, two-way sentiment analysis is performed by using the Sentistrength algorithm. At first the binary classification that generates positive or negative polarity to the given text. Secondly emotional temperatures are calculated for each poem in the dataset. The idea behind this approach is that the depressive text is more likely to have negative temperature than positive. We used Sentistrength algorithm that generates two scores between 5 to -5 indicating the stress/negative and relaxation/ positive emotional temperature for each poem. The Wordcloud in Figure 3 provides insights about the sentiment supporting words occurrences in poem data.

Table 2. Polarity and emotional temperature analysis

Poem text	class	positive	negative	polarity
The fear of the unknown weighs me down and mostly I would want to curl up into a ball and hide out	depressive	1	-4	Negative

The calculated emotional temperatures are considered as features that are fed to the classifier for prediction (see Table 2).

RESULTS

Classification model is developed in Rapidminer with SVM, RF, Fast Large Margin, and Generalized Linear Model. We implemented 10-fold cross validation with 70-30 splits for the classification evaluation. Figure 4 explains the classification results based on four classifiers. The accuracy is measured in terms of F1 score which is best achieved with SVM (72%) followed by Fast Large Margin (70%). The results show that emotional temperatures as a feature can be used to detect depression. The classification is satisfactory, which implies that depressive poem data contains high stress or negative emotions.

Figure 4. Classification results

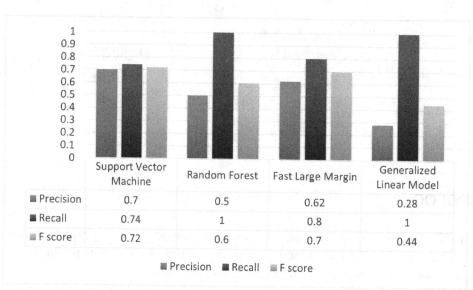

	Support Vector Machine	Random Forest	Fast Large Margin	Generalized Linear Model
■ Precision	0.7	0.5	0.62	0.28
■ Recall	0.74	1	0.8	1
■ F score	0.72	0.6	0.7	0.44

■ Precision   ■ Recall   ■ F score

FUTURE RESEARCH DIRECTIONS

This chapter provides depression recognition approaches in popular social media platforms including Facebook, Twitter, and Reddit while focusing on textual features. Other social media platforms such as Instagram, Tumblr, and online blogs are yet to be explored. Apart from text, images and facial expressions are also found in studies excluded as this chapter only focuses on NLP. In addition, most of the NLP approaches are language-dependent as these are presented to explore only English text. Language dependency is the primary limitation of most NLP approaches that cannot detect depression in other languages. Further, identifying required social media users' data is highly proportional to the correct classification results. For instance, users can control what they share on social media. Therefore, the post that appears depressive may be shared in a different context. Moreover, the noise in raw data reduces an adequate amount of data which may be useful in prediction, i.e., pronouns. Another aspect is that classification depends upon the appropriate annotation. This problem can be settled by asking the psychiatrist or other domain experts to annotate the dataset. On the other hand, DL methods may be incorporated for larger datasets to detect fine-grained depression contents and subsequently the depressive individuals.

In addition to the limitations mentioned earlier, future directions are also necessitated to be presented. For instance, NLP approaches to handle multilingual and heterogeneous datasets may be put forward. Another aspect could be to explore the Spatio-temporal and cross-cultural contents to explore the depression. Multimodalities may be explored for even fine-grained depression detection. The evolution of depression and its stages could be explored from the shared content on OSM. Multitask learning may be explored since depression may lead to suicide attempts; hence the relationship between depression and suicide may be explored. Moreover, depression causes in different environments (offices, educational institutes, etc.) may be researched.

CONCLUSION

This chapter provides hierarchical segmentation of depression detection in social media users. The research works take knowledge from different areas such as psychology, sociology, health informatics, and computer science. Accordingly, the datasets collection methods, platforms, features, classification, and evaluation methods vary across different studies, making it challenging to know which study outperformed. Besides, the researchers have used similar or different features with multiple NLP, ML, DL, and hybrid methods. In general, each study revolves around data collection, feature extraction, and classification model generation. In addition, most of the authors have not specified the age groups of users. Therefore, most of the studies are placed in Generic group rather than in the Early detection group. Furthermore, both groups adopted similar approaches, features, and social media platforms. In ML approaches, SVM is prominent with better accuracy. In DL, CNNs are used with different ML and DL combinations. Hybrid approaches are based on lexical and ML combinations or ML and DL combinations. Similarly, NLP features are also quite common in all studies. For example, each study reports linguistic features, behavioral features, and positive or negative sentiment analysis. Whereas very few studies considered time, social connections, and geolocation data of social media posts. As well as English is the only language in all studies except one study that worked on the Chinese language. Likewise, Twitter is the most researched social media. On the other hand, few studies used Facebook and Reddit, and some have not reported the platform. While few studies used blogs, questionnaire and other datasets that do not come under the scope of this chapter, so we ignored. At last, we brief communities which are unique as compared to the general Community.

ACKNOWLEDGMENT

This research received no specific grant from any funding agency in the public, commercial, or not-for-profit sectors.

REFERENCES

Abboute, A., Boudjeriou, Y., Entringer, G., Azé, J., Bringay, S., & Poncelet, P. (2014, June). Mining twitter for suicide prevention. In *International Conference on Applications of Natural Language to Data Bases/Information Systems* (pp. 250-253). Springer.

Acharya, U. R., Oh, S. L., Hagiwara, Y., Tan, J. H., Adeli, H., & Subha, D. P. (2018). Automated EEG-based screening of depression using deep convolutional neural network. *Computer Methods and Programs in Biomedicine, 161*, 103–113. doi:10.1016/j.cmpb.2018.04.012 PMID:29852953

AlSagri, H. S., & Ykhlef, M. (2020). Machine learning-based approach for depression detection in twitter using content and activity features. *IEICE Transactions on Information and Systems, 103*(8), 1825–1832. doi:10.1587/transinf.2020EDP7023

Arora, P., & Arora, P. (2019, March). Mining twitter data for depression detection. In *International Conference on Signal Processing and Communication (ICSC)* (pp. 186-189). IEEE. 10.1109/ICSC45622.2019.8938353

Back, M. D., Stopfer, J. M., Vazire, S., Gaddis, S., Schmukle, S. C., Egloff, B., & Gosling, S. D. (2010). Facebook profiles reflect actual personality, not self-idealization. *Psychological Science, 21*(3), 372–374. doi:10.1177/0956797609360756 PMID:20424071

Bader, C. S., Skurla, M., & Vahia, I. V. (2020). Technology in the assessment, treatment, and management of depression. *Harvard Review of Psychiatry, 28*(1), 60–66. doi:10.1097/HRP.0000000000000235 PMID:31913982

Bonner, A. (2019). *You Are What You Tweet Detecting Depression in Social Media via Twitter Usage.* Towards Data Science. Retrieved 14 September 2021, from https://towardsdatascience.com/you-are-what-you-tweet-7e23fb84f4ed

Calvo, R. A., Milne, D. N., Hussain, M. S., & Christensen, H. (2017). Natural language processing in mental health applications using non-clinical texts. *Natural Language Engineering, 23*(5), 649–685. doi:10.1017/S1351324916000383

Cortis, K., & Davis, B. (2021). Over a decade of social opinion mining: A systematic review. *Artificial Intelligence Review, 54*(7), 4873–4965. doi:10.100710462-021-10030-2 PMID:34188346

Cuadros, D. F., Tomita, A., Vandormael, A., Slotow, R., Burns, J. K., & Tanser, F. (2019). Spatial structure of depression in South Africa: A longitudinal panel survey of a nationally representative sample of households. *Scientific Reports, 9*(1), 1–10. doi:10.103841598-018-37791-1 PMID:30700798

De Choudhury, M., Counts, S., Horvitz, E. J., & Hoff, A. (2014, February). Characterizing and predicting postpartum depression from shared facebook data. In *Proceedings of the 17th ACM conference on Computer supported cooperative work & social computing* (pp. 626-638). 10.1145/2531602.2531675

De Choudhury, M., Gamon, M., Counts, S., & Horvitz, E. (2013, June). Predicting depression via social media. *Health Information Science and Systems, 6*(1), 1–12.

Depression Tests and Diagnosis. (n.d.). *Healthline.* Retrieved 14 September 2021, from https://www.healthline.com/health/depression/tests-diagnosis

Deshpande, M., & Rao, V. (2017, December). Depression detection using emotion artificial intelligence. In International Conference on Intelligent Sustainable Systems (ICISS) (pp. 858-862). doi:10.1109/ISS1.2017.8389299

Dreisbach, C., Koleck, T. A., Bourne, P. E., & Bakken, S. (2019). A systematic review of natural language processing and text mining of symptoms from electronic patient-authored text data. *International Journal of Medical Informatics, 125*, 37–46. doi:10.1016/j.ijmedinf.2019.02.008 PMID:30914179

Efron, M., & Winget, M. (2010). Questions are content: A taxonomy of questions in a microblogging environment. *Proceedings of the American Society for Information Science and Technology, 47*(1), 1–10. doi:10.1002/meet.14504701208

Eichstaedt, J. C., Smith, R. J., Merchant, R. M., Ungar, L. H., Crutchley, P., Preoţiuc-Pietro, D., & Schwartz, H. A. (2018). Facebook language predicts depression in medical records. *Proceedings of the National Academy of Sciences of the United States of America, 115*(44), 11203–11208. doi:10.1073/pnas.1802331115 PMID:30322910

Garland, E., & Solomons, K. (n.d.). Early Detection of Depression in Young and Elderly People. *BCMJ, 44*(9), 469-472. Retrieved 14 September 2021, from https://bcmj.org/articles/early-detection-depression-young-and-elderly-people

Geraci, J., Wilansky, P., de Luca, V., Roy, A., Kennedy, J. L., & Strauss, J. (2017). Applying deep neural networks to unstructured text notes in electronic medical records for phenotyping youth depression. *Evidence-Based Mental Health, 20*(3), 83–87. doi:10.1136/eb-2017-102688 PMID:28739578

Ghosh, S., Ekbal, A., & Bhattacharyya, P. (2021). A multitask framework to detect depression, sentiment and multi-label emotion from suicide notes. *Cognitive Computation*, 1–20.

Giuntini, F. T., Cazzolato, M. T., dos Reis, M. D. J. D., Campbell, A. T., Traina, A. J., & Ueyama, J. (2020). A review on recognizing depression in social networks: Challenges and opportunities. *Journal of Ambient Intelligence and Humanized Computing, 11*(11), 4713–4729. doi:10.100712652-020-01726-4

Guntuku, S. C., Yaden, D. B., Kern, M. L., Ungar, L. H., & Eichstaedt, J. C. (2017). Detecting depression and mental illness on social media: An integrative review. *Current Opinion in Behavioral Sciences, 18*, 43–49. doi:10.1016/j.cobeha.2017.07.005

Havigerová, J. M., Haviger, J., Kučera, D., & Hoffmannová, P. (2019). Text-based detection of the risk of depression. *Frontiers in Psychology, 10*, 513. doi:10.3389/fpsyg.2019.00513 PMID:30936845

Hawn, C. (2009). Take two aspirin and tweet me in the morning: How Twitter, Facebook, and other social media are reshaping health care. *Health Affairs, 28*(2), 361–368. doi:10.1377/hlthaff.28.2.361 PMID:19275991

He, Q., Veldkamp, B. P., Glas, C. A., & de Vries, T. (2017). Automated assessment of patients' self-narratives for posttraumatic stress disorder screening using natural language processing and text mining. *Assessment, 24*(2), 157–172. doi:10.1177/1073191115602551 PMID:26358713

Higuera, V. (2021). *Everything You Want to Know About Depression*. Retrieved 27 November 2021, from https://www.healthline.com/health/depression

Homan, C., Johar, R., Liu, T., Lytle, M., Silenzio, V., & Alm, C. O. (2014, June). Toward macro-insights for suicide prevention: Analyzing fine-grained distress at scale. In *Proceedings of the Workshop on Computational Linguistics and Clinical Psychology: From Linguistic Signal to Clinical Reality* (pp. 107-117). 10.3115/v1/W14-3213

Hu, H. W., Hsu, K. S., Lee, C., Hu, H. L., Hsu, C. Y., Yang, W. H., ... Chen, T. A. (2019). Keyword-Driven Depressive Tendency Model for Social Media Posts. In *International Conference on Business Information Systems* (pp. 14-22). Springer. 10.1007/978-3-030-20482-2_2

Karmen, C., Hsiung, R. C., & Wetter, T. (2015). Screening internet forum participants for depression symptoms by assembling and enhancing multiple NLP methods. *Computer Methods and Programs in Biomedicine, 120*(1), 27–36. doi:10.1016/j.cmpb.2015.03.008 PMID:25891366

Katchapakirin, K., Wongpatikaseree, K., Yomaboot, P., & Kaewpitakkun, Y. (2018). Facebook social media for depression detection in the Thai community. In *2018 15th International Joint Conference on Computer Science and Software Engineering (JCSSE)* (pp. 1-6). 10.29007/tscc

Kholifah, B., Syarif, I., & Badriyah, T. (2020). Mental Disorder Detection via Social Media Mining using Deep Learning. *Kinetik: Game Technology, Information System, Computer Network, Computing, Electronics, and Control, 5*(4), 309–316. doi:10.22219/kinetik.v5i4.1120

Kim, Y. M., & Delen, D. (2018). Medical informatics research trend analysis: A text mining approach. *Health Informatics Journal, 24*(4), 432–452. doi:10.1177/1460458216678443 PMID:30376768

Kumar, P., Garg, S., & Garg, A. (2020). Assessment of anxiety, depression and stress using machine learning models. *Procedia Computer Science, 171*, 1989–1998. doi:10.1016/j.procs.2020.04.213

Lee, Y., Ragguett, R. M., Mansur, R. B., Boutilier, J. J., Rosenblat, J. D., Trevizol, A., Brietzke, E., Lin, K., Pan, Z., Subramaniapillai, M., Chan, T. C. Y., Fus, D., Park, C., Musial, N., Zuckerman, H., Chen, V. C.-H., Ho, R., Rong, C., & McIntyre, R. S. (2018). Applications of machine learning algorithms to predict therapeutic outcomes in depression: A meta-analysis and systematic review. *Journal of Affective Disorders, 241*, 519–532. doi:10.1016/j.jad.2018.08.073 PMID:30153635

Liakata, M., Kim, J. H., Saha, S., Hastings, J., & Rebholz-Schuhmann, D. (2012). Three hybrid classifiers for the detection of emotions in suicide notes. *Biomedical Informatics Insights, 5*, BII-S8967.

Lin, C., Hu, P., Su, H., Li, S., Mei, J., Zhou, J., & Leung, H. (2020). Sensemood: Depression detection on social media. In *Proceedings of the 2020 International Conference on Multimedia Retrieval* (pp. 407-411). 10.1145/3372278.3391932

Luby, M. D. J. (2017). *Diagnosing Early-Onset Depression in Young Children*. Retrieved 27 November 2021, from https://www.bbrfoundation.org/blog/diagnosing-early-onset-depression-young-children

Ma, L., Wang, Z., & Zhang, Y. (2017). Extracting depression symptoms from social networks and web blogs via text mining. In *International Symposium on Bioinformatics Research and Applications* (pp. 325-330). Springer. 10.1007/978-3-319-59575-7_29

Marerngsit, S., & Thammaboosadee, S. (2020). A Two-Stage Text-to-Emotion Depressive Disorder Screening Assistance based on Contents from Online Community. In *2020 8th International Electrical Engineering Congress (iEECON)* (pp. 1-4). 10.1109/iEECON48109.2020.229524

Mathioudakis, M., & Koudas, N. (2010). Twittermonitor: trend detection over the twitter stream. In *Proceedings of the 2010 ACM SIGMOD International Conference on Management of data* (pp. 1155-1158). 10.1145/1807167.1807306

Morales, M. R. (2018). *Multimodal depression detection: An investigation of features and fusion techniques for automated systems*. City University of New York.

Morales, M. R., & Levitan, R. (2016). *Speech vs. text: A comparative analysis of features for depression detection systems. In 2016 IEEE spoken language technology workshop.* SLT.

O'dea, B., Wan, S., Batterham, P. J., Calear, A. L., Paris, C., & Christensen, H. (2015). Detecting suicidality on Twitter. *Internet Interventions: the Application of Information Technology in Mental and Behavioural Health*, 2(2), 183–188. doi:10.1016/j.invent.2015.03.005

Orabi, A. H., Buddhitha, P., Orabi, M. H., & Inkpen, D. (2018). Deep learning for depression detection of twitter users. In *Proceedings of the Fifth Workshop on Computational Linguistics and Clinical Psychology: From Keyboard to Clinic* (pp. 88-97). 10.18653/v1/W18-0609

Oyebode, O., & Orji, R. (2020). Deconstructing Persuasive Strategies in Mental Health Apps Based on User Reviews using Natural Language Processing. BCSS@ PERSUASIVE.

Pachouly, S. J., Raut, G., Bute, K., Tambe, R., & Bhavsar, S. (2021). *Depression Detection on Social Media Network (Twitter) using Sentiment Analysis*. Academic Press.

Park, A., Conway, M., & Chen, A. T. (2018). Examining thematic similarity, difference, and membership in three online mental health communities from Reddit: A text mining and visualization approach. *Computers in Human Behavior*, 78, 98–112. doi:10.1016/j.chb.2017.09.001 PMID:29456286

Reece, A. G., & Danforth, C. M. (2017). Instagram photos reveal predictive markers of depression. *EPJ Data Science*, 6, 1–12.

Rude, S., Gortner, E. M., & Pennebaker, J. (2004). Language use of depressed and depression-vulnerable college students. *Cognition and Emotion*, 18(8), 1121–1133. doi:10.1080/02699930441000030

Seal, A., Bajpai, R., Agnihotri, J., Yazidi, A., Herrera-Viedma, E., & Krejcar, O. (2021). DeprNet: A Deep Convolution Neural Network Framework for Detecting Depression Using EEG. *IEEE Transactions on Instrumentation and Measurement*, 70, 1–13. doi:10.1109/TIM.2021.3053999

Shah, F. M., Ahmed, F., Joy, S. K. S., Ahmed, S., Sadek, S., Shil, R., & Kabir, M. H. (2020). Early Depression Detection from Social Network Using Deep Learning Techniques. In *2020 IEEE Region 10 Symposium (TENSYMP)* (pp. 823-826). 10.1109/TENSYMP50017.2020.9231008

Shen, G., Jia, J., Nie, L., Feng, F., Zhang, C., Hu, T., . . . Zhu, W. (2017). Depression Detection via Harvesting Social Media: A Multimodal Dictionary Learning Solution. In IJCAI (pp. 3838-3844). doi:10.24963/ijcai.2017/536

Smys, S., & Raj, J. S. (2021). Analysis of Deep Learning Techniques for Early Detection of Depression on Social Media Network-A Comparative Study. *Journal of Trends in Computer Science and Smart Technology, 3*(1), 24-39.

Sokratous, S., Merkouris, A., Middleton, N., & Karanikola, M. (2013). The association between stressful life events and depressive symptoms among Cypriot university students: A cross-sectional descriptive correlational study. *BMC Public Health, 13*(1), 1–16. doi:10.1186/1471-2458-13-1121 PMID:24304515

Stankevich, M., Isakov, V., Devyatkin, D., & Smirnov, I. V. (2018). Feature Engineering for Depression Detection in Social Media. In ICPRAM (pp. 426-431). doi:10.5220/0006598604260431

Stankevich, M., Latyshev, A., Kuminskaya, E., Smirnov, I., & Grigoriev, O. (2019). Depression detection from social media texts. In *Data Analytics and Management in Data Intensive Domains: XXI International Conference DAMDID/RCDL,* (p. 352). Academic Press.

Stirman, S. W., & Pennebaker, J. W. (2001). Word use in the poetry of suicidal and nonsuicidal poets. *Psychosomatic Medicine, 63*(4), 517–522. doi:10.1097/00006842-200107000-00001 PMID:11485104

Syarif, I., Ningtias, N., & Badriyah, T. (2019). Study on Mental Disorder Detection via Social Media Mining. In *2019 4th International Conference on Computing, Communications and Security (ICCCS)* (pp. 1-6). 10.1109/CCCS.2019.8888096

Tadesse, M. M., Lin, H., Xu, B., & Yang, L. (2019). Detection of depression-related posts in rcddit social media forum. *IEEE Access: Practical Innovations, Open Solutions, 7,* 44883–44893. doi:10.1109/ACCESS.2019.2909180

Thomas, K. M., & Duke, M. (2007). Depressed writing: Cognitive distortions in the works of depressed and nondepressed poets and writers. *Psychology of Aesthetics, Creativity, and the Arts, 1*(4), 204–218. doi:10.1037/1931-3896.1.4.204

Trotzek, M., Koitka, S., & Friedrich, C. M. (2018). Utilizing neural networks and linguistic metadata for early detection of depression indications in text sequences. *IEEE Transactions on Knowledge and Data Engineering, 32*(3), 588–601. doi:10.1109/TKDE.2018.2885515

What causes depression? (2019). *Harvard Health.* Retrieved 14 September 2021, from https://www.health.harvard.edu/mind-and-mood/what-causes-depression

What Is Depression? (n.d.). Retrieved 27 November 2021, from https://www.psychiatry.org/patients-families/depression/what-is-depression

WHO. (n.d.). Retrieved 27 November 2021, from https://www.who.int/health-topics/depression#tab=tab_1

Wołk, A., Chlasta, K., & Holas, P. (2021). *Hybrid approach to detecting symptoms of depression in social media entries.* arXiv preprint:2106.10485.

Wolohan, J. T., Hiraga, M., Mukherjee, A., Sayyed, Z. A., & Millard, M. (2018,). Detecting linguistic traces of depression in topic-restricted text: Attending to self-stigmatized depression with NLP. In *Proceedings of the First International Workshop on Language Cognition and Computational Models* (pp. 11-21). Academic Press.

Wongkoblap, A., Vadillo, M., & Curcin, V. (2021). Depression Detection of Twitter Posters using Deep Learning with Anaphora Resolution: Algorithm Development and Validation. *JMIR Mental Health*. Advance online publication. doi:10.2196/19824

Wongkoblap, A., Vadillo, M. A., & Curcin, V. (2018). A multilevel predictive model for detecting social network users with depression. In *IEEE International Conference on Healthcare Informatics (ICHI)* (pp. 130-135). 10.1109/ICHI.2018.00022

Wongkoblap, A., Vadillo, M. A., & Curcin, V. (2021). Deep Learning With Anaphora Resolution for the Detection of Tweeters With Depression: Algorithm Development and Validation Study. *JMIR Mental Health*, *8*(8), e19824. doi:10.2196/19824 PMID:34383688

Wu, M. Y., Shen, C. Y., Wang, E. T., & Chen, A. L. (2020). A deep architecture for depression detection using posting, behavior, and living environment data. *Journal of Intelligent Information Systems*, *54*(2), 225–244. doi:10.100710844-018-0533-4

Yang, L., Jiang, D., Xia, X., Pei, E., Oveneke, M. C., & Sahli, H. (2017). Multimodal measurement of depression using deep learning models. In *Proceedings of the 7th Annual Workshop on Audio/Visual Emotion Challenge* (pp. 53-59). 10.1145/3133944.3133948

Yang, W., & Mu, L. (2015). GIS analysis of depression among Twitter users. *Applied Geography (Sevenoaks, England)*, *60*, 217–223. doi:10.1016/j.apgeog.2014.10.016

Yarkoni, T. (2010). Personality in 100,000 words: A large-scale analysis of personality and word use among bloggers. *Journal of Research in Personality*, *44*(3), 363–373. doi:10.1016/j.jrp.2010.04.001 PMID:20563301

Yazdavar, A. H., Al-Olimat, H. S., Ebrahimi, M., Bajaj, G., Banerjee, T., Thirunarayan, K., ... Sheth, A. (2017). Semi-supervised approach to monitoring clinical depressive symptoms in social media. In *Proceedings of the IEEE/ACM International Conference on Advances in Social Networks Analysis and Mining* (pp. 1191-1198). 10.1145/3110025.3123028

Zucco, C., Calabrese, B., & Cannataro, M. (2017). Sentiment analysis and affective computing for depression monitoring. In *IEEE international conference on bioinformatics and biomedicine* (pp. 1988–1995). BIBM. doi:10.1109/BIBM.2017.8217966

Chapter 14
Assessing Together the Trends in Newspaper Topics and User Opinions:
A Co-Evolutionary Approach

Elise Noga-Hartmann
ETIS UMR 8051, CY Cergy Paris University, France

Dimitris Kotzinos
ETIS UMR 8051, CY Cergy Paris University, France

ABSTRACT

This chapter proposes and explores all features of a model capable of capturing trends within large corpora of texts. Not only are trends assessed through a numerical index, but they are displayed alongside rhetorical and attitudinal information on all topics concerned for all relevant epochs. This way, trend evolutions can be analyzed in the light of wordings and thinking evolutions, thus allowing for a co-evolutionary approach to trend assessing. Each and every step is methodologically explained, as well as the interactions between them. Variations and adaptations are also discussed for a greater adaptability of the model to all use cases.

INTRODUCTION

The news is a window with a view to and from many layers of the society. The multiple forces that concur to its formation, through a relentless battle for prevalence, leave behind them a great deal of clues. Once collected, they can be used to understand the state of the world at a certain time or over some period. Whether these forces are market based (a newspaper has to sell copies and generate clicks to survive financially), opinion based (angles are chosen to carry editorial orientations) or truth based (one can consider journalism as an attempt to an objective description of reality and its events), they meddle, up until an article is written, submitted and published. From there on, they are exposed to public opinion.

DOI: 10.4018/978-1-7998-9594-7.ch014

This precious encounter between news makers and news consumers is where trends emerge, sometimes from as little as a small semantic shift.

User perception on the other hand, is formed based on personal beliefs, news posts and societal influence and changes over time, even for the same topic. When these personal opinions on a specific topic converge, they form (opinion) trends. Trends can be defined as elements that generate or are subjected to a peak of interest of a certain group of individuals at a certain time ("To be one of the words, subjects, or names that is being mentioned most often on a social media website or a news website at a particular time", according to the Cambridge Dictionary). If one wants to study trends, numerous questions arise: further than the object of the trend, forces behind its advent bear very insightful information about societal context at that time. Doing so automatically, prevents from risks linked to a subjective analysis. In the current work, user opinions are extracted, as they appear in user comments, at the corresponding articles of popular newspapers, like the New York Times. This would allow to present a model combining metadata analysis and topic modeling (from the articles) and opinion mining and trend computation (from the comments) in order to offer an efficient framework for understanding the interplay between articles and the evolution of opinions in the society. Based on newspaper articles, their comments and tweets the articles are quoted in, the model aims at recognizing trends, qualifying their momentary importance and their duration. Once a trend is identified, the model provides useful information on both parties (news provider and news consumer) involved, thus enabling it to inform about its emergence.

The goal of this work is to identify, report and explore the interplay between the articles that appear in traditional media, like newspapers, and the interactions of the people online who either react to the articles by commenting or discussing them on social media platforms. The main objective is to understand the evolution of the topics covered and if this evolution is in any way correlated between the two.

BACKGROUND

Prior to technically construct the model that will be discussed in this chapter, some theoretical foundations have had to be laid. Assuming a large enough but fixed number of topics, for a newspaper like the New York Times, it can be hypothesized that all topics are discussed at all time in a minimal form. Hence, all regular subtopics aren't changing the words distribution within the way every topic is covered (even more so if data are preprocessed to remove under- and over- occurring words). Henceforth no punctual trend can emerge without a variation in either the way the topic is addressed or the way it is perceived (although the latter would end up influencing the former). The model proposed here is able to capture these variations. Whilst they, on their own, can enhance the comprehension of all events by identifying the link between semantic and attitudes' shifts, a whole new dimension is brought to the analysis by the introduction of the trend index. Being able to quantify both in duration and in valence one of those shifts adds to society's understanding of the way discussions emerge. To examine trends as defined hereabove (that is to say peaks of interest in online discussions/publications), it is necessary to observe shifts in relatively short time slices. Scaling down in time, while it might soften punctual trends, will show general dynamics and lead to deduce relative importance of a topic over the others. Hence, the temporal component of such an analysis is both key to the understanding of evolving power balances and a tool to displace the examination's perspective.

To capture both semantic, attitude and trends shifts through time, the present model combines two text analysis techniques and an indexation one. Although it has three layers of calculations, the first two are closely related and require to operate together, whereas the third one will add an angle of analysis while being able to work autonomously. This model uses algorithms of topic modeling and opinion mining, as well as a formula that builds an index out of metadata. It can thus be divided in two parts Figure 1, below, shows its general structure.

The first part of the model allows for a joint representation of rhetorical and perception shifts. It combines topic modeling and opinion mining. Thus, introducing a dynamic way to define the target of the automated opinion mining techniques, which subsequently can be used to extract opinions and/or sentiments around a topic from texts and user comments associated with the texts. Text corpora coming from newspaper archives are a good example for applying such techniques because they combine the description of topics in the form of long or short articles in a daily basis over long time periods with the ability to provide user (reader) opinions on them in the form of letters or more recently web site comments. This combination provides new ways to look into the information and to identify relationships between the evolution of the topics' descriptions and this of opinions.

A temporal topic modeling algorithm is applied to a large corpus of press articles (6,969 articles, belonging to 24 time slices, with a vocabulary size of 3,445 after lemmatization) in order to extract a list of topics, their evolutions through following epochs, articles and vocabulary associated with each and every one of them. All words used to describe a topic at different times will be used in the final representation to capture and understand semantic shifts. Given a list of articles for a topic at an epoch, all the user-generated comments around them are gathered and analyzed. Using opinion mining, each is given a sentiment rating (from very negative to very positive). Theses scores, once aggregated, allow to follow closely attitude shifts around the studied topic.

Figure 1. General structure of the co-evolutionary model

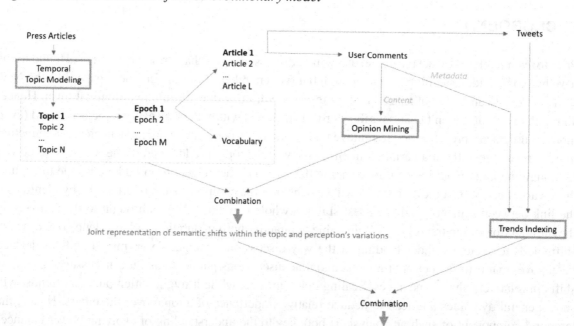

Results of these two analyses are then combined to obtain a joint representation of semantic and attitude variations for all topics through all epochs. That is for the first part of the model. The second one aims at extracting a measure of importance of a given topic at a certain time, that is to say, understand how trending has been a particular combination of vocabulary in public opinion at a given period. Whether this trend is negative, neutral or positive in the climate of opinion can be distinguished on a case-by-case basis, once all results are rendered by the model.

In order to construct the trend index, all tweets quoting each article of each epoch for each topic are added to the database, and their metadata, alongside comments metadata, are being mobilized. Hence, user comments' metadata (both the number of comments on the topic and the time frame over which the topic has been commented) and metrics from social media (the number of tweets mentioning the article -not counting those from the NYT accounts- and average numbers of retweets and likes) are at the core of this second part of the model. Their multiple facets are used as indicators of momentary and temporal importance, weighted and combined into a score over ten. Combined with the previously obtained representation, it allows the framework to analyze co-evolutionarily the rise and fall of trends in newspapers' topics towards which this model is intended. This trend index computed for each epoch within a topic gives insights on internal trends; compared with those of other topics, gives insights on the relative importance of one topic amongst the others.

Overall, the evolution and description of topics in a traditional news media outlet is compared with the evolution of opinions/trends of the users/commenters, in order to try to understand the relation and the interplay among the two. Correlations and deviations that could signify new ways on how public opinion is formed are targeted within the results.

MAIN FOCUS OF THIS CHAPTER

Topic Modeling

Topic modeling allows the extraction of a topic or topics from a given collection of texts. If the exercise is rather simple for a human being, it requires an understanding of every layer of meaning that can be given to words, which makes it hard for automatic computation. To achieve an efficient computation, on the matter that is of interest here, one needs a strong statistical model, able to overpass polysemous issues and to link topics even though the semantics are slightly switching from one article to another. Time is also at high stakes here, as rhetorical variations within topics need to be monitored through epochs. If the state of the art gives out multiple algorithms able to achieve the needed computation, technical choices have had to be made in order to yield efficient, relevant and appropriate results.

Historically, the first widely used algorithm of topic modeling was introduced in the late 1990's by T. Landauer and S. Dumais (Laundauer & Dumais, 1997) in a series of papers and presentations. The Latent Semantic Analysis (LSA), an extension of the Latent Semantic Indexing (that can be dated back to the late 1980's) proposes to create a vectorial representation of the lexicon used in a text corpus. The main intuition behind this algorithm is to exploit mutual constraints between words of a document collection, based on the idea that the meaning of a text is the sum of the meanings of the words that compose it. This first atemporal method's main flaw was it did not rely on any strong statistical model, a probabilistic version of it was introduced shortly after (Hofmann, 1999). As the interest grew around the field of topic modeling, the most widely used and known algorithm emerged (Blei, Ng, & Jordan,

2001). The Latent Dirichlet Allocation (LDA), apart from being central to topic modeling, has been a prolific basis of reflection for all researchers and the development they brought.

Still, time needed to be taken into account and LDA posed a condition on document exchangeability that prevented it from doing so - as it meant all documents in the training base were drawn from the same pool of topics. This problem was fixed with the introduction of Dynamic Topic Model (DTM) (Blei & Lafferty, 2006). DTM asserts markovian assumptions on state transitions and uses a discrete definition of time, as well as replaces the dirichlet distribution in the generation process by a normal one, averaged on the distribution of the previous time sequence. It also suppresses the hypothesis of document exchangeability posed in LDA, that would otherwise imply that all documents are drawn from a single topic pool (hence neglecting the evolution over time). The removal of this exchangeability assumption allows to model underlying topics' dynamics and underlines the importance of the sequential organization of the documents. Thus, one needs to determine time slicing for the corpora (in their example, authors decided on a yearly sequencing). Figure 2 presents a graphical representation of DTM - which appears as a serialized LDA, expanded by β and α - to capture evolution over time.

Figure 2. Graphical model representation of DTM extracted from (Blei & Lafferty, 2006), originally described "Each topic's natural parameter $\beta_{t,k}$ evolves over time, together with the mean parameter αt of the logistic normal distribution for the topic proportions"

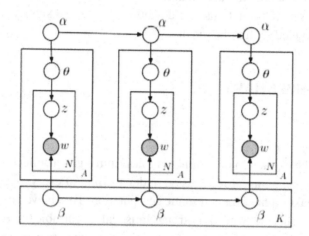

In the field of temporal topic modeling (as opposed to atemporal - according to the importance given to time in the topic modeling process), DTM appears quite as crucial as LDA, and many other algorithms derive from it. Another way of incorporating time in the computation is to consider it as continuous. This assumption is the base for the Topic over Time algorithm (ToT) (Wang & McCallum, 2006). The authors state that topics are responsible for generating both words and timestamps, hence the continuous aspect of time in their model.

Although literature gives a wide variety of algorithms that could be used to perform topic modeling on a database composed of news articles, the model developed here puts emphasis on the evolution and the variations through time. Henceforth, all non-temporal ones - LSA, its probabilistic version and LDA - have to be forsaken. A technical choice has then to be made between DTM and ToT. While a continuous conception of time is appealing, ToT is not modeling changes of words within topics through time *per se* and as phrased in (Hall, Jurafsky, & Manning, 2008): « the beta distributions in Topics over Time are relatively inflexible» (whereas they also state that «the Dynamic Topic Model penalizes large changes from year to year»). The Dynamic Topic Model algorithm, as implemented for (Greene & Cross, 2017) - slightly modified, in order to correct file outcomes and to adapt it to the pipeline structure created for the co-evolutionary model presented here - presents the crushing advantage of producing a list of words per topic per epoch, as well as a classification per topic of each article.

Table 1. Overall column for topic #1, revolving around the US presidency

Rank	Overall
1	biden
2	president
3	administration
4	washington
5	house
6	white
7	american
8	plan
9	federal
10	right

Therefore, DTM is to be used in the proposed implementation of the present model. Further discussions can argue in favor of the usage of any other temporal topic modeling algorithm. Even atemporal, given one finds a different way to adapt their computation to the time constraint - although this would be much more debatable. As presented in the general overview of the model, the chosen algorithm needs to take as entries a corpus of news articles and to produce a list of topics, which are described by epoch by a series of words (their individual vocabulary, used to monitor rhetorical variations in the treatment of a particular topic between two epochs) and a way to classify all entry-articles with a pair of topic-epoch stamps (used to build a bridge with the opinion mining part and the trends indexing).

Using a temporal topic modeling algorithm such as DTM on a wide base of timed short texts produces numerous files. Amongst them, for every topic, a table is created, in which, for each epoch where the topic is present, a list of the ten most relevant words, ordered by relevance, is displayed (other files created are used to connect the different parts of the model, such as a list of the most relevant articles for each epoch within each topic). This table also contains an "overall" column, made of the most relevant words for the topic, all epochs combined. The overall column can be used to establish what is the topic about. Table 1 gives an example of such a column, on a topic labeled as #1 after computation, that follows all things related to the US presidency (see words such as Biden - Joe Biden, 46th president of the United States of America-, white and house - the White House, official residence and workplace of the president -, administration and federal - setting the fact that this topic concerns matters of politics at the US federal level).

However useful this column is for human understanding of the stakes of each topic, it will not be used in any other way in the model. Focus will rather be on the per epoch columns, each labeled with a window number. Continuing with topic #1, Table 2 gives an overview of the results obtained with DTM. A line "Dates" was manually added in order to facilitate comprehension. Only four windows are being displayed here, for the sake of readability. The choice has been made to slice time into windows covering two consecutive days, to adapt to the available database and observe with the utmost precision all variations. Any other slicing is practicable, according to one's objectives and database. It would be part of the future development of this work to experiment with different time windows to understand and demonstrate the different granularity of the various topics over time and the possible effects of the different choices.

Table 2. Overview of the semantic evolution within topic #1 for a sample of epochs, treating of US presidency

Rank	Window 1	Window 2	Window 4	Window 5
Dates	Jul. 3 - Jul. 4	Jul. 5 - Jul. 6	Jul. 9 - Jul. 10	Jul. 11 - Jul. 12
1	biden	biden	biden	white
2	president	house	american	statue
3	meet	white	plan	house
4	family	day	family	take
5	house	holiday	president	robert
6	job	celebration	administration	south
7	worker	july	illinois	director
8	surfside	president	rally	season
9	white	independence	college	removed
10	independence	pandemic	support	gave

The semantic evolution shown through epochs in Table 2 follows quite precisely the events of the month of July in the United States. The first epoch (or window), running from July 3rd to July 4th, echoes the meeting between the President and families of victims of the collapse of a building in Surfside (Florida) - collapse that happened on the 24th of June - as well as the celebration of Independence Day (4th of July, national day of the United States). The second window tells the story of how the pandemic weights in on this year's Independence Day celebrations at the White House. The fourth epoch (9th - 10th of July) recounts the first stop in Illinois of Joe Biden as President. He notably visited a college in Crystal Lake - where he presented a support plan for working families with children to be able to send them to college -, and Trump supporters organized a rally nearby to protest. Lastly, window 5, shown in Table 2, follows a declaration by Joe Biden, where he cheered the removal of a statue of confederate general Robert E. Lee in Charlottesville (Virginia).

Ultimately, the Dynamic Topic Models algorithm is able to identify broad topics within a large database of short texts and to then pinpoint small scale semantic changes in the way they are addressed.

Opinion Mining

Simultaneously to the topic modeling part, the opinion mining can be achieved on the database of all comments retrieved alongside their corresponding articles. Then one can begin to use an algorithm to classify the emotions conveyed, and their valence. Multiple challenges arise here, the main one residing in being able to understand users' opinion based on short to very short text (sometimes as short as a simple "YES"). This part of the model will help establish how a particular subject was perceived at a given time according to the vocabulary used to describe it. One will be specifically interested in the evolution of the distribution of the opinions gathered.

Opinion mining and sentiment analysis have raised interest amongst the scientific community as early as 1966, when Philip Stone first described his General Inquirer system, considered to be the first attempt at textual sentiment extraction (Stone, Dunphy, Smith, & Ogilvie, 1966). First machine learning approaches were developed nearly 40 years later, motivated by the sentiment lexicon proposed in (Pang, Lee, & Vaithyanathan, 2002). In the meantime, different approaches have been explored, tried and used, with variable results in terms of accuracy. They all fell under the category of manual classification, whether the emphasis was placed on nouns, adverbs or verbs. For a more accurate description of the field between its beginnings and the introduction of machine learning, one can read (Kaur & Gupta, 2013). On the whole, context has always been, and continues to be, a broad challenge in the field.

With the introduction of artificial intelligence in the domain of opinion mining, a consequent number of papers were published, applying and testing machine learning techniques to it. (Sidorov & Miranda-Jiménez, 2012), for example, are using and comparing Naïve Bayes, Support Vector Machines and Decision Trees. Generally speaking, all AI methods used in sentiment classification derive from one of three categories: supervised, unsupervised and case-based. Analysis can be run on document level, paragraph (or short text) level and feature level (one can think here of a review of a smartphone, qualifying differently its battery capacities and the quality of the pictures it takes). A precise comparative of a great number of machine learning techniques that have been applied to this field can be found in (Rashid, Anwer, Iqbal, & Sher, 2013). One of the most used solution for short text sentiment classification was first presented in 2010, in (Thelwall, Buckley, Paltoglou, Cai, & Kappas, 2010). Toping most of the pre-existing methods, SentiStrength shows human accuracy on short text, so much that it is used by the famous user rating website TripAdvisor. Finally, hybrid combinations of methods are able to perform well on this matter, such as part-of-speech (manual marking of grammatical components of the text) combined to a machine learning or a lexicon-based approach, as shown in (Meddeb, Lavandier, & Kotzinos, 2020).

Working with short texts really narrows down the number of options available to perform efficiently opinion mining. On average, user-generated comments on press articles are about five hundred signs long, a majority of them stands between two hundred and fifty and seven hundred signs, although they can be as short as two signs or exceed a thousand signs. These features bring them closer to comments on rating website such as TripAdvisor. Seeing the human-like performances of SentiStrength (Thelwall, Buckley, Paltoglou, Cai, & Kappas, 2010) on short texts, its usage by a behemoth of the field and the great variety of options provided by its authors, the choice was made to pursue with this solution. As people tend to express contrasted opinion in developed argumentations, the dual form of the algorithm has been chosen to evaluate sentiments in the comments. This form gives out two ratings, each corresponding to the most extreme value encountered in both positive and negative evaluation of the text. For example, if a user states that he or she likes one part of the topic discussed in the article but that he or she absolutely hates another one, the algorithm will evaluate this comment as with a great valence in negativity and a somewhat important in positivity.

In this manner, all comments are graded either before, in parallel or after the topic modeling step. The emphasis has to be put, during the maneuver, on keeping track of which comments belong to which article, so that when articles are classified between topics and epochs, all aggregation calculations can be run smoothly. For a given lot of articles, corresponding to a certain epoch within a certain topic, all ratings attributed to their comments are counted by value, on a scale from minus five (very negative) to plus five (very positive), and normalized, in order to be able to display the comments' sentiment distribution.

Once both computations are complete, one can begin to parallelize results in order to get a clean display. This combination ensues a joint representation of semantic shifts and perception variations within each topic throughout epochs. Henceforth, a visual interpretation of results is already possible, as this part of the model is able to produce concrete results autonomously. However, going further and integrating the trends indexing step gives a whole new dimension to the newly obtained data.

Figure 3. Extract of opinion mining results (bars), represented parallelly to a normal distribution (curve)

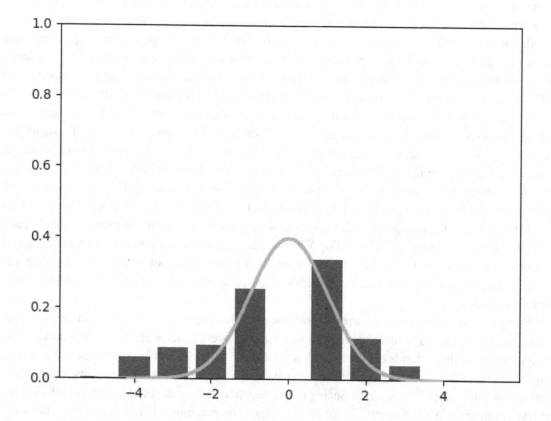

With every rating returned by SentiStrength counted by value and normalized, it is possible to realize visually efficient bar charts. The reduced length of the scale allows for a global visualization at once, and a good perception of the distribution of opinions. Figure 3 is a good sample of what can be obtained this way. It also shows how the ratings tend to follow a normal distribution. Two remarks can be drawn from this point. Firstly, the imperfectness of this following is proof of the existence of tendencies within public opinion: there is not a single vocabulary at a single epoch used to describe a single topic that raises perfectly balanced reactions, some are viewed more positively, some more negatively, some are more polarizing, some stun public opinion in such a way that observed distributions have become too far from a normal one to even think of creating a link between the two in the first place. Secondly, being able to observe an average behavior (*i.e.*, resemblance to the normal distribution) will largely contribute to the analysis. Henceforth, all empirically observed distributions are to be compared to this reference and variations will be identified much easily.

Figure 4. Extract of opinion mining results for a topic on covid vaccines

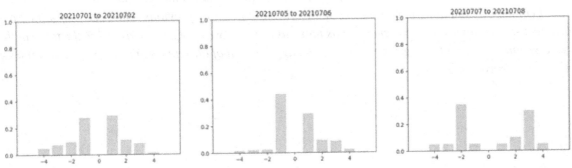

On that matter, Figure 4 is an illustration of some variations that can be observed. If the first window represented shows a somewhat normal distribution (although it may be said that public opinion is slightly displaced to neutral negativity - as the extremely positive values are lessen and the neutral ones are mildly higher than expected), the second and the third ones are representatives of very identifiable shifts. The second epoch relates a displacement to the neutral part of the opinion spectrum. One can observe an almost disappearance of the negative and very negative values, to the benefit of the neutral negative. A possible interpretation of such a phenomenon, without any other information, could be that the associated semantics have stabilized to something rather acceptable for the opinion (i.e., people are getting used to the reality described). They may have already provoked enthusiastic reactions that are not fading with the stabilization. Whatever the case may be, there seems to be no strong debate within public opinion on this particular subject, expressed in this particular form, at this particular time. On the opposite, the third epoch shown here is paradigmatic of an argumentative and nuanced debate. Not only more extreme positions represent the majority of the opinion expressed, but both neutrals have faded. Given the dual form of the algorithm used here, this can only mean that a wide portion of the comments present both a very positive and a marked negative point of view, hence the interpretation in favor of a nuanced debate.

Still, on their own, these opinion graphs are hardly interpretable. Drawing conjectures on public opinion solely based on bar charts is at best borderline. For a more solid and complete analysis, one needs to look at the combination of both hereabove exposed steps, which happens in the next section.

Combination of Topic Modeling and Opinion Mining results

In order to obtain a joint representation of rhetorical and perception shifts, results from the topic modeling part and from the opinion mining part need to be put in perspective with respect to the timestamps. Figure 5 gives an example of what can be obtained from this parallelization. Not only is the distribution of opinion evaluations put in perspective with the vocabulary for the concerned epoch, but evolutions through time can be monitored. Thus, impacts of a rhetorical shift can be observed directly on the opinion, and the other way around, modifications on the opinion can be interpreted with regards to the vocabularies employed.

Figure 5. Example of joint representation of semantic and attitudes' shifts. DTM discovered a topic around the building that collapsed in Surfside (Florida, near Miami) in late June 2021. Words in the second column are annotated according to their evolution from the previous time slice (+: gained importance; -: lost importance; =: remained as important; none: was not used to describe the topic in the previous time slice). Both bar graphs represent an aggregation of all sentiment ratings of the comments on the associated articles

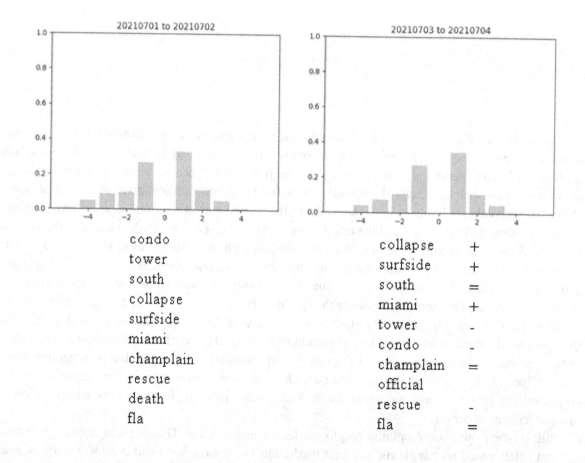

A quick analysis of the results displayed on Figure 5 shows a slight drop in extremely positive attitude, coinciding with the emergence of the word "official" and the loss of importance of the term "rescue" - which could indicate that public opinion started to develop negative feelings as an accusative finger was pointed towards officials and the hope of saving another soul from the collapsed building vanished. This kind of hypothesis could not have been drawn from either one of the parts alone. Nevertheless, another layer can be added to these results, in order to bring out a more complete analysis. Hitherto, all topics are looked as if they had the same importance at all time. Being able to assess a trend indicator would not only permit to rank topics amongst them, but to add some meaningful information to opinion shifts' observations.

Trends Indexing

The last part of the model involves the creation of an index capable of assessing trends. It really is where the model differentiates itself from what can be found in the literature, as it takes into account long-term impacts as well as momentary ones. Knowing which words are used to describe a topic at a given moment, and the reaction of public opinion to those, is not enough to truly understand if that said vocabulary shift has had a meaningful impact or was simply an inconsequential intellectual verbose effect. The ability to gauge how trending has been a certain topic expressed in certain words -while raising certain reactions from the opinion- allows to measure that effect. The fact that the model computes the index over time, epoch after epoch, enhances all the more the impact of the analysis that can be drawn from the results. Finally, a careful consideration has to be given to the choice of the coefficients, with regards to both the aim of the computation and the specificities of the data.

Literature contains many references on trends finding. However, almost all of them are solely focusing on vocabulary to determine what part of a topic was trending (whether it is in general or according to time). These works rely on topic modeling algorithm, just like (Shiryaev, Dorofeev, Fedorov, Gagarina, & Zaycev, 2017) in which LDA is used to analyze technical knowledge domain in order to capture, through important keywords, multiple trends in different fields. As reported in (Mathew, Agrawal, & Menzies, 2018), "text mining methods can detect large scale trends within [the software research] community", and this type of work is extremely important for researchers to get some perspective on their field and its evolutions.

However, few works relate to trend mining based on metrics derived from user-generated comments or shares. Some, as presented in (Crisci, Grasso, Nesi, & al, 2018), have used such metrics to understand trends and predict the evolution of their related subjects. More specifically, Crisci and al. have selected a set of metrics to characterize trends among tweets, such as "volume of tweets, the distribution of linguistic elements, the volume of distinct users involved in tweeting, and the sentiment analysis of tweets". Notwithstanding how close this type of research can be from the model developed here, there is not, to the best of the authors' knowledge, in the actual literature, any work that utilizes a time component in the metrics selected to assess trends.

The third (and last) part of the model is designed to enhance the understanding acquired through the first two. It consists in creating a trend index, based on several metrics, from both comments and tweets quoting the articles from the database, so as to get a deep understanding of the resonance of the semantic and attitudes shifts formerly identified. Among the metrics used, and that is truly where the innovation stands in this model, some are directly linked to time. In such manner, a distinction between momentary and long-lasting craze can be operated, leading to a more precise trend ranking. This consideration is based on the idea that if a topic is really trending, not only does it raise a lot of comments, but they spread through time, as long as the trend remains. This is visible in both user-generated comment on the website, as well as in content creation on twitter, and discussions on the platform.

Metrics

Metrics were chosen in order to construct equivalencies between comments-based and tweets-based metadata. To that end, four families were assembled: simple count, average interest, maximum engagement and maintenance over time. Thus, comments and tweets are counted, replies to the comments and retweets are averaged, the maximum number of recommendations for a single comment and of favs/likes for a single comment is taken and the total period during which articles were commented and during which articles were quoted in tweets are finally computed.

Each and every one of these metrics is of some specific interest for the present object of study. They are listed below, per family, and commented with regard to the specificities of the context under which the model was developed.

1. **Simple Counts**: The number of comments can be a good indicator *per se*. It allows to measure the interest that was raised by the article - more comments are to be found under articles that are part of a hot topic, ones that echo public opinion's interests. However, it has to be considered with a certain distance because some articles are not available for comment on the newspaper's website (due to moderation/editorial choices). This last remark is not applicable to the number of tweets, as every article has a link and can be shared on social media. Though, the rest of the analysis remains, except that a tweet represents a stronger engagement, as it is a public statement of the topic on a platform where users are easily identifiable and recognizable (other people have to dig more to find a precise person's comment on the newspaper's website than on Twitter), it is also a click further than just writing in the comments section (the number of click necessary to accomplish an action is a recognized metric for engagement).

2. **Average Interest**: The number of replies gives an indication on the importance of the debate of which the article is a part. It also quantifies public opinion engagement towards this debate (in the sense that the number of steps between the notification of the article and the sending of a reply to another user's comment is significant and that people will not go all the way through for some random topic). It makes then a lot of sense to average it over all articles of the said topic at the said epoch, to ensure a global level of highly engaged interactions. The same goes for the averaged number of retweets: it gives an indication on the importance of the debate - through communities' engagement -, but has to be averaged as some user centered communities tend to be more active than others.

3. **Maximum Engagement**: The number of recommendations gives another indication on real engagement with the topic and the article. Not only does one user have to read the article, he also has to go through the comments' section and get a particularly positive reaction to what is written in order to go a click further and issue the recommendation. As the objective here is not to understand if an article has had only useful comments, the choice has been made to take as a metric the maximum number of recommendations reached by a comment under an article of a said epoch for a said topic. If some could argue that the fav/like option on Twitter is of less consequences than the retweet one, it still gives an insight on effective engagement towards the topic, given that a tweet

that was faved/liked by a user is more likely to appear in one of its followers' timelines tagged "Liked by *username*". This metric is also a popularity measure, as information tends to travel within users' bubbles, one that transcends bubbles can be considered as really popular - hence the use of the maximum, the goal here is not to approximate bubbles' sizes.

4. **Maintenance over Time**: The total period over which comments and tweets have run are the last two metrics taken into account. They give a great idea on the importance of the topic in the long run. They help distinguish between momentary fame (or topics becoming hot because not a single hot topic was addressed at the same epoch or in the database) and trends rooted in public opinion's list of high concerns. A popular topic will fuel the conversation for much longer than a simple fad effect. Looking at how long the conversation was maintained enables a reflection based on numbered and timed components, that gives a more precise analysis because it has this additional layer.

All these metrics are then combined into an equation in order to create the trend index that will be used in the final render. Depending on one's ambition and/or research subject, multiple formulas can be considered:

Formula A:

$$T_{index} = a * (Nb_{comments} + Avg_{replies} + Max_{recommendations} + Period_{comments}) + (1 - a) * (Nb_{tweets} + Avg_{Fav} + Period_{tweets})$$

1.

This form allows for a weighting between tweets and comments importance in the construction of the index. One might favorize it if there is an apparent gap between both database quality.

Formula B:

$$T_{index} = a * (Nb_{comments} + Nb_{tweets}) + b * (Avg_{replies} + Avg_{Fav}) + c * (Max_{recommendations} + Max_{RT}) + d * (Period_{comments} + Period_{tweets})$$

2.

This form allows for a weighting per family. One might prefer it if timed metrics are more relevant to one's analysis than static ones (if the interest of one's research is oriented toward momentary or lasting trends), or if one is more interested in interaction than in engagement.

Formula C:

$$T_{index} = a * (x_1 * Nb_{comments} + y_1 * Avg_{replies} + z_1 * Max_{recommendations} + g_1 * Period_{comments}) + (1 - a) * (x_2 * Nb_{tweets} + y_2 * Avg_{Fav} + z_2 * Max_{RT} + g_2 * Period_{tweets})$$

3.

This third form is a combination of both previous ones, allowing for a complete freedom in weightings. Once all calculations are done, and numbers are normalized, the trend index will appear (one whatever scale was decided, here numbers have been normalized to form a grade between zero and ten). A computation at the epoch scale will enable to parallelize the index with results from the previous steps of the model, however one can also compute per epoch at the topic scale (averaging over the whole topic) in order to rank topics per importance at each epoch, or, finally, one can decide to compute a single leaderboard computing at the topic scale, averaging over all epochs within each topic.

The diversity of formulas proposed for this part of the model gives a wide range of configurations for testing and comparing part-specific results. Hereunder will be measured indexes for an all-neutral configuration (reference scenario, α=0.5, a=b=c=d=x_1=x_2=y_1=y_2=z_1=z_2=g_1=g_2=1), a comment-oriented configuration (scenario #2, α=0.8, all other equal to 1), a tweet-oriented configuration (scenario #3, α=0.2, all other equal to 1), a momentary-trend-oriented configuration (scenario #4, α = 0.5 ; a, b, c, x_1, x_2, y_1, y_2 z_1, z_2 are given high values ; d, g_1, g_2 are given low values) and a long-term-trend-oriented configuration (scenario #5, α = 0.5 ; a, b, c, x_1, x_2, y_1, y_2 z_1, z_2 are given low values ; d, g_1, g_2 are given high values) that will also be tested in an extreme form (scenario #6, α = 0.5 ; a, b, c, x_1, x_2, y_1, y_2 z_1, z_2 are given very low values ; d, g_1, g_2 are given very high values).

Figure 6. Comparison between all three formulas for each scenario mentioned (reference = neutral, 2 = comment-oriented, 3 = tweet-oriented, 4 = momentary-oriented, 5 = long-term, 6 = extreme long-term), noted *Formula*_*Scenario*, e.g., A_2 stands for all results obtained through the use of the first formula -weighting with α- with factor values described in the comment-oriented scenario. Redundant data have been deleted (e.g., in scenario #2, the first and third formulas - respectively A and C - are giving the same results) for clarity

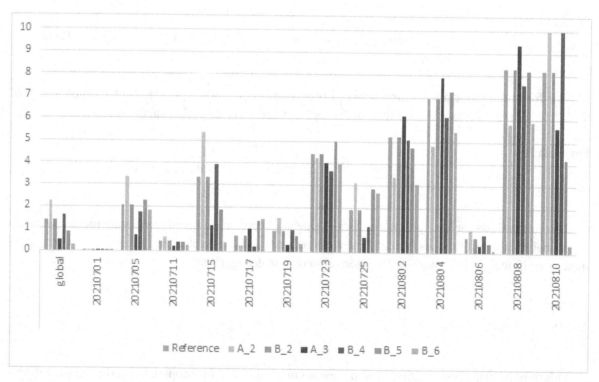

This comparison, visible on Figure 6, shows at first glance that, if globally all formulas in all tests tend to stick to a low/high tendency, some seem to have certain behavior that emphasis on the importance of adapting the formula to the desired analysis. B_6, for example, that gives extremely high importance to temporal metrics is regularly out of trend. At the epoch beginning on the 10th of August 2021, when all other formulas are giving a grade above four out of ten, it is giving a very low trend index to the topic, whereas it scores the highest for the epoch beginning on the 17th of July 2021. This can be explained by, for the first case, a high number of comments and/or tweets concentrated on very few days (A_2 being really high and A_3 being relatively low in comparison, one might expect higher figures for all comments-related metrics). For the second case, B_4 scores the lowest, A_3 scores higher than A_2, so there has to be a higher number of tweets than of comments, both remaining quite low, and these are relatively well spread over time. Once again, and since the ranking totally differs from one formula to another, this comparison is really proof that both formulas and factors have to be adapted to one's database and objectives. However, whatever choice is made, the algorithm is capable of producing a coherent index that will fit perfectly with the rest of the model, and that will permit to obtain the co-evolutionary approach to trends assessing aimed.

Table 3. Top 15 topic trend ranking, as per all three formulas - changes induced by the third formula are highlighted in italics

Rank	1	2	3	4	5	6	7	8	9	10	11	12	13	14	15
Per A	19	16	8	15	7	14	20	10	2	5	17	1	4	11	9
Per B	19	16	8	15	7	14	20	10	2	5	17	1	4	11	9
Per C	19	16	8	15	*14*	*10*	*5*	*17*	2	*7*	*20*	1	*9*	4	*11*

Changes between formulas and factors choices can also be observed on a higher scale, when computing ranking amongst topics (all epochs combined). This topic level trend indicator is visible on Table 3. A and B are displaying the same values as all a, b, c and d were equal to 1 and changes were introduced within the values of the third equation factors. Still, these changes can be considered as minor, given that they are mostly inversion (see topics #9, #4 and #11, at the thirteenth, fourteenth and fifteenth positions), although the seventh topic loses five positions in the transition. This type of information about the data gives a hint about an overall ranking of the topics detected, which can prove itself useful, depending on one's objectives.

Another representation that can be extracted from this part of the model lies somewhere between the two mentioned hereabove. It is neither within a topic assessing trend index per epoch, nor outside every topic giving a global rank. This third representation ranks topics periodically, each epoch has a trend index for each topic represented in it and a ranking is possible on this basis. An example of such results is presented on Figure 7. Not all topics are present at all epochs, so lines can be discontinuous, nevertheless it gives a comprehensive understanding of global trends evolution. Some topics are to remain afloat whilst other will only have fifteen minutes of glory and fade away for the rest of the time slice studied - this contrast tends to be more pronounced with a combination of factors favorizing temporal metrics. All in all, this type of representation can be used to identify strong discontinuances to dig into with the co-evolutionary illustration provided by the whole model. For instance, on Figure 7, topic #2 (Covid, delta variant and vaccination) is of some importance throughout the whole period, except in the epoch starting on the 15th of July 2021, where it suddenly drops. Multiple hypothesis can be drawn from hereon, that would be verified or invalidated thanks to the precise in-topic results of the model. One could wonder whether the angle used to describe the subject suddenly changed and did not please nor interest public opinion, or whether numerous topics gained a sudden (and brief, as topic #2 goes back to its regular trend index values two epochs later) interest (did some event happen on that day? Did the newspaper try to push the discussion on some other topics? Did other topics become hotter due to a semantic change?).

Figure 7. Evolution of topics #1 to #4's importance rank according to trend index through time. Topics refer to: 1- US Presidency 2- Covid (delta variant and vaccination) 3- Others (part of the daily briefing) 4- Tokyo Olympics

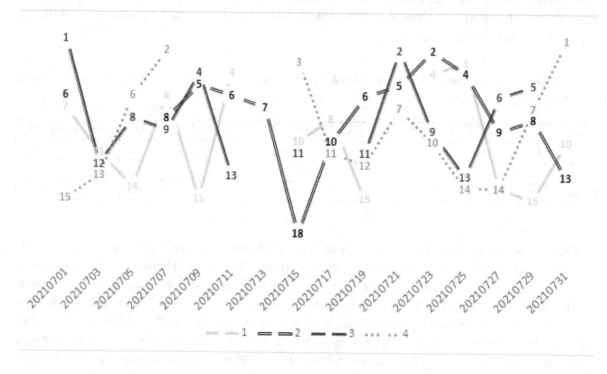

This last part of the model offers various tools to add up to the analysis began with the topic modeling and the opinion mining parts. Once gathered in a single representative form, the co-evolutionary approach in trends assessing takes shape and is ready for human (or automated - however this could quickly be proved limited) analysis.

With the completion of the trend indexing step of the model, all results are ready for a final combination, according to topics and epochs. This last step allows to visualize all at once attitude, semantic and trend evolutions within each topic. After reviewing how these results can be rendered, one might wonder about this model's adaptability to slightly different research subjects and areas for improvement, that will be discussed before the general conclusion.

SOLUTIONS AND RECOMMENDATIONS

The final combination of all three big steps of the model (topic modeling, opinion mining and trend indexing) is all about displaying altogether their results in order to be able to follow each topic's evolutions through time.

Figure 8. Final form of the results of the model, extracted from topic #1. The trend index was obtained with the neutral form of the formulas, where α=0.5 and all other factors are equal to 1

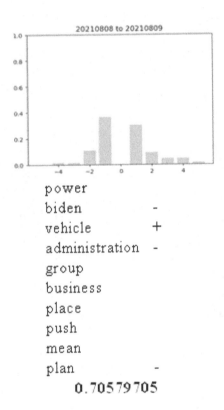

Figure 8 shows an example of such a visualization. For each topic, a picture (jpeg) file is produced grouping all epochs. Each epoch is characterized by its beginning and ending dates, as well as its opinion distribution graph, its vocabulary list (the choice has been made here to color words according to their position in the list of words from the previous epoch, marking their gain or loss of importance within the topic or their appearance) and its trend index (of the three formulas discussed earlier, only one result is displayed, as it has been decided to select the neutral form where they all produce the same result, hence inducing a form of neutrality within the analysis - as it might have been detrimental to choose one of the three values displayed were they not to be the same, hence risking missing valuable and relevant data). This way, Figure 8 shows the computation's results for topic #1 (treating of the US presidency) for the period running from the 8th of August 2021 to the 9th of August 2021. This topic at this epoch for this vocabulary was perceived relatively positively by the opinion (there are some very positive comments, ranked five, and no very negative comments - that would have been ranked minus five - compared to the normal distribution, the category "minus three" is underrepresented and the category "four" is over-represented). The words "biden", "administration" and "plan" have lost in importance, whereas the word vehicle, which was already part of the discussion at the previous epoch, gained in importance within the topic. The trend index of 0.7 shows that it had very little impact on the opinion (nor gravity or even meaningfulness, the trend grade being normalized out of ten).

Figure 9. Two following epochs in the final form of the results of the model, extracted from topic #4. The trend index was obtained with the neutral form of the formulas, where α=0.5 and all other factors are equal to 1

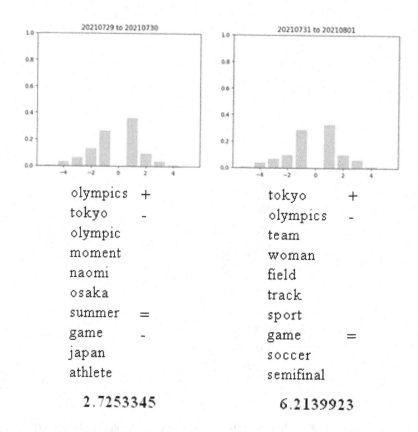

If each epoch can be analyzed on its own, as hereabove, more sense can be extracted through a comparative and evolutive analysis. For instance, Figure 9 shows two following epochs from a single topic result file and more precise conclusions can be drawn from all three aggregates about the state of the world (from an American perspective) at this time. A descriptive glance at these results shows that opinion, although mildly negative, slightly improved between the two epochs (category "4" is absent from the first graph and appears in the second one), that the first epoch refers to the Tokyo Olympics in a "naomi osaka" perspective when the second epoch expresses the subject in terms of "woman soccer semifinal", and that the interest has increased significantly.

Now, what does it say about the New York Times readers' and followers' point of view on the Tokyo Olympics between the 29th of July and the 1st of August 2021? Firstly, the interest in the topic is certain, compared to the index on Figure 8 (0.7), even 2.7 is a mark of relevance to the general discussion. Secondly, the interest increases when the topic is discussed around winning athletes, even more if they appear to be American: Naomi Osaka is a Japanese tennis player who lost in the third round of the Olympics, while the American feminine football team had just qualified for the semifinals (then lost to Canada, but the opinion was unaware of it at this time, the semifinals were played on the 2nd of August).

This way, although a more precise analyze would require information about all commenters, a comparative view of the results has helped highlighting a larger interest (and positive attitude towards) American accomplishments within the readers and followers of the New York Times - which could not have been done analyzing solely the results for one of these epochs.

FUTURE RESEARCH DIRECTIONS

This model is intended as a flexible framework, a global canvas, that can be adapted to the needs of the user. It has been used here on a corpus of nearly 7,000 texts - it could have been larger and was limited by data retrieval issues (i.e., tweets are only freely available for thirty days). It is very scalable, as every part can be run separately (hence not overloading the random-access memory). The main limitation to consider is on the topic modeling part, which is the only aspect of the model that takes into account the whole database at once and performs wide calculations on its data. On that aspect, whereas as originally described, DTM took approximately four hours to run on 30,000 articles (vocabulary size of 15,955) with a 20-topics model (Blei & Lafferty, 2006), ten years later, (Bhadury, Chen, Zhu, & Liu, 2016) used Gibbs sampling and stochastic gradient Langevin dynamic to compute a 1000-topics DTM on a corpora of 2.6 million documents, in less than half an hour.

Some variations, other than scalability-related, can also be considered. One could, *exempli gratia* use another topic modeling algorithm, provided that results ensure the liaison with the comments base for the sake of the rest of the computations ; or adjust the opinion mining part, employing another grading method (SentiStrength has many options in that direction), another algorithm (although the authors would not recommend a by-hand method - working on such large bases) or integrating the tweets in the opinion analysis (using them as part of the comments' base; it was not the case in this implementation because considering how many bots are retweeting news article - especially political ones - the risk of a bias was too large to be taken) ; or operate changes on the trend indexing method, trying different variations around the values of the factors or by mining other metrics (the timed layer is the most prolific in ideas - a potential bias of the present implementation is that a conversation going strongly for a long time and a conversation that stopped and started again much later are worth the same ; this could be done either by associating a negative factor to a long time without comment or by assessing more finely the strength of the debate through time).

This way, the model can be applied to a lot of different databases, as long as public opinion (or an equivalent) can be retrieved one way or another. However, one might not forget to adapt the metrics used if the database used stands too far from the one presented here - e.g., a database that lacks either comments or tweets on the articles should force the remodeling of the trend indexing formula; a database focused on a single time slice should, on another hand, be analyzed through an atemporal topic modeling algorithm, results for all topic could be displayed on the same document, although one might still want to make sure that the said database is large enough to avoid overfitting issues.

CONCLUSION

This chapter presents a new approach to assess trends in newspaper's articles, by trying to establish the coevolution taking place as the articles are published and the users react to them. For this, a model is proposed, combining three algorithmic technologies. First, a topic modeling step, that separates the database into topics (and these topics into epochs) characterized by a certain vocabulary. Then, the comments associated with each article are graded thanks to an opinion mining phase. The combination of these two first steps produces a joint representation of semantic (from the articles' topics) and attitudes (from the users' comments) evolutions through time. Finally, a trend index is computed by extracting information from the comments metadata and the tweets quoting the articles in question. Notably, some of these metrics are giving a temporal dimension to this index, as they take into account, measure and weight the maintenance of the discussion over time. Combined with the mid-computation representation, it produces a co-evolutionary way to analyze trends and their internal components.

Not only does this model allow for a profound understanding of the discussion topics in the society at a given time regarding all, some or one subject, but it is patternable enough to be applied to a wide variety of research subjects. The examples shown have helped outlining the possible existence of a national American chauvinistic sentiment (that may not have gone unnoticed, but still shows in the model results) within a population of readers and followers of the newspaper. A wider analysis of the results permits to see which aspect of the American administration are the most considered by the opinion as well as how it has reacted to slight changes in their handling. This model can pose as a tool for computer scientist as well as for sociologist. The innovative approach proposed here, combined to the variety of fields that could benefit from it is intended to create bridges between research spheres and to profit the largest number.

REFERENCES

Bhadury, A., Chen, J., Zhu, J., & Liu, S. (2016). Scaling up dynamic topic models. *Proceedings of the 25th International Conference on World Wide Web WWW'16* (pp. 381-390). International World Wide Web Steering Committee. 10.1145/2872427.2883046

Blei, D., & Lafferty, J. D. (2006). Dynamic topic models. *Proceedings of the 23rd International Conference on Machine Learning* (pp. 113-120). Association for Computing Machinery. 10.1145/1143844.1143859

Blei, D., Ng, A., & Jordan, M. (2001). Latent dirichlet allocation. *Journal of Machine Learning Research, 3*, 601–608.

Crisci, A., Grasso, V., Nesi, P., Pantaleo, G., Paoli, I., & Zaza, I. (2018). Predicting TV programme audience by using twitter based metrics. *Multimedia Tools and Applications, 77*(10), 12203–12232. doi:10.100711042-017-4880-x

Greene, D., & Cross, J. (2017). Exploring the Political Agenda of the European Parliament Using a Dynamic Topic Modeling Approach. *Political Analysis, 25*(1), 77–94. doi:10.1017/pan.2016.7

Hall, D., Jurafsky, D., & Manning, C. D. (2008). Studying the history of ideas using topic models. *Proceedings of the Conference on Empirical Methods in Natural Language Processing* (pp. 363-371). Association for Computational Linguistics. 10.3115/1613715.1613763

Hofmann, T. (1999). Probabilistic latent semantic indexing. *Proceedings of the 22nd Annual International ACM SIGIR Conference on research and Development in Information Retrieval* (pp. 50-57). Association for Computing Machinery.

Kaur, A., & Gupta, V. (2013). A Survey on Sentiment Analysis and Opinion Mining Techniques. *Journal of Emerging Technologies in Web Intelligence*, *5*(4), 367–371. doi:10.4304/jetwi.5.4.367-371

Laundauer, T., & Dumais, S. T. (1997). A solution to plato's problem: The latent semantic analysis theory of acquisition, induction and representation of knowledge. *Psychological Review*, *104*(2), 211–240. doi:10.1037/0033-295X.104.2.211

Mathew, G., Agrawal, A., & Menzies, T. (2018). Finding Trends in Software Research. *IEEE Transactions on Software Engineering*.

Meddeb, I., Lavandier, C., & Kotzinos, D. (2020). Using Twitter Streams for Opinion Mining: A case study on Airport Noise. *Communications in Computer and Information Science*, *1197*, 145–160. doi:10.1007/978-3-030-44900-1_10

Pang, B., Lee, L., & Vaithyanathan, S. (2002). Thumbs up? Sentiment Classification using Machine Learning Techniques. *Proceedings of the Empirical Methods on Natural Language Processing*, 79-86.

Rashid, A., Anwer, N., Iqbal, M., & Sher, M. (2013). A survey paper: Areas, techniques and challenges of opinion mining. *International Journal of Computer Science Issues*, *10*(2), 18–32.

Shiryaev, A. P., Dorofeev, A. V., Fedorov, A. R., Gagarina, L. G., & Zaycev, V. V. (2017). LDA models for finding trends in technical knowledge domain. *2017 IEEE Conference of Russian Young Researchers in Electrical and Electronic Engineering*, 551-554. 10.1109/EIConRus.2017.7910614

Sidorov, G., & Miranda-Jiménez, S. (2012). Empirical Study of Machine Learning BAsed Approach for Opinion Mining in Tweets. In I. Batyrshin & M. Gonzalez Mendoza (Eds.), Lecture Notes in Computer Science: Vol. 7629. *Advances in Artificial Intelligence. MICAI 20212* (pp. 1–14). Springer.

Stone, P., Dunphy, D., Smith, M., & Ogilvie, D. (1966). *The General Inqiurer - A computer approach to content analysis*. MIT Press.

Thelwall, M., Buckley, K., Paltoglou, G., Cai, G., & Kappas, A. (2010). Sentiment strength detection in short informal text. *Journal of the American Society for Information Science and Technology*, *61*(12), 2544–2558. doi:10.1002/asi.21416

Wang, X., & McCallum, A. (2006). Topics over time: A non-markov continuous time model of topical trends. *Proceedings of the 12th ACM SIGKDD International Conference on Knowledge Discovery and Data Mining* (pp. 424-433). Association for Computing Machinery. 10.1145/1150402.1150450

KEY TERMS AND DEFINITIONS

Attitude: A person's or a group of person's feelings towards a subject. Attitudes have an impact on and are reflected in individual or group behavior.

Engagement: A measure of the importance of something for someone in terms of how much energy this person is capable to invest in this object of interest.

Polysemous: Quality of a word that has multiple meanings (e.g., light).

Semantic Shift: Modification over time in the vocabulary used to describe a specific object.

Time Slicing: Manually cutting a database into portions of the same duration.

Trend: An object receiving a lot of attention over a given period of time.

Valence: Measure of the magnitude of an emotion. Rage has a more important valence than frustration.

Chapter 15
Sentiment Analysis and Stance Detection in Turkish Tweets About COVID-19 Vaccination

Doğan Küçük
Gazi University, Turkey

Nursal Arıcı
iD https://orcid.org/0000-0002-4505-1341
Gazi University, Turkey

ABSTRACT

Public health surveillance has gained more importance recently due the global COVID-19 pandemic. It is important to track public opinions and positions on social media automatically, so that this information can be used to improve public health. Sentiment analysis and stance detection are two social media analysis methods that can be applied to health-related social media posts for this purpose. In this chapter, the authors perform sentiment analysis and stance detection in Turkish tweets about COVID-19 vaccination. A sentiment- and stance-annotated Turkish tweet dataset about COVID-19 vaccination is created. Different machine learning approaches (SVM and Random Forest) are applied on this dataset, and the results are compared. Widespread COVID-19 vaccination is claimed to be useful in order to cope with this pandemic. Therefore, results of automatic sentiment and stance analysis on Twitter posts on COVID-19 vaccination can help public health professionals during their decision-making processes.

INTRODUCTION

The novel Coronavirus Disease 2019 (COVID-19) pandemic is a global pandemic that has affected many people and countries. Many studies are being published in medical journals based on patient examinations. People are also expressing their ideas and opinions about the pandemic on social media like Twitter, Facebook, Instagram, and Reddit. There are also studies that publish social media datasets about the COVID-19 pandemic. In addition to the pandemic itself, social media users are expressing

DOI: 10.4018/978-1-7998-9594-7.ch015

their opinions about various aspects of the pandemic as well. For instance, they are expressing their ideas about using face masks, about social distancing, COVID-19 vaccines, remote working and online education in order to prevent the spread of the disease.

Automatic social media analysis can be used to extract useful information from the related datasets and social media platforms about the pandemic. In several studies, it is pointed out that social media analysis can facilitate automatic public health surveillance and can provide useful and timely information for public health professionals (Küçük et al., 2017; Edo-Osagie et al., 2020; Küçük et al., 2021).

Sentiment analysis is a social media analysis method and it is also commonly known as opinion mining in the related literature (Liu, 2010; Agarwal et al., 2011; Sun et al., 2017). At the end of the sentiment analysis process, the input text is generally classified as Positive, Negative, or Neutral (Liu, 2010; Agarwal et al., 2011; Sun et al., 2017). In several related studies, None (or, Neither) is also added to the list of sentiment class labels.

Stance detection is another social media analysis problem like sentiment analysis. Stance detection classifies stance (position) of the input text (like tweets) towards a given target. The input text is usually classified as Favor, Against, or None (Neither) at the end of the stance detection procedure (Mohammad et al., 2016a; Mohammad et al., 2016b; Küçük & Can, 2020). Stance detection is also known as stance prediction, stance analysis, stance classification, and stance identification in the related literature. In some studies, Neutral is also used as a stance class.

In this book chapter, we create a Turkish tweet dataset on COVID-19 vaccination. We first annotate this dataset with sentiment labels (Positive, Negative, None) and stance labels (Favor, Against, None). Next, we perform sentiment analysis and stance detection on this dataset using different machine learning approaches. These automatic sentiment and stance classification results can be used by public health experts. Contributions of our study are listed below:

1. To the best of our knowledge, we present the first Turkish tweet dataset about COVID-19 vaccination which is annotated with both sentiment and stance classes. The dataset can be used by sentiment analysis and stance detection researchers. The dataset has been annotated with the common polarity classes of "Positive", "Negative", and "None", as well as with the common stance classes of "Favor", "Against", and "None". Previous work on stance detection on Turkish tweets has only considered the two stance classes: Favor and Against classes (binary classification) (Küçük & Can, 2020). In our work, multi-class stance classification towards COVID-19 vaccination (target) is performed using our dataset labeled with three stance classes.
2. Two different machine learning approaches (SVM and Random Forest) are tested on this dataset and their performance results are compared. These learning approaches are selected because of their common use by the related work on stance detection and sentiment analysis. The dataset and the corresponding test results can be used for research purposes by other researchers as test dataset and baseline system for comparison, respectively.

To sum up, we believe that our book chapter will contribute to sentiment analysis and stance detection on COVID-19 vaccination. Based on our work, other classification techniques can also be tested and compared with our results.

Because of the global impact of the COVID-19 pandemic, social media analysis on tweets about COVID-19 vaccination like our work will help public health experts and other related authorities.

BACKGROUND

Sentiment analysis is an important research topic and it is mostly performed on online texts including social media posts, user reviews of products, and newspaper articles (Liu, 2010; Agarwal et al., 2011; Sun et al., 2017).

Sentiment analysis is considered as one of the subproblems of the more general research problem of affective computing (Picard, 2003). Based on related work, affective computing is about the recognition and modeling of emotional information (Picard, 2003). Emotion recognition (Saxena et al., 2020; Yousaf et al., 2020) is similarly another subproblem of affective computing. Therefore, affective computing is considered as a research problem at the intersection of computer science, psychology, engineering, and neuroscience, among others (Calvo et al., 2015).

There are several practical tools of sentiment analysis, including VADER (Valence Aware Dictionary for sEntiment Reasoning) presented in (Hutto & Gilbert, 2014). VADER is a rule-based sentiment analyzer and its performance is compared with several other sentiment analyzers and learning-based approaches. It is reported that VADER outperforms individual human raters (Hutto & Gilbert, 2014).

SentiWordNet is an important lexical resource for sentiment analysis (Baccianella et al., 2010). SentiWordNet is created by annotating all WordNet (Miller, 1995; Fellbaum, 2010) synsets as Positive, Negative, and Neutral (Baccianella et al., 2010).

An important and popular subproblem of sentiment analysis is aspect-based sentiment analysis (Do et al., 2019). In aspect-based sentiment analysis, the sentiment (or polarity) towards an aspect of an entity is identified, usually as Positive, Negative, or Neutral, similar to the case of generic sentiment analysis. There are studies that present aspect-based sentiment analysis tools, such as ABSApp sentiment analyzer proposed in (Pereg et al., 2019).

Singh et al. (2017) have performed sentiment analysis using several learning algorithms such as Naïve Bayes, decision trees, OneR, in order to optimize the performance of sentiment analysis. It is found that OneR learning algorithm performs better than the other algorithms achieving an F-Measure of 97% on the compiled datasets used in the study (Singh et al., 2017). In another study, sentiment analysis is consider as equivalent to emotion recognition (López-Chau et al., 2020) and machine learning based approaches are tested on tweets about an earthquake in Mexico in 2017. It is reported in the study that Naïve Bayes and SVM show the highest performance at the end of the related experiments (López-Chau et al., 2020). In another study on sentiment analysis, different algorithms such as Logistic Regression, SVM, Voted Perceptron and Hyper Pipes are tested for sentiment analysis on Albanian texts (Biba & Mane, 2014). It is reported that Hyper Pipes is on average the best performing classifier (Biba & Mane, 2014).

There are also several studies conducted on sentiment analysis of texts about the COVID-19 pandemic, which are very relevant to content of our current book chapter.

Sentiment analysis on Twitter after the announcement of lockdown in India because of the COVID-19 pandemic is presented in (Barkur & Vibha, 2020). The results show that overall sentiment in India at the time of lockdown was positive (Barkur & Vibha, 2020). Opinions of different nations to COVID-19 pandemic and lockdowns are examined in (Imran et al., 2020). Opinion mining is performed using deep learning (Long Short Term Memory - LSTM) in this study (Imran et al., 2020). Similarly, in another related study (Chakraborty et al., 2020), sentiment analysis is conducted on COVID-19 related tweets, using different deep learning classifiers.

Pastor (2020) uses an existing sentiment analysis tool (called Aylien[1]) to analyze the tweets of Filipinos about the community quarantine as a measure to prevent the COVID-19 pandemic. The evaluation results demonstrate that the sentiments of the Twitter users are mostly negative (reaching up to 83.42%) because of the negative results of the quarantine period (Pastor, 2020).

In (Hussain et al., 2021), sentiment analysis is performed on tweets and Facebook posts from UK and US on COVID-19 vaccines. The sentiment analysis method uses BERT (Bidirectional Encoder Representations from Transformers) (Devlin et al., 2018) which is a deep learning based language model. They use more than 300K social media posts published in nine months in 2020. They provide positive and negative sentiment graphs for different COVID-19 vaccines (Hussain et al., 2021).

The study by Singh et al. (2021) also presents sentiment analysis results on COVID-related tweets using the BERT (Devlin et al., 2018). The study is performed on two different datasets, one of them is collected without location constraint and the other data set includes tweets from India (Singh et al., 2021). Validation accuracy reported in the study is approximately 94% (Singh et al., 2021).

Supervised machine learning approaches are compared in (Rustam et al., 2021) for sentiment analysis on COVID-19 related tweets. A systematic review of sentiment analysis studies on infectious diseases like COVID-19 is presented in (Alamoodi et al., 2020). In another related study (Boon-Itt and Skunkan, 2020); around 108K tweets in English (on COVID-19) are examined. The sentiments (positive, negative) and emotions (joy, fear, trust, etc.) in the tweets are extracted using a lexicon-based approach. It is found that most of the tweets have negative sentiment and most tweets have fear, trust, and anticipation as the extracted emotions (Boon-Itt & Skunkan, 2020). Kaur et al. (2021) perform sentiment analysis tests on tweets related to COVID-19 using SVM machine learning algorithm and Recurrent Neural Network (RNN) which is a deep learning algorithm. An existing COVID-19 tweet dataset (Lamsal, 2021) is used during the related sentiment analysis tests (Kaur et al., 2021).

Topic modeling and sentiment analysis on tweets about online education during the COVID-19 pandemic are explored in (Mujahid et al., 2021). About 17.000 tweets about online education are used in the study. Different sentiment analyzers and resources (such as VADER (Hutto & Gilbert, 2014), TextBlob[2], and SentiWordNet (Baccianella et al., 2010)) in addition to machine learning and deep learning methods are tested and compared within the course of the study (Mujahid et al., 2021).

In (Ghasiya & Okamura, 2021); topic modeling and sentiment analysis are performed on about 100,000 news articles about COVID-19. Top2vec (Angelov, 2020) is used in this study for topic modeling and RoBERTa (Liu et al., 2019) is used for sentiment analysis. It is reported that about 90% validation accuracy is achieved for sentiment analysis (Ghasiya & Okamura, 2021).

In (Jang et al., 2021), topic modeling and aspect-based sentiment analysis are performed on tweets about COVID-19, from North America (particularly, Canada). For aspect-based sentiment analysis, ABSApp tool presented in (Pereg et al., 2019) is utilized. As the result of the study, negative sentiment is observed towards the pandemic (Jang et al., 2021).

Another topic modeling and sentiment analysis study on tweets about COVID-19 has been carried out in Brazil in (de Melo & Figueiredo, 2021). In this work, news articles are also analyzed in addition to the tweets. VADER (Hutto & Gilbert, 2014) sentiment analyzer is used during sentiment analysis, which is a rule-based tool (de Melo & Figueiredo, 2021).

In (Batra et al., 2011), the sentiments of people from six countries are analyzed, based on their tweets in English (about COVID-19 vaccination). Both sentiment analysis and emotion recognition are performed during tweet classification. Different deep learning methods are utilized. The study states that neighboring countries have similar sentiments about the vaccination (Batra et al., 2011).

The attitudes of Twitter users after the announcement of COVID-19 vaccines are studied in (Boucher et al., 2011). English and French tweets are analyzed using unsupervised learning (categorization/clustering) approaches. The results show that about 31.2% of people have concerns about safety, efficacy, freedom, and they have mistrust in the related institutions (Boucher et al., 2011).

Again, sentiment analysis towards COVID-19 vaccination during the first months of vaccine announcements is performed in (Malagoli et al., 2021). About 12 million tweets are considered. It is determined that negative sentiment exists towards tweets which are against vaccination (Malagoli et al., 2021). Another study about sentiment analysis on tweets about COVID-19 vaccines (Sattar & Arifuzzaman, 2021) that sentiments of most tweets are positive. Existing two sentiment analyzers are used in the study and the percentage of vaccinated population is also forecasted. Tsai & Wang (2021) explore the sentiments of Twitter users towards public health policies during the COVID-19 pandemic. These policies include stay-at-home, mask wearing, and social distancing policies (Tsai & Wang, 2021).

Melton et al. (2021) uses a lexicon-based sentiment analysis method on Reddit social media posts about COVID-19 vaccines. The results show that positive opinions in these texts are more common than negative opinions (Melton et al., 2021). In particular, it is reported that about 56.7% of the posts are found to be positive, about 27.7% of the posts have a negative sentiment, and finally about 15.6% of them have a neutral sentiment (Melton et al., 2021).

Yin et al. (2021) have also performed sentiment analysis on tweets about COVID-19 vaccines using VADER (Hutto & Gilbert, 2014) sentiment analysis tool. They have worked on tweets from different countries including India, the US, the UK, and Canada. It is reported in the study that positive sentiment is more prevalent compared to negative sentiment towards the vaccines. It is claimed that Twitter users mostly have a positive attitude towards the vaccines (Yin et al., 2021).

The change of sentiments towards COVID-19 vaccines in South Korea is analyzed using natural language processing techniques in (Shim et al., 2021). Sentiment analysis is performed on the collected tweets, using a sentiment analysis lexicon for Korean (Park et al., 2020). At the end of the study, it is concluded that the ratios of positive and negative sentiments are similar before and after the emergence of the vaccines (Shim et al., 2021).

In (Yousefinaghani et al., 2021); public sentiments towards COVID-19 vaccines are analyzed. About 4 million tweets are utilized in the study. It is observed that positive sentiment towards vaccines is more common compared to negative sentiment. It is also pointed out that popular organizations and people are usually expressing positive sentiment towards COVID-19 vaccines on Twitter (Yousefinaghani et al., 2021).

Finally, in (Bonneville et al., 2021), the change of COVID-19 vaccine opposition on Twitter is explored. It is found that vaccine opposition has increased by 80% on Twitter, during the period considered in the study (Bonneville et al., 2021).

As mentioned above, stance detection is a social media analysis task that is related to sentiment analysis. There are recent studies conducted to address various aspects of stance detection. For instance, a tweet dataset annotated with stance labels is presented in (Mohammad et al., 2016a) where this dataset is made publicly available for research purposes. Another annotated dataset is proposed in (Sobhani et al., 2017) for multi-target stance detection. Recent surveys on stance detection (mostly) on textual content are presented in (Küçük & Can, 2020; Küçük & Can, 2021). We should also note that, initial studies on stance detection usually employ traditional machine learning approaches while more recent studies mostly use deep learning based approaches.

Stance detection is also applied to health-related and (in particular, COVID-19 related) tweets, similar to the case of sentiment analysis.

A stance detection approach on the general vaccination topic is presented in 2017 by (Skeppstedt et al., 2017). The stance classes are for, against, and undecided. The F-score of the stance detection approach based on Support Vector Machine (SVM) on online forum posts for vaccination is 62% when binary classification (between for and against classes). When three classes are used, the F-score is 44% (Skeppstedt et al., 2017). In (D'Andrea et al., 2019), stance detection on general vaccination topic is investigated on Italian tweets. The stance classes in this study are `in favor of vaccination`, `not in favor of vaccination`, and `neutral`. Their best performing approach is based on SVM, stemmed n-grams, and bag-of-words representation. Deep learning methods are also tested in the study. It is claimed that real-time opinion monitoring about vaccination is possible on Twitter (D'Andrea et al., 2019). Similarly, a stance detection approach towards vaccination in Italy is described in (Bechini et al., 2020). In (Mutlu et al., 2020) a stance dataset of tweets is presented about the efficacy of hydroxychloroquine for treating COVID-19.

Cotfas et al. (2021) have also analyzed the stances of Twitter users after the announcement of the first COVID-19 vaccine on the 9th of November 2020. Machine learning and deep learning approaches are applied to around 2,35 million tweets. The results indicate that neutral stance is the most common and more Twitter users are in favor of the vaccine that users who are against the vaccine (Cotfas et al., 2021). Using BERT (Devlin et al., 2019), an accuracy of 78.94% is attained (Cotfas et al., 2021).

In another related study, He et al. (2021) search for reasons of not wearing face masks at the time of COVID-19 pandemic. They have analyzed around 267K tweets for this purpose using different machine learning and deep learning approaches. LSTM is chosen because it performs better than other approaches. At the end of the study, reasons of not wearing face masks are found as physical discomfort, negative effects, and lack of effectiveness (He et al., 2021). Another study (Sanders et al., 2021) on using face masks during the COVID-19 pandemic performs clustering and sentiment analysis on tweets. It is stated that clustering can improve the analysis of public opinion about mask wearing for preventing COVID-19 (Sanders et al., 2021).

Finally, in a recent study by Tsao et al. (2021) a review of studies about COVID-19 and social media is presented. Five themes are found after reviewing the related literature which focus on public attitude surveys, infodemics identification, mental health assessment, COVID-19 detection and prediction, evaluation of government responses to the pandemic, and evaluation of prevention videos (Tsao et al., 2021).

MAIN FOCUS OF THE CHAPTER

In this chapter, we present our sentiment and stance analysis experiments on Turkish tweets about COVID-19 vaccination.

In the following subsection, we first present our Turkish tweet dataset annotated for this purpose. The actual sentiment and stance experiments are presented in the upcoming section of the chapter.

Data Collection: Turkish Tweet Dataset

The tweet dataset includes 600 tweets collected with Twitter Streaming API, using the Turkish keyword "*aşı*" ("*vaccine*") during data collection.

Before actual annotation of the tweets, they are preprocessed as follows: tweets about vaccination or vaccines related to other diseases are removed from the collected tweets. So, all of the tweets in the dataset are about COVID-19 vaccination or vaccines.

300 tweets (part-1) are collected on 12/18/2020 and 300 tweets are (part-2) are downloaded on 07/18/2021. Thereby, we do not limit ourselves to a single period of time but instead use social media data published in different seasons.

The tweets are annotated by a single native Turkish annotator, both with sentiment and stance classes. Three sentiment (polarity) classes are considered: Positive, Negative, and None. Similarly, three stance classes are considered: Favor, Against, and None. There is a single target for the stance detection task, which is *COVID-19 Vaccination.*

The annotator is given annotation guidelines similar to the guidelines presented in (Mohammad et al., 2017). At the end of the annotation process; in part-1 (consisting of tweets of 12/18/2020) of the dataset, 122 tweets are annotated as Favor, 123 as Against, 55 as None (stance), and, at the same time 19 as Positive, 124 as Negative, and 157 as None (sentiment). For part-2 (consisting of tweets posted on 12/18/2020), 137 tweets are annotated as Favor, 122 as Against, and 41 as None (stance), and at the end of polarity/sentiment annotation, 25 tweets are annotated as Positive, 161 as Negative and 114 as None (sentiment).

The annotation results are summarized as percentages in the pie charts given in Figure 1 and Figure 2, respectively, for part-1 and part-2 of the annotated dataset.

Figure 1. Percentages of stance and sentiment annotation classes in part-1 of the Turkish tweet dataset about COVID-19 vaccination

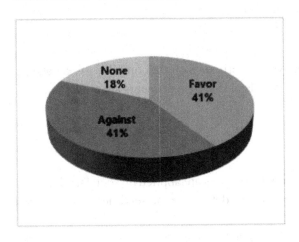
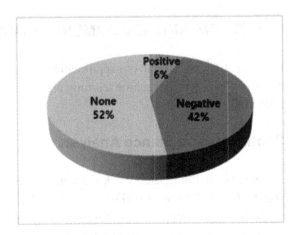

Figure 2. Percentages of stance and sentiment annotation classes in part-2 of the Turkish tweet dataset about COVID-19 vaccination

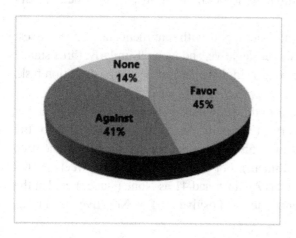 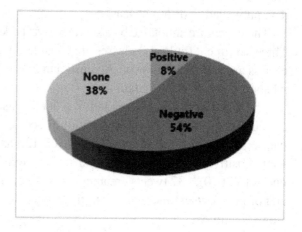

The authors plan to share the sentiment and stance annotations (together with tweet ids) of the dataset with the research community. After sharing these annotations, the dataset can be used by other researchers and different approaches can be compared on this dataset.

SOLUTIONS AND RECOMMENDATIONS

In this section, we present our sentiment and stance analysis experiments on the compiled tweet dataset, using two supervised machine learning algorithms. The details of these experiments are provided in the following subsection.

Sentiment and Stance Analysis

As reviewed in the Related Work section, different learning algorithms are applied on social media posts about COVID-19 and COVID-19 vaccines. These studies aim to determine the sentiments and stances of social media users towards these important issues.

In this book chapter, we test two different supervised learning algorithms on our sentiment- and stance-annotated dataset on COVID-19 vaccination.

The first algorithm is Support Vector Machine (SVM) which is a traditional machine learning algorithm that has been used extensively for sentiment and stance analysis. It is reported in the literature that SVM is by far one of the best performing algorithms applied to stance detection.

The second learning model used is Random Forest algorithm which is an ensemble learning algorithm and is again commonly used in the related literature. The implementations of Weka[3] machine learning tool are used for both learners (Frank et al., 2009). The SVM classifier in the Weka environment used polynomial kernel functions.

For both of our models, we use unigrams, hashtag use, and emoticon use, as features. These features have been used by different learning models for different natural language processing problems.

In Table 1, we present the performance evaluation results of our two learning models on the first and second parts of our dataset, for sentiment analysis and stance detection. 10-fold cross-validation is used during these evaluation procedures. Weighted F-Measure is used as the evaluation metric for these multi-class classification tasks. As commonly known, F-Measure is calculated as the harmonic mean of Precision and Recall metrics.

Table 1. Performance evaluation results of the learners on the compiled Turkish tweet datasets on COVID-19 vaccination

	Sentiment Analysis (F-Measure)		Stance Detection (F-Measure)	
	SVM	**Random Forest**	**SVM**	**Random Forest**
Part-1 of the Dataset	54.1%	40.9%	53.3%	49.6%
Part-2 of the Dataset	57.2%	45.3%	56.7%	49.4%

The evaluation results given in Table 1 are low. These low performance rates could be due to the following reasons:

1. The number of tweets in the annotated dataset is limited. We used 10-fold cross-validation during the evaluation process. Hence, at each fold, the number tweets used for training is limited which is reflected as low performance rates.
2. The feature set used for sentiment analysis and stance detection is the same and includes unigrams, hashtag use, and emoticon use. Other lexical, contextual, and word vector features (like word2vec (Mikolov et al., 2013) and GloVe (Pennington et al., 2014) vectors) can be added to the feature set to be used by the learning algorithms.

Based on the results given in Table 1, the following additional conclusions can be drawn.

The SVM learner performs better than the Random Forest learner for both of the problems. The performance rates of the SVM learners for both tasks are quite close to each other on the first and second part of the dataset. However, sentiment analysis performance of Random Forest learner on both parts of the dataset is quite lower than its stance detection performance.

The dataset compiled and utilized in this book chapter is important since it is the first Turkish tweet corpus annotated with the three classes (Favor, Against, and None) of stance detection. Previous work on Turkish stance detection includes a sports-related tweet dataset annotated with two stance classes only, i.e., Favor and Against (Küçük & Can, 2020). It is also significant for its being one of the first datasets on COVID-19 vaccination.

Therefore, we believe that our results are promising and can be used by future related work for comparison purposes.

FUTURE RESEARCH DIRECTIONS

Future work based on our study includes the following:

1. First of all, the number of tweets in the annotated Turkish tweet dataset (compiled within the course of the current book chapter) can be increased from 600 tweets to more than 1,000 tweets. In future work based on the current book chapter, the extended version of the tweet dataset will be annotated by at least two annotators. During these studies, inter-annotator agreement values will also be computed and presented. The extended versions of the dataset will also be shared publicly (by the authors) for research purposes.

2. Secondly, other high-performance learning algorithms like Multilayer Perceptron (MLP) and other neural network based learners, ensemble learning algorithms, and deep learning algorithms (like RNN, LSTM, CNN, and GRU) and trained models will be tested on the existing dataset and the extended versions of the dataset.

3. During these tests, new lexical and contextual features can be added to the existing feature set. For instance, named entities can also be used as additional features, using the outputs of a named entity recognizer for Turkish (Küçük & Arıcı, 2016; Küçük et al., 2017). Using contextual features in addition to the existing feature set is also an important future research direction. Other plausible features include word vector features such as word2vec (Mikolov et al., 2013) and GloVe (Pennington et al., 2014) vectors.

4. There are several other research problems closely related to sentiment analysis and stance detection. These problems include emotion recognition (Saxena et al., 2020; Yousaf et al., 2020) where the actual emotion class labels are explored such as Joy, Sadness, Anger, and Disgust. As stated previously, emotion recognition and sentiment analysis are usually considered as subproblems of the more general research problem of affective computing (Picard, 2003). Performing emotion recognition on tweets about COVID-19 vaccination, using different machine learning and deep learning based approaches, will be an important contribution to the existing body of work.

5. Another related research problem is rumour detection (Gorrel et al., 2017; Tian et al., 2020). It is often emphasized in the related literature that there are numerous rumours about the COVID-19 pandemic circulating on social media platforms. Therefore, identification of such rumours and analyzing the veracity of these rumours is an important future research direction.

6. Fake news detection is also a related and significant topic (Shu et al., 2017; Reis et al., 2019). Fake news is defined as new that intentionally include false information (Shu et al., 2017). Due to the possible negative impact of fake news about COVID-19 pandemic on society, it is important to automatically detect fake news about the pandemic. As fake news is known to spread very fast on social media platforms, fake news detection within the context of COVID-19 is an important future research direction to follow.

7. Another research topic closely related to fake news detection is automatic fact checking (Vlachos & Riedel, 2014). Fact checking is defined in the related literature as the determination of the truth value of a claim (Vlachos & Riedel, 2014). Due to the large volumes of unverified claims being posted on social media platforms every day, fact checking and fake news detection are important research directions particularly on textual content about the COVID-19 pandemic. Automatic fact checking and fake news detection on social media posts about the COVID-19 pandemic can prevent public health problems that may result due to the spreading unverified claims about the pandemic.

As stated previously, we plan to make the annotations of the dataset (with tweet ids) available for public use. After this sharing of the annotated dataset, the dataset and evaluation results can be used by other researchers to compare their own approaches to sentiment and stance analysis on social media.

CONCLUSION

Both sentiment analysis and stance detection are important problems in natural language processing. They are mostly applied to social media posts. As reviewed in the current book chapter, there are several studies conducted on social media like Twitter, Reddit, and Facebook about COVID-19 related issues. One of these issues is vaccination and there are debates on social media about this topic. In the current book chapter, we present an annotated tweet dataset including tweets on COVID-19 vaccination or vaccines. The first part of the dataset includes 300 tweets published on 12/18/2020 while the second part includes 300 tweets published on 07/18/2021. The dataset is annotated both with the three polarity classes for sentiment analysis, and three classes of stance detection. After the compilation of the dataset, we perform sentiment analysis and stance detection experiments on both parts of the dataset using SVM and Random Forest classifiers. The results obtained are promising and can be used by future work on the same dataset for comparison purposes. COVID-19 is a global pandemic affecting many people and governments. Social media analysis studies similar to our work can help related decision-makers about controversial health-related issues like COVID-19 vaccination.

REFERENCES

Agarwal, A., Xie, B., Vovsha, I., Rambow, O., & Passonneau, R. J. (2011). Sentiment analysis of Twitter data. *Proceedings of the Workshop on Language in Social Media (LSM)*, 30-38.

Alamoodi, A., Zaidan, B., Zaidan, A., Albahri, O., Mohammed, K., Malik, R., Almahdi, E. M., Chyad, M. A., Tareq, Z., Albahri, A. S., Hameed, H., & Alaa, M. (2020). Sentiment analysis and its applications in fighting COVID-19 and infectious diseases: A systematic review. *Expert Systems with Applications*, *167*, 114155. doi:10.1016/j.eswa.2020.114155 PMID:33139966

Angelov, D. (2020). *Top2vec: Distributed representations of topics.* arXiv preprint arXiv:2008.09470.

Baccianella, S., Esuli, A., & Sebastiani, F. (2010). Sentiwordnet 3.0: an enhanced lexical resource for sentiment analysis and opinion mining. In *Proceedings of the International Language Resources and Evaluation Conference (LREC)* (*Vol. 10*, No. 2010, pp. 2200-2204). Academic Press.

Barkur, G., Vibha, G. B. K., & Kamath, G. B. (2020). Sentiment analysis of nationwide lockdown due to COVID 19 outbreak: Evidence from India. *Asian Journal of Psychiatry*, *51*, 102089. doi:10.1016/j.ajp.2020.102089 PMID:32305035

Batra, R., Imran, A. S., Kastrati, Z., Ghafoor, A., Daudpota, S. M., & Shaikh, S. (2021). Evaluating Polarity Trend Amidst the Coronavirus Crisis in Peoples' Attitudes toward the Vaccination Drive. *Sustainability*, *13*(10), 5344. doi:10.3390u13105344

Bechini, A., Ducange, P., Marcelloni, F., & Renda, A. (2020). Stance analysis of Twitter users: The case of the vaccination topic in Italy. *IEEE Intelligent Systems*.

Biba, M., & Mane, M. (2014). Sentiment analysis through machine learning: An experimental evaluation for Albanian. In *Recent Advances in Intelligent Informatics* (pp. 195–203). Springer. doi:10.1007/978-3-319-01778-5_20

Bonnevie, E., Gallegos-Jeffrey, A., Goldbarg, J., Byrd, B., & Smyser, J. (2021). Quantifying the rise of vaccine opposition on Twitter during the COVID-19 pandemic. *Journal of Communication in Healthcare*, *14*(1), 12–19. doi:10.1080/17538068.2020.1858222

Boon-Itt, S., & Skunkan, Y. (2020). Public perception of the COVID-19 pandemic on Twitter: Sentiment analysis and topic modeling study. *JMIR Public Health and Surveillance*, *6*(4), e21978. doi:10.2196/21978 PMID:33108310

Boucher, J. C., Cornelson, K., Benham, J. L., Fullerton, M. M., Tang, T., Constantinescu, C., Mourali, M., Oxoby, R. J., Marshall, D. A., Hemmati, H., Badami, A., Hu, J., & Lang, R. (2021). Analyzing social media to explore the attitudes and behaviors following the announcement of successful COVID-19 vaccine trials: Infodemiology study. *JMIR Infodemiology*, *1*(1), e28800. doi:10.2196/28800 PMID:34447924

Calvo, R. A., D'Mello, S., Gratch, J. M., & Kappas, A. (Eds.). (2015). *The Oxford Handbook of Affective Computing*. Oxford Library of Psychology. doi:10.1093/oxfordhb/9780199942237.001.0001

Chakraborty, K., Bhatia, S., Bhattacharyya, S., Platos, J., Bag, R., & Hassanien, A. E. (2020). Sentiment analysis of COVID-19 tweets by deep learning classifiers—A study to show how popularity is affecting accuracy in social media. *Applied Soft Computing*, *97*, 106754. doi:10.1016/j.asoc.2020.106754 PMID:33013254

Cotfas, L. A., Delcea, C., Roxin, I., Ioanăş, C., Gherai, D. S., & Tajariol, F. (2021). The longest month: Analyzing COVID-19 vaccination opinions dynamics from tweets in the month following the first vaccine announcement. *IEEE Access: Practical Innovations, Open Solutions*, *9*, 33203–33223. doi:10.1109/ACCESS.2021.3059821 PMID:34786309

D'Andrea, E., Ducange, P., Bechini, A., Renda, A., & Marcelloni, F. (2019). Monitoring the public opinion about the vaccination topic from tweets analysis. *Expert Systems with Applications*, *116*, 209–226. doi:10.1016/j.eswa.2018.09.009

de Melo, T., & Figueiredo, C. M. (2021). Comparing news articles and tweets about COVID-19 in Brazil: Sentiment analysis and topic modeling approach. *JMIR Public Health and Surveillance*, *7*(2), e24585. doi:10.2196/24585 PMID:33480853

Devlin, J., Chang, M. W., Lee, K., & Toutanova, K. (2018). *BERT: Pre-training of deep bidirectional transformers for language understanding*. arXiv preprint arXiv:1810.04805.

Do, H. H., Prasad, P. W. C., Maag, A., & Alsadoon, A. (2019). Deep learning for aspect-based sentiment analysis: A comparative review. *Expert Systems with Applications*, *118*, 272–299. doi:10.1016/j.eswa.2018.10.003

Edo-Osagie, O., De La Iglesia, B., Lake, I., & Edeghere, O. (2020). A scoping review of the use of Twitter for public health research. *Computers in Biology and Medicine, 122*, 103770. doi:10.1016/j. compbiomed.2020.103770 PMID:32502758

Fellbaum, C. (2010). WordNet. In *Theory and Applications of Ontology: Computer Applications* (pp. 231–243). Springer. doi:10.1007/978-90-481-8847-5_10

Frank, E., Hall, M., Holmes, G., Kirkby, R., Pfahringer, B., Witten, I. H., & Trigg, L. (2009). Weka-a machine learning workbench for data mining. In *Data Mining and Knowledge Discovery Handbook* (pp. 1269–1277). Springer. doi:10.1007/978-0-387-09823-4_66

Ghasiya, P., & Okamura, K. (2021). Investigating COVID-19 news across four nations: A topic modeling and sentiment analysis approach. *IEEE Access: Practical Innovations, Open Solutions, 9*, 36645–36656. doi:10.1109/ACCESS.2021.3062875 PMID:34786310

Gorrell, G., Kochkina, E., Liakata, M., Aker, A., Zubiaga, A., Bontcheva, K., & Derczynski, L. (2019). SemEval-2019 task 7: RumourEval, determining rumour veracity and support for rumours. In *Proceedings of the 13th International Workshop on Semantic Evaluation* (pp. 845-854). 10.18653/v1/S19-2147

He, L., He, C., Reynolds, T., Bai, Q., Huang, Y., Li, C., Zheng, K., & Chen, Y. (2021). Why do people oppose mask wearing? A comprehensive analysis of US tweets during the COVID-19 pandemic. *Journal of the American Medical Informatics Association: JAMIA, 28*(7), 1564–1573. doi:10.1093/jamia/ocab047

Hussain, A., Tahir, A., Hussain, Z., Sheikh, Z., Gogate, M., Dashtipour, K., Ali, A., & Sheikh, A. (2021). Artificial intelligence–enabled analysis of public attitudes on Facebook and Twitter toward covid-19 vaccines in the United Kingdom and the United States: Observational study. *Journal of Medical Internet Research, 23*(4), e26627. doi:10.2196/26627 PMID:33724919

Hutto, C., & Gilbert, E. (2014). VADER: A parsimonious rule-based model for sentiment analysis of social media text. In *Proceedings of the International AAAI Conference on Web and Social Media* (*Vol. 8*, No. 1). AAAI.

Imran, A. S., Daudpota, S. M., Kastrati, Z., & Batra, R. (2020). Cross-cultural polarity and emotion detection using sentiment analysis and deep learning on COVID-19 related tweets. *IEEE Access: Practical Innovations, Open Solutions, 8*, 181074–181090. doi:10.1109/ACCESS.2020.3027350 PMID:34812358

Jang, H., Rempel, E., Roth, D., Carenini, G., & Janjua, N. Z. (2021). Tracking COVID-19 discourse on Twitter in North America: Infodemiology study using topic modeling and aspect-based sentiment analysis. *Journal of Medical Internet Research, 23*(2), e25431. doi:10.2196/25431 PMID:33497352

Kaur, H., Ahsaan, S. U., Alankar, B., & Chang, V. (2021). A proposed sentiment analysis deep learning algorithm for analyzing COVID-19 tweets. *Information Systems Frontiers, 23*(6), 1–13. doi:10.100710796-021-10135-7 PMID:33897274

Küçük, D., & Arıcı, N. (2016). Türkçe için Wikipedia tabanlı varlık ismi tanıma sistemi (Wikipedia-based named entity recognition system for Turkish). *Politeknik Dergisi, 19*(3), 325–332.

Küçük, D., Arıcı, N., & Küçük, D. (2017). Named entity recognition in Turkish: Approaches and issues. In *Proceedings of the International Conference on Applications of Natural Language to Information Systems* (pp. 176-181). Springer.

Küçük, D., Arıcı, N., & Küçük, E. E. (2021). Sosyal medyada otomatik halk sağlığı takibi: Güncel bir derleme [Automatic public health monitoring on social media: A recent survey]. *Niğde Ömer Halisdemir Üniversitesi Mühendislik Bilimleri Dergisi, 10*(2).

Küçük, D., & Can, F. (2020). Stance detection: A survey. *ACM Computing Surveys, 53*(1), 1–37. doi:10.1145/3369026

Küçük, D., & Can, F. (2021). Stance detection: Concepts, approaches, resources, and outstanding issues. In *Proceedings of the 44th International ACM SIGIR Conference on Research and Development in Information Retrieval* (pp. 2673-2676). ACM.

Küçük, E. E., Yapar, K., Küçük, D., & Küçük, D. (2017). Ontology-based automatic identification of public health-related Turkish tweets. *Computers in Biology and Medicine, 83*, 1–9. doi:10.1016/j.compbiomed.2017.02.001 PMID:28187367

Lamsal, R. (2021). Design and analysis of a large-scale COVID-19 tweets dataset. *Applied Intelligence, 51*(5), 2790–2804. doi:10.100710489-020-02029-z PMID:34764561

Liu, B. (2010). Sentiment analysis and subjectivity. Handbook of Natural Language Processing, 627-666.

Liu, Y., Ott, M., Goyal, N., Du, J., Joshi, M., & Chen, D. (2019). *RoBERTa: A robustly optimized BERT pretraining approach.* arXiv preprint arXiv:1907.11692.

López-Chau, A., Valle-Cruz, D., & Sandoval-Almazán, R. (2020). Sentiment analysis of Twitter data through machine learning techniques. In *Software Engineering in the Era of Cloud Computing* (pp. 185–209). Springer. doi:10.1007/978-3-030-33624-0_8

Malagoli, L. G., Stancioli, J., Ferreira, C. H., Vasconcelos, M., Couto da Silva, A. P., & Almeida, J. M. (2021). A look into COVID-19 vaccination debate on Twitter. In *Proceedings of the 13th ACM Web Science Conference* (pp. 225-233). 10.1145/3447535.3462498

Melton, C. A., Olusanya, O. A., Ammar, N., & Shaban-Nejad, A. (2021). Public sentiment and topic modeling regarding COVID-19 vaccines on Reddit social media platform: A call to action for strengthening vaccine confidence. *Journal of Infection and Public Health, 14*(10), 1505–1512. doi:10.1016/j.jiph.2021.08.010 PMID:34426095

Mikolov, T., Chen, K., Corrado, G., & Dean, J. (2013). *Efficient estimation of word representations in vector space.* arXiv preprint arXiv:1301.3781.

Miller, G. A. (1995). WordNet: A lexical database for English. *Communications of the ACM, 38*(11), 39–41. doi:10.1145/219717.219748

Mohammad, S., Kiritchenko, S., Sobhani, P., Zhu, X., & Cherry, C. (2016a). A dataset for detecting stance in tweets. In *Proceedings of the Tenth International Conference on Language Resources and Evaluation (LREC)* (pp. 3945-3952). Academic Press.

Mohammad, S., Kiritchenko, S., Sobhani, P., Zhu, X., & Cherry, C. (2016b). SemEval-2016 task 6: Detecting stance in tweets. In *Proceedings of the 10th International Workshop on Semantic Evaluation* (pp. 31-41). 10.18653/v1/S16-1003

Mohammad, S. M., Sobhani, P., & Kiritchenko, S. (2017). Stance and sentiment in tweets. *ACM Transactions on Internet Technology, 17*(3), 1–23. doi:10.1145/3003433

Mujahid, M., Lee, E., Rustam, F., Washington, P. B., Ullah, S., Reshi, A. A., & Ashraf, I. (2021). Sentiment analysis and topic modeling on tweets about online education during COVID-19. *Applied Sciences (Basel, Switzerland), 11*(18), 8438. doi:10.3390/app11188438

Mutlu, E. C., Oghaz, T., Jasser, J., Tutunculer, E., Rajabi, A., Tayebi, A., Ozmen, O., & Garibay, I. (2020). A stance data set on polarized conversations on Twitter about the efficacy of hydroxychloroquine as a treatment for COVID-19. *Data in Brief, 33*, 106401. doi:10.1016/j.dib.2020.106401 PMID:33088880

Park, H. M., Kim, C. H., & Kim, J. H. (2020). Generating a Korean sentiment lexicon through sentiment score propagation. *KIPS Transactions on Software and Data Engineering, 9*(2), 53–60.

PastorC. K. (2020). Sentiment analysis of Filipinos and effects of extreme community quarantine due to coronavirus (COVID-19) pandemic. SSRN, 3574385. doi:10.2139/ssrn.3574385

Pennington, J., Socher, R., & Manning, C. (2014). GloVe: Global vectors for word representation. *Proceedings of the 2014 Conference on Empirical Methods in Natural Language Processing (EMNLP)*. 10.3115/v1/D14-1162

Pereg, O., Korat, D., Wasserblat, M., Mamou, J., & Dagan, I. (2019). ABSApp: A portable weakly-supervised aspect-based sentiment extraction system. In *Proceedings of the 2019 Conference on Empirical Methods in Natural Language Processing and the 9th International Joint Conference on Natural Language Processing (EMNLP-IJCNLP): System Demonstrations* (pp. 1-6). 10.18653/v1/D19-3001

Picard, R. W. (2003). Affective computing: Challenges. *International Journal of Human-Computer Studies, 59*(1-2), 55–64. doi:10.1016/S1071-5819(03)00052-1

Reis, J. C., Correia, A., Murai, F., Veloso, A., Benevenuto, F., & Cambria, E. (2019). Supervised learning for fake news detection. *IEEE Intelligent Systems, 34*(2), 76–81. doi:10.1109/MIS.2019.2899143

Rustam, F., Khalid, M., Aslam, W., Rupapara, V., Mehmood, A., & Choi, G. S. (2021). A performance comparison of supervised machine learning models for COVID-19 tweets sentiment analysis. *PLoS One, 16*(2), e0245909. doi:10.1371/journal.pone.0245909 PMID:33630869

Sanders, A. C., White, R. C., Severson, L. S., Ma, R., McQueen, R., Paulo, H. C. A., ... (2021). Unmasking the conversation on masks: Natural language processing for topical sentiment analysis of COVID-19 Twitter discourse. medRxiv, 2020-08.

Sattar, N. S., & Arifuzzaman, S. (2021). COVID-19 vaccination awareness and aftermath: Public sentiment analysis on Twitter data and vaccinated population prediction in the USA. *Applied Sciences (Basel, Switzerland), 11*(13), 6128. doi:10.3390/app11136128

Saxena, A., Khanna, A., & Gupta, D. (2020). Emotion recognition and detection methods: A comprehensive survey. *Journal of Artificial Intelligence and Systems, 2*(1), 53–79. doi:10.33969/AIS.2020.21005

Shu, K., Sliva, A., Wang, S., Tang, J., & Liu, H. (2017). Fake news detection on social media: A data mining perspective. *SIGKDD Explorations*, *19*(1), 22–36. doi:10.1145/3137597.3137600

Shim, J. G., Ryu, K. H., Lee, S. H., Cho, E. A., Lee, Y. J., & Ahn, J. H. (2021). Text mining approaches to analyze public sentiment changes regarding COVID-19 vaccines on social media in Korea. *International Journal of Environmental Research and Public Health*, *18*(12), 6549. doi:10.3390/ijerph18126549 PMID:34207016

Singh, M., Jakhar, A. K., & Pandey, S. (2021). Sentiment analysis on the impact of coronavirus in social life using the BERT model. *Social Network Analysis and Mining*, *11*(1), 1–11. doi:10.100713278-021-00737-z PMID:33758630

Singh, J., Singh, G., & Singh, R. (2017). Optimization of sentiment analysis using machine learning classifiers. Human-Centric Computing and Information Sciences, 7(1), 1-12. doi:10.118613673-017-0116-3

Skeppstedt, M., Kerren, A., & Stede, M. (2017). Automatic detection of stance towards vaccination in online discussion forums. In *Proceedings of the International Workshop on Digital Disease Detection using Social Media 2017* (pp. 1-8). Academic Press.

Sobhani, P., Inkpen, D., & Zhu, X. (2017). A dataset for multi-target stance detection. In *Proceedings of the 15th Conference of the European Chapter of the Association for Computational Linguistics:* Volume 2, *Short Papers* (pp. 551-557). Academic Press.

Sun, S., Luo, C., & Chen, J. (2017). A review of natural language processing techniques for opinion mining systems. *Information Fusion*, *36*, 10–25. doi:10.1016/j.inffus.2016.10.004

Tian, L., Zhang, X., Wang, Y., & Liu, H. (2020). Early detection of rumours on Twitter via stance transfer learning. *Advances in Information Retrieval*, *12035*, 575–588. doi:10.1007/978-3-030-45439-5_38

Tsai, M. H., & Wang, Y. (2021). Analyzing Twitter data to evaluate people's attitudes towards public health policies and events in the era of COVID-19. *International Journal of Environmental Research and Public Health*, *18*(12), 6272. doi:10.3390/ijerph18126272 PMID:34200576

Tsao, S. F., Chen, H., Tisseverasinghe, T., Yang, Y., Li, L., & Butt, Z. A. (2021). What social media told us in the time of COVID-19: a scoping review. *The Lancet Digital Health*.

Vlachos, A., & Riedel, S. (2014). Fact checking: Task definition and dataset construction. In *Proceedings of the ACL 2014 Workshop on Language Technologies and Computational Social Science* (pp. 18-22). 10.3115/v1/W14-2508

Yin, H., Song, X., Yang, S., & Li, J. (2021). *Sentiment analysis and topic modeling for COVID-19 vaccine discussions.* arXiv preprint arXiv:2111.04415.

Yousaf, A., Umer, M., Sadiq, S., Ullah, S., Mirjalili, S., Rupapara, V., & Nappi, M. (2020). Emotion recognition by textual tweets classification using voting classifier (LR-SGD). *IEEE Access: Practical Innovations, Open Solutions*, *9*, 6286–6295. doi:10.1109/ACCESS.2020.3047831

Yousefinaghani, S., Dara, R., Mubareka, S., Papadopoulos, A., & Sharif, S. (2021). An analysis of COVID-19 vaccine sentiments and opinions on Twitter. *International Journal of Infectious Diseases*, *108*, 256–262. doi:10.1016/j.ijid.2021.05.059 PMID:34052407

ENDNOTES

1   https://aylien.com/
2   https://textblob.readthedocs.io/en/dev/index.html
3   https://www.cs.waikato.ac.nz/~ml/weka/

Chapter 16
Teleworker Experiences in #COVID-19:
Insights Through Sentiment Analysis in Social Media

Rigoberto García-Contreras
Autonomous University of the State of Mexico, Mexico

J. Patricia Muñoz-Chávez
Technological University of the Metropolitan Area of the Valley of Mexico, Mexico

David Valle-Cruz
Autonomous University of the State of Mexico, Mexico

Asdrúbal López-Chau
Autonomous University of the State of Mexico, Mexico

ABSTRACT

The COVID-19 pandemic has become a critical and disruptive event that has substantially changed the way people live and work. Although several studies have examined the effects of remote work on organizational outcomes and behaviors, only a few have inquired into how its opportune implementation impacts aggregate emotions over time. This chapter aims to conduct a sentiment analysis with public reactions on Twitter about telework during the pandemic period. The results showed fluctuations in emotional polarity, starting with a higher positive charge in the early pandemic scenarios that became weaker, and the negative polarity of emotions increased. Fear, sadness, and anger were the emotions that increased the most during the pandemic. Knowledge about people's sentiments about telework is important to complement organizational research and to complement the framework for the development of efficient telework implementation strategies.

DOI: 10.4018/978-1-7998-9594-7.ch016

INTRODUCTION

In early 2020, the coronavirus (SARS-CoV-2) began its imminent spread around the world. Since then, these have been atypical times for all humankind. COVID-19 pandemic disease preventive measures have been a hurdle for millions of people and have led to disruptive changes in day-to-today activities (Palumbo, 2020). Many countries have implemented quarantine and social distancing measures to reduce the number of infections and protect the health of their populations. These included the shutdown of schools, universities, workplaces, businesses, mass events, and all activities non-essential activities (Kraus et al., 2020). However, by the end of the year, more than 70 million people were reported to be infected around the world (WHO, 2020), creating a landscape of uncertainty and mayhem.

Although these measures are guaranteed to stem the spread of infection and suggest that they will keep people safe, several studies have shown a negative impact on people's psychological well-being (Shofiya & Abidi, 2021). Furthermore, the whirlwind of changes and fears triggered by the COVID-19 pandemic has led to a tendency for people to experience a variety of emotions and psychological ailments. For example, a study carried out in Hong Kong revealed that 70% of the people surveyed were anxious about the idea of being infected by COVID-19 (Ren et al., 2020). While there is also a concern for economic and job security. In this regard, Lippens et al. (2021) found that 35% of Belgian respondents are afraid of losing their job due to the crisis.

In terms of the work environment, responses to the pandemic also brought about rapid changes in how people worked. With the world almost at a standstill; the only viable option was the massive relocation of workers to their homes and forcing a large part of them to adapt to the telework' features (Toleikienė et al., 2020). Indeed, by the end of the third quarter of 2020, most workers (71%) reported that they could perform their work tasks remotely (Parker et al., 2021). Teleworking or remote work is a method of working in which the employee works full-time or partial time outside the conventional company workplace and is not a foreign practice for many companies, organizations, and individuals in multiple industries, but past efforts have not been as successful as expected for everyone (Messenger, 2019). Even the abrupt implementation since last spring has been difficult for those employees who rarely performed work at home (Parker et al., 2021). Nevertheless, the imminent threat of the coronavirus in the environment and the concern for a probable economic collapse in industries and governments; gave a new opportunity to test, at an unprecedented level, its virtues, and limitations and to be able to look forward to a better future for their operation.

Due to the large-scale change that remote work represents for employees, it is necessary to explore how they feel. Over the last two years (2020-2021), the conditions and effects of telework in individuals have been evaluated: exploring the presence of occupational fears from the COVID-19 crisis such as fear of job loss and the importance of perceived job insecurity on organizational and individual outcomes, for instance, job satisfaction or employee well-being (Lippens et al., 2021). In addition, evidence suggests that forced remote work can have negative consequences on the psychosocial and sentimental aspects of employees (Bentley et al., 2016; Palumbo, 2020; Vega et al., 2015). On the other hand, the effects of telework in organizations and workers have been evaluated through conventional methods and techniques (qualitative and quantitative). Collecting data in interviews, surveys, and indicators and with traditional analysis tools (Abdel et al., 2021; Edelmann et al., 2021; Garcia-Contreras et al., 2021), being less frequent the studies with alternative techniques such as sentiment analysis (Zhang et al., 2021a). This opens up a wide range of alternatives for the use of new unconventional computational methods, such as cloud technologies, machine learning, and sentiment analysis (Ozcan et al., 2021; Tyagi et al., 2021); which enable the analysis of large volumes of data (Big Data) such as banking applications, email, blogs, and social networks (López-Chau et al., 2020a).

Nowadays, with the rapid Internet development and disruptive technologies, modern society uses social media (e.g., Twitter, Tik Tok, Instagram, and Facebook), most of the day, to disseminate and share information with their close and not-so-close contacts. Since the COVID-19 outbreak, social networking sites have proven to be a useful tool in disseminating and obtaining messages and news related to the pandemic situation (Tsao et al., 2021). For instance, Han et al. (2021) note a striking increase in the number of tweets about COVID-19 issued by citizens, organizations, and governments. Sometimes, users spill their emotions into opinions that they freely express on social and this information can be used for various applications in market research, business intelligence, prediction of consumption patterns, and sentiment analysis (Mostafa, 2013).

Sentiment analysis or opinion mining is a tool that has attracted attention due to its application in several fields. This technique consists of a process of collecting opinions about a specific target (topic) and classifying them according to the emotions observed in the selected content, which are then analyzed using machine learning techniques (Cyril et al., 2021) or lexicons (Valle-Cruz et al., 2021). Emotion processing is important for the detection of human behaviors in the face of social events such as the COVID-19 or massive implementation of telework during the pandemic period (Shofiya & Abidi, 2021; Valle-Cruz et al., 2021). In this regard, COVID-19 became a trending topic in digital media and social media because many people around the world share their sentiments and interests about how their current life is going in the light of the coronavirus. People have expressed themselves on Twitter using general hashtags on the topic: #Covid-19, #Coronavirus, #SocialDistancing; on positive sentiments: #StayHome, #QuarantineandChill, #TogetheratHome, and on negative sentiments: #Covidiots, #FuckCovid19 (Lacsa, 2021). Furthermore, the shift from work to telework has intensified the interest in understanding its emotional effects on employees. Social media also have received reactions related to telework accompanied by hashtags: #Workathome, #Teleworking, #HomeOffice. These reactions include opinions that can be measured on a scale from negative to positive sentiments about teleworking. For example, it is likely that many people who were not used to or willing to work remotely were left with no choice and experienced different sentiments than those who had antecedents of teleworking (Zhang et al., 2021a).

Therefore, considering the gaps, this chapter conducts a multimodal sentiment analysis in social media (Twitter) through the trending topic analysis, regarding the implementation of telework during the COVID-19 crisis to find its positive and negative emotional effects on workers. The study contributes in the following ways. First, it proposes a model for assessing the informational content of tweets and validate the insights from large amounts of data in social networks. Second, it contributes to organizational knowledge, specifically to the literature on telework, by reporting the emotional advantages and disadvantages of telework insights to improve and give continuity to its practice. Finally, it incorporates a multimodal sentiment analysis approach applied to a contemporary organizational phenomenon and complements the knowledge of the field: telework in times of COVID-19.

This chapter includes four sections from now on. The first section consists of the literature review related to teleworking in the COVID-19 era, social media (Twitter), and sentiment analysis. The second section describes the method based on multimodal sentiment analysis techniques with a sentimental lexicon approach and the emotion hourglass. The fourth section outlines the results of sentiment classification. The last section presents conclusions and future research.

BACKGROUND

This section is threefold. The first subsection discusses literature for the understanding of telework in times of COVID-19. The second subsection presents research on social media and sentiment analysis in the pandemic period. The third subsection states the hypotheses guiding the study.

Towards Understanding Teleworking in Times of COVID-19

Numerous activities, that traditionally took place in a physical environment, such as work, shopping, learning, recreation, socializing, and so on, have been incorporated into the virtual world because of changes in ICT, the rapid digitization, and expansion of the Internet. These activities that occur remotely supported by Information and Communication Technologies (ICT) are called teleactivities, among them, telework (Mouratidis et al., 2021). Telework or remote work is not new. It has its origins in the mid-1970s, created to reduce travel, traffic, and therefore fuel consumption during the oil crisis, as well as an environmental strategy to reduce air pollution (Nilles, 1975, 1994). In this way, workers who seek greater freedom based on their personal needs could decide on this option, since teleworking helps to decrease spatial and temporal limitations (Wang & Ozbilen, 2020). However, evaluating the benefits of remote work is difficult, since for decades studies have shown both the positive effects and its disadvantages, for example, those related to transport, emotional well-being, and work-life balance private (Anderson et al., 2015; Gajendran & Harrison, 2007; Hook et al., 2020; Kim, 2017; Pendyala et al., 1991).

Recently, since the emergence of the COVID-19 pandemic, telework had rapid and substantial growth, in order to reduce the spread of the virus and preserve health. For this reason, the governments implemented various non-medical measures: including social distancing, isolation, and shutdown of schools and organizations. Thus, teleworking, as an emerging practice, became the only viable option to continue business and activities (Figliozzi & Unnikrishnan, 2021). Therefore, organizations around the world have embraced remote working, and thousands of employees who had never worked from home before switched to this form of work overnight. This situation affected the work environment since many employees did not have the equipment, spaces, skills, and knowledge required for it. This phenomenon has motivated the development of research that explores the theoretical foundations combined with empirical analysis in various scenarios related to telework during the pandemic (De' et al., 2020).

In this regard, studies have shown that teleworking during the pandemic has involved various challenges, including psychological ones because the presence of family at home has been associated with greater sentiments of cognitive overload and perceived demands regardless of the use of digital tools (Schmitt et al., 2021). Likewise, the adequacy and satisfaction with remote work, home study, and lockdown have been analyzed. The findings showed that in some cases the adequacy of the spaces has been insufficient, mainly due to the lack of exclusive spaces for teleworking or very small spaces, poor lighting, and lack of availability of digital resources due to the number of family members who study or work at home (Cuerdo-Vilches & Navas-Martín, 2021). All of this highlighted the existed imbalance between men and women due to the time they spend on household chores and even caring for dependent people such as children and the elderly (Eurofound, 2020).

On the other hand, the benefits that teleworking during the COVID-19 pandemic has provided both employees and organizations have also been evidenced, with flexibility playing an important role. The main evidence that account for the benefits of working at home is those related to health, by reducing the risk of infection and those that address the reduction of travel and its consequent environmental benefits (Alipour et al., 2021; Jenelius & Cebecauer, 2020; Shakibaei et al., 2021). However, there is an increasing interest in analyzing the benefits it offers to human resources and management (Stiles, 2020). In this context, research has shown that teleworking is highly appreciated by employees, and particularly the combination of working at home and working in the office, as an optimum solution, could increase organizational performance, as well as social and professional networks (Davidescu et al., 2020).

In the organizational landscape, studies disclose that teleworking during the pandemic has generated both positive and negative results in their behavior in employees. Although it produces a higher level of vigor, it promotes autonomy and influences the job motivation that is highly related to engagement, it also amplifies the negative effect of burnout on turnover intentions, due to the lack of psychological and social relationships, sentiments of belonging, in addition to the impossibility of disconnecting from work (Chi et al., 2021). Besides, Kazekami (2020) found that teleworking increases happiness, job satisfaction, and productivity, the latter increases when telework is carried out at appropriate hours but decreases if they are prolonged. Likewise, trying to balance work and household chores increases stress, which affects life satisfaction but not productivity.

Social Media (Twitter) and Sentiment Analysis in Times of COVID-19

Social media changed the way people communicate. Currently, millions of users use them to share any kind of information all around the world. In addition, they use it to communicate ideas, opinions, as well as to express sentiments and emotions about their everyday lives (Kydros et al., 2021; López-Chau et al., 2020b). Twitter is one of the most popular and widely used social media for sharing messages (over 300 million monthly users). These messages are called "tweets" and have the main characteristic of being short (less than 280 characters). In addition, Twitter is microblogging where users can publish their posts and interact with others, which provides valuable linguistic information and becomes an important source of Big Data (Kydros et al., 2021; Medford et al., 2020).

The information posted on Twitter reflects public attitudes and it is useful for a range of purposes. For example, to predict stock market fluctuations (Mostafa, 2013), consumer preferences (Zhang et al., 2021b), political campaigns (Valle-Cruz et al., 2021), among other applications. In the same way, people use Twitter to express their day-to-day actions and reactions, which has motivated them to explore people's sentiments and emotions. Sentiment analysis is one of the practical tools used in the Twitter dataset to identify emotions (positive or negative) and opinions (favorable or unfavorable) towards a subject or issue through a mathematical calculation (Cyril et al., 2021; Shofiya & Abidi, 2021).

Social media are useful in critical situations because they become communication tools for times of high uncertainty (e.g., pandemics, natural disasters, and terrorist attacks). Furthermore, social media helps to broadcast critical information and provide first-person narratives of what is happening in real-time (Han et al., 2021). This information is collected to gain insight into users' perspectives and reactions to critical events. For example, Murthy and Gross (2017) identified the reactions in tweets of the population of New Jersey during and after Hurricane Sandy; or López Chau et al. (2020b) who performed a sentiment analysis in response to the Mexico City earthquake through Twitter posts.

During the times of COVID-19, social distancing policies limited contact between people, who relied on social media to obtain information and uphold contact with family and friends, sharing emotions, stresses, and fears. On the other hand, governments and news organizations used them to disseminate information about the disease to soothe and advise society. This increased the amount of data about the disease and its consequences on people, making it a trending topic (Han et al., 2021; Kydros et al.,

2021). Like in previous critical events, Twitter has been effective in disseminating information and understanding public opinion, fostering sentiment analysis with data mined from those tweets of topic: #coronavirus #COVID-19. In this regard, some authors carry out studies using sentiment analysis to understand emotions during the pandemic period. Some examples are presented below:

- Shofiya and Abidi (2021) analyzed the sentiment of Canadians expressed on Twitter towards social distancing related to COVID-19.
- Han et al. (2021) identified that citizen's display changing patterns and concerns over time in response to the information posted on Twitter (media, influential profiles, and individuals).
- Medford et al. (2020) showed that tweets predominantly expressed negative sentiments, mainly linked to emotions of fear, surprise, and anger due to the risk of contagion and economic uncertainty.
- Samuel et al. (2020), identified on Twitter public sentiment about socio-economic consequences and the severity of COVID-19 in the development of extreme sentiments, emotional challenges, and mental health (extreme fear and confusion mixed with confidence and anticipation).
- Boon-Itt and Skunkan (2020) found in their results two main aspects of public concern about the pandemic in Twitter: concern about spread and symptom trends and negative outlook towards COVID-19 (fear and anxiety).

Sentiment Analysis Telewoking, and COVID-19

The COVID-19 pandemic has become one of the greatest challenges that humankind has faced. One of the priorities was to preserve an active workforce to avoid economic, political, and social collapse. Thereby, teleworking or remote work has led employees around the world to change the way they work on a daily routine (Parker et al., 2021). However, in drastic cases, it has been impossible to keep employees, increasing unemployment (Lippens et al., 2021). Both situations are part of working life in the COVID-19 era and showed an impact on individual aspects such as well-being, health, safety, work-life balance, and economic situation. In addition, the lapses of the pandemic (first wave, second wave, or arrival of vaccines) also affected these individual dimensions. In this regard, the Eurofound (2021) identified fluctuations in people's mental well-being along with the progression of the pandemic.

Remote work has been noted for displaying a paradox (Zhang et al., 2021a). On the one hand, it can have positive results due to work flexibility and autonomy; reduced expenses, and individual work-life balance (Schuster et al., 2020). Furthermore, it was associated with high levels of job attitudes, satisfaction, performance, and commitment, as well as low levels of stress (Davidescu et al., 2020; Garcia-Contreras et al., 2021; Ofei-Dodoo et al., 2020). These results can be mirrored in emotional loads and positive sentiments that are interpreted from the perspective of the SenticNet-Hourglass of Emotions (Wang et al., 2020). In other words, the consequences of teleworking could be categorized within the affective dimensions (sensitivity, aptitude, pleasantness, and attention); specifically, be placed within the basic positive emotions of this model such as surprise, anticipation, joy, and trust (Samuel et al., 2020; Valle-Cruz et al., 2021). The above leads to the following prediction:

Hypothesis One: Teleworking has a positive effect on the sentiments analyzed on Twitter.

On the other side of the paradox, remote work can have negative considerations. Studies show that teleworking can adversely affect the boundary between work and personal life; technological and personal limitations; increase workload; role ambiguity and job confusion; family conflicts, and isolation, which leads to negative consequences such as burnout, depression, anxiety, and weak relationships between co-workers and supervisors (Armas-Elguera et al., 2021; Palumbo, 2020; Suh & Lee, 2017; Topi, 2004). As well as with the positive consequences of teleworking, the negative consequences also can be categorized within the hourglass of emotions (Wang et al., 2020). In this sense, can be included within the basic emotions of this model. These sentiments can be disgust, sadness, and fear (Samuel et al., 2020; Valle-Cruz et al., 2021). Based on the above, the following hypothesis is proposed:

Hypothesis Two: Teleworking has a negative effect on the sentiments analyzed on Twitter.

Finally, as mentioned above, the stages of the pandemic caused fluctuations in the emotional response of people (Kydros et al., 2021). In other words, the early phase of the pandemic brought the closure of many activities and the shift to forced telework. This brought a scenario of uncertainty (disgust, sadness, or fear) and with the course of time, people valued the opportunity to work in the safety of their homes and keep their jobs (anticipation, joy, or trust). Similarly, with the advent of the next phases (e.g., vaccination and the potential back to normal life), sentiments and emotions could be changing in remote workers (Eurofound, 2021; Kraus et al., 2020; Zhang et al., 2021b). According to these considerations, the following hypothesis is proposed:

Hypothesis three: There is a variation in the sentiments presented on Twitter regarding telework during the COVID-19 pandemic.

METHOD TO SENTIMENT ANALYSIS

To study the teleworkers' experience during COVID-19: the authors conducted a sentiment analysis approach on Twitter based on the emotional charge (Valle-Cruz et al., 2021) and lexicon: SenticNet-Hourglass of Emotions (Wang et al., 2020). Sentiment lexicons are lists of words and phrases that are associated with positive and negative sentiments. Some of them are quantified with a score to assess their intensity (Valle-Cruz et al., 2021). The sentiment analysis consisted of the following six steps (Figure 1).

Figure 1. Method: collection and data analysis
Source: Authors' Own Elaboration

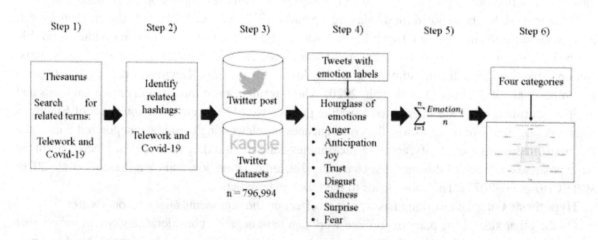

Step 1: First, the authors searched, in a thesaurus, for words and terms related to telework and COVID-19. Related to telework, they found the terms "remote work" and "home office". Related to COVID-19, they found the terms: "coronavirus", "pandemic", and "quarantine".

Step 2: In a second place, the authors identified the hashtags related to the terms used in the first step. Were found 20 hashtags, were discarded 4, and left 16 by its contents: #corona, #coronavirus, #covid, #coworking, #digitalnomad, #homeoffice, #lockdown, #pandemic, #quarantine, #remotework, #remoteworking, #socialdistancing, #stayhome, #staysafe, #wfh, and #workfromhome.

Step 3: Tweets were downloaded directly from Twitter for each hashtag. To complement the data collection, the authors downloaded the datasets, of Twitter posts, related to telework and COVID-19 stored in Kaggle. The number of tweets per dataset are shown in Table 1.

Table 1. Analyzed data sets about telework and COVID-19

Dataset	Tweets
#corona	10,000
#coronavirus	10,000
#covid	10,000
#coworking	2,665
#digitalnomad	3,003
#homeoffice	6,292
#lockdown	10,000
#pandemic	10,000
#quarantine	5,072
#remotework	10,000
#remoteworking	3,626
#socialdistancing	4,336
#stayhome	10,000
#staysafe	10,000
#wfh	9,235
#workfromhome	10,000
Corona_NLP_test	3,798
Corona_NLP_train	41,157
covid19_tweets	179,108
covidvaccine	279,939
vaccination_all_tweets	168,763
Total	**796,994**

Source Authors' Own Elaboration.

Step 4: The SenticNet Hourglass of Emotions lexicon (Figure 2) is a tool used to represent, detect and describe affective states through labels and is able to indicate the polarity of feelings with acceptable accuracy (Gupta & Agrawal, 2020). Moreover, this novel model has gained confidence for this kind of studies (Valle-Cruz et al., 2021). Consequently, the lexicon allowed screening the emotional charge of each Twitter post with the corpus-semantic-based approach. During the analysis, the following emotions were identified: Anger, Trust, Disgust, Anticipation, Fear, Joy, Surprise, and Sadness, taking into consideration the second sentimental level of the Emotion Hourglass Framework (Wang et al., 2020).

Figure 2. SenticNet-hourglass of emotions
Source: Wang et al. (2020)

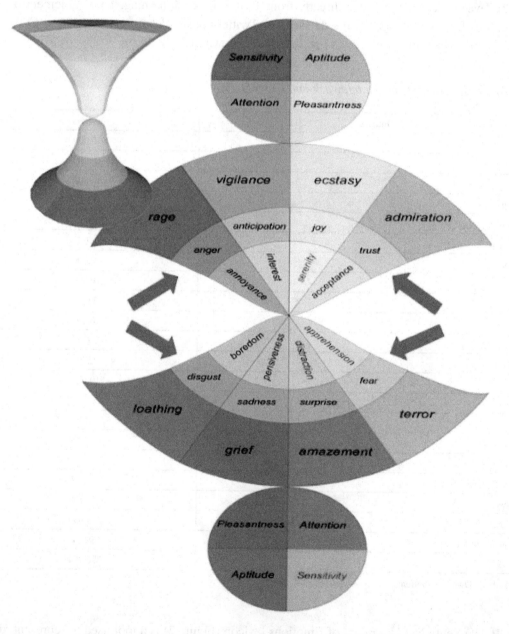

Step 5: For this step, a function based on the lexicon made it possible to count the terms with a sentiment load in each publication (tweet). Based on these frequencies, it was possible to obtain the derived features, as well as to determine the ratio of the frequencies of the terms in the body of the text, and to know the value of the difference between the ratios in order to build a multi-emotional sentiment classifier model and predominant emotions. Likewise, the authors calculated and standardized the emotional charge based on the average results of the sentiment lexicons on a scale from "0" to "1", to make them comparable. At this level, the authors found some datasets with similar behavior ratios, for this reason, it was decided to join them. Then, were created four main categories: *Coronavirus and Pandemic, Teleworking and Quarantine, Vaccination,* and *Other Issues* related to services, news, businesses (supermarkets and pharmacies), and massive purchase of toilet paper, among others. The categories explain four scenarios of teleworking and the pandemic.

Step 6: Finally, following the previous steps, the emotional charge and predominant emotions of each dataset were calculated in order to compare them and analyze the results of the four categories.

SOLUTIONS AND RECOMMENDATIONS

Telework and COVID-19 Sentiment Scenarios

Based on the sentiment analysis performed, the authors identified four scenarios that have been played out during the period of the coronavirus pandemic: 1) the pandemic beginning, 2) teleworking and quarantine stage, 3) vaccination period, and 4) other issues related to the pandemic. This section describes the details of each scenario and some final connotations regarding the hypotheses raised during the COVID-19 pandemic that is used to discuss the results.

Global Disruption: The Pandemic Beginning

The first scenario comprises posts referring to the new coronavirus and the beginning of the pandemic. Initially, the data showed high levels of anticipation and sadness, as well as joy (since a portion of the posts is memes[1] and jokes related to the pandemic). On a second level, found sentiments related to trust, disgust, and surprise. To a lesser extent, we identified anger caused by the spread of COVID-19. Figure 3 shows an early scenario of tweet opinions. Sentiments showed slightly balanced values (positive and negative). It is evident that sentiments of anticipation (excitement, alertness, and anxiety), sadness, and disgust in front of the unknowns about the new virus, as well as uncertainty about economic and labor aspects, are identified in social media (Kraus et al., 2020; Samuel et al., 2020). However, when the effects of the pandemic were not so alarming at the beginning, positive values such as joy, confidence, and surprise were observed due to the significant sentiment of staying safe at home, satisfying economic needs, and maintaining their professional activities (Parker et al., 2021; Schmitt et al., 2021). Even at this stage, the changes caused by the coronavirus were included in situations of sarcasm and irony; for instance, the memes published about coronavirus and primary changes in people's activities. In addition, humor is a useful tool for coping with sentiments arising from uncertainty, the likelihood of losing jobs, and the horror of death (Flaherty & Rughiniş, 2021; Kertcher & Turin, 2020).

Figure 3. First scenario: the new coronavirus and the beginning of pandemic
Source: Authors' Own Elaboration

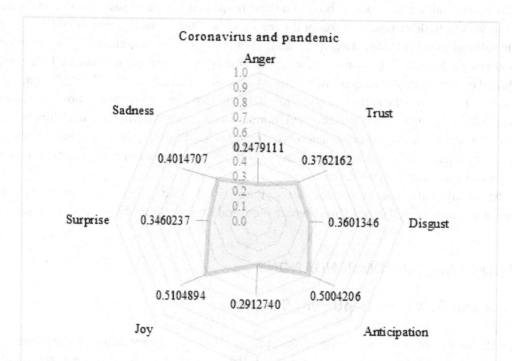

In addition, a word cloud was generated using the Twitter handle and revealed the word cloud depicted in Figure 4. In it, the most salient points or themes are displayed. Several posts of the pandemic are centered on remote work, lockdown, working from home, pleasure, and new job forms. In this way, the semantics of the conversations reveal, on the one hand, the anticipation and sadness of staying home, but at the same time the confidence of maintaining their job through teleworking; on the other hand, sentiments of joy at being safer and in a job that involves flexibility and freedom.

Figure 4. Word cloud related to the new coronavirus and beginning of pandemic
Source: Authors' Own Elaboration

Advancing the Pandemic: Teleworking and quarantine

The second scenario shows similar emotional levels to the first scenario. Similarly, measures related to telework and quarantine, in essence, the emotions are charged with anticipation and joy. Although this situation can be confusing (due to the consequences of the pandemic), joy predominates because of the customary use of Twitter: users are looking for fun and leisure, as well as information (Figure 5). Consequently, even as the effects of the pandemic intensified, the sentiments expressed on Twitter remained slightly homogeneous. On the one hand, negative sentiments involved staying in quarantine, persistent uncertainty, information security, risk of contagion, and frustration (Zhang et al., 2021a). On the other hand, positive themes continued to be present in work-life balance, staying employed, and sentiment relief from the threats of the pandemic (Flaherty & Rughiniş, 2021; Schmitt et al., 2021).

Figure 5. Second scenario: teleworking and quarantine
Source: Authors' Own Elaboration

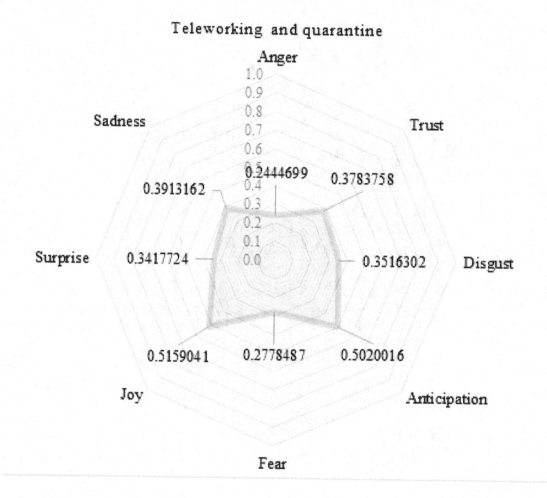

In this sense, having similar results to the first scenario, word clusters from scenario two suggest the presence of some recurring themes, such as the telework, pleasure, digital nomad, among others (Figure 6).

Figure 6. Word cloud related to teleworking and the quarantine
Source: Authors' Own Elaboration

Time to Get Vaccinated

The third scenario shows a considerable increase, concerning the second scenario, in fear (89%), anger (57%), and sadness (43%). Some causes are related to the lack of vaccines, deaths, the failure of measures to contain the pandemic, as well as the working and economic conditions of teleworkers. At this level, the conditions at the world level generate uncertainty in the economy as well as in health (Figure 7). In this scenario, negative sentiments prevailed. Fear over the lack of accurate public information about the virus and the increase in infections, deaths, and job losses in a large part of the countries was reflected in the tweets posted (Kydros et al., 2021; Parker et al., 2021). On the other hand, many people were angry about the lock-in time and the increase in workloads of those who kept their jobs; meanwhile, sentiments of sadness corresponded to posts about total closures of workplaces, firms in crisis, and unemployment (Abdel Hadi et al., 2021; Garcia-Contreras et al., 2021).

Figure 7. Third scenario: Vaccination period
Source: Authors' Own Elaboration

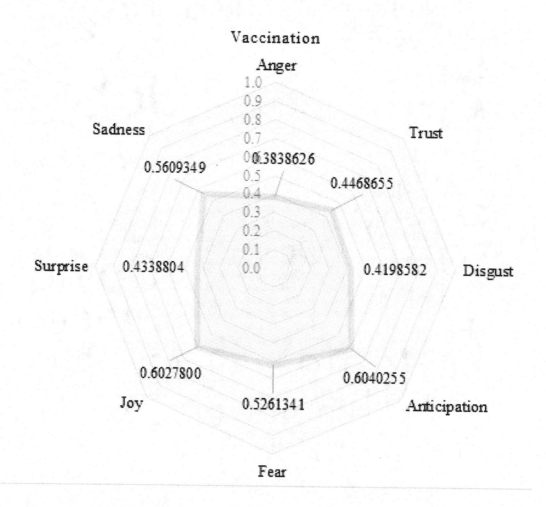

Figure 8 shows the word cloud depicting the most common monograms occurring in tweets about the vaccination category. Among them are vaccine marks, as well as the words COVID, vaccine, first, feel, death.

Figure 8. Word cloud related to the vaccination period
Source: Authors' Own Elaboration

Other Aspects of the Pandemic

The fourth scenario is similar to the third one. In these kinds of Twitter posts, there are diverse topics about the pandemic such as questions about available businesses and services, news, and media information, as well as some products needed or thought to be needed to survive the pandemic. Compared to the second scenario, there is an increase in fear (106%), sadness (52%), and anger (50%) (Figure 9). In the last scenario, sentiments with negative polarity persisted and increased substantially. Fear was the most common emotion expressed on Twitter during the last two scenarios. The information continues to reflect fear of death, contagion, and the need for resources to overcome the pandemic; however, there is also emotional anxiety and fear regarding the effect on the economic and political crisis that may affect people's work environment (Chi et al., 2021; Medford et al., 2020). Sadness and anger followed and included themes of isolation, lack of information, and uncertainty about continuing to work remotely or returning to the office (Samuel et al., 2020; Shofiya & Abidi, 2021; Topi, 2004).

Figure 9. Fourth scenario: other issues related to the pandemic
Source: Authors' Own Elaboration

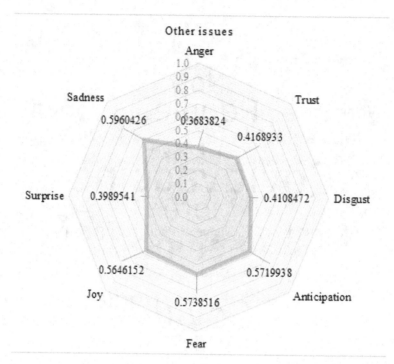

Regarding the last category, Figure 10 shows the word cloud where the most frequent words were covid, coronavirus, price, store, food, shop, and grocery.

Figure 10. Word cloud related to other issues related to the pandemic
Source: Authors' Own Elaboration

Final Connotations Regarding the Hypotheses Raised

The behavior of scenarios and emotions, identified during the pandemic, is shown in Figure 11. Fear, sadness, and anger increased, the most, during the crisis period. Despite this, the social media essence of posting is filled with anticipation, true and joy. Twitter continued to be used as a social media for fun and entertainment.

Figure 11. Behavior of themes and sentiments during the pandemic
Source: Authors' Own Elaboration

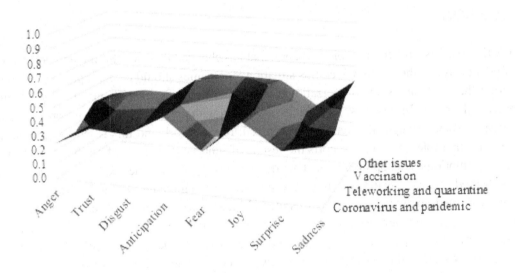

The sentiment analysis results show a dual polarity of emotions during four different scenarios. First, the results show three positive emotions in tweets related to telework and teleworkers: confidence, anticipation, and joy. These findings are congruent with the benefits of remote work such as flexibility, autonomy, productivity, resource savings, and job satisfaction (Albro & McElfresh, 2021; Bentley et al., 2016; Edelmann et al., 2021). In addition, the ability to work at home for COVID-19 made the transition to virtual social connections for information and the opportunity to hold jobs in order to meet personal and family needs without exposing themselves and their loved ones to the risk of contagion (Lippens et al., 2021; Schmitt et al., 2021; Vega et al., 2015). These events reinforce sentiments of anticipation and confidence, as well as allow them to show joy despite the critical situation (Kazekami, 2020; Min et al., 2021). These results support Hypothesis one by demonstrating that Twitter posts during the COVID-19 pandemic reflect positive sentiments toward telework.

Second, the results show three negative emotions that affected teleworkers during the pandemic period: fear, sadness, and anger, mainly in the most recent periods of the pandemic. The results of the analysis confirm the paradox of teleworking by pointing out the disadvantages of its forced implementation (Figliozzi & Unnikrishnan, 2021; Topi, 2004; Zhang et al., 2021a). In this regard, organizations around the world embraced telework and a large number of workers were not prepared for this method of working and did not have the equipment, space, and knowledge to do it (De' et al., 2020). Moreover, isolation and workloads can have a negative effect on the sentiments (fear, sadness, and anger) expressed by employees in their online postings (Chi et al., 2021; Palumbo, 2020; Shofiya & Abidi, 2021; Truchot et al., 2021). These findings support Hypothesis two because sentiment analysis on Twitter suggests negative effects of teleworking on publications.

Lastly, Hypothesis three proposed the variation in sentiments expressed on Twitter about telework during the pandemic. The results of sentiment analysis showed fluctuations in emotions overtime during the pandemic. Specifically, the incremental ravages of the pandemic weakened the positive polarity shown in early pandemic scenarios, while negative emotions increased over time in Twitter posts. This is consistent with the findings of Samuel et al. (2020) and Kydros et al. (2021). This supports Hypothesis three.

CONCLUSION

The COVID-19 crisis has become a phenomenon that has changed the way of think and behaves of millions of people around the world. Given this situation, companies should be equipped with meaningful information that will have some organizational value, and that will create contributed to obtaining a competitive advantage. In this sense, it is necessary to know the feelings of the workforce towards one of the greatest social changes that have ever occurred: remote work and this is where opinion mining plays an important role. This study reports the results of sentiment analysis of Twitter posts to identify perceptions, emotions, and opinions about working remotely during the COVID-19 pandemic. The findings showed fluctuations in the sentiment expressed in social media (Twitter) as the impacts of the pandemic worsened. In the first two scenarios identified, a positive polarity of sentiments is presented, and the study discovered high levels of anticipation and joy mixed with lower levels of fear, anger, and sadness. However, as the pandemic progressed, positive sentiments became weaker and sentiments with negative polarity increased in frequency, especially for the two later scenarios identified.

Therefore, tweets related to teleworking allowed describing the teleworker's emotions and sentiments. It is observed that some of them are joyful and trustful because they spend time at home with the family and keep their work in a safe environment. On the other hand, many people show fear, anger, and other negative thoughts because of the conflicts of the emerging telework implementation and the conflicts they experience such as work-life balance management, isolation, and work overload.

These findings are valuable to complement organizational studies on telework because they provide insight into the positive and negative impacts on work, and the broad emotional reactions of employees. This with the objective that managers have elements that allow them to generate strategies to improve work conditions, increase work autonomy and give value to employees, and thereby, make remote work more effective and efficient to improve productivity rates, as well as to visualize its future institutionalization that does not only work to get out of the COVID-19 crisis.

REFERENCES

Abdel Hadi, S., Bakker, A. B., & Häusser, J. A. (2021). The role of leisure crafting for emotional exhaustion in telework during the COVID-19 pandemic. *Anxiety, Stress, and Coping, 34*(5), 530–544. doi:10.1080/10615806.2021.1903447 PMID:33769142

Albro, M., & McElfresh, J. M. (2021). Job engagement and employee-organization relationship among academic librarians in a modified work environment. *Journal of Academic Librarianship, 47*(5), 102413. doi:10.1016/j.acalib.2021.102413

Alipour, J. V., Fadinger, H., & Schymik, J. (2021). My home is my castle – The benefits of working from home during a pandemic crisis. *Journal of Public Economics, 196*, 104373. doi:10.1016/j.jpubeco.2021.104373

Anderson, A. J., Kaplan, S. A., & Vega, R. P. (2015). The impact of telework on emotional experience: When, and for whom, does telework improve daily affective well-being? *European Journal of Work and Organizational Psychology, 24*(6), 882–897. doi:10.1080/1359432X.2014.966086

Armas-Elguera, F., Talavera-Ramírez, J. E., Cárdenas, M., & De la Cruz-Vargas, J. A. (2021). Trastornos del sueño y ansiedad de estudiantes de Medicina del primer y último año en Lima, Perú. *Revista de La Fundación Educación Médica, 24*(3), 133–138. doi:10.33588/fem.243.1125

Bentley, T. A., Teo, S. T. T., McLeod, L., Tan, F., Bosua, R., & Gloet, M. (2016). The role of organisational support in teleworker wellbeing: A socio-technical systems approach. *Applied Ergonomics, 52*, 207–215. doi:10.1016/j.apergo.2015.07.019 PMID:26360212

Boon-Itt, S., & Skunkan, Y. (2020). Public Perception of the COVID-19 Pandemic on Twitter: Sentiment Analysis and Topic Modeling Study. *JMIR Public Health and Surveillance, 6*(4), e21978. doi:10.2196/21978 PMID:33108310

Chi, O. H., Saldamli, A., & Gursoy, D. (2021). Impact of the COVID-19 pandemic on management-level hotel employees' work behaviors: Moderating effects of working-from-home. *International Journal of Hospitality Management, 98*, 103020. doi:10.1016/j.ijhm.2021.103020 PMID:34493887

Cuerdo-Vilches, T., Navas-Martín, M., March, S., & Oteiza, I. (2021). Adequacy of telework spaces in homes during the lockdown in Madrid, according to socioeconomic factors and home features. *Sustainable Cities and Society, 75*, 103262. doi:10.1016/j.scs.2021.103262

Cyril, C. P. D., Beulah, J. R., Subramani, N., Mohan, P., Harshavardhan, A., & Sivabalaselvamani, D. (2021). An automated learning model for sentiment analysis and data classification of Twitter data using balanced CA-SVM. *Concurrent Engineering, 29*(4), 386–395. doi:10.1177/1063293X211031485

Davidescu, A. A., Apostu, S.-A., Paul, A., & Casuneanu, I. (2020). Work Flexibility, Job Satisfaction, and Job Performance among Romanian Employees—Implications for Sustainable Human Resource Management. *Sustainability, 12*(15), 6086. doi:10.3390u12156086

De', R., Pandey, N., & Pal, A. (2020). Impact of digital surge during Covid-19 pandemic: A viewpoint on research and practice. *International Journal of Information Management, 55*, 102171. https://doi.org/10.1016/j.ijinfomgt.2020.102171

Edelmann, N., Schossboeck, J., & Albrecht, V. (2021). RemoteWork in Public Sector Organisations: Employees' Experiences in a Pandemic Context. *ACM International Conference Proceeding Series*, 408–415. doi:10.1145/3463677.3463725

Eurofound. (2020). *Living, working and COVID-19*. Publications Office of the European Union. doi:10.2806/467608

Eurofound. (2021). *Living, working and COVID-19 (Update April 2021) : Mental health and trust decline across EU as pandemic enters another year*. Publications Office of the European Union. doi:10.2806/76802

Figliozzi, M., & Unnikrishnan, A. (2021). Home-deliveries before-during COVID-19 lockdown: Accessibility, environmental justice, equity, and policy implications. *Transportation Research Part D, Transport and Environment*, *93*, 102760. https://doi.org/https://doi.org/10.1016/j.trd.2021.102760

Flaherty, M. G., & Rughiniş, C. (2021). Online Memes and COVID-19. *Contexts*, *20*(3), 40–45. https://doi.org/10.1177/15365042211035338

Gajendran, R. S., & Harrison, D. A. (2007). The Good, the Bad, and the Unknown About Telecommuting: Meta-Analysis of Psychological Mediators and Individual Consequences. *The Journal of Applied Psychology*, *92*(6), 1524–1541. https://doi.org/10.1037/0021-9010.92.6.1524

Garcia-Contreras, R., Munoz-Chavez, P., Valle-Cruz, D., Ruvalcaba-Gomez, E. A., & Becerra-Santiago, J. A. (2021). Teleworking in Times of COVID-19. Some Lessons for the Public Sector from the Emergent Implementation during the Pandemic Period: Teleworking in times of COVID-19. *ACM International Conference Proceeding Series*, 376–385. doi:10.1145/3463677.3463700

Gupta, N., & Agrawal, R. (2020). Application and techniques of opinion mining. In Hybrid Computational Intelligence (pp. 1–23). Academic Press. https://doi.org/10.1016/b978-0-12-818699-2.00001-9.

Han, C., Yang, M., & Piterou, A. (2021). Do news media and citizens have the same agenda on COVID-19? an empirical comparison of twitter posts. *Technological Forecasting and Social Change*, *169*, 120849. https://doi.org/10.1016/j.techfore.2021.120849

Hook, A., Court, V., Sovacool, B. K., & Sorrell, S. (2020). A systematic review of the energy and climate impacts of teleworking. *Environmental Research Letters*, *15*(9), 093003. https://doi.org/10.1088/1748-9326/ab8a84

Jenelius, E., & Cebecauer, M. (2020). Impacts of COVID-19 on public transport ridership in Sweden: Analysis of ticket validations, sales and passenger counts. *Transportation Research Interdisciplinary Perspectives*, *8*, 100242. doi:10.1016/j.trip.2020.100242

Kazekami, S. (2020). Mechanisms to improve labor productivity by performing telework. *Telecommunications Policy*, *44*(2), 101868. https://doi.org/10.1016/j.telpol.2019.101868

Kertcher, C., & Turin, O. (2020). 'Siege Mentality' Reaction to the Pandemic: Israeli Memes During Covid-19. *Postdigital Science and Education*, *2*(3), 581–587. doi:10.1007/s42438-020-00175-8

Kim, S. N. (2017). Is telecommuting sustainable? An alternative approach to estimating the impact of home-based telecommuting on household travel. *International Journal of Sustainable Transportation*, *11*(2), 72–85. https://doi.org/10.1080/15568318.2016.1193779

Kraus, S., Clauss, T., Breier, M., Gast, J., Zardini, A., & Tiberius, V. (2020). The economics of CO-VID-19: Initial empirical evidence on how family firms in five European countries cope with the corona crisis. *International Journal of Entrepreneurial Behaviour & Research*, 26(5), 1067–1092. https://doi.org/10.1108/IJEBR-04-2020-0214

Kydros, D., Argyropoulou, M., & Vrana, V. (2021). A content and sentiment analysis of greek tweets during the pandemic. *Sustainability*, *13*(11), 6150. https://doi.org/10.3390/su13116150

Lacsa, J. E. M. (2021). #COVID19: Hashtags and the power of social media. *Journal of Public Health*. doi:10.1093/pubmed/fdab242

Lippens, L., Moens, E., Sterkens, P., Weytjens, J., & Baert, S. (2021). How do employees think the COVID-19 crisis will affect their careers? *PLoS One*, *16*(5), 1–19. https://doi.org/10.1371/journal.pone.0246899

López-Chau, A., Valle-Cruz, D., & Sandoval-Almazán, R. (2020a). Sentiment Analysis of Twitter Data Through Machine Learning Techniques. In M. Ramachandran & Z. Mahmood (Eds.), Software Engineering in the Era of Cloud (pp. 185–209). Springer International Publishing. https://doi.org/10.1007/978-3-030-33624-0_8.

López Chau, A., Valle-Cruz, D., & Sandoval-Almazán, R. (2020b). Sentiment Analysis in Crisis Situations for Better Connected Government. In Z. Mahmood (Ed.), *Web 2.0 and Cloud Technologies for Implementing Connected Government* (pp. 162–181). IGI Global. doi:10.4018/978-1-7998-4570-6.ch008

Medford, R. J., Saleh, S. N., Sumarsono, A., Perl, T. M., & Lehmann, C. U. (2020). An "Infodemic": Leveraging High-Volume Twitter Data to Understand Early Public Sentiment for the Coronavirus Disease 2019 Outbreak. *Open Forum Infectious Diseases*, *7*(7). https://doi.org/10.1093/ofid/ofaa258

Messenger, J. C. (2019). *Telework in the 21st Century: An Evolutionary Perspective*. Edward Elgar Publishing.

Min, H., Peng, Y., Shoss, M., & Yang, B. (2021). Using machine learning to investigate the public's emotional responses to work from home during the COVID-19 pandemic. *The Journal of Applied Psychology*, *106*(2), 214–229. https://doi.org/10.1037/apl0000886

Mostafa, M. M. (2013). More than words: Social networks' text mining for consumer brand sentiments. *Expert Systems with Applications*, *40*(10), 4241–4251. https://doi.org/10.1016/j.eswa.2013.01.019

Mouratidis, K., Peters, S., & van Wee, B. (2021). Transportation technologies, sharing economy, and teleactivities: Implications for built environment and travel. *Transportation Research Part D, Transport and Environment*, *92*, 102716. https://doi.org/https://doi.org/10.1016/j.trd.2021.102716

Murthy, D., & Gross, A. J. (2017). Social media processes in disasters: Implications of emergent technology use. *Social Science Research*, *63*, 356–370. https://doi.org/10.1016/j.ssresearch.2016.09.015

Nilles, J. (1975). Telecommunications and Organizational Decentralization. *IEEE Transactions on Communications*, *23*(10), 1142–1147. https://doi.org/https://doi.org/ 10.1109/TCOM.1975.1092687

Nilles, J. (1994). *Making telecommuting happen: A guide for telemanagers and telecommuters*. Van Nostrand Reinhold Editors.

Ofei-Dodoo, S., Long, M. C., Bretches, M., Kruse, B. J., Haynes, C., & Bachman, C. (2020). Work engagement, job satisfaction, and turnover intentions among family medicine residency program managers. *International Journal of Medical Education, 11*, 47–53. https://doi.org/10.5116/ijme.5e3e.7f16

Ozcan, S., Suloglu, M., Sakar, C. O., & Chatufale, S. (2021). Social media mining for ideation: Identification of sustainable solutions and opinions. *Technovation, 107*, 102322. https://doi.org/10.1016/j.technovation.2021.102322

Palumbo, R. (2020). Let me go to the office! An investigation into the side effects of working from home on work-life balance. *International Journal of Public Sector Management, 33*(6–7), 771–790. https://doi.org/10.1108/IJPSM-06-2020-0150

Parker, K., Horowitz, J., Minkin, R., & Arditi, T. (2021). *How the Coronavirus Outbreak Has-and Hasn't-Changed the Way Americans Work.* https://www.pewresearch.org/social-trends/2020/12/09/how-the-coronavirus-outbreak-has-and-hasnt-changed-the-way-americans-work/

Pendyala, R. M., Goulias, K. G., & Kitamura, R. (1991). Impact of telecommuting on spatial and temporal patterns of household travel. *Transportation, 18*, 383–409. https://doi.org/10.1007/BF00186566

Ren, S.-Y., Gao, R.-D., & Chen, Y.-L. (2020). Fear can be more harmful than the severe acute respiratory syndrome coronavirus 2 in controlling the corona virus disease 2019 epidemic. *World Journal of Clinical Cases, 8*(4), 652–657. https://doi.org/10.12998/wjcc.v8.i4.652

Samuel, J., Rahman, M. M., Ali, G. G. M. N., Samuel, Y., Pelaez, A., Chong, P. H. J., & Yakubov, M. (2020). Feeling Positive About Reopening? New Normal Scenarios From COVID-19 US Reopen Sentiment Analytics. *IEEE Access: Practical Innovations, Open Solutions, 8*, 142173–142190. https://doi.org/10.1109/ACCESS.2020.3013933

Schmitt, J. B., Breuer, J., & Wulf, T. (2021). From cognitive overload to digital detox: Psychological implications of telework during the COVID-19 pandemic. *Computers in Human Behavior, 124*, 106899. https://doi.org/10.1016/j.chb.2021.106899

Schuster, C., Weitzman, L., Sass Mikkelsen, K., Meyer-Sahling, J., Bersch, K., Fukuyama, F., Paskov, P., Rogger, D., Mistree, D., & Kay, K. (2020). Responding to COVID-19 through Surveys of Public Servants. *Public Administration Review, 80*(5), 792–796. https://doi.org/10.1111/puar.13246

Shakibaei, S., de Jong, G. C., Alpkökin, P., & Rashidi, T. H. (2021). Impact of the COVID-19 pandemic on travel behavior in Istanbul: A panel data analysis. *Sustainable Cities and Society, 65*, 102619. https://doi.org/10.1016/j.scs.2020.102619

Shofiya, C., & Abidi, S. (2021). Sentiment Analysis on COVID-19-Related Social Distancing in Canada Using Twitter Data. *International Journal of Environmental Research and Public Health, 18*(11), 5993. https://doi.org/10.3390/ijerph18115993

Stiles, J. (2020). Strategic niche management in transition pathways : Telework advocacy as groundwork for an incremental transformation. *Environmental Innovation and Societal Transitions, 34*, 139–150. https://doi.org/10.1016/j.eist.2019.12.001

Suh, A., & Lee, J. (2017). Understanding teleworkers' technostress and its influence on job satisfaction. *Internet Research*, 27(1), 140–159. https://doi.org/10.1108/IntR-06-2015-0181

Toleikienė, R., Rybnikova, I., & Juknevičienė, V. (2020). Whether and how does de Crisis-Induced Situation Change e-Leadership in the Public Sector. *Transylvanian Review of Administrative Sciences*, 10(41), 149–166. https://dx.doi.org/10.24193/tras.SI2020.9

Topi, H. (2004). Supporting Telework: Obstacles and Solutions. *Information Systems Management*, 21(3), 79–85. https://doi.org/10.1201/1078/44432.21.3.20040601/82481.12

Truchot, D., Andela, M., & Takhiart, H. (2021). Stressors met by quarantined French students during the covid-19 pandemic. Their links with depression and sleep disorders. *Journal of Affective Disorders*, 294, 54–59. https://doi.org/10.1016/j.jad.2021.06.059

Tsao, S. F., Chen, H., Tisseverasinghe, T., Yang, Y., Li, L., & Butt, Z. A. (2021). What social media told us in the time of COVID-19: a scoping review. *The Lancet Digital Health, 3*(3), e175–e194. doi:10.1016/S2589-7500(20)30315-0

Tyagi, P., Javalkar, D., & Chakraborty, S. (2021). Sentiment analysis of twitter data using hybrid classification methods and comparative analysis. *Journal of Jilin University*, 40(6). https://doi.org/10.17605/OSF.IO/2NVJK

Valle-Cruz, D., Lopez-Chau, A., & Sandoval-Almazan, R. (2021). How much do Twitter posts affect voters? Analysis of the multi-emotional charge with affective computing in political campaigns. *ACM International Conference Proceeding Series*, 1–14. doi:10.1145/3463677.3463698

Vega, R. P., Anderson, A. J., & Kaplan, S. A. (2015). A Within-Person Examination of the Effects of Telework. *Journal of Business and Psychology*, 30(2), 313–323. https://doi.org/10.1007/s10869-014-9359-4

Wang, K., & Ozbilen, B. (2020). Synergistic and threshold effects of telework and residential location choice on travel time allocation. *Sustainable Cities and Society*, 63, 102468. https://doi.org/10.1016/j.scs.2020.102468

Wang, Z., Ho, S. B., & Cambria, E. (2020). A review of emotion sensing: Categorization models and algorithms. *Multimedia Tools and Applications*, 79(47–48), 35553–35582. https://doi.org/10.1007/s11042-019-08328-z

WHO. (2020). *Weekly epidemiological update - 27 December 2020*. https://www.who.int/publications/m/item/weekly-epidemiological-update---29-december-2020

Zhang, C., Yu, M. C., & Marin, S. (2021a). Exploring public sentiment on enforced remote work during COVID-19. *The Journal of Applied Psychology*, 106(6), 797–810. https://doi.org/10.1037/apl0000933

Zhang, J., Zhang, A., Liu, D., & Bian, Y. (2021b). Customer preferences extraction for air purifiers based on fine-grained sentiment analysis of online reviews. *Knowledge-Based Systems*, 228, 107259. https://doi.org/10.1016/j.knosys.2021.107259

ENDNOTE

[1] Memes are popular and humorous cultural products created that are distributed virally via the Internet and therefore each has exponential distribution potential (Kertcher & Turin, 2020).

Compilation of References

Abboute, A., Boudjeriou, Y., Entringer, G., Azé, J., Bringay, S., & Poncelet, P. (2014, June). Mining twitter for suicide prevention. In *International Conference on Applications of Natural Language to Data Bases/Information Systems* (pp. 250-253). Springer.

Abdel Hadi, S., Bakker, A. B., & Häusser, J. A. (2021). The role of leisure crafting for emotional exhaustion in telework during the COVID-19 pandemic. *Anxiety, Stress, and Coping, 34*(5), 530–544. doi:10.1080/10615806.2021.1903447 PMID:33769142

Abdelrahman, A. M., & Kayed, A. (2015). A survey on semantic similarity measures between concepts in health domain. *American Journal of Computational Mathematics, 5*(02), 204–214. doi:10.4236/ajcm.2015.52017

Acharya, U. R., Oh, S. L., Hagiwara, Y., Tan, J. H., Adeli, H., & Subha, D. P. (2018). Automated EEG-based screening of depression using deep convolutional neural network. *Computer Methods and Programs in Biomedicine, 161*, 103–113. doi:10.1016/j.cmpb.2018.04.012 PMID:29852953

Adomavicius, G., & Tuzhilin, A. (2005). Toward the next generation of recommender systems: a survey of the state-of-the-art and possible extensions. *Transactions on Knowledge and Data Engineering, 17*(6), 734–749. https://ieeexplore.ieee.org/abstract/document/1423975/

Agarwal, A. (2011). Sentiment analysis of Twitter data. *Proceedings of the Workshop on Languages in Social Media,* 30–38. Available at: https://dl.acm.org/citation.cfm?id=2021114

Agarwal, A., Xie, B., Vovsha, I., Rambow, O., & Passonneau, R. J. (2011, June). Sentiment analysis of twitter data. In *Proceedings of the workshop on language in social media (LSM 2011)* (pp. 30-38). Academic Press.

Agarwal, A., Xie, B., Vovsha, I., Rambow, O., & Passonneau, R. J. (2011). Sentiment analysis of Twitter data. *Proceedings of the Workshop on Language in Social Media (LSM),* 30-38.

Agarwal, B., & Mittal, N. (2017). Machine Learning Approaches for Sentiment Analysis. *Artificial Intelligence: Concepts, Methodologies, Tools, and Applications, 3*, 1740–1756.

Agarwal, B., & Mittal, N. (2017). Machine Learning Approaches for Sentiment Analysis. In *Artificial Intelligence, Concepts, Methodologies, Tools, and Applications.* doi:10.4018/978-1-5225-1759-7.ch070

Ahmed, W., & Graduate, D. (n.d.). *Using Social Media Data for Research: An Overview of Tools* Published by the Communication Technology Division of the Association for Education in Journalism and Mass Communication. Available at: http://www.joctec.org/wp-content/uploads/2018/04/A6_WA_v2.pdf

Ahsaee, M. G., Naghibzadeh, M., & Naeini, S. E. Y. (2014). Semantic similarity assessment of words using weighted WordNet. *International Journal of Machine Learning and Cybernetics, 5*(3), 479–490. doi:10.100713042-012-0135-3

Ain, Q. T., Ali, M., Riaz, A., Noureen, A., Kamran, M., Hayat, B., & Rehman, A. (2017). Sentiment analysis using deep learning techniques: A review. *International Journal of Advanced Computer Science and Applications*, *8*(6), 424.

Akef, I., Arango, J. S. M., & Xu, X. (2016). Mallet vs GenSim: Topic modeling for 20 news groups report. *Univ. Ark. Little Rock Law J.*

Akhtar, M. S., Gupta, D., Ekbal, A., & Bhattacharyya, P. (2017). Feature selection and ensemble construction: A two-step method for aspect based sentiment analysis. *Knowledge-Based Systems*, *125*, 116–135. doi:10.1016/j.knosys.2017.03.020

Alamoodi, A., Zaidan, B., Zaidan, A., Albahri, O., Mohammed, K., Malik, R., Almahdi, E. M., Chyad, M. A., Tareq, Z., Albahri, A. S., Hameed, H., & Alaa, M. (2020). Sentiment analysis and its applications in fighting COVID-19 and infectious diseases: A systematic review. *Expert Systems with Applications*, *167*, 114155. doi:10.1016/j.eswa.2020.114155 PMID:33139966

Albalawi, R., Yeap, T. H., & Benyoucef, M. (2020). Using Topic Modeling Methods for Short-Text Data: A Comparative Analysis. *Frontiers in Artificial Intelligence*, *3*(42), 42. Advance online publication. doi:10.3389/frai.2020.00042 PMID:33733159

Albro, M., & McElfresh, J. M. (2021). Job engagement and employee-organization relationship among academic librarians in a modified work environment. *Journal of Academic Librarianship*, *47*(5), 102413. doi:10.1016/j.acalib.2021.102413

Alessia, D., Ferri, F., Grifoni, P., & Guzzo, T. (2015). Approaches, tools and applications for sentiment analysis implementation. *International Journal of Computers and Applications*, *125*(3).

Aletras, N., & Stevenson, M. (2013, June). Representing topics using images. In *Proceedings of the 2013 Conference of the North American Chapter of the Association for Computational Linguistics: Human Language Technologies* (pp. 158-167). Academic Press.

Aletras, N., & Stevenson, M. (2015). A Hybrid Distributional and Knowledge-based Model of Lexical Semantics. SEM@ NAACL-HLT, 20-29. doi:10.18653/v1/S15-1003

Al-Ghadir, A. I., Azmi, A. M., & Hussain, A. (2021). A novel approach to stance detection in social media tweets by fusing ranked lists and sentiments. *Information Fusion*, *67*, 29–40. doi:10.1016/j.inffus.2020.10.003

Ali, L., & Shears, R. (2009). Betrayed: A terrifying true story of a young woman dragged back to Iraq (1st ed.). Academic Press.

Alipour, J. V., Fadinger, H., & Schymik, J. (2021). My home is my castle – The benefits of working from home during a pandemic crisis. *Journal of Public Economics*, *196*, 104373. doi:10.1016/j.jpubeco.2021.104373

AlSagri, H. S., & Ykhlef, M. (2020). Machine learning-based approach for depression detection in twitter using content and activity features. *IEICE Transactions on Information and Systems*, *103*(8), 1825–1832. doi:10.1587/transinf.2020EDP7023

Alvanita, A. (2018). The Character Development of Neville Longbottom in the Harry Potter Series. *Lexicon*, *1*(3). Advance online publication. doi:10.22146/lexicon.v1i3.42080

Alwan, J. K., Hussain, A. J., Abd, D. H., Sadiq, A. T., Khalaf, M., & Liatsis, P. (2011). Political Arabic Articles Orientation Using Rough Set Theory with Sentiment Lexicon. *IEEE Access: Practical Innovations, Open Solutions*, *9*, 24475–24484. doi:10.1109/ACCESS.2021.3054919

Amasyah, M. F. (2006). *An Approach for Word Categorization Based on Semantic Similarity Measure Obtained from Search Engines. 2006 IEEE 14th Signal Processing and Communications Applications.*

Anderson, A. J., Kaplan, S. A., & Vega, R. P. (2015). The impact of telework on emotional experience: When, and for whom, does telework improve daily affective well-being? *European Journal of Work and Organizational Psychology*, *24*(6), 882–897. doi:10.1080/1359432X.2014.966086

Angelov, D. (2020). *Top2vec: Distributed representations of topics.* arXiv preprint arXiv:2008.09470.

Anoop, V. S., & Asharaf, S. (2020). Aspect-Oriented Sentiment Analysis: A Topic Modeling-Powered Approach. *Journal of Intelligent Systems*, *29*(1), 1166–1178. doi:10.1515/jisys-2018-0299

Anwar, A., Ilyas, H., Yaqub, U., & Zaman, S. (2021). Analyzing QAnon on Twitter in Context of US Elections 2020: Analysis of User Messages and Profiles Using VADER and BERT Topic modeling. *DG. O2021: The 22nd Annual International Conference on Digital Government Research*, 82–88.

Apachae Software Foundation. (2021). *Apache Tika - A content analysis toolkit.* https://tika.apache.org/

Apache OPEN NLP Documentation. (2017). https://opennlp.apache.org/docs/

Aparicio, J. T., de Sequeira, J. S., & Costa, C. J. (2021). Emotion analysis of Portuguese Political Parties Communication over the covid-19 Pandemic. *2021 16th Iberian Conference on Information Systems and Technologies (CISTI)*, 1–6.

Armas-Elguera, F., Talavera-Ramírez, J. E., Cárdenas, M., & De la Cruz-Vargas, J. A. (2021). Trastornos del sueño y ansiedad de estudiantes de Medicina del primer y último año en Lima, Perú. *Revista de La Fundación Educación Médica*, *24*(3), 133–138. doi:10.33588/fem.243.1125

Arora, P., & Arora, P. (2019, March). Mining twitter data for depression detection. In *International Conference on Signal Processing and Communication (ICSC)* (pp. 186-189). IEEE. 10.1109/ICSC45622.2019.8938353

Artetxe, M., Labaka, G., & Agirre, E. (2017). Learning bilingual word embeddings with (almost) no bilingual data. *Proceedings of the 55th Annual Meeting of the Association for Computational Linguistics*, *1*, 451-462. 10.18653/v1/P17-1042

Aslam, F., Awan, T. M., Syed, J. H., Kashif, A., & Parveen, M. (2020). Sentiments and emotions evoked by news headlines of coronavirus disease (COVID-19) outbreak. *Humanities and Social Sciences Communications*, *7*(1), 1–9. doi:10.105741599-020-0523-3

Asl, M. P. (2019). Foucauldian rituals of justice and conduct in Zainab Salbi's Between Two Worlds. *Journal of Contemporary Iraq & the Arab World*, *13*(2-3), 227–242. doi:10.1386/jciaw_00010_1

Asl, M. P. (2020). Micro-Physics of discipline: Spaces of the self in Middle Eastern women life writings. *International Journal of Arabic-English Studies*, *20*(2), 223–240. doi:10.33806/ijaes2000.20.2.12

Asl, M. P. (2021). Gender, space and counter-conduct: Iranian women's heterotopic imaginations in Ramita Navai's City of Lies. *Gender, Place and Culture*, 1–21. Advance online publication. doi:10.1080/0966369X.2021.1975100

Asl, M. P. (2022). Truth, space, and resistance: Iranian women's practices of freedom in Ramita Navai's City of Lies. *Women's Studies*. Advance online publication. doi:10.1080/00497878.2022.2030342

Awadallah, R., Ramanath, M., & Weikum, G. (2011). Opinionetit: Understanding the opinions-people network for politically controversial topics. *Proceedings of the 20th ACM International Conference on Information and Knowledge Management*, 2481–2484. 10.1145/2063576.2063997

Baccianella, S., Esuli, A., & Sebastiani, F. (2010). Sentiwordnet 3.0: an enhanced lexical resource for sentiment analysis and opinion mining. In *Proceedings of the International Language Resources and Evaluation Conference (LREC)* (Vol. *10*, No. 2010, pp. 2200-2204). Academic Press.

Bach, N. X., Van, P. D., Tai, N. D., & Phuong, T. M. (2015). Mining vietnamese comparative sentences for sentiment analysis. In *Proceedings of Seventh International Conference on Knowledge and Systems Engineering* (pp. 162-167). IEEE. 10.1109/KSE.2015.36

Back, M. D., Stopfer, J. M., Vazire, S., Gaddis, S., Schmukle, S. C., Egloff, B., & Gosling, S. D. (2010). Facebook profiles reflect actual personality, not self-idealization. *Psychological Science, 21*(3), 372–374. doi:10.1177/0956797609360756 PMID:20424071

Bader, C. S., Skurla, M., & Vahia, I. V. (2020). Technology in the assessment, treatment, and management of depression. *Harvard Review of Psychiatry, 28*(1), 60–66. doi:10.1097/HRP.0000000000000235 PMID:31913982

Bai, S., Bai, X., Latecki, L. J., & Tian, Q. (2017). Multidimensional Scaling on Multiple Input Distance Matrices. AAAI, 1281-1287.

Bandorski, D., Kurniawan, N., Baltes, P., Hoeltgen, R., Hecker, M., Stunder, D., & Keuchel, M. (2016). Contraindications for video capsule endoscopy. *World Journal of Gastroenterology, 22*(45), 9898–9908. doi:10.3748/wjg.v22.i45.9898 PMID:28018097

Bao, W., Yue, J., & Rao, Y. (2017). A deep learning framework for financial time series using stacked autoencoders and long-short term memory. *PLoS One, 12*(7), 1–24. doi:10.1371/journal.pone.0180944 PMID:28708865

Bar, D., Zesch, T., & Gurevych, I. (2015). *Composing Measures for Computing Text Similarity*. Academic Press.

Barbier, G., & Liu, H. (2011). Data mining in social media. In C. C. Aggarwal (Ed.), *Social Network Data Analytics* (pp. 327–352). Springer US. doi:10.1007/978-1-4419-8462-3_12

Bar, D., Zesch, T., & Gurevych, I. (2012). Text reuse detection using a composition of text similarity measures. *Proceedings of COLING, 2012*, 167–184.

Barkur, G., Vibha, G. B. K., & Kamath, G. B. (2020). Sentiment analysis of nationwide lockdown due to COVID 19 outbreak: Evidence from India. *Asian Journal of Psychiatry, 51*, 102089. doi:10.1016/j.ajp.2020.102089 PMID:32305035

Barton, G. (2017). *Harry Potter and the translator's nightmare*. VOX. https://www.vox.com/culture/2016/10/18/13316332/harry-potter-translations

Basave, A. E. C., He, Y., & Xu, R. (2014, June). Automatic labelling of topic models learned from twitter by summarisation. In *Proceedings of the 52nd Annual Meeting of the Association for Computational Linguistics (*Volume 2: *Short Papers)* (pp. 618-624). Academic Press.

Basiri, M. E., Nemati, S., Abdar, M., Cambria, E., & Acharya, U. R. (2021). ABCDM: An Attention-based Bidirectional CNN-RNN Deep Model for sentiment analysis. *Future Generation Computer Systems, 115*, 279–294. doi:10.1016/j.future.2020.08.005

Batet, M., Sanchez, D., Valls, A., & Gibert, K. (2013). Semantic similarity estimation from multiple ontologies. *Applied Intelligence, 38*(1), 29–44. doi:10.100710489-012-0355-y

Batra, R., Imran, A. S., Kastrati, Z., Ghafoor, A., Daudpota, S. M., & Shaikh, S. (2021). Evaluating Polarity Trend Amidst the Coronavirus Crisis in Peoples' Attitudes toward the Vaccination Drive. *Sustainability, 13*(10), 5344. doi:10.3390u13105344

Batrinca, B., & Treleaven, P. C. (2014). Social media analytics: A survey of techniques, tools and platforms. *AI & Society, 30*(1), 89–116. doi:10.100700146-014-0549-4

Bechini, A., Ducange, P., Marcelloni, F., & Renda, A. (2020). Stance analysis of Twitter users: The case of the vaccination topic in Italy. *IEEE Intelligent Systems*.

Bele, N., Panigrahi, P. K., & Srivastava, S. K. (2017). Political sentiment mining: A new age intelligence tool for business strategy formulation. *International Journal of Business Intelligence Research, 8*(1), 55–70. doi:10.4018/IJBIR.2017010104

Beleveslis, D., Tjortjis, C., Psaradelis, D., & Nikoglou, D. (2019). A hybrid method for sentiment analysis of election related tweets. *2019 4th South-East Europe Design Automation, Computer Engineering, Computer Networks and Social Media Conference (SEEDA-CECNSM)*, 1–6.

Belohlavek, R., & Mikula, T. (2020). Typicality in Conceptual Structures Within the Framework of Formal Concept Analysis. CLA, 33-45.

Belohlavek, R. (2008). *Introduction to formal concept analysis*. Palacky University, Department of Computer Science.

Bener, A., Misirli, A. T., Caglayan, B., Kocaguneli, E., & Calikli, G. (2015). Lessons Learned from Software Analytics in Practice. In C. Bird, T. Menzies, & T. Zimmermann (Eds.), *The Art and Science of Analyzing Software Data* (pp. 453–489). Morgan Kaufmann. doi:10.1016/B978-0-12-411519-4.00016-1

Benlahbib, A., & Nfaoui, E. H. (2021). Mtvrep: A movie and tv show reputation system based on fine-grained sentiment and semantic analysis. *Iranian Journal of Electrical and Computer Engineering, 11*(2), 1613. doi:10.11591/ijece.v11i2.pp1613-1626

Bentley, T. A., Teo, S. T. T., McLeod, L., Tan, F., Bosua, R., & Gloet, M. (2016). The role of organisational support in teleworker wellbeing: A socio-technical systems approach. *Applied Ergonomics, 52*, 207–215. doi:10.1016/j.apergo.2015.07.019 PMID:26360212

Berry, M. W., Dumais, S. T., & O'Brien, G. W. (1995). Using Linear Algebra for Intelligent Information Retrieval. *SIAM Review, 37*(4), 573–595. doi:10.1137/1037127

Bhadane, C., Dalal, H., & Doshi, H. (2015). Sentiment analysis: Measuring opinions. *Procedia Computer Science, 45*, 808–814. doi:10.1016/j.procs.2015.03.159

Bhadury, A., Chen, J., Zhu, J., & Liu, S. (2016). Scaling up dynamic topic models. *Proceedings of the 25th International Conference on World Wide Web WWW'16* (pp. 381-390). International World Wide Web Steering Committee. 10.1145/2872427.2883046

Bhatia, S., Lau, J. H., & Baldwin, T. (2016). *Automatic labelling of topics with neural embeddings*. arXiv preprint arXiv:1612.05340.

Biba, M., & Mane, M. (2014). Sentiment analysis through machine learning: An experimental evaluation for Albanian. In *Recent Advances in Intelligent Informatics* (pp. 195–203). Springer. doi:10.1007/978-3-319-01778-5_20

Bing, L., Liu, B., & Zhang, L. (2012). A survey of opinion mining and sentiment analysis. *Mining Text Data*, 415–463.

Bing, L. (2012). *Sentiment Analysis and Opinion Mining (Synthesis Lectures on Human Language Technologies)*. University of Illinois.

Bird, C., Menzies, T., & Zimmermann, T. (2015). The Art and Science of Analyzing Software Data. In C. Bird, T. Menzies, & T. Zimmermann (Eds.), *The Art and Science of Analyzing Software Data*. Morgan Kaufmann. doi:10.1016/B978-0-12-411519-4.00001-X

Bird, S., Klein, E., & Loper, E. (2009). *Natural language processing wiht python: analysing text with the natural language toolkit*. O'Reilly Media.

Blei, D. M., Ng, A. Y., & Jordan, M. I. (2003). Latent dirichlet allocation. *The Journal of Machine Learning Research,* *3*, 993-1022.

Blei, D. M., Ng, A. Y., & Jordan, M. I. (2003). Latent dirichlet allocation. *Journal of Machine Learning Research, 3,* 993–1022.

Blei, D., & Lafferty, J. D. (2006). Dynamic topic models. *Proceedings of the 23rd International Conference on Machine Learning* (pp. 113-120). Association for Computing Machinery. 10.1145/1143844.1143859

Boiy, E., & Moens, M. F. (2009). A machine learning approach to sentiment analysis in multilingual web texts. *Information Retrieval, 12*(5), 526–558. doi:10.100710791-008-9070-z

Bollegala, D., Matsuo, Y., & Ishizuka, M. (2011). A web search engine-based approach to measure semantic similarity between words. *IEEE Transactions on Knowledge and Data Engineering, 23*(7), 977–990. doi:10.1109/TKDE.2010.172

Bonaccorsi, A., Chiarello, F., & Fantoni, G. (2021). Impact for whom? Mapping the users of public research with lexicon-based text mining. *Scientometrics, 126*(2), 1745–1774. doi:10.100711192-020-03803-z

Bonn, U. (2019). *Venema P-Model algorithm.* Retrieved from https://www2.meteo.uni-bonn.de/staff/venema/themes/surrogates/

Bonner, A. (2019). *You Are What You Tweet Detecting Depression in Social Media via Twitter Usage.* Towards Data Science. Retrieved 14 September 2021, from https://towardsdatascience.com/you-are-what-you-tweet-7e23fb84f4ed

Bonnevie, E., Gallegos-Jeffrey, A., Goldbarg, J., Byrd, B., & Smyser, J. (2021). Quantifying the rise of vaccine opposition on Twitter during the COVID-19 pandemic. *Journal of Communication in Healthcare, 14*(1), 12–19. doi:10.1080/17538068.2020.1858222

Bonta, V., & Janardhan, N. K. N. (2019). A comprehensive study on lexicon based approaches for sentiment analysis. *Asian Journal of Computer Science and Technology, 8*(S2), 1–6. doi:10.51983/ajcst-2019.8.S2.2037

Boon-Itt, S., & Skunkan, Y. (2020). Public perception of the COVID-19 pandemic on Twitter: Sentiment analysis and topic modeling study. *JMIR Public Health and Surveillance, 6*(4), e21978. doi:10.2196/21978 PMID:33108310

Boucher, J. C., Cornelson, K., Benham, J. L., Fullerton, M. M., Tang, T., Constantinescu, C., Mourali, M., Oxoby, R. J., Marshall, D. A., Hemmati, H., Badami, A., Hu, J., & Lang, R. (2021). Analyzing social media to explore the attitudes and behaviors following the announcement of successful COVID-19 vaccine trials: Infodemiology study. *JMIR Infodemiology, 1*(1), e28800. doi:10.2196/28800 PMID:34447924

Bourequat, W., & Mourad, H. (2021). Sentiment Analysis Approach for Analyzing iPhone Release using Support Vector Machine. *International Journal of Advances in Data and Information Systems, 2*(1), 36–44. doi:10.25008/ijadis.v2i1.1216

Boussaadi, S., Aliane, H., Cerist, A., & Abdeldjalil, P. O. (2020). *Modeling of scientists profiles based on LDA.* Academic Press.

Brownlee, J. (2017, May 24). *A Gentle introduction to long short-term memory networks by the experts.* Retrieved from Machine Learning Mastery: https://machinelearningmastery.com/gentle-introduction-long-short-term-memory-networks-experts/

Brownlee, J. (2017). *Machine Learning Mastery with Python: Understand Your Data, Create Accurate Models and Work Projects End-To-End.* Jason Brownlee.

Bruni, E., Tran, N. K., & Baroni, M. (2014). Multimodal distributional semantics. *Journal of Artificial Intelligence Research, 49,* 1–47. doi:10.1613/jair.4135

Bruns, A., & Liang, Y. E. (2012). Tools and methods for capturing Twitter data during natural disasters. *First Monday*, *17*(4). Advance online publication. doi:10.5210/fm.v17i4.3937

Brush, K. (2020). *Data Visualization*. https://searchbusinessanalytics.techtarget.com/definition/data-visualization

Burton, D. (2020). *textacy: NLP, before and after spaCy*. https://github.com/Joiike/textacy

Calefato, F., Lanubile, F., Maiorano, F., & Novielli, N. (2018). Sentiment polarity detection for software development. *Empirical Software Engineering*, *23*(3), 1352–1382. doi:10.100710664-017-9546-9

Calvo, R. A., D'Mello, S., Gratch, J. M., & Kappas, A. (Eds.). (2015). *The Oxford Handbook of Affective Computing*. Oxford Library of Psychology. doi:10.1093/oxfordhb/9780199942237.001.0001

Calvo, R. A., Milne, D. N., Hussain, M. S., & Christensen, H. (2017). Natural language processing in mental health applications using non-clinical texts. *Natural Language Engineering*, *23*(5), 649–685. doi:10.1017/S1351324916000383

Cambria, E., Das, D., Bandyopadhyay, S., Feraco, A., & ... (2017). *A practical guide to sentiment analysis*. Springer. doi:10.1007/978-3-319-55394-8

Cambria, E., Li, Y., Xing, F. Z., Poria, S., & Kwok, K. (2020). SenticNet 6: Ensemble application of symbolic and sub-symbolic AI for sentiment analysis. *Proceedings of the 29th ACM International Conference on Information & Knowledge Management*, 105–114. 10.1145/3340531.3412003

Canhasi, E. (2013). Measuring the sentence level similarity. In *Proceedings of 2nd International Symposium of Computing in Informatics and Mathematics* (pp. 35-42). Academic Press.

Carly. (2020). The Big Six Translations of Harry Potter. *The Rowling Magazine*. https://www.therowlinglibrary.com/2020/07/22/the-six-translations-of-harry-potter/

Castillo, J. J. (2011). A WordNet-based semantic approach to textual entailment and cross-lingual textual entailment. *International Journal of Machine Learning and Cybernetics*, *2*(3), 177–189. doi:10.100713042-011-0026-z

Ceci, F., Gonçalves, A. L., & Webe, R. (2016). A model for sentiment analysis based on ontology and cases. *IEEE Latin America Transactions*, *14*(11), 4560–4566. doi:10.1109/TLA.2016.7795829

Cederman, L., & Weidmann, N. (2017). Predicting armed conflict: Time to adjust our expectations? *Science*, *355*(6324), 474–476. doi:10.1126cience.aal4483 PMID:28154047

Chakraborty, K., Bhatia, S., Bhattacharyya, S., Platos, J., Bag, R., & Hassanien, A. E. (2020). Sentiment analysis of COVID-19 tweets by deep learning classifiers—A study to show how popularity is affecting accuracy in social media. *Applied Soft Computing*, *97*, 106754. doi:10.1016/j.asoc.2020.106754 PMID:33013254

Chandrasekaran, D., & Mago, V. (2021). Evolution of Semantic Similarity—A Survey. [CSUR]. *ACM Computing Surveys*, *54*(2), 1–37. doi:10.1145/3440755

Charalabidis, Y., Maragoudakis, M., & Loukis, E. (2015). Opinion Mining and Sentiment Analysis in Policy Formulation Initiatives: The EU-Community Approach. In E. Tambouris, P. Panagiotopoulos, Ø. Sæbø, K. Tarabanis, M. A. Wimmer, M. Milano, & T. Pardo (Eds.), *Electronic Participation: Proceedings of the 7th IFIP 8.5 International Conference on Electronic Participation (ePart 2015)* (pp. 147–160). Springer International Publishing.

Chau, A. L., Valle-Cruz, D., & Sandoval-Almazán, R. (2021). Sentiment Analysis in Crisis Situations for Better Connected Government: Case of Mexico Earthquake in 2017. In *Web 2.0 and Cloud Technologies for Implementing Connected Government* (pp. 162–181). IGI Global.

Chen, H. C., Guo, X. H., Liu, L. Q., & Zhu, X. H. (2017). A Short Text Similarity Measure Based on Hidden Topics. *Computer Science and Technology: Proceedings of the International Conference (CST2016)*, 1101-1108. 10.1142/9789813146426_0124

Chi, O. H., Saldamli, A., & Gursoy, D. (2021). Impact of the COVID-19 pandemic on management-level hotel employees' work behaviors: Moderating effects of working-from-home. *International Journal of Hospitality Management*, 98, 103020. doi:10.1016/j.ijhm.2021.103020 PMID:34493887

Chiu, S.-I., & Hsu, K.-W. (2018). Predicting political tendency of posts on Facebook. *Proceedings of the 2018 7th International Conference on Software and Computer Applications*, 110–114. 10.1145/3185089.3185094

Chollet. (2015). *Keras: The Python deep learning library*. Retrieved from Keras: https://keras.io/

Chowdhury, G. G. (2003). Natural language processing. *Annual Review of Information Science & Technology*, 37(1), 51–89. doi:10.1002/aris.1440370103

Church, K. W. (2017). Word2Vec. *Natural Language Engineering*, 23(1), 155–162. doi:10.1017/S1351324916000334

Cimiano, P., Hotho, A., & Staab, S. (2005). Learning concept hierarchies from text corpora using formal concept analysis. *Journal of Artificial Intelligence Research*, 24, 305–339. doi:10.1613/jair.1648

Cioffi-Revilla, C. (2010). *A methodology for complex social simulations*. Available at: https://papers.ssrn.com/sol3/papers.cfm?abstract_id=2291156

Clauset, A. (2018). Trends and fluctuations in the severity of interstate wars. *SciencesAdvances -. Social Sciences*, 4(2), 1–10. doi:10.1126ciadv.aao3580 PMID:29507877

CNN. (2020). *CNN - breaking news, latest news and videos*. Retrieved from CNN: https://edition.cnn.com

Codocedo, V., Lykourentzou, I., & Napoli, A. (2014). A semantic approach to concept lattice-based information retrieval. *Annals of Mathematics and Artificial Intelligence*, 72(1-2), 169–195. doi:10.100710472-014-9403-0

Collomb, A., Costea, C., Joyeux, D., Hasan, O., & Brunie, L. (2014). A study and comparison of sentiment analysis methods for reputation evaluation. *Rapport de recherche RR-LIRIS-2014-002*.

Correia, R. B., Wood, I. B., Bollen, J., & Rocha, L. M. (2020). Mining Social Media Data for Biomedical Signals and Health-Related Behavior. *Annual Review of Biomedical Data Science*, 3(1), 433–458. doi:10.1146/annurev-biodatasci-030320-040844 PMID:32550337

Cortis, K., & Davis, B. (2021). Over a decade of social opinion mining: A systematic review. *Artificial Intelligence Review*, 54(7), 4873–4965. doi:10.100710462-021-10030-2 PMID:34188346

Cossu, J. V., Torres-Moreno, J. M., SanJuan, E., & El-Bèze, M. (2020). *Intweetive Text Summarization*. arXiv preprint arXiv:2001,11382.

Cotfas, L. A., Delcea, C., Roxin, I., Ioanăş, C., Gherai, D. S., & Tajariol, F. (2021). The longest month: Analyzing COVID-19 vaccination opinions dynamics from tweets in the month following the first vaccine announcement. *IEEE Access: Practical Innovations, Open Solutions*, 9, 33203–33223. doi:10.1109/ACCESS.2021.3059821 PMID:34786309

Criado, J. I., Sandoval-Almazan, R., & Gil-Garcia, J. R. (2013). Government innovation through social media. *Government Information Quarterly*, 30(4), 319–326. doi:10.1016/j.giq.2013.10.003

Crisci, A., Grasso, V., Nesi, P., Pantaleo, G., Paoli, I., & Zaza, I. (2018). Predicting TV programme audience by using twitter based metrics. *Multimedia Tools and Applications*, 77(10), 12203–12232. doi:10.100711042-017-4880-x

Cuadrado, J. C., & Gómez-Navarro, D. P. (2011). *Un modelo lingüístico-semántico basado en emociones para la clasificación de textos según su polaridad e intensidad.* Facultad de Informática Universidad Complutense de Madrid, Departamento de Ingeniería del Software e Inteligencia Artificial . Madri: Facultad de Informática Universidad Complutense de Madrid.

Cuadros, D. F., Tomita, A., Vandormael, A., Slotow, R., Burns, J. K., & Tanser, F. (2019). Spatial structure of depression in South Africa: A longitudinal panel survey of a nationally representative sample of households. *Scientific Reports*, *9*(1), 1–10. doi:10.103841598-018-37791-1 PMID:30700798

Cuerdo-Vilches, T., Navas-Martín, M., March, S., & Oteiza, I. (2021). Adequacy of telework spaces in homes during the lockdown in Madrid, according to socioeconomic factors and home features. *Sustainable Cities and Society*, *75*, 103262. doi:10.1016/j.scs.2021.103262

Cyril, C. P. D., Beulah, J. R., Subramani, N., Mohan, P., Harshavardhan, A., & Sivabalaselvamani, D. (2021). An automated learning model for sentiment analysis and data classification of Twitter data using balanced CA-SVM. *Concurrent Engineering*, *29*(4), 386–395. doi:10.1177/1063293X211031485

D'Andrea, A., Ferri, F., Grifoni, P., & Guzzo, T. (2015). Approaches, Tools and Applications for Sentiment Analysis Implementation. *International Journal of Computers and Applications*, *125*(3), 26–33. doi:10.5120/ijca2015905866

D'Andrea, E., Ducange, P., Bechini, A., Renda, A., & Marcelloni, F. (2019). Monitoring the public opinion about the vaccination topic from tweets analysis. *Expert Systems with Applications*, *116*, 209–226. doi:10.1016/j.eswa.2018.09.009

Das, D. (2019). *Social Media Sentiment Analysis using Machine Learning : Part — II.* https://towardsdatascience.com/social-media-sentiment-analysis-part-ii-bcacca5aaa39

Davidescu, A. A., Apostu, S.-A., Paul, A., & Casuneanu, I. (2020). Work Flexibility, Job Satisfaction, and Job Performance among Romanian Employees—Implications for Sustainable Human Resource Management. *Sustainability*, *12*(15), 6086. doi:10.3390u12156086

De Choudhury, M., Counts, S., Horvitz, E. J., & Hoff, A. (2014, February). Characterizing and predicting postpartum depression from shared facebook data. In *Proceedings of the 17th ACM conference on Computer supported cooperative work & social computing* (pp. 626-638). 10.1145/2531602.2531675

De Choudhury, M., Gamon, M., Counts, S., & Horvitz, E. (2013, June). Predicting depression via social media. *Health Information Science and Systems*, *6*(1), 1–12.

De Deyne, S., Navarro, D. J., Perfors, A., & Storms, G. (2012). *Strong structure in weak semantic similarity: A graph based account.* Cognitive Science Society.

de Melo, T., & Figueiredo, C. M. (2021). Comparing news articles and tweets about COVID-19 in Brazil: Sentiment analysis and topic modeling approach. *JMIR Public Health and Surveillance*, *7*(2), e24585. doi:10.2196/24585 PMID:33480853

De', R., Pandey, N., & Pal, A. (2020). Impact of digital surge during Covid-19 pandemic: A viewpoint on research and practice. *International Journal of Information Management*, *55*, 102171. https://doi.org/10.1016/j.ijinfomgt.2020.102171

Deerwester, S., Dumais, S. T., Furnas, G. W., Landauer, T. K., & Harshman, R. (1990). Indexing by latent semantic analysis. *Journal of the American Society for Information Science*, *41*(6), 391–407. doi:10.1002/(SICI)1097-4571(199009)41:6<391::AID-ASI1>3.0.CO;2-9

Deguchi, T., & Ishii, N. (2021). Document Similarity by Word Clustering with Semantic Distance. *International Conference on Hybrid Artificial Intelligence Systems*, 3-14. 10.1007/978-3-030-86271-8_1

Dejevsky, M. (2017, june). *As Syria's war enters its endgame, the risk of a US-Russia conflict escalates.* Retrieved from The Guardian: https://www.theguardian.com/commentisfree/2017/jun/21/syria-war-endgame-us-russia-conflict-washington-moscow-accidental-war

Demaine, E., Hesterberg, A., Koehler, F., Lynch, J., & Urschel, J. (2021). Multidimensional scaling: Approximation and complexity. *International Conference on Machine Learning,* 2568-2578.

Department of Peace and Conflict Research at Uppsala University. (1980). *Uppsala Conflict Data.* Retrieved from Uppsala Conflict Data Program - UCDP: https://ucdp.uu.se/

Depression Tests and Diagnosis. (n.d.). *Healthline.* Retrieved 14 September 2021, from https://www.healthline.com/health/depression/tests-diagnosis

Deshpande, M., & Rao, V. (2017, December). Depression detection using emotion artificial intelligence. In International Conference on Intelligent Sustainable Systems (ICISS) (pp. 858-862). doi:10.1109/ISS1.2017.8389299

Devereux, B. J., Clarke, A., Marouchos, A., & Tyler, L. K. (2013). Representational similarity analysis reveals commonalities and differences in the semantic processing of words and objects. *The Journal of Neuroscience: The Official Journal of the Society for Neuroscience, 33*(48), 18906–18916. doi:10.1523/JNEUROSCI.3809-13.2013 PMID:24285896

Devika, M., Sunitha, C., & Ganesh, A. (2016). Sentiment analysis: A comparative study on different approaches. *Procedia Computer Science, 87,* 44–49. doi:10.1016/j.procs.2016.05.124

Devlin, J., Chang, M. W., Lee, K., & Toutanova, K. (2018). *Bert: Pre-training of deep bidirectional transformers for language understanding.* arXiv preprint arXiv:1810.04805.

Devlin, J., Chang, M. W., Lee, K., & Toutanova, K. (2018). *BERT: Pre-training of deep bidirectional transformers for language understanding.* arXiv preprint arXiv:1810.04805.

Dhaoui, C., Webster, C., & Tan, L. (2017, August). Social media sentiment analysis: Lexicon versus machine learning. *Journal of Consumer Marketing, 34*(6), 480–488. Advance online publication. doi:10.1108/JCM-03-2017-2141

Diao, H., Zhang, Y., Ma, L. & Lu, H., (2021). *Similarity Reasoning and Filtration for Image-Text Matching.* Technical Report.

Ding, S., Cong, G., Lin, C. Y., & Zhu, X. (2008). Using conditional random fields to extract contexts and answers of questions from online forums. In *Proceedings of ACL-08: HLT* (vol. 8, pp. 710-718). Association for Computational Linguistics.

Ding, X., & Liu, B. (2010). Resolving object and attribute coreference in opinion mining. In *Proceedings of the 23rd International Conference on Computational Linguistics* (pp. 268-276). Association for Computational Linguistics.

Ding, X., Liu, B., & Yu, P. S. (2008). A holistic lexicon-based approach to opinion mining. In *Proceedings of the 2008 International Conference on Web Search and Data Mining* (pp. 231-240). ACM. 10.1145/1341531.1341561

Do, H. H., Prasad, P. W. C., Maag, A., & Alsadoon, A. (2019). Deep learning for aspect-based sentiment analysis: A comparative review. *Expert Systems with Applications, 118,* 272–299. doi:10.1016/j.eswa.2018.10.003

Dorle, S., & Pise, N. (2018). Political sentiment analysis through social media. *2018 Second International Conference on Computing Methodologies and Communication (ICCMC),* 869–873. 10.1109/ICCMC.2018.8487879

Dos Santos, C., & Gatti, M. (2014, August). Deep convolutional neural networks for sentiment analysis of short texts. In *Proceedings of COLING 2014, the 25th International Conference on Computational Linguistics: Technical Papers* (pp. 69-78). Academic Press.

Dreisbach, C., Koleck, T. A., Bourne, P. E., & Bakken, S. (2019). A systematic review of natural language processing and text mining of symptoms from electronic patient-authored text data. *International Journal of Medical Informatics*, *125*, 37–46. doi:10.1016/j.ijmedinf.2019.02.008 PMID:30914179

Dueñas-Fernández, R. (n.d.). *Detecting trends on the Web: A multidisciplinary approach*. Elsevier. Available at: https://www.sciencedirect.com/science/article/pii/S1566253514000116

Dumais, S. T., Furnas, G. W., Landauer, T. K., Deerwester, S., & Harshman, R. (1988, May). Using latent semantic analysis to improve access to textual information. In *Proceedings of the SIGCHI conference on Human factors in computing systems* (pp. 281-285). 10.1145/57167.57214

Du, X., Kowalski, M., Varde, A. S., Melo, G., & Taylor, R. W. (2020). Public opinion matters: Mining social media text for environmental management. *SIGWEB Newsl.*, (Autumn), 5. Advance online publication. doi:10.1145/3352683.3352688

Ebaid, H. A. (2018). Adjectives as Persuasive Tools: The Case of Product Naming. *Open Journal of Modern Linguistics*, *8*(6), 262–293. doi:10.4236/ojml.2018.86022

Edelmann, N., Schossboeck, J., & Albrecht, V. (2021). Remote Work in Public Sector Organisations: Employees' Experiences in a Pandemic Context. *ACM International Conference Proceeding Series*, 408–415. doi:10.1145/3463677.3463725

Edo-Osagie, O., De La Iglesia, B., Lake, I., & Edeghere, O. (2020). A scoping review of the use of Twitter for public health research. *Computers in Biology and Medicine*, *122*, 103770. doi:10.1016/j.compbiomed.2020.103770 PMID:32502758

Efron, M., & Winget, M. (2010). Questions are content: A taxonomy of questions in a microblogging environment. *Proceedings of the American Society for Information Science and Technology*, *47*(1), 1–10. doi:10.1002/meet.14504701208

Eichstaedt, J. C., Smith, R. J., Merchant, R. M., Ungar, L. H., Crutchley, P., Preoţiuc-Pietro, D., & Schwartz, H. A. (2018). Facebook language predicts depression in medical records. *Proceedings of the National Academy of Sciences of the United States of America*, *115*(44), 11203–11208. doi:10.1073/pnas.1802331115 PMID:30322910

Ekman, P. (1999). Basic emotions. Handbook of Cognition and Emotion, 98(45–60), 16. doi:10.1002/0470013494.ch3

El Badry, H. (2014). Rain Over Baghdad: An Egyptian Novel (1st ed.). The American University in Cairo Press.

Elavarasi, S. A., Akilandeswari, J., & Menaga, K. (2014). A survey on semantic similarity measure. *International Journal of Research in Advent Technology*, *2*, 389–398.

Elbadrawy, A., & Karypis, G. (2014). *Feature-based similarity models for top-n recommendation of new items. Department of Computer Science, University of Minnesota*. Tech. Rep.

Elekes, A., Schaler, M., & Bohm, K. (2017). On the Various Semantics of Similarity in Word Embedding Models. *Digital Libraries (JCDL), 2017 ACM/IEEE Joint Conference on*, 1-10. 10.1109/JCDL.2017.7991568

Elghazaly, T., Mahmoud, A., & Hefny, H. A. (2016). Political sentiment analysis using twitter data. *Proceedings of the International Conference on Internet of Things and Cloud Computing*, 1–5.

Elsayed, T., Lin, J., & Oard, D. W. (2008). Pairwise document similarity in large collections with MapReduce. In *Proceedings of the 46th Annual Meeting of the Association for Computational Linguistics on Human Language Technologies: Short Papers*. Association for Computational Linguistics. 10.3115/1557690.1557767

Emmert-Strib, F., Yang, Z., Feng, H., Tripathi, S., & Dehmer, M. (2018). An introductory review of deep learning for prediction models with big data. *Frontiers in Artificial Intelligence - Deep Learning in Computational Social Science*, *27*, 16-32. doi:10.3389/frai.2020.00004

Enck, W., & Xie, T. (2014). Tutorial: Text analytics for security. *Proceedings of the ACM Conference on Computer and Communications Security, 1*, 1540–1541. 10.1145/2660267.2660576

Eurofound. (2020). *Living, working and COVID-19.* Publications Office of the European Union. doi:10.2806/467608

Eurofound. (2021). *Living, working and COVID-19 (Update April 2021) : Mental health and trust decline across EU as pandemic enters another year.* Publications Office of the European Union. doi:10.2806/76802

Fang, X., & Zhan, J. (2015). Sentiment analysis using product review data. *Journal of Big Data, 2*(1), 1–14. doi:10.118640537-015-0015-2

fastText. (2016). *What is fastText?* https://fasttext.cc/docs/en/support.html

fastText. (2020). *Wiki word vectors.* https://fasttext.cc/docs/en/pretrained-vectors.html

Fayyad, U. M. (n.d.). *Summary from the KDD-03 Panel-Data Mining: The Next 10 Years.* Available at: www.DMXgroup.comwww.Kdnuggets.comwww.gm.com

Fayyad, U., Piatetsky-Shapiro, G., & Smyth, P. (1996). From Data Mining to Knowledge Discovery in Databases. *AI Magazine, 17*(3), 37–37. doi:10.1609/AIMAG.V17I3.1230

Fellbaum, C. (1998). *WordNet.* John Wiley & Sons, Inc. doi:10.7551/mitpress/7287.001.0001

Fellbaum, C. (2010). WordNet. In *Theory and Applications of Ontology: Computer Applications* (pp. 231–243). Springer. doi:10.1007/978-90-481-8847-5_10

Ferrara, E. (2014). *Web Data Extraction, Applications and Techniques: A Survey.* Available at: https://arxiv.org/pdf/1207.0246.pdf

Figliozzi, M., & Unnikrishnan, A. (2021). Home-deliveries before-during COVID-19 lockdown: Accessibility, environmental justice, equity, and policy implications. *Transportation Research Part D, Transport and Environment, 93*, 102760. https://doi.org/https://doi.org/10.1016/j.trd.2021.102760

Flaherty, M. G., & Rughiniş, C. (2021). Online Memes and COVID-19. *Contexts, 20*(3), 40–45. https://doi.org/10.1177/15365042211035338

Frank, E., Hall, M., Holmes, G., Kirkby, R., Pfahringer, B., Witten, I. H., & Trigg, L. (2009). Weka-a machine learning workbench for data mining. In *Data Mining and Knowledge Discovery Handbook* (pp. 1269–1277). Springer. doi:10.1007/978-0-387-09823-4_66

Gajendran, R. S., & Harrison, D. A. (2007). The Good, the Bad, and the Unknown About Telecommuting: Meta-Analysis of Psychological Mediators and Individual Consequences. *The Journal of Applied Psychology, 92*(6), 1524–1541. https://doi.org/10.1037/0021-9010.92.6.1524

Galley, M. (2006). A skip-chain conditional random field for ranking meeting utterances by importance. In *Proceedings of the 2006 Conference on Empirical Methods in Natural Language Processing* (pp. 364-372). Association for Computational Linguistics. 10.3115/1610075.1610126

Ganapathibhotla, M., & Liu, B. (2008). Mining opinions in comparative sentences. In *Proceedings of the 22nd International Conference on Computational Linguistics* (vol. 1, pp. 241-248). Association for Computational Linguistics.

Gandomi, A., & Haider, M. (2015). Beyond the hype: Big data concepts, methods, and analytics. *International Journal of Information Management, 35*(2), 137–144. doi:10.1016/j.ijinfomgt.2014.10.007

Gao, X., & Ichise, R. (2017). Adjusting Word Embeddings by Deep Neural Networks. ICAART, (2), 398-406. doi:10.5220/0006120003980406

Garcia-Contreras, R., Munoz-Chavez, P., Valle-Cruz, D., Ruvalcaba-Gomez, E. A., & Becerra-Santiago, J. A. (2021). Teleworking in Times of COVID-19. Some Lessons for the Public Sector from the Emergent Implementation during the Pandemic Period: Teleworking in times of COVID-19. *ACM International Conference Proceeding Series*, 376–385. doi:10.1145/3463677.3463700

Garland, E., & Solomons, K. (n.d.). Early Detection of Depression in Young and Elderly People. *BCMJ, 44*(9), 469-472. Retrieved 14 September 2021, from https://bcmj.org/articles/early-detection-depression-young-and-elderly-people

Geraci, J., Wilansky, P., de Luca, V., Roy, A., Kennedy, J. L., & Strauss, J. (2017). Applying deep neural networks to unstructured text notes in electronic medical records for phenotyping youth depression. *Evidence-Based Mental Health, 20*(3), 83–87. doi:10.1136/eb-2017-102688 PMID:28739578

Ghasiya, P., & Okamura, K. (2021). Investigating COVID-19 news across four nations: A topic modeling and sentiment analysis approach. *IEEE Access: Practical Innovations, Open Solutions, 9*, 36645–36656. doi:10.1109/ACCESS.2021.3062875 PMID:34786310

Ghosh, S., & Mitra, P. (2008). Combining content and structure similarity for XML document classification using composite SVM kernels. *Pattern Recognition, 2008. ICPR 2008. 19th International Conference on*, 1-4. 10.1109/ICPR.2008.4761539

Ghosh, S., Ekbal, A., & Bhattacharyya, P. (2021). A multitask framework to detect depression, sentiment and multi-label emotion from suicide notes. *Cognitive Computation*, 1–20.

Giuntini, F. T., Cazzolato, M. T., dos Reis, M. D. J. D., Campbell, A. T., Traina, A. J., & Ueyama, J. (2020). A review on recognizing depression in social networks: Challenges and opportunities. *Journal of Ambient Intelligence and Humanized Computing, 11*(11), 4713–4729. doi:10.100712652-020-01726-4

Giusti, R., & Batista, G. E. (2013, Oct 19). An empirical comparison of dissimilarity measures for time series classification. *Brazilian Conference on Intelligent System*, 82-88. 10.1109/BRACIS.2013.22

Gleditsch, N. P. (2020). *Lewis Fry Richardson: His Intellectual Legacy and Influence in the Social Sciences*. Springer. doi:10.1007/978-3-030-31589-4

Goldstone, R. L., Medin, D. L., & Gentner, D. (1991). Relational similarity and the nonindependence of features in similarity judgments. *Cognitive Psychology, 23*(2), 222–262. doi:10.1016/0010-0285(91)90010-L PMID:2055001

Gomaa, W. H., & Fahmy, A. A. (2013). A survey of text similarity approaches. *International Journal of Computers and Applications, 68*, 13–18. doi:10.5120/11638-7118

Goncalves, J., Liu, Y., Xiao, B., Chaudhry, S., Hosio, S., & Kostakos, V. (2015). Increasing the reach of government social media: A case study in modeling government-citizen interaction on Facebook. *Policy & Internet, 7*(1), 80–102.

Gonçalves, P., Araújo, M., Benevenuto, F., & Cha, M. (2013). Comparing and Combining Sentiment Analysis Methods. *Proceedings of the First ACM Conference on Online Social Networks*, 27–38. 10.1145/2512938.2512951

Goodfellow, I., Benbio, Y., & Courville, A. (2016). *Deep learning – adaptive computation and machine learning series*. MIT Press.

Google, L. L. C. (1998, September 4). *Google*. Retrieved July 2016, from Google Search: www.google.com

Google, L. L. C. (2016). *API cloud natural language*. Retrieved February 25, 2017, from Google cloud: https://cloud.google.com/natural-language?hl=pt-br

Google. (2021). *Cloud Natural Language.* https://cloud.google.com/natural-language/docs/quickstart

Gorrell, G., Kochkina, E., Liakata, M., Aker, A., Zubiaga, A., Bontcheva, K., & Derczynski, L. (2019). SemEval-2019 task 7: RumourEval, determining rumour veracity and support for rumours. In *Proceedings of the 13th International Workshop on Semantic Evaluation* (pp. 845-854). 10.18653/v1/S19-2147

Graham, S. (2019). *A history of the bildungsroman.* Cambridge University Press. doi:10.1017/9781316479926

Greene, D., & Cross, J. (2017). Exploring the Political Agenda of the European Parliament Using a Dynamic Topic Modeling Approach. *Political Analysis*, 25(1), 77–94. doi:10.1017/pan.2016.7

Grishman, R. (2015). Information Extraction. *IEEE Intelligent Systems*, 30(5), 8–15.

Gujjar, J. P., & HR, P. K. (2021). Sentiment Analysis: Textblob For Decision Making. *International Journal of Scientific Research & Engineering Trends*, (7), 1097–1099.

Gujjar, J. P., & Manjunatha, T. (2018). Profitability Analysis of Indian Information Technology Companies using DuPont Model. *Asian Journal of Management*, 9(3), 1105–1108. doi:10.5958/2321-5763.2018.00176.2

Gundecha, P., & Liu, H. (2012). Mining Social Media: A Brief Introduction. *2012 TutORials in Operations Research, Dmml*, 1–17. doi:10.1287/educ.1120.0105

Guntuku, S. C., Yaden, D. B., Kern, M. L., Ungar, L. H., & Eichstaedt, J. C. (2017). Detecting depression and mental illness on social media: An integrative review. *Current Opinion in Behavioral Sciences*, 18, 43–49. doi:10.1016/j.cobeha.2017.07.005

Guo, W., & Diab, M. (2012). A simple unsupervised latent semantics based approach for sentence similarity. In *Proceedings of the Sixth International Workshop on Semantic Evaluation.* Association for Computational Linguistics.

Guo, C., Lu, M., & Wei, W. (2021). An improved LDA topic modeling method based on partition for medium and long texts. *Annals of Data Science*, 8(2), 331–344. doi:10.100740745-019-00218-3

Gupta, M. (2019). *ML | What is Machine Learning?* https://www.geeksforgeeks.org/ml-machine-learning/

Gupta, N., & Agrawal, R. (2020). Application and techniques of opinion mining. In Hybrid Computational Intelligence (pp. 1–23). Academic Press. https://doi.org/10.1016/b978-0-12-818699-2.00001-9.

Gupta, A., Kumar, M. A., & Gautam, J. (2017). A Survey on Semantic Similarity Measures. *IJIRST-International Journal for Innovative Research in Science & Technology*, 3, 12.

Gupta, A., & Yadav, K. (2014). Semantic similarity measure using information content approach with depth for similarity calculation. *International Journal of Scientific & Technology Research*, 3, 165–169.

Gupta, V., & Lehal, G. (2009). A Survey of Text Mining Techniques and Applications. *Journal of Emerging Technologies in Web Intelligence*, 1(1). Advance online publication. doi:10.4304/jetwi.1.1.60-76

Haddi, E., Liu, X., & Shi, Y. (2013). The Role of Text Pre-processing in Sentiment Analysis. *Procedia Computer Science*, 17, 26–32. doi:10.1016/j.procs.2013.05.005

Hajian, B., & White, T. (2011). Measuring semantic similarity using a multi-tree model. CEUR Workshop Proceedings, 756.

Halkia, M., Ferri, S., Schiellens, M. K., & Papazoglou, M. (2020). The global conflict risk index: A quantitative tool for policy support on conflict prevention. *Progress in Disaster Science*, 6, 100069. Advance online publication. doi:10.1016/j.pdisas.2020.100069

Hall, D., Jurafsky, D., & Manning, C. D. (2008). Studying the history of ideas using topic models. *Proceedings of the Conference on Empirical Methods in Natural Language Processing* (pp. 363-371). Association for Computational Linguistics. 10.3115/1613715.1613763

Halsey, T. C., Jensen, M. H., Kadanoff, L. P., Procaccia, I., & Shraiman, B. I. (1987). Fractal measures and their singularities: The characterization of strange sets. *Nuclear Physics B - Proceedings Supplement, 2*, 501–511. doi:10.1016/0920-5632(87)90036-3

Han, C., Yang, M., & Piterou, A. (2021). Do news media and citizens have the same agenda on COVID-19? an empirical comparison of twitter posts. *Technological Forecasting and Social Change, 169*, 120849. https://doi.org/10.1016/j.techfore.2021.120849

Hao, D., Zuo, W., Peng, T., & He, F. (2011). An approach for calculating semantic similarity between words using WordNet. *Digital Manufacturing and Automation (ICDMA), 2011 Second International Conference on*, 177-180. 10.1109/ICDMA.2011.50

Hatzivassiloglou, V., Klavans, J. L., & Eskin, E. (1999). Detecting text similarity over short passages: Exploring linguistic feature combinations via machine learning. *Proceedings of the 1999 joint sigdat conference on empirical methods in natural language processing and very large corpora*, 203-212.

Havigerová, J. M., Haviger, J., Kučera, D., & Hoffmannová, P. (2019). Text-based detection of the risk of depression. *Frontiers in Psychology, 10*, 513. doi:10.3389/fpsyg.2019.00513 PMID:30936845

Hawn, C. (2009). Take two aspirin and tweet me in the morning: How Twitter, Facebook, and other social media are reshaping health care. *Health Affairs, 28*(2), 361–368. doi:10.1377/hlthaff.28.2.361 PMID:19275991

Haykin, S. O. (2008). *Neural networks and learning machines*. Pearson.

Hegre, H., Allansson, M., Basedau, M., Colaresi, M., Croicu, M., Fjelde, H., ... Schneider, G. (2018). Views: A political violence early-warning system. *Journal of Peace Research, 56*(2), 474–476. https://journals.sagepub.com/doi/full/10.1177/0022343319823860

He, L., He, C., Reynolds, T., Bai, Q., Huang, Y., Li, C., Zheng, K., & Chen, Y. (2021). Why do people oppose mask wearing? A comprehensive analysis of US tweets during the COVID-19 pandemic. *Journal of the American Medical Informatics Association: JAMIA, 28*(7), 1564–1573. doi:10.1093/jamia/ocab047

Helle, V., Negus, A., & Nyberg, J. (2018). *Improving armed conflict prediction using machine learning: views+*. Retrieved from https://pdfs.semanticscholar.org/3008/beffb4496316bb1677253de89eb4b2a695c3.pdf

He, Q., Veldkamp, B. P., Glas, C. A., & de Vries, T. (2017). Automated assessment of patients' self-narratives for posttraumatic stress disorder screening using natural language processing and text mining. *Assessment, 24*(2), 157–172. doi:10.1177/1073191115602551 PMID:26358713

Higuera, V. (2021). *Everything You Want to Know About Depression*. Retrieved 27 November 2021, from https://www.healthline.com/health/depression

Hinterberger, K. (2020). *The portrayal of villains in J.K. Rowling's "Harry Potter."* doi:10.25365/thesis.62071

Hoang, M., Bihorac, O. A., & Rouces, J. (2019). Aspect-based sentiment analysis using bert. In *Proceedings of the 22nd Nordic Conference on Computational Linguistics* (pp. 187-196). Academic Press.

Hochreiter, S., & Schmidhuber, J. (1997). Long short-term memory. *Neural Computation, 9*(8), 1735–1780. doi:10.1162/neco.1997.9.8.1735 PMID:9377276

Hoffman, T. (1999). Probabilistic latent semantic analysis. *Proc. of the 15th Conference on Uncertainty in AI.*

Hofmann, T. (1999). Probabilistic latent semantic indexing. *Proceedings of the 22nd Annual International ACM SIGIR Conference on research and Development in Information Retrieval* (pp. 50-57). Association for Computing Machinery.

Homan, C., Johar, R., Liu, T., Lytle, M., Silenzio, V., & Alm, C. O. (2014, June). Toward macro-insights for suicide prevention: Analyzing fine-grained distress at scale. In *Proceedings of the Workshop on Computational Linguistics and Clinical Psychology: From Linguistic Signal to Clinical Reality* (pp. 107-117). 10.3115/v1/W14-3213

Hong, L., & Davison, B. D. (2010). Empirical study of topic modeling in Twitter. *Proceedings of the First Workshop on Social Media Analytics.* 10.1145/1964858.1964870

Hook, A., Court, V., Sovacool, B. K., & Sorrell, S. (2020). A systematic review of the energy and climate impacts of teleworking. *Environmental Research Letters*, 15(9), 093003. https://doi.org/10.1088/1748-9326/ab8a84

Hossain, E., Sharif, O., & Hoque, M. M. (2021). Sentiment polarity detection on bengali book reviews using multinomial naive bayes. In *Progress in Advanced Computing and Intelligent Engineering* (pp. 281–292). Springer.

Hout, M. C., Godwin, H. J., Fitzsimmons, G., Robbins, A., Menneer, T., & Goldinger, S. D. (2016). Using multidimensional scaling to quantify similarity in visual search and beyond. *Attention, Perception & Psychophysics*, 78(1), 3–20. doi:10.375813414-015-1010-6 PMID:26494381

Hu, M., & Liu, B. (2004). Mining and summarizing customer reviews. *KDD-2004 - Proceedings of the Tenth ACM SIGKDD International Conference on Knowledge Discovery and Data Mining*, 168–177. 10.1145/1014052.1014073

Hu, Q., & Cho, Y. R. (2015). An integrative measure of graph-and vector-based semantic similarity using information content distance. *Bioinformatics and Biomedicine (BIBM), 2015 IEEE International Conference on*, 517-522.

Huang, H. H., Yang, H. C., & Kuo, Y. H. 2008, November. A Sense Based Similarity Measure for Cross-Lingual Documents. *Intelligent Systems Design and Applications, 2008.ISDA'08.Eighth International Conference on, 1*, 9-13. 10.1109/ISDA.2008.284

Huang, H. H., & Kuo, Y. H. (2010). Cross-lingual document representation and semantic similarity measure: A fuzzy set and rough set based approach. *IEEE Transactions on Fuzzy Systems*, 18(6), 1098–1111. doi:10.1109/TFUZZ.2010.2065811

Hu, H. W., Hsu, K. S., Lee, C., Hu, H. L., Hsu, C. Y., Yang, W. H., ... Chen, T. A. (2019). Keyword-Driven Depressive Tendency Model for Social Media Posts. In *International Conference on Business Information Systems* (pp. 14-22). Springer. 10.1007/978-3-030-20482-2_2

Hu, M., & Liu, B. (2004). Mining and summarizing customer reviews. In *Proceedings of the tenth ACM SIGKDD International Conference on Knowledge Discovery and Data Mining* (pp. 168-177). ACM.

Hu, M., & Liu, B. (2006). Opinion feature extraction using class sequential rules. In *AAAI Spring Symposium: Computational Approaches to Analyzing Weblogs* (pp. 61-66). American Association for Artificial Intelligence.

Hume, D. (2004). *Disertación sobre las pasiones y otros ensayos morales* (Vol. 5). Anthropos Editorial.

Hussain, A., & Cambria, E. (2018). Semi-supervised learning for big social data analysis. *Neurocomputing*, 275, 1662–1673.

Hussain, A., Tahir, A., Hussain, Z., Sheikh, Z., Gogate, M., Dashtipour, K., Ali, A., & Sheikh, A. (2021). Artificial intelligence–enabled analysis of public attitudes on Facebook and Twitter toward covid-19 vaccines in the United Kingdom and the United States: Observational study. *Journal of Medical Internet Research*, 23(4), e26627. doi:10.2196/26627 PMID:33724919

Hussein, D. M. E.-D. M. (2018). A survey on sentiment analysis challenges. *Journal of King Saud University-Engineering Sciences*, *30*(4), 330–338. doi:10.1016/j.jksues.2016.04.002

Hutto, C., & Gilbert, E. (2014). VADER: A parsimonious rule-based model for sentiment analysis of social media text. In *Proceedings of the International AAAI Conference on Web and Social Media* (*Vol. 8*, No. 1). AAAI.

Ibañez, M. M., Rosa, R. R., & Guimarães, L. N. (2020). Sentiment Analysis Applied to Analyze Society's Emotion in Two Different Context of Social Media Data. *Inteligencia Artificial*, 66-84. doi:10.4114/submission/intartif.vol23iss66pp66-84

Ibañez, M. M., Rosa, R. R., & Guimarães, L. N. (2021). *Análise de emoções em mídias sociais utilizando aprendizado de máquina e séries temporais considerando informações de eventos extremos sociais e naturais*. Instituto Nacional de Pesquisas Espaciais - INPE. Retrieved from http://urlib.net/rep/8JMKD3MGP3W34R/44H7S82

IBM Cloud Education. (2020). *Machine learning*. https://www.ibm.com/in-en/cloud/learn/machine-learning

IBM. (n.d.). *IBM Watson*. https://www.ibm.com/watson/about

Ilyas, S. H. W., Soomro, Z. T., Anwar, A., Shahzad, H., & Yaqub, U. (2020, June). Analyzing Brexit's impact using sentiment analysis and topic modeling on Twitter discussion. In *The 21st Annual International Conference on Digital Government Research* (pp. 1-6). 10.1145/3396956.3396973

Imran, A. S., Daudpota, S. M., Kastrati, Z., & Batra, R. (2020). Cross-cultural polarity and emotion detection using sentiment analysis and deep learning on COVID-19 related tweets. *IEEE Access: Practical Innovations, Open Solutions*, *8*, 181074–181090. doi:10.1109/ACCESS.2020.3027350 PMID:34812358

Iosif, E., & Potamianos, A. (2010). Unsupervised semantic similarity computation between terms using web documents. *IEEE Transactions on Knowledge and Data Engineering*, *22*(11), 1637–1647. doi:10.1109/TKDE.2009.193

Islam, A., & Inkpen, D. (2008). Semantic text similarity using corpus-based word similarity and string similarity. *ACM Transactions on Knowledge Discovery from Data*, *2*(2), 10. doi:10.1145/1376815.1376819

Islam, T. (2019). Yoga-veganism: Correlation mining of twitter health data. *8th KDD Workshop on Issues of Sentiment Discovery and Opinion Mining (WISDOM)*.

Isnain, A. R., Supriyanto, J., & Kharisma, M. P. (n.d.). Implementation of K-Nearest Neighbor (K-NN) Algorithm For Public Sentiment Analysis of Online Learning. *Indonesian Journal of Computing and Cybernetics Systems*, *15*(2), 121-130. doi:10.1007/978-981-33-4299-6_23

Jackson, S., Zhang, F., Boichak, O., Bryant, L., Li, Y., Hemsley, J., Stromer-Galley, J., Semaan, B., & McCracken, N. (2017). Identifying political topics in social media messages: A lexicon-based approach. *Proceedings of the 8th International Conference on Social Media & Society*, 1–10. 10.1145/3097286.3097298

Jackson, P., & Mouliner, I. (2002). *Natural language processing for online applications: Text retrieval, extraction and categorization*. John Benjamins B.V. doi:10.1075/nlp.5(1st)

Jacobs, A. M. (2015). Neurocognitive poetics: Methods and models for investigating the neuronal and cognitive-affective bases of literature reception. *Frontiers in Human Neuroscience*, *9*(APR), 1–22. doi:10.3389/fnhum.2015.00186 PMID:25932010

Jacobs, A. M. (2019). Sentiment Analysis for Words and Fiction Characters From the Perspective of Computational (Neuro-)Poetics. *Frontiers in Robotics and AI*, *6*, 53. doi:10.3389/frobt.2019.00053 PMID:33501068

Jacobs, A. M., Schuster, S., Xue, S., & Lüdtke, J. (2017). What's in the brain that ink may character…. *Scientific Study of Literature*, *7*(1), 4–51. doi:10.1075sol.7.1.02jac

Jagdale, R. S., Shirsat, V. S., & Deshmukh, S. N. (2016). Sentiment analysis of events from Twitter using open source tool. *International Journal of Computer Science and Mobile Computing*, 5(4), 475–485.

Jang, H., Rempel, E., Roth, D., Carenini, G., & Janjua, N. Z. (2021). Tracking COVID-19 discourse on Twitter in North America: Infodemiology study using topic modeling and aspect-based sentiment analysis. *Journal of Medical Internet Research*, 23(2), e25431. doi:10.2196/25431 PMID:33497352

Jannati, R., Mahendra, R., Wardhana, C. W., & Adriani, M. (2018). Stance classification towards political figures on blog writing. *2018 International Conference on Asian Language Processing (IALP)*, 96–101. 10.1109/IALP.2018.8629144

Jelodar, H., & Frank, R. (2021). *Semantic Knowledge Discovery and Discussion Mining of Incel Online Community: Topic modeling.* arXiv preprint arXiv:2104.09586.

Jelodar, H., Wang, Y., Yuan, C., Feng, X., Jiang, X., Li, Y., & Zhao, L. (2019). Latent Dirichlet allocation (LDA) and topic modeling: Models, applications, a survey. *Multimedia Tools and Applications*, 78(11), 15169–15211.

Jenelius, E., & Cebecauer, M. (2020). Impacts of COVID-19 on public transport ridership in Sweden: Analysis of ticket validations, sales and passenger counts. *Transportation Research Interdisciplinary Perspectives*, 8, 100242. doi:10.1016/j.trip.2020.100242

Jiang, J. J., & Conrath, D. W. (1997). *Semantic similarity based on corpus statistics and lexical taxonomy.* arXiv preprint cmp-lg/9709008.

Jindal, N., & Liu, B. (2006). Identifying comparative sentences in text documents. In *Proceedings of the 29th Annual International ACM SIGIR Conference on Research and Development in Information Retrieval* (pp. 244-251). ACM.

Jindal, N., & Liu, B. (2006b). Mining comparative sentences and relations. In *Proceedings of the 21st International Conference on Artificial Intelligence* (vol. 22, pp. 1331-1336).

Jockers, M. L. (2016). The ancient world in nineteenth-century fiction; or, correlating theme, geography, and sentiment in the nineteenth century literary imagination. *DHQ: Digital Humanities Quarterly*, 10(2), 1–17.

Jose, R., & Chooralil, V. S. (2016). Prediction of election result by enhanced sentiment analysis on twitter data using classifier ensemble Approach. *2016 International Conference on Data Mining and Advanced Computing (SAPIENCE)*, 64–67. 10.1109/SAPIENCE.2016.7684133

Joyce, B., & Deng, J. (2017). Sentiment analysis of tweets for the 2016 US presidential election. *2017 Ieee Mit Undergraduate Research Technology Conference (Urtc)*, 1–4. 10.1109/URTC.2017.8284176

Julia, S., & David, R. (n.d.). *6 Topic modeling | Text Mining with R.* Retrieved January 1, 2022, from https://www.tidytextmining.com/topicmodeling.html

Kalra, P. (2013). Text mining: Concepts, process and applications. *Journal of Global Research in Computer Science*, 4, 36–39.

Karamizadeh, S., Abdullah, S. M., Manaf, A. A., Zamani, M., & Hooman, A. (2013). An overview of principal component analysis. *Journal of Signal and Information Processing*, 4(03, 3B), 173–175. doi:10.4236/jsip.2013.43B031

Karimi, A., Rossi, L., & Prati, A. (2020). *Improving BERT Performance for Aspect-Based Sentiment Analysis.* arXiv preprint arXiv:2010.11731.

Karmen, C., Hsiung, R. C., & Wetter, T. (2015). Screening internet forum participants for depression symptoms by assembling and enhancing multiple NLP methods. *Computer Methods and Programs in Biomedicine*, 120(1), 27–36. doi:10.1016/j.cmpb.2015.03.008 PMID:25891366

Katchapakirin, K., Wongpatikaseree, K., Yomaboot, P., & Kaewpitakkun, Y. (2018). Facebook social media for depression detection in the Thai community. In *2018 15th International Joint Conference on Computer Science and Software Engineering (JCSSE)* (pp. 1-6). 10.29007/tscc

Kaur, A., & Gupta, V. (2013). A Survey on Sentiment Analysis and Opinion Mining Techniques. *Journal of Emerging Technologies in Web Intelligence, 5*(4), 367–371. doi:10.4304/jetwi.5.4.367-371

Kaur, H., Ahsaan, S. U., Alankar, B., & Chang, V. (2021). A proposed sentiment analysis deep learning algorithm for analyzing COVID-19 tweets. *Information Systems Frontiers, 23*(6), 1–13. doi:10.100710796-021-10135-7 PMID:33897274

Kazekami, S. (2020). Mechanisms to improve labor productivity by performing telework. *Telecommunications Policy, 44*(2), 101868. https://doi.org/10.1016/j.telpol.2019.101868

Kermanidis, K. L., & Maragoudakis, M. (2013). Political sentiment analysis of tweets before and after the Greek elections of May 2012. *International Journal of Social Network Mining, 1*(3–4), 298–317. doi:10.1504/IJSNM.2013.059090

Kertcher, C., & Turin, O. (2020). 'Siege Mentality' Reaction to the Pandemic: Israeli Memes During Covid-19. *Postdigital Science and Education, 2*(3), 581–587. doi:10.1007/s42438-020-00175-8

Keshavarz, H., & Abadeh, M. S. (2017). ALGA: Adaptive lexicon learning using genetic algorithm for sentiment analysis of microblogs. *Knowledge-Based Systems, 122*, 1–16. doi:10.1016/j.knosys.2017.01.028

Keylock, C. J. (2017). Multifractal surrogate-data generation algorithm that preserves pointwise hölder regularity structure, with initial applications to turbulence. *Physical Review. E, 95*(3), 032123. doi:10.1103/PhysRevE.95.032123 PMID:28415176

Khakimova, A.K., Charnine, M.M., Klokov, A.A. & Sokolov, E.G. (2020). *Approaches to assessing the semantic similarity of texts in a multilingual space.* Academic Press.

Khan, A., Younis, U., Kundi, A. S., Asghar, M. Z., Ullah, I., Aslam, N., & Ahmed, I. (2020). Sentiment classification of user reviews using supervised learning techniques with comparative opinion mining perspective. In *Proceedings of Advances in Computer Vision* (Vol. 944, pp. 23–29). Springer.

Khanday, A. M. U. D., Khan, Q. R., & Rabani, S. T. (2021). SVMBPI: support vector machine-based propaganda identification. In Cognitive Informatics and Soft Computing (pp. 445-455). Springer. doi:10.1007/978-981-16-1056-1_35

Kherwa, P., & Bansal, P. (2020). Topic modeling: a comprehensive review. *EAI Endorsed Transactions on Scalable Information Systems, 7*(24).

Kherwa, P., & Bansal, P. (2020). Topic modeling: A comprehensive review. *EAI Endorsed Transactions on Scalable Information Systems, 7*(24), 1–12.

Kholifah, B., Syarif, I., & Badriyah, T. (2020). Mental Disorder Detection via Social Media Mining using Deep Learning. *Kinetik: Game Technology, Information System, Computer Network, Computing, Electronics, and Control, 5*(4), 309–316. doi:10.22219/kinetik.v5i4.1120

Kim, S. N. (2017). Is telecommuting sustainable? An alternative approach to estimating the impact of home-based telecommuting on household travel. *International Journal of Sustainable Transportation, 11*(2), 72–85. https://doi.org/10.1080/15568318.2016.1193779

Kim, Y. M., & Delen, D. (2018). Medical informatics research trend analysis: A text mining approach. *Health Informatics Journal, 24*(4), 432–452. doi:10.1177/1460458216678443 PMID:30376768

Kiritchenko, S., Zhu, X., & Mohammad, S. M. (2014). Sentiment analysis of short informal texts. *Journal of Artificial Intelligence Research*, *50*, 723–762. doi:10.1613/jair.4272

Kite. (2018). *doc2bow*. https://www.kite.com/python/docs/gensim.corpora.Dictionary.doc2bow

Koehn, P. (2009). *Statistical machine translation*. Cambridge University Press. doi:10.1017/CBO9780511815829

Kraus, S., Clauss, T., Breier, M., Gast, J., Zardini, A., & Tiberius, V. (2020). The economics of COVID-19: Initial empirical evidence on how family firms in five European countries cope with the corona crisis. *International Journal of Entrepreneurial Behaviour & Research*, *26*(5), 1067–1092. https://doi.org/10.1108/IJEBR-04-2020-0214

Küçük, D., Arıcı, N., & Küçük, E. E. (2021). Sosyal medyada otomatik halk sağlığı takibi: Güncel bir derleme [Automatic public health monitoring on social media: A recent survey]. *Niğde Ömer Halisdemir Üniversitesi Mühendislik Bilimleri Dergisi*, *10*(2).

Küçük, D., & Arıcı, N. (2016). Türkçe için Wikipedia tabanlı varlık ismi tanıma sistemi (Wikipedia-based named entity recognition system for Turkish). *Politeknik Dergisi*, *19*(3), 325–332.

Küçük, D., Arıcı, N., & Küçük, D. (2017). Named entity recognition in Turkish: Approaches and issues. In *Proceedings of the International Conference on Applications of Natural Language to Information Systems* (pp. 176-181). Springer.

Küçük, D., & Can, F. (2020). Stance detection: A survey. *ACM Computing Surveys*, *53*(1), 1–37. doi:10.1145/3369026

Küçük, D., & Can, F. (2021). Stance detection: Concepts, approaches, resources, and outstanding issues. In *Proceedings of the 44th International ACM SIGIR Conference on Research and Development in Information Retrieval* (pp. 2673-2676). ACM.

Küçük, E. E., Yapar, K., Küçük, D., & Küçük, D. (2017). Ontology-based automatic identification of public health-related Turkish tweets. *Computers in Biology and Medicine*, *83*, 1–9. doi:10.1016/j.compbiomed.2017.02.001 PMID:28187367

Kumar, P., Garg, S., & Garg, A. (2020). Assessment of anxiety, depression and stress using machine learning models. *Procedia Computer Science*, *171*, 1989–1998. doi:10.1016/j.procs.2020.04.213

Kurach, K., Gelly, S., & Jastrzebski, M. (2017). *Better Text Understanding Through Image-To-Text Transfer*. arXiv preprint arXiv:1705.08386.

Kwak, H. (n.d.). *What is Twitter, a Social Network or a News Media?* Available at: http://bit.ly

Kydros, D., Argyropoulou, M., & Vrana, V. (2021). A content and sentiment analysis of greek tweets during the pandemic. *Sustainability*, *13*(11), 6150. https://doi.org/10.3390/su13116150

L, H. J. V. (2019). Opinion Mining using Machine Learning Techniques. *International Journal of Engineering and Advanced Technology*, *9*(2), 4287–4292. doi:10.35940/ijeat.B4108.129219

Lacsa, J. E. M. (2021). #COVID19: Hashtags and the power of social media. *Journal of Public Health*. doi:10.1093/pubmed/fdab242

Lafferty, J., McCallum, A., & Pereira, F. (2001) Conditional random fields: Probabilistic models for segmenting and labeling sequence data. In *Proceedings of the 8th International Conference on Machine Learning* (vol. 1, pp. 282-289). doi:10.1007/978-3-030-17798-0_3

Lamsal, R. (2021). Design and analysis of a large-scale COVID-19 tweets dataset. *Applied Intelligence*, *51*(5), 2790–2804. doi:10.100710489-020-02029-z PMID:34764561

Lateral Gmb, H. (2019). *NewsBot - Give me 5*. Retrieved March 2018, from Related news at the click of a button: https://getnewsbot.com/

Lau, J. H., Newman, D., Karimi, S., & Baldwin, T. (2010, August). Best topic word selection for topic labelling. In *Coling 2010* (pp. 605–613). Posters.

Laundauer, T., & Dumais, S. T. (1997). A solution to plato's problem: The latent semantic analysis theory of acquisition, induction and representation of knowledge. *Psychological Review*, *104*(2), 211–240. doi:10.1037/0033-295X.104.2.211

Lavanya, S., & Arya, S. S. (2012). An approach for measuring semantic similarity between words using SVM and LS-SVM. *Computer Communication and Informatics (ICCCI), 2012 International Conference on*, 1-4. 10.1109/ICCCI.2012.6158835

Lazer, D. (n.d.). *Computational social science*. Available at: https://science.sciencemag.org/content/323/5915/721.short

Lee, J., Park, D. H., & Han, I. (2008). The effect of negative online consumer reviews on product attitude: An information processing view. *Electronic Commerce Research and Applications*, *7*(3), 341–352. doi:10.1016/j.elerap.2007.05.004

Lee, Y., Ragguett, R. M., Mansur, R. B., Boutilier, J. J., Rosenblat, J. D., Trevizol, A., Brietzke, E., Lin, K., Pan, Z., Subramaniapillai, M., Chan, T. C. Y., Fus, D., Park, C., Musial, N., Zuckerman, H., Chen, V. C.-H., Ho, R., Rong, C., & McIntyre, R. S. (2018). Applications of machine learning algorithms to predict therapeutic outcomes in depression: A meta-analysis and systematic review. *Journal of Affective Disorders*, *241*, 519–532. doi:10.1016/j.jad.2018.08.073 PMID:30153635

Li, W., Zheng, S., Liu, D., & Jiao, S. (2010). A novel computational approach to concept semantic similarity. *Computer, Mechatronics, Control and Electronic Engineering (CMCE), 2010 International Conference on*, *1*, 89-92. 10.1109/CMCE.2010.5610535

Liakata, M., Kim, J. H., Saha, S., Hastings, J., & Rebholz-Schuhmann, D. (2012). Three hybrid classifiers for the detection of emotions in suicide notes. *Biomedical Informatics Insights*, *5*, BII-S8967.

Liddy, E. D. (2001). *Natural language processing*. Academic Press.

Lim, B., & Zohren, S. (2021). *Time-series forecasting with deep learning: a survey*. The Royal Society Publishing. doi:10.1098/rsta.2020.0209

Lin, C., Hu, P., Su, H., Li, S., Mei, J., Zhou, J., & Leung, H. (2020). Sensemood: Depression detection on social media. In *Proceedings of the 2020 International Conference on Multimedia Retrieval* (pp. 407-411). 10.1145/3372278.3391932

Lin, F.-M., & Horng, W.-S. (2010). The housekeeper and the professor by Yoko Ogawa. *The Mathematical Intelligencer*, *2*(32), 75–76. doi:10.100700283-009-9100-8

Lippens, L., Moens, E., Sterkens, P., Weytjens, J., & Baert, S. (2021). How do employees think the COVID-19 crisis will affect their careers? *PLoS One*, *16*(5), 1–19. https://doi.org/10.1371/journal.pone.0246899

Li, R., Feng, F., Wang, X., Lu, P., & Li, B. (2015). Obtaining cross modal similarity metric with deep neural architecture. *Mathematical Problems in Engineering*, *2015*, 2015. doi:10.1155/2015/293176

Liu, B. (2010). Sentiment analysis and subjectivity. Handbook of Natural Language Processing, 627-666.

Liu, B. (2010). Sentiment analysis and subjectivity. Handbook of Natural Language Processing, Second Edition, 627–666.

Liu, B. (2015). Sentiment analysis: Mining opinions, sentiments, and emotions. *Sentiment Analysis: Mining Opinions, Sentiments, and Emotions*, 1–367. doi:10.1017/CBO9781139084789

Liu, P., Yuan, W., Fu, J., Jiang, Z., Hayashi, H., & Neubig, G. (2021). *Pre-train, prompt, and predict: A systematic survey of prompting methods in natural language processing.* arXiv preprint arXiv:2107.13586.

Liu, Y., Ott, M., Goyal, N., Du, J., Joshi, M., & Chen, D. (2019). *RoBERTa: A robustly optimized BERT pretraining approach.* arXiv preprint arXiv:1907.11692.

Liu, B. (2010). Sentiment analysis and subjectivity. In *Handbook of natural language processing* (2nd ed., pp. 627–666). Taylor and Francis Group.

Liu, B. (2012). Sentiment analysis and opinion mining. *Synthesis Lectures on Human Language Technologies, 5*(1), 1–167. doi:10.2200/S00416ED1V01Y201204HLT016

Liu, C. L., Hsaio, W. H., Lee, C. H., Lu, G. C., & Jou, E. (2012). Movie rating and review summarization in mobile environment. *IEEE Transactions on Systems, Man and Cybernetics. Part C, Applications and Reviews, 42*(3), 397–407. doi:10.1109/TSMCC.2011.2136334

Liu, J., Huang, M., & Zhu, X. (2010). Recognizing biomedical named entities using skip-chain conditional random fields. In *Proceedings of the 2010 Workshop on Biomedical Natural Language Processing* (pp. 10-18). Association for Computational Linguistics.

Liu, S. M., & Chen, J. H. (2015). A multi-label classification based approach for sentiment classification. *Expert Systems with Applications, 42*(3), 1083–1093.

Liu, Y. H. (2017). *Python Machine Learning By Example.* Packt Publishing Ltd.

Liu, Y., & Liang, Y. (2013). A Sentence Semantic Similarity Calculating Method based on Segmented Semantic Comparison. *Journal of Theoretical and Applied Information Technology, 48,* 231–235.

Liu, Y., Sun, C., Lin, L., Wang, X., & Zhao, Y. (2015). Computing Semantic Text Similarity Using Rich Features. PACLIC.

Liu, Z. (2013). *High performance latent dirichlet allocation for text mining.* Brunel University School of Engineering and Design PhD Theses.

Li, X., Fu, X., Xu, G., Yang, Y., Wang, J., Jin, L., ... Xiang, T. (2020). Enhancing BERT representation with context-aware embedding for aspect-based sentiment analysis. *IEEE Access : Practical Innovations, Open Solutions, 8,* 46868–46876.

Lochbaum, K., & Management, L. S.-I. P. (1989). *Comparing and combining the effectiveness of latent semantic indexing and the ordinary vector space model for information retrieval.* Elsevier. Available at: https://www.sciencedirect.com/science/article/pii/0306457389901003

Loper, E., & Bird, S. (2002). NLTK: The natural language toolkit. In *Proceedings of the ACL-02 Workshop on Effective Tools and Methodologies for Teaching Natural Language Processing and Computational Linguistics* (vol. 1, pp. 63-70). Association for Computational Linguistics.

López Chau, A., Valle-Cruz, D., & Sandoval-Almazán, R. (2020b). Sentiment Analysis in Crisis Situations for Better Connected Government. In Z. Mahmood (Ed.), *Web 2.0 and Cloud Technologies for Implementing Connected Government* (pp. 162–181). IGI Global. doi:10.4018/978-1-7998-4570-6.ch008

López-Chau, A., Valle-Cruz, D., & Sandoval-Almazán, R. (2020). Sentiment Analysis of Twitter Data Through Machine Learning Techniques. In Software Engineering in the Era of Cloud Computing (pp. 185–209). Springer. doi:10.1007/978-3-030-33624-0_8

López-Chau, A., Valle-Cruz, D., & Sandoval-Almazán, R. (2020a). Sentiment Analysis of Twitter Data Through Machine Learning Techniques. In M. Ramachandran & Z. Mahmood (Eds.), Software Engineering in the Era of Cloud (pp. 185–209). Springer International Publishing. https://doi.org/10.1007/978-3-030-33624-0_8.

Lopez-Gazpio, I., Maritxalar, M., Lapata, M., & Agirre, E. (2019). Word n-gram attention models for sentence similarity and inference. *Expert Systems with Applications*, *132*, 1–11. doi:10.1016/j.eswa.2019.04.054

Loria, S. (2018). textblob Documentation. *Release 0.15, 2*, 269.

Luby, M. D. J. (2017). *Diagnosing Early-Onset Depression in Young Children*. Retrieved 27 November 2021, from https://www.bbrfoundation.org/blog/diagnosing-early-onset-depression-young-children

Luo, J. M., Vu, H. Q., Li, G., & Law, R. (2020). Topic modelling for theme park online reviews: Analysis of Disneyland. *Journal of Travel & Tourism Marketing*, *37*(2), 272–285. doi:10.1080/10548408.2020.1740138

Ma, B., Yang, Y., Zhao, F., Dong, R., & Zhou, X. (2015). Semantic Similarity Computation Based on Multi-Features Fusion. *International Journal of Hybrid Information Technology*, *8*(5), 31–40. doi:10.14257/ijhit.2015.8.5.04

Madylova, A., & Oguducu, S. G. (2009), September. A taxonomy based semantic similarity of documents using the cosine measure. *Computer and Information Sciences, 2009.ISCIS 2009. 24th International Symposium on,* 129-134.

Mahajan, P., & Rana, A. (2018). Sentiment Classification-How to Quantify Public Emotions Using Twitter. *International Journal of Sociotechnology and Knowledge Development*, *10*(1), 57–71. doi:10.4018/IJSKD.2018010104

Ma, L., Wang, Z., & Zhang, Y. (2017). Extracting depression symptoms from social networks and web blogs via text mining. In *International Symposium on Bioinformatics Research and Applications* (pp. 325-330). Springer. 10.1007/978-3-319-59575-7_29

Malagoli, L. G., Stancioli, J., Ferreira, C. H., Vasconcelos, M., Couto da Silva, A. P., & Almeida, J. M. (2021). A look into COVID-19 vaccination debate on Twitter. In *Proceedings of the 13th ACM Web Science Conference* (pp. 225-233). 10.1145/3447535.3462498

Malik, E. F., Keikhosrokiani, P., & Asl, M. P. (2021). Text mining life cycle for a spatial reading of Viet Thanh Nguyen's *The Refugees* (2017). *The 2021 International Congress of Advanced Technology and Engineering (ICOTEN)*. 10.1109/ICOTEN52080.2021.9493520

Malik, E. F., Keikhosrokiani, P., & Asl, M. P. (2021). Text mining life cycle for a spatial reading of Viet Thanh Nguyen's *The Refugees* (2017). *2021 International Congress of Advanced Technology and Engineering (ICOTEN)*.

Manda, K. R. (2019). Sentiment Analysis of Twitter Data Using Machine Learning and Deep Learning Methods. In *Blekinge Institute of Technology*. Faculty of Computing, Department of Computer Science.

Manosso, F. C. (2021). *Using sentiment analysis in tourism research : A systematic, bibliometric, and integrative review*. Academic Press.

Marcus, J. (2020, April). *US-Iran war of words raises fresh fears of Gulf clash*. Retrieved from BBC News: https://www.bbc.com/news/world-middle-east-52399283

Marerngsit, S., & Thammaboosadee, S. (2020). A Two-Stage Text-to-Emotion Depressive Disorder Screening Assistance based on Contents from Online Community. In *2020 8th International Electrical Engineering Congress (iEECON)* (pp. 1-4). 10.1109/iEECON48109.2020.229524

Martus, T. (2009). A Guide to the Harry Potter Novels. *Children's Literature Association Quarterly*, *27*(4), 233–234. doi:10.1353/chq.0.1431

Mathew, G., Agrawal, A., & Menzies, T. (2018). Finding Trends in Software Research. *IEEE Transactions on Software Engineering*.

Mathioudakis, M., & Koudas, N. (2010). Twittermonitor: trend detection over the twitter stream. In *Proceedings of the 2010 ACM SIGMOD International Conference on Management of data* (pp. 1155-1158). 10.1145/1807167.1807306

Meddeb, I., Lavandier, C., & Kotzinos, D. (2020). Using Twitter Streams for Opinion Mining: A case study on Airport Noise. *Communications in Computer and Information Science, 1197*, 145–160. doi:10.1007/978-3-030-44900-1_10

Medford, R. J., Saleh, S. N., Sumarsono, A., Perl, T. M., & Lehmann, C. U. (2020). An "Infodemic": Leveraging High-Volume Twitter Data to Understand Early Public Sentiment for the Coronavirus Disease 2019 Outbreak. *Open Forum Infectious Diseases, 7*(7). https://doi.org/10.1093/ofid/ofaa258

Medhat, W., Hassan, A., & Korashy, H. (2014). Sentiment analysis algorithms and applications: A survey. *Ain Shams Engineering Journal, 5*(4), 1093–1113.

Mei, Q., Shen, X., & Zhai, C. (2007, August). Automatic labeling of multinomial topic models. In *Proceedings of the 13th ACM SIGKDD international conference on Knowledge discovery and data mining* (pp. 490-499). 10.1145/1281192.1281246

Melton, C. A., Olusanya, O. A., Ammar, N., & Shaban-Nejad, A. (2021). Public sentiment and topic modeling regarding COVID-19 vaccines on Reddit social media platform: A call to action for strengthening vaccine confidence. *Journal of Infection and Public Health, 14*(10), 1505–1512. doi:10.1016/j.jiph.2021.08.010 PMID:34426095

Meneveau, C., & Sreenivasan, K. R. (1987). Simple multifractal cascade model for fully developed turbulence. *Physical Review Letters, 59*(13), 1424–1427. doi:10.1103/PhysRevLett.59.1424 PMID:10035231

Meng, L., Huang, R., & Gu, J. (2013). *An Effective Algorithm for Semantic Similarity Metric of Word Pairs*. Academic Press.

Messenger, J. C. (2019). *Telework in the 21st Century: An Evolutionary Perspective*. Edward Elgar Publishing.

Mihalcea, R., Corley, C., & Strapparava, C. (2006). Corpus-based and knowledge-based measures of text semantic similarity. AAAI, 6, 775-780.

Mihardi, M., & Budi, I. (2018). Public sentiment on political campaign using Twitter data in 2017 Jakarta's governor election. *2018 International Conference on Applied Information Technology and Innovation (ICAITI)*, 67–72. 10.1109/ICAITI.2018.8686740

Mikhail, D. (2018). *The beekeeper: Rescuing the stolen women of Iraq* (1st ed.). New Directions Publishing.

Mikolov, T., Chen, K., Corrado, G., & Dean, J. (2013). *Efficient estimation of word representations in vector space*. arXiv preprint arXiv:1301.3781.

Mikolov, T., Sutskever, I., Chen, K., Corrado, G. S., & Dean, J. 2013b. Distributed representations of words and phrases and their compositionality. Advances in Neural Information Processing Systems, 3111-3119.

Mikolov, T., Yih, W. T., & Zweig, G. (2013a). Linguistic regularities in continuous space word representations. *Proceedings of the 2013 Conference of the North American Chapter of the Association for Computational Linguistics: Human Language Technologies*, 746-751.

Miller, G. A. (1995). WordNet: A lexical database for English. *Communications of the ACM, 38*(11), 39–41. doi:10.1145/219717.219748

Min, H., Peng, Y., Shoss, M., & Yang, B. (2021). Using machine learning to investigate the public's emotional responses to work from home during the COVID-19 pandemic. *The Journal of Applied Psychology, 106*(2), 214–229. https://doi.org/10.1037/apl0000886

Minkov, E., & Cohen, W. W. (2012). Graph based similarity measures for synonym extraction from parsed text. *Workshop Proceedings of TextGraphs-7 on Graph-based Methods for Natural Language Processing, Association for Computational Linguistics,* 20-24.

Mohammad, S., & Hirst, G. (2005). *Distributional measures as proxies for semantic relatedness.* Academic Press.

Mohammad, S., Kiritchenko, S., Sobhani, P., Zhu, X., & Cherry, C. (2016a). A dataset for detecting stance in tweets. In *Proceedings of the Tenth International Conference on Language Resources and Evaluation (LREC)* (pp. 3945-3952). Academic Press.

Mohammad, S. M., Sobhani, P., & Kiritchenko, S. (2017). Stance and sentiment in tweets. *ACM Transactions on Internet Technology, 17*(3), 1–23. doi:10.1145/3003433

Mohammad, S. M., Zhu, X., Kiritchenko, S., & Martin, J. (2015). Sentiment, emotion, purpose, and style in electoral tweets. *Information Processing & Management, 51*(4), 480–499. doi:10.1016/j.ipm.2014.09.003

Mohammad, S., Kiritchenko, S., Sobhani, P., Zhu, X., & Cherry, C. (2016b). SemEval-2016 task 6: Detecting stance in tweets. In *Proceedings of the 10th International Workshop on Semantic Evaluation* (pp. 31-41). 10.18653/v1/S16-1003

Morales, M. R. (2018). *Multimodal depression detection: An investigation of features and fusion techniques for automated systems.* City University of New York.

Morales, M. R., & Levitan, R. (2016). *Speech vs. text: A comparative analysis of features for depression detection systems. In 2016 IEEE spoken language technology workshop.* SLT.

Mostafa, M. M. (2013). More than words: Social networks' text mining for consumer brand sentiments. *Expert Systems with Applications, 40*(10), 4241–4251. https://doi.org/10.1016/j.eswa.2013.01.019

Mouratidis, K., Peters, S., & van Wee, B. (2021). Transportation technologies, sharing economy, and teleactivities: Implications for built environment and travel. *Transportation Research Part D, Transport and Environment, 92,* 102716. https://doi.org/https://doi.org/10.1016/j.trd.2021.102716

Moyer, J. D., & Kaplan, O. (2020, June 6). *Will the Coronavirus fuel conflict projections based on economic and development data show an increased.* Retrieved from Foreign Policy – the Global Magazine of News and Ideas: https://foreignpolicy.com/2020/07/06/coronavirus-pandemic-fuel-conflict-fragile-states-economy-food-prices/

Muchlinski, D., Siroky, D., He, J., & Kocher, M. (n.d.). Comparing random forest with logistic regression for predicting class-imbalanced civil war onset data. *Political Analysis, 24*(1), 87-103. Retrieved from https://www.jstor.org/stable/24573207

Muhic, A., Rupnik, J., & Skraba, P. (2012). Cross-lingual document similarity. *Information Technology Interfaces (ITI), Proceedings of the ITI 2012 34th International Conference on,* 387-392.

Mujahid, M., Lee, E., Rustam, F., Washington, P. B., Ullah, S., Reshi, A. A., & Ashraf, I. (2021). Sentiment analysis and topic modeling on tweets about online education during COVID-19. *Applied Sciences (Basel, Switzerland), 11*(18), 8438. doi:10.3390/app11188438

Murthy, D., & Gross, A. J. (2017). Social media processes in disasters: Implications of emergent technology use. *Social Science Research, 63,* 356–370. https://doi.org/10.1016/j.ssresearch.2016.09.015

Mutlu, E. C., Oghaz, T., Jasser, J., Tutunculer, E., Rajabi, A., Tayebi, A., Ozmen, O., & Garibay, I. (2020). A stance data set on polarized conversations on Twitter about the efficacy of hydroxychloroquine as a treatment for COVID-19. *Data in Brief, 33*, 106401. doi:10.1016/j.dib.2020.106401 PMID:33088880

Nalisnick, E. T., & Baird, H. S. (2013). Character-to-Character Sentiment Analysis in Shakespeare's Plays. *ACL*, 479–483. http://www.ibiblio.org/xml/examples/shakespeare/

Nandi, V., & Agrawal, S. (2016). Political sentiment analysis using hybrid approach. *International Research Journal of Engineering and Technology, 3*(5), 1621–1627.

Nasukawa, T., & Yi, J. (2003). Sentiment analysis: Capturing favorability using natural language processing. *Proceedings of the 2nd International Conference on Knowledge Capture, K-CAP 2003*, 70–77. 10.1145/945645.945658

Nieminen, E. (2021). *The Character Development of Neville Longbottom in J.K. Rowling's Harry Potter Novel Series*. https://trepo.tuni.fi/handle/10024/124797

Nilles, J. (1994). *Making telecommuting happen: A guide for telemanagers and telecommuters*. Van Nostrand Reinhold Editors.

Nilles, J. (1975). Telecommunications and Organizational Decentralization. *IEEE Transactions on Communications, 23*(10), 1142–1147. https://doi.org/https://doi.org/ 10.1109/TCOM.1975.1092687

Niu, L., Dai, X., Zhang, J., & Chen, J. (2015). Topic2Vec: learning distributed representations of topics. *Asian Language Processing (IALP), 2015 International Conference on*, 193-196.

NLTK. (2021). *Natural Language Toolkit*. https://www.nltk.org/

Nussbaum, M. C. (2006). *El ocultamiento de lo humano: repugnancia, vergüenza y ley* (Vol. 77). Katz editores.

O'dea, B., Wan, S., Batterham, P. J., Calear, A. L., Paris, C., & Christensen, H. (2015). Detecting suicidality on Twitter. *Internet Interventions: the Application of Information Technology in Mental and Behavioural Health, 2*(2), 183–188. doi:10.1016/j.invent.2015.03.005

O'Sullivan, K. (2020). *25 Best Romance Novels to Make You Believe in Love Again*. https://www.thepioneerwoman.com/news-entertainment/g32157911/best-romance-novels/

Ofei-Dodoo, S., Long, M. C., Bretches, M., Kruse, B. J., Haynes, C., & Bachman, C. (2020). Work engagement, job satisfaction, and turnover intentions among family medicine residency program managers. *International Journal of Medical Education, 11*, 47–53. https://doi.org/10.5116/ijme.5e3e.7f16

Oliveira, C. A. (1990). *IDEAL - uma interface dialógica em linguagem natural para sistemas especialistas*. São José dos Campos: Instituto Nacional de Pesquisas Espaciais (INPE). Retrieved from http://urlib.net/rep/6qtX3pFwXQZ3r59YCT/GUpqq

Orabi, A. H., Buddhitha, P., Orabi, M. H., & Inkpen, D. (2018). Deep learning for depression detection of twitter users. In *Proceedings of the Fifth Workshop on Computational Linguistics and Clinical Psychology: From Keyboard to Clinic* (pp. 88-97). 10.18653/v1/W18-0609

Oyebode, O., & Orji, R. (2020). Deconstructing Persuasive Strategies in Mental Health Apps Based on User Reviews using Natural Language Processing. BCSS@ PERSUASIVE.

Ozcan, S., Suloglu, M., Sakar, C. O., & Chatufale, S. (2021). Social media mining for ideation: Identification of sustainable solutions and opinions. *Technovation, 107*, 102322. https://doi.org/10.1016/j.technovation.2021.102322

Ozyurt, B., & Akcayol, M. A. (2021). A new topic modeling based approach for aspect extraction in aspect based sentiment analysis: SS-LDA. *Expert Systems with Applications*, *168*, 114231. doi:10.1016/j.eswa.2020.114231

Pachouly, S. J., Raut, G., Bute, K., Tambe, R., & Bhavsar, S. (2021). *Depression Detection on Social Media Network (Twitter) using Sentiment Analysis*. Academic Press.

Pagliardini, M., Gupta, P., & Jaggi, M. (2017). *Unsupervised learning of sentence embeddings using compositional n-gram features*. arXiv preprint arXiv:1703.02507.

Pak, A., & Paroubek, P. (2010, May). Twitter as a corpus for sentiment analysis and opinion mining. In LREc (Vol. 10, No. 2010, pp. 1320-1326). Academic Press.

Palumbo, R. (2020). Let me go to the office! An investigation into the side effects of working from home on work-life balance. *International Journal of Public Sector Management*, *33*(6–7), 771–790. https://doi.org/10.1108/IJPSM-06-2020-0150

Pang, B., & Lee, L. (2004). A Sentimental Education: Sentiment Analysis Using Subjectivity Summarization Based on Minimum Cuts. *Computing Research Repository - CORR*, 271–278. doi:10.3115/1218955.1218990

Pang, B., Lee, L., & Vaithyanathan, S. (2002). *Thumbs up? Sentiment classification using machine learning techniques*. arXiv preprint cs/0205070.

Pang, B., & Lee, L. (2008). Opinion mining and sentiment analysis. *Foundations and Trends in Information Retrieval*, *2*(1-2), 1–135. doi:10.1561/1500000011

Pang, B., Lee, L., & Vaithyanathan, S. (2002). Thumbs up? Sentiment Classification using Machine Learning Techniques. *Proceedings of the Empirical Methods on Natural Language Processing*, 79-86.

Pang, B., Lee, L., & Vaithyanathan, S. (2002). Thumbs up?: sentiment classification using machine learning techniques. In *Proceedings of the ACL-02 Conference on Empirical Methods in Natural Language Processing* (vol. 10, pp. 79-86). Association for Computational Linguistics. 10.3115/1118693.1118704

Park, A., Conway, M., & Chen, A. T. (2018). Examining thematic similarity, difference, and membership in three online mental health communities from Reddit: A text mining and visualization approach. *Computers in Human Behavior*, *78*, 98–112. doi:10.1016/j.chb.2017.09.001 PMID:29456286

Parker, K., Horowitz, J., Minkin, R., & Arditi, T. (2021). *How the Coronavirus Outbreak Has-and Hasn't-Changed the Way Americans Work*. https://www.pewresearch.org/social-trends/2020/12/09/how-the-coronavirus-outbreak-has-and-hasnt-changed-the-way-americans-work/

Park, H. M., Kim, C. H., & Kim, J. H. (2020). Generating a Korean sentiment lexicon through sentiment score propagation. *KIPS Transactions on Software and Data Engineering*, *9*(2), 53–60.

Park, S., Bier, L. M., & Park, H. W. (2021). The effects of infotainment on public reaction to North Korea using hybrid text mining: Content analysis, machine learning-based sentiment analysis, and co-word analysis. *El Profesional de la Información*, *30*(3), 300306. doi:10.3145/epi.2021.may.06

PastorC. K. (2020). Sentiment analysis of Filipinos and effects of extreme community quarantine due to coronavirus (COVID-19) pandemic. *SSRN*, 3574385. doi:10.2139/ssrn.3574385

Pathak, P., Goswami, R., Joshi, G., Patel, P., & Patel, A. (2013). CRF-based clinical named entity recognition using clinical NLP. *Proceedings of the 10th International Conference on Natural Language Processing*.

Pedregosa, F., Varoquaux, G., Gramfort, A., Michel, V., Thirion, B., Grisel, O., Blondel, M., Prettenhofer, P., Weiss, R., Dubourg, V., Vanderplas, J., Passos, A., Cournapeau, D., Brucher, M., Perrot, M., & Duchesnay, É. (2011). Scikit-learn: Machine Learning in Python. *Journal of Machine Learning Research*, *12*(85), 2825–2830.

Pendyala, R. M., Goulias, K. G., & Kitamura, R. (1991). Impact of telecommuting on spatial and temporal patterns of household travel. *Transportation*, *18*, 383–409. https://doi.org/10.1007/BF00186566

Pennington, J., Socher, R., & Manning, C. (2014). GloVe: Global vectors for word representation. *Proceedings of the 2014 Conference on Empirical Methods in Natural Language Processing (EMNLP)*. 10.3115/v1/D14-1162

Pereg, O., Korat, D., Wasserblat, M., Mamou, J., & Dagan, I. (2019). ABSApp: A portable weakly-supervised aspect-based sentiment extraction system. In *Proceedings of the 2019 Conference on Empirical Methods in Natural Language Processing and the 9th International Joint Conference on Natural Language Processing (EMNLP-IJCNLP): System Demonstrations* (pp. 1-6). 10.18653/v1/D19-3001

Perez, E., Kiela, D., & Cho, K. (2021). *True Few-Shot Learning with Language Models*. arXiv preprint arXiv:2105.11447.

Perikos, I., Kardakis, S., & Hatzilygeroudis, I. (in press). Sentiment analysis using novel and interpretable architectures of Hidden Markov Models. *Knowledge-Based Systems*.

Phang, Y. C., Kassim, A. M., & Mangantig, E. (2021). Concerns of Thalassemia Patients, Carriers, and their Caregivers in Malaysia: Text Mining Information Shared on Social Media. *Healthcare Informatics Research*, *27*(3), 200–213. doi:10.4258/hir.2021.27.3.200 PMID:34384202

Picard, R. W. (2003). Affective computing: Challenges. *International Journal of Human-Computer Studies*, *59*(1-2), 55–64. doi:10.1016/S1071-5819(03)00052-1

Pickell, D. (2019). *Social Media Data Mining – How it Works and Who's Using it*. G2 Company.

Pirro, G., & Euzenat, J. (2010). A feature and information theoretic framework for semantic similarity and relatedness. *The Semantic Web–ISWC*, *2010*, 615–630. doi:10.1007/978-3-642-17746-0_39

Piryani, R., Madhavi, D., & Singh, V. K. (2017). Analytical mapping of opinion mining and sentiment analysis research during 2000–2015. *Information Processing & Management*, *53*(1), 122–150. doi:10.1016/j.ipm.2016.07.001

Pollak, S., Martinc, M., & Poniz, K. M. (2020). Natural Language Processing for Literary Text Analysis: Word-Embeddings-Based Analysis of Zofka Kveder's Work. In DHandNLP@ PROPOR (pp. 33-42). Academic Press.

Pontiki, M., Galanis, D., Papageorgiou, H., Androutsopoulos, I., Manandhar, S., Al-Smadi, M., ... Eryiğit, G. (2016, January). Semeval-2016 task 5: Aspect based sentiment analysis. In *International workshop on semantic evaluation* (pp. 19-30). 10.18653/v1/S16-1002

Porter, M. F. (1980). An algorithm for suffix stripping. *Program*, *14*(3), 130–137. Available at: http://www.emeraldinsight.com/doi/10.1108/eb046814

Pota, M., Esposito, M., Palomino, M. A., & Masala, G. L. (2018). A subword-based deep learning approach for sentiment analysis of political tweets. *2018 32nd International Conference on Advanced Information Networking and Applications Workshops (WAINA)*, 651–656.

Pozzi, F. A., Fersini, E., Messina, E., & Liu, B. (2016). *Sentiment analysis in social networks*. Morgan Kaufmann.

Prabhakaran, S. (2018). *Topic Modeling with Gensim (Python)*. Machine Learning Plus.

Prathvi Kumari, R. K. (2013). Measuring Semantic Similarity between Words using Page-Count and Pattern Clustering Methods. *International Journal of Innovative Technology and Exploring Engineering*.

Rajagopal, D., Cambria, E., Olsher, D., & Kwok, K. (2013). A graph-based approach to commonsense concept extraction and semantic similarity detection. *Proceedings of the 22nd International Conference on World Wide Web*, 565-570. 10.1145/2487788.2487995

Rajman, M. (1998). *Text mining-knowledge extraction from unstructured textual data*. Springer. Available at: https://link.springer.com/chapter/10.1007/978-3-642-72253-0_64

Ramón-Hernández, A., Simón-Cuevas, A., Lorenzo, M. M. G., Arco, L., & Serrano-Guerrero, J. (2020). Towards Context-Aware Opinion Summarization for Monitoring Social Impact of News. *Information (Basel)*, *11*(11), 535. doi:10.3390/info11110535

Rangapuram, S. S., Seeger, M. W., Gasthaus, J., Stella, L., Wang, Y., & Januschowski, T. (2018). Deep State Space Models for Time Series Forecasting. In Advances in Neural Information Processing Systems. Curran Associates, Inc. Retrieved from https://proceedings.neurips.cc/paper/2018/file/5cf68969fb67aa6082363a6d4e6468e2-Paper.pdf

Rashid, A., Anwer, N., Iqbal, M., & Sher, M. (2013). A survey paper: Areas, techniques and challenges of opinion mining. *International Journal of Computer Science Issues*, *10*(2), 18–32.

Reece, A. G., & Danforth, C. M. (2017). Instagram photos reveal predictive markers of depression. *EPJ Data Science*, *6*, 1–12.

Reis, J. C., Correia, A., Murai, F., Veloso, A., Benevenuto, F., & Cambria, E. (2019). Supervised learning for fake news detection. *IEEE Intelligent Systems*, *34*(2), 76–81. doi:10.1109/MIS.2019.2899143

Rejito, J., Atthariq, A., & Abdullah, A. (2021). Application of text mining employing k-means algorithms for clustering tweets of Tokopedia. *Journal of Physics: Conference Series*.

Ren, S.-Y., Gao, R.-D., & Chen, Y.-L. (2020). Fear can be more harmful than the severe acute respiratory syndrome coronavirus 2 in controlling the corona virus disease 2019 epidemic. *World Journal of Clinical Cases*, *8*(4), 652–657. https://doi.org/10.12998/wjcc.v8.i4.652

Resnik, P. (1999). Semantic similarity in a taxonomy: An information-based measure and its application to problems of ambiguity in natural language. *Journal of Artificial Intelligence Research*, *11*, 95–130. doi:10.1613/jair.514

Reuters. (2019). *Reuters news agency: World's largest news agency*. Retrieved from Reuters: https://www.reuters.com/

Reyes-Menendez, A., Saura, J., & Alvarez-Alonso, C. (2018, November). Understanding #worldenvironmentday user opinions in twitter: A topic-based sentiment analysis approach. *International Journal of Environmental Research and Public Health*, *15*(11), 2537. Advance online publication. doi:10.3390/ijerph15112537 PMID:30428520

Rhodes, R. A. W. (2014). Public administration. In The Oxford Handbook of Political Leadership. OUP.

Richardson, L. F. (1960). *Arms and Insecurity: A Mathematical Study of the Causes and*. Boxwood.

Riggs, F. W. (1965). Relearning an old lesson: The political context of development administration. *Public Administration Review*, *25*(1), 70–79. doi:10.2307/974009

Rodríguez-Ibáñez, M., Gimeno-Blanes, F.-J., Cuenca-Jiménez, P. M., Soguero-Ruiz, C., & Rojo-Álvarez, J. L. (2021). Sentiment Analysis of Political Tweets From the 2019 Spanish Elections. *IEEE Access: Practical Innovations, Open Solutions*, *9*, 101847–101862. doi:10.1109/ACCESS.2021.3097492

Rodriguez, M. A., & Egenhofer, M. J. (2003). Determining semantic similarity among entity classes from different ontologies. *IEEE Transactions on Knowledge and Data Engineering*, *15*(2), 442–456. doi:10.1109/TKDE.2003.1185844

Roger, L., & Manning, C. D. (2004). Deep dependencies from context-free statistical parsers: correcting the surface dependency approximation. In *Proceedings of the 42nd Annual Meeting of the Association for Computational Linguistics (ACL-04)* (pp. 327–334). Academic Press.

Roostaee, M., Fakhrahmad, S. M., Sadreddini, M. H., & Khalili, A. (2014). Efficient calculation of sentence semantic similarity: A proposed scheme based on machine learning approaches and NLP techniques. *Scientific Journal of Review*, *3*, 94–106.

Rosa, R. R., Neelakshi, J., Pinheiro, G. A., Barchi, P. H., & Shiguemori, H. (2019). Modeling social and geopolitical disasters as extreme events: a case study considering the complex dynamics of international armed conflicts. In L. Santos, R. G. Negri, & T. J. Carvalho (Eds.), *Towards mathematics, computers and environment: a disasters perspective* (pp. 233–254). Springer. doi:10.1007/978-3-030-21205-6_12

Rosenthal, S., Farra, N., & Nakov, P. (2017, August). SemEval-2017 task 4: Sentiment analysis in twitter. In S. Bethard, M. Carpuat, M. Apidianaki, S. M. Mohammad, D. Cer, & D. Jurgens (Eds.), *Proceedings of the 11th international workshop on semantic evaluation (SemEval-2017)* (pp. 502–518). Association for Computational Linguistics. 10.18653/v1/S17-2088

Ross, J. (2009). *IraqiGirl: Diary of a teenage girl in Iraq*. Haymarket Books.

Rowling, J. K. (1998). *Harry Potter and the chamber of secrets*. Bloomsbury Pub.

Rowling, J. K. (2000). *Harry Potter and the Goblet of Fire*. Bloomsbury.

Rude, S., Gortner, E. M., & Pennebaker, J. (2004). Language use of depressed and depression-vulnerable college students. *Cognition and Emotion*, *18*(8), 1121–1133. doi:10.1080/02699930441000030

Rupapara, V., Rustam, F., Amaar, A., Washington, P. B., Lee, E., & Ashraf, I. (2021). Deepfake tweets classification using stacked Bi-LSTM and words embedding. *PeerJ. Computer Science*, *7*, e745. doi:10.7717/peerj-cs.745 PMID:34805502

Russell, S., & Norvig, P. (2020). *Artificial Intelligence: A Modern Approach*. Pearson. http://aima.cs.berkeley.edu/global-index.html

Rustam, F., Khalid, M., Aslam, W., Rupapara, V., Mehmood, A., & Choi, G. S. (2021). A performance comparison of supervised machine learning models for COVID-19 tweets sentiment analysis. *PLoS One*, *16*(2), e0245909. doi:10.1371/journal.pone.0245909 PMID:33630869

Sabin, D. (2017). *Facebook Makes A.I. Program Available in 294 Languages*. https://www.inverse.com/article/31075-facebook-machine-learning-language-fasttext

Saif, H., He, Y., & Alani, H. (2012, November). Semantic sentiment analysis of twitter. In *International semantic web conference* (pp. 508–524). Springer. 10.1007/978-3-642-35176-1_32

Salas-Zárate, M. D. P., Medina-Moreira, J., Lagos-Ortiz, K., Luna-Aveiga, H., Rodriguez-Garcia, M. A., & Valencia-Garcia, R. (2017). Sentiment analysis on tweets about diabetes: An aspect-level approach. *Computational and Mathematical Methods in Medicine*, *2017*, 2017. doi:10.1155/2017/5140631 PMID:28316638

Salbi, Z., & Becklund, L. (2006). *Between two worlds: Escape from tyranny: Growing up in the shadow of Saddam*. Penguin.

Salim, H., & Saad, N. N. (2016). Portraying the Protagonists: A Study of the Use of Adjectives in Harry Potter and the Deathly Hallows. *Undefined*, *5*(6), 259–264. doi:10.7575/aiac.ijalel.v.5n.6p.259

Salinas, D., Flunkert, V., & Gasthaus, J. (2018). *DeepAR: Probabilistic Forecasting with Autoregressive Recurrent Networks*. Cornell University. arXiv:1704.04110

Salton, G., Wong, A., & Yang, C. S. (1975). A vector space model for automatic indexing. *Communications of the ACM*, *18*(11), 613–620. doi:10.1145/361219.361220

Samuel, J., Rahman, M. M., Ali, G. G. M. N., Samuel, Y., Pelaez, A., Chong, P. H. J., & Yakubov, M. (2020). Feeling Positive About Reopening? New Normal Scenarios From COVID-19 US Reopen Sentiment Analytics. *IEEE Access: Practical Innovations, Open Solutions*, 8, 142173–142190. https://doi.org/10.1109/ACCESS.2020.3013933

Sanchez, D., Batet, M., Isern, D., & Valls, A. (2012). Ontology-based semantic similarity: A new feature-based approach. *Expert Systems with Applications*, *39*(9), 7718–7728. doi:10.1016/j.eswa.2012.01.082

Sanders, A. C., White, R. C., Severson, L. S., Ma, R., McQueen, R., Paulo, H. C. A., . . . Bennett, K. P. (2021). Unmasking the conversation on masks: Natural language processing for topical sentiment analysis of COVID-19 Twitter discourse. medRxiv, 2020-08.

Sanders, A. C., White, R. C., Severson, L. S., Ma, R., McQueen, R., Paulo, H. C. A., . . . (2021). Unmasking the conversation on masks: Natural language processing for topical sentiment analysis of COVID-19 Twitter discourse. medRxiv, 2020-08.

Sandoval-Almazan, R., & Valle-Cruz, D. (2020). Sentiment Analysis of Facebook Users Reacting to Political Campaign Posts. *Digital Government: Research and Practice*, *1*(2), 1–13. doi:10.1145/3382735

Santorini, B. (1990). *Part-of-speech Tagging Guidelines for the Penn Treebank Project (3rd revision)*. Academic Press.

Saruladha, K., Aghila, G., & Raj, S. (2010). A survey of semantic similarity methods for ontology based information retrieval. *2010 Second International Conference on Machine Learning and Computing*, 297-301. 10.1109/ICMLC.2010.63

Sasson, J. (2003). *Mayada, daughter of Iraq* (1st ed.). Dutton Adult.

Sattar, N. S., & Arifuzzaman, S. (2021). COVID-19 vaccination awareness and aftermath: Public sentiment analysis on Twitter data and vaccinated population prediction in the USA. *Applied Sciences (Basel, Switzerland)*, *11*(13), 6128. doi:10.3390/app11136128

Saxena, A., Khanna, A., & Gupta, D. (2020). Emotion recognition and detection methods: A comprehensive survey. *Journal of Artificial Intelligence and Systems*, *2*(1), 53–79. doi:10.33969/AIS.2020.21005

Sazzed, S., & Jayarathna, S. (2021). SSentiA: A Self-supervised Sentiment Analyzer for classification from unlabeled data. *Machine Learning with Applications*, 4, 100026. doi:10.1016/j.mlwa.2021.100026

Scao, T. L., & Rush, A. M. (2021). *How Many Data Points is a Prompt Worth?* arXiv preprint arXiv:2103.08493.

Schick, T., & Schütze, H. (2020). *Exploiting cloze questions for few shot text classification and natural language inference*. arXiv preprint arXiv:2001.07676.

Schmitt, J. B., Breuer, J., & Wulf, T. (2021). From cognitive overload to digital detox: Psychological implications of telework during the COVID-19 pandemic. *Computers in Human Behavior*, *124*, 106899. https://doi.org/10.1016/j.chb.2021.106899

Schuhmacher, M., & Ponzetto, S. P. (2014). Knowledge-based graph document modeling. *Proceedings of the 7th ACM international conference on Web search and data mining*, 543-552. 10.1145/2556195.2556250

Schuster, C., Weitzman, L., Sass Mikkelsen, K., Meyer-Sahling, J., Bersch, K., Fukuyama, F., Paskov, P., Rogger, D., Mistree, D., & Kay, K. (2020). Responding to COVID-19 through Surveys of Public Servants. *Public Administration Review*, *80*(5), 792–796. https://doi.org/10.1111/puar.13246

Schwering, A. (2005). Hybrid model for semantic similarity measurement. *On the Move to Meaningful Internet Systems 2005: CoopIS, DOA, and ODBASE*, 1449-1465.

scikit learn. (2011a). *Ensemble methods.* https://scikit-learn.org/stable/modules/ensemble.html#

scikit learn. (2011b). *Support Vector Machines.* https://scikit-learn.org/stable/modules/svm.html#svm

Seal, A., Bajpai, R., Agnihotri, J., Yazidi, A., Herrera-Viedma, E., & Krejcar, O. (2021). DeprNet: A Deep Convolution Neural Network Framework for Detecting Depression Using EEG. *IEEE Transactions on Instrumentation and Measurement, 70*, 1–13. doi:10.1109/TIM.2021.3053999

Severyn, A., & Moschitti, A. (2015, August). Twitter sentiment analysis with deep convolutional neural networks. In *Proceedings of the 38th international ACM SIGIR conference on research and development in information retrieval* (pp. 959-962). 10.1145/2766462.2767830

Shah, F. M., Ahmed, F., Joy, S. K. S., Ahmed, S., Sadek, S., Shil, R., & Kabir, M. H. (2020). Early Depression Detection from Social Network Using Deep Learning Techniques. In *2020 IEEE Region 10 Symposium (TENSYMP)* (pp. 823-826). 10.1109/TENSYMP50017.2020.9231008

Shakibaei, S., de Jong, G. C., Alpkökin, P., & Rashidi, T. H. (2021). Impact of the COVID-19 pandemic on travel behavior in Istanbul: A panel data analysis. *Sustainable Cities and Society, 65*, 102619. https://doi.org/10.1016/j.scs.2020.102619

Sharma, Y., Mittal, E., & Garg, M. (2016). Political Opinion Mining from Twitter. *International Journal of Information Systems in the Service Sector, 8*(4), 47–56. doi:10.4018/IJISSS.2016100104

Shelke, N., Deshpande, S., & Thakare, V. (2017). Domain independent approach for aspect oriented sentiment analysis for product reviews. In *Proceedings of the 5th international conference on frontiers in intelligent computing: Theory and applications* (pp. 651-659). Springer. 10.1007/978-981-10-3156-4_69

Shen, G., Jia, J., Nie, L., Feng, F., Zhang, C., Hu, T., . . . Zhu, W. (2017). Depression Detection via Harvesting Social Media: A Multimodal Dictionary Learning Solution. In IJCAI (pp. 3838-3844). doi:10.24963/ijcai.2017/536

Shepard, R. N. (1980). Multidimensional scaling, tree-fitting, and clustering. *Science, 210*(4468), 390–398. doi:10.1126cience.210.4468.390 PMID:17837406

Shibata, N., Kajikawa, Y., & Sakata, I. (2010). How to measure the semantic similarities between scientific papers and patents in order to discover uncommercialized research fronts: A case study of solar cells. *Technology Management for Global Economic Growth (PICMET), 2010 Proceedings of PICMET'10*, 1-6.

Shim, J. G., Ryu, K. H., Lee, S. H., Cho, E. A., Lee, Y. J., & Ahn, J. H. (2021). Text mining approaches to analyze public sentiment changes regarding COVID-19 vaccines on social media in Korea. *International Journal of Environmental Research and Public Health, 18*(12), 6549. doi:10.3390/ijerph18126549 PMID:34207016

Shirakawa, M., Nakayama, K., Hara, T., & Nishio, S. (2015). Wikipedia-based semantic similarity measurements for noisy short texts using extended naive bayes. *IEEE Transactions on Emerging Topics in Computing, 3*(2), 205–219. doi:10.1109/TETC.2015.2418716

Shiryaev, A. P., Dorofeev, A. V., Fedorov, A. R., Gagarina, L. G., & Zaycev, V. V. (2017). LDA models for finding trends in technical knowledge domain. *2017 IEEE Conference of Russian Young Researchers in Electrical and Electronic Engineering*, 551-554. 10.1109/EIConRus.2017.7910614

Shofiya, C., & Abidi, S. (2021). Sentiment Analysis on COVID-19-Related Social Distancing in Canada Using Twitter Data. *International Journal of Environmental Research and Public Health, 18*(11), 5993. https://doi.org/10.3390/ijerph18115993

Shu, K., Sliva, A., Wang, S., Tang, J., & Liu, H. (2017). Fake news detection on social media: A data mining perspective. *SIGKDD Explorations*, *19*(1), 22–36. doi:10.1145/3137597.3137600

Sidorov, G., & Miranda-Jiménez, S. (2012). Empirical Study of Machine Learning BAsed Approach for Opinion Mining in Tweets. In I. Batyrshin & M. Gonzalez Mendoza (Eds.), Lecture Notes in Computer Science: Vol. 7629. *Advances in Artificial Intelligence. MICAI 20212* (pp. 1–14). Springer.

Singh, J., Singh, G., & Singh, R. (2017). Optimization of sentiment analysis using machine learning classifiers. Human-Centric Computing and Information Sciences, 7(1), 1-12. doi:10.118613673-017-0116-3

Singh, J., Saini, M., & Siddiqi, S. (2013). Graph Based Computational Model for Computing Semantic Similarity. *Emerging Research in Computing, Information, Communication and Applications, ERCICA, 2013*, 501–507.

Singh, M., Jakhar, A. K., & Pandey, S. (2021). Sentiment analysis on the impact of coronavirus in social life using the BERT model. *Social Network Analysis and Mining*, *11*(1), 1–11. doi:10.100713278-021-00737-z PMID:33758630

Singh, T., & Kumari, M. (2016). Role of Text Pre-processing in Twitter Sentiment Analysis. *Procedia Computer Science*, *89*, 549–554. doi:10.1016/j.procs.2016.06.095

Skeppstedt, M., Kerren, A., & Stede, M. (2017). Automatic detection of stance towards vaccination in online discussion forums. In *Proceedings of the International Workshop on Digital Disease Detection using Social Media 2017* (pp. 1-8). Academic Press.

Smys, S., & Raj, J. S. (2021). Analysis of Deep Learning Techniques for Early Detection of Depression on Social Media Network-A Comparative Study. *Journal of Trends in Computer Science and Smart Technology, 3*(1), 24-39.

Sobhani, P., Inkpen, D., & Zhu, X. (2017). A dataset for multi-target stance detection. In *Proceedings of the 15th Conference of the European Chapter of the Association for Computational Linguistics:* Volume 2, *Short Papers* (pp. 551-557). Academic Press.

Socher, R., Perelygin, A., Wu, J., Chuang, J., Manning, C. D., Ng, A. Y., & Potts, C. (2013, October). Recursive deep models for semantic compositionality over a sentiment treebank. In *Proceedings of the 2013 conference on empirical methods in natural language processing* (pp. 1631-1642). Academic Press.

Sokratous, S., Merkouris, A., Middleton, N., & Karanikola, M. (2013). The association between stressful life events and depressive symptoms among Cypriot university students: A cross-sectional descriptive correlational study. *BMC Public Health*, *13*(1), 1–16. doi:10.1186/1471-2458-13-1121 PMID:24304515

Sornette, D. (2006). Endogenous versus exogenous origins of crises. In S. Albeverio, V. Jentsch, & H. Kantz (Eds.), Extremes events in nature and society (pp. 107-131). Springer. doi:10.1007/3-540-28611-X_5

spaCy. (2018). *Industrial-strength Natural Language*. https://spacy.io/

SpaCy. (2019). *Industrial-strength natural language processing*. Retrieved June 2018, from SpaCy: https://spacy.io/

spaCy. (2020). *Available trained pipelines for English*. https://spacy.io/models/en#en_core_web_lg

Stankevich, M., Isakov, V., Devyatkin, D., & Smirnov, I. V. (2018). Feature Engineering for Depression Detection in Social Media. In ICPRAM (pp. 426-431). doi:10.5220/0006598604260431

Stankevich, M., Latyshev, A., Kuminskaya, E., Smirnov, I., & Grigoriev, O. (2019). Depression detection from social media texts. In *Data Analytics and Management in Data Intensive Domains: XXI International Conference DAMDID/RCDL*, (p. 352). Academic Press.

Stiles, J. (2020). Strategic niche management in transition pathways : Telework advocacy as groundwork for an incremental transformation. *Environmental Innovation and Societal Transitions*, *34*, 139–150. https://doi.org/10.1016/j.eist.2019.12.001

Stirman, S. W., & Pennebaker, J. W. (2001). Word use in the poetry of suicidal and nonsuicidal poets. *Psychosomatic Medicine*, *63*(4), 517–522. doi:10.1097/00006842-200107000-00001 PMID:11485104

Stone, P., Dunphy, D., Smith, M., & Ogilvie, D. (1966). *The General Inqiurer - A computer approach to content analysis.* MIT Press.

Suh, A., & Lee, J. (2017). Understanding teleworkers' technostress and its influence on job satisfaction. *Internet Research*, *27*(1), 140–159. https://doi.org/10.1108/IntR-06-2015-0181

Sultan, M. A., Bethard, S., & Sumner, T. (2015). DLS @ CU: Sentence Similarity from Word Alignment and Semantic Vector Composition. SemEval@ NAACL-HLT, 148-153.

Sun, C., Huang, L., & Qiu, X. (2019). *Utilizing BERT for aspect-based sentiment analysis via constructing auxiliary sentence.* arXiv preprint arXiv:1903.09588.

Sun, X. (n.d.). *Empirical studies on the nlp techniques for source code data preprocessing.* Available at: https://dl.acm.org/citation.cfm?id=2627514

Sun, S., Luo, C., & Chen, J. (2017). A review of natural language processing techniques for opinion mining systems. *Information Fusion*, *36*, 10–25. doi:10.1016/j.inffus.2016.10.004

Suresh, H., & Raj, D. G. (2015). Analysis of Machine Learning Techniques for Opinion Mining. *Advances in Research*, *3*(12), 375–381.

Sutton, C., & McCallum, A. (2006). An introduction to conditional random fields for relational learning. *Introduction to Statistical Relational Learning*, *2*, 93–128.

Syahputra, H. (2021). Sentiment Analysis of Community Opinion on Online Store in Indonesia on Twitter using Support Vector Machine Algorithm (SVM). *Journal of Physics: Conference Series*.

Syarif, I., Ningtias, N., & Badriyah, T. (2019). Study on Mental Disorder Detection via Social Media Mining. In *2019 4th International Conference on Computing, Communications and Security (ICCCS)* (pp. 1-6). 10.1109/CCCS.2019.8888096

Taboada, M. (2016). Sentiment Analysis: An Overview from Linguistics. *Annual Review of Linguistics*, *2*(1), 325–347. doi:10.1146/annurev-linguistics-011415-040518

Taboada, M., Brooke, J., Tofiloski, M., Voll, K., & Stede, M. (2011). Lexicon-Based Methods for Sentiment Analysis. *Computational Linguistics*, *37*(2), 267–307. doi:10.1162/COLI_a_00049

Tadesse, M. M., Lin, H., Xu, B., & Yang, L. (2019). Detection of depression-related posts in reddit social media forum. *IEEE Access: Practical Innovations, Open Solutions*, *7*, 44883–44893. doi:10.1109/ACCESS.2019.2909180

Takagi, N. M. T. (2015). WSL: Sentence similarity using semantic distance between words. In *Proceedings of the 9th International Workshop on Semantic Evaluation* (pp.128-131). Academic Press.

Taku910.github.io. (2017). *CRF++: Yet Another CRF toolkit.* https://taku910.github.io/crfpp/

Tally, R. T. (2012). The Way of the Wizarding World: Harry Potter and the Magical Bildungsroman. In J. K. Rowling: Harry Potter. Macmillan Education UK. doi:10.1007/978-1-137-28492-1_4

Tally, R. T. Jr., (Ed.). (2017). *The Routledge handbook of literature and space.* Taylor & Francis. doi:10.4324/9781315745978

Tan, A.-H. (1999). Text mining: The state of the art and the challenges. *Proceedings of the pakdd 1999 workshop on knowledge discovery from advanced databases.*

Tang, S., & Cai, Z. (2010). Tourism domain ontology construction from the unstructured text documents. *Cognitive Informatics (ICCI), 2010 9th IEEE International Conference on,* 297-301. 10.1109/COGINF.2010.5599723

Tang, X., Qu, W., & Chen, X. (2016). Semantic change computation: A successive approach. *World Wide Web (Bussum),* *19*(3), 375–415. doi:10.100711280-014-0316-y

Tavenard, R., Fouzi, J., Vandewiele, G., Divo, F., Androz, G., Holtz, C., ... Woods, E. (2020). Tslearn, a machine learning toolkit for time series data. *Journal of Machine Learning Research, 21*(118), 1–6. https://jmlr.org/papers/v21/20-091.html

The Guardian. (2020). *News, sport and opinion from the guardian's US edition.* Retrieved from The Guardian: https://www.theguardian.com/international

Thelwall, M., Buckley, K., Paltoglou, G., Cai, G., & Kappas, A. (2010). Sentiment strength detection in short informal text. *Journal of the American Society for Information Science and Technology, 61*(12), 2544–2558. doi:10.1002/asi.21416

Thet, T. T., Na, J. C., & Khoo, C. S. (2010). Aspect-based sentiment analysis of movie reviews on discussion boards. *Journal of Information Science, 36*(6), 823–848. doi:10.1177/0165551510388123

Thomas, K. M., & Duke, M. (2007). Depressed writing: Cognitive distortions in the works of depressed and nondepressed poets and writers. *Psychology of Aesthetics, Creativity, and the Arts, 1*(4), 204–218. doi:10.1037/1931-3896.1.4.204

Tian, L., Zhang, X., Wang, Y., & Liu, H. (2020). Early detection of rumours on Twitter via stance transfer learning. *Advances in Information Retrieval, 12035,* 575–588. doi:10.1007/978-3-030-45439-5_38

Titov, I., & McDonald, R. A joint model of text and aspect ratings for sentiment summarization. In *Proceedings of ACL-08: HLT* (pp. 308-316). Association for Computational Linguistics.

Toleikienė, R., Rybnikova, I., & Juknevičienė, V. (2020). Whether and how does de Crisis-Induced Situation Change e-Leadership in the Public Sector. *Transylvanian Review of Administrative Sciences, 10*(41), 149–166. https://dx.doi.org/10.24193/tras.SI2020.9

Topi, H. (2004). Supporting Telework: Obstacles and Solutions. *Information Systems Management, 21*(3), 79–85. https://doi.org/10.1201/1078/44432.21.3.20040601/82481.12

Tripathy, A., Agrawal, A., & Rath, S. K. (2016). Classification of sentiment reviews using n-gram machine learning approach. *Expert Systems with Applications, 57,* 117–126. doi:10.1016/j.eswa.2016.03.028

Trotzek, M., Koitka, S., & Friedrich, C. M. (2018). Utilizing neural networks and linguistic metadata for early detection of depression indications in text sequences. *IEEE Transactions on Knowledge and Data Engineering, 32*(3), 588–601. doi:10.1109/TKDE.2018.2885515

Truchot, D., Andela, M., & Takhiart, H. (2021). Stressors met by quarantined French students during the covid-19 pandemic. Their links with depression and sleep disorders. *Journal of Affective Disorders, 294,* 54–59. https://doi.org/10.1016/j.jad.2021.06.059

Tsai, M. H., & Wang, Y. (2021). Analyzing Twitter data to evaluate people's attitudes towards public health policies and events in the era of COVID-19. *International Journal of Environmental Research and Public Health, 18*(12), 6272. doi:10.3390/ijerph18126272 PMID:34200576

Tsao, S. F., Chen, H., Tisseverasinghe, T., Yang, Y., Li, L., & Butt, Z. A. (2021). What social media told us in the time of COVID-19: a scoping review. *The Lancet Digital Health, 3*(3), e175–e194. doi:10.1016/S2589-7500(20)30315-0

Tsao, S. F., Chen, H., Tisseverasinghe, T., Yang, Y., Li, L., & Butt, Z. A. (2021). What social media told us in the time of COVID-19: a scoping review. *The Lancet Digital Health*.

Turney, P. D. (2002). Thumbs Up or Thumbs Down? Semantic Orientation Applied to Unsupervised Classification of Reviews. *Proceedings of 40th Meeting of the Association for Computational Linguistics*, 417. 10.3115/1073083.1073153

Turney, P. D., & Pantel, P. (2010). From frequency to meaning: Vector space models of semantics. *Journal of Artificial Intelligence Research*, 37, 141–188. doi:10.1613/jair.2934

Tversky, A., & Gati, I. (1978). Studies of similarity. *Cognition and Categorization*, 1, 79-98.

Tyagi, P., Javalkar, D., & Chakraborty, S. (2021). Sentiment analysis of twitter data using hybrid classification methods and comparative analysis. *Journal of Jilin University*, 40(6). https://doi.org/10.17605/OSF.IO/2NVJK

University of Harvard. (2019). *Detrended fluctuation analysis (DFA)*. Retrieved from University of Harvard: http://reylab.bidmc.harvard.edu/download/DFA/intro/

UOL. (2017). *EUA ataca síria com mais de 50 mísseis*. Retrieved from UOL: https://noticias.uol.com.br/ultimas-noticias/ansa/2017/04/06/

Uysal, A. K., & Gunal, S. (2014). The impact of preprocessing on text classification. *Information Processing & Management*, 50(1), 104–112. doi:10.1016/j.ipm.2013.08.006

Vajjala, S., Gupta, A., Surana, H., & Majumder, B. (2020). *Practical Natural Language Processing: A Comprehensive Guide to Building Real-World NLP Systems*. O'Reilly Media Inc.

Valdez, D., Pickett, A. C., & Goodson, P. (2018). Topic modeling: Latent semantic analysis for the social sciences. *Social Science Quarterly*, 99(5), 1665–1679.

Valle-Cruz, D., Lopez-Chau, A., & Sandoval-Almazan, R. (2021). How much do Twitter posts affect voters? Analysis of the multi-emotional charge with affective computing in political campaigns. *ACM International Conference Proceeding Series*, 1–14. doi:10.1145/3463677.3463698

Valle-Cruz, D., Lopez-Chau, A., & Sandoval-Almazan, R. (2021). How much do Twitter posts affect voters? Analysis of the multi-emotional charge with affective computing in political campaigns. *DG. O2021: The 22nd Annual International Conference on Digital Government Research*, 1–14.

Valle-Cruz, D. (2019). Public value of e-government services through emerging technologies. *International Journal of Public Sector Management*, 32(5), 530–545. doi:10.1108/IJPSM-03-2018-0072

Valle-Cruz, D., Fernandez-Cortez, V., López-Chau, A., & Sandoval-Almazán, R. (2021). Does Twitter Affect Stock Market Decisions? Financial Sentiment Analysis During Pandemics: A Comparative Study of the H1N1 and the COVID-19 Periods. *Cognitive Computation*, 1–16. PMID:33520006

Valle-Cruz, D., López-Chau, A., & Sandoval-Almazán, R. (2020). Impression analysis of trending topics in Twitter with classification algorithms. *Proceedings of the 13th International Conference on Theory and Practice of Electronic Governance*, 430–441. 10.1145/3428502.3428570

van Atteveldt, W., van der Velden, M. A., & Boukes, M. (2021). The Validity of Sentiment Analysis: Comparing Manual Annotation, Crowd-Coding, Dictionary Approaches, and Machine Learning Algorithms. *Communication Methods and Measures*, 15(2), 121–140. doi:10.1080/19312458.2020.1869198

Varathan, K. D., Giachanou, A., & Crestani, F. (2017). Comparative opinion mining: A review. *Journal of the Association for Information Science and Technology*, 68(4), 811–829. doi:10.1002/asi.23716

Vayansky, I., & Kumar, S. A. P. (2020). A review of topic modeling methods. *Information Systems, 94*, 101582.

Vega, R. P., Anderson, A. J., & Kaplan, S. A. (2015). A Within-Person Examination of the Effects of Telework. *Journal of Business and Psychology, 30*(2), 313–323. https://doi.org/10.1007/s10869-014-9359-4

Verma, Y., & Jawahar, C. V. (2014). Im2Text and Text2Im: Associating Images and Texts for Cross-Modal Retrieval. BMVC, 1, 2.

Vigneshvaran, P., Jayabalan, E., & Vijaya, K. (2013). A predominant statistical approach to identify semantic similarity of textual documents. *Pattern Recognition, Informatics and Mobile Engineering (PRIME), 2013 International Conference on*, 496-499. 10.1109/ICPRIME.2013.6496721

Vinodhini, G., & Chandrasekaran, R. M. (2012). Sentiment analysis and opinion mining: A survey. *International Journal (Toronto, Ont.), 2*(6), 282–292.

Vlachos, A., & Riedel, S. (2014). Fact checking: Task definition and dataset construction. In *Proceedings of the ACL 2014 Workshop on Language Technologies and Computational Social Science* (pp. 18-22). 10.3115/v1/W14-2508

Wang, J., & Dong, Y. (2020). Measurement of text similarity: A survey. *Information (Basel), 11*(9), 421. doi:10.3390/info11090421

Wang, K., & Ozbilen, B. (2020). Synergistic and threshold effects of telework and residential location choice on travel time allocation. *Sustainable Cities and Society, 63*, 102468. https://doi.org/10.1016/j.scs.2020.102468

Wang, X., & McCallum, A. (2006). Topics over time: A non-markov continuous time model of topical trends. *Proceedings of the 12th ACM SIGKDD International Conference on Knowledge Discovery and Data Mining* (pp. 424-433). Association for Computing Machinery. 10.1145/1150402.1150450

Wang, Y., Huang, M., Zhu, X., & Zhao, L. (2016, November). Attention-based LSTM for aspect-level sentiment classification. In *Proceedings of the 2016 conference on empirical methods in natural language processing* (pp. 606-615). 10.18653/v1/D16-1058

Wang, Z., Ho, S.-B., & Cambria, E. (2020). A review of emotion sensing: Categorization models and algorithms. *Multimedia Tools and Applications, 79*(47-48), 1–30. doi:10.100711042-019-08328-z

Webster, J. J., & Kit, C. (1992). Tokenization as the initial phase in NLP. In *Proceedings of the 14th conference on Computational linguistics* (p. 1106). Association for Computational Linguistics. doi:10.3115/992424.992434

What causes depression? (2019). *Harvard Health*. Retrieved 14 September 2021, from https://www.health.harvard.edu/mind-and-mood/what-causes-depression

What Is Depression? (n.d.). Retrieved 27 November 2021, from https://www.psychiatry.org/patients-families/depression/what-is-depression

WHO. (2020). *Weekly epidemiological update - 27 December 2020.* https://www.who.int/publications/m/item/weekly-epidemiological-update---29-december-2020

WHO. (n.d.). Retrieved 27 November 2021, from https://www.who.int/health-topics/depression#tab=tab_1

Wille, R. (2005). Formal concept analysis as mathematical theory of concepts and concept hierarchies. *Formal Concept Analysis, 3626*, 1-33.

Wilson, T., Wiebe, J., & Hoffmann, P. (2005). Recognizing contextual polarity in phrase-level sentiment analysis. In *Proceedings of the Conference on Human Language Technology and Empirical Methods in Natural Language Processing* (pp. 347-354). Association for Computational Linguistics. 10.3115/1220575.1220619

Wołk, A., Chlasta, K., & Holas, P. (2021). *Hybrid approach to detecting symptoms of depression in social media entries.* arXiv preprint:2106.10485.

Wolohan, J. T., Hiraga, M., Mukherjee, A., Sayyed, Z. A., & Millard, M. (2018,). Detecting linguistic traces of depression in topic-restricted text: Attending to self-stigmatized depression with NLP. In *Proceedings of the First International Workshop on Language Cognition and Computational Models* (pp. 11-21). Academic Press.

Wongkar, M., & Angdresey, A. (2019). Sentiment analysis using Naive Bayes Algorithm of the data crawler: Twitter. *2019 Fourth International Conference on Informatics and Computing (ICIC).*

Wongkoblap, A., Vadillo, M. A., & Curcin, V. (2018). A multilevel predictive model for detecting social network users with depression. In *IEEE International Conference on Healthcare Informatics (ICHI)* (pp. 130-135). 10.1109/ICHI.2018.00022

Wongkoblap, A., Vadillo, M., & Curcin, V. (2021). Depression Detection of Twitter Posters using Deep Learning with Anaphora Resolution: Algorithm Development and Validation. *JMIR Mental Health.* Advance online publication. doi:10.2196/19824

WordNet. (2005). *WordNet Search - 3.1.* http://wordnetweb.princeton.edu/perl/webwn?s=cow

Wu, Z., & Ong, D. C. (2020). Context-guided bert for targeted aspect-based sentiment analysis. Association for the Advancement of Artificial Intelligence, 1-9.

Wu, M. Y., Shen, C. Y., Wang, E. T., & Chen, A. L. (2020). A deep architecture for depression detection using posting, behavior, and living environment data. *Journal of Intelligent Information Systems, 54*(2), 225–244. doi:10.100710844-018-0533-4

Xanthopoulos, P., Pardalos, P. M., & Trafalis, T. B. (2013). *Robust data mining.* Springer.

Xie, L., Pan, P., & Lu, Y. (2015). Analyzing semantic correlation for cross-modal retrieval. *Multimedia Systems, 21*(6), 525–539. doi:10.100700530-014-0397-6

Xu, H., Liu, B., Shu, L., & Yu, P. S. (2019). *BERT post-training for review reading comprehension and aspect-based sentiment analysis.* arXiv preprint arXiv:1904.02232.

Xue, X. (2008). *Distributional features for text categorization.* https://ieeexplore.ieee.org/abstract/document/4589210/

Xu, K., Liao, S. S., Li, J., & Song, Y. (2011). Mining comparative opinions from customer reviews for competitive intelligence. *Decision Support Systems, 50*(4), 743–754. doi:10.1016/j.dss.2010.08.021

Yadav, A., & Vishwakarma, D. K. (2020). Sentiment analysis using deep learning architectures: A review. *Artificial Intelligence Review, 53*(6), 4335–4385.

Yadav, R. K., Jiao, L., Granmo, O. C., & Goodwin, M. (2021, May). Human-level interpretable learning for aspect-based sentiment analysis. In *The Thirty-Fifth AAAI Conference on Artificial Intelligence (AAAI-21).* AAAI.

Yang, S., & Ko, Y. (2011). Extracting comparative entities and predicates from texts using comparative type classification. In *Proceedings of the 49ᵗʰ Annual Meeting of the Association for Computational Linguistics* (pp. 1636–1644). Academic Press.

Yang, L., Jiang, D., Xia, X., Pei, E., Oveneke, M. C., & Sahli, H. (2017). Multimodal measurement of depression using deep learning models. In *Proceedings of the 7th Annual Workshop on Audio/Visual Emotion Challenge* (pp. 53-59). 10.1145/3133944.3133948

Yang, W., & Mu, L. (2015). GIS analysis of depression among Twitter users. *Applied Geography (Sevenoaks, England), 60*, 217–223. doi:10.1016/j.apgeog.2014.10.016

Yarkoni, T. (2010). Personality in 100,000 words: A large-scale analysis of personality and word use among bloggers. *Journal of Research in Personality, 44*(3), 363–373. doi:10.1016/j.jrp.2010.04.001 PMID:20563301

Yazdavar, A. H., Al-Olimat, H. S., Ebrahimi, M., Bajaj, G., Banerjee, T., Thirunarayan, K., ... Sheth, A. (2017). Semi-supervised approach to monitoring clinical depressive symptoms in social media. In *Proceedings of the IEEE/ACM International Conference on Advances in Social Networks Analysis and Mining* (pp. 1191-1198). 10.1145/3110025.3123028

Ye, Q., Zhang, Z., & Law, R. (2009). Sentiment classification of online reviews to travel destinations by supervised machine learning approaches. *Expert Systems with Applications, 36*(3), 6527–6535. doi:10.1016/j.eswa.2008.07.035

Yin, H., Song, X., Yang, S., & Li, J. (2021). *Sentiment analysis and topic modeling for COVID-19 vaccine discussions.* arXiv preprint arXiv:2111.04415.

Ying, S. Y., Keikhosrokiani, P., & Asl, M. P. (2020). Comparison of data analytic techniques for a spatial opinion mining in literary works: A review paper. *International Conference of Reliable Information and Communication Technology,* 523–535.

Ying, S. Y., Keikhosrokiani, P., & Asl, M. P. (2021). Comparison of data analytic techniques for a spatial opinion mining in literary works: A review paper. In F. Saeed, F. Mohammed, & A. Al-Nahari (Eds.), *Innovative Systems for Intelligent Health Informatics* (pp. 523–535). Springer International Publishing. doi:10.1007/978-3-030-70713-2_49

Ying, S. Y., Keikhosrokiani, P., & Asl, M. P. (2022). Opinion mining on Viet Thanh Nguyen's The Sympathizer using topic modelling and sentiment analysis. *Journal of Information Technology Management, 14*(Special Issue), 163–183. doi:10.22059/jitm.2022.84895

Young, P., Lai, A., Hodosh, M., & Hockenmaier, J. (2014). From image descriptions to visual denotations: New similarity metrics for semantic inference over event descriptions. *Transactions of the Association for Computational Linguistics, 2*, 67–78. doi:10.1162/tacl_a_00166

Younis, U., Asghar, M. Z., Khan, A., Khan, A., Igbal, J., & Jilani, N. (2020). Applying machine learning techniques for performing comparative opinion mining. *Open Computer Science, 10*(1), 461–477. doi:10.1515/comp-2020-0148

Yousaf, A., Umer, M., Sadiq, S., Ullah, S., Mirjalili, S., Rupapara, V., & Nappi, M. (2020). Emotion recognition by textual tweets classification using voting classifier (LR-SGD). *IEEE Access: Practical Innovations, Open Solutions, 9*, 6286–6295. doi:10.1109/ACCESS.2020.3047831

Yousefinaghani, S., Dara, R., Mubareka, S., Papadopoulos, A., & Sharif, S. (2021). An analysis of COVID-19 vaccine sentiments and opinions on Twitter. *International Journal of Infectious Diseases, 108*, 256–262. doi:10.1016/j.ijid.2021.05.059 PMID:34052407

Yousefpour, A., Ibrahim, R., Hamed, H. N. A., & Hajmohammadi, M. S. (2014). A comparative study on sentiment analysis. *Advances in Environmental Biology, 8*(13), 53–68.

Yue, L., Chen, W., Li, X., Zuo, W., & Yin, M. (2019). A survey of sentiment analysis in social media. *Knowledge and Information Systems, 60*(2), 617–663. doi:10.100710115-018-1236-4

Zafarani, R., Abbasi, M. A., & Liu, H. (2014). *Social media mining - an introduction.* Cambridge University Press. doi:10.1017/CBO9781139088510

Zhang, N., Li, L., Chen, X., Deng, S., Bi, Z., Tan, C., . . . Chen, H. (2021). *Differentiable prompt makes pre-trained language models better few-shot learners.* arXiv preprint arXiv:2108.13161.

Zhang, Q., Yi, G. Y., Chen, L.-P., & He, W. (2021). *Text mining and sentiment analysis of COVID-19 tweets.* https://arxiv.org/abs/2106.15354

Zhang, Z., Miao, D., & Yue, X. (2013). *Similarity measure for short texts using topic models and rough sets*. Academic Press.

Zhang, C., Yu, M. C., & Marin, S. (2021a). Exploring public sentiment on enforced remote work during COVID-19. *The Journal of Applied Psychology*, *106*(6), 797–810. https://doi.org/10.1037/apl0000933

Zhang, J., Zhang, A., Liu, D., & Bian, Y. (2021b). Customer preferences extraction for air purifiers based on fine-grained sentiment analysis of online reviews. *Knowledge-Based Systems*, *228*, 107259. https://doi.org/10.1016/j.knosys.2021.107259

Zhang, K., Xie, Y., Yang, Y., Sun, A., Liu, H., & Choudhary, A. (2014). Incorporating conditional random fields and active learning to improve sentiment identification. *Neural Networks*, *58*, 60–67. doi:10.1016/j.neunet.2014.04.005 PMID:24856246

Zhang, L., & Liu, B. (2014). Aspect and entity extraction for opinion mining. In *Proceedings of Data Mining and Knowledge Discovery for Big Data* (pp. 1–40). Springer Berlin Heidelberg. doi:10.1007/978-3-642-40837-3_1

Zhao, W. (n.d.). *Topical keyphrase extraction from twitter*. Available at: https://dl.acm.org/citation.cfm?id=2002521

Zhen, Z., Shen, J., & Lu, S. (2008). WCONS: An ontology mapping approach based on word and context similarity. *Proceedings of the 2008 IEEE/WIC/ACM International Conference on Web Intelligence and Intelligent Agent Technology, IEEE Computers & Society*, *3*, 334–338.

Zhu, G., & Iglesias, C. A. (2017). Computing semantic similarity of concepts in knowledge graphs. *IEEE Transactions on Knowledge and Data Engineering*, *29*(1), 72–85. doi:10.1109/TKDE.2016.2610428

Zucco, C., Calabrese, B., & Cannataro, M. (2017). Sentiment analysis and affective computing for depression monitoring. In *IEEE international conference on bioinformatics and biomedicine* (pp. 1988–1995). BIBM. doi:10.1109/BIBM.2017.8217966

About the Contributors

Pantea Keikhosrokiani received the Bachelor of Science degree in electrical and electronics engineering, the master's degree in information technology from the School of Computer Sciences, Universiti Sains Malaysia (USM), Malaysia, and the Ph.D. degree in service system engineering, information system. She was a Teaching Fellow with the National Advanced IPv6 Centre of Excellence (Nav6), USM, where she is currently a Senior Lecturer with the School of Computer Sciences. Her recent book was published entitled Perspectives in the Development of Mobile Medical Information Systems: Life Cycle, Management, Methodological Approach and Application, in 2019. Her articles were published in distinguished edited books and journals, including Telematics and Informatics (Elsevier), Cognition, Technology, and Work (Springer), Taylors and Francis, and IGI Global. She was indexed by ISI, Scopus, and PubMed. Her research and teaching interests include information systems development, database systems, health and medical informatics, business intelligence, text analytics, location-based mobile applications, big data, and technopreneurship.

Moussa Pourya Asl is a Senior Lecturer in literary studies at Universiti Sains Malaysia, where he also obtained his PhD (English Literature) from School of Humanities. His primary research area is in diasporic literature and gender and cultural studies, and he has published several articles in the above-mentioned areas in Asian Ethnicity, American Studies in Scandinavia, Cogent: Arts & Humanities, Gema Online, and 3L.

* * *

Haseeb Ahmad received the B.S. degree from G.C. University, Faisalabad, Pakistan, in 2010, the Master's degree from the Virtual University of Pakistan in 2012, and Ph.D. in 2017 from Beijing University of Posts and Telecommunications, Beijing, China. Currently, he is serving as Assistant Professor at National Textile University, Faisalabad, Pakistan. His current research interest includes data mining, information retrieval, natural language processing, and information security.

Shahbaz Ahmad graduated with distinction at the GC University, Faisalabad, and completed his master's degree in Computer Science with honors at the National Textile University. Currently, he is pursuing his Ph.D. in Computer Science from Capital University of Science and Technology Islamabad. Shahbaz received multiple distinctions throughout his studies. He is the recipient of Chancellor's roll of honor and the gold medal in his Ph.D. and MS. His research interests are bibliometrics, scientometrics, and data science. Much of his work has been on improving research paper recommender systems' accuracy using co-citation and metadata analysis. He is serving as a lecturer at the Department of Computer Science (DCS) since 2016 and responsible for teaching undergraduate courses and supervising student projects.

Nur Ain Nasuha Anuar is a graduate student in the English literature section of School of Humanities, Universiti Sains Malaysia. Her primary research interests are South Asian literature, and gender and cultural studies. She has published an article related to the mentioned areas in PERTANIKA Journal of Social Sciences & Humanities.

Nursal Arıcı is a Professor at Department of Computer Engineering of Gazi University.

Nurfatin Binti Sofian is currently student at School of Computer Sciences, Universiti Sains Malaysia.

Nikmatul Husna Binti Suhendra is currently student at School of Computer Sciences, Universiti Sains Malaysia.

Nikhil V. Chandran is a full-time PhD research scholar at Data Engineering Lab, Kerala University of Digital Sciences, Innovation and Technology, Thiruvananthapuram, India. He received his M.Tech from MAHE in 2015 and M.Phil from CUSAT, Kerala in 2017. His research interests include Deep Learning, Kernel Methods, Information Retrieval, Text Mining, Blockchain and NLP.

Htet Naing Chuu received his first Master's degree in Computer Science from the Asian Institute of Technology University (Thailand, 2018). Later, he was interested in Machine Learning, and he continued his second Master's degree in Data Science and Analytics from Universiti Sains Malaysia (USM, 2021).

Rigoberto R. G. C. Contreras, Ph.D., is an assistant professor at the Autonomous University of the State of Mexico. His research interests are related to the Management of Intangibles and the Economics of Knowledge in Organizations. He holds a Ph.D. in Economic and Administrative Sciences, a Master's Degree in Administration with a specialization in Organizational Management, and a Bachelor's Degree in Administration. He has been a visiting researcher at the Laboratory of Personality Psychology, National University of Córdoba, Argentina. He received the award for best paper of the Chapter: Knowledge Management by the Mexican Academy of Administrative Sciences. He has publications in several national and international journals and publishing houses. Member of the Mexican National Council of Science and Technology – CONACyT.

Chaudhry Mhammad Nadeem Faisal received BS degree in Information Technology from Pakistan in 2005, MS degree in computer science from Blekinge Institute of Technology, Sweden in 2009, and a Ph.D. degree in computer engineering from the University of Oviedo, Spain in 2017. He is an Assistant Professor at National Textile University, Pakistan. His research interests include Human-Computer Interaction, visual ergonomics, web accessibility, and usability evaluation of industrial systems.

Keng Hoon Gan is a senior lecturer in School of Computer Sciences, Universiti Sains Malaysia. She received her Ph. D. degree from Universiti of Malaya (UM) in 2013. She is current the Program Manager of Research Ecosystem and Innovation at the School of Computer Sciences. Her domains of specialization include information retrieval, structured retrieval, structured document representation and query optimization. She has initiated a research platform SIIR (Semantics in Information Retrieval @ ir.cs.usm.my) which is a research initiative related to semantically enhanced information retrieval, and its related applications.

T. V. Geetha completed her Ph.D in Natural Language Processing from Anna University, Chennai. She is currently, retired Senior Professor and UGC-BSR Faculty Fellow, Computer Science and Engineering Department, CEG Campus, Anna University, Chennai, Tamil Nadu, India. Her research interests include Biomedical Text Mining, Music Processing, Tamil Computing, Text Mining, Search Engines, Deep Learning, Semantic Computing, etc.

Lamartine Nogueira Frutuoso Guimarães earned his Ph.D. in Nuclear Engineering from The University of Tennessee, Knoxville, TN in 1992. He has been a Researcher at the Institute for Advanced Studies since 1984. He has been a full researcher since 1992, and has served as head of the Nuclear Energy Division from 2005 to 2021. Also has been a professor at the graduate level of Applied Computing at the National Institute for Space Research in Applied Artificial Intelligence since 1998, teaching the disciplines of Artificial Intelligence and Intelligent Control Theory. Additionally, is a professor at the graduate level of Space Science and Technology at the Aeronautical Institute of Technology in Space Propulsion and Hypersonics, having as research line Nuclear Propulsion, since 2012, teaching the disciplines Nuclear Power Generation in Space and Nuclear Systems. He is also a full professor at Universidade Paulista since 2015. He teaches courses of Computer Science, Computer Engineering, Systems Analysis and Development, Artificial Intelligence, Mathematics for Computing, Computable Systems, and Basic Physics. He worked for 9 years at Faculdade de Tecnologia São Francisco in the Control and Automation Engineering course. He worked for 2 years at the IBTA College in the Decision Making course. He worked for 13 years at Universidade Braz Cubas, in basic physics, numerical calculus, transport phenomena, advanced calculus, linear algebra, analytic geometry and artificial intelligence. He received 2 awards and/or honors. He received the Santos Dumont Medal of Merit, in 2009. Between 1994 and 2008 he coordinated 6 research projects. Currently, he coordinates 4 scientific projects. He works in the area of Nuclear Engineering, with emphasis on Dynamic Simulation of Systems and Processes. In his "Lattes" curriculum the most frequent terms in the contextualization of scientific, technological and artistic-cultural production are: nuclear technology applied to space, numerical simulation, liquid metal cooled reactor, nuclear microreactor technology, fast reactor, applied nuclear technology and AI in aerospace and nuclear applications (fuzzy logic, genetic algorithms, neural networks, deep learning, big data, data mining, computer vision, defense analysis using threat emotion analysis in social medias and their combinations). Since 2008, he is the manager and was the creator of the TERRA - Advanced Fast Reactor Technology project, which aims to research the key technologies of advanced high-temperature fast microreactors, planned to be used in space nuclear propulsion. His main current interest is in the application of nuclear technology in space exploration, such as: space nuclear propulsion, nuclear reactors as a power source for facilities, satellites and space vehicles, Radioisotope Thermoelectric Generators and IA applications in space and defense.

Nurfarah Hadira Abdul Hadi is a graduate student in English literature at School of Humanities, Universiti Sains Malaysia. Her research interests are in South Asian diasporic literature, gender and cultural studies, and she has published an article in the above-mentioned areas in Gema Online.

Thasnim Humida is currently a Assistant Professor at Dept. of Mass Communication and Journalism, Begum Rokeya University, Rangpur, Bangladesh.

Marilyn Ibañez is a PhD in Applied Computing at the National Institute for Space Research in the area of Machine Learning, with emphasis in sentiment analysis. Master in Applied Computing, with emphasis in image analysis, from the National Institute for Space Research and Bachelor in Computer Science from the Federal University of Itajubá. Moreover, has already worked as a substitute teacher in basic, technical, and technological education at the Federal Institute of São Paulo. She has also worked in the area of software analysis, development, and testing in companies. Additionally, has experience in analysis and development of commercial automation software in C++ language under Linux operating environment, analysis, and testing of embedded software in C++ language under QNX operating environment, GIS software testing, scientific mathematical development in C++ programming language under Linux operating environment, in image analysis and machine learning.

Vijayarani J. is currently working as Teaching Fellow in Computer Science and Engineering Department, CEG Campus, Anna University, Chennai, Tamil Nadu, India. She completed her Ph.D. in Text Mining from Anna University, Chennai. Her research interests include NLP, Text Mining, Machine Learning, Deep Learning, and Semantic Computing.

Nurul Najiha Jafery has finished her master's degree in Master of Science (Data Science& Analytic) from School of Computer Sciences, Universiti Sains Malaysia. Currently, she is perusing her PhD at the Faculty of Electrical Engineering, Universiti Teknologi Mara (UiTM).

Dimitris Kotzinos's main research interests include data management algorithms, techniques and tools; development of methodologies, algorithms and tools for web based information systems, portals and web services; and the understanding of the meaning (semantics) of interoperable data and services on the web. In that respect, he is interested in providing conceptual models for the cultural domain and analyzing information collected by personal devices by visitors of cultural organizations. Since recently, he is also working on studying the formation and evolution of discussions in online social networks and he is interested in using such techniques to identify and analyze opinions around various types of events. Dimitris has published in various journals, books, conferences, and workshops and serves as a program committee member and reviewer for various conferences and journals.

Doğan Küçük is a Ph.D. Student at the Department of Computer Engineering of Gazi University.

Asdrúbal López-Chau: Ph.D. in Computer Science; Master in Computer Engineering, and M.S. in Communications and Electronics Engineering for National Polytechnic Institute (IPN). He is currently an Associate Professor at the Autonomous University of the State of Mexico (UAEM). His research interests include machine learning, data mining, computer vision and embedded systems. His scientific production includes more than 12 articles with impact factor and more than 8 book chapters in international publishers. He is a reviewer of articles in JCR journals and has participated in several research projects in Mexico. He is a member of the Mexican National Council of Science and Technology – CONACyT.

Md Habib Al Mamun is a PhD student at School of Computer Sciences, Universiti Sains Malaysia (USM), Malaysia. He works as Senior manager of Computer and Information System in GAZI Communications, Bangladesh after graduating from Master of Informatics.

J. Patricia Muñoz-Chávez is a Ph.D. Associate Professor at the Technological University of the Metropolitan Area of the Valley of Mexico. Her research interests are related to Organizations, Higher Education, and Organizational Behavior. She holds a Ph.D. in Strategic Planning and Technology Management (Popular Autonomous University of the State of Puebla.), a Master's Degree in Management, and a Bachelor's Degree in Accountant (Autonomous University of the State of Hidalgo). She did a research stay at the University of Malaga, Spain. She has publications in several national and international journals and publishers.

Faiza Nasir earned her MS degree in Computer Science from National Textile University, Faisalabad, Pakistan.

Ajaypradeep Natarajsivam received his B.E., Degree from Ganathipathy Tulsis Jain Engineering College, Tamilnadu, India in the year 2014 and M.E., Degree from Global Institute of Engineering and Technology, Tamilnadu, India in the year 2016. He is currently a research scholar under School of Computer Science and Engineering in Vellore Institute of Technology, Tamilnadu, India. His areas of interest include Machine Learning, Data Analytics, Mobile Computing and Deep Learning.

Elise Noga-Hartmann is a Master's degree graduate of both political sciences and computer science. She specialized in economics and finance on the first hand, and in data science and machine learning, on the other hand. She worked at the ETIS lab. during her last year of computer science Master's degree, where she focused on AI subjects regarding the analysis of large text corpora.

Sasikala R. received the B.E. degree from Kongu Engineering College, Tamilnadu, India in 1994, the M.E degree from Govt. College of Technology, Coimbatore, Tamilnadu in 2003, and the Ph.D. degree from the Anna University, Chennai, Tamilnadu in 2011. She is currently an Associate Professor, Department of Computational Intelligence in School of Computer Science and Engineering at VIT University, Vellore, Tamilnadu, India. Her research interests include: Cloud Computing, Big Data, Wireless Networks, Body Sensor Networks and Optical Switching Networks. He has published many research papers in various conferences and reputed journals. She is a life member of Computer Society of India and Indian Society for Technical Education.

Reinaldo Rosa is a Technician in Electronics and Telecommunications (ITJ-1982). Graduated in Physics and Astronomy at the Federal University of Rio de Janeiro (1988), MS (1991) and PhD (1995) in Astrophysics and Space Science from INPE with research conducted at the University of Maryland, USA (SW-CNPq scholarship) from Nov 1993 to Nov 1995. He did post-doctoral research in Computational Space Physics at Nagoya University (1997) under FAPESP sponsorship. Created the Nucleus for Simulation and Analysis of Complex Systems in the Laboratory of Computation and Applied Mathematics (LABAC) at INPE as a FAPESP young researcher fellow in an emerging center (1998-2002). He is a full time S&T civil servant at LABAC-INPE-MCTIC, hired in 2002, 40 hours regime, where he works as a professor of the Post-Graduation Course in Applied Computing (CAP). He was Coordinator of PG

457

of CAP (2003-2004/2012-2013). Former Secretary General of SBMAC (2003-2005). He is a Council Member of the Pan-American Association of Interdisciplinary Computational Sciences. He is Deputy Head of LABAC-INPE. Chair of COSPAR (2012/2014/2016). He has experience in Space Science and Technology, with emphasis on Applied Computing, working mainly on the following topics: statistical physics of nonlinear processes, computational physics for simulation and signal analysis, Big Data and Artificial Intelligence Technologies. In the last eight years he has been dedicated to computational space physics, with focus on Data Science and HPC. He works in R&D with a predominantly interdisciplinary profile having published about 90 articles in international journals and 02 books. Collaborates on projects with institutional partnerships in Brazil and abroad, with emphasis on applied computing (machine learning and neurocomputing with pyCUDA and R) to space physics and environmental physics. He is Principal Investigator (PI) of FAPESP Thematic Project (Case No. 14/11156-4). He is a member of the advisory committee for evaluation of FAPESP's PIPE Program.

Nur-Hana Samsudin was born in Kuala Lumpur, Malaysia. She received her Ph.D. degree in Computer Science from the University of Birmingham, United Kingdom in 2017. She was a researcher in MIMOS (M) Bhd. Currently she is a Senior Lecturer at the Universiti Sains Malaysia in Penang Malaysia. She currently hold one patent and five copyrights. Her research interest covers the domain of Natural Language Processing, speech processing, text processing, sustainable under-resourced language studies and polyglot speech synthesis.

Rodrigo Sandoval-Almazán (PhD) is Associate Professor at the Political Sciences and Social Sciences Department in the Autonomous University of the State of Mexico, in Toluca City. Dr. Sandoval-Almazan is the author or co-author of articles in Government Information Quarterly, Information Polity, First Monday, Government; Journal of Information Technology for Development; Journal of Organizational Computing and Electronic Commerce; International Journal of E-Politics IJEP. His research interests include artificial intelligence, social media in government. Public innovation, digital government, and open government.

Anoop V. S. has completed his Doctor of Philosophy (Ph.D.) and Master of Philosophy (M.Phil.) from the Indian Institute of Information Technology and Management - Kerala (IIITM-K) under Cochin University of Science and Technology (CUSAT). In the very previous role, he has worked as an Assistant Professor in Computer Science at Rajagiri College of Social Sciences (Autonomous), Kochi, India. He has also worked as a Senior Data Scientist with CogTalk at Dubai Future Accelerator for implementing Artificial Intelligence solutions for Etisalat Digital and Etihad Airways. Anoop is an experienced Software Engineer with more than five years of experience working with US-based MNCs in Technopark, Thiruvananthapuram. He has completed many industry internships on Artificial Intelligence and implemented text mining algorithms to solve complex business problems. Anoop's research interests are primarily in Applied Text Mining, Information Retrieval, and Blockchain. He has several publications in his credit that include edited books, book chapters, articles in international journals, and conference proceedings.

David Valle-Cruz, Ph.D., is an Assistant Professor at the Universidad Autónoma del Estado de México and is a member of the Mexican National System of Researchers. David is a Computer Engineer and a Computer Scientist; he holds a Ph.D. in Economics and Management. He has been a visiting researcher at the Center for Technology in Government (CTG), SUNY Albany, NY, and at the Computer Science and Multi-Agent Systems Laboratory of CINVESTAV, Guadalajara, Mexico. His articles have been published in leading journals, including Government Information Quarterly, Cognitive Computation, First Monday, Information Polity, and the International Journal of Public Sector Management (among others). His research interests are related to Applied Artificial Intelligence, Social Media, and Emerging Technologies in the Public Sector.

Teck Keat Yeow is currently working as Data Scientist in Acronis Singapore. He holds a Master in Computer Science at Universiti Sains Malaysia.

Xian Zhao received the Bachelor of Engineering degree in Metallurgical Engineering from the School of Material Science and Engineering, Jiangsu University (JUS), China, in 2018, and the Master of Science degree in Data Science and Analytics from the School of Computer Science, Universiti Sains Malaysia (USM), Malaysia, in 2021. Currently he is a PhD student in School of Computer Science, USM. His research interests include financial transaction, business informatics, customer service, and health and medical informatics.

Index

 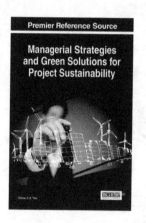  

IGI Global Author Services

Providing a high-quality, affordable, and expeditious service, IGI Global's Author Services enable authors to streamline their publishing process, increase chance of acceptance, and adhere to IGI Global's publication standards.

Benefits of Author Services:

- **Professional Service:** All our editors, designers, and translators are experts in their field with years of experience and professional certifications.

- **Quality Guarantee & Certificate:** Each order is returned with a quality guarantee and certificate of professional completion.

- **Timeliness:** All editorial orders have a guaranteed return timeframe of 3-5 business days and translation orders are guaranteed in 7-10 business days.

- **Affordable Pricing:** IGI Global Author Services are competitively priced compared to other industry service providers.

- **APC Reimbursement:** IGI Global authors publishing Open Access (OA) will be able to deduct the cost of editing and other IGI Global author services from their OA APC publishing fee.

Author Services Offered:

 English Language Copy Editing
Professional, native English language copy editors improve your manuscript's grammar, spelling, punctuation, terminology, semantics, consistency, flow, formatting, and more.

 Scientific & Scholarly Editing
A Ph.D. level review for qualities such as originality and significance, interest to researchers, level of methodology and analysis, coverage of literature, organization, quality of writing, and strengths and weaknesses.

 Figure, Table, Chart & Equation Conversions
Work with IGI Global's graphic designers before submission to enhance and design all figures and charts to IGI Global's specific standards for clarity.

 Translation
Providing 70 language options, including Simplified and Traditional Chinese, Spanish, Arabic, German, French, and more.

Hear What the Experts Are Saying About IGI Global's Author Services

"Publishing with IGI Global has been *an amazing experience* for me for sharing my research. The *strong academic production* support ensures quality and timely completion." – **Prof. Margaret Niess, Oregon State University, USA**

"The service was *very fast, very thorough, and very helpful* in ensuring our chapter meets the criteria and requirements of the book's editors. I was *quite impressed and happy* with your service." – **Prof. Tom Brinthaupt, Middle Tennessee State University, USA**

Learn More or Get Started Here:

For Questions, Contact IGI Global's Customer Service Team at cust@igi-global.com or 717-533-8845

IGI Global
PUBLISHER of TIMELY KNOWLEDGE
www.igi-global.com

Printed in the USA
by BookBaby Publishing

Printed in the United States
by Baker & Taylor Publisher Services